By Alison Weir

FICTION

Six Tudor Queens

Katharine Parr, The Sixth Wife
Katheryn Howard, The Scandalous Queen
Anna of Kleve, The Princess in the Portrait
Jane Seymour, The Haunted Queen
Anne Boleyn, A King's Obsession
Katherine of Aragon, The True Queen

The King's Pleasure
The Last White Rose
The Marriage Game
A Dangerous Inheritance
Captive Queen
The Lady Elizabeth
Innocent Traitor
The Passionate Tudor
The Cardinal

NONFICTION

England's Medieval Queens

Queens at War
Queens of the Age of Chivalry
Queens of the Crusades
Queens of the Conquest

The Lost Tudor Princess: The Life of Lady Margaret Douglas
Elizabeth of York: A Tudor Queen and Her World
Mary Boleyn: The Mistress of Kings
The Lady in the Tower: The Fall of Anne Boleyn
Mistress of the Monarchy: The Life of Katherine Swynford, Duchess of Lancaster
Queen Isabella: Treachery, Adultery, and Murder in Medieval England
Mary Queen of Scots and the Murder of Lord Darnley
Henry VIII: The King and His Court
Eleanor of Aquitaine: A Life
The Life of Elizabeth I
The Children of Henry VIII
The Wars of the Roses
The Princes in the Tower
The Six Wives of Henry VIII

Queens at War

Queens

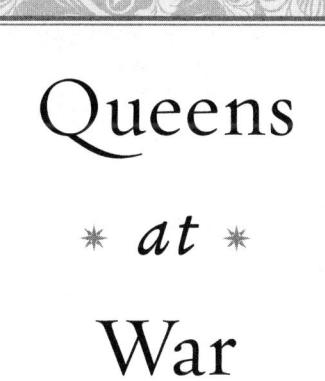

✷ at ✷

War

England's Medieval Queens

BOOK FOUR

ALISON WEIR

Ballantine Books | New York

Ballantine Books
An imprint of Random House
A division of Penguin Random House LLC
1745 Broadway, New York, NY 10019
randomhousebooks.com
penguinrandomhouse.com

Copyright © 2025 by Alison Weir

Penguin Random House values and supports copyright. Copyright fuels creativity, encourages diverse voices, promotes free speech, and creates a vibrant culture. Thank you for buying an authorized edition of this book and for complying with copyright laws by not reproducing, scanning, or distributing any part of it in any form without permission. You are supporting writers and allowing Penguin Random House to continue to publish books for every reader. Please note that no part of this book may be used or reproduced in any manner for the purpose of training artificial intelligence technologies or systems.

BALLANTINE BOOKS & colophon are registered trademarks of Penguin Random House LLC.

Originally published in the United Kingdom by Jonathan Cape,
an imprint of Penguin Random House UK, London.

Hardcover ISBN 978-1-101-96675-4
Ebook ISBN 978-1-101-96676-1

Printed in the United States of America

1st Printing

First US Edition

BOOK TEAM: Production editor: Luke Epplin • Managing editor: Pamela Alders • Production manager: Sarah Feightner • Proofreaders: Barb Jatkola, Pam Feinstein, Deb Bader

Book design by Caroline Cunningham after Virginia Norey's original design

The authorized representative in the EU for product safety and compliance is Penguin Random House Ireland, Morrison Chambers, 32 Nassau Street, Dublin D02 YH68, Ireland. https://eu-contact.penguin.ie

*This book is dedicated, with all my love,
to the cherished memory of my dear husband,
Rankin Alexander Lorimer Weir
(1948–2023)*

Contents

✳

List of Illustrations   xiii

Maps   xvii

Family Trees   xx

Preface   xxiii

Introduction   xxvii

Part One: Joan of Navarre, Queen of Henry IV

1 "Mutual affection and delight"   3
2 "This blessed sacrament of marriage"   15
3 "His beloved consort"   22
4 "Cruelly tormented"   29
5 "A woman of great prudence and judgment"   36

Part Two: Katherine of Valois, Queen of Henry V

1 "Your fair and noble daughter"   43
2 "Our dearest and best-beloved son"   48
3 "The superstitious deeds of necromancers"   54
4 "My dear Englishman"   60
5 "His bed of pain"   69
6 "That godly, faithful, true Princess"   75

    7 "Following more her own appetite"   85

    8 "I did kiss a queen"   91

    9 "A king greatly degenerated from his father"   98

Part Three: Margaret of Anjou, Queen of Henry VI

    1 "The magnificent and very bright Margaret"   107

    2 "A queen not worth ten marks"   116

    3 "Of stomach and courage more like to a man"   123

    4 "The solicitation and exhortation of the Queen"   132

    5 "A harvest of heads"   144

    6 "In the hands of a woman"   150

    7 "A sudden and thoughtless fright"   155

    8 "An infirmity of mind"   161

    9 "Wars of the Roses"   169

   10 "By fair means or foul"   174

   11 "A great and strong labor'd woman"   181

   12 "A dolt and a fool"   192

   13 "Madam, your war is done"   200

   14 "Captain Margaret"   207

   15 "Great slaughter"   217

   16 "Traitors and rebels"   222

   17 "The handsomest prince my eyes ever beheld"   226

   18 "I will either conquer or be conquered"   232

   19 "Dire vicissitude"   241

Part Four: Elizabeth Widville, Queen of Edward IV

    1 "Now take heed what love may do"   255

    2 "Governed by lust"   260

    3 "The Rivers run so high"   268

    4 "Very great division"   277

    5 "Secret displeasure"   284

6	"A most deadly hatred" 290
7	"The marriage of the Queen of England and the Earl of Warwick" 300
8	"Forsaken of all her friends" 311
9	"My cousin of York, you are very welcome" 317
10	"The last hope of thy race" 326
11	"He has, in short, chosen to crush the seed" 334
12	"More like a death than a life" 342
13	"Privy pleasures" 348

PART FIVE: ANNE NEVILLE, QUEEN OF RICHARD III

1	"Violent dissensions" 355
2	"The world seemeth queasy" 363
3	"A rondolet of Malmsey" 370
4	"An unknown disease" 377
5	"Demanding rather than supplicating" 381
6	"The present danger" 389
7	"Seditious and disgraceful proceedings" 397
8	"God save King Richard!" 405
9	"Assemblies and confederacies" 411
10	"The rightful inheritor" 419
11	"On the word of a king" 424
12	"An incestuous passion" 431
13	"A burden to her husband" 439

Afterword: "Without any worldly pomp"   443

Epilogue   461

Appendix: Notes on Some of the Chief Sources   465

Select Bibliography   475

Sources of Quotes in the Text   501

Index   511

List of Illustrations

✴

While every effort has been made to trace copyright holders, if any have been inadvertently overlooked the publishers would be happy to acknowledge them in future editions.

Church roof boss depicting Joan of Navarre. (St. Andrew's Church in Sampford Courtenay © Lionel Wall, greatenglishchurches.co.uk)

Joan's father, Charles II "the Bad," King of Navarre. (© Bibliothèque Nationale de France)

Joan of Navarre with her first husband, John IV, Duke of Brittany, and their children. (© Princeton University Library, Department of Rare Books and Special Collections, Manuscript. Garrett MS 40)

Historiated initial "H"(enry) of Henry IV, with a full foliate border, at the beginning of his Statutes. (Yates Thompson 48, folio 147 © British Library archive/Bridgeman Images)

An imaginary portrait of King Henry IV. (Anglesey Abbey, National Trust © National Trust Photographic Library/Bridgeman Images)

The coronation of Joan of Navarre, wife of King Henry IV of England, 26 January 1403, *c.*1483 (ink on vellum). (Pageant IV from Cotton Julius E. IV, art. 6, from the "Beauchamp Pageant" © British Library archive/Bridgeman Images)

Pevensey Castle, where Joan was imprisoned for witchcraft. (© john/Alamy Stock Photo)

Leeds Castle, owned by several medieval queens of England. (© Ian G Dagnall/Alamy Stock Photo)

Tomb of Henry IV and Joan of Navarre. (Canterbury Cathedral © Angelo Hornak/Alamy Stock Photo)

Tomb effigy of Charles VI, King of France. (Basilica of Saint-Denis, fifteenth century © Photo Josse/Bridgeman Images)

Tomb effigy of Isabeau of Bavaria, Queen of France. (Basilica of Saint-Denis © Bridgeman Images)

Portrait of Henry V (oil on panel). (National Portrait Gallery © Bridgeman Images)

The marriage of King Henry V of England and Katherine of Valois. (British Library Royal MS. 20 E. VI folio 9v © British Library archive/Bridgeman Images)

Katherine of Valois, Queen to Henry V, giving birth to Henry VI at Windsor. (© Smith Archive/Alamy Stock Photo)

Statue of King Henry V. (Part of the Kings Screen inside the historic York Minster in York, England, on 19 July 2017 © Chris Dorney/Alamy Stock Photo)

Bermondsey Abbey, where Katherine of Valois died. (*The History of London* by Walter Besant, New York, Harper & Brothers, 1892 © The Library of Congress)

Katherine of Valois, funeral effigy. (Westminster Abbey © Dean and Chapter of Westminster)

The tomb of Katherine of Valois. (Westminster Abbey © Dean and Chapter of Westminster)

Portrait of King René of Anjou (1409–80), also called René I of Naples or René of Sicily, 1475 (oil on canvas). (Detail of triptych, Cathédrale Saint-Sauveur, Aix-en-Provence © Photo Josse/Bridgeman Images)

Margaret of Anjou, medal by Pietro da Milano, 1463. (Victoria and Albert Museum © Jimlop collection/Alamy Stock Photo)

King Henry VI. (National Portrait Gallery © CBW/Alamy Stock Photo)

The ruins of Titchfield Abbey, Hampshire, where Henry VI married Margaret of Anjou. (© Kevin Allen/Alamy Stock Photo)

The marriage of Henry VI and Margaret of Anjou. (Illuminated manuscript entitled "Mariage d'Henri VI et de Marguerite d'Anjou"

List of Illustrations

c.1484, Bibliotèque Nationale, Paris, MS. Français 5054, folio 126v © IanDagnall Computing/Alamy Stock Photo)

Margaret of Anjou, drawing of lost window in the church of the Cordeliers, Angers. (Bibliothèque Nationale de France as part of the collection of Roger de Gaignières, who assembled a large collection of drawings of monuments nationwide during the late seventeenth and early eighteenth centuries. The drawings of the Gaignières collection were published in 1729–33 in *Les Monuments de la Monarchie Françoise* by Bernard de Montfaucon, Volume 3, Plate LXIII © Photo Vault/Alamy Stock Photo)

John Talbot, Earl of Shrewsbury, presenting the Talbot Shrewsbury Book to Henry VI and Margaret of Anjou. (Illustration from "Shrewsbury Talbot Book of Romances," c.1445, ink, color, and gold on vellum, British Library Royal MS. 15 E. VI, folio 2v © British Library archive/Bridgeman Images)

The prayer roll of Margaret of Anjou. (Bodleian Library, Jesus College, Oxford MS. 124 © Jesus College, Oxford)

The château of Amboise, where Margaret of Anjou was reconciled to Warwick, and Anne Neville married Edward of Lancaster. (Loire Valley, Touraine, France © Ian G Dagnall/Alamy Stock Photo)

Margaret of Anjou, from the Roll of the Fraternity of Our Lady, of the Skinners Company of London. (From *Some Account of the Worshipful Company of Skinners of London,* by James Foster Wadmore, 1902 © by kind permission of the Worshipful Company of Skinners)

Elizabeth Widville (c.1437–92). (Portrait in oil on panel, Queens' College, Cambridge © incamerastock/Alamy Stock Photo)

Edward IV. (© With the kind permission of the Master and Fellows of Corpus Christi College, Cambridge)

The marriage of Edward IV and Elizabeth Widville. (Illuminated manuscript page from Volume 6 of the *Anciennes chroniques d'Angleterre* by Jean de Waurin, Bibliothèque Nationale, Paris, MS. Français 85, folio 215 © The Picture Art Collection/Alamy Stock Photo)

Elizabeth Widville, from the guild book of the London Skinners' Fraternity, of the Assumption of the Virgin. (Guildhall Library MS. 31692 © Bridgeman Images)

Frontispiece of the Luton Guild Book showing the Holy Trinity, the founders of the Guild, and Edward IV and Elizabeth Widville. (From the frontispiece of the Luton Guild Register, Wardown Park Museum © Courtesy of the Culture Trust)

King Edward IV of England (1461–83), and Queen Elizabeth Widville. (Royal Window, Northwest Transept, Canterbury Cathedral © GRANGER—Historical Picture Archive/Alamy Stock Photo)

Anne Neville and her two husbands, Edward of Lancaster, Prince of Wales, and Richard III; and Edward of Middleham, Prince of Wales. (Cotton Julius E. IV, art. 6, folio 28, Descendants of Countess Anne of Warwick, from the "Beauchamp Pageant," *c.*1483 [ink on vellum] © British Library archive/Bridgeman Images)

Anne Neville, Richard III, and their son, Edward of Middleham. (Section of the "Rous Rolls," an illustrated armorial roll-chronicle by John Rous, British Library, Additional MS. 48976, folios 62–65 © World History Archive/Alamy Stock Photo)

Portrait of King Richard III (Oil on panel, National Portrait Gallery © Bridgeman Images)

Elizabeth of York. (East window at Little Malvern Priory, Worcs, 1480s, depicting King Edward IV and Elizabeth Widville © G. P. Essex/Alamy Stock Photo)

King Henry VII (1457–1509). (Hardwick Hall © National Trust Images)

The tomb of Edward IV and Elizabeth Widville in St. George's Chapel, Windsor. (© By permission of the Dean and Canons of Windsor)

Britain

SCOTLAND
- Falkland
- Dunfermline
- Linlithgow
- Edinburgh
- Dunstanburgh
- Alnwick
- Warkworth
- Dumfries
- Lincluden
- Kirkudbright
- Wark
- Hexham
- Newcastle
- Durham
- Barnard Castle

Solway Firth

Irish Sea

North Sea

- Middleham
- Sheriff Hutton
- York
- Towton
- Wakefield
- Sandal
- Doncaster
- Ravenspur

ENGLAND
- Penmynydd
- *ANGLESEY*
- Denbigh
- Chester
- Sheen
- Lincoln
- Harlech
- Eccleshall
- Tutbury
- Shrewsbury
- Nottingham
- Walsingham
- King's Lynn
- Norwich
- Leicester
- Bosworth
- Groby
- Stamford
- Fotheringhay

Trent

WALES
- Brecon
- Carmarthen
- Abergavenny
- Raglan
- Chepstow
- Pembroke
- Hereford
- Gupshill
- Tewkesbury
- Worcester
- Coventry
- Kenilworth
- Warwick
- Northampton
- Cambridge
- Bury St. Edmunds
- Stony Stratford
- Berkhamsted
- Ware
- Pleshey
- St. Albans
- Hertford
- Barnet
- Havering
- Ewelme
- Eton
- **London**
- Blackheath
- Wallingford
- Windsor
- Bristol
- Bath
- Reading
- Bermondsey
- Rochester
- Sandwich
- Eltham
- Leeds
- Canterbury
- Greenwich
- Maidstone
- Ightham
- Dover
- Heytesbury
- Winchester
- Cerne
- Southampton
- Titchfield
- Pevensey
- Exeter
- Portsmouth
- Plymouth
- Dartmouth

Severn

River Thames

English Channel

0 — 50 — 100 miles
0 — 50 — 100 — 150 km

France and the Low Countries

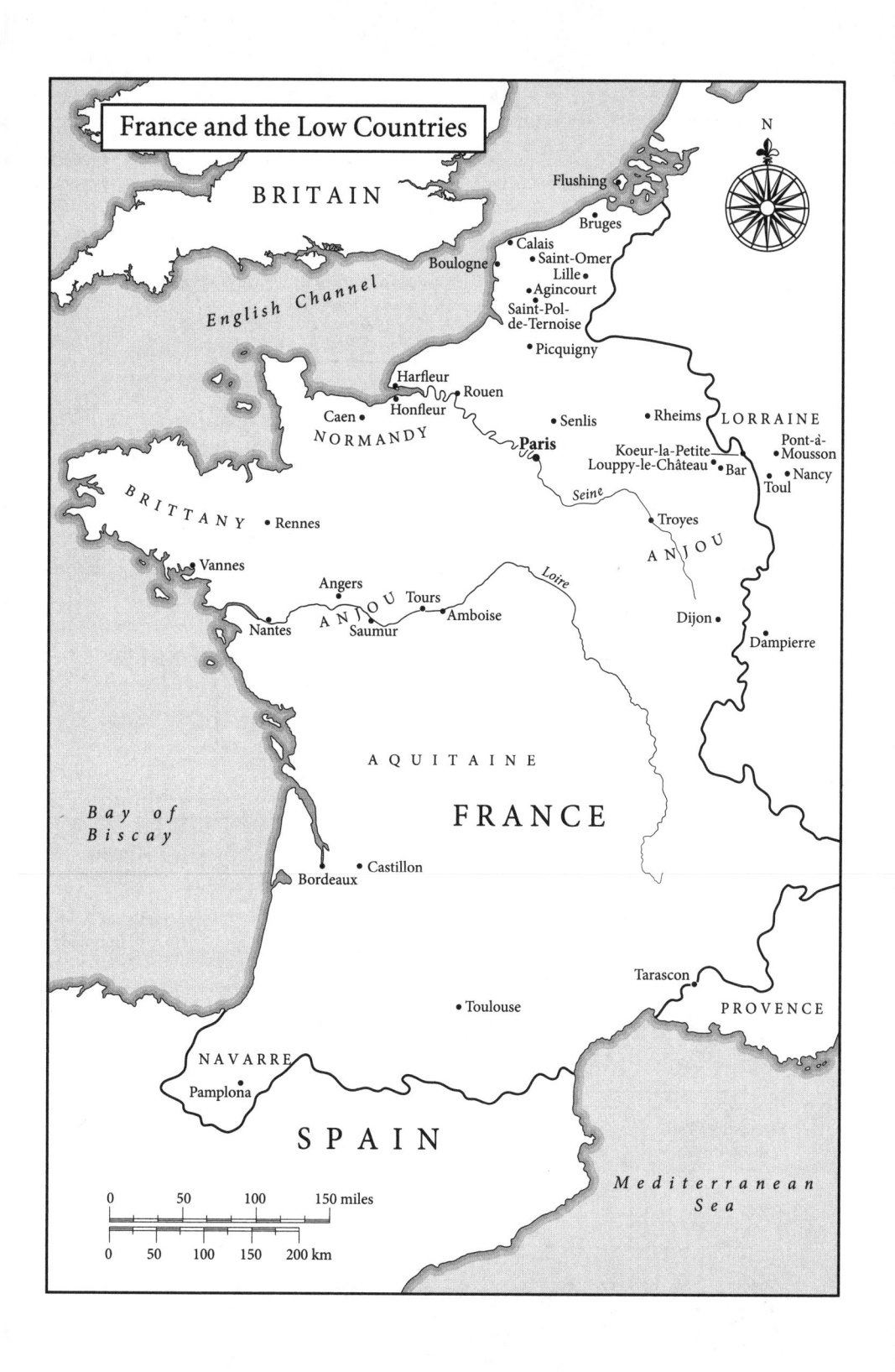

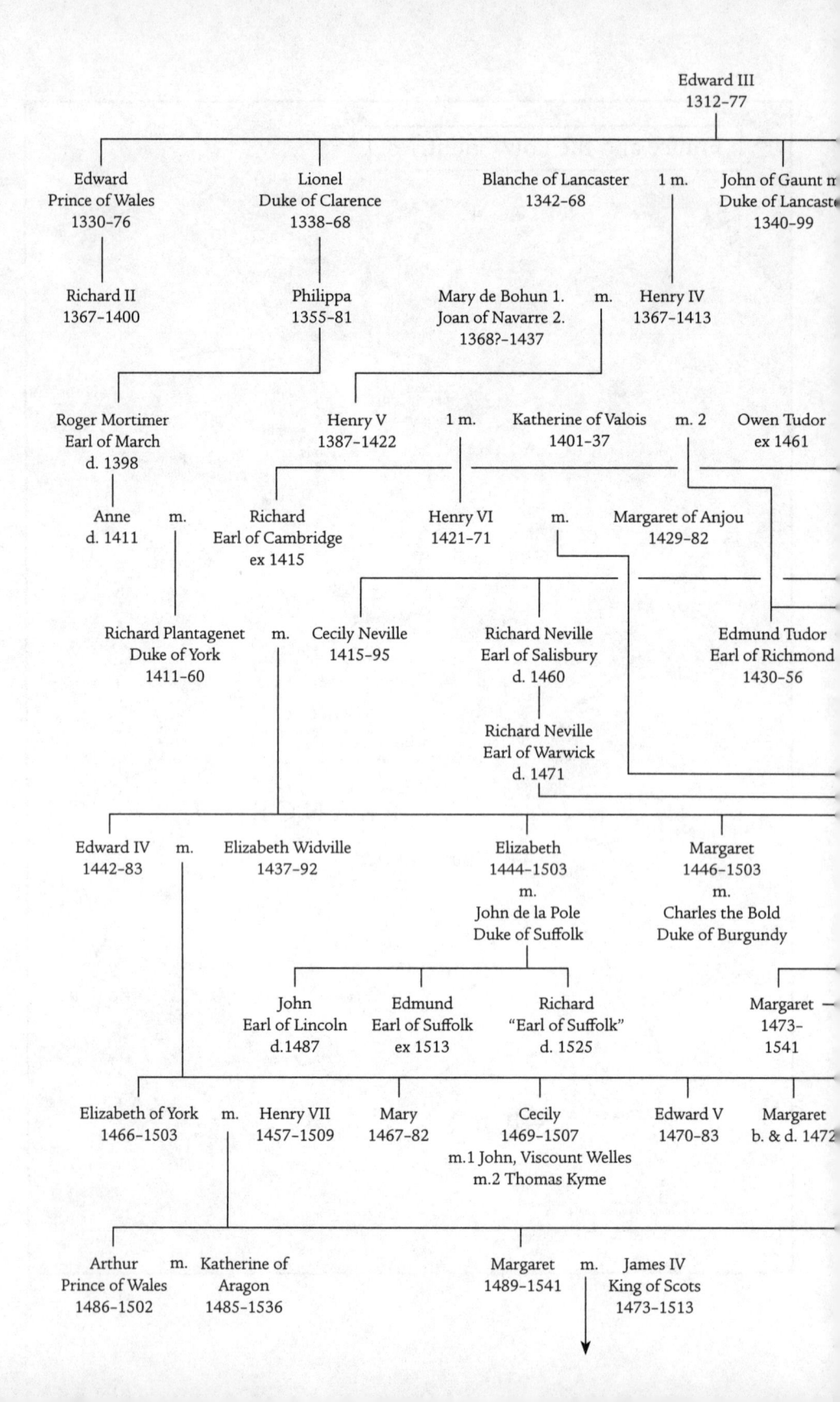

```
                                                                Edward III
                                                                  1312-77
         ┌────────────────┬──────────────────────────────────────────┬────────────────────┐
     Edward              Lionel              Blanche of Lancaster  1 m.   John of Gaunt m.
 Prince of Wales     Duke of Clarence            1342-68                  Duke of Lancaster
    1330-76              1338-68                                              1340-99
       │                    │                        │
   Richard II           Philippa         Mary de Bohun 1.  m.   Henry IV
    1367-1400           1355-81          Joan of Navarre 2.     1367-1413
                          │              1368?-1437
   ┌──────────────────────┴─────┐                     │
 Roger Mortimer              Henry V      1 m.   Katherine of Valois   m. 2   Owen Tudor
  Earl of March             1387-1422              1401-37                      ex 1461
    d. 1398
       │
    Anne      m.    Richard               Henry VI       m.    Margaret of Anjou
   d. 1411       Earl of Cambridge        1421-71                 1429-82
                    ex 1415
       │
 Richard Plantagenet  m.   Cecily Neville    Richard Neville              Edmund Tudor
   Duke of York             1415-95          Earl of Salisbury            Earl of Richmond
    1411-60                                      d. 1460                     1430-56
                                                    │
                                              Richard Neville
                                              Earl of Warwick
                                                  d. 1471

 ┌──────────┬──────────────────────┬──────────────────────────┬──────────────────┐
 Edward IV   m.   Elizabeth Widville        Elizabeth               Margaret
  1442-83          1437-92                   1444-1503              1446-1503
                                                m.                     m.
                                           John de la Pole      Charles the Bold
                                           Duke of Suffolk      Duke of Burgundy
                              ┌─────────────────┼───────────────┐
                            John           Edmund          Richard            Margaret
                        Earl of Lincoln  Earl of Suffolk  "Earl of Suffolk"   1473-
                            d.1487         ex 1513           d. 1525          1541

 ┌───────────────┬──────────────┬────────────┬────────────┬──────────┐
 Elizabeth of York  m.  Henry VII    Mary        Cecily       Edward V    Margaret
    1466-1503           1457-1509  1467-82     1469-1507      1470-83    b. & d. 1472
                                           m.1 John, Viscount Welles
                                           m.2 Thomas Kyme

 ┌──────────────────────────────┬──────────────┐
 Arthur       m.   Katherine of         Margaret    m.   James IV
 Prince of Wales    Aragon               1489-1541      King of Scots
   1486-1502       1485-1536                              1473-1513
                                              │
                                              ↓
```

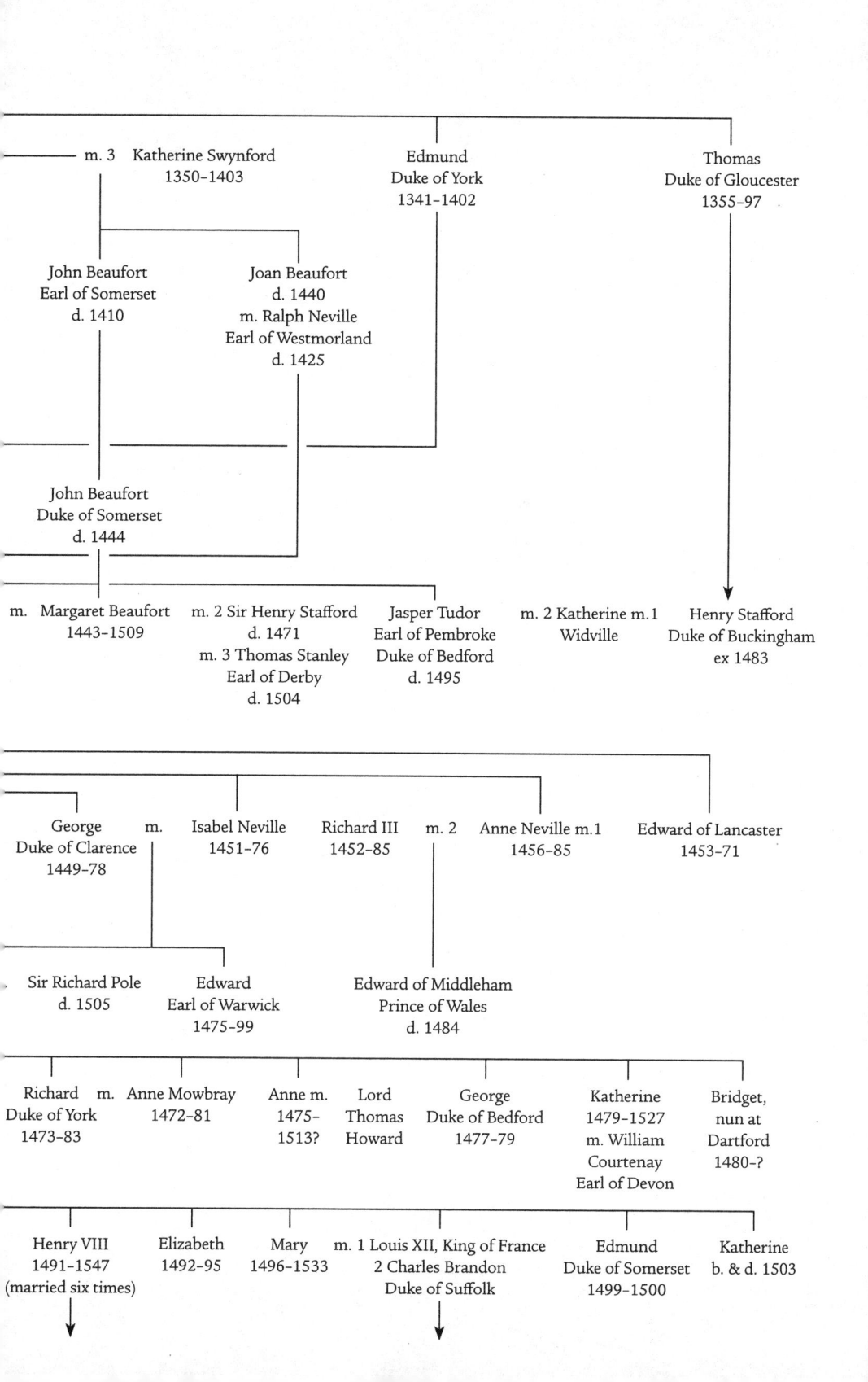

		m. 3	Katherine Swynford 1350-1403		Edmund Duke of York 1341-1402		Thomas Duke of Gloucester 1355-97

John Beaufort
Earl of Somerset
d. 1410

Joan Beaufort
d. 1440
m. Ralph Neville
Earl of Westmorland
d. 1425

John Beaufort
Duke of Somerset
d. 1444

m. Margaret Beaufort
1443-1509

m. 2 Sir Henry Stafford
d. 1471
m. 3 Thomas Stanley
Earl of Derby
d. 1504

Jasper Tudor
Earl of Pembroke
Duke of Bedford
d. 1495

m. 2 Katherine
Widville

m. 1 Henry Stafford
Duke of Buckingham
ex 1483

George
Duke of Clarence
1449-78

m. Isabel Neville
1451-76

Richard III
1452-85

m. 2 Anne Neville m. 1
1456-85

Edward of Lancaster
1453-71

Sir Richard Pole
d. 1505

Edward
Earl of Warwick
1475-99

Edward of Middleham
Prince of Wales
d. 1484

Richard
Duke of York
1473-83

m. Anne Mowbray
1472-81

Anne
1475-1513?

m. Lord Thomas Howard

George
Duke of Bedford
1477-79

Katherine
1479-1527
m. William Courtenay
Earl of Devon

Bridget,
nun at Dartford
1480-?

Henry VIII
1491-1547
(married six times)

Elizabeth
1492-95

Mary
1496-1533

m. 1 Louis XII, King of France
2 Charles Brandon
Duke of Suffolk

Edmund
Duke of Somerset
1499-1500

Katherine
b. & d. 1503

Preface

✳

On 13 October 1399, the coronation of Henry IV, first sovereign of the House of Lancaster, took place at Westminster. His accession heralded almost a century of dynastic conflict, for up to 1485 and beyond, as will be related in this book, the English crown was to be the object of feuds, wars, and conspiracies—not because of a dearth of heirs, but because there were too many powerful magnates with a claim to the throne. During this period, might would largely prevail over right in determining who should be king. Alliances were made and broken, or shifted bewilderingly in the wake of events. Strength and success were what counted: an effective ruler was more likely to hold on to the throne and bring stable government, however dubious his title.

English queenship did not change significantly during this period; consorts were still expected to produce heirs, exercise charity and patronage, play a ceremonial role, and be the very mirror of the Virgin Mary: virtuous, submissive, yet regal. Nevertheless, England's queens would be caught up in the dynastic conflicts and wars. The fifteenth century was a turbulent age that witnessed the latter stages of the Hundred Years War between England and France and the English civil wars between the royal houses of Lancaster and York, known as the Wars of the Roses, which dragged on intermittently from 1455 to 1487.

Since the Norman Conquest of 1066, English kings had chosen brides from European royal and noble houses in the interests of forging dynastic connections and political alliances. But the fifteenth century was to witness a radical change in that respect, for in 1464, Edward IV married Elizabeth Widville for love, which scandalized his subjects because it brought no material benefits, while Richard III wed an heiress from the English nobility, although he did gain a great landed inheritance.

Each of the five queen consorts who lived in this period was involved in one way or another in the Hundred Years War or the Wars of the Roses. The marriage of Joan of Navarre to Henry IV was meant to give England an advantage against France; those of Katherine of Valois, to Henry V, and Margaret of Anjou, to Henry VI, were supposed to bring about a peace, while Margaret of Anjou, Elizabeth Widville, and Anne Neville were all deeply involved in the Wars of the Roses. It was a perilous time for queens, and all, in one way or another, were overtaken by tragedy.

The sources for the period are rich and give more insights into the personal lives and personalities of these women than those written in earlier centuries. Yet good as the sources are, they lack the personal detail of those documenting, for example, the wives of Henry VIII, in the 1530s, so my approach to the book, as in earlier volumes, is to focus on what information we do have and infer what I can from that, which means that the narrative may not always be chronological.

Aside from Edward IV marrying for love, there is good evidence that the marriages of all the Lancastrian monarchs, Henry IV, Henry V, and Henry VI, were love matches too, even if they were contracted for political reasons. We know too little about the marriage of Richard III and Anne Neville to draw many conclusions, yet there are pointers to its being the least successful of the royal marriages in this period.

Her fierce loyalty to the weak Henry VI drove Margaret of Anjou to be fiercely proactive in the Lancastrian cause and to fight for her son's rights, but she was criticized and slandered for her unfeminine assumption of leadership, and Edward IV thought her more a threat than any Lancastrian general, while Shakespeare later called her a "she-wolf." Elizabeth Widville wielded considerable power as Queen, but was ruthlessly deprived of any influence when Edward died. Foreign-born consorts were at a disadvantage from the outset because the insular English had long memories of extravagant queens who had brought no dowry or secured the aggrandizement of greedy kinsfolk; with the exception of

Katherine of Valois and, perhaps, Anne Neville, none of these queens was very popular, and most suffered some disparagement of their reputations, creating a mythology that has sometimes endured for centuries.

I should like to acknowledge the fantastic support and creative input that I have received from my brilliant editor, Anthony Whittome, my commissioning editors, Bea Hemming and Susanna Porter, and the amazing publishing teams at Jonathan Cape in the United Kingdom and Ballantine in the United States. Huge thanks also go to Lucy Chaudhuri of Cape, for managing the publication process; Mary Chamberlain, for the copyedit; Louise Navarro-Cann, for sourcing the many images I asked for; and Jessica Spivey, for publicity.

I wish also to express my warmest thanks and appreciation to my agents, Julian Alexander, Ben Clark, Abby Koons, and Sarah Stamp. You're the best, and I feel very privileged as an author to have such a great team behind me.

Lastly, but never least, I am indebted to my family and friends for all their love and support, especially my daughter, Kate, and her husband, Jason; my cousin Christine, who has been like a sister to me; my uncle and aunt, John and Joanna Marston; my brother-in-law, Kenneth, and my cousins David and Peter and their families; and Wendy and Brian. You're all stars!

Introduction

✳

IN 1340, HENRY IV'S GRANDFATHER, EDWARD III, HAD LAID claim to the crown of France, asserting that he was the true heir by virtue of descent from his mother, the sister of the last king of the House of Capet. The French held that the Salic law prevented a woman from succeeding to their throne, or transmitting a claim, in consequence of which the House of Valois was now ruling France.

Edward's defiant quartering of the lilies of France with the leopards of England on his coat of arms had led to what later became known as the Hundred Years War. When he died in 1377, all that remained of the territories he had wrested from the French were the duchy of Aquitaine, five towns and the land around Calais known as the Pale.

Edward had provided for his sons by marrying them to English heiresses and creating them dukes. Their descendants would one day challenge each other for the throne itself. The eldest son, Edward of Woodstock, Prince of Wales (known from the sixteenth century as the "Black Prince"), had predeceased his father, and it was his son, Richard II, who succeeded Edward III, but remained childless. Edward's second son, Lionel of Antwerp, Duke of Clarence, had sired one daughter, Philippa, who married Edmund Mortimer, 3rd Earl of March. The House of York would one day claim the throne on the basis of its descent from Edward III through Philippa of Clarence.

Edward III's third surviving son was John of Gaunt, Duke of Lancaster, whose marriage to Blanche, the heiress of Lancaster, made him a fabulously wealthy magnate with vast estates throughout England. Blanche was the mother of his heir, Henry of Bolingbroke, the future Henry IV. After her death in 1368, Lancaster wed Constance of Castile, in an unsuccessful attempt to claim the crown of Castile. When she died in 1394, he married his mistress, Katherine Swynford, who had borne him four bastards, all surnamed Beaufort after a lordship he had once owned in France.

The Beauforts would dominate English politics for the next century. From the eldest, John Beaufort, were descended the Beaufort dukes of Somerset. The only daughter, Joan, was married to the powerful Ralph Neville, 1st Earl of Westmorland, and would become matriarch of the prolific Neville family.

Edward III's fourth surviving son was Edmund of Langley, Duke of York, the founder of the male line of the royal House of York. He fathered two sons: Edward, his heir, who was killed in 1415 in the Battle of Agincourt, and Richard, Earl of Cambridge, who married Anne Mortimer, the great-granddaughter of Lionel of Antwerp, Duke of Clarence.

Edward III's youngest son was Thomas of Woodstock, Duke of Gloucester, whose descendants became the dukes of Buckingham. Gloucester was Henry of Bolingbroke's brother-in-law. At thirteen, Henry had been married to eleven-year-old Mary de Bohun (pronounced Boon), younger daughter and co-heiress of Humphrey de Bohun, Earl of Hereford, Essex, and Northampton. The Bohuns were of ancient Norman stock, one of England's great noble families. Eleanor de Bohun, Mary's elder sister and co-heiress, was married to Gloucester.

Not being content with his share of the Bohun inheritance, Gloucester was determined to lay his hands on the rest, and put relentless pressure on Mary to give it up and take the habit of a Poor Clare nun. But, in July 1380, with the connivance of Lancaster, Mary's aunt kidnapped her while Gloucester was campaigning in France and spirited her away to Arundel Castle in Sussex. That month, Lancaster obtained from Richard II a grant of Mary's marriage, thus thwarting his brother's ambitions. A furious Gloucester "never after loved the Duke as he had hitherto done."[1] By March 1381, Henry and Mary had been married with great ceremony and rejoicing at Rochford Hall in Essex.

Afterward, Mary remained there with her mother, with Lancaster paying for her maintenance; it had been agreed that the consummation of the marriage should be delayed until Mary reached fourteen on 15 February 1382. But the young couple breached this rule and in April 1382, Mary bore a son who lived for four days.

The young couple were finally given their own establishment and began cohabiting in November 1385. On 16 September 1386, at Monmouth Castle, Mary gave birth to the future Henry V. Thomas followed in 1387, John in 1389, Humphrey in 1390, and Blanche in 1392. The marriage appears to have been happy, with the couple sharing a love of chess, dogs, parrots, and music. Mary, who came from a cultivated family, played the harp and cithar, Henry the recorder. His faithfulness to her was commented on throughout the courts of Europe, and he was assiduous in sending gifts of food to satisfy her cravings during pregnancy.

Mary de Bohun did not survive the birth of her last child, Philippa, in 1394, and Henry sincerely mourned her death.

By then, a deadly enmity had flared between Henry and Richard II. Alienated by the King's high-handed misgovernment and his unpopular favorites, Henry had united in opposition with Gloucester and the earls of Arundel, Nottingham, and Warwick. Because they were appealing to Richard to restore good government, they called themselves the "Lords Appellant." In the "Merciless" Parliament of 1388, they had purged the court of favorites and curbed the King's autonomy. Two years later, Richard had wrested the reins of government from the Lords Appellant, and for the next eight years ruled England himself.

In 1396, he signed a truce with France and sealed it by marrying Isabella, the six-year-old daughter of Charles VI. Both peace and marriage were unpopular with his subjects, who would have preferred to see England's claim to France reasserted, but Richard's resources could not support another war.

In the face of vociferous opposition from his magnates, he was anxious to retain Lancaster's loyalty and in 1396, he persuaded Pope Boniface XI to issue a bull confirming the Duke's marriage to Katherine Swynford and legitimizing the Beauforts. In 1397, Richard issued letters patent declaring the Beauforts legitimate under English law, which was afterward confirmed by Act of Parliament.

That year, Richard showed himself determined to be an absolute monarch and rule without Parliament. He ordered the murder of his uncle, Gloucester, then moved against the other former Lords Appellant. When Henry and Nottingham fell out and accused each other of treason, the King ordered that the issue should be settled according to trial by combat, an ancient European custom whereby God was invited to intervene by granting a victory to the righteous party. But, just as the combat was about to begin, the King threw down his baton, halted the proceedings, and sentenced both men to exile. Henry sought refuge in Paris.

Grieved by the exile of his son, Lancaster died in 1399. In Paris, Henry learned that Richard had sequestered the vast estates he should have inherited, and immediately returned to England, burning with a desire for vengeance. In July, he landed in Yorkshire, claiming that he had come to safeguard his inheritance and reform the government. There was a huge tide of popular feeling against Richard, especially in London, where Henry was well liked. As he progressed south, nobles and commons flocked to his banner and he quickly gathered a large army, meeting little resistance. Richard was unable to rouse much support and many of his followers deserted him. At Conwy Castle, he surrendered to a deputation sent by Henry.

In September, Henry entered London to a tumultuous reception, while Richard, a prisoner in his train, was greeted with jeers, pelted from the rooftops with rubbish, and confined in the Tower of London. Henry now appointed a commission to consider who should be king. Many magnates were unhappy at the prospect of his seizing the throne, yet there were reasons enough for setting Richard aside. Henry, it seemed, was the only realistic alternative, for the legitimate heir, the Earl of March, was just a child.

Henry used every means in his power to force Richard to abdicate. Knowing that his own claim was precarious, the official line was to be that Richard's misgovernment justified his deposition. Coercion and threats were used to persuade the King to cooperate and on 29 September 1399, he signed an instrument of abdication, in which he requested that he be succeeded by his cousin of Bolingbroke, who took the crown as Henry IV.

Introduction

* * *

Some believed that Henry IV was a usurper who had gained a crown by deposing England's lawful, anointed sovereign. The legitimacy of his title would remain a sensitive issue. His claim to rule by right of blood was a bald lie, for he had falsely asserted that his ancestor, Edmund Crouchback, Earl of Lancaster, had been the eldest son of Henry III, not the second son, and had been overlooked because of bodily deformity in favor of his "younger" brother, Edward I. This deceived no one. Henry's title really derived from his already being de facto King of England, having taken the throne by force. Yet, his birth, wealth, abilities, and four strapping sons had made him the only viable candidate for the throne, the only man capable of restoring law, order, and firm government.

No one had supported the superior claim of the legitimate heir, the Earl of March. Indeed, Archbishop Arundel took it upon himself to preach a sermon stating that England would from now on be ruled by men, not boys. As a result, the claim of the rightful heirs to the throne would remain dormant for sixty years.

Henry IV soon discovered that it was less easy to hold on to the crown than to usurp it. He had promised to provide good and just government, but the first decade of his reign would be troubled by conspiracies to overthrow him. He did his best to demonstrate that he was ruling with the advice and support of Parliament, sanctioning laws giving it unprecedented powers, establishing the privileges of free debate and the immunity of members from arrest, leaving them free to criticize him as they pleased.

Yet the charisma that had attracted people to his cause, and the heady burst of popularity that had greeted his accession, were not so much in evidence after it, especially when people realized that the evils of Richard's misgovernment could not be put right overnight. Henry might be an industrious man of business and ruthless when it came to dealing with rebels; he might have enjoyed the support of the Church, having authorized the passing of the statute De Heretico Comburendo, which condemned heretics to be burned to death. But the distrust of various magnates and a permanent shortage of money, exacerbated by the cost of putting down rebellions, were problems he could not surmount; consequently, his reign was a time of continual tension.

In France, the government of the mad Charles VI steadfastly refused to recognize Henry as King, denouncing him as a traitor to his lawful sovereign and referring to him, when addressing English envoys, as "the lord who sent you." This would lead, in 1401, to the resumption of the Hundred Years War. The Valois court was at that time riven by opposing factions led by Charles VI's powerful relatives, the dukes of Burgundy and Orléans, whose followers were called Burgundians and Armagnacs. Henry became adept at playing these two nobles off against each other, but little military action was seen in France during his reign.

Parliament had condemned the former King Richard to perpetual imprisonment in a secret place from which no one could rescue him, and he was taken north to Pontefract Castle. The order for his murder was probably sent there in January 1400. The chronicler Adam of Usk stated that death came miserably to the former King as "he lay in chains in the castle of Pontefract, tormented with starving fare."

By the spring of 1400, Henry IV may have felt more secure on his throne, but he was shortly to be disabused of that comfortable illusion. Impersonations of his dead rival were not all that he had to contend with. Shakespeare called the first decade of his reign "a scrambling and unquiet time" because it witnessed a series of rebellions. In Wales, Owen Glendower, a descendant of the princes of Powys, inspired the Welsh people to revolt against English rule. Then hostilities erupted between the King and the Percy family, who were a great power in the North. This was the situation when Henry decided to take a second wife.

PART ONE

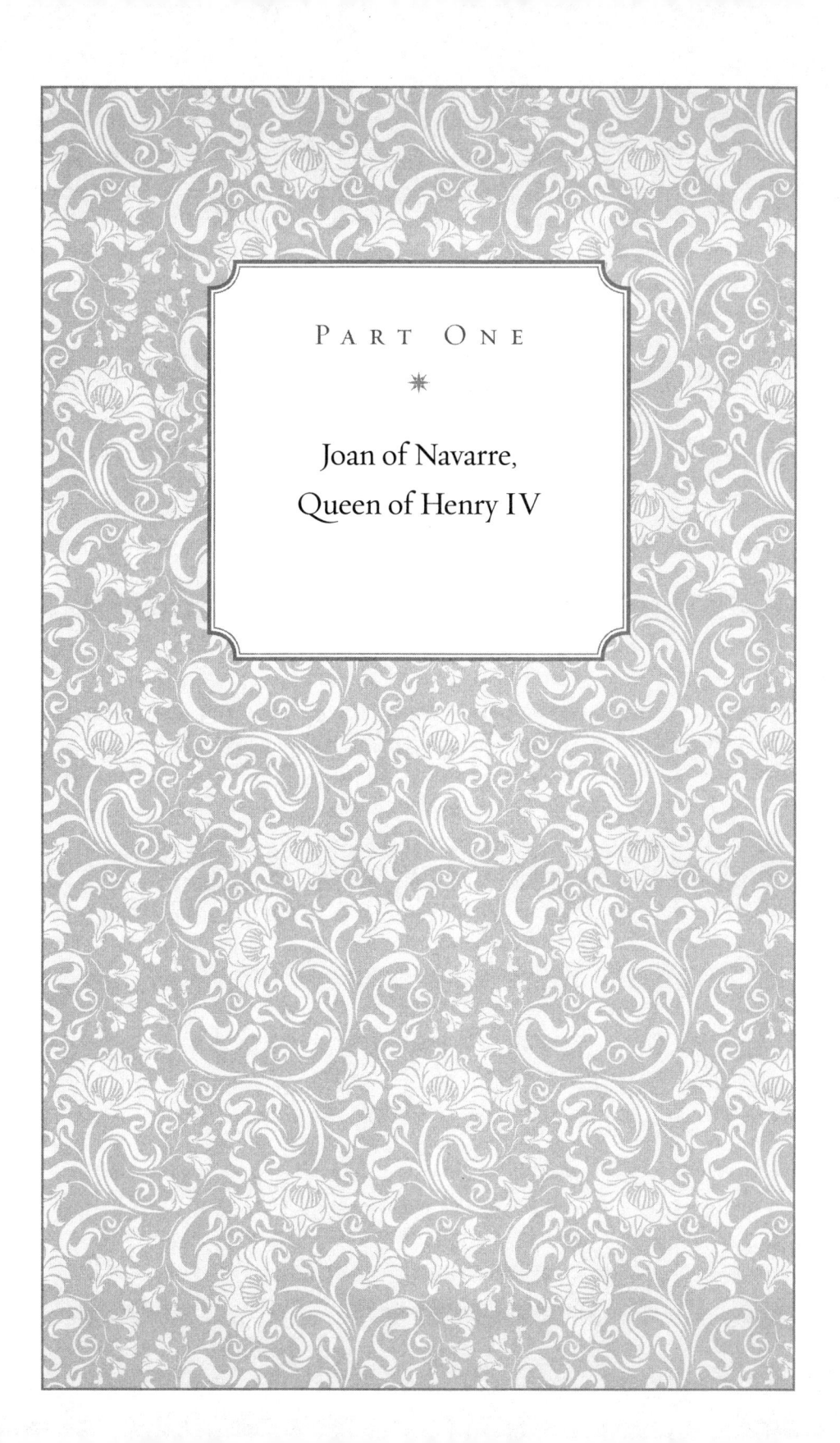

✺

Joan of Navarre,
Queen of Henry IV

I

"Mutual affection and delight"

✳

THE STORY OF FIFTEENTH-CENTURY ENGLISH QUEENSHIP began in February 1400, when Joan of Navarre, Dowager Duchess of Brittany, was residing at De La Motte, her château at Vannes, and received a proposal of marriage from Henry IV.

Henry had then been a widower for six years. In Paris, he had considered marrying Lucia, daughter of Gian Galeazzo Visconti, Duke of Milan, or Marie, Countess of Eu, a niece of Charles VI, but Richard II had scuppered those plans. Now, as King, Henry needed a great marriage alliance with political advantages, and he saw Joan as the ideal choice. He was hoping for an ally against Charles VI. Brittany seemed ideal, as it enjoyed virtual independence from France, while owing fealty to its King, and dynastic blood ties between Brittany and England were close.

A new alliance between England and Brittany would be advantageous in terms of enlisting Breton support against France and encircling that kingdom with Henry's allies, while England could profit from the Breton salt trade. Doubtless the King also had his eye on Joan's rich Breton dower, the financial settlement with which a man endowed his wife on marriage (as opposed to the dowry she brought to him). He believed that her illustrious dynastic connections would benefit him; being a usurper, he was in need of powerful allies and may have felt that marriage with Joan would equate to recognition of his right to rule and his acceptance in European royal circles.

It is possible that they had met in the autumn of 1396 at a royal wedding at Calais, or in England in 1398, or in Brittany in 1399, when Henry was Duke of Lancaster. At thirty-three, he would surely have made an impression on Joan, being a powerfully built man of five foot ten, always richly and elegantly garbed. He was handsome, with a curled mustache, good teeth, deep russet hair, and the short, forked beard fashionable in that period, as was seen when his tomb was opened in 1832. He was well educated and proficient in Latin, French, and English, although, for preference, he spoke Norman French, the traditional language of the English court. A skillful jouster, he loved tournaments and feats of arms, and his reputation as a knight was widespread. Devout and markedly orthodox in his religious views, he had been twice on crusade, first in 1390 with the German Order of Teutonic Knights against Lithuanian pagans in Poland, and then in 1392, to Jerusalem. He loved literature, poetry, and music, and a consort of drummers, trumpeters, and pipers accompanied him wherever he went, while he himself was a musician of note.

Joan might have detected that he was a man of great ability, energetic, tenacious, courageous, and strong. He was popular and respected, having a charismatic personality, being humorous, courteous, even-tempered, generous, reserved, and dignified. People were impressed by his courtesy, chivalry, and affability. He was conventional in outlook, staunch and devout. It may not have been apparent to Joan that he was also ambitious and restless, or that he could be a devious and calculating opportunist. But when the couple met, he was an exile, having been banished from the realm of England by Richard II. Attraction there may have been between the Dowager Duchess and her visitor, but his prospects were then uncertain.

The Infanta Joan of Navarre had already led a somewhat turbulent existence. She was the sixth of the seven children of Charles II "the Bad," King of Navarre. She had been born around 1368–9, probably at Estella, where her mother, Jeanne of Valois, lived from 1368 to 1373. She was exceptionally well connected, being related to most of the ruling families of Europe. Queen Jeanne was the daughter of John II of France, and Joan's grandmother, another Jeanne, who had died in 1349 and had been the daughter of Louis X of France. Having been barred by the Salic law and the adultery of her mother from succeeding to the throne of France, the elder Jeanne had inherited only the small kingdom of Navarre, which bestrode the Pyrenees.

Joan was named for her mother, grandmother, and great-grandmother, all reigning queens of Navarre. Her name is given variously in contemporary sources but has been anglicized here to Joan. Her infancy coincided with an invasion of Navarre by the armies of Castile, and she was placed for safety with her cousin Jeanne de Beaumont in the monastery of Santa Clara at Estella, which had nurtured earlier Navarrese princesses and was now paid a florin a day for a teacher and a servant for the two girls. There, the young Joan grew up and received an elementary education befitting her sex and her rank.

Following the loss of a score of castles, King Charles had to make peace with the invaders. After her mother's death in childbirth in 1373, Joan returned to his court, where she and her sisters were looked after by their aunt, Agnes, Countess of Foix, and saw their father frequently. They kept dogs and birds, ate a lot of fish, meat, and poultry, made offerings on feast days, enjoyed court entertainments, and were provided with new clothes and shoes as they outgrew their old ones. They were given writing materials, indicating that they were literate. They would have enjoyed visiting the King's small menagerie at Pamplona, where he kept lions, a camel, an ostrich, monkeys, and parrots.

Because he was descended from Louis X of France, the turbulent Charles the Bad considered he had a claim to the French throne, which inevitably set him at odds with the Valois kings, especially Charles V, who once claimed that his disreputable brother-in-law had used necromancy to murder him. Joan's childhood was overshadowed by her father's dangerous intrigues and the upheavals they caused, and in 1381, she and her brothers were placed in the castle of Breteuil in Normandy for their protection. But it wasn't secure and, on the orders of the regents of France, their maternal uncles, the dukes of Berri and Burgundy, the children were captured by French soldiers and carried off to Paris, where they were held for five years as hostages for their father's good behavior. The regents looked after them well and they received honorable treatment until their father managed to procure their release in 1386.

In 1384, Berri and Burgundy had proposed a marriage between Joan, then about sixteen, and the widowed, childless John IV de Montfort,

Duke of Brittany, who was a French vassal, but an autonomous ruler. He was forty-six, an irascible man with a long mustache who had strong links to England. He had been brought up at the court of Edward III, whose daughter Mary had been his first wife; his second was Joan Holland, half-sister to Richard II. Edward III had made John a Knight of the Garter, and he was then also Earl of Richmond, his family having held the title since the thirteenth century. But there had been a coolness between John IV and Richard II since Brittany had made peace with France in 1381 and Richard had confiscated the earldom. John, however, was now inclining toward England again. Charles the Bad was eager to secure him as a husband for Joan because he needed allies against France, and Duke John was eager for the match because he desperately wanted an heir; if he failed to produce one, his duchy would pass to his dynastic rival and enemy, the Count of Penthièvre. Marriage to Joan might also bring about a rapprochement with her French relatives. John was so eager for the match that in November 1384, he entered into negotiations immediately after his second wife's death.

Joan's marriage was agreed upon in May 1386. Viscount and Viscountess de Rohan, her beloved paternal aunt and uncle, were instrumental in arranging the alliance, for which Joan was enduringly grateful. Years later, as a widow, she rewarded her aunt Jeanne with a pension of £1,000 (£936,380) "in remuneration of the good pains and diligence she used to procure our marriage with our very dear and beloved lord, whom God assoil, of which marriage it has pleased our Lord and Savior that we should continue a noble line, to the great profit of the county of Bretagne and our other children, sons and daughters. And for this, it was the will and pleasure of our said very dear and beloved lord, if he had had a longer life, to have bestowed many gifts and benefits on our said aunt, to aid her in her sustenance and provision."[1] On 27 July, the marriage contract was signed at Pamplona. Under its terms, Charles the Bad promised an extravagant dowry of 120,000 gold livres (£73:5 million) in French coinage and 6,000 livres (£3:7 million) from rents due to him.

We have no record of Joan's meeting with her future husband. She and John were married on 11 September 1386, in the chapel at Saillé, on the salt marshes near Guérande, Brittany. A host of Breton nobles attended the ceremony. The wedding party then traveled to Nantes for the feasts and pageants that had been arranged in their honor.

"Mutual affection and delight"

Joan's dowry was never paid in full. Her father, who had made superhuman efforts to raise just under 47,000 livres (£28:8 million) of it, was suffering a decline in health that caused paralysis in all his limbs, but seems not to have affected his propensity to make trouble. In December, from his sickbed at Pamplona, he dropped hints to Duke John that a powerful Breton warlord, Oliver de Clisson, who supported the House of Penthièvre, had conceived a criminal passion for Joan. John and the one-eyed Clisson had once been friends but had recently fallen out after Clisson intrigued with the Duke's enemies and made an unsuccessful attempt to invade England on behalf of the French. Fearing that Clisson was plotting to abduct Joan, John wrote a friendly letter inviting him to attend a parliament at Vannes, where the young Duchess would be holding court at her château of De La Motte.

Meanwhile, King Charles's condition had deteriorated to the point where his doctor had felt bound to wrap him from neck to foot in linen cloth impregnated with brandy or aqua vitae. According to one source, the woman ordered to sew up the cloth knotted it at the top, but rather than cutting off the thread with scissors, she used a candle, which ignited the alcohol. Another contemporary, the chronicler Jean Froissart, stated that a brazier of coals was used to warm the bed and, "by the pleasure of God, or of the devil, the fire caught to his sheets, and from that to his person, swathed as it was in matter highly inflammable, and the King was horribly burnt as far as his navel." The fire was doused, but Charles lingered in agony for a fortnight before dying on 1 January 1387.

Some had seen his decay as a punishment for his dissolute life, but there was shock throughout Christendom at his horrific death. The Bretons, however, rejoiced that the world had been delivered from such a monster.

John's suspicions of Clisson did not extend to Joan. Despite his being known as the most irascible prince in Europe, he and his bride were delighted with each other. In February 1387, "in token of their mutual affection and delight in their union, the Duke and Duchess exchanged gifts of gold, sapphires, pearls and other costly gems, with horses, falcons and various sorts of wines."[2] A child was quickly conceived, the first of nine children. In 1395, John would enlarge Joan's dower handsomely.

Despite having had to fight off rival claimants to his duchy, John IV had brought peace to Brittany and made it prosperous. He favored friendship with England over an alliance with France, which sometimes brought him into conflict with Charles VI and the French duke, who had been hoping for his support, not to mention powerful opponents like Oliver de Clisson. In consequence, Joan would soon suffer further upheavals in her life.

Unaware of the insinuations made by Charles the Bad, Oliver de Clisson arrived at Vannes and was warmly welcomed by the Duke and the heavily pregnant Duchess. John invited him to view the massive new château of l'Hermine, which he had rebuilt for Joan on the city's ramparts. But when Clisson arrived there on 27 June, he was suddenly arrested, imprisoned in chains, and condemned to death. The Duke ordered that he be sewn into a sack and thrown in the river.

When his jailer refused to comply, John relented and kept Clisson in prison, demanding a large ransom. The following year, the French King bought his freedom and Clisson fled to France, where he very loudly complained about the way he had been treated, and was later made Constable of France. The French believed that Joan had been behind a plot to get rid of him, yet there is no evidence to support that. In fact, she and the Duke were clearly unnerved by the affair because they shut themselves up at De La Motte, fearing a retaliatory ambush, and it was some time before they again ventured beyond Vannes.

Joan saw her marriage as a noble alliance and believed it to be the will of God that "we should continue a noble line, to the great profit of the county of Bretagne."[3] Her eldest child, another Joan, was born on 12 August 1387 at Nantes, after the furor over Clisson had quietened. Isabella arrived in October 1388, in the midst of more political turmoil, but both she and her sister died in December that year. By then, on the advice of his council, John had reluctantly made peace with France and gone there to pay homage to Charles VI.

When Joan was nearing her time with her third pregnancy, she took up residence at the château of l'Hermine. Her palatial apartments were on the second floor of the central donjon, and included a bedchamber and two rooms for steam-bathing; a staircase ascended to John IV's suite above. The Breton council, concerned about potential threats from France or Oliver de Clisson, warned the Duke: "Your lady is now far advanced in her pregnancy and you should pay attention that she be not alarmed." But all went well and Joan gave birth to her first son on 24 December 1389, which "made the Duke very happy."[4] The baby was initially going to be called Peter, after Joan's brother, but the Duke had him christened John after himself. In tribute to Joan, he created the Order of the Hermine in her honor and made her its first member.

In 1390, relations with France again became strained. Toward the end of 1391, Joan's kinsman, John, Duke of Berri, visited Nantes at the behest of Charles VI to broker a peace between Duke John and his enemies, Oliver de Clisson and the House of Penthièvre. Attended by "a large cortège of illustrious ladies," Joan "graciously welcomed her beloved uncle and gave him the kiss of peace," telling him how much she welcomed his coming.[5] She plied him with rich gifts and laid on entertainments. But Berri's tactless, heavy-handed approach to the peace talks offended Duke John, who was about to pull out and hold the French envoys hostage when Joan's brother Peter, Count of Mortmain, arrived at Nantes. Alarmed, he sought out the Duchess, who was again pregnant, and found her being washed by her attendants. She agreed to dissuade the Duke, being inclined—as King Charles's cousin—to favor the French. "Setting aside her modesty," she "took her children in her arms, in spite of the encumbrance at the end of her term," and, wearing her nightgown, with her hair loose, she "went that night, unexpected, to the room of the Duke, followed only by a few of her ladies. She went down on her knees before [him] and, in a voice broken by sobs, she begged him to take pity on her and her children and earnestly pleaded that he renounce his plans so as not to alienate himself by an act of felony toward his King and the princes of the blood, who might, after his death, protect his children."

"Lady," he replied, "how you come by your information I know not, but rather than be the cause of such distress to you, I will revoke my order."[6]

Joan persuaded him to meet the ambassadors the next day in Nantes Cathedral, and then to accompany them peaceably to Tours. The chronicler monk of Saint-Denis "heard this [tale] from the ambassadors themselves, who related to him the peril from which they escaped through the prudence of Joan." At Tours, in February 1392, Charles VI received the Duke royally and offered the Duchess his two-year-old daughter Jeanne as a bride for her son John. Sadly, Jeanne died that year, but the King substituted his newborn infant of the same name in her place.

Joan's daughter Marie was born on 18 February 1391, at Nantes. Marguerite followed in 1392, Arthur on 24 August 1393, at Château de Suscinio at Sarzeau, Gilles in 1394, Richard in 1395, at Château de Clisson, and Blanche in 1397. The Duchess's frequent pregnancies and maternal responsibilities must have limited her influence at the Breton court, yet still she exercised a subtle agency, especially after she produced male heirs, which strengthened her position.

When Oliver de Clisson narrowly escaped assassination in France in June 1392, Duke John gave asylum to Peter de Craon, the man who had made the attempt. An angry Charles VI sent messengers to demand that he give him up. They were shocked to find Craon being treated as an honored guest at Joan's court at l'Hermine—as was Clisson, when he heard. Enraged, he incited a civil war in Brittany, and John, Joan, and their children were again obliged to seek refuge at Vannes. Meanwhile, their jewels and plate were seized by their enemies. Urged on by Clisson, Charles VI himself marched on Brittany at the head of an army, but suffered the first attack of the madness that was to bedevil his life, and had to withdraw.

The rule of France was now entrusted to Joan's uncle, Philip the Bold, Duke of Burgundy, who was friendly toward Brittany and broke the opposition to Duke John's rule, obliging Clisson to renounce the office of Constable of France. At the plea of her cousin, Viscount de Rohan, who acted as her intermediary, Joan made efforts to win round those Breton nobles who had rebelled against the Duke. But, his heir being only four years old, John feared what might ensue if he was killed, and wrote to Clisson, offering peace terms. Clisson would only treat with him if he handed over his son as a hostage, but Joan protested, and it was some days before she could be persuaded to allow Rohan to take the child to Château Joscelin, where Clisson was under siege. To her great joy, Clisson immediately sent her son back to her and agreed to make peace. Joan was praised by the Breton chroniclers for having brought it about through the good offices of Rohan. In 1393, she was further applauded when she prevailed on the Duke to raise the siege and extend concessionary terms to Clisson. The reconciliation, however, was only temporary.

In 1395, when Joan's daughter Marie was three, her father offered her in marriage to Henry of Monmouth, son and heir of the newly widowed Henry of Bolingbroke. The castle of Brest was then in the possession of the English, but, "at the especial desire of the Duchess Joan," it was "appointed for the solemnisation of the nuptials and the residence of the youthful pair. After the cession of this important town had been guaranteed by Richard II, who was against the Lancastrian marriage, the King of France contrived to break the proposed alliance by inducing the heir of Alençon to offer to marry the Princess with a smaller dower than the heir of Lancaster was to have received with her."[7] This strategy proved successful. In June 1396, Marie, now five, was betrothed to John of Perche, son of Peter, Duke of Alençon, at Saint-Aubin-du-Cormier, Ille-et-Vilaine, near Fougères. The marriage took place in July. John succeeded his father as Duke in 1404.

In March 1396, in the hope of restoring good relations and recovering the earldom of Richmond, of which Duke John still felt he had been unjustly deprived, Joan wrote to Richard II in the formal style then used in royal letters:

> My most dear and redoubted lord,
> I desire every day to be certified of your good estate, which God grant that it may ever be as good as your heart desires, and as I should wish it for myself. If it would please you to let me know of it, you would give me great rejoicings in my heart, for every time that I hear good news of you, I am most perfectly glad of heart. And if to know tidings from this side would give you pleasure, when this was written, my lord, I and our children were together in good health of our persons, thanks to our Lord, who, by His grace, ever grant you the same. I pray you, my dearest and most redoubted lord, that it would ever please you to have the affairs of my said lord well recommended, as well in reference to the deliverance of his lands as other things, which lands in your hands are the cause why he sends his people promptly toward you. So may it please you hereupon to provide him with your gracious remedy, in such manner that he

may enjoy his said lands peaceably, even as he and I have our perfect surety and trust in you more than in any other. And let me know your good pleasure, and I will accomplish it willingly and with a good heart, to my power. My dearest and most redoubted lord, I pray the Holy Spirit that He will have you in His holy keeping.

Written at Vannes, the 15th day of March, The Duchess of Brittany.[8]

That year, Joan and John traveled to Paris to see their eldest son, John, Count of Montfort, married to Jeanne, the daughter of Charles VI. The wedding took place at the Hôtel de Saint-Pol, with the Archbishop of Rouen officiating. It was a splendid gathering of royalty, which included the King and Queen of France, the Queen of Sicily, and Joan's uncles, the dukes of Berri and Burgundy.

The Duke and Duchess traveled north to Saint-Omer, where they banqueted with a gathering of royalties who were on their way to Calais, where Richard II was to be married to Isabella of Valois. It was here that Joan probably met Henry of Bolingbroke for the first time. In November, John and Joan were among the congregation in the church of St. Nicholas at Calais to witness the royal wedding.

Back in Vannes, on 15 February 1397, Joan wrote again to Richard II:

My very dear and most honorable lord and cousin,
Since I am desirous to hear of your good estate, which our Lord grant that it may ever be as good as your noble heart knows best how to desire, and indeed as I would wish it for myself, I pray you, my most dear and honored lord and cousin, that it would please you very often to let me know the certainty of it, for the very great joy and gladness of my heart; for every time that I can hear good news of you, it rejoices my heart very greatly. And if, of your courtesy, you would hear the same from across here, thanks to you, at the writing of these presents, I and my children were together in good health of our persons, thanks to God, who grant you the same, as Johanna of Bavalen, who is going over to you, can tell you more fully, whom please it you to have recommended in the business on which she is going over.

This letter was misdated to 1400 by Mary Anne Wood, its Victorian editor, which has led many to suppose that it was sent to Henry IV, and that

Johanna of Bavalen was acting as a go-between in the brokering of a marriage between Joan and Henry. But it was sent on the same day, and expressed the same sentiments, as a letter from John IV to Richard II, and Johanna of Bavalen's mission may have concerned the restitution of the earldom of Richmond. It has been suggested that she is to be identified with Joanna of Bavaria, Duchess of Austria, but there is no record of that lady visiting England in 1397, the year she bore her first child, so it is likely that Johanna was one of Joan's ladies.

In April 1398, the Duke—and probably the Duchess—traveled to England to attend the annual feast of the Order of the Garter at Windsor. During this visit, Richard II restored the earldom of Richmond to John IV. This could have afforded Joan another opportunity to meet Henry of Bolingbroke.

Three contemporary sources—Froissart, Bouchart, and Fernando de Ybarra—stated that in June 1399, just before his momentous invasion of England, the exiled Bolingbroke, who was staying in Paris, paid a brief visit to the court of Brittany at Nantes, where he was warmly welcomed by the Duke and the Duchess, to whom, according to Breton chroniclers, he was personally attracted from the first, for she was "a very beautiful princess."[9] Froissart stated that John IV gave him arms and three warships and wished him well before he sailed away, while Ybarra claimed that Joan gave him a posy of forget-me-nots that inspired him to adopt his motto, "Souveignez" or "Soverayne" ("Remember me"). But not three weeks elapsed between Henry leaving Paris and arriving at England on 30 June or 4 July (sources differ as to the date). Given that the distance from Paris to Nantes and then from Nantes to Boulogne, whence he sailed, was 810 miles, he would have had to ride a punishing forty miles a day to complete the journey; and Froissart was in error in stating that he landed at Plymouth, when he arrived at Ravenspur on the Yorkshire coast, so he may also have been wrong in claiming that Henry had visited Brittany. However, it is possible that Henry had done so earlier that year.

The autumn of 1399 saw Joan tending her husband in his final sickness. He died on 1 November. In a codicil to his will dated 26 October, he had confirmed Joan's dower and "all his former gifts to his beloved companion." He dictated it from his sickbed, in the absence of others and in the presence of the Duchess, and it was given under his seal in the castle tower near Nantes, about the hour of Vespers. He demonstrated his trust in Joan by appointing her and their son John, who now succeeded as John V, as chief executors. Because the new Duke was only eleven, Joan was to rule as regent and have the entire care of him and her other children. She was present at her late husband's funeral in Nantes Cathedral.

Peace was foremost on her list of priorities, and one of her first acts, in which she was aided by the clergy, was to stage a public reconciliation with Oliver de Clisson, Penthièvre, and other rebel lords. This took place on 1 January 1400 at the château of Blein, where Clisson and his supporters all swore to obey Joan during her son's minority. She also took oaths of loyalty on her son's behalf from other prominent men and secured the fidelity of Brittany's chief cities and towns.

On 22 March, accompanied by his mother, the young Duke made a state entry into Rennes, where, in the presence of a large gathering of nobles and prelates, he swore solemn oaths to govern righteously before keeping vigil all night before the altar of the cathedral. The next day, he was knighted by Clisson, after which he knighted his brothers Arthur and Gilles. He was then invested with the ducal regalia and borne in procession through the city before attending a feast hosted by Joan at the château of Rennes.

2

"This blessed sacrament of marriage"

※

IN FEBRUARY 1400, JOAN HAD SENT HER TRUSTED SQUIRE, Antoine Riczi (later her attorney and secretary), and one Nicholas Aldrewick, to London. They had been in England the previous year on business connected with the earldom of Richmond. Before February was out, they returned "by command of the King, with letters on his behalf addressed to the Duchess"[1] and written by John Norbury, Henry IV's Treasurer, who addressed her as his "very dear and good friend." These letters related to English and Breton pirates operating in the Channel, but there were almost certainly others in which Henry made discreet approaches to Joan.

Joan was interested. She may have felt attracted to Henry as a man, but that was not the prime consideration for a woman of her rank. As a monarch, he could offer her a crown, wealth, and a new sphere of influence, whereas her role as regent of Brittany would soon be redundant when her son reached his majority. Negotiations proceeded covertly and slowly, because both parties were aware that a marriage between them would not be popular in Brittany, France, Burgundy, or England, and Joan, while keen on the prospect of becoming Queen of England, may have stalled at the thought of what would happen to her children in her absence.

In November 1401, Joan's envoys returned to England, sailing back to Brittany in December, bearing gifts for her (a bejeweled pax and costly rings that had been owned by Richard II's child bride, Isabella of Valois) and accompanied by English messengers. On 15 March 1402, Joan appointed Riczi and John Rhys as her proctors; John Norbury was to act for Henry. Soon afterward, the Breton envoys crossed to England with letters under Joan's signet empowering them to conclude the marriage treaty. A betrothal was secretly agreed upon, although Joan stipulated that she could not travel to England until she had set her affairs in order in Brittany.

She also needed to secure a dispensation, since she and Henry were third cousins twice over. Since 1378, the Church had been riven by what was known as the Great Schism, with rival pontiffs in Rome and Avignon. Joan supported Benedict XIII, who presided at Avignon. On 20 March 1402, he granted a dispensation permitting her to marry anyone she pleased within the fourth degree of consanguinity, a generous concession given that Henry IV supported the Roman Pope, Boniface IX. Joan had been warned by canon lawyers that marrying him would be a deadly sin, but Benedict assured her that this would be rendered void by the great benefits to be gained by her becoming Queen of England. On 23 June, he would issue another dispensation that sanctioned her living with schismatics and receiving Holy Communion from them, as long as she remained loyal to him.

Joan instantly dispatched ambassadors, Anthony and John Rhys, to conclude the alliance. The marriage contract was signed on 2 April 1402 at Eltham Palace, the proxy wedding taking place the next day in the presence of Thomas Arundel, Archbishop of Canterbury, the Privy Council, the earls of Somerset and Northumberland, and the latter's heir, Sir Henry Percy, popularly known as "Hotspur." Henry Bowet, Bishop of Bath and Wells, officiated, and Riczi stood in for Joan. The King placed a ring on his finger and the proxy bride vowed: "I, Antoine Riczi, in the name of my worshipful lady, Joan, the daughter of Charles, lately King of Navarre, Duchess of Brittany and Countess of Richmond, take you, Henry of Lancaster, King of England and Lord of Ireland, to my husband, and thereto I, Antoine, in the spirit of my said lady, plight you my troth." It was the first recorded instance of the final sentence being used in a betrothal ceremony. Joan now began styling herself Queen of England.

She brought no dowry to the marriage, but she had been left a large sum of money by Duke John and she had the income from her Breton dower lands; therefore, she was financially independent. After the proxy ceremony, she wrote to Henry to ask for compensation for the master of a Navarrese vessel that had been robbed of its cargo of wine by a captain in the Earl of Arundel's fleet. "At the request of his dearest consort," the King enjoined his Admiral "to see that proper satisfaction be made to the master of the wine ship,"[2] and warned that anyone who refused to obey him would be arrested.

The cat was now out of the bag. In May, rumor had it that the King intended to travel to Brittany to marry Joan, and there were fears that there would be an uprising in favor of Richard II in his absence. But on 25 June, the King directed Thomas, Lord Camoys, and other commissioners to safely conduct Queen Joan to England and paid him £100 (£76,200) in expenses, despite Parliament having insisted that Joan pay the cost of her journey from Brittany.

There was little enthusiasm for the marriage in England. It was highly unpopular in Brittany and—contrary to what Henry had evidently hoped—sparked a conflict with England, for the Breton lords feared that their duchy would be subsumed into the English Crown and were aghast when it became known that Joan wanted to take her children to England with her, to be brought up under the King's tutelage. Outraged, they hastened to appeal to Burgundy for support.

Joan's forthcoming marriage set alarms ringing in France too, which now found itself surrounded by England and its allies. On 1 October 1402, Burgundy arrived at Nantes, intent on resolving matters to King Charles's advantage. Joan welcomed him amiably and they dined together in great splendor. The Duke gave her costly crowns and scepters, one set of crystal, the other of gold, pearls, and precious stones, and he also had presents for her sons, her aunt Rohan, her ladies-in-waiting, and the officers of her household. It was a clever ruse that soon had those ladies begging him to accept the guardianship of the duchy and the ducal princes.

The pleasantries disposed of, he put pressure on Joan to abandon her projected marriage, but she remained adamant. She did, however, allow herself to be persuaded that it would be better to leave her four sons under his guardianship than to alienate the Bretons by taking them abroad. He was, after all, her uncle and the boys' kinsman. Joan agreed, although it must have been with a heavy heart. Ceding control of the duchy to Burgundy, she required him to swear on the Holy Evangelists to protect her sons and respect the laws and privileges of Brittany, then made him put these promises in writing and herself signed the document and enjoined "the young princes to be obedient to him and to attend diligently to his advice."[3] She had to make protracted efforts to get the Bretons to agree to her taking her unmarried daughters Marguerite and Blanche, aged ten and five, to England, to which Henry had given his consent.

On 3 November, Joan bade farewell to her sons when Burgundy left with them for Paris. There, John V was required to pay homage to Charles VI. Joan would continue to keep in contact with the boys by letter.

At last, the way was clear for her to leave Brittany. In December, Henry sent his half-brothers, John Beaufort, Earl of Somerset, and Henry Beaufort, Bishop of Lincoln, with the earls of Worcester and Northumberland, Lord Camoys, and many other lords to Brittany to receive Joan.

On 26 December, Joan left Nantes for Vannes with her daughters and their nurses, attended by a great retinue of Bretons and Navarrese. Plans for the assembly of a fleet to carry her to England had been afoot for months, and the Earl of Arundel "had provided, by royal command, a ship well-appointed with victuals, arms and thirty-six mariners for the service of bringing our lady the Queen from Brittany."[4] Sumptuous quarters had been prepared on board for her, hung with Imperial cloth of gold and containing a bed with curtains of crimson satin.

On 13 January, Joan and her daughters set sail from Camaret-sur-Mer near Brest for Southampton. The winter weather being atrocious, they endured a grueling five-day voyage in storms that caused structural damage to the vessel and blew it off course to Cornwall. Joan was horribly seasick. Making land at Falmouth on 19 January 1403, she rested awhile before being escorted by the lords across Bodmin Moor and via Okehampton to Exeter, arriving there on 27 January. She had come, observed the chronicler Thomas Walsingham, "from a smaller Brittany to a greater Britain, from a dukedom to a kingdom, from a fierce tribe to a peace-loving people."

Apprised of Joan's coming, Henry IV set out with a small retinue and rode for Exeter, where he welcomed her to England. They were lavishly

"This blessed sacrament of marriage"

entertained by the civic authorities, who provided them with a chariot and horses to take them to Bridport. While the King rode on toward Winchester, where they were to be married, Nicholas Aldrewick accompanied Joan via Dorchester and Salisbury to Winchester, where she met up again with Somerset, Worcester, and Bishop Beaufort, who had had to race ahead to borrow money for the rest of the journey.

Joan had taken up residence in Wolvesey Castle, the Bishop of Winchester's residence, by 5 February, when she and the King presided over a feast attended by a host of lords and ladies. In all, sixty-six dishes were served in three courses. It being Lent (the season when the devout were meant to abstain from meat, eggs, and dairy produce), fish predominated, including roasted salmon, sturgeon, pike, bream, crab, lampreys, trout, eels, and perch. Meat was also served: roast cygnets, capons, venison, griskins (pork tenderloin), rabbits, bitterns, pheasants, stuffed pullets, partridges, kid, woodcock, plover, quails, snipe, fieldfares, brawn, and pottage. In addition, cream of almonds, pears in syrup, custards, milk fritters, and elaborate sugar sculptures, or "subtleties," were presented to the high table after each course: a crowned panther breathing flames, and Lancastrian crowned eagles made of marzipan.

Henry's chief wedding gift to Joan was a crown costing £1,313:6s.8d. (£1,133,550), which may have been the one Richard II had given Anne of Bohemia for their wedding in 1382. It had ten fleurons (flower-shaped ornaments) and was studded with emeralds, sapphires, rubies, pearls, and diamonds. She also received a gem-encrusted cup and ewer of gold, ten armlets lavishly adorned with gems, a triangular clasp, and a rich jeweled gold collar of linked S's bearing Henry's motto, "Souveignez." Costing £333:6s.8d. (£287,490), the collar was delivered to Winchester in time for the wedding and is perhaps to be identified with the one on Joan's tomb effigy. The King's sons John and Humphrey gave her two gold tablets they had commissioned for her, although their father paid for them.[5] The Prince of Wales was unable to attend the wedding, but wrote to Henry, "beseeching God in all wise, my sovereign lord, to send you in this blessed sacrament of marriage joy [and] prosperity, long to endure."[6]

On 7 February, the marriage was solemnized with great ceremony in the priory of St. Swithun (now Winchester Cathedral). The bride and groom processed along the striped cloth that had been laid down the nave, and Henry Beaufort, Bishop of Lincoln, officiated (he would become Bishop of Winchester the following year, replacing William of Wykeham, who had been too infirm to officiate at the wedding). Among those present were the King's children John and Philippa. The celebrations continued for three days. The bill for the wedding itself came to £433:6s.8d. (£373,830), with an extra £522:12s. (£451,520) for the feast that followed, at which meat and game were served in abundance, as well as fish for the clergy, followed by pears in syrup, cream of almonds, and a subtlety in the form of a crowned eagle. The royal couple stayed in Winchester for three days before making their way in slow stages via Farnham Castle to Eltham Palace.

On 22 February, "messengers and couriers [were] sent to divers counties of England with letters to divers lords and ladies," commanding them "to come to the coronation of the Lady Queen Joan, Queen of England."[7]

Two days later, as the royal couple approached the capital, the Lord Mayor, alderman, and sheriffs, with members of the City's guilds wearing liveries of brown and blue and hoods of scarlet, rode out in procession to Blackheath to welcome Joan and escort her into London. They were preceded by six minstrels who had been paid £4 (£3,450) each to play for her.

Joan spent that night in the royal palace of the Tower of London, where, by tradition, kings and queens stayed before their coronations. The next day, 25 February, she rode in procession to Westminster Abbey. As she passed through Cheapside, a band of minstrels played for her. She was crowned by Archbishop Arundel, with the diadem the King had given her. A manuscript drawing of her coronation in the Beauchamp Pageant,[8] dating from c.1485-90, shows a queen enthroned on a raised platform beneath a canopy of estate bearing the royal arms, with two archbishops placing the crown on her head, and lords, ladies, and damsels wearing chaplets of roses standing around the foot of the steps. She wears traditional ceremonial dress of a style dating back to the fourteenth century: a sideless surcoat—probably purple—with a kirtle beneath, and a mantle fastened across the upper chest with cords and tassels. In her hands—unusually for a queen consort, as they signify sovereignty—are a scepter and an orb surmounted by a cross.

Her hair is loose, symbolic of queenly virginity. Only unmarried girls could wear their hair loose; it had to be covered after marriage, a custom that endured into the nineteenth century. But queens, who were supposed to be the mirror of the Virgin Mary in their piety and mercifulness, were the exception. As the Mother of Christ was the Queen of Heaven and mediatrix supreme, earthly queens exercised their influence through intercession.

Henry had outlaid £631 (£544,760) on a great feast and tournaments in celebration of the coronation. Joan's champion, the Earl of Warwick, "kept joust on the Queen's part against all other comers, and so notably and knightly behaved himself as redounded to his noble fame and perpetual worship."[9] A miniature in the Beauchamp Pageant shows Henry and Joan seated on a cushioned bench in an open gallery, watching the tournament. Attended by her ladies, Joan appears in a close-fitting gown and a headdress with wired veiling that must have been two feet tall, and which may have looked slightly incongruous, given that she was petite in stature, like her effigy; when their tomb was opened in 1832, her leaden shroud—probably an anthropomorphic (body-shaped) coffin—was found to be much smaller than Henry IV's.

3

"His beloved consort"

✳

When the celebrations were over, Henry moved with Joan, his sons, and his daughter Philippa to Eltham Palace for Easter. On 8 March, at the petition of Parliament, Henry set Joan's dower as Queen of England at 10,000 marks (£5,754,920) annually, larger than that granted to most earlier consorts, making her one of the richest magnates—possibly the richest—in England. But Henry would struggle to maintain his Queen so lavishly; the Crown's total annual income was just £56,000 (£48,346,200)—and the extra expense would cause financial problems that lasted the whole reign.

The sources are largely silent on the personal relationship between the King and Queen, but external evidence suggests that the marriage proved happy. The couple spent much time together, and Henry treated Joan well. Praised for his chaste life, he was faithful and generous and always solicitous in ascertaining that her needs and those of her household were met. They shared a love of music. Their stone heads can be seen on either side of the great east window of Naish Priory in Somerset.

Joan was lauded for her beauty, grace, and majesty. Her tomb effigy at Canterbury shows her in a fashionable gown and surcoat with a low, gold-edged neckline leaving the shoulders bare, with gold buttons down the front. She wears her rich Lancastrian SS collar—the earliest-surviving example of one—and an elaborate crown. Her hair is confined in crespines on either side of her fashionably shaven forehead. Her impassive face has a slight double chin and a prominent pointed nose, although this has been restored at some point and may not be the same shape as the original.

Joan was apparently welcomed by the King's family. She established good relationships with his children and was to champion the Prince of Wales when he quarreled with his father. Edward, Duke of York, the King's thirty-year-old married cousin, was much taken with Joan and expressed his admiration for her in courtly verses extolling her beauty and virtues:

> *Excellent sovereign, seemly to see.*
> *Proved prudence, peerless of price;*
> *Bright blossom of benignity,*
> *Of figure fairest, and freshest of days! . . .*
>
> *Your womanly beauty delicious*
> *Hath me all bent unto its chain;*
> *But grant to me your love gracious,*
> *My heart will melt as snow in rain.*
>
> *If ye but wist my life and knew*
> *Of all the pains that I y-feel,*
> *I wis ye would upon me rue,*
> *Although your heart were made of steel . . .*
>
> *And though ye be of high renown,*
> *Let mercy rule your heart so free;*
> *From you, lady, this is my boon,*
> *To grant me grace in some degree.*
>
> *To mercy, if you will me take,*
> *If such your will be for to do,*
> *Then would I truly, for my sake,*
> *Change my cheer and slake my woe.*

The poem was written in the spirit of courtly love, the aristocratic game in which a knight dedicated himself to the service of a lady usually higher in rank (and often married) and swore undying love. Queens were often the objects of courtly desire, although the game was supposed to stop short of consummation, for while a lover might strive to win his lady's love, she would not normally deign to grant the final favor; in theory, she was meant to remain unattainable. In 1411, York expanded the college of chantry priests founded by his father, York's younger brother, at Fotheringhay, Northamptonshire, the purpose being that they would pray for the souls of Henry IV, Joan, and the royal family.

Joan was fashion-conscious, as her effigy shows. She ordered luxury fabrics to be made up into sumptuous clothes. She enjoyed good food, including lampreys imported from Brittany, with wine, costly spices, and other delicacies. She kept exotic animals and birds, and also gave birds as gifts. She owned beautiful illuminated manuscripts, including a psalter that still survives in the library of the University of Manchester. She prevailed on the King to support scholars at the universities of Oxford and Cambridge. She made several successful intercessions over the years, obtaining favors for clergymen, and pardons for the abbots of Colchester and Byleigh, tenants of hers accused of murder, and even, in 1404, for Maud de Ufford, Countess of Oxford, the mother of Richard II's favorite, Robert de Vere. The Countess had incited a conspiracy against Henry IV, claiming that Richard II was still alive, and had been imprisoned in the Tower.

The marriage might have been happy, but the hoped-for support from Brittany never materialized. Henry had married Joan "hoping through her to gain some assistance" against his many foes. "His hopes were promptly dashed, however, because the Bretons, disapproving of the marriage, allied themselves with the French."[1] Even as Joan was celebrating her wedding, Breton ships were attacking English merchant vessels sailing from Bordeaux. It was not an auspicious start, although Joan had the good sense not to become involved in what turned out to be a two-year-long conflict between England and Brittany. In August, Breton pirates caused a conflagration in Plymouth, provoking the townsfolk to attack their ships.

These were not the only clouds on the horizon. Henry IV now urgently had to deal with the rebellious Percies in the North and the rising of Owen Glendower in Wales, which the Bretons were aiding. On 21 July

1403, he vanquished his enemies at the Battle of Shrewsbury, where Sir Henry "Hotspur" Percy was killed.

The year ended badly. According to the contemporary Northern Chronicle,[2] Joan gave birth to stillborn twins (*"genuit duos abortios"*) late in 1403, presumably after she and Henry visited Cirencester in November. After that, there were no more children.

In England, Joan's was a life of luxury. Richard II had carried out improvements to the royal residences on a vast scale, having them modernized, decorated, and gilded. The walls of the royal apartments at Westminster, Windsor, and the Tower of London were now painted with heraldic or allegorical designs in brilliant colors. Richard had also refurbished Eltham Palace in Kent, a favorite residence of English queens since the early fourteenth century. Here he had built a bathhouse, a painted chamber, and a dancing chamber, while the windows were of stained glass and the surrounding gardens laid with turf. Henry IV rebuilt much of the inner court at Eltham, creating new apartments for himself and Queen Joan. Her lodging, erected in 1404–7, was two floors high and thirty-five feet long. It comprised a parlor and withdrawing chamber at ground level, with a hall, kitchen, chapel, farther chambers, and a privy upstairs.

In the royal apartments in the Tower, Richard II had installed 105 square feet of glass painted with fleurs-de-lis and the royal arms of England, as well as floor tiles depicting heraldic leopards and white harts, and murals of popinjays (parrots) and fleurs-de-lis worked in gold and vermilion.

Westminster was the foremost royal residence and the administrative center of government. It extended along the Thames shore, southwest of the City of London. A royal residence had stood on this site opposite Westminster Abbey since the sainted King Edward the Confessor had built both in the eleventh century, and the magnificent Westminster Hall had been completed by William II in 1099; Richard II had added the splendid oak hammer-beam roof. The sprawling palace was the chief seat of royal government. Parliament often met there, usually in the vast Painted Chamber (the walls of which were covered with frescos of scenes from the Bible) or the White Hall or St. Stephen's Chapel. Westminster Hall was used for state occasions and coronation banquets. Daily, it housed the busy law courts—the Court of Common Pleas and the Court of King's Bench—and stalls selling books and other goods. In December 1404, Henry IV granted Joan, for life, a newly built tower that stood by the entrance of Westminster Hall, for meetings of her council, the storage of charters and other documents, and the auditing of her accounts. It was effectively her office.

Visitors would gaze in wonder at the beautiful St. Stephen's Chapel, decorated in 1350-61 with murals depicting the family of Edward III, and at the Star Chamber, built by Edward III, so called because of its ceiling, which was painted blue like the night sky and patterned with gilded stars. The private chambers of the royal family were sumptuous, boasting beds hung with cloth of gold and satin, and made up with deep feather mattresses, pillows embroidered with the arms of England, and coverlets furred with ermine. The whole effect of the state apartments was one of magnificent color and splendor, calculated to impress foreigners and so convince them of the wealth and might of the island kingdom.

Joan did intercede with the King on behalf of needy petitioners and prisoners, but if she tried to influence him politically, she went about it subtly. Even so, the Earl of Westmorland, for one, believed her patronage to be worth having, as evidenced by the pensions he paid to her secretary, Antoine Riczi, and two esquires of her chamber.

Joan's honeymoon with Henry's subjects did not last long. Her dower was not paid regularly or in full because of the difficulties her officers encountered in wresting rents from her manors; after a year, it was nearly £5,000 (£4,877,110) in arrears and she had to petition Parliament for payment. The traditional English grumbles about an alien queen soon surfaced. There were complaints that she was avaricious and that she had appropriated the estates of her wards. Although Joan worked to maintain good relations between England and Brittany, there was general disappointment that the duchy remained neutral and failed to support England in the war against France. Indeed, with Joan's sons under the control of France and Burgundy, England was soon in conflict with

Brittany, and there was little likelihood of that situation changing in the foreseeable future. Naturally, Joan supported the young Duke John, both morally and financially; in 1404, she assigned him rents worth 6,000 livres (£5,852,530) and the reversion of 70,000 livres (£68:3 million) owing to her from the time of her first marriage. Since she managed her own finances with determined acumen, Henry, for all his expectations, received nothing from her Breton revenues.

In January 1404, Parliament was moved to complain about the proliferation of foreigners in the households of the King and Queen and ordered that all aliens leave the kingdom. Joan was allowed to keep her Breton cook, two knights (including Nicholas Aldrewick), one lady, one damsel, one maid, two chamberers, two esquires, twelve Breton launderers, and a nurse and a chamberer for her daughters. Antoine Riczi was permitted to travel between England and Brittany, but not to live in England. Joan made no complaint but largely ignored the order to dismiss everyone else.

Soon afterward, her son Arthur, now eight, was brought to England so that Henry could invest him with the earldom of Richmond. The King had bypassed John V because he had given his allegiance to Charles VI, his father-in-law.

Around March, the Breton government, in John's name, sent envoys to ask for the return of Joan's daughters, but she refused to give them up, even when the envoys emphasized that they were the property of Brittany. The Bretons were angered and made noises about confiscating Joan's dower, but she had cannily placed much of it in the hands of friendly lords, who transferred her revenues via her English officers. On 18 November, however, she paid John V the sum of 70,000 ducats (£1,444,800), which she had received from her brother, the King of Navarre, and £6,000 (£5,852,530) from her rents from Normandy. In October, Parliament had suspended all annuities for a year, but those that had been made to the Queen and the King's sons were allowed to stand.

It was perhaps to further mollify her former husband's countrymen that, in January 1405, Joan persuaded Henry to pardon and release Breton pirates he had captured and incarcerated. The King, "at the mediation and earnest solicitation of his beloved consort, Queen Joan, forgave and liberated, without ransom, all the prisoners taken in arms against him at Dartmouth by John Cornwall" in 1404, when Breton forces had raided the coast.[3] This made Joan even more unpopular in England.

In 1405, Henry compensated her for the arrears of her dower with a substantial grant of properties confiscated from the Percies, among them the manor of Petworth, Sussex, and a great house on the west side of St. Martin's Lane, near Aldersgate, London, "commonly called Northumberland House" because it had belonged to Henry Percy. Joan used it as her wardrobe.[4] However, the grant was deemed illegal and revoked, and provision was made for her from other sources.

In April 1405, the court moved to Windsor for the feast of St. George. By then, the King was too ill to ride a horse.

4

"Cruelly tormented"

✷

Joan did not long enjoy an untroubled married life. Even before they were married, Henry had begun to experience short blackouts, like epileptic fits, which may have been caused by a blow to the head during his jousting days. From 1405, the year he finally subdued his rebels, he suffered ill health, which may have been the reason why he fathered no more children. The first attack of what appeared to be a skin disease made him scream with pain and cry out that he was on fire.

With pain came disfigurement. "The King lost the beauty of his face. He was a leper, and ever fouler and fouler."[1] The Brut Chronicle asserts that he actually was smitten with leprosy. His face and hands were covered with large pustules and his nose became misshapen. The swellings and rashes on his skin were so vile that few people could bring themselves to look at him. From 1406, he had a bad leg. Later, a tumor grew beneath his nose, and in 1408 the chronicler Adam of Usk stated that his flesh was rotting.

The doctors could do nothing for him. Rumors about his condition were widespread. The French believed that his toes and fingers had fallen off, the Scots that he had shrunk to the size of a child. Most people, including the King himself, regarded his illness as evidence of God's wrath.

What was this terrible disease? It was unlikely to have been leprosy, though that was common in Europe at that time, segregation not being as rigorously enforced as Victorian scholars believed. And the condition of Henry's well-preserved face, seen during his exhumation in 1832, proved that contemporary descriptions of his skin disease were exaggerated. Whatever it was, though, his illness made him increasingly incapacitated.

In February 1406, Parliament raised the issue of the "great discontents engendered in the minds of all classes of men on account of the influx of foreigners which the King's late marriage has introduced into the realm, the disorderly state of the royal household and the evil influence exercised over public affairs by certain individuals supposed to be about the persons of the King and Queen." The Speaker, John Tiptoft, complained that the order Parliament had earlier given "for removing aliens from the Queen's court had been very ill observed, [and] that certain strangers who did seem to be officers about the Queen should, by a certain day, depart the realm." Consequently, "all French persons, Bretons, Lombards, Italians and Navarrese whatsoever" were to "be removed out of the palace from the King and Queen, except the Queen's two daughters and Maria St. Parensy, excepting likewise Nicholas Aldrewick and John Purian and their wives." All were to relinquish any grants made to them by the King or Queen. Parliament also asked "that the Queen would be pleased to pay for her journeys to the King's houses, as Queen Philippa [wife of Edward III] had been pleased to do."[2]

The King asked Parliament to grant suitable dower properties to Joan to make up for the arrears due to her. The Lords voted her all the revenues once enjoyed by Anne of Bohemia, Richard II's Queen, which made up the dower to the promised 10,000 marks (£5,754,920) yearly. Among the properties she received was Leeds Castle in Kent.

In 1395, the chronicler Jean Froissart had written of "the beautiful palace in Kent called Leeds Castle." Built on two islands in the middle of a lake, it had been the property of several queens of England, and it clearly became one of Joan's favorite residences; she spent a lot of time there during her marriage to Henry. Today, the only remains from her time are the thirteenth-century Gloriette built for Eleanor of Castile, the gatehouse, and the wall surrounding the larger island, which was thirty-two feet high in Joan's day and enclosed a moat. The rest of the castle was rebuilt in the 1820s. In 1412, the King gave Joan permission to grant Leeds to Archbishop Arundel. It is from his inventory that we know something of Leeds when it was in Joan's possession. By 1419, the castle had reverted to the Crown.

Joan's other favored residences were Devizes Castle and Holme Park, the Bishop of Salisbury's Thames-side palace at Sonning, near Reading, Berkshire. The fortified house predated the Norman Conquest of 1066, but was demolished in the seventeenth century, when a new mansion was built on the site. Then there was Pirgo Palace at Havering atte Bower, which stood in a thousand-acre hunting park in Essex. It had been built by Edward the Confessor in the eleventh century and had since formed part of the dower of several queens of England. The main palace at Havering was used by kings.

In 1405, Henry IV had betrothed his daughter Philippa to Eric IX, King of Denmark, Norway, and Sweden. On 7 August 1406, Henry and Joan traveled with her to the port of Lynn "to take ship there. And in that town he lay nine days [with] the two queens, three sons of the King and many other lords and ladies."[3] In the middle of August, Philippa's ship sailed. She and Eric were married at Lund on 26 October.

Joan could no longer keep her own daughters with her. Great marriages had been arranged for them by the Breton government, and they had to be sent home to Brittany; it seems she never saw them again. From the marriages of all her children, Joan had nineteen grandchildren. She maintained an affectionate correspondence with her daughters as well as her sons.

Joan worked tirelessly to foster better relations with Brittany. In July 1407, in a letter to John V, Henry IV expressed "his earnest wish, on account of the close tie existing between them through his dearest consort, that peace and amity may be established." John, now nineteen, replied, "As our very dear and redoubtable mother, the Queen of England, has several times signified her wish that all good friendship should subsist between our very redoubted lord and father Henry, King of England, her lord and spouse, on one part, and ourselves on the other, we desire to enter into an amicable treaty."[4] A truce was proclaimed on 13 September.

* * *

In 1407, Henry IV took further steps to ensure the future security of his dynasty by excluding his Beaufort half-siblings from their rightful place in the succession. Although he confirmed Richard II's statute legitimizing them, he added an amendment by his own letters patent, inserting the words *"excepta dignitate regali,"* which effectively barred the Beauforts and their descendants from inheriting the throne of England. The amendment was of dubious legality and caused some controversy because it was never incorporated into an Act of Parliament, nor approved by Parliament. Yet it had the effect of debasing the status of the Beauforts, and it was not until much later in the fifteenth century that lawyers acting on their behalf would assert that letters patent could not supersede an Act of Parliament and that consequently they should not have been excluded from the succession. That Henry's bar was not highly regarded was proved in 1485, when the son of a Beaufort became King of England.

Joan had commissioned "an alabaster tomb" for her first husband, John IV, which had been made in England. In February 1408, "at the request of our dearest consort," Henry arranged for it "to be conveyed in the barge of St. Nicholas of Nantes"[5] to Nantes Cathedral. Joan sent with it a jewel-encrusted reliquary of the Trinity, made for John V and now in the Louver. Around this time, she also sent him a gold, gem-studded sculpture of the Holy Trinity, five tiers high and finished in white enamel, which had once belonged to Anne of Bohemia. In April, she was made a Lady of the Order of the Garter.

In June 1408, while visiting Archbishop Arundel at Mortlake, the King suffered a seizure—possibly a mild stroke—and lay unconscious for so long that his attendants feared he was dying, but he recovered. A renowned Italian doctor was taken into his service, but fears for his life resurfaced when he again became very unwell in December, and he was so convinced he was dying that he recalled his son Thomas from Ireland. On 21 January 1409, having moved with Joan to Greenwich in the hope that a change of air would be beneficial, he made his will, directing that his Queen be endowed with the duchy of Lancaster, which instituted a custom that lasted until the reign of Henry VII. In July, when staying with Joan at Havering, he granted her lands and revenues to make up the value of her dower. That year, he also gave her six lead mines in Cornwall and the workmen to load her ship with their yield. It was an appropriate gift, for the mines supplied Brittany. Easter and Christmas that year were spent at Eltham.

Thereafter, Henry's health deteriorated. He suffered more fainting fits and bouts of illness and seems to have had a heart complaint; at times, he was unable to walk and he rarely ventured beyond London. As he grew worse, the Beauforts' influence at court increased, and the balance of power swung from the King to the Prince of Wales. Shakespeare portrays "Prince Hal" as a riotous and dissolute frequenter of taverns with the disreputable Sir John Falstaff, and indeed the real Prince "was in his youth an assiduous cultor of lasciviousness; passing the bounds of modesty, he was the servant of Venus" and "found leisure for the excesses common to ungoverned age."[6] But there was more to him than that. Having fought his first battle at fifteen, Henry of Monmouth had gained an early and wholly justified reputation as a brilliant soldier and military strategist.

Impatient to wear the crown, the Prince sought to gain control of the kingdom and allied himself with his Beaufort uncles in an attempt to seize power. This led eventually to total estrangement between father and son. Despite his illness, the King refused to abdicate. He was determined to hold on to power even though he was becoming increasingly enfeebled. When, at times, the burden of sovereignty became too much, he relied on Archbishop Arundel, his Chancellor, who tried unsuccessfully to ensure that the Prince and the Beauforts did not gain control of the government. In 1409, Arundel was forced through young Henry's machinations to resign as Chancellor, and the Prince and his faction became the dominant power on the Privy Council.

France was still riven by the raging conflict between the Burgundians and the Armagnacs. Joan's son Arthur supported the latter and lost his earldom of Richmond for it. Like her stepson, Prince Henry, Joan supported Burgundy, to the extent that John the Fearless accredited his ambassador to her, as well as to the King and the Prince of Wales. Joan did her best to deter Henry from entangling himself in the feud. Instead, he sent the Duke of York on a secret mission to France to propose a marriage between the Prince of Wales and Katherine, the eleven-year-old daughter of Charles VI, as a means of cementing a peace between England and France. Charles VI had already suggested the match in 1406, 1408, and 1409, but nothing had come of any of those proposals. Again, it was an abortive effort. Henry's ambassadors deliberated with Charles without arriving at any conclusion consistent with Henry's honor or advantage, and returned home.

By 1411, the King was becoming increasingly immobile. For five years now, he had been "cruelly tormented" by "festering of the flesh, dehydration of the eyes and rupture of the internal organs."[7] In the spring of 1412, he was said to be unable to walk. Even so, he refused to heed his half-brother Bishop Beaufort's suggestion that he abdicate, and threw his weight behind the Armagnacs, whereupon the Duke of Berri did his best to wean Joan away from the Burgundians. The quarrel left many of Joan's kinsfolk distressingly divided. Joan's son Gilles was for Burgundy, like her, but on 19 July, he died of dysentery alongside her brother Peter while fighting for the Duke at Auxerre. He was buried near his father at Nantes.

The King and Queen kept the Christmas of 1412 at Eltham with the Prince of Wales and Humphrey, Duke of Gloucester, Henry's youngest son. The King had recently been so ill that he had lain in bed looking quite dead, and when he did recover a little, he would see no one but Joan. Yet at the festive season, he summoned "as much cheerfulness as he could muster."[8]

In January, the royal couple moved to Westminster, but Henry was unable to attend Parliament. That month, wishing to secure provision for Joan in her widowhood, he issued letters patent confirming that she was to have the dower he had assigned her.

On 20 March 1413, the King walked painfully to the shrine of St. Edward the Confessor in Westminster Abbey, but when he knelt to make his offering, he suffered a stroke and collapsed. His attendants carried him into the Jerusalem Chamber in the Abbot's house, so called because tapestries depicting the history of Jerusalem hung there. The Queen was summoned, as was Prince Henry. When he could speak, the King recalled that he had once expressed a desire to go on a final crusade and die in Jerusalem.

They laid him on a pallet by the fire, but despite the warmth, he complained that his arms and legs felt cold. Guilt seems to have weighed heavily on him, for he was heard to whisper, "Only God knows by what right I took the crown." His confessor arrived and begged him to repent of his usurpation of the throne.

He was obviously dying. Custom decreed that the crown be placed by his side on a cushion of cloth of gold, and it was brought at once. By then, the King appeared to be dead, and a napkin was laid over his face. When the Prince arrived, he picked up the crown and made to place it on his head, at which moment the King stirred. Instead of reproving his son, as Shakespeare has him doing in *Henry IV Part 2,* he talked for a while with him and was heard to say that he repented of ever having charged himself with the crown of England, for it had proved too heavy a burden for him. At the last, he made his peace with his heir and died blessing him, with Joan at his side. He was forty-seven.

Henry was buried in the Trinity Chapel behind the high altar of Canterbury Cathedral, near to the tomb of the Black Prince and the shrine of St. Thomas Becket. There is no record of Joan attending his funeral, but later she commissioned a fine tomb, in which she would one day be buried beside him. Their effigies of marble and gilt were to lie on it, beneath a tester embossed with their coats of arms, badges, and mottoes. Joan's effigy, which was not placed on the tomb until after her death, was probably made at this time because it shows her in queenly robes, not as a widow.

5

"A woman of great prudence and judgment"

✳

AT FORTY-FIVE, JOAN FACED HER SECOND WIDOWHOOD. HER requests to the Pope for the right to have a portable altar for the saying of Mass, and to choose a confessor to absolve her of sin and impose penance, may reflect a need for spiritual consolation to assuage the guilt that can come with grief. She chose to stay in England, where she could be supported financially by her dower and spend a comfortable life in retirement. She lived well at Havering and her other houses. An inventory of her possessions, taken in 1419, lists costly ornaments for her chapel, a Sarum missal, cameos set with gold and pearls, gold beads, several rings, including a silver one in the form of a serpent, spoons in a silk case bearing the arms of Brittany, and some pieces of jewelry that may have been gifts from John IV or Henry IV: a gold chain with a florette inscribed "To love and serve" in French, a heart-shaped gold brooch bearing the legend "I am bound to you," and another brooch declaring "You have my whole heart for my life." Joan also owned an "adamant stone" that symbolized love, a silver penholder that hung from her girdle, silver cups with lids of enamel adorned with leaves, acorns, and roses, silver bottles, and silver forks.

Her wardrobe was not as luxurious as might have been expected. In 1419, it was recorded that she had a russet gown and matching sideless surcoat lined with polecat fur, an old russet cloak, a black gown and matching mantle of lambskin, with a surcoat of black lyraigne (a light woolen Flemish cloth) and a red Breton nightcap. She slept in a bed with canopies and hangings of red and green, and a coverlet of red and white tapestry. In her coffers were napery, towels of Paris work, and books on "art and other sciences."[1] She is known to have owned at least eight illuminated manuscripts and psalters, most of them devotional works.

Joan was horrified when she heard that her son, the Duke of Brittany, was contemplating the appropriation of her Breton dower lands for himself. Early in 1414, she approached the French ambassador and wept as she confided her fears that the Duke, "who she had always found to be a true, natural, loyal, humble and obedient son to her," had been persuaded by evil counselors to abandon her. She begged him to take a message "in true love and maternal affection" to John, "the creature whom she loved best in the world," expressing her hope that "he would act toward her as an obedient son, a true and loyal friend," and declaring that she could never believe he had proposed the changes to her dower that were causing her such dismay and displeasure. However, she let it be known that she was thinking of taking a third husband, a powerful prince of England, France, or another land who had the means to assert her rights, by force if necessary.

The threat was effective. John V wrote: "We swear and promise in good faith to [her], on pain of incurring her perpetual indignation," to uphold the grant of her dower lands, although he insisted on retaining the right to have them administered by his own captains and officials, declaring that he wished "to repair and improve the situation [and] we desire with all our heart and power to serve and obey our very formidable lady and mother."[2] Nevertheless, wrangles between mother and son over Joan's dower would continue almost to the end of her life.

Henry IV left England in a more prosperous and settled state than he had found it. While he had achieved nothing to bring glory upon himself, he had successfully vanquished his enemies and driven baronial opposition underground; and although some still regarded him as an upstart with a dubious right to the crown, his son succeeded unchallenged to the throne.

On Passion Sunday, 9 April 1413, Henry V was crowned in Westminster Abbey. "As soon as he was made king he changed suddenly into another man, zealous for honesty, modesty and gravity, there being no sort of virtue that he was not anxious to display."[3] His biographer, Titus Livius, says that he reformed and amended his life, and "had no carnal knowledge of women" until he married. He abandoned his dissolute young friends and paid heed to the experienced men of affairs on his Council. His first objective was to distance himself from his father's style of government and thereby earn fresh popularity and support for the House of Lancaster.

Henry cherished the memory of his mother, Mary de Bohun, and had Masses offered for her at Syon Abbey in the name of "Queen Mary." However, anxious to secure Brittany as an ally against France, he showed friendship to Joan, protecting her rights and addressing her in official documents as "his dearest mother, Joan, Queen of England" or "our most dear mother." There being no other queen in England, she remained the first lady in the land.

Henry had "an oval, handsome face with a broad, open forehead, a straight nose, ruddy cheeks and lips, a deeply indented chin, small, well-formed ears, hair brown and thick, bright hazel eyes, and stature above the average."[4] Clean-shaven, he wore his hair short and straight in the Norman military fashion. He was of lean, muscular build, agile, and very strong. French envoys once described him as a prince of distinguished appearance and commanding stature, with an expression that seemed to hint at pride. One observer thought he looked more like a priest than a soldier.

He was deeply pious and orthodox, spending hours at prayer each day and making many pilgrimages to the shrines of saints. One of his ambitions was to wrest Jerusalem back from the Turks. He was severe with heretics and virtually stamped out Lollardy.

Books were his greatest treasure. He had an extensive library and was literate in English, French, Latin, and Welsh. He enjoyed books on history, theology, and hunting, as well as contemporary works by Geoffrey Chaucer, Thomas Hoccleve, and John Lydgate. He was also a connoisseur of the arts and architecture, although not on the same scale as Richard II. He had a passion for singing and was an accomplished musician. An enthusiastic sportsman, he enjoyed hawking, fishing, wrestling, leaping, and running, in which he excelled, being faster, it was said, than a dog or even an arrow. Surprisingly, he had little interest in jousting.

English chroniclers were unanimous in their praise of Henry V, excelling themselves in superlatives. Walsingham described him as "prudent, far-seeing, magnanimous, firm, persistent, war-like and distinguished." Though taciturn in speech, he could be a good listener and was gifted with a dry wit. Yet those who knew him found him a cold man who inspired respect rather than love. He was highly self-disciplined and expected others to be so, too. He had a formidable presence, a lordly and severe manner, and was somewhat melancholy in temperament, tending to look serious at moments of triumph.

Henry had common sense, being perceptive and a wise judge of character; he could be persuasive and often aggressive when it came to asserting his rights. He was discreet, even secretive, but made it a point of honor to treat everyone with the utmost affability. "He went straight to the point," wrote a French envoy. On occasion he could appear sanctimonious and pedantic, parading his virtues. His worst fault would prove to be a ruthless brutality that was only unleashed when his authority was challenged. Once, during a siege, a man danced on the wall of the fortress, mocking the King and blowing a trumpet to imitate a fart; when the town was captured Henry had him executed. His justice was strictly impartial, meted out to friend and foe, high and low alike. He was not a merciful king, and his enemies feared his vengeance, which made his conquests easier since his reputation rode before him.

Henry inherited the same insecurities his father had faced. Some still regarded the House of Lancaster as a usurping dynasty and looked upon Edmund Mortimer, Earl of March, as the rightful king; some even believed that Richard II was still alive. However, people had become used to the new order, and it had gained a considerable degree of acceptance. Shakespeare would later portray Henry V as the vindicator of the House of Lancaster, whose deeds and reputation removed the taint of usurpation that adhered to his dynasty.

Henry was fortunate in possessing the attributes required of a successful medieval ruler. He was a brilliant general, a courageous leader who took a personal interest in his men and the practicalities of warfare. His contemporaries saw him as the embodiment of the "parfit, gentil knight" described by Chaucer, a Christian hero-king to whose name legends swiftly attached themselves. His magnificent reputation made a powerful impression on his contemporaries, and indeed on English history. Not for nothing was he called the flower of Christian chivalry.

Henry was a born leader who ascended the throne with astonishing confidence, determined to provide England with good government. He proved an adept administrator and a superb politician, believing that the prosperity of the realm depended on the integrity of its king and that any threat to the monarchy was a threat to a divinely ordered society. Even his enemies praised him as a wise ruler. He was careful in his spending, avoided borrowing money, and planned well ahead, all of which resulted in a significant recovery of the royal finances.

He made consistent efforts to win the support and cooperation of his magnates. His aggressive war policy united them behind him and brought England to the forefront of European politics. England had not been so well governed since the time of Edward III.

Having established himself firmly on the throne, Henry turned his attention to the fulfillment of an ambition he had long cherished: the conquest of France. He firmly believed that God was on his side, that his claim to the French throne was just, and that he was undertaking a sacred duty. By unifying his people in such a great cause, he could channel their energies and interests into a profitable enterprise and so avert any threat of rebellion.

The magnates, and the people at large, supported him enthusiastically, as did Parliament, which did not hesitate to vote funds for an invasion force. This seemed the ideal moment to strike: the mad King Charles VI reigned in France and the country was divided by factional rivalries.

On 30 June 1414, Henry gave Queen Joan permission to reside in the royal castles of Windsor, Wallingford, Berkhamsted, and Hertford during his forthcoming absence in France. In the sixteenth century, the chronicler Raphael Holinshed claimed that he appointed her, as "a woman of great prudence and judgment in national affairs, to be regent in his absence, with the advice of the Privy Council." But there is no contemporary evidence for this, and it was Henry's brother, John, Duke of Bedford, whom Joan called "our dearest and best-beloved son,"[5] who was made lord protector of the realm.

PART TWO

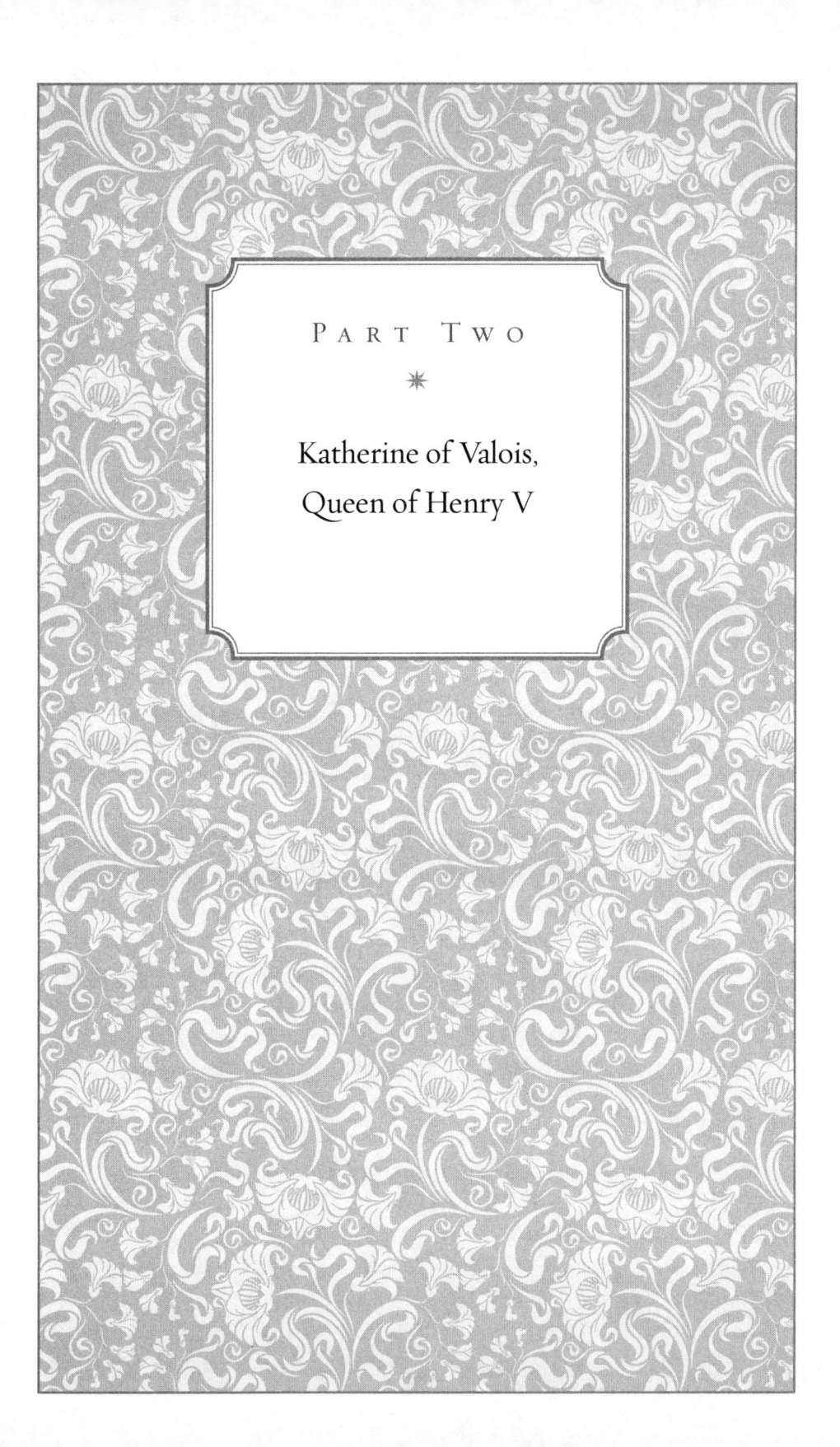

✸

Katherine of Valois,
Queen of Henry V

I

"Your fair and noble daughter"

✳

WHEN PARLIAMENT MET IN APRIL 1414, "THE SUBJECT OF this most illustrious King's marriage was broached, and he consented, provided such a consort could be found for him as would conduce to the peace and harmony and quietness of the realm."[1] Henry saw that at least parts of France might become his through an alliance, rather than war. In May, Thomas Chaucer, son of the poet Geoffrey, was commissioned to travel to France to propose—once more—a marriage between the King and Charles VI's youngest daughter, Katherine; he was to treat with the French and inform them that Henry would not consider marrying anyone else for a year. Between July and October, the Earl of Salisbury was in France, pushing forward the negotiations, which were to be among the most protracted in English royal history. On 28 July, Henry himself wrote to Charles VI: "We are disposed to lead an innocent life with your fair and noble daughter Katherine, our very dear cousin." Talks were resumed in December, when another embassy arrived in Paris. The Holy Roman Emperor Sigismund was keen to see the marriage go ahead, and Charles VI's government asked him to use his influence in that behalf. Sigismund informed Henry that he would be meeting with Charles to discuss the matter, but nothing came of his intervention.

On 12 March 1415, an English embassy led by bishops Langley and Courtenay met Charles's representatives in France, and informed them that their master was demanding all the lands ceded by France to England in 1360 under the terms of the Treaty of Brétigny, which included Aquitaine, Gascony, Poitou, Saintonge, the Agenais, the Périgord, the Limousin, Quercy, Bigorre, the Angoumois, Montreuil-sur-Mer, Ponthieu, Calais, Sangatte, and Guînes, along with a dowry of two million gold crowns (£315 million). The bishops stated that Parliament was prepared to offer a dower of a million crowns, on condition that Katherine's father provided her trousseau in return.

The French refused to recognize Henry's claims or agree to his extortionate terms. Instead, in July, they offered territorial concessions in Aquitaine and a dowry of 600,000 gold crowns (£96:5 million)—greater than that of any previous French princess—with clothes and jewels. The English bishops were not authorized to agree to the territorial proposals, but they lowered their demand for the dowry to one million crowns (£154:5 million). The French, however, would only go to 850,000 crowns (£133:9 million), while Henry was adamant that he be given full sovereignty of the territories he had demanded. With no agreement, the English envoys returned home at the end of March.

Katherine of Valois had been born on 27 October 1401 at the Hôtel de Saint-Pol, a Parisian royal residence built in 1360 by her grandfather, Charles V. (It was demolished in the sixteenth century.) She was the tenth child and youngest daughter of Charles VI and Isabeau of Bavaria, and she was brought up with her sister Michelle at the Hôtel de Saint-Pol, where her mentally unstable father lived from 1403.

In 1392, Charles VI had experienced an attack of raging mania, run berserk with a lance, and killed four people before being overcome by his attendants. Since then, he had been subject to violent fits and delusions, sometimes believing he was made of glass and would shatter if touched; at other times he announced that his name was George and seemed unable to recognize his wife and children.

Charles did have periods of lucidity, as when Katherine was born. But when he was in the grip of insanity, he foamed at the mouth, refused to wash, and quickly became filthy, infested with vermin, and covered in sores. Like a dog, he would eat his food off the floor. He "suffered fits of madness which recurred every year at the same season."[2]

Katherine's diminutive, dark-haired mother, Isabeau of Bavaria, came from the German House of Wittelsbach; her mother was a Visconti of Milan. Isabeau did not deserve her later reputation for being a nymphomaniac and neglecting her children. In the seventeenth century, François Timoléon, Abbé de Choisy, a writer not known for historical accuracy, asserted that Katherine and her sister Michelle were filthy, sometimes starving, and frequently abandoned by their unpaid attendants, and that they had to scavenge for food or rely on the charity of servants. He claimed that when Charles VI came out of one of his stupors, he taxed Katherine's governess with the appalling state of his daughters, and that she told him that the Queen was responsible.

"I myself am not better treated, you perceive," he allegedly replied, and gave her a gold cup to sell, so that she could buy necessities for the princesses.

It has recently been demonstrated that these calumnies have their roots in Burgundian and English propaganda, none of which is substantiated by contemporary evidence. Isabeau was the victim of a campaign of character assassination, which has continued down the centuries. Significantly, she had fallen out with Burgundy, who also acted as regent when his nephew, the King, was incapacitated, and wanted her influence neutralized. She was in fact a respected and competent regent during her husband's spells of insanity. Her accounts show that she was a loyal wife and a good mother who bought clothing, toys, and books for her children and paid for Masses for those who died in infancy. In 1404, when there was an outbreak of plague in Paris, she moved them to Melun for safety. Katherine was taught to read, and perhaps to write. Her Book of Hours, now in the British Library, contains prayers that may have been written in her own hand.

Katherine's eldest sister, Isabella, had been married to Richard II of England in 1396, but had returned to France in 1401 after his deposition and death, and been found a second husband in Charles, Duke of Orléans. She had died in childbirth in 1409. Katherine's brother, Charles, two years her junior, was the Dauphin, the heir to France. Of her two surviving sisters, Jeanne and Michelle were respectively married to John V, Duke of Brittany (the son of Joan of Navarre), and Philip, heir to John the Fearless, Duke of Burgundy, after the death of Philip the Bold in 1404. Another sister, Marie, became Prioress of Poissy. The royal children were brought up with Burgundy's offspring, of whom Anne and

Agnes would have been Katherine's closest companions, although they were younger than her.

There was fierce rivalry for the regency between the King's younger brother, Louis, Duke of Orléans, and John the Fearless. Rumors claimed that Orléans was the Queen's lover, and attempts were made to kidnap the royal children. On one occasion, learning that the King was restored to his senses, the Queen and Orléans were said to have plotted to flee to Milan and take the girls with them, but were overtaken on the road by Burgundy. Another time, when the King was again lucid, Isabeau deserted Orléans and asked her brother, Louis of Bavaria, to escort her children and Burgundy's daughters to her. Burgundy sent men in pursuit, for Michelle was betrothed to his son. At Juvisy, they captured his daughters and Michelle, and ordered the Dauphin, Katherine, and the other royal children to be taken back to the King in Paris.

After Orléans was murdered in 1407, Isabeau was imprisoned at Tours. Katherine was taken from her and sent to be educated at the convent at Poissy, where her sister Marie was shortly to take the veil. There, she perhaps learned some Latin and emerged with the most engaging manners.

Money was needed for the war, and concern was expressed in Parliament that, despite having been banished, "many Bretons had come into the kingdom again, some of whom were then dwelling in the Queen's house, and others very near it." Some were believed to be spies who had learned state secrets there and sold them abroad. "It was requested that the King would constrain all such to depart."[3] Bedford, determined to avoid unnecessary outlay on Queen Joan's retinue, may have stirred up feeling against these foreigners.

In the middle of June, as he prepared to leave for France, Henry went in procession to St. Paul's Cathedral and made an offering, and "from thence to the Queen [Joan], the self-same day, and took his leave full reverently."[4]

Early in July, a French embassy led by the Archbishop of Bourges came to London to say that King Charles was willing to dismember his kingdom by ceding to England many important territories and towns, and to give Henry his daughter Katherine in marriage with 800,000 gold crowns (£126 million), a dowry that was unprecedented. But Henry, who feasted the envoys royally, demanded 900,000 crowns (£141:8 million), while the envoys stalled at setting a date for the Princess to come to England, and did not help matters when they challenged the validity of Henry's claim to France and even asserted that he had no right to the crown of England either, and that they ought to be treating with the rightful heirs of Richard II. A furious Henry declared that he would take France by force, to which the envoys replied that, if that was his intention, King Charles would do his best to receive him; but it would be a strange way of wooing Katherine, covered with the blood of her countrymen. At that, negotiations abruptly broke down and the French went home.

In late summer, having left Bedford as regent of England, Henry crossed the English Channel with an army of 10,000 men to win his rights in France, and his Princess. He laid siege to the port of Harfleur and took it. In October 1415, the English scored an unexpected and spectacular victory over the flower of French chivalry at the Battle of Agincourt. As at Crécy and Poitiers in the reign of Edward III, it was the skill of the English archers that proved the decisive factor. Among the French casualties were Queen Joan's brother Charles of Navarre, and John, Duke of Alençon, husband of her daughter Marie, a young mother of five, who was forced to flee from the English forces in Normandy. Joan's son Arthur had also fought for the French, but had been wounded before being captured by Henry V.

The importance of Agincourt cannot be overestimated. Apart from demoralizing the French, it fired the imagination of every Englishman, made Henry V a popular hero, and bolstered the growing nationalism of his subjects. Few now questioned the title of Lancaster to the throne, for both Henry and his people believed that God had vindicated his right by granting such a decisive victory.

2

"Our dearest and best-beloved son"

※

ONE OF HENRY'S FIRST ACTS AFTER THE BATTLE WAS TO INform his stepmother of his triumph. He "dispatched a messenger to the Queen with news of his victory, which filled the nation with universal joy." Joan was with Bishop Beaufort at a service in St. Paul's Cathedral when the news was brought to her. She must have had very mixed feelings about the English victory, and had to conceal them, but she ensured that *"Te Deum* was sung in all the churches, and a mighty procession consisting of the Queen, prelates and nobility, with the Mayor and corporation of the City of London, walked from St. Paul's to Westminster on the following day to return public thanks to Almighty God."[1]

On 10 November, addressing him as "high and puissant Prince, our dearest and best-beloved son," Joan wrote to Bedford from Langley on behalf of her "dear and good friend John Faringdon, our attorney general, that he may be paid his fee, and thus this our hearty prayer may take full effect in accomplishment of our desire in this matter, according to the entire confidence that we have in you. And if there be anything on our part that we can do to your pleasure, be pleased to signify it, and we will accomplish it with very good heart, according to our power."[2] Her signature on this letter—"Royne Jahanne"—is the earliest surviving signature of a queen of England.

That November, Henry returned to England. As the bells of London pealed out, he was received in the City with wild rejoicing and fêted with nine hours of pageantry and processions culminating in a service of thanksgiving in St. Paul's, where Queen Joan was waiting to greet him. Not once, in all that celebration, was the austere King seen to smile, even though his people were ebullient with joy and shouting their acclaim. When the day's celebrations drew to a close, Joan accompanied Henry to Westminster.

A grateful Parliament happily voted further subsidies to finance the continuation of the war, even though the cost of the campaign had been enormous and placed some strain on an already overburdened treasury. Parliament also petitioned the King for the removal of all Bretons residing in England, including those who remained in the Queen's household, on the grounds that they were enemies of the realm and selling state secrets to the French. Joan made no complaint.

Henry had brought to England his captive, Arthur of Brittany, who was allowed a meeting with his mother. Joan had not seen him since 1404, when he was eleven; he was now twenty-two. According to a Breton lord, she was hoping that he might instinctively recognize her and had one of her ladies-in-waiting sit in her place when Arthur was brought to her chamber. When he greeted the lady as his mother, Joan railed at him, then "both began to cry because they were so dear to each other. And the Queen gave him a thousand nobles, and also shirts and garments, and he did not afterward dare to speak to her or visit her, as he would have wished,"[3] for the King packed him off to the Tower, and then to Fotheringhay Castle, and would not let Joan see him again. It was impossible for her to intercede for his release or ransom, lest her own loyalty come under suspicion, so she wisely did her best to work for peace between England and Brittany, and remained in favor. When, in 1416, the Council "banished strangers about Queen Joan, who give information to the enemy and carry much treasure out of the kingdom,"[4] suspicion did not attach to her.

Between 1415 and 1418, Henry made several grants and concessions to Joan. In 1416, at the feast of St. George, she and other Ladies of the Garter—the queens of Spain, Portugal, and Denmark, and the Duchess of Holland—each received from him eight ells of blue cloth, two luxurious furs made up of 300 bellies of miniver, and 170 Garter stripes, all to make new Garter robes. In 1418, Henry ordered the collectors at the Port of London to waive the dues on three sealed cases of money, sixty pipes of wine, seven baskets of lamps, two bales of Joscelin cloth, and one barrel of anchovies that had been brought to England on the *St. Nicholas of Nantes* for Joan. That same day, orders went to the ports of Plymouth and Dartmouth to allow John V's man, Johan de Moine, to bring eight large barrels of wine into the country for the Queen Dowager, free of duty. The King also allowed the *St. Nicholas of Nantes* to import animals, an organ player, and other items for her. Jacotin de Hasse, her horsemaster, brought her four horses, three smaller palfreys, a popinjay, and London cloth.

Clearly, relations between Joan and her stepson were warm, even though her son John V was hostile to Henry's ambitions in France. However, the year before, thanks in part to Joan's influence, the two rulers had signed a truce in which they had agreed to refrain from all acts of war against each other. In 1418, Joan sent gifts of a popinjay and three horses to John's wife, Jeanne.

In 1417, Henry V launched a campaign to conquer Normandy, the patrimony of his ancestors. Caen and Lisieux fell to him that year, Falaise, Domfront, and Louviers in 1418.

Months later, the Dauphin Charles, heir to Charles VI, had hinted about resurrecting a marriage alliance between England and France, and in November an English embassy traveled to Alençon to reopen negotiations. But after Henry demanded Normandy, Aquitaine, Ponthieu, and other lands once held by the English, along with a dowry now back up to a million gold crowns, the meeting ended in deadlock.

The following month, an English delegation met with the French and the Burgundians at Pont-de-l'Arche. Burgundy's envoy, Cardinal Orsini, brought a portrait of Katherine for Henry and asked whether so beautiful a princess required a great dowry. When shown the portrait, Henry said he liked it well and thought the Princess "surpassing fair." But he still demanded a million crowns as dowry, plus the lands ceded at Brétigny, and again negotiations broke down.

In 1418, Queen Isabeau was imprisoned at Tours by the Count of Armagnac, father-in-law of the Dauphin, but after Burgundy came to her rescue, she went to Troyes and again established herself as regent, taking control of the King and her daughter Katherine. She would cede the regency to Burgundy later that year.

The Norman capital, Rouen, capitulated in January 1419 after a long and bitter siege, occasioning great celebrations in London. Henry, meanwhile, had pressed on to take Paris, the capital. On 7 April, representatives of both kingdoms arranged for him to meet with Katherine, her parents, and Burgundy. The meeting opened on 29 May in a large, palisaded field at Meulan, opposite Isle Belle on the River Seine. Henry arrived with Burgundy, while Isabeau and Katherine came in a brightly painted barge. The French camp was set up at one end of the field—Isabeau and her daughter stayed in a tent of blue velvet embroidered with the fleurs-de-lis of France—while the English pavilions were at the opposite end. A tent set up in the middle was to be used for the negotiations. King Charles could not attend—he was suffering another episode of madness.

On 1 June, after three days of feasting and negotiations, Henry was introduced to Katherine for the first time. He was reportedly overwhelmed by her beauty and charm. It was love at first sight, wrote Waurin, "that fired the heart of this martial King."[5] According to the Burgundian chronicler Monstrelet, "King Henry was very desirous to marry her, and not without cause, for she was very handsome, of high birth, and with the most engaging manners." Her beauty, it was said, more than justified her portrait. At eighteen, she had blossomed into "a very handsome lady to look at, of graceful figure and pleasing countenance."[6] In the *Bedford Hours*, she is depicted with fair hair, like most representations of the Virgin Mary. Her wooden funeral effigy at Westminster Abbey shows her to have had a long neck, good bone structure, and the elongated Valois nose.

There are other images of Katherine. Monstrelet's chronicle has a woodcut of her based on a carved image on an oak chest in York Minster. A stone head from the church at Stackallan, County Meath, found in a field and auctioned in Dublin in 2018, has been identified as her, the features being strikingly similar to the effigy at Westminster.

"With a most respectful obeisance," Henry "saluted the Queen and then kissed her and her daughter." Some chroniclers noted Katherine's blushes and her sweetness. Shakespeare's delightful scene between the King and his "French Kate" is fiction, but "it was plainly to be seen that

King Henry was desperately in love with her."[7] Katherine, who left the gathering at the end of the day, also felt a strong attraction. "She had passionately longed to be married to King Henry and, from the moment she saw him, constantly solicited her mother, with whom she could do anything, until her marriage took place." But when Henry asked to meet her a second time, Isabeau refused, probably assuming that keeping her daughter tantalizingly out of reach would increase his ardor and make him more amenable in negotiations.

Still he continued to press his claims. He even offered to surrender his right to the crown of France in return for the lands ceded by treaty in 1360. The French were having none of it. They insisted that 600,000 crowns (£96:5 million) be deducted from the dowry of 800,000 crowns (£126 million) they were now offering, because that sum should have been reimbursed when Katherine's sister Isabella, widow of Richard II, had returned to France in 1401. Henry countered by demanding a rebate of 400,000 crowns for the jewels assigned to Katherine, which he asserted were not worth a quarter of that sum. The arguments continued until early July, when Burgundy refused to negotiate any further and made peace with the Armagnacs. An angry Henry warned that he would have the Princess Katherine and all he demanded, or he would drive Charles and Burgundy out of France.

On 11 July, John the Fearless signed a peace treaty with Charles VI. At the end of the month, Henry seized Pontoise in retaliation. Fearing that Paris would be next, Charles and Isabeau fled with Katherine to Troyes. But on 10 September, Burgundy was murdered at Montereau by supporters of the Dauphin Charles, an act of violence that proved advantageous to England because it drove John's son Philip, the new Duke of Burgundy (later known as Philip the Good), toward a stronger alliance with the English. When the news was brought to Henry, he vowed that, with the help of God and St. George, he would have the Lady Katherine, though every Frenchman said him nay. He assured the messengers that he would aid Philip, but only if he himself married Katherine and succeeded Charles VI as King of France.

On 20 September, Queen Isabeau appealed to Henry V to avenge the Duke's death and resume the marriage negotiations. Henry did an about-turn. On 27 October, at Mantes, he received Charles VI's representatives and told them he was prepared to take Katherine without a dowry—if her father recognized him as the heir to France. He also informed Duke Philip that if he agreed to support that compromise, Henry would avenge his father's murder. At Christmas, Henry and Philip concluded a new alliance, in which it was agreed that Henry would marry Katherine and one of his brothers would marry Philip's sister Anne (John, Duke of Bedford, would marry Anne of Burgundy in 1423) and that Henry and Katherine would have France when Charles died.

3

"The superstitious deeds of necromancers"

✵

IN 1419, HENRY CONCLUDED A TRUCE WITH THE DUKE OF BRITtany, "at the prayer of Joan, that excellent and most dear lady, the Queen our mother, as she desires peace and tranquillity."[1] Joan's influence had secured Brittany's neutrality, and she did all she could to maintain it, with the result that the truce was extended later that year.

Until now, relations between the King and his stepmother had evidently been warm and cordial. But in August 1419, when Henry was fighting hard to conquer Normandy and his brother Bedford was in charge in England, two members of the Queen Dowager's household, Roger Colles and Petronelle Brocart, laid information against her confessor, a Franciscan friar called John Randolf. On 16 August, "the King's kinswoman," Joan Fitzalan, the widowed Lady Bergavenny, who lived near the Franciscan priory in Shrewsbury, was ordered to "seize all gold, silver things, goods and jewels of any kind" in the friar's possession "or committed by him to any other person to keep, and bring them before the King and Council"[2] to be confiscated. The inventory in *The Rolls of Parliament* shows that many were high-status items, such as jewels and plate and a woman's nightcap, "red after the guise of Brittany," suggesting they had belonged to Joan. Some—chalices and images of the Trinity—obviously came from the Queen's chapel and were properly in the care of her confessor.

Randolf had tried to flee abroad but was arrested in Guernsey and sent to Henry V in Normandy. The Parliament Rolls recorded that, "upon information given to the King, our sovereign lord, as well by relation and confession of one Friar John Randolf, as by other credible evidences, that Joan, Queen of England, had compassed and imagined the death and destruction of our said lord the King in the most high and horrible manner that could be devised." There is no mention of witchcraft in this shocking accusation. Walsingham didn't mention it either, writing only that Joan "was accused by certain persons of some wickedness that would have tended to the King's harm." However, on 25 September, the Archbishop of Canterbury would relay to the English clergy the King's order that they offer prayers "to preserve and protect him from the superstitious deeds of necromancers" who were plotting his destruction,[3] from which it might be inferred that Joan was indeed suspected of witchcraft. Later, it was openly stated that Randolf, "at the exciting of the said Queen, by sorcery and necromancy wrought for to destroy the King; but, as God would, his falseness was at last espied."[4]

We do not know what evidence was produced against Joan, how she allegedly intended to harm the King, or what Randolf actually said in his confession, but news of her "compassing, imagination and destruction" was "published throughout all England."[5]

With so little evidence to go on, it is hard to determine Joan's guilt. We have no record of her inner feelings, but she had long had reason to resent the King, who had been instrumental in bringing about the death of her brother and the imprisonment of her son. She was joined by kinship to England's ancient enemy, and she had never been popular in her adopted land. Yet what would she have gained from destroying or harming Henry V? He had no son to succeed him, and his death might have precipitated a civil war between rival claimants for the throne. That Joan, who had striven to establish peace in Brittany, would not have thought of that seems unlikely. If she had wanted revenge on Henry for refusing to heed her pleas for Arthur's release, she had waited a long time to take it. Besides, her comfortable life in England depended on his favor.

A century later, under Henry VIII, Joan would have faced the death penalty for compassing the death of the King. But Henry V did not go so far. On 27 September, an Order in Council decreed that all the lands, property, goods, and chattels of the Queen, "and also all the goods and chattels of Roger Colles of Salisbury and of Petronelle Brocart, lately residing with the said Queen, who are notoriously suspected of the said treason, should be received and kept by the Treasurer of England, or his deputy, for the time being, who should have the custody of the said goods and chattels, and that letters patent should be passed under the Great Seal in that behalf; and that the Treasurer should provide for the support of the Queen and the servants assigned to her, according to the advice of the Council, openly read in this Parliament. And because it was doubted whether persons bound to pay rents to the Queen could be discharged, it was ordained in Parliament, at the request of the Commons assembled, that all such persons, upon payment to the Treasurer, shall be protected against the said Queen in all time to come."[6] In other words, Joan would not be able to proceed against them for nonpayment of their dues. The chief beneficiary of her forfeiture was the King, but others profited also, including Jacqueline of Hainault, wife of Humphrey, Duke of Gloucester, and Margaret, Duchess of Bavaria, widow of John the Fearless.

Joan did not face trial, which is probably significant in itself. Had she been condemned, the law would have demanded her execution. Plotting regicide was treason, for which women were burned at the stake. But Henry V did not prosecute her, possibly out of respect for his father's memory, or because he feared reprisals from Brittany—or because he knew that the charges were baseless.

What is likely is that Henry dared not risk a court finding her innocent, because he would have had to return her dower, which represented a large proportion of government revenues. This suggests that Joan had been deliberately framed so that he could use her revenues to raise more much-needed money for the war—and to dower his bride. Significantly, early in 1419, Henry had exhorted his "dear chevalier, William Kynwolmersh, to send all the sums of money he possibly can borrow of the dower of Joan the Queen." "Let these sums be sent from time to time without fail," he commanded, "leaving her only money enough for her reasonable expenses, and to pay any annuities she might have granted."[7]

Despite being deprived of her English income, Joan still had the rents from her Breton dower, so she was not impoverished. But she was to lose her freedom. On 1 October, on Bedford's order, she was arrested at Havering, charged with "treasonous imagining" and "seeking by sorcery and necromancy to have destroyed the King."[8] Having been "committed (all her attendants being removed) to the governance and safe custody"[9] of Sir John Pelham, a friend of her late husband, who seems to have been a lenient jailer, she found herself confined in a moated manor house at Rotherhithe that had been built by Edward III in 1350, but was now owned by Bermondsey Abbey. Here she was allowed nine serving women and kept in some comfort, £52:6s.9d. (£45,300) being outlaid in the first week alone of her confinement.

In December, having hired five new attendants, Pelham escorted Joan via Dartford and Rochester to Leeds Castle before confining her in Pevensey Castle, near the Sussex coast, later that month, "there to be kept under his control."[10] It had originally been built around AD 290 as the last of the Roman forts of the Saxon shore, to guard the kingdom against invaders. Within its massive walls, the Normans had built a castle, now ruined, although parts of the towers, keep, and chapel remain. In 1268, it had been granted to Eleanor of Provence, Queen of Henry III, and remained in the hands of the Crown, passing to John of Gaunt, who had appointed Sir John Pelham as its constable in 1394. Pelham had later supported Henry IV's coup against Richard II and been granted Pevensey Castle in reward. By then, it was in poor condition, having been rarely used by royalty, although James I of Scots had been imprisoned there in Pelham's custody in 1415, and repairs and maintenance would be undertaken in the years that followed. The strongly fortified inner bailey was enclosed by a large moat; it had a keep in one corner, ranges of lodgings and a hall, a chapel where Mass would be celebrated in the Queen's presence on all the major feast days of the Church, and a kitchen in the courtyard.

£37 (£32,230) a week was allocated for her expenses. That sum, however, gradually dwindled to £11 (£9,580) because she ran up a high expenditure, although her friends were allowed to send money to her. It appears that her imprisonment was not oppressive, which again suggests that the charges were trumped up, since a witch who had compassed the King's death would have merited a far harsher punishment.

Daily sums were spent on her kitchen, buttery, stables, and wardrobe. She was provided with horses, suggesting that she was allowed to ride out, presumably under guard. She was assigned a large household of between twenty-eight and thirty-six servants, including four officers, four ladies, nineteen grooms, and seven pages. She employed a clerk, Thomas Lilbourne, whose accounts survive, and two serjeants-at-law to ensure that she received all moneys due to her, including queengold, her share of fines payable to the King. The King's own physician, the Portuguese Pedro de Alcobaça (known in England as Peter de Offball), was appointed to attend to her ailments and charged expensive medicines to the Exchequer.

She had been stripped of her goods, including her beds—always the most costly items of furniture in a medieval household—and her clothes; it appears (from an address made by Henry V to his Council in July 1422) that she was made—at least initially—to dress in black, in the garb of a penitent. A London mercer was paid to supply nine yards of black cloth, costing 36s. (£1,150) for two kirtles for her, and a further eight yards for a gown. These, and hose, were made up by a tailor. More bolts of fabric were provided for Joan's male and female attendants.

John V was furious when he heard the news of his mother's arrest. He sent a deputation headed by the Bishop of Nantes to Henry V at Melun to demand her immediate release, but their journey was in vain. The King was implacable. In December, he had Randolf imprisoned in Château Gaillard, but soon moved him to the Tower of London, where he was guarded by nine men, which shows how dangerous he was considered to be.

In February 1420, John V himself, along with his brother Richard, was captured by the Count of Penthièvre and the Dauphin in a bid to make him renounce the duchy of Brittany, which meant that Joan and three of her sons were all prisoners at the same time. Appeals to Henry V fell on deaf ears, but the brothers were soon released, thanks to the efforts of John's Duchess, Jeanne de Valois.

In March 1420, Joan was moved to the greater comfort of Leeds Castle. Her Wardrobe Book, now in the castle archives, records her expenditure for the period from 8 March to 21 July. She had an allowance of food, drink, and firewood. She was able to send to Flanders for furs, silks, lace, linens, and a rich silk material called tartaire, and to Scandinavia for aqua vitae. Her harp was repaired and she was provided with a new cage for her popinjay. The luxuries provided for her included a girdle and garters of gold, silk laces, a silver-gilt buckle, 400 clasps, gold rosaries, a gold chain with a pendant Lamb of God, a buckle and pendant of silver gilt, a gilt basin, silver-gilt knives, a silver candlestick, a gold rosary, rose water, and a pot of citrus. Other purchases included shoes, gloves, and boots. Joan still dressed chiefly in black garments, among them a black satin mantle lined with squirrel fur; she had thirty pairs of shoes and, in the bath, wore "stewing" clothes made of nineteen ells of cloth. She had a thirteenth-century psalter, which she inscribed with her name, and a book of hours, now in the Philadelphia Free Library.

Her larders were stocked with wheat, barley, beans, peas, oats, ale, oxen, beef, veal, lamb, pork, capons, poultry, geese, ducks, pheasants, partridges, rabbit, salted and fresh fish, treacle, and costly spices including pepper, cinnamon, green ginger, and myrrh. There were ample stores of hay, litter, coal, firewood, and rushes for the floors. Joan kept a wine cellar for which she purchased wines from Gascony, La Rochelle, and the Rhineland.

She was given no new Garter robes, and never would be again, but she was permitted to receive and entertain visitors, among them Archbishop Chichele, Bishop Beaufort (twice), and—on three occasions—her stepson Humphrey, Duke of Gloucester, who were all entertained by Nicholas, Joan's minstrel. Had the charges against her been credible, these guests would probably have given her a wide berth.

Thomas, Lord Camoys, arrived in April 1420 and stayed as Joan's guest until January 1421. She had known him since he escorted her to England in 1403, and it has been suggested that they were close. He was around seventy and had been a widower for three years; she was perhaps fifty-two. The length of his stay shows that they were at least good friends. When he died on 28 March 1421, Joan wore a mourning gown made from seven yards of black cloth, with a fur-trimmed collar, and a satin cloak. That Easter, she bought a new outfit and ordered several bolts of black cloth to be made up into gowns and mantles, squirrel fur, and fur for a collar and to line a cloak.

During the year ending March 1421, the government outlaid £700 (£637,760) on Joan's maintenance, notably less than the 10,000 marks (£5,754,920) of her dower.

4

"My dear Englishman"

✳

As the war dragged on, Henry V's reputation for cruelty grew. At the siege of Rouen, his harsh treatment of noncombatants—women, children, and old men—resulted in 12,000 dying from hunger and exposure. Anyone bearing arms who refused to surrender was put to death, and Henry once had a deserter buried alive before his horrified companions. When Caen fell, 2,000 people were rounded up in the marketplace and slaughtered, their blood running in rivulets through the streets. Henry turned a deaf ear to the cries of the doomed citizens until he came upon the corpse of a decapitated woman with a dead baby at her breast. Only then did he call a halt to the killing, although he allowed his men to continue to plunder and rape. As he rode by on his charger, stern and implacable, hordes of terrified people fell to their knees, crying for mercy.

By 1420, Henry was master of Normandy, Brittany, Maine, Champagne, and the duchy of Aquitaine. The greatest prize of all was within his grasp, but he had had enough of negotiating with the French and declared that he had been deceived and baffled so many times that he would treat with no one but the Princess Katherine herself, whose innocence, he was sure, would not try to deceive him. His words were reported to the Queen, who sent the Bishop of Arras to Henry to say that if he came to Troyes, Katherine would marry him there, and that, as her inheritance, he should have the crown of France after the death of King

Charles. Charles had already disinherited his one surviving son, the Dauphin, for ordering the murder of John the Fearless.

Isabeau took Charles and Katherine to Troyes, where they lodged at an inn called La Couronne, on the market square. When the English army arrived, they moved to a Franciscan convent.

On 23 March 1420, Henry rode into Troyes in state, "longing for the sight of his darling,"[1] and was received by Charles VI, Queen Isabeau, and Philip of Burgundy. On 9 April, a peace treaty was drawn up. Henry informed the Lord Mayor of London of "the bond of matrimony made for the good of peace between us and our dear and most beloved Katherine," who was to have a dower of 10,000 marks, the same sum as Joan of Navarre. In her husband's name, Isabeau agreed that Henry would inherit France on Charles VI's death and that the French throne would devolve upon his heirs and successors. Normandy was formally ceded to Henry, and he was to be regent of France if the need arose before he succeeded to the throne. Arthur of Brittany was released; he would be appointed Constable of France in 1422.

The treaty was signed on 15 May at Troyes. Five days later, Katherine was present when Henry visited the court of Charles VI at the convent. He bowed low to her, "kissing her with great joy."[2] There followed "a joyous meeting, honorable receiving, and a loving embracing of both parties."[3]

When the treaty was ratified and sealed on 21 May 1420 in the cathedral, in the presence of the flower of the English and French nobility, Katherine sat enthroned with her mother, whose signature on the document damned her reputation in France for centuries to come. When Henry knelt before Katherine and the Queen, they apologized that the King was indisposed, Charles having lapsed into madness again. Henry took Katherine's hand and led her and Isabeau to the high altar, where the articles of the treaty were read out and they all appended their seals. Then Henry plighted his troth, placing on Katherine's finger a costly ring. She timidly assented. Then he presented her to Sir Louis de Robart, whom he had appointed to defend her person whenever he himself was away at war. Afterward, Henri de Savoisy, Archbishop of Sens, conducted the betrothal ceremony, and a banquet was held in celebration; wishing to avoid drunken misbehavior, Henry ordered his soldiers to drink only watered wine.

Thenceforth, he called Katherine "our wife." She sent him a love letter, which was delivered by the Bishop of Arras.

Six days later, peace between England and France was proclaimed—one of the most contentious peaces in French history, for the Treaty of Troyes effectively disinherited the House of Valois and marked the pinnacle of Henry V's achievement in France. Yet hostilities continued as before, when the Dauphin Charles, a penniless exile, set up a rival court at Bourges, determined to fight for the throne.

Escorted by the Count of Saint-Pol, Katherine came again to Troyes on 1 June. She was richly garbed, Burgundy having outlaid 3,000 florins (about £20,000) on her bridal gown and trousseau. She looked "right good and fair, of grace intrepid in her womanhood," the bringer of peace "with bright beams shining."[4] When her bridegroom greeted her and kissed her hand, his nobles saw her blush.

The "magnificent espousals" of Henry V and "that excellent, glorious lady, Dame Katherine" took place "with great solemnity" at noon on Trinity Sunday, 2 June.[5] Walsingham wrote that the setting was Troyes Cathedral, but the contemporary French chronicler Jean Juvénal des Ursins stated that the King "willed that the ceremony should be carried out entirely according to the custom of France in the parish church of St. John at Troyes"—the church of Saint-Jean-au-Marché, where the King made a handsome offering of 213 nobles (£45,654) on his wedding day, having walked there from his hotel across the marketplace, attended by a strong military presence, James I, King of Scots (then being held in honorable captivity by the English), and many lords in sumptuous finery. "Great pomp and magnificence were displayed by [Henry] and his princes, as if he were at that moment king of all the world."[6] Katherine arrived in a chariot drawn by eight white English horses, a gift from her husband-to-be. Her mother and sisters were present in church, with only a few French peers. Burgundy was among them, wearing deepest mourning.

An illustration of the wedding appears in the Beauchamp Pageant. After the ceremony, which was conducted by the Archbishop of Sens, the royal couple made offerings at the altar, then sipped wine from a wooden mazer. Music was provided by sixteen singers and thirty-eight musicians brought by the King.

His English knights had wanted to mark the nuptials with a tournament, but Henry had refused. "Playing at fighting was not to be the amusement of his wedding, but the actual siege of Sens,"[7] which Henry's forces had encircled. As soon as the ceremony was over, a public proclamation was made that everyone should be ready armed and equipped by the following day. In the meantime, there was a feast in the archiepiscopal palace, and the blessing of the nuptial bed by the Archbishop. Later that night, the guests formed a grand procession and brought wine and soup to the newlyweds. A nuptial hymn was sung and there was much merrymaking. Then everyone left the couple alone until a fanfare of trumpets sounded a *réveil* at dawn.

On 3 June, Henry marched out of Troyes to besiege Sens. Katherine, her parents, and Burgundy accompanied him. On 11 June, after Sens fell, he and Katherine rode in state through its gates together with the Archbishop of Sens, to whom Henry said, "You have given me a wife, and now I restore you yours—your church."

The King left Katherine with her mother at Bray-sur-Seine when he rode to nearby Montereau, where the Armagnacs were holding the body of John the Fearless. Having laid siege to the town, he made several visits to Katherine. Montereau fell on 24 June and the corpse was exhumed and retrieved for burial at Dijon. By then, Henry Chichele, Archbishop of Canterbury, had arrived in France, come to congratulate the King on his marriage.

The court moved to Corbeil. Henry had already assembled a household for Katherine. She was not permitted any French servants except three ladies and two damsels; the rest of the women were English, among them Margaret Holland, Duchess of Clarence (the wife of Henry's youngest brother, Thomas), who was appointed Katherine's chief lady-in-waiting. They arrived from England in July, with many other noblewomen who came to pay their respects. Katherine's seal survives in King's Lynn Museum.

On 13 July, Henry laid siege to Melun. He visited Katherine on occasion at Corbeil, and sent her jewels worth 100,000 crowns (£16 million), although they were seized by French brigands before they reached her.

As the siege dragged on, Henry had a house built for her within his encampment and sent for her to join him. She came with her parents and stayed for a month. Every morning, she was woken by the sound of minstrels playing for her, and every evening, they played for an hour to soothe her to sleep. This was a tender gesture on Henry's part, as was his purchase of harps costing £8:13s.4d. (£8,850) for them both in October. Theirs was a dynastic match, yet there was clearly more to it than that. All the evidence suggests that he was pleased with his bride.

When Melun fell on 18 November, Henry had Isabeau proclaimed regent of France. On 1 December, he, Charles VI, and Burgundy rode in state into Paris, where they were ceremoniously received by the Parlement, the university, and the burgesses of the city. The next day, attended by a train of noblewomen, "Queen Katherine and her mother made their grand entry into Paris," their ermine cloaks borne before their litter. They entered through the Porte Saint-Antoine, where they were received by Burgundy and the King's brothers, John, Duke of Bedford, and Thomas, Duke of Clarence. "Great magnificence was displayed at the arrival of the Queen of England, but it would take up too much time to relate all the rich presents that were offered to her by the citizens of Paris. The streets and houses were hung with tapestry the whole of that day, and wine was constantly running from brass cocks and in conduits, and more rejoicings than tongues can tell were made in Paris for the peace and for the marriage of Katherine the Fair."[8] She and Isabeau were present when Henry held a magnificent court at the palace of the Louver, where he and Katherine were staying. "It is scarcely possible to tell in detail of the state they kept that day, the feasts and ceremony, and the luxury of their court."[9] It was in stark contrast to the shabby court of Charles VI at the Hôtel de Saint-Pol and the dearth of food in the city.

That month, Parliament petitioned the King "that he, with the gracious lady, his companion, would please to return to England to comfort, support and refresh them by their presence."[10] He and Katherine left Paris on 27 December, accompanied by Bedford and an army of 6,000 men. They received a state welcome in Rouen on 31 December and stayed for three weeks. On 19 January 1421, they departed with a vast retinue that included Bedford and James I, and traveled north to Amiens, arriving on 22 January to a splendid civic welcome. Here, they stayed in the house of the bailiff, Robert le Jeune, who gave Katherine an array of fine gifts. Then it was on to Saint-Pol, Thérouanne, and English-owned Calais, where the Merchants of the Staple and the citizens came out to receive their new Queen and present her with more luxury presents. Meanwhile, on 30 January, messengers were dispatched all over England with writs summoning the lords spiritual and temporal to her coronation.

After waiting for a favorable wind, the royal couple embarked for England, making port on 1 February at Dover, where they were carried ashore in triumph on the shoulders of the Barons of the Cinque Ports before large crowds who—according to Monstrelet—received Henry "as if he had been an angel of God." To them, as to him, the new Queen was a trophy, the living embodiment of his victory over the French.

Crowds flocked to see them that day as they traveled to Canterbury, where they were welcomed by Archbishop Chichele. After making offerings at the shrine of St. Thomas Becket, Henry traveled ahead to London to approve the City's state welcome. Katherine left Canterbury on 20 February for Eltham Palace, where Henry was awaiting her. They rode together toward London the next day. At Blackheath, the Lord Mayor, aldermen, and chief citizens, all clad in white cloaks with red hoods, received them as 30,000 spectators looked on. The sound of "clarions and other loud minstrelsies"[11] accompanied them as they approached the City. At the gates of London Bridge, statues of the legendary giants Gog and Magog stood guard, bowing to the Queen as she passed through. Beside them were model lions with moving eyes and limbs, eight pairs of singing angels, nineteen virgins (one for every year of the Queen's life), and an image of St. Petronilla, the patron saint of the House of Valois. That night, Katherine lodged at the Tower of London.

On the following day, 22 February, dressed in white, she was borne along the streets in a splendid chariot, escorted by lords, aldermen, and representatives of the craft guilds, and greeted by a throng eager to see "the glorious and royal sight of strangers that came with them from overseas." Buildings had been decorated with greenery, and windows and roofs were hung with cloth of gold, silks, velvet, and Arras tapestries, while bunting stretched from house to house. Music sounded as the citizens showed their Queen the sights of London and performed pageants depicting stories of the saints "for her comfort and pleasure."[12] The Lord Mayor presented her with two basins and 1,000 marks (£592,200). That night, she slept in the Palace of Westminster. Her reception had cost, in total, £80 (£72,890).

On the morning of 23 February, two bishops escorted Katherine on foot from Westminster Hall to Westminster Abbey, where she was crowned by Archbishop Chichele "with such splendid magnificence that the like had never been seen at any coronation since the time of that noble knight Arthur, King of the English."[13] By custom, the King was not present: this was to be the Queen's triumph alone. Afterward, she sat enthroned on the King's Bench in Westminster Hall and presided over a feast attended by a host of lords, ladies, judges, and the Lord Mayor and chief citizens of London. To Katherine's right at the marble high table sat Archbishop Chichele and Henry Beaufort, Bishop of Winchester; to her left, under his own canopy of estate, was James I, and next to him sat the Dowager Duchess of York and the Dowager Countess of Huntingdon. The Dowager Countess of Kent sat at the Queen's feet, holding a napkin in case she felt ill. Katherine's brothers-in-law, the dukes of Bedford and Gloucester, were also present, Gloucester acting as overseer and standing bareheaded before the Queen. The Earl of March and the Earl Marshal, both holding the Queen's scepters, knelt on the steps of the dais.

Because it was Lent, the royal cooks had been creative. Apart from brawn served with mustard, the feast consisted of seafood: freshwater crayfish, pike with herbs, spiced roasted lampreys, eels in black butter, trout, codling, fried plaice, whiting, crab, sea bream, conger, sole, mullet, chub, barbel, roach, fresh salmon, halibut, roasted gurnard, fried smelt, prawns, lobster, carp, dory, turbot, tench, gudgeon, perch, fresh sturgeon, whelks, shrimps, and roasted porpoise. Among the sweetmeats were leche Lombard (honey cakes with wine syrup) fashioned with the arms of the King and Queen, jelly garnished with columbine flowers, date compote, cream motley, white pottage (cream of almonds), "cheven flampayne" (meatballs) decorated with the royal arms and three gold crowns, and white leche garnished with hawthorn leaves.[14]

At the end of each course, a subtlety was presented to the high table, the first in the form of a pelican on her nest symbolizing Christ's sacrifice on the Cross; the second represented St. Catherine, the Queen's patron saint, disputing with the doctors of the Church, and holding in her hands a book and the legend: "This sign to the King great joy will bring, and all his people she will content." Another subtlety showed St. Barnabas attended by angels. The last was fashioned as a tiger looking in a mirror and a man on horseback holding a whelp, with the motto: "By force of arms, and not by that of reason, I have captured this beast"—a snide allusion to the Dauphin.[15] At the end of the feast, the subtleties were broken up and handed around to the company, while free food and drink were given out to the people.

During the feast, Katherine begged Henry to liberate King James, it being customary for queens to make an intercession at their coronations; he consented, on condition that James fought for him in France. Learning that the Scots King was enamored of Henry's cousin, Joan Beaufort, daughter of the late Earl of Somerset, Katherine pressed Henry to agree to their marriage. According to Stow, they were betrothed before the coronation celebrations ended. The Queen also presented Sir James Stewart with the gilt cup with which he had served her at the feast.

After a progress through the kingdom, Henry and Katherine arrived at Westminster in May, when Parliament met. In London, they were entertained in Hart Street at the house of the celebrated Richard Whittington, a former Lord Mayor who was so fabulously wealthy that he was said to have fed his fire with expensive spices and cedarwood. When Katherine commented on the cost, before their astonished eyes he threw into the flames bonds worth £60,000 (£54:5 million), owed to him by the King.

In March, Jacqueline, sovereign Countess of Hainault, Holland, and Zeeland, fled from the Low Countries to escape the ambitions of her estranged husband, John IV of Brabant, who was a creature of Burgundy. She arrived in England to beg aid from Henry V, who welcomed her warmly, granted her asylum, and installed her in the Queen's household, outlaying £100 (£91,110) monthly for her maintenance. The two women were the same age and evidently became friends.

In May, Katherine gave the King a loan of £1,333:6s.8d. (£1,214,480) toward upholding the Treaty of Troyes. She was pregnant when, on 10 June, he sailed from Dover to resume campaigning in France and avenge the death of his brother Clarence, who had been killed at the Battle of Baugé. A contemporary song imagines Katherine's sadness at the King's departure:

Retourne-toi, embrasse-moi,
Mon cher Anglais!
Puisque Dieu nous a assemblés,
Faut nous aimer.

("Return and embrace me / my dear Englishman! / Since God has brought us together / we must love each other.")

5

"His bed of pain"

✳

Again, Henry left his Queen and his kingdom in the charge of Bedford. A century later, the chronicler Hall stated that, before he departed, he forbade Katherine to go to Windsor for her confinement because of an old prophecy foretelling that "Henry of Windsor shall long reign and lose all." There is no contemporary evidence for this, and Katherine is unlikely to have disobeyed him. She moved to Windsor in the autumn and took up residence in sumptuous apartments hung with tapestries embroidered in gold.

Windsor Castle was one of the foremost royal residences in England. A great fortress had stood here since the days of William the Conqueror, and successive monarchs had converted it into a great palace. Edward III had built a stately range of stone lodgings in the upper ward and converted the old ones in the lower ward into a college dedicated to St. George to create the perfect setting for his new Order of the Garter. To the south of the main quadrangle, which served as the tournament ground, stood St. George's Hall, a masterpiece of gothic splendor with seventeen tall arched windows, and the Royal Chapel. To the north there were separate sets of first-floor chambers for the King and Queen, arranged around two inner courtyards, Brick Court and Horn Court.

A holy relic, the Silver Jewel, said to be the foreskin of Christ, was sent from France to aid Katherine in her labor. At four o'clock in the afternoon of St. Nicholas's Day, 6 December, she bore a son, who was styled

Duke of Cornwall from birth. A manuscript drawing in the Beauchamp Pageant depicts the scene, showing the Queen, crowned (although she would not have been in reality) and lying in a great bed, tended by four ladies, one of whom holds the swaddled infant, who is also crowned; another smooths the sheets; at the doorway, a third passes on the good news of the birth to a messenger waiting outside. Bells rang out as London erupted in celebration, and the Lord Mayor of London ordered that the *Te Deum* be sung in the City's churches.

Henry V was besieging Meaux when his chamberlain brought him the news that he had a male heir, filling his heart with great gladness. He sent word that the child be christened Henry, commanding that, without delay, the Queen must attend the Mass of the Holy Trinity and present her son before the Lord. Archbishop Chichele officiated at the baptism, while Bedford, Bishop Beaufort, and Jacqueline of Hainault stood as sponsors, with Jacqueline holding the heir in her arms. Hall later claimed that a guilty Katherine wrote an affectionate letter to the King, craving his forgiveness for having disobeyed him in bearing her child at Windsor, but again there is no contemporary record of his having expressed any displeasure with her.

On 20 December, royal messengers were dispatched to many lords and ladies, commanding them to be present at Windsor on 12 January for the Queen's solemn purification, a ceremony known as "churching" that marked the end of her confinement and return to everyday life.

The little Prince thrived, and in January 1422, Joan Astley was appointed his nurse, on a salary of £20 (£19,160). That spring, evidently missing Henry, Katherine wrote to him, saying that she earnestly longed to behold him once more. In response, he invited her to join him in France. In the middle of May, when her son was six months old, Katherine left him behind in England in the care of Duke Humphrey. With Bedford, his wife, and an army of 20,000 reinforcements for the King, she took ship at Southampton and crossed the Channel to be reunited with her husband.

On 21 May, she landed at Harfleur and, escorted by Bedford, made her stately way up the Seine to Rouen, where King James was waiting to conduct them toward Paris. At Mantes, Katherine was welcomed by peals of bells and presented with two great silver cups. Meaux fell to Henry that month and when he met up with Katherine on 26 May at the royal château of Bois de Vincennes, in the presence of King Charles and Queen Isabeau and cheering crowds, he greeted her as joyfully "as if she had been an angel from God."[1] They had not seen each other for nearly a year, and Katherine may have been dismayed at the change in her husband, for the stresses of war and endless campaigning had prematurely aged him. From 1419, he had suffered various maladies, but recently he had contracted a lengthy illness as a result of his long and excessive labors during the siege of Meaux, and was clearly not a well man. He looked different too, for he had grown a beard and let his severely cut hair grow long and bushy. A stone effigy of him on the Kings Screen in York Minster, executed around 1425 and recently identified as a true likeness, portrays him thus, as does the obverse of his great seal.

On 30 May, he and Katherine rode into Paris with a magnificent train, but their reception was more muted this time. Pageants were mounted in celebration of the birth of an heir to France, but the festivities were low-key because smallpox was rampant in the city. Katherine offended some French people by having two ermine robes carried before her chariot, as if she had been crowned Queen of France already, but one can perhaps sympathize with her desire to remind the people of Paris that Henry owed his crown to her, their Princess, and that she was the mother of their future King. Her reaction to the Treaty of Troyes, the disinheriting of her brother, and the loss of France to the English is not recorded, but these developments must have caused her some heart-searching.

Charles VI and Queen Isabeau arrived the same day. After attending Mass at Notre-Dame, Henry and Katherine spent Whitsun at the palace of the Louvre, while her parents again stayed at the run-down Hôtel de Saint-Pol. "On Whit-Sunday, [she] sat at table in the Louvre, gloriously apparelled, having her crown on her head. The English princes and nobles were partakers with the great lords of France of this feast, each seated according to his rank, while the tables were covered with the richest viands and wines. Queen Katherine next day held a great court, and all the Parisians went to see their Princess and her lord sitting enthroned, crowned with their most precious diadems. But, as no meat or drink was offered to the populace, they went away much discontented, [for] King Charles had once been as liberal and courteous as any of his predecessors, but now he was seated at a table with his Queen, quite forsaken by his nobles, who all flocked to pay their court to his daughter and her husband, at which the common people grieved much."[2]

At the beginning of June, Henry and Katherine visited the Hôtel de Nesle, where the citizens of Paris performed a play entitled *The Mystery of the Passion of St. George*. On 11 June, the royal party visited the abbey of Saint-Denis before departing for Compiègne. On the way, Henry left Katherine at Senlis with her parents and, defying his doctors' advice, rode on alone. On the way, he learned that the Dauphin's forces were besieging Cosne and, despite feeling unwell, promised to come to its aid, but on 7 July, he fell ill with a high fever and violent diarrhea. He was too weak to mount a horse, yet he insisted on being carried by litter at the head of his men to direct the relief of Cosne, but was forced to rest for a fortnight at Corbeil. There, in agony and unable to go on, he resigned his command to his brother Bedford and had himself conveyed back by boat along the Seine to Vincennes, near Paris. It is often said that he had contracted dysentery, but his physicians gave up treating him because he had an incurable "cancer,"[3] possibly of the rectum.

By 13 July, aware of encroaching mortality, Henry had had a change of heart toward Queen Joan, prompted by fears for the health of his soul and the exhortations of his confessor. He informed his Council: "Howbeit we have taken into our hand till a certain time, and for such causes as ye know, the dowers of our mother, Queen Joan, except a certain pension thereof yearly, which we assigned for the expense reasonable of her, and of a certain meinie [retinue] that should be about her, we, doubting lest it should be a charge unto our conscience for to occupy forth longer the said dower in this wise, the which charge we be advised no longer to bear on our conscience, will and charge you that ye make deliverance unto our said mother the Queen wholly of her said dower, and suffer her to receive it as she did heretofore; and that she make her officers whom she list [desires], so they be our liegemen and good men; and that therefore we have given in charge and commandment at this time to make her full restitution of the dower. Furthermore, we will and charge you that her beds and all other things movable that we had of her, ye deliver her again. And we ordain that she have of such cloth and of such color as she will devise herself, five or six gowns, such as she useth to wear. And because we suppose she will soon remove from the palace where she now is, that ye ordain her horses for eleven chairs [chariots], and let her remove them whatsoever place within our realm that her list, and when her list."[4] No reason for Joan's imprisonment was given.

On 21 July, just eight days after the King had given the order, Joan was released from Leeds Castle, but her dower and most of her possessions were restored to her only piecemeal because Henry V had sold, mortgaged, or reassigned most of her lands, mainly to Queen Katherine. The Council outlaid £100 (£95,780) on horses to transport her and her belongings wherever she wished to go. She established her court chiefly at Kings Langley, Hertfordshire, where she made extensive improvements.

Katherine and her parents were still at Senlis when, on 10 August 1422, Henry arrived at Vincennes. Refusing this time to be carried, which he said was for women and children, he insisted on riding to the castle on horseback and forced himself into the saddle, but he was in such agony that he could endure no more than a few steps, so his attendants were obliged to lift him, half fainting, into a litter, and bore him into the castle, where they laid him upon "his bed of pain."

There he remained until 31 August, when he demanded to know the truth about his condition, and his physicians told him that he had, at most, two hours to live. Bedford came to say farewell, as did his other captains.

As that evening wore on, the dying King's sufferings increased. His intestines, genitalia, and lungs were already in a state of putrefaction. Around two o'clock in the morning of 1 September, he whispered that his constant desire had been to recapture Jerusalem from the Turks and expressed remorse for his treatment of Queen Joan. He dictated his will, in which he left Katherine a golden scepter, precious ornaments, and jewels, and confirmed her dower.

"Comfort my dear wife, the most afflicted creature living," he enjoined Bedford.[5] Clutching a crucifix, he murmured, *"In manus tuas, Domine, ipsum terminum redemisti"* ("Into Thy hands, Lord, you have redeemed me at the end") and died.

His death, wrote Walsingham, "was deservedly mourned" for "it left no one like him among Christian kings or princes. Thinking of his memorable deeds, people felt awe at his sudden and terrible removal."

Monstrelet says that Katherine and her mother were with Henry at Vincennes when he died, but other evidence shows that she was still at Senlis when the news was broken to her. She took charge of the funeral arrangements. Henry's body was so skeletal that there was little flesh left to decompose. His corpse was embalmed, placed in a lead coffin, and laid on a black-draped bier surmounted by a stuffed leather effigy wearing royal robes and a crown. It was taken to Saint-Denis, where it rested for the night of 15 September before being escorted by the late King's household, wearing black and white mourning, and a mighty host of mourners, in a doleful procession through France.

On 24 September, Katherine joined it at Rouen. "At a distance from the corpse of about two miles followed the widow, Queen Katherine, right honorably accompanied." The body rested at the church of St. Vulfran in Abbeville, where Masses were sung, by the Queen's orders, for the repose of Henry's soul. The procession moved on and "the Queen, with a mighty retinue, came after at a mile's distance."[6] The cortège traveled north via Hesdin, Montreuil, and Boulogne, reaching Calais early in November. On the way, Katherine learned that her little son was now the inheritor of two crowns, for her father had died on 21 October. Henry VI was duly proclaimed King of France, in accordance with the terms of the Treaty of Troyes. Most French people refused to acknowledge him, holding that the Dauphin should succeed his father. But the English had the advantage, for the Duke of Burgundy was a staunch friend to England and all-powerful in France. Not yet twenty-one, Katherine was now the Queen Mother of both England and France.

6

"That godly, faithful, true Princess"

※

The Privy Council had sent ships to convey the cortège across the sea, and ladies to attend Katherine. At Dover, the Archbishop of Canterbury and fourteen other bishops were waiting to receive the coffin and the Queen when they made land on 31 October 1422. The mournful procession made its way via Canterbury, Ospringe, Rochester, and Dartford to Blackheath, where, on 5 November, the coffin was met by fifteen more bishops, a host of mitred abbots, and the chief citizens of London. To the accompaniment of dirges, it was brought through London to St. Paul's Cathedral. As it passed, the citizens stood by their doors holding lighted torches. On 6 November, Henry was taken in procession to his final resting place in Westminster Abbey.

The Queen and King James were chief mourners at the funeral the next day, when a solemn congregation assembled in the abbey and the King's three favorite chargers were led up to the altar. He was interred in the chapel of St. Edward the Confessor. It was Katherine—according to the Latin inscription—who raised and paid for a fine tomb of Caen stone and Purbeck marble in a new H-shaped chantry next to the shrine of St. Edward. Henry had left strict instructions for its design, and the chantry was completed in 1431. On the tomb was placed a costly oak effigy plated with silver and gilt, with a head of solid silver. During the Reformation of the 1530s, Henry VIII's commissioners stripped the tomb of its silver, leaving only a headless effigy. A new head, based on contemporary portraits, was added in 1971.

As King, Henry V had been extremely successful: he had maintained peace at home by governing with firmness, justice, and mercy, and had united his people behind him in a common endeavor. His victories had added luster to the name of Lancaster, and he had restored the prestige and authority of the Crown. His achievements were regarded by his contemporaries as little short of miraculous, and his early biographers wrote extravagantly flattering accounts of him, thus giving rise to the legend of a hero-king that found its greatest expression in Shakespeare's play and has influenced writers of English history to this day.

His death was an unmitigated disaster for England. Much of France remained to be conquered, a forbidding task. Ruled by an infant king, however diligent his regents, England could not hope to win the war, for her resources could no longer support it. Henry V's campaigns had brought the Crown near to bankruptcy and burdened it with crippling debts. It was inevitable that divided opinion about the continuance or otherwise of the war with France would split the English magnates into factions: those in favor of prosecuting the war, and those who believed that a peace was essential. These differences would institute decades of government by factions, which would undermine law and order, the stability of the realm, and the Crown itself. There were fervent hopes that Henry VI would grow up to emulate the auspicious example of his father, but he was a helpless infant of nine months, and England faced years of minority rule. Not for nothing was it commonly said, "Woe to thee, O land, when thy king is a child."

The magnates had already sworn allegiance to Henry VI and made plans for the minority government, summoning Parliament in the King's name and establishing a regency council made up of the most influential lords and bishops in the kingdom. As Henry V had directed in his will, Bedford was to be governor of Normandy and, soon, regent of France, and Gloucester protector of England and guardian of the young King. The lords of the Council were reluctant to allow the ambitious Gloucester sovereign power and his duties were restricted to keeping the peace and summoning and dissolving Parliament; when Bedford was in England,

Gloucester was to give precedence to him. For these limitations, Gloucester blamed his uncle, Bishop Beaufort, whose influence was never to be underestimated and who had himself wished to be named regent. Having opposed this vociferously, Gloucester was now convinced that Beaufort had had his revenge. The squabbles between them were to influence English politics for the next twenty-five years. Gloucester was convinced that the war with France should be continued, but Beaufort became increasingly sure that an honorable peace was the best solution.

The provisions of Henry V's will denied the Queen any political role in the regency and, at his behest, the young King's great-uncles, Thomas Beaufort, Duke of Exeter, and Bishop Beaufort, were given responsibility for his safekeeping and nurture. Katherine was permitted to have her son with her during his early years. On the day after her husband's funeral, she moved to Windsor, where she remained in seclusion with the boy for a year, both maintaining separate households. Thereafter, they often stayed at Hertford Castle or Waltham Palace, residing at the Palace of Westminster only on state occasions. Katherine played the part of Queen Dowager to perfection. Her roles were purely domestic and ceremonial. She never involved herself in politics and was in turn accorded all the honors due to her rank. Since her dower lands were—ostensibly—being restored to Queen Joan, Katherine lived on the yearly income of about £2,400 (£2,298,620) from estates Henry had assigned her from the duchy of Lancaster, and an annuity of 20,000 livres (£19,155,130) paid by the French government, but her dower payments—confirmed in November 1422 and meant to amount to 10,000 marks (£5,746,540)—often fell short of what was due to her. She did not return to France, which was still torn by war, but spent much of her time at Hertford Castle, clearly a favorite residence.

Queen Joan bought mourning weeds for herself and her maids on the death of Henry V. Superseded in status by Queen Katherine, the young King's mother, Joan lived quietly during her retirement, attending as diligently as ever to her financial affairs, but troubled by the inefficiency of her staff at Havering. Her children had evidently been hoping that, once freed, she would return to Brittany. In a treaty between John V and Philip of Burgundy, concluded on 18 April 1422, John had stated that he and his siblings hoped to see their mother pardoned, "who for such a long time has been far away from her children, and they so want to see her that there is nothing that would bring them more comfort or rejoicing until she can come here to see and visit them, and be here in innocence and liberty."[1] But Joan never returned to Brittany, probably because she was concerned about losing her English income.

Joan seems not to have been ostracized on account of the stigma of witchcraft, which suggests that most people did not credit the charges against her. The truth behind them lies in the figures. The King had benefited from her dower revenues by £8,000 (£7,662,050) for the period from June 1421 to August 1422, whereas he had outlaid only £1,000 (£957,760) a year on her maintenance during her imprisonment.

According to Joan's household book for 1423, Cardinal Beaufort dined with her at Leeds in June and Gloucester in July. Joan made a few minor charitable donations, among them alms to the chapel at Leeds Castle, and gave small monetary gifts to those who had done her good service. In contrast, she outlaid £56:4d. (£53,630) on her cellar, purchasing wines from Gascony, La Rochelle, and the Rhine. In 1423, her dower was finally restored to her. That year, she visited Leeds Castle, "living in all princely prosperity"[2] as the guest of Queen Katherine, who had been granted Leeds that year as part of her dower and immediately set about making repairs. She kept a chamber for her son the King in the Gloriette, where there was also a study and a cloister. In 1435, Katherine had a clock with a bell installed at Leeds, which rang out the hours.

Joan probably never attended the court of Henry VI, and although there is no record of his visiting her, he showed great favor to her grandson Gilles, the son of John V, paying him an annuity and making him a Knight of the Garter.

She was still in mourning for Henry V when, at Easter 1423, she purchased fourteen and a half yards of black cloth for two new gowns. She also bought black silk loops and 400 clasps for a black cape; black satin and gray squirrel fur for a collar and mantle; and three dozen shoes at 6d. per pair. In 1428, she owned seven black gowns (including one of Florence damask), ten kirtles, sixteen pairs of hose, various fur biliments, a silk cap, and templars, the bejeweled cylindrical headwear that framed the face on each side.

By 1424, Joan was enjoying a comfortable lifestyle, although she struggled to obtain payments of her Breton dower because the duchy's alliance with England had broken down. In 1432, John V sent his son Gilles to England to make friendly overtures to Henry VI. Queen Joan was involved in their peace talks. In 1433, to smooth the way to a peace, she instructed her officers in Brittany to ransom English prisoners of war with the revenues of her dower lands.

At Langley, she played host to Gloucester's duchess, Jacqueline of Hainault, in 1425; to Gloucester himself in 1427; and to Bishop Beaufort the following year. From 1427, she patronized the composer John Dunstable. In March 1431, some rooms at Langley were badly damaged by a destructive fire in which Joan lost furniture, plate, and household stuff "through the want of care and drowsiness of a minstrel and the heedless keeping of a candle."[3] Thereafter, she resided mainly at Pirgo Palace in Havering.

Friar Randolf had remained in prison, despite Gloucester's efforts to free him, which were opposed by Bishop Beaufort. In 1429, he was killed in a brawl in the Tower. That year, having recovered from a long illness in 1427-8, Joan began to distance herself from worldly luxuries and in 1429 she gave all the rich contents of her chapel to Gloucester's second wife, Eleanor Cobham. Thereafter, Joan lived frugally—for a queen—on 500 marks (£265,040) a year. In 1427, she embarked on a pilgrimage to shrines at Walsingham, Norwich, Peterborough, and St. Albans. In 1433-4, she stayed at the Cistercian abbey of St. Mary at Stratford Langthorne in Essex, a house that enjoyed her patronage, as did Chertsey Abbey in Surrey.

Langley was again habitable by 1432; Joan spent the Christmas of 1436 there, although the house was still in poor repair. In January 1437, Henry VI, now fifteen, sent Joan a New Year's gift of a gold tablet adorned with four balas rubies, eight pearls, and a great sapphire, which had been given to him by Eleanor Cobham.

England's other widowed Queen, Katherine, was treated "reverently with all friendship and courtesy"[4] by Gloucester, but he and the Council were aware that an attractive girl in her early twenties would perhaps wish to remarry at some stage, which might cause difficulties. There was no precedent for a queen dowager remarrying in England, and if Katherine married an English lord, he might have political ambitions and seek to exercise inappropriate influence over the young King, while her marrying abroad could cause equally serious complications. Fortunately, the Queen was preoccupied with her son, who stayed with her during his infancy; Henry V had commanded that they share a household, although Katherine had her own apartments where she lived in royal state. She paid the royal Wardrobe £7 (£6,700) a day for her keep. She and the King spent much of their time at Windsor.

In accordance with the wishes of his father and his widowed mother, young Henry's attendants were largely chosen from those who had loyally served them both. Early in 1423, the redoubtable Richard de Beauchamp, Earl of Warwick, became the King's legal guardian. On 21 February, Dame Alice Boteler, a wise, experienced woman who had served Katherine, was appointed his governess, and the Council, in the King's name, gave her "power to chastise us reasonably from time to time" because "in our tender age it behooves us to be taught and instructed in courtesy and nurture and other matters becoming a royal person." Nor would Dame Alice be "molested, hurt or injured" in years to come for beating her sovereign.[5] George Arthurton, clerk of the Queen's closet, was appointed the young King's confessor.

Henry VI's first public appearance was at the opening of Parliament in 1423, when he was nearly two. On Saturday 13 November, Katherine brought him from Windsor, and they lodged at an inn near Staines for the night. On Sunday morning, as Henry was carried to her chariot, which was waiting to take him to Kingston, "he shrieked, he cried, he sprang, and would be carried no farther. Nothing the Queen could devise might content him." She thought he was ill, so "they bore him again to the inn and there he abode all day. On the Monday he was borne to his mother's car, he then being merry or glad of cheer, and so they came to Kingston and rested that night. On the Tuesday, Queen Katherine brought him to Kennington Palace." This account, which appeared in the London Chronicle of c.1430, was later seen as an early manifestation of Henry VI's sanctity, for it was believed that his refusal to travel on a Sunday betokened incipient holiness. Modern parents might well describe it as a temper tantrum typical of a two-year-old, but people in the fifteenth century were apt to see portents in such things.

On 18 November, Henry went in procession to Parliament, riding on

Katherine's lap on a wheeled throne drawn by white horses. "It was a strange sight, and the first time it was ever seen in England, an infant sitting on the mother's lap, before it could tell what English meant, to exercise the place of sovereign direction in open Parliament. And those pretty hands, which could not yet feed himself, were made capable of wielding a scepter; and he, who was beholden to his nurse for milk, did distribute sustenance to the law and justice of his nation. The Queen, with her infant on her knee, was enthroned among the lords, whom, by the Chancellor, the little King saluted and spoke to them his mind by means of another's tongue."[6] The similarity to the Virgin and Child was probably deliberate.

Katherine and her son spent the Christmas of 1423 at Hertford Castle with the King of Scots as their guest. On 12 February 1424, Katherine may have attended his wedding to Bishop Beaufort's niece, Joan Beaufort, at the priory of St. Mary Overie in Southwark. Afterward, there was a feast at nearby Winchester Palace, hosted by Cardinal Beaufort. That year, James was allowed to return to Scotland.

According to "The King's Quair," an autobiographical dream-sequence poem composed by James during his captivity,[7] he had fallen in love with a lady of high birth and beauty whom he had espied from his window at Windsor Castle. He did not name her in the poem, or even meet her, but called her his "heart's queen" and adored her from afar, according to the prevailing code of courtly love. He wrote of "her golden hair and rich attire," her fretwork gown adorned with pearls, the great balas rubies, emeralds, and sapphires she wore, and her chaplet of red, white, and blue plumes with "spangles bright as gold," like love knots, and four "jonettes," or pear tree blossoms. The word "jonette" has been seen as a play on Joan Beaufort's name. He may first have seen the young lady at Windsor around March 1423, the time of year when pear trees blossom.

Mary McGrigor, however, has credibly suggested that the object of his devotion was the widowed Queen Katherine, who was then in residence at Windsor. She was blond, and the rich jewels mentioned in the poem were perhaps more appropriate for a queen than the unmarried daughter of an earl, while red and blue, the colors of her plumes, were those of Paris's saints, St. Denis and St. Martin, and of the Virgin Mary, the patroness of France, and also the colors of the Oriflamme, the sacred battle standard of the kings of France. Katherine had been a good patroness and friend to James, and it would have been entirely appropriate for him to express his devotion to her in courtly vein, even if it was not reciprocated. Nevertheless, the Beaufort arms are also red, white, and blue, and unmarried girls did wear chaplets on their loose hair, so the young lady could well have been Joan Beaufort.

In 1424, Parliament again confirmed Katherine's dower, putting her in possession of all the dower lands of the queens of England except Langley and Havering, which remained in the hands of Queen Joan. They would bring Katherine an income of 40,000 crowns (£643,200).

Gloucester had married Jacqueline of Hainault, whose marriage to John IV of Brabant had been annulled by the Anti-Pope, Benedict XIII, whose decrees were not universally recognized, and certainly not by John's cousin, Philip of Burgundy. Gloucester, however, was determined to keep Jacqueline as his wife. Jacqueline had appealed to Katherine for protection, and when Philip challenged Gloucester to mortal combat, Katherine and her mother, Queen Isabeau, were asked in to mediate on behalf of England and France. They found for Brabant and asked that Parliament compensate Gloucester. That year, Katherine also mediated in a quarrel between Gloucester and Bedford.

Two days before the opening of Parliament in April 1425, the Queen once again brought the King to London, riding through the City on her wheeled throne with her son on her knee. When the procession stopped at St. Paul's Cathedral, Gloucester lifted Henry down, and he and Exeter led the three-year-old to the high altar, where the child dutifully said his prayers and looked gravely about him. He was then carried out into the churchyard and, to the people's delight, placed on a white horse and taken in procession through Cheapside and St. George's Bar at Southwark to his palace of Kennington, where he and his mother lodged that night. Two days later, they went in procession to Westminster to open Parliament, with Henry riding on a large white horse, as the crowds cried out their blessings, saying that he appeared to be the very image of his famous father, and expressing hopes that he would grow up to display the same martial zeal.

In 1425, the Council granted Katherine the use of Baynard's Castle, a

Thames-side palace in the City of London, which she could use during the minority of Richard of Cambridge, nephew of Edward, Duke of York. Richard's father, the Earl of Cambridge, York's younger brother, had been executed for treason in 1415. The Council had decided that Henry VI needed some companions of his own age, decreeing that all noble boys in royal wardship be brought up with him at court. In May 1426, the King was knighted by Bedford, then he himself conferred knighthood on some of his young companions and on Richard of Cambridge, who on that same day was formally restored to the dukedom of York.

The King and his mother spent the Christmases of 1426, 1427, and 1428 at Eltham. It was on one of these occasions that the poet John Lydgate wrote a *ballade* for Katherine, "that godly, faithful, true Princess," wishing her joy and gladness, with "care and sorrow forever set aside" and the love and loyalty of the people.[8] Lydgate also composed "A New Year's Ballad" addressed to the Queen and her son at Hertford Castle; it was written as if from Katherine to the young King, to accompany her gift of an eagle. Lydgate may also have written one of the plays performed at court during these festive seasons, and he certainly composed a poem, "That now is hay sometime was grass," "at the commandment of Queen Katherine, as in her sports she walked by the meadows that were mown in the month of July."[9] Katherine may have been the Queen to whom he dedicated his "Life of Our Lady."

Little is known of Katherine's personal life during her widowhood. She and her retinue lived in the King's household until at least 1430. Henry never failed to choose pretty gifts for her at New Year, such as the ruby ring given him by Bedford, which he presented to her on 1 January 1428, on the advice of Alice Boteler.

In 1427, as he approached his sixth birthday, the young King was removed from the care of women, to reside at Windsor, Eltham, Berkhamsted, Wallingford, or Hertford, the latter being his mother's dower properties. In June 1428, the King's guardian, the Earl of Warwick, was given sole charge of him and ordered by the Council, in the King's name, to instruct him in good manners, courtesy, letters, and languages. Like Alice Boteler before him, Warwick was authorized "to chastise us from time to time, according to his good advice and discretion." He did not spare the rod, but Henry VI had the advantage of being educated by one of the finest minds of the age.

There is no evidence that during his childhood, Henry VI suffered the mental instability that would visit him in later life. Yet there was pressure on him to live up to the example set by his illustrious, victorious father, and as he grew older, it must have become increasingly obvious to those around him that the young King was never going to excel as a warrior.

7

"Following more her own appetite"

✸

IN 1438, THE AUTHOR OF THE CHRONICLE EDITED BY J. A. GILES (and known as Giles's Chronicle) stated that Gloucester had once persuaded the Council to forbid a marriage between Katherine and Edmund Beaufort, a younger son of John Beaufort, Earl of Somerset. She is said to have reacted angrily, declaring, "Then I shall marry a man so basely, yet so gently born, that my lord regents may not object!" Although Giles's Chronicle contains the only contemporary reference to the matter, it has been suggested that Katherine and Edmund had an affair and even that her son, another Edmund, was the result of this union; it has also been claimed that it was because of this affair that Katherine was made to live in her son's household, so that she could be kept under supervision. Yet Henry V had ordered that she and her son share a household, and there is no other evidence that she had a liaison with Beaufort. In 1426, Parliament formally petitioned the Lord Chancellor to grant widowed queens permission to "marry at their will."[1] If this was presented at Katherine's request, then there may have been some truth in the assertion that she was involved with Beaufort, although that is pure speculation.

Sometime between 1425 and 1429, she did become romantically involved with a Welshman called Owain ap Maredudd ap Tewdwr. Owen Tudor, as he is more commonly known—although he did not adopt the anglicized version of his surname until 1459—came from a landed gentry family in Anglesey, north Wales, and he could trace his descent back to the thirteenth century. The genealogies later commissioned by his grandson Henry VII to show that the Tudors were descended from ancient Welsh and British princes through Rhys ap Tewdwr, Prince of Deheubarth, Wales (d. 1093), cannot be substantiated.

Owen's father, Maredudd (Meredith), the fourth son of a younger son, had been butler and shield-bearer to the Bishop of Bangor. The Tudors, as they later became known, supported Owen Glendower's rebellion. Outlawed for killing a man, Maredudd had fled with his wife to Glendower at Snowden. Owen himself was perhaps born there, around 1400; tradition has it that Glendower, for whom he may have been named, was his godfather. In 1403, after the Battle of Shrewsbury and the defeat of Glendower, Maredudd and his family were dispossessed of all their lands. A senior branch of the family eventually had the estate at Penmynydd restored to them and, taking the name Theodore, lived there in obscurity until the seventeenth century, ignored by their more famous relatives.

Owen perhaps came to England with his father to plead for the restitution of their lands. One source has him fighting bravely for Henry V at Agincourt, for which the King made him a Squire of the Body, entitling him to bear arms. From around 1420, Owen served in France in the retinue of Sir Walter Hungerford, who later became steward of Henry VI's household.

From 1422, Owen was a member of the guard at Windsor, where Queen Katherine and the young King were in residence. The first mention of his serving in her household dates only from *c.*1484:[2] According to the Welsh chronicler Elis Gruffydd (1490–1552), he was appointed the Queen's sewer, or server at table. Later, he was made keeper or clerk of the Queen's wardrobe, in which capacity he would have settled accounts for her clothes and safeguarded her jewels. Hall described Owen as "a goodly gentleman and a beautiful person, garnished with many gifts, both of nature and of grace," while Polydore Vergil stated that he was "adorned with wonderful gifts of body and mind." The chronicler Gregory called him "no man of birth, neither of livelihood." Owen was never knighted, and in 1425 his annual income was at most £40 (£38,030); therefore, the assertion that he owned property worth £3,000 (£2,852,280) a year seems highly unlikely, although he may have owned a house at Glengauny in Anglesey, a tradition mentioned by Daniel Defoe and Agnes Strickland. Perhaps his humble status was one of the things that appealed to Katherine. Not having noble or royal blood, or political influence, he could not be regarded by the Council as a threat.

Owen's love affair with the Queen is surrounded by mystery and unsubstantiated tales. According to the Welsh chronicle of Ellis Griffith,[3] she was attracted to him when she watched him swimming nude in the moat at Leeds Castle. But he was then pursuing one of her maids, who did not fancy him. Disguising herself as the maid, Katherine contrived an encounter, but when Owen, not recognizing her, gave her a love-bite on her cheek, she drew back. That evening, when he served her at supper and saw the mark, he realized who she was and that she had sought him out because she was attracted to him.

Stow claimed that, when Katherine was staying at Windsor, Owen was required to dance before her as she sat on a low seat, surrounded by her ladies. He tripped and fell into her lap, and her reaction gave rise to speculation that she favored him. One version of the story had it that Owen did not trip, but that, while dancing, his knee touched the Queen's, and he next appeared with a ribbon tied around it.

"Why do you use that ribbon, Sir?" Katherine asked.

"Please, your Grace, to avoid touching you."

"Perhaps you may touch me in another part," she is supposed to have replied.

Robin of Anglesey (Robin Ddu), writing in 1461, claimed that Owen, "once on holiday, clapped his ardent, humble affection on the daughter of the King of the land of wine." Such affection must have had great appeal for a young woman who had been starved of love for several years.

One apocryphal legend asserted that Katherine's ladies reminded her "how much she lowered herself by paying attention to a person who, though possessing some personal accomplishments and advantages, had no princely nor even gentle alliances, but belonged to a barbarous clan of savages reckoned inferior to the lowest English yeoman. She replied that, being a Frenchwoman, she had not been aware that there was any difference of race in the British island." She secretly sent messengers into Anglesey to discover what they could about Owen's past, but he got wind of it and sent a warning to his mother. Another version of the story had it that she repeated what her ladies had said to him and asked him to bring his relations to Windsor to prove them wrong. "He brought into her presence John ap Meredith and Howel ap Llywelyn, his near cousins, men of the goodliest stature and personage, but wholly destitute of bringing-up and nurture. For when the Queen had spoken to them in divers languages, and they were not able to answer, she said they were the goodliest dumb creatures she ever saw."[4]

Katherine was evidently unaware that Glendower's rising had left the English suspicious of the Welsh, or that they had imposed all kinds of humiliating restrictions on them. The Charter of Brecon of 1409 had rescinded many of their liberties and forbidden them to carry arms, form assemblies, own land in England, or hold high office. The marriage of a Welshman to the Queen Mother would have been unthinkable—even if it had been legal. Owen was fortunate in having gained sufficient royal favor to circumvent some of these laws, but Katherine evidently had no idea how unpopular her connection with him might prove.

Although she was of the highest rank, it was quite within the bounds of the aristocratic conventions of courtly love for Owen to worship her from afar and even pay chaste court to her. But it did not stop there, and she may well have seized the initiative. "Being but young in years," she was "of less discretion to judge what was decent to her estate."[5] According to Giles's Chronicle, she was not "able to fully curb her carnal passions."

Katherine married Owen "privily,"[6] meaning in secret, probably because she was taking a husband so far beneath her in rank. That alone would have warranted secrecy, for Owen, the lowly clerk of her wardrobe, "had been so presumptuous as by marriage with the young Queen to intermix his blood with the noble race of kings."[7] In marrying a man so far below her, the Queen, "being young and lusty," had been "following more her own appetite than friendly counsel, and regarding more her private affection than her open honor."[8] Maybe she had fears that the Council would not permit them to wed, although in Tudor times it would be asserted that their marriage was acknowledged around 1428, but there is no contemporary evidence for this.

Katherine's contributions to the upkeep of the King's household ceased after 1430, indicating when her marriage to Owen probably took place; she was then twenty-nine. Owen's Welshness would have been another reason to keep the marriage secret. It has been suggested that John

Lydgate's poem *The Temple of Glass,* a dream sequence that took its inspiration from Chaucer and told of a lady who secretly marries a man forbidden to her, may allude to Katherine; it was written at an unnamed lover's request.

The earliest reference to the couple being married appears in Gregory's Chronicle for 1438, where it is stated that the common people knew nothing of it. It is clear from this that secrecy was maintained until after Katherine's death. In 1428, when Katherine sued the Bishop of Carlisle for encroaching on her dower lands, she did so in her own name, while the epitaph on her lost tomb described her as a widow at her death, although at that time Owen was alive. And when Owen Tudor was summoned to see the King after her death, he was not described as her husband, but as someone who "dwelled with Queen Katherine."[9]

Nevertheless, the Act of Parliament that raised "the illustrious and magnificent princes" Edmund and Jasper Tudor to the nobility in 1452, stated that they were the "natural and legitimate sons of the most serene lady the Queen" and "begotten and born in lawful matrimony, as is sufficiently well known both to your most serene Majesty and to all the lords spiritual and temporal of your realm," and "conceived and born in a lawful marriage."[10] The legitimacy of the union was not questioned until the seventeenth century.

The Council—and the King—were clearly aware of the marriage, but probably left the couple unmolested to avoid a scandal. The author of Giles's Chronicle claimed that in 1428, Gloucester, suspecting that Katherine and Owen were romantically involved, persuaded Parliament to pass a law prohibiting anyone to marry the Queen Dowager without license of the King (when he came of age) and the Council, on pain of forfeiture. The clergy were said to have consented to this only so far "as it contradicted not the laws of God and the Church, and that no deadly sin should be occasioned by it." The Act does not survive in the Parliament Rolls because, according to Sir Edward Coke, Lord Chief Justice from 1613 to 1616, it was never printed. In 1943, the Welsh barrister, judge, and politician Sir Thomas Artemus Jones and officials from the Public Record Office proved conclusively that the Rolls had not been tampered with and that the Act had never existed.

Katherine left Windsor around 1430 and spent the rest of her life in quiet obscurity, residing with Owen at her dower properties, chiefly

Waltham and Hertford. She was at Waltham for Christmas 1430 and in November 1431; Bishop Beaufort visited her there. Owen was naturalized by Parliament in May 1432 and treated thereafter as an English subject; John Leland stated that he had seen a genealogy proving his descent that Katherine had had to show the Lords. In 1434, she assigned him control of her dower lands in Flintshire, Wales.

The couple had several children, which was not known to "the common people till that she were dead and buried."[11] The eldest was Edmund, perhaps born in 1430, or early 1431, at Much Hadham Palace in Hertfordshire, a brick-built twelfth-century manor owned by the bishops of London that still stands today. The second son, Jasper, arrived in November or December 1431 at the Bishop of Ely's manor at Hatfield in Hertfordshire. Clearly the two bishops were sympathetic to Katherine's need for privacy and discretion.

In 1432, Katherine's third pregnancy was near term when she visited the King at Westminster, but her labor began prematurely, obliging her to seek refuge in Westminster Abbey. The child she bore, who was called Owen or Thomas, was taken away to be reared by the brethren under a new name, Edward Bridgewater. Polydore Vergil says he became a Benedictine monk at Westminster. He died in 1502 and was buried there in the abbey. Vergil also states that Katherine and Owen had four children, while *The Great Chronicle of London* asserts there were three or four, and mentions a daughter (perhaps called Margaret, Jacinda, or Tacina) who became a nun, although no other source refers to her.

Katherine celebrated the New Year of 1435 at Gloucester with the King. In February, at Hertford, she instructed Jehan le Sac, her receiver general in France and Normandy, to pay a Parisian goldsmith £26 (£24,720) for a pair of silver flagons, giving strict instructions about exchange rates, a subject on which she was clearly knowledgeable, and ordering him to take care that there were no shortcomings.

8

"I did kiss a queen"

※

Throughout the 1420s the war with France was continuing under Bedford's direction. The Dauphin Charles had refused to recognize Henry VI as King of France and was bent on pursuing his own claim to the throne. In 1428, the Earl of Salisbury laid siege to the city of Orléans, which was in the Dauphin's hands. The latter's prospects were dismal when there appeared at his court a peasant girl, Joan of Arc, who claimed to have heard angelic voices instructing her to free France from English rule. At length, the Dauphin was persuaded to allow her to lead the defense of Orléans. What followed was a resounding victory for the French, which marked a turning point in their fortunes, whereas the English could date the decline of their hold on France to the appearance of Joan of Arc. Their defeat at Orléans in 1429 was the first major setback they had suffered since the death of Henry V.

After another victory at Patay in 1429, Joan led the Dauphin to Rheims. There, on 18 June, in the cathedral that had seen the hallowing of his royal ancestors, he was crowned as Charles VII. Even now, the English might have retrieved the situation, but their war effort was hampered by bitter squabbling between the nobles in council.

In England, on 5 November 1429, Henry VI was crowned in Westminster Abbey, with Queen Katherine occupying a seat of honor nearby. It was a long ordeal for a child not yet eight, but Henry bore it well and with gravity, despite the crown being too heavy for him to wear with comfort. The coronation should have marked his assumption of personal rule, but at eight he was still too young to exercise sovereign power. The Council would continue to govern for him for several more years under the authority of Gloucester and Beaufort, who were often at each other's throats.

In 1430, much to the relief of the English, Joan of Arc was captured by the Duke of Burgundy, who sold her to his ally, Bedford. In May 1431, after being convicted of witchcraft, she was handed over by the Church to the secular authorities and burned at the stake at Rouen in the presence of Cardinal Beaufort. Yet her death did not herald a revival of English fortunes in France.

Henry VI was in Rouen at the time of Joan's trial, but he was not present at her execution. There is no direct evidence of Katherine accompanying him to France, although some of her servants were in Rouen in February that year. She was possibly pregnant at the time.

Bedford, desperate to retrieve the situation in France before it was too late, had decided that Henry should be crowned King of France in Paris to counter the impact of Charles VII's coronation the year before. Accordingly, Henry's took place at the cathedral of Notre-Dame on 16 December 1431. There is no record of Katherine being present.

The French did not want an English king. Fired by a new and vibrant spirit of nationalism, they were determined to oust the invaders. Even as Henry was being crowned in Paris, crowds were rioting in the streets and some of the nobility were hastening to Charles's aid. The coronation was one of Bedford's few failures, and he knew it. Judging the mood of the French people to be dangerous, he sent Henry home to England almost immediately.

By 1434, it was obvious that England no longer had the resources to support the war. Bedford was ill, and he urged that England negotiate an honorable peace with France before she was ignominiously defeated. Burgundy was already negotiating his own peace with Charles VII, and before the year was out had written to Henry VI formally breaking their alliance. Cardinal Beaufort and many others on the Council agreed with Bedford, but Gloucester was adamant: Henry V's policies must be carried out until their final objective was achieved. A deadlock had been reached. But in September 1435, Bedford died at Rouen. Six days later the Treaty of Arras was signed by Philip and Charles, heralding the end of English dominion over France. When Henry VI heard the news, he wept uncontrollably. As a French princess whose line had been disinherited, his mother must have had very mixed feelings.

Early in 1436 the Council decided that Richard, Duke of York, should replace Bedford as governor of Normandy and regent of France. Aged twenty-five, he was the premier magnate of the realm and eager for high office.

In September 1434, Katherine had been assigned £10,500 (£9,911,130) in arrears of her dower, but there was still money outstanding. In May 1436, she wrote from Hertford Castle to Jehan le Sac, as payment had been held up and "we cannot obtain any answer or settlement" due to "the hindrances and differences which have sprung up in our son's lordship of France and Normandy. Very great obstacles have always intervened, and daily do intervene, going on from bad to worse"; but she was hoping that her affairs would be settled speedily.

That year, her health began to decline, and it has been suggested that she was suffering from cancer. It was probably because she was unwell that she withdrew to the abbey of Bermondsey, a foundation favored by royal and noble ladies. There is no contemporary evidence to substantiate later allegations that the Council had just discovered her marriage and had her incarcerated at Bermondsey as punishment. The King, now fourteen, was kept informed of her progress and may have visited her.

By order of the Council, William de la Pole, Earl of Suffolk, was entrusted with the care of her children by Owen and placed her sons in the "custody" of his sister, Catherine de la Pole, Abbess of Barking. On 16 July, the Abbess was assigned £50 (£47,410) for the keep of "Edmund ap Meredith ap Tudor" and "Jasper ap Meredith ap Tudor."[1] Oddly, they were not correctly named as "ap Owen ap Tudor," although clearly the connection was known. Abbess Catherine provided them with food, clothing, and lodging, and both were allowed servants to wait upon them, as befitted their status as the King's half-brothers. But there was a long delay in the payment of the promised allowance and, in 1440, the Abbess was to complain to the King, who removed his half-brothers and placed them in the care of a tutor.

At Bermondsey, Katherine's health deteriorated fast. As 1436 drew to its end, she prepared for death. On 1 January 1437, Henry VI sent her a tablet of gold adorned with a crucifix inlaid with pearls and sapphires as a New Year's gift. That day, clearly of sound mind, she made her will, stating that she was "in so piteous point of so grievous a malady" and knew she was approaching "the silent and fearful conclusion" of her illness, "in the which I have been long, and yet am, troubled and vexed by the visitation of God, to whom be thanking and laud in all His gifts."

She addressed the will to her "full entirely beloved son," to whom she gave her "full hearty natural blessing," and nominated him as her sole executor, with Beaufort and Gloucester as supervisors. "I purpose," she dictated, "by the grace of God and under your succor, protection and comfort, in whom only, among all other earthly, stands my trust." There was no mention of Owen Tudor or their children. "And I am right sure that ye will best tender and favor my will in ordaining for my soul and body, in seeing that my debts be paid and my servants guerdoned [rewarded], in tender and favorable fulfilling of my intent." She declared that her soul would pass into eternity "as naked, as desolate, as willing to be scourged as the poorest soul God ever formed."[2]

Katherine died on 3 January 1437. The King was enthroned in Parliament when they brought him the news. Immediately, he appointed his closest male relatives, Beaufort and Gloucester, and the Bishop of Lincoln to act alongside himself as his mother's executors. Contemporary chroniclers asserted, nevertheless, that he never forgave Gloucester for the way he had treated Katherine. He did his best to ensure that "the memory of the blessed princess, Queen Katherine" was revered, "chiefly because she was worthy to give birth by divine gift to [his] most handsome form and illustrious royal person."[3]

The inscription on Henry V's tomb in Westminster Abbey reads: "Henry V, Hammer of the Gauls, lies here. Henry was put in the urn 1422. Virtue conquers all. The fair Katherine finally joined her husband in 1437. Flee idleness."

But Katherine was not buried in his tomb. Her corpse badly dressed, she was laid in a rough coffin. Her wooden funeral effigy was placed upon it, painted and robed in a satin mantle, surcoat, and tunic, all trimmed with ermine, and furnished with a crown, scepter, and rings; the indentation for the crown can still be seen. The effigy is now on display in the Queen's Diamond Jubilee Gallery at Westminster Abbey; it was probably modeled on a death mask: the face is gaunt, the neck emaciated, the face tragic. Katherine looks older than her thirty-five years, although that was quite middle-aged in the fifteenth century.

The coffin, beneath a black velvet canopy hung with bells, was conveyed on a magnificent hearse to lie in state in the church of St. Katharine by the Tower. It then rested in St. Paul's Cathedral, before being taken in procession to Westminster Abbey, where, on 9 February, after a solemn dirge and Mass, Katherine was buried with royal honors before the altar of the Lady Chapel. The King was chief mourner.

Henry raised a fine altar tomb to his mother's memory. On it was placed a Latin epitaph: "Death, daring spoiler of the world, has laid within this tomb the noble clay that shrined Queen Katherine's soul. From the French King derived, our fifth Henry, wife; of the sixth Henry, mother. As a maid and widow, both a perfect flower of modesty esteemed. Here, happy England, brought she forth that King on whose auspicious life thy weal depends, and rift of whom, thy bliss would soon decay. Joy of this land, and brightness of her own; glory of mothers, to her people dear; a follower sincere of the true faith: Heaven and Earth combined alike to praise this woman who adorns them both e'en now—Earth by her offspring; by her virtues, Heaven! In the fourteen hundred [and] thirty-seventh year, first month's third day, her life drew to its close, and this Queen's soul, beyond the starry sphere, in Heaven received, for aye reigns blissfully."[4]

Katherine's grandson, Henry VII, ordered that new hearse verses be hung above her tomb. They extolled his own descent and described her as Owen Tudor's wife:

> *Here lies Queen Katherine, closed in grave, the French King's daughter,*
> *And of thy kingdom, Charles VI, the true, undoubted heir.*
> *Twice joyful wife in marriage, matched to Henry V by name,*
> *Because through her he [en]nobled was and shined in double fame:*

> *The King of England by descent, and by Queen Katherine's right,*
> *The realm of France he did enjoy, triumphant king of might.*
> *A happy Queen to Englishmen, she came right grateful here,*
> *And four days' space they honored God, with lips and reverent fear.*
> *Henry VI this Queen brought forth, with painful labor plight,*
> *In whose empire France was then, and he an English wight;*
> *Under no lucky planet born unto himself, or throne,*
> *But equal with his parents both in pure religion.*
> *Of Owen Tudor, after this, thy next son Edmund was,*
> *O Katherine! A renowned prince that did in glory pass.*
> *Henry VII, a Britain pearl, a gem of England's joy,*
> *A peerless prince was Edmund's son, a good and gracious* roi.
> *Therefore, a happy life was this, a happy mother pure,*
> *Thrice happy child, but grand-dame she, more than thrice happy sure!*

Katherine's tomb and epitaph were dismantled between October 1502 and January 1503 when Henry VII had the old Lady Chapel demolished to make way for the Henry VII Chapel, where he intended to be buried. Her coffin was found much decayed, but her bones, which (according to the contemporary historian David Henry) were "firmly united and thinly covered with flesh," were laid in "a coffin of boards"[5] and placed on the pavement beside Henry V's tomb, both locked behind a decorative grille.

Henry VII died in 1509. In his will, he had directed that, "as the body of our grand-dame of right noble memory, Queen Katherine, is interred within our monastery of Westminster, and we propose shortly to translate thither the relics of our uncle of blessed memory, Henry VI, our body is to be buried in the same monastery in the chapel where our said grand-dame lies buried."[6]

Katherine lay aboveground for three centuries as one of the curiosities shown to visitors. In 1585, one observer recorded that she looked like an Egyptian mummy. In 1631, the antiquarian John Weever described her as lying "in a chest or coffin with a loose cover, to be seen or handled of any who much desire it." In 1669, the diarist Samuel Pepys saw, "by particular favor, the body of Queen Katherine of Valois, and I had the upper part of her body in my hands, and I did kiss her mouth, reflecting that I did kiss a queen." By then, the body was like leather and the limbs were movable, like a puppet's. In 1711, a German scholar, John Crull, saw Katherine's remains. "Part of her skeleton is still to be seen in a wooden chest, standing on the south side of her husband's monument," he recorded.

During the reign of George II (1727–60), the antiquarian Thomas Hearne recorded that part of Katherine's skeleton was to be seen aboveground in a wooden chest; at that time, her bones were still firmly united and thinly clothed with flesh, like scrapings of tanned leather. In 1776, the old coffin was partly hidden from view when it was placed in a new one and moved beneath the Villers monument in St. Nicholas's Chapel, although visitors could ask the verger for permission to view it. In 1778, the Dean ordered it to be buried in the Percy vault, but nothing was done, and in 1793, Katherine's body in its decaying coffin was described as one of the sights of London. Three years later, it was reported that "of late years, the Westminster scholars amused themselves with tearing [it] to pieces."[7] It was probably in the wake of this desecration that Katherine was finally moved into the Percy vault in 1798.

In 1878, Queen Victoria gave permission for Dean Stanley to have the Queen's remains decently laid to rest beneath an ancient altar slab in Henry V's chantry chapel, a move recommended by Sir Walter Scott. It was no easy matter to transfer the disintegrating coffin. The rotten pieces of wood were gradually and gently lifted off, and the remains of Queen Katherine were then exposed to view. A drawing by Sir George Scharf shows them scattered in the coffin, the broken skull and pelvis at the head, and the legs, with muscle and skin still attached, at the bottom. Several parts were missing, but enough of the skeleton remained to show that the Queen had been five foot six or five foot seven inches tall. A simple epitaph was mounted on the new tomb.

Katherine's historical importance lies chiefly in her marriage to Henry V, which brought him the throne of France. She made little political impact in England and did not exercise power, yet her second marriage, made at her own choice, was to have long-term significance for the English monarchy, for from it sprang the Tudors, who were to rule England for 118 years.

9

"A king greatly degenerated from his father"

✳

In the July following Katherine's death, Henry VI "willed that Owen Tudor, the which dwelled with his mother, Queen Katherine, should come into his presence," and informed him he was "free to come and free to go."[1] But Owen was then summoned before the Council. He had heard that there were those who had spread calumnies about him in the King's hearing, and knew Gloucester for his enemy, so he took sanctuary in Westminster Abbey. What he feared is not known, but possibly the Council, having been reluctant to move against him while the King's mother was alive, now wanted him punished for compromising her honor—the reason given by Vergil, writing in the reign of Tudor's grandson, Henry VII—and probably for flouting the laws against Welshmen prior to his naturalization.

Gloucester eventually persuaded him to leave sanctuary and refute the tales told of him, and issued him with a safe-conduct. Once at liberty, Owen made for Wales, taking with him a hoard of gold and silver plate. Overtaken by Gloucester's men in Warwickshire, probably on account of fears that he would foment rebellion in Wales, he was imprisoned in Newgate with just his confessor and a servant for company, and his goods and the plate were confiscated. His offense is not recorded, but while he was in Newgate, news of his arrest, and his marriage to the late Queen, quickly became public knowledge.

* * *

On 18 July 1437, having briefly again enjoyed the status of first lady in the land, Joan of Navarre passed away at Pirgo Palace, Havering, aged about sixty-nine. She never had recouped the whole of the dower that had been seized from her.

Her passing was expected. In the week beforehand, the King made grants of some of her properties, to take effect after her death. On 23 July, he "appointed the funeral of our grandmother Queen Joan (whom God assoil) to be holden and solemnized at Canterbury, the 6th day of August next coming." He commanded the Duke and Duchess of Gloucester, the earls of Huntingdon, Northumberland, and Oxford, "and other lords and ladies of our realm to be ready for the same day, to the worship of God and our said grandmother, at the solemnity of the said funeral."[2] Gloucester took charge of the arrangements.

Joan's body rested at Bermondsey Abbey on its way to Canterbury Cathedral, where the funeral service was conducted on 11 August by the Archbishop of Canterbury, assisted by the bishops of Norwich and Winchester, the Prior of Christchurch, Canterbury, the Abbot of St. Augustine's, and the Abbot of Battle. Attended by the full panoply of church and state, Joan was buried with Henry IV in a vault beneath the magnificent tomb of Nottingham alabaster she had commissioned. The tomb and the fine effigies placed on it were originally painted in vivid colors, although they have faded over the centuries and the scepters have disappeared. Joan's effigy shows her as a young woman with bared shoulders, the Lancastrian livery collar with "SS" links, and an elaborate crown. On the cornice and canopy can be seen her device, the ermine of Brittany, chained and collared, with her motto "Temperance." In 1832, the vault was opened in the presence of the Dean. Joan's coffin lay on top of Henry's on a rough wooden bench beneath a pile of rubble. The King's remains were exposed, but Joan's were not.

For centuries after her death, the taint of her alleged offense clung. In the nineteenth century, it was claimed that "Joan, the witch queen," haunted the site of Pirgo Palace. Even today, people associate her with witchcraft. Yet there is no good evidence to support that calumny. In fact, Joan was an accomplished stateswoman and diplomat who has largely been overlooked by historians, probably because her power was chiefly exercised in Brittany or behind the scenes in England, and she had no children with Henry IV. She was liked within the royal family, but unpopular with the people of England. Yet she was more competent and experienced than many other medieval queens, and for this alone she deserves to be better remembered.

On 12 November 1437, Henry VI declared himself of age and assumed control of the government. Although he firmly supported Beaufort's peace policy, he was prepared to relinquish neither the French lands still held by England nor the title of King of France. He was too weak and inexperienced to stand up to Gloucester, especially when the Duke warmed to his favorite theme, the sacred duty of fulfilling the wishes of Henry's mighty father.

A mature, strong, and determined ruler might have saved the situation, with the power of the nobles being diverted to other causes. Henry VI, "his mother's stupid offspring and a king greatly degenerated from his father, did not cultivate the art of war,"[3] was not a strong king, and was never interested in winning military glory. Therein lay the tragedy of the House of Lancaster.

In 1910, Henry VI's skeleton was exhumed at Windsor. Examination showed that he had been a strongly built man, about five foot nine inches tall, with brown hair and a small head. A portrait of him in the National Portrait Gallery, which is probably a copy of an original from life, shows a chubby-faced, clean-shaven youth. He wore fashionable clothes, but as he grew older, he came to see rich apparel as a worldly vanity, and took to wearing broad-toed shoes like those of a countryman, a long gown with a round hood, and a long tunic, all in dark gray. This drew criticism from his subjects, who expected their sovereign to look and dress like a king.

John Whethamstede, Abbot of St. Albans, described Henry as a simple and upright man. Philippe de Commines called him "ignorant and almost simple"; even John Blacman, who wrote a hagiography of Henry at the behest of Henry VII, used the word "simple" to describe him, and in 1461 Whethamstede accused Henry of "excessive simplicity in his acts." The word "simplex" then meant gullible or guileless; not until the seventeenth century was the word used to describe a feebleminded person. Nevertheless, gullibility was not a desirable quality in a king: Jean de Waurin stated that all the evils that befell England during Henry's reign were due to his simplemindedness.

Although Henry had been well educated and had a love of learning, John Hardyng described him as being "of small intelligence." Yet he had a strong sense of fairness, wished to see justice available to all, and was accessible to his subjects. He was generally a kindly soul, gentle, generous, honest, and well-intentioned, and too humble and virtuous to govern a country sliding slowly into political anarchy. His qualities were manifold, but they were not the qualities required of a sovereign.

During early manhood, he suffered from spells of excessive melancholy and depression. In the 1440s, he was described as "not steadfast of wit as other kings have been" and some of his subjects were hauled before the justices and punished for having called the King a lunatic. Given the state of England at that time, they might have been forgiven for believing it.

Henry's piety is legendary, yet was he as pious as was later claimed when Henry VII tried to have him canonized as a Lancastrian saint? There is no doubt that his personal piety was genuine. At the great feasts of the year, he wore a rough hair shirt under his robes, "so that his body might be restrained from excess."[4] He feared God and avoided evil. He would not transact any business on Sundays or holy days, nor would he allow his courtiers to speak during services, bring their hawks into church, or wear their swords or daggers there, and he would remain on his knees throughout the service in perfect silence, his head bowed. When going about his daily duties he was constantly engaged in meditation and prayer, withdrawn into a world of his own to which he could retreat from the harsh realities of political life. Because he was the King, his piety attracted attention. By the time he was twenty-five he was famed for it throughout Europe, and Pope Eugenius IV, impressed by the King's charities and care for the poor, awarded him the highest Papal honor, the Golden Rose. But John Blacman, Henry's great Tudor apologist, tended to see piety in everything that he did and interpreted many of his acts as saintly.

Henry saw himself as a guardian of public morality. He never took the Lord's name in vain and could not abide swearing. He held that the revealing clothes of the period led people into promiscuity, an opinion shared by many contemporary moralists. Blacman says that as a youth he was "a pupil of chastity." He was "chaste and pure from the beginning of his days and eschewed all licentiousness in word or deed while he was young." "At the age of sixteen, [he] avoided the sight and conversation of women, affirming them to be the work of the Devil. He was firmly resolved to have intercourse with no woman unless within the bounds of matrimony."[5] Shortly before he married at the age of twenty-three, a Papal envoy reported that he lived more like a monk than a king and "avoided the company of women."

"He took great precautions to secure not only his own chastity but that of his servants," and was so concerned about immorality at his court that he was not above keeping "careful watch through hidden windows of his chamber" on ladies entering his palace, "lest any foolish impertinence of women cause the fall of any of his household."[6] He was excessively prudish and much offended by nudity, often quoting Petrarch on the subject, saying, "The nakedness of a beast is in men unpleasing, but the decency of raiment makes for modesty." Therefore he "was wont utterly to avoid the unguarded sight of naked persons." When he visited the Roman baths at Bath and saw men "wholly naked, with every garment cast off," he fled in embarrassment. One Christmas, a certain lord brought before him some young ladies who danced with bared bosoms, but he angrily averted his eyes, turned his back on them, and went out to his chamber, muttering, "Fie, fie, for shame!"

Henry's chief interest was in his two great academic foundations, Eton College and King's College, Cambridge. He spent lavishly on them, and on his palaces and his favorites, with little regard for his depleted treasury. He was easily manipulated and exploited by unscrupulous courtiers, who took advantage of his extravagant generosity; he, in turn, lacked the perception to judge the worthiness of its recipients.

His chief weakness was allowing himself to be dominated by political factions, who frequently manipulated him into making unwise decisions and who were chiefly concerned with promoting their own interests. He had a peculiar talent for surrounding himself with the most rapacious, self-seeking, and unpopular magnates, in heeding whose advice he showed a marked lack of political judgment. Whoever controlled the

King controlled the country; throughout his reign, therefore, the government of England was carried out according to the wishes of whichever faction was able at any given time to influence him.

Yet few kings can have inherited so many problems: a kingdom near bankruptcy, a Council divided by factions, a legal system corrupted by local magnates and their armed retainers, an aristocracy that was growing ever mightier and losing its integrity, and a war that could not be won, but which was draining the country of its resources. None of these problems was Henry's fault, but his failure to address them effectively made their escalation his responsibility.

One night in January or February 1438, Owen Tudor escaped from Newgate Jail. In March he was returned to prison. That summer, the King set him at liberty, but Gloucester had him recaptured and incarcerated in Wallingford Castle, claiming he had broken jail. He was then returned to Newgate, but again escaped "through help of his priest, and went his way, hurting foul his keeper."[7] By July, Owen was in the custody of the constable of Windsor Castle. He remained there for a year before being released in July 1439 on a huge bail of £2,000 (£1,378,970), on condition that he agreed not to attempt to go anywhere near Wales. On 10 November, once the King had attained his majority, he granted his stepfather a general pardon for all offenses committed before the previous October; again, Owen's original offense was not specified.

From then on, Owen Tudor never looked back. The King, by special favor, granted him a pension of £40 (£27,580) out of his own privy purse, and for the next twenty years, Owen enjoyed a life of comfortable obscurity. Lodged in the royal household until around 1455, he was treated with respect and kindness by the King, who made him several grants of land and in 1459 increased his annuity to £100 (£94,570). In February 1460, he was appointed Keeper of the King's Parks in the county of Denbigh, and we can assume that by then he had been allowed once more to take up residence in his native Wales.

In 1459, an unnamed Welshwoman bore him a bastard son, David Owen, at Pembroke Castle. When Owen Tudor's grandson, Henry Tudor, invaded Wales in 1485, David joined him and was knighted; after Henry became Henry VII a few days later, Sir David Owen grew in prosperity, married an heiress, and probably settled in Sussex, where he is buried in the priory church of Easebourne, near Midhurst.

As well as providing for his stepfather, Henry VI also took care of his half-brothers, Edmund and Jasper Tudor. Sometime after March 1442, he arranged for them to be brought to court and was at great pains to do his best for "the Lords Edmund and Jasper in their boyhood and youth, providing for them most strict and safe guardianship, putting them under the care of virtuous and worthy priests, both for teaching and for right living and conversation, lest the untamed practices of youth should grow rank if they lacked any to prune them."[8] The King's concern and affection fostered fraternal bonds that would endure for life. The young Tudors were "of most noble character of a most refined nature" with "other natural gifts, endowments, excellent and heroic virtues, and other merits of a laudable life and of the best manners and of probity."[9]

Part Three

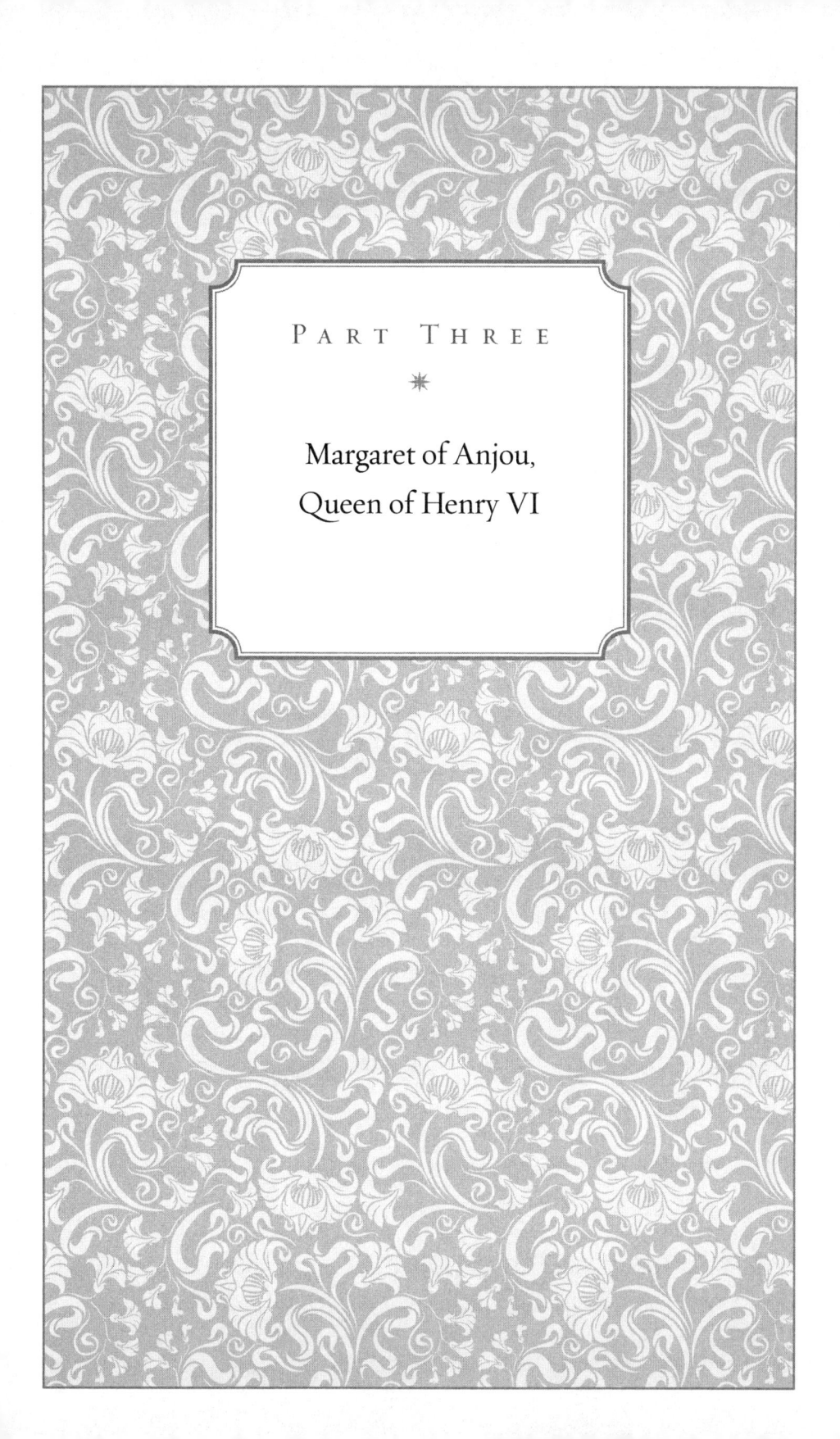

✻

Margaret of Anjou, Queen of Henry VI

I

"The magnificent and very bright Margaret"

✳

By 1441, the nineteen-year-old Henry VI had conceived "an earnest desire to live under the holy sacrament of marriage." Anxious to secure an attractive bride, he insisted on being sent portraits of suitable candidates. None of these likenesses has survived.

Henry wanted a marriage alliance to cement the hoped-for peace with France. From 1441 to 1443, he was considering a match with the daughter of the Count of Armagnac, Burgundy's rival. Then, in the autumn of 1443, either Charles, Duke of Orléans, or Cardinal Beaufort proposed Margaret of Anjou, Charles VII's niece by marriage, a suggestion enthusiastically received by the King and the powerful William de la Pole, Earl of Suffolk, who was called England's "second king."[1] Suffolk had little difficulty in persuading the Council to agree to the match. Philip of Burgundy had suggested Margaret as far back as 1436, but Charles VII had vetoed the idea. Now, apparently, Orléans was urging the union. Naturally, Gloucester opposed it, if only because Beaufort had suggested it, but Gloucester had no influence with the King.

Margaret of Anjou had been born on 23 March 1430 at the château of Pont-à-Mousson, Lorraine, of which only ruins survive. The date of her birth was recorded in her father's book of hours. He was René, Duke of Anjou and Count of Lorraine, a descendant of the counts of Anjou, ancestors of the Plantagenets. Her mother was Isabella, daughter of Charles the Bold, Duke of Lorraine, whom René succeeded in 1431. René and

Isabella had married in 1420 and Margaret was the fifth of their ten children; six died in childhood. Her two surviving brothers were John of Calabria, six years her senior, who would later succeed to their father's titles, and Louis, who died at the age of fifteen in 1444. Her older sister Yolande would, centuries later, be mythically immortalized by Tchaikovsky in his opera *Iolanthe*.

Margaret was baptized with due pomp in Toul Cathedral in Lorraine, and named after her maternal grandmother, Margaret of Bavaria. It is often said that she was reared in infancy by her father's old nurse, Théophanie la Magine, whose tomb effigy at Saumur shows her holding the swaddled René and his sister Marie, later the wife of Charles VII of France; but her epitaph does not mention her caring for Margaret or her siblings.

René of Anjou has been described as a man of many crowns, but no kingdoms. Born in 1408, he was the second son of Louis II, Count of Anjou, by the formidable Yolande of Aragon. Said to be the wisest and most beautiful princess in Christendom, she was described by Louis XI of France as having a man's heart in a woman's body. She had brought up Charles VII, acted as his adviser, and married him to her daughter Marie. She had introduced Joan of Arc to him. She had been regent of Provence during René's minority, and was now highly respected and powerful.

René's political career had been checkered. During Margaret's childhood, he was a prisoner of the Burgundians, who were backing Antoine de Vaudémont, a rival claimant to Lorraine and a client of the Duke of Burgundy. The infant Margaret was with her mother at Nancy when news of her father's capture at the Battle of Bulgnéville arrived in July 1431. Isabella was indefatigable. She tried unsuccessfully to negotiate with Vaudémont for his release, then she and Yolande raised an army to protect themselves from him and appealed to the Emperor Sigismund to rule favorably on René's claim, which he eventually did in 1434. Isabella may have taken her children with her when she rode to the court of Charles VII at Vienne and begged him to help, but he had limited resources and too many troubles of his own. She then made an appeal to Burgundy, to no avail; René remained in prison at Rouen. Margaret must have learned much from the example of her redoubtable mother, who had ruled Lorraine jointly with René and continued to do so in his absence, although her efforts to raise his ransom left the duchy impoverished.

In 1433, still Burgundy's prisoner, René was constrained to arrange a marriage between the infant Margaret and Pierre of Luxembourg, heir of the Count of Saint-Pol, a supporter of Vaudémont, but the negotiations fizzled out. The following year, René inherited the duchy of Anjou (with Provence and Maine), although it was occupied by the English. Having betrothed his daughter Yolande to Vaudémont's heir, Ferry (or Frederick), he ransomed himself, leaving his two sons as hostages, and was reunited with his wife. Four-year-old Margaret, his "little creature," must initially have wondered who this stranger was, yet René was not around for long because he was unable to meet the conditions of his release and had to hand himself over to Duke Philip to be returned to captivity at Dijon. His parting from Isabella and Margaret was heartbreakingly emotional.

When René's widowed sister-in-law, Joanna II, Queen of the Two Sicilies (as the kingdoms of Naples and Sicily were known), died in February 1435, she left him her crown, her county of Provence, and her claims to the kingdoms of Jerusalem and Hungary. Being in captivity, René had to cede his title to Alfonso of Aragon, but he nevertheless continued to call himself King of Naples and Sicily, though it was as empty a pretense as were his claims to be King of Jerusalem and Hungary. His authority held good only in Anjou, Lorraine, and Provence, although Isabella, now styling herself Queen of the Two Sicilies, had to exercise it while he was a prisoner.

In 1435, Margaret was living with her mother at the castle of Tarascon on the River Rhône. It was a pleasant existence, for the family were loved by the local people, who brought them humble gifts and built bonfires by the castle walls to ward off the plague when it struck. Isabella saw that Margaret was well educated, tutoring her herself and perhaps arranging for her to have lessons with the scholar Antoine de la Salle, who taught her brother. It was a happy childhood, for Margaret was deeply loved by her family.

It is sometimes stated that when Isabella left Tarascon with her children to pursue René's claim to the Two Sicilies, she took five-year-old Margaret with her, but in fact she sent her north to Saumur to be raised in the household of her grandmother Queen Yolande. Isabella then hastened to Marseilles, where she boarded a ship bound for Naples and there took up residence in the old royal palace at Capua. Staging a grand ceremony, she had the absent René proclaimed King, and was then carried in procession through Naples in a triumphal chair of velvet embroidered with gold; later accounts state incorrectly that Margaret and Louis were seated beside her.

René had been considering possible husbands for Margaret. Around 1435–6, Burgundy demanded that she marry his infant son, Charles, Count of Charolais, but the plan came to nothing because René did not want to hand over Bar and Pont-à-Mousson as dowry. In November 1436, he regained his liberty and traveled south to Naples, where he was publicly reunited with Isabella. They lived in Capua in some luxury until Naples fell to the Spaniards in 1441, when they returned to France.

Saumur was a fairy-tale château, painted white with pepperpot towers, as it appears in the contemporary manuscript "Les Très Riches Heures du Duc de Berry." Margaret spent seven years there with the pious and cultivated Queen Yolande, a strong female role model. Her education progressed and she developed a passion for romances and Boccaccio's *Decameron*. She was also influenced by the works of Christine de Pisan, an early advocate of equality for women. Yolande ensured that Margaret was well versed in court etiquette and able to keep accounts, useful assets in a princess.

In 1442, the Emperor Frederick III asked Yolande for Margaret's hand, whereupon Yolande, on René's instructions, had her granddaughter beautifully dressed and presented to the Imperial envoys, who were sent away laden with gifts. Negotiations nevertheless foundered.

Margaret was twelve when her grandmother died in November 1442. With Yolande's bequest of jewels, Margaret returned to her parents, who were living in the château at Angers in some style, surrounded by luxuries such as silks and porcelain imported from as far away as China.

René was a highly cultivated and talented man, a musician of some renown, and a gifted artist and poet whose illuminated manuscripts are arguably the best-executed of the period. His library contained over 200 books on theology, history, law, and science. He kept a menagerie of exotic beasts. His small but brilliant court, which moved between Angers and Saumur, attracted many talented people seeking patronage. It was famed for its entertainments and its tournaments, which René raised to an art form, and for its artificial creation of a pastoral idyll inspired by the new Humanism sweeping across Europe from Italy. He wrote a manual on jousting, and an allegorical romance, the *Livre de Coeur de l'Amour Epris* ("The Book of the Heart Seized by Love").

Thanks to his sister Marie being Queen of France, René was able to build up a sphere of influence at the French court. The friendship between Charles VII and René dated back to childhood, when they had been as brothers at the court of René's father at Angers. Now René found himself a member of the King's council and an honored courtier who was constantly at Charles's side at tournaments, courtly ceremonies, and banquets. He also campaigned on the French King's behalf in Normandy and Lorraine. By 1444, despite his landless status, René was a considerable power at the French court, and the Milanese ambassador observed that he was "the one who governs this entire realm."

Late in 1442, Burgundy entered negotiations with Margaret's mother for her marriage to his nephew, Charles I, Count of Nevers. The couple were betrothed on 4 February 1443 at Tarascon, and it was agreed that the bride would have a dowry of 50,000 livres (£51,880,400) and that her children would inherit Sicily, Provence, and Bar. This provoked Antoine de Vaudémont, who held that these territories should be his by virtue of his son's betrothal to Margaret's older sister, and he complained to Charles VII, who promptly scuppered the match.

Margaret also had an admirer in the courtly tradition. Pierre de Brézé, Sieur de la Varenne and Seneschal of Anjou, who was old enough to be her father and reputed to be "the best warrior of all that time."[2] He served as seneschal of the château of Angers and had there conceived an entirely proper and chivalrous passion for her, carrying her colors at jousts and calling himself her "Chevalier Servant."

René's ancestral territories of Maine and Anjou were still in the hands of the English, and when he learned from Suffolk of the King of England's interest in his daughter, he realized that a marriage alliance would be an excellent means of getting them back. And so private negotiations went forward.

At some point, René sent Margaret to live with her aunt, Queen Marie, at the French court, where she won golden opinions for her beauty and character. The Burgundian chronicler Barante wrote: "There was no princess in Christendom more accomplished than my lady Margaret of Anjou. She was already renowned in France for her beauty and wit and her lofty spirit of courage."

In January 1444, it seemed that peace with France was within England's grasp, for an agreement was reached between Henry VI, Charles VII, and Philip of Burgundy that their commissioners should meet shortly at Tours to discuss peace terms and a marriage alliance between England and France. Also present would be René of Anjou, father of the prospective bride.

In February, an English embassy headed by Suffolk arrived at the French court at Tours. Magnificently equipped at great cost to the Exchequer, Suffolk appears to have been unenthusiastic about his mission, having belatedly realized that peace with France would not be popular with the English people; consequently, he did not wish to be too closely associated with it. On 17 April, he was courteously received by Charles and King René, who had traveled over from Angers, and afforded a state welcome. Peace talks then commenced. Suffolk made a formal request for the hand of Margaret, to which René readily agreed, although he warned the Earl that he was penniless and could not provide his daughter with a dowry. He then demanded that England return to him Maine and Anjou as part of the terms of the marriage treaty, a demand backed by King Charles. Suffolk referred the matter back to the Council in England, knowing full well that the cession of Maine and Anjou in return for a queen who brought no financial advantage would be deeply unpopular. But Henry VI had just learned that the Count of Nevers was on the point of offering again for Margaret, and knew he had to act quickly.

He empowered Suffolk to agree to the cession of Maine and Anjou in return for the English being allowed to retain Aquitaine, Normandy, and all the other territories conquered by Henry V. He agreed to waive Margaret's dowry and undertook to pay for the wedding out of his own privy purse, while Suffolk was to conduct the bride to England at the King's expense. Already, Henry was making strenuous efforts to raise money for this purpose. Meanwhile, at Tours, Suffolk could only arrange a two-year truce, for Charles's stringent demands rendered a peace treaty impossible at this stage. The marriage, however, was to be a stepping stone to such a treaty.

Throughout the negotiations, Margaret stayed at the castle of Angers with her mother. In early May, they traveled to Tours, where they stayed with King René in the abbey of Beaumont-les-Tours. On 4 May, in the great hall of the nearby castle of Reculée, Suffolk paid his respects to his future Queen, and was much impressed by her beauty and bearing. On 22 May, the Treaty of Tours was signed at Châlons, providing for the marriage of Henry and Margaret and a two-year truce with France, and including a secret clause committing the English to the surrender of Maine and Anjou. The impoverished René had at the last minute appealed to the clergy of Anjou, who donated part of their revenues to provide the bride with a trousseau and fund the betrothal celebrations. René's estates granted him a further 33,000 livres (£21:2 million). He now settled a dowry of 20,000 livres (£12:9 million) on Margaret, with the rights she would inherit from him to the islands of Majorca and Minorca, although they were not in his possession and Henry would have to conquer them. Margaret herself renounced all claims to any other territories.

Two days later, on 24 May, she was betrothed to Henry VI in the church of St. Martin at Tours (now the cathedral). King Charles led Margaret to the Papal legate, Piero da Monte, Bishop of Brescia, who officiated at the ceremony, and Suffolk stood proxy for King Henry, who had charged him to "engage verbally the excellent and magnificent and very bright Margaret" and make the promises on his behalf.[3]

Afterward, the betrothal party proceeded through cheering crowds, ecstatic at the prospect of peace, until they came to the abbey of Saint-Julien. There a great feast was held, at which Margaret was accorded the same honors as the Queen of France. "Queen Margaret was set in the middle of the hall as principal of the feast and royally by her own as queen of England. The lords and ladies were worthily served, and all the commons that followed them had great cheer of meat and drink." There was dancing "until an untimely hour" and even a joust with camels.[4]

On 27 June 1444, Suffolk returned to London, where he was received with great rejoicing. The Treaty of Tours and the truce were laid before Parliament for ratification, and Gloucester made a speech thanking Suffolk for arranging them, believing that both had been negotiated on terms advantageous to England and without making any substantial concessions. Henry VI rewarded Suffolk by raising him to the rank of marquess. He wrote to his bride, expressing his eagerness to see her. In an exchange of cordial letters, King Charles warned him that it would take time to equip her as a queen. Meanwhile, Henry had written to the Goldsmiths' Company, one of London's great livery guilds, "entreating them to do their devoir at the coming of his entirely well-beloved wife the Queen, whom he expected, through God's grace, to have with him in right brief time." They probably supplied the plate he gave her as wedding gifts: a covered saltcellar of gold, enameled with the royal arms and marguerites, its boss adorned with a balas ruby; and a golden pitcher decorated with sapphires.

Charles prepared a safe-conduct for Margaret to take on her journey. On 7 November, Suffolk again crossed to France with an embassy as splendid as before, accompanied by the earls of Shrewsbury and Salisbury, and by his wife, Alice Chaucer (granddaughter of the poet Geoffrey Chaucer), who was to act as principal lady-in-waiting to the Queen on the journey home. They arrived at Nancy in January. Margaret and her parents were there to welcome Queen Marie and the Dauphine. In March, Charles VII and King René joined them, and the proxy wedding ceremony took place on 7 March in Nancy Cathedral. Louis de Heraucourt, Bishop of Toul, officiated, and again, Suffolk represented his sovereign. The bride wore a gown of white satin embroidered with silver and gold marguerites, her personal emblem, which appeared everywhere, on clothing, hangings, canopies, and banners. Her train bearer was Alice Chaucer, Marchioness of Suffolk, who became a friend for life.

After the wedding, a ceremonial banquet was attended by the King and Queen of France, the Dauphin Louis, King René, and a host of French lords. There were magnificent celebrations, and Charles and René led the nobility of France in procession through the city. The feasting continued for a week, and there were miracle plays and eight days of tournaments, hosted by René and presided over by Charles VII's mistress, Agnes Sorel, who appeared as "the Lady of Beauty." All the combatants wore garlands or devices of marguerites in honor of the bride, who presented the prizes with Queen Marie. King Charles himself entered the lists in Margaret's honor, once in contest with her father, who was dramatically dressed in black, while her champion Pierre de Brézé broke a lance with Suffolk. The celebrations ended with a lavish ball.

One of the contestants was Ferry de Vaudémont, who had succeeded his father, Antoine, as count. Frustrated because his marriage to Margaret's sister, Yolande, had been continually delayed, due to an ongoing dispute between their fathers over her rights to Lorraine, he gathered a group of his jousting comrades and abducted her, intending to hide her in a safe place until René and Isabella agreed to the wedding going ahead. René was furious, but when the King and Queen of France interceded for the young couple, he backed down, and there was more cause for rejoicing. Ferry and Yolande were married the following year.

2

"A queen not worth ten marks"

✳

WHEN CHARLES RECEIVED HENRY'S RATIFICATION OF THE marriage contract, it was time for Margaret to leave for England, accompanied by an impressive escort of 1,500 persons, including five barons with their baronesses, seventeen knights, sixty-five squires, 174 valets, eighty-two yeomen, and twenty sumptermen to look after her baggage; yet strangely she had only four personal servants, which was hardly in keeping with her new status.

Two miles from Nancy, King Charles formally took leave of her, saying he feared he had done nothing for her by placing her on one of the greatest thrones of Europe, for it was scarcely worthy of her. After he had commended her to God, uncle and niece wept bitterly on parting, and Queen Marie could not speak for emotion, kissing Margaret repeatedly. At Bar-le-Duc, Margaret said farewell to her parents; it was a heartrending leave-taking, and they were all so overcome that they too were struck dumb. After these partings, Margaret suffered severe abdominal pains, and doctors had to be summoned.

On 15 March, she entered Paris, and on the following day, she received a stately welcome at the cathedral of Notre-Dame. Afterward, her brother, John of Calabria, formally delivered her into the safekeeping of Suffolk. The governor of Normandy, Richard, Duke of York, attended by an escort of 600 archers, welcomed his new Queen on behalf of King Henry, and presented her with a palfrey caparisoned with crimson and gold velvet sewn with golden roses, a gift from her husband. Cannon saluted and church bells pealed as the Queen's cavalcade rode through Paris.

On 17 March, the Duke of Orléans accompanied Margaret to Poissy, and from there York escorted them along the River Seine to Rouen, the English capital in Normandy, where she was greeted by another salute of cannon-fire and more joyful peals of bells. But she was still unwell and had to absent herself from the state entry into the city on 22 March, being represented by Alice Chaucer, who wore the Queen's bridal robes, and the countesses of Salisbury and Shrewsbury. She would have been cheered by the arrival of a fine mare trapped in gold, another gift from King Henry, one she had asked for.

In Rouen, she had to pawn some silver-gilt plate to the Duchess of Somerset to make up the wages of the sailors who would bring her to England. She then had to buy cheap, secondhand plate to replace it, and she was also obliged to purchase shoes and clothing for fifteen poor women.

After a week in Rouen, Margaret arrived at Pontoise, and was York's guest at two state dinners paid for by King Henry, there and in Mantes. Relations between the thirty-three-year-old Duke and the fifteen-year-old Queen were noticeably cordial, and there was no hint of the deadly enmity that would one day divide them.

Henry VI was eagerly contemplating "the coming of our most beloved wife the Queen into our presence."[1] Parliament had voted £5,129:2s.5d. (£5,389,650) toward the cost of bringing the new Queen to England, and applauded the marriage and the truce, "by which two happy events, through God's grace, justice and peace should be firmly established throughout the realm."[2] The Council had dispatched an escort of fifty-six ships to bring the bride home.

On 3 April, Margaret arrived at Harfleur, then sailed along the coast in a ship called *The Trinity* to Cherbourg, where the English fleet was waiting. Margaret's ship, *The Cock John,* had been refitted with new chambers for her and her attendants, and a bridge on which she could board and disembark.

Prior to their departure, Suffolk did his best to prepare Margaret for her future role and advise what was expected of her. He was concerned about her comparative poverty. Henry VI might have been content to take a queen without a dowry, but there had been complaints in England that, for all René's magnificent titles, he had "too short a purse to send his daughter honorably to the King, her spouse." Gloucester had openly deplored the lack of dowry and accused Parliament of having "bought a queen not worth ten marks."[3] René had provided his daughter with a trousseau of sorts. A furrier had supplied 120 pelts of white fur for trimming robes, and a merchant of Angers had provided eleven ells of violet and crimson cloth of gold, plus a thousand small pieces of fur. But that was all.

Margaret endured a rough crossing to England; the sea was turbulent, and the rolling of the ship not only broke its masts but also made her ill. On 9 April, *The Cock John* beached at Portchester, Hampshire, in the midst of a storm, but no reception awaited the new Queen's arrival because she was not yet expected. Braving thunder and lightning, the mayor and other local worthies, apprised of her coming, hastened to lay carpets on the beach, while large crowds came running to cheer her and strew rushes on the sand, as church bells rang out a welcome. But Margaret was too sick to walk, and Suffolk had to carry her ashore. Her clothes, the assembled dignitaries were dismayed to see, looked like rags. Suffolk bore her to a nearby cottage, where she fainted; when she felt better, she was taken to the convent of God's House at Portsmouth to recuperate. Henry later rewarded the ship's master for having "conveyed his beloved consort safely to England."

The next day, the weather improved, and Margaret was sufficiently restored to make an offering in the convent chapel and be rowed in state along the coast to Southampton. The King had paid for Italian trumpeters to play on the decks of two Genoese galleys as her ship passed, but it is doubtful if she paid them much heed as she was feeling ill again. Once they docked at Southampton, Suffolk installed Margaret in God's House Hospital, a refuge for travelers, and paid Master Francis, her physician, £3:3s.2d. (£3,310) to purchase "divers spices, confections and powders for making medicines" for her.[4] Suffolk was so concerned at Margaret's lack of decent apparel that he summoned a London tiremaker (dressmaker), Margaret Chamberlayne, to attend her.

Henry waited five days at Southwick Priory until Margaret finally arrived on 14 April, much restored. According to the account of a Milanese ambassador in France, written years later, he disguised himself as a squire and took her a letter written, he said, by the King of England. As Margaret read it, he took stock of her, saying to himself that a woman may be seen over well when she reads a letter. Margaret had no idea who he was, being so engrossed in the letter, and she never looked at him as he knelt before her in his squire's dress. After the King had gone, Suffolk asked, "Most serene Queen, what do you think of the squire who brought the letter?"

"I did not notice him," Margaret replied.

"Most serene Queen, the person dressed as a squire was the most serene King of England," the Earl revealed. "And the Queen was vexed at not having known it, because she had kept him on his knees. Afterward the King wrote to her, and they made great triumphs."[5]

Despite his efforts, Henry had raised very little money to pay for his wedding; the cost would amount to £5,500 (£6,071,660), £2,500 over budget, which attracted criticism. He had even pawned the crown jewels, but then realized he needed them for the ceremony, and had to pawn his personal jewelry and plate to retrieve them.

On 22 April 1445, Henry and Margaret were married in a quiet ceremony at Titchfield Abbey in Hampshire. William Ayscough, Bishop of Salisbury and confessor to the King, officiated. Henry placed on Margaret's finger a gold ring set with an enormous ruby which had been given to him at his French coronation by Bishop Beaufort and refashioned for his bride. His wedding gifts to her were a gold collar sparkling with precious stones, a costly pendant, and the plate already mentioned. Margaret also received a lion from an unknown admirer, who had perhaps heard of her father's menagerie; it was promptly dispatched at considerable expense to the royal menagerie at the Tower of London. Another gift of an eagle was commemorated by John Lydgate in a ballad.

The chronicler John Capgrave, for whom Henry could do no wrong, commented: "This marriage the whole people believe will be pleasing to God and to the realm because peace and abundant crops came to us with it."[6] The auguries were promising.

Henry was delighted with his bride. All contemporary sources agree that Margaret was beautiful. Chastellain called her the exemplification of "all that is majestic" in woman, and "one of the most beautiful persons in the world. She was indeed a very fair lady, altogether well worth the looking at, and of high bearing withal." She had, he added, excellent manners. According to Vergil, she was "a young lady exceeding others of her time, as well in beauty as wisdom, imbued with a high courage above the nature of her sex." The French chronicler Thomas Basin called her "a good-looking and well-developed girl." The Milanese ambassador informed Bianca Maria Visconti, Duchess of Milan, that Margaret was "a most handsome woman, though somewhat dark and not as beautiful as your serenity."[7] Surviving manuscript illustrations of Margaret portray her as blond or auburn-haired. So he may have been referring to her complexion.

The best surviving image of Margaret is a head and shoulders profile relief on a medal struck in 1463 by Pietro da Milano, now in the Victoria and Albert Museum (a copy is in the Bibliothèque Nationale in Paris.) It shows her with upswept hair, wearing a crown. This sitter bears more than a passing resemblance to a noble lady painted by René of Anjou in a tournament scene in his manuscript *Le Livre de Tournois,* now in the Bibliothèque Nationale. She is evidently of high rank, for she is attended by a bevy of well-dressed ladies and is shown standing at the right of the page, inspecting the helms of jousters. Did René depict his own daughter? It is tempting to think so.

Margaret appears in several manuscript illustrations. The most famous shows her and Henry VI being presented with an illuminated copy of John Talbot's *Poems and Romances,* and dates from c.1450–3.[8] In his dedication, Talbot praised the Queen: "Though you speak English so well, you have not forgotten your French." He lauded her marriage for bringing peace to England and expressed the hope that she would bear an heir to continue her husband's illustrious line.

There is a fanciful portrayal of Margaret's wedding in the Royal MSS in the British Library, and a beautiful picture of her and Henry kneeling before the altar in Eton College Chapel in the manuscript of Ranulf Higden's *Polychronicon,* now in Eton College Library. Margaret appears as an older woman, hooded and at prayer, in a manuscript owned by the Worshipful Company of Skinners of the City of London, of whose guild—then the Fraternity of Our Lady's Assumption—she was patroness.

There are fifteenth-century carvings of Henry and Margaret at Lambeth Palace in London. A worn corbel head of a woman with flowing hair, said to portray Margaret, is in the porch of the parish church of St. John the Baptist, Henley-in-Arden, while her head and Henry's are shown in crude relief on a 500-year-old bell that once hung in Valle Crucis Abbey in North Wales and is now at Great Ness Church, Shropshire. Nearby Wrockwardine Church has an ancient chair carved with an illustration of Queen Margaret confronting a robber, a famous episode from the Wars of the Roses. An eighteenth-century drawing of a lost stained-glass window from the Church of the Cordeliers at Angers shows Margaret kneeling in prayer, wearing a sideless surcoat furred with ermine and long hair beneath her crown. A painting in the Toledo Museum of Art, Ohio, was once thought, incorrectly, to depict the marriage of Henry and Margaret.

After the wedding, the King and Queen spent five nights at Titchfield Abbey, and the Charter Rolls record that the Abbot and convent were well rewarded for their hospitality and courtesy. But the union looked not to be fruitful. Henry was twenty-three, Margaret sixteen; their wedding night is unlikely to have seen the flowering of any grand passion. Margaret was still unwell; in May, the King informed the Archbishop of Canterbury: "Our dear and best beloved wife the Queen is yet sick of the labor and indisposition of the sea, by occasion of which the pox been broken out upon her, for which cause we may not in our own person hold the feast of St. George in our castle of Windsor."[9] In 1446, rumor had it that Bishop Ayscough, the King's confessor, had warned him against self-indulgence and having his "sport" with his bride, advising him not to "come nigh her" any more than was necessary for the procreation of heirs. As Margaret did not produce an heir for eight years, Henry may have taken his confessor's advice to heart. Yet the couple publicly received gifts while lying in bed together one New Year in the early years of their marriage and were evidently close.

Henry was "a man of a meek spirit and of a simple wit, but the Queen was of a great wit."[10] For all the disparity in their characters, Margaret became devoted to Henry and fiercely supportive of him. Blacman says that he "kept his marriage vow wholly and sincerely, never dealing unchastely with any woman, even in the absences of the lady," which in later years "were sometimes very long," through force of circumstances. Nor, "when they lived together, did he use his wife unseemly, but with all honesty and gravity." He was a generous husband, anxious to ensure that she lacked for nothing. Margaret addressed him in her letters as "my most redoubted lord." From the first, they were deeply loyal to each other, spending as much time as possible together.

The physical side of marriage was perhaps of no great importance to Henry, although he knew that it was a king's responsibility to provide for the succession. Yet Margaret's failure to conceive may not have been so much his fault as hers, for her accounts show that she fasted several times each week. The nonappearance of a son was to rebound on her because infertility in a marriage was invariably regarded as the fault of the wife. Barrenness in a queen was a national disaster, for the provision of an heir was crucial to the well-being and stability of the realm.

3

"Of stomach and courage more like to a man"

✷

AFTER LEAVING TITCHFIELD ABBEY, THE ROYAL COUPLE MOVED to Bishop's Waltham in Hampshire, where Margaret stayed as the guest of Cardinal Beaufort while Henry rode on to Westminster. She then made a progress through Sussex and Surrey to Eltham Palace. Henry had ordered that the Queen's apartments there be rebuilt with a new hall, scullery, and range of lodgings, and they were now ready for her. Her lodgings at Westminster and Sheen had been renovated, as they had not been used for more than a decade.

On Friday 28 May 1445, she traveled from Eltham Palace to Blackheath, where she was officially welcomed by "an equestrian procession"[1] of the Lord Mayor of London, the aldermen and the sheriffs, all clad in scarlet and attended by guildsmen in blue gowns with embroidered sleeves and red hoods. Gloucester, attended by 500 retainers sporting ostrich feathers, then escorted her to his palace at Greenwich, where he hosted a banquet in her honor. Relations between them were frosty, for Margaret knew he had opposed her marriage; she had already decided that she would be guided by his rival, Bishop Beaufort.

On the following day, Margaret made her state entry into London, coming upriver by barge to Southwark and entering the City by London Bridge. She was warmly received, all the nobility sporting daisies (marguerites) in her honor. That night, she stayed at the Tower of London, in keeping with ancient custom. "And there the King, at the reverence of the Queen, made 46 Knights of the Bath. On the morrow at afternoon, the Queen came from the Tower in a horse bier [litter] with two steeds trapped all in white damask powdered with gold, and so was the vesture that she had on, and the pillows and all the bier in one suite; and her hair combed down about her shoulders with a coronal of gold, rich pearls and precious stones. There were lords on horseback and nineteen chariots of ladies and their gentlewomen, and all the crafts of the City of London going on foot in their best array unto St. Paul's."[2]

Margaret was borne through the streets of the capital, which were decorated with a profusion of marguerites, and passed beneath triumphal arches. Fountains and conduits spouted ale and wine for all to drink freely. At several points, the cavalcade halted so that the Queen could watch miracle plays and "many costly pageants made of divers old histories, to her great comfort."[3] They featured "angels and other heavenly things, with song and melody in divers places."[4] "At the bridge-foot toward Southwark was a pageant of 'Peace and Plenty,' and at every street corner two puppets in a moving pageant called 'Justice and Peace' were made to kiss each other. Noah's ship [was] upon the bridge with verses in English; at Leadenhall, Madam Grace, the chancellor of God; at the inn in Cornhill; St. Margaret; at the great conduit in Cheapside; 'The Five Wise and Foolish Virgins' at the cross in the Chepe; 'The Heavenly Jerusalem,' with verses; at Paul's Gate; 'The General Resurrection and Judgment.'"[5] All extolled Margaret as the bringer of peace.

In St. Paul's Cathedral, she made an offering at the high altar. Some of those watching were less than enthusiastic about their new Queen, for Gloucester's supporters had already stirred up anger over her lack of a dowry and capitalized on their distrust of "the Frenchwoman." Others greeted her merrily, sporting daisies in their caps or hoods. Thus she came to the Palace of Westminster to be reunited with the King, who had spent the day at the house of a London goldsmith.

On Sunday 30 May, Margaret was crowned "royally and worthily"[6] in Westminster Abbey by John Stafford, Archbishop of Canterbury, and received the homage of the lords. The coronation was followed by a splendid banquet in Westminster Hall and three days of tournaments. Soon afterward, Margaret's escort were sent home with gifts from the King.

* * *

Parliament now conferred upon the Queen a dower of 10,000 marks (£7,175,590) per annum, the same as Queen Joan's and Queen Katherine's. However, it was not paid in its entirety and was soon in arrears. This was one reason why Margaret found it hard to cover the expenses of her large household.

On 13 July, a French embassy arrived at Westminster to discuss a permanent peace. Henry told them "that he did not hold them as strangers as they belonged to the household of his uncle of France, whom, of all persons in the world, after the Queen his wife, he loved the best." The envoys apologized "for the long delay of the Queen's arrival. They now came to inquire after her health and to wish them both much joy and a long-continued prosperity."[7]

They asked Henry VI to cede Maine and Anjou to King René without delay, as secretly provided for in the Treaty of Tours. Henry prevaricated, even when the envoys produced letters from King Charles to him and the Queen, urging him to honor his promise and saying this would be the best means of achieving a permanent peace. He played for time, and the only benefit to result from the meeting was an extension of the truce until July 1446.

The King's marriage might have seemed a triumph for Beaufort and Suffolk, but the English people in general did not want peace with France: they wanted glorious victories over their old enemy. Margaret represented a peace they regarded as ignominious, and they disliked her for it. Later, when it ultimately led to England's defeat and humiliation, she was held responsible. Although she always acted as she thought best in Henry's interests, she never learned to understand the prejudices and fears of her husband's subjects. Indeed, it was her belief in the peace policy that strengthened Henry's resolve to pursue it in the face of public opposition.

Later it would be said that, from the time of his marriage, King Henry never profited. Gloucester seized every opportunity to voice his disapproval and, although he did not personally show himself hostile to Margaret, he did his best to engender distrust of her in the minds of the people. As a result of this, and the inbred Francophobia of the English, the marriage was never popular. Gloucester and many others felt that the truce constituted a threat to England, in that it gave the French time in which to rearm and plan a decisive assault on England's remaining territories in France.

The royal marriage also gave rise to increasing bitterness between court factions. In France, where Margaret had spent her formative years, rule by factions was accepted as a necessary evil, but in England it was bitterly resented. From the first, however, she zealously identified herself with Beaufort's party, in the belief that she was helping her husband. Her willingness to support a particular faction did much to exacerbate the divisions in the court and the household. By placing herself in opposition to Gloucester, she made an enemy of him. From the first, she and Suffolk were determined to overthrow him.

Yet, in the opinion of the Duke of Orléans, "England had never seen a queen more worthy of a throne than Margaret. It seemed as if she had been formed by Heaven to supply to her royal husband the qualities which he required in order to become a great king." The Milanese ambassador wrote in awe-inspired tones of "the magnificence of the Queen of England." From the first, Margaret was every inch a queen, having a commanding presence. She was competent in transacting business and in safeguarding her rights and made the most of the financial advantages of her position. She obtained a license to export wool and tin wherever she pleased, thereby evading customs duties and the strict rules of the Merchants of the Staple at Calais. She paid for ships to be fitted out to trade in the Mediterranean. She attempted, with some success, to boost England's wool trade by importing skilled craftsmen from Flanders and Lyon, and tried to introduce silk weaving into England, bringing in foreign craftsmen, encouraging women to join the trade, and becoming patron of the Sisterhood of Silk Women, a guild based in Spitalfields, London.

One servant praised her "wise and charitable disposition,"[8] and there is plenty of evidence for her kindnesses and her good ladyship. She was generous in her gifts. In 1452–3, for example, she gave presents to ninety-eight persons, plus others to lowly servants. She afforded generous financial help to members of her household who were ill or getting married, or to those who had suffered bad luck, such as two Newmarket men whose stable had burned down during a royal visit.

The Queen's Wardrobe Book for the year 1452–3 survives. It shows that she did not lavish large sums on clothes, buying only bolts of silk and cloth of gold, imported from Venice, and jewelry. She was devout, attending Mass daily. On a pilgrimage to Canterbury in the year of her marriage, she heard choirboys singing Mass by Our Lady's altar in the cathedral undercroft and visited the shrine of St. Thomas Becket; she stayed at Le Hale, a pavilion made of white woolen cloth, set up in Blean Woods, just north of the city. She loved hunting and frequently gave orders that the game in her forests be reserved for her own use.

Much of Margaret's copious correspondence from the early years of her marriage survives. It reveals her preoccupation with matchmaking, dower and estate matters, hunting, wine, clothes, and obtaining preferment for her friends and members of her household. She was active in pursuing justice and in involving herself in the affairs of well-born families, influencing opinions, and promoting the interests of her friends and servants. Her patronage extended far and wide, and she was not averse to commanding favors.

Margaret quickly learned to speak English. She was highly literate, loved Italian romances, and was a "devout pilgrim to the shrine of Boccaccio,"[9] whose racy *Decameron* was in lighthearted contrast to the pious tomes her husband read.

In many respects, she took after her mother and grandmother, both strong, capable women. She was intelligent and courageous and had great strength of character, which was apparent even in youth. She was undoubtedly talented, valiant, and imbued with the chivalric culture of her father's court, but she had also inherited the hauteur and pride of her royal forebears. Etiquette at her court was rigorously formal. Duchesses, even princes of the blood, were obliged to approach her on their knees.

Margaret has been credited, incorrectly, with being the foundress of Queens' College, Cambridge. The college was founded in 1446 as St. Bernard's College by Andrew Docket, Rector of St. Botolph's, Cambridge, who urged Margaret to become patroness the following year. She petitioned the King to allow her to grant a new charter to the college and rename it "the Queens' College of St. Margaret and St. Bernard," to "the laud and honor of the feminine sex," and asked that it be dedicated "to the conservation of our faith and augmentation of poor clergy, namely of the empress of all sciences and faculties of theology." Henry agreed, and her charter was granted to the college on 15 April, the first stone being laid that day by Sir John Wenlock, the Queen's chamberlain; Margaret herself was not present, probably because of an outbreak of plague in Cambridge. There is no evidence that she gave any financial endowment beyond the £200 (£201,240) she donated in 1448—it was Docket who bore the lion's share of the cost of the foundation—yet she certainly took an interest in the college. The foundation stone of its chapel was inscribed: "The Lord shall be a refuge to our sovereign lady, Queen Margaret, and this stone shall be for a token of the same."

Margaret was the complete antithesis of Henry, and probably viewed his willingness to forgive his enemies and opponents as a weakness. Instinctively, she began to shoulder his burdens and responsibilities, and he let her, being content to have someone else take the initiative. Margaret quickly became the dominant partner in the marriage. According to Gregory's Chronicle, the English nobility soon learned that "all the workings that were done grew by her because she was far wittier than the King." She had energy and drive enough for two, and Henry accepted her tutelage without protest.

Margaret's motto was "Humble and loyal," but this belied her ambition and her love of power. She used her rank and influence to secure the advancement of her favorites, thereby ensuring that the court party remained dominant. Headstrong and inexperienced, she was unable to assess the damage she was doing to her reputation.

According to *The Paston Letters,* Margaret grew into "a great and strong labored [hardworking] woman." Charles, Duke of Orléans, was of the opinion that "this woman excelled all others, as well in beauty and favor as in wit and policy, and was of stomach and courage more like to a man than to a woman." The Tudor chronicler Hall stated that she was "of haute character, desirous of glory and covetous of honor and of reason, policy, counsel and other gifts and talents of nature belonging to a man"; she wanted "to rule and not be ruled." Polydore Vergil called her "a woman of sufficient forecast, very desirous of renown, full of policy counsel, comely behavior and all manly qualities, in whom appeared great wit, great diligence, great heed and great carefulness." For "diligence, circumspection and speedy execution of causes," she was "comparable to a man."

She could be domineering, ruthless, autocratic, and impulsive. Her quick temper and changeable moods often irritated her male contemporaries, who complained that, when she was vehemently bent on something, she was like a weathercock. She could be vindictive, quick to repay a slight or insult, and was not a person to be trifled with.

These personality traits may not have been evident early in the marriage, but as time passed, the Queen's eagerness to involve herself in politics began to draw adverse comment, because it was regarded as unwomanly. The more she realized how inept Henry was, the more she was driven to make decisions for him. Not since the time of Isabella of France, wife of Edward II, had a queen of England ventured to involve herself to any great degree in politics. Margaret made it clear from the first that she was to be no passive consort, content to remain in her husband's shadow. She had a fine brain and meant to use it, even though the business of government was considered a male preserve. By thrusting herself forward, taking the initiative on the King's behalf, and refusing to compromise, she confirmed the suspicions of those who suspected that she would have preferred the ineffectual Henry to concentrate his energies exclusively on his prayers and his foundations, having "determined with herself to take upon her the rule and regiment both of the King and his kingdom."[10] But until 1453, when the whole political scene shifted and changed, her critics did not seriously challenge her influence because, notwithstanding her prayers to the Virgin and saints, she was childless and would have no power whatsoever if the King died.

The Queen maintained a large establishment, and financing it trebled the outgoings of the royal household. She paid £7 (£7,040) a day to the treasurer of the King's household toward the cost, although she often found to her dismay that some of the money due to her as part of her dower was paid late. She therefore had to stretch such resources as she had to the limit, especially as she was generous to those in her service, and assiduous in obtaining promotion for them. Those in holy orders could realistically hope to be preferred to a prebend or deanery if they gave good service, while the brothers William and Laurence Booth became successive archbishops of York thanks to her favor.

Among the officers of the Queen's household were the Clerk of the Closet, the Private Secretary, the Clerk of the Signet, and the Clerk of the Jewels. She had five ladies-in-waiting, one of whom was listed in Queen Margaret's Wardrobe Book for 1452-3 as "Lady Isabella Grey." The names Elizabeth and Isabella were sometimes interchangeable in contemporary records, and it was incorrectly stated by Sir Thomas More and Edward Hall that this was the future Queen Elizabeth Widville, eldest daughter of Sir Richard Widville and wife of Sir John Grey; in fact, she was Elizabeth FitzHugh, wife of Sir Ralph Grey, and she had been one of the ladies who attended Margaret on her journey to England in 1445 and who had received several gifts from her. Another attendant was Elizabeth, wife of the powerful James Butler, Earl of Wiltshire, one of the foremost members of the court faction and a great admirer of the Queen.

In the lower ranks of Margaret's servants were ten damsels, two chamberwomen, grooms, pages of the robes, pages of the beds, pages of the bakery, scullions, kitchen staff who worked in the buttery and pantry, the Queen's "herbman" or gardener, twenty-seven esquires, and twenty-seven valets.

Margaret's influence made the court once again the hub of fashionable society. She entertained royally and hunted frequently, ordering that the game in her forests be preserved exclusively for her use, and that bloodhounds be especially trained for her.

Her chief mentor after her marriage was Suffolk. A poem he wrote to her survives as a typical example of the kind of courtly verse that was then fashionable:

> *How ye lover is set to serve ye flower . . .*
> *Mine heart is set and all mine whole intent*
> *To serve this flower in my most humble wise*
> *As faithfully as can be thought or meant*
> *Without feigning or sloth in my service.*
> *For wit thee well, it is a paradise*
> *To see this flower when it begin to spread*
> *With colors fresh enewed, white and red.*[11]

In the context of the time-honored aristocratic game of courtly love, it was perfectly proper and socially acceptable for a man to address admiring verses to a lady of rank, but in the sixteenth century, the chronicler Edward Hall asserted that Margaret and Suffolk were lovers, and that Gloucester later accused Cardinal Beaufort of turning a blind eye to the fact and even encouraging them. Shakespeare gave traction to the calumny. But no contemporary chronicler, however hostile, hinted that there was anything improper in the relationship. Suffolk was forty-eight and Margaret fifteen. He was a suave, experienced man of the world with cultivated charm, while she was a young, untried girl. He was kindly and avuncular, and made no secret of his admiration; she was flattered and susceptible. His party had arranged her marriage and therefore she supported it. Moreover, she enjoyed an enduring friendship with his wife, Alice.

What Suffolk did do was use Margaret's confidence and loyalty to his own advantage. In return, he did his best to protect her from criticism, keeping her in ignorance of public opinion and dissident voices in Council and Parliament. Together they made a formidable political team, for the court faction headed by Beaufort and Suffolk controlled both King and government.

4

"The solicitation and exhortation of the Queen"

✻

Edmund Beaufort, Earl of Somerset (whose name had been linked with Katherine of Valois), was another favorite of the Queen, who referred to him in her Wardrobe Book as "our dearest cousin." He ranked foremost among the lords who despised York and schemed to bring him down. On his advice, in the late summer of 1445, Margaret persuaded Henry to recall York to England, since the Duke's five-year term of duty was at an end. On his arrival, he was stripped of his authority to govern Normandy, which he had done well, having acted commendably throughout the English conquest of France. This is the first instance of Margaret showing hostility toward York.

In October 1445, King René wrote to Henry VI, urging him to surrender Maine and Anjou. That same month a second French embassy arrived in London in response to Henry's request for a further extension of the truce. Urged by her father and uncle, Queen Margaret began to exert pressure on Henry to do as they wished and honor the treaty. She pleaded, cajoled, nagged, raged, and threw tantrums, but still Henry prevaricated. On 17 December, Margaret wrote to Charles VII and promised to do all she could to obtain Henry's compliance, "for better pleasure we could not have than to see appointment of final peace between him and you." At length, in December, the King gave Charles a solemn written undertaking to cede Maine and Anjou to René by 30 April 1446, "to please the King of France and at the request of his wife." But rumors of his secret arrangement somehow leaked out, unleashing a storm of protest. It was Suffolk upon whom most of the opprobrium fell, for it was he who had arranged the Treaty of Tours.

Henry ignored the storm and did nothing until the last minute. On 30 April, knowing he could delay no longer, he sent orders to the governor of Maine and Anjou to evacuate the provinces, preparatory to ceding them to the French. This confirmation of the rumors sparked a further wave of outrage, and when the governor refused to obey the King's command, there was general jubilation. Such was the mood of the people that Henry dared not force the issue.

Margaret was not so timid. In May, she reminded him of his promise, begging him to keep his word. He would not listen, being too fearful of his subjects' reaction. Margaret now found herself under a barrage of pressure from the French King, and tried to placate him:

> We have hope, most high and puissant Prince, our very dear uncle, that it will be the pleasure of my lord that, by the grace of God, we shall effectively see a fruitful conclusion to the matter of the general peace. In all worldly things, we desire to be guided by cordial affection for the maintaining and fostering of union and true concord between you two, who are so near in kindred. And do you always signify unto us all things agreeable to you that we may accomplish, such as are within our power, joyfully and with all our heart.[1]

But Margaret could do nothing to move her husband, and the squabble over Maine and Anjou dragged on throughout the rest of the year without reaching a conclusion satisfactory to either side. Charles became increasingly exasperated by Henry's dilatoriness and tried to force him to surrender the territories. In December, Margaret wrote to her uncle again:

> In that you pray and exhort us perseveringly to hold our hand toward my most redoubted lord that on his part he be still inclined to the benefit of peace, may it please you to know that, in truth, we are employed at it, and shall be with good heart, so far as it shall be possible. For better pleasure could we not have in this world than to see appointment of final peace between him and you. And in this, at our lord's pleasure, we

shall on our part extend our hand and shall employ ourselves to the utmost of our power in such manner as that, in reason, you and all other must be content. In this, we shall, for your pleasure, do the best that we can do, as we have always done.[2]

Not until 1448 would Maine be formally ceded to France, whereupon it was observed that England had received with Margaret "nothing of goods, but the loss of Maine and Anjou, which lands her husband gave in perpetuity to the Queen's father. And this the King granted and gave away Maine and Anjou at the request of his Queen, [who] begged that they be given to her father at the urging of William de la Pole, Earl of Suffolk, and his wife, who earlier had promised to request it."[3] Suffolk protested that he had never done anything prejudicial to the King's interests, but Margaret certainly had urged the handover of the territories, as attested by Henry himself, who wrote in December 1445 that she had requested this many times.

In 1446, in the hope of cementing further the truce between England and France, Margaret proposed a marriage between York's four-year-old heir, Edward, Earl of March, and Madeleine, daughter of Charles VII, but although Suffolk gave the proposal his backing, nothing came of it. Nevertheless, the suggestion was a tacit acknowledgment of the dynastic importance of York.

In December 1446, an incident occurred that gave the court party cause to wonder if York was secretly plotting to seize the throne. His armorer, John Davies, had an apprentice, William Catour, who claimed to have heard Davies say that the crown belonged by right to York. Suffolk had Catour hauled before the Council to repeat his accusation, while York, who feared being implicated in Davies's treasonable assertion, demanded that the armorer be brought to justice and punished. Davies denied having said any such thing, but his judges decreed that he and Catour should undergo trial by combat, using staves. The trial took place at Smithfield, in the presence of the King, the Queen, and the whole court. Catour was victorious, and it was therefore deemed that God had given His verdict. Davies was hanged and his body burned.

From now on, the Queen and her party would be suspicious of York and his dynastic intentions.

Gloucester, far from heeding warnings to temper his criticisms, had become ever more outspoken. Margaret saw his censures as insults to herself which could not be forgiven or forgotten, and most of his fellow councillors had fallen out with him. He was causing so much dissension that Henry VI decided that he must be silenced once and for all. The Queen, Suffolk, Beaufort, and Somerset all agreed, and managed to convince Henry that Gloucester was plotting a coup with the intention of setting himself up as King and immuring Henry and Margaret in religious houses. Margaret was so fearful of his evil intentions that she begged Henry to order his arrest. The King summoned his uncle to answer certain charges before Parliament.

In the bitter February of 1447, accompanied by a great force, the King and Queen arrived at Bury St. Edmunds in Suffolk, where the King formally opened Parliament in St. Edmund's Abbey. When Gloucester met with Henry at Bury, he was confronted, not only by his unsmiling sovereign, but also by a hostile group that included the Queen, Suffolk, and Somerset, and the latter's old enemy Beaufort. Suffolk charged him with plotting treason and spreading rumors against the Queen's honor. Gloucester hotly denied everything, but Margaret said coldly, "The King knows your merits, my lord."

The Duke was arrested by a deputation of lords including the Queen's steward, Viscount Beaumont, Lord High Constable of England, who charged him in the King's name with high treason and placed him under house arrest. Gloucester remained in his lodgings for twelve days. On 23 February 1447, he died there. The cause of his death has never been properly established. Contemporary rumor had it that he had been strangled, suffocated with a featherbed, or had a red-hot spit thrust into his bowels. Public opinion deemed Suffolk guilty of his enemy's alleged murder, although he would hardly have acted without the King's sanction, for Gloucester was a prince of the blood and heir presumptive to the throne.

No one pointed a finger of suspicion at the King or Queen, although some lamented the coming of the Queen to England. Much later, the Tudor chronicler Grafton would claim that "the Queen, minding to preserve her husband in honor, and herself in authority, procured and consented to the death of this noble man." In the seventeenth century, Richard Baker asserted that Margaret "had a special hand" in it. Yet neither Margaret nor Beaufort was likely to have ordered Gloucester's assassination without Henry's knowledge or approval.

There is no evidence, however, that Gloucester was murdered. His great friend Abbot Whethamstede believed he had died from natural causes. The Duke was fifty-seven and had ruined his constitution by years of physical excesses and debauchery. There is no doubt that his arrest came as a shock to him, and there is every possibility that it may have hastened his end, perhaps from a stroke, for he lay for three days in a coma before expiring. But many in high places had wanted him out of the way, and his death was timely. It left York heir presumptive to the throne until such time as the Queen bore a son. In 1448, a farmhand was arrested for saying that she should not be Queen because she had failed to bear an heir, and that York should be named heir for the future security of the realm. Margaret must have been aware of the vulnerability of her situation.

York was wealthy, experienced in warfare and government, and the father of a growing family with healthy sons. Arguably, he had a better claim to the throne than Henry VI, being descended through the female line from the second son of Edward III, whereas Henry was descended from the male line of the fourth surviving son; yet York was loyal to the King and there is no evidence at this time that he had ambitions to wear the crown. Nevertheless, he had the resources and the ability to pursue his claim if he so wished, as the court party was well aware, which was why York was not acknowledged as Henry's heir. Instead, the question of the succession passing to the Beauforts was raised, and York's rights were overlooked.

York succeeded Gloucester as leader of the opposition to the court party. He was a political conservative, proud, serious, and remote, and unpopular among his fellow magnates, who resented his arrogance, even as they respected him. Like Gloucester, he desired to see the government formulate an aggressive war policy against France, as Henry V would have wished. He was genuinely concerned about the misgovernment of the court faction and resolved to eliminate the endemic corruption and indiscriminate patronage of its régime. To York, loyalty to the King meant demanding the reform of the government and the dismissal of all the corrupt advisers and time-servers who were dragging the reputation of the Crown into the dust. Soon, the common people began to hail him as the champion of good government and reform.

After Gloucester's death, Margaret was given Bella Court, his manor at Greenwich, a magnificent house set in lovely gardens, which he had built after acquiring the large hunting park surrounding it in 1433. Margaret renamed it Placentia, meaning a pleasant place, and immediately began converting it into one of the first double-courtyard palaces in England, with ranges of brick and timber, and black and white stone. It had floors paved with Flemish terra-cotta tiles bearing her monogram, beautiful glass or latticed windows decorated with marguerites and Henry's hawthorn buds, pillars and arcades adorned with sculpted marguerites, a vestry that served as a jewel house, a "bathing vat" for the Queen, and a gallery overlooking a garden she created herself, with a shaded arbor. New tapestries were hung. In the refurbished house, pageants were mounted for the entertainment of the King and court.

By 1447, Cardinal Beaufort had virtually retired from political life, although his party remained dominant under the leadership of his protégés, Suffolk and Somerset. When he died on 15 March 1447, he bequeathed to Margaret "the blue bed of gold and damask wherein the Queen used to lie when she was at the palace of Waltham,"[4] the Hampshire residence of the bishops of Winchester. Soon afterward, Margaret was made a Lady Companion of the Order of the Garter.

The Cardinal's demise left Somerset as head of the powerful Beaufort family. Again, there were rumors that he would be named heir presumptive. Having inherited his uncle's fortune, he was now a very wealthy man, and was accorded precedence as a full prince of the blood. The King relied heavily on his counsel and showered him with gifts and honors, which aroused the resentment of other magnates, especially York, who justifiably regarded Somerset as a threat to his own position.

Together with Suffolk, Somerset now led the court party, both men enjoying the full confidence of the King and Queen. Suffolk was at the zenith of his power, rejoicing in many high offices. Margaret, irrevocably associated with him and the loss of Maine and Anjou, was hated accordingly, especially when she and Suffolk attempted to evade customs duties on the export of wool, alienating English merchants who had hitherto been staunch supporters of the Crown.

With the deaths of Gloucester and Beaufort, Margaret's influence grew. Every letter signed by the King was now backed up by a similar one from the Queen. She demanded to be kept informed on all political matters, especially negotiations with France and military and financial affairs. State papers and reports on seditious persons were submitted for her inspection, and the court party would not act without her approval.

The emergence of the Queen onto the political stage gave birth to a new factional rivalry to replace that of Gloucester and Beaufort. Beaufort's peace party had become the court party, headed by the Queen, Suffolk, and Somerset, which controlled the King and the government. The opposing faction comprised the lords who had been excluded from this charmed circle, mainly because they upheld the ideals for which Gloucester had fought for most of his career or were critical of the ruling party. This faction now looked to York to lead them.

The court party feared York. It had consistently blocked his attempts to participate in government. In December 1447, to get him out of the way, he was appointed the King's Lieutenant in Ireland for a term of ten years. This ill-conceived appointment was the brainchild of Suffolk. It was obvious to York that he was being sentenced to virtual exile, and he managed to delay his departure for two years. But the King and his advisers were now treating him as an enemy.

In February 1448, Charles VII, angered because Henry had still not handed over Maine and Anjou, led his armies into Maine and laid siege to the city of Le Mans. The garrison could not hold out and Henry agreed on a formal surrender that was greeted with anger and bitterness in England. A worried Margaret persuaded him to promise financial compensation to dispossessed English landowners returning from Maine, but the money was never forthcoming, which created more ill feeling. So did the news that the Queen's father had fought on the French side in Maine, which did not endear Margaret any more to the English, even though it had caused her great distress. Inevitably, it was she and Suffolk who bore the brunt of public opprobrium.

In spring 1448, the King demonstrated his confidence in the leaders of the court party by creating Edmund Beaufort Duke of Somerset and William de la Pole Duke of Suffolk. Possibly Henry wished to raise them to equal rank with York, and it may have been in response that York began using the surname Plantagenet, which had been in abeyance since the twelfth century, when it had been borne as a nickname by Geoffrey, Count of Anjou, father of Henry II, after the sprig of broom (*planta genista*) he wore in his hat. York adopted the name to emphasize his royal connections and proximity to the throne, doubtless implying that it should have been he who was advising the King, not an upstart like Suffolk, whose grandfather had been a wool merchant, or a magnate tainted by bastard descent such as Somerset.

York's chief concern was that the King would repudiate Henry IV's letters patent and declare Somerset his heir. He saw the elevation of Somerset as a deliberate attempt to block his own political and dynastic ambitions, and knew that it was Suffolk and Somerset, and not the King, who were responsible for his political exile. Thus the rivalry of York with the two new dukes crystallized into a deadly political feud that would have serious repercussions.

Somerset and the Queen began a whispering campaign, spreading rumors that, in calling himself Plantagenet, York was plotting treason, intending to mount a coup and take the throne. Tainted with suspicion and impeded by his own aloofness and arrogance, York found it increasingly difficult to win the support of his fellow magnates. In 1449, he was expelled from court and exiled to Ireland, this being the work of Suffolk and Somerset, who were "overjoyed" at the Duke's departure.[5] York's post was no sinecure, for Ireland at that time was riven by tribal feuds and struggles. His achievements there were modest, but he won the favor and affection of the Anglo-Irish settlers and even some of the native Irish, establishing a long-standing affinity between Ireland and the House of York.

That same year, Somerset, as governor of Normandy and chief commander of the English forces in France, took up residence at Rouen, the capital of the duchy. His appointment was "due to the solicitation and exhortation of the Queen and of some of the barons in power." But he proved a failure, having neither ability nor capacity for the job, and carried out his duties "so negligently that afterward, due to his misconduct, the whole country was returned to the control of the King of France."[6] In March 1449, urged on by Suffolk, Henry VI broke the truce and reopened hostilities, which made a nonsense of his much-vaunted desire for peace and effectively amounted to a new declaration of war. It gave the French a pretext to launch a full-scale attack on Normandy, which they were determined to reconquer. In July, Charles VII formally declared war on England. The peace that Margaret's marriage was supposed to have cemented had been shattered.

There were fears that the French offensive would lead to the loss of Normandy, the hub of English power in France. By 15 August, "about thirty fortified towns in Normandy were lost."[7] Charles VII's status among the monarchs of Europe was now in the ascendant, and his victories gave him new confidence and the impetus to carry the war to a successful conclusion. In the late summer of 1449, his armies overran Normandy and launched an assault upon Rouen. Somerset agreed to discuss terms and withdraw from the city if the French left the English in possession of the towns they held along the Norman coast. This was agreed, and in October the Duke surrendered Rouen to the victorious French. In December, the ports of Harfleur and Honfleur fell to Charles VII.

The disastrous effects of the peace policy were plain to see, and the mood of the English people was ugly. Rumor had it that Margaret was not René's daughter but a bastard and therefore unfit to be Queen. But Suffolk was the chief target of the people's hatred. The virulent criticism leveled at him greatly alarmed the Queen, who urged Henry to deal forcefully with his fractious subjects. He summoned Parliament, as Suffolk's supporters hastened to dissociate themselves from him and his enemies poised for the kill.

In Ireland, York was kept informed of what was happening in England, holding himself in readiness to support the attack on Suffolk, anticipating that the fall of the favorite would provide an opportunity for him to elbow his way onto the Council. He knew there were others of like mind who desired reform of the administration and would be glad to see Suffolk go.

Suffolk was frantically trying to consolidate his position. Early in 1450, with the help of the Queen, he secured a great matrimonial prize for his son John—his ward, the seven-year-old Margaret Beaufort, a wealthy little girl who had a better claim to the throne than her uncle, the Duke of Somerset. Born in 1443, Margaret was the daughter of John Beaufort, Duke of Somerset, and descended through him from Edward III through a line tainted with bastardy. Her grandfather, John Beaufort, Earl of Somerset, had been the eldest son of John of Gaunt, Duke of Lancaster, and Katherine Swynford. Their four Beaufort children had been born before their marriage in 1396 and had been legitimized the following year by a statute of Richard II. But in 1407, in letters patent confirming their legitimacy, Henry IV had added a qualification that the Beauforts could not inherit the crown. Although letters patent could not overturn a statute, a doubt remained, and the question of the Beauforts' right to the succession was greatly to exercise legal minds in the decades to come. Margaret Beaufort's claim had until now largely been overlooked because she was female and a child, but an ambitious husband with means and determination might be ready to press it.

The significance of this betrothal was not lost on Suffolk's contemporaries, some of whom drew the unlikely conclusion that he was plotting the overthrow of Henry VI in order to secure a crown for his son and establish the de la Poles on the throne of England. Others believed that the Duke hoped to persuade the King to recognize Margaret Beaufort as his heir. The confusion surrounding the succession shows that the people of England had no clear idea as to who had the best claim to succeed a childless Henry VI.

When Parliament finally assembled on 22 January, Suffolk tried to justify his rule, reminding everyone how loyally his family had served the Crown and asserting that he had been the victim of great infamy and defamation. He swore he had never betrayed his King or his country. But an angry Parliament petitioned the King that he be arrested and impeached, and the Duke was sent to the Tower of London while the Commons prepared a Bill of Indictment, in which, among other things, it was alleged that he had urged the King "not to come nigh" the Queen, which accounted for her failure to bear an heir. Margaret was then at Eltham, and she was still there in February, when lightning struck the west front of the palace and destroyed the great hall, kitchen, and storehouse.

Henry VI refused to allow any of the charges to be formally examined by Parliament. Instead, he called upon Suffolk to answer them. The Duke denied all, describing them as utterly false and untrue. The Chancellor informed him that the King held him to be no traitor. But the

Commons were baying for Suffolk's blood, so Henry conceded that there might be some truth in the charges. Margaret, anxious to save the man who had arranged her marriage and been a fatherly support to her ever since, persuaded the King that a sentence of exile should be sufficient to satisfy the Commons. When the storm had blown over, Suffolk could be brought back and restored to favor. Henry agreed, and sentenced Suffolk to exile for five years from 1 May.

The Commons and the people were furious. To them, it seemed that parliamentary justice had been circumvented by those whose proper function it was to enforce it. The mood of Parliament was such that, had the Duke stood trial, he would undoubtedly have been condemned to a traitor's death. The Lords were angry because they had not been consulted as to Suffolk's fate. The Londoners were particularly incensed by the sentence; when the Duke was released from the Tower on 18 March, a mob tried to force entry to his house, intent on lynching him, and he had to escape by a back door. Frustrated of their prey, the Londoners seized his horse and assaulted his servants.

On 30 April, Suffolk sailed from Ipswich for Calais. In the straits of Dover, his ship was intercepted by *The Nicholas of the Tower,* a vessel that had been lying in wait. She was in fact part of the royal fleet, and under Somerset's orders. When Suffolk saw her approaching, his heart failed him. He was made to board her, whereupon the master greeted him with the words, "Welcome, Traitor!" He was subjected to a mock trial and found guilty of treason. At dawn the next day, he was hustled off the ship and into a small boat, and there beheaded with six strokes of a rusty sword. His body was left to rot on the sands of Dover, until the King found out and ordered his burial.

Many rejoiced at Suffolk's end. Political songs gloatingly recounted his fall. The identity of his killers was never established; presumably, they acted on the orders of those who felt he should suffer a just punishment for his crimes, a punishment the law had failed to impose.

Suffolk's widow, the indomitable Alice Chaucer, broke the news of his death to the Queen, who was so grief-stricken that she could not eat for three days and wept continually. Then anger surfaced, with a burning desire for justice and retribution. Suffolk might be dead, but she still had Somerset and other powerful supporters to help her avenge him. In ignorance of his role in Suffolk's murder, she now turned to Somerset to take his place as leader of the court party, her friendship extending also to his wife, Eleanor Beauchamp. Suffolk's widow, Alice Chaucer, stayed on at court as Margaret's lady-in-waiting.

The days when the court party could rule unchallenged were numbered. Now the deadly enmity between York and Somerset remained the gravest threat to peace between the factions.

5

"A harvest of heads"

※

By 1450, the Lancastrian government had lost much of its credibility and was bankrupt, with massive debts. Under the influence of the court party, Henry VI had given away royal lands and estates on an unprecedented scale and thus lost their revenues. The court faction, the chief beneficiaries of Henry's generosity, were milking the country dry, and had strongly resisted all attempts by Parliament to deprive them of their ill-gotten gains. There was no likelihood, therefore, of any immediate improvement to the Crown's financial problems.

The people of England were largely united in their desire for political stability, firm government, and the restoration of law and order. They were aware that the court party was manipulating the administration of law to the benefit of its individual members and their affinities, and that it so monopolized the King and the Council that there was little hope of any effective opposition emerging.

People were also appalled by what had been happening in France. Early in 1450, English troops began returning from Normandy, having fled before the victorious advance of the French. In misery and poverty, they trudged along the roads that led from the Channel ports, begging and stealing as they went. Some terrorized the countryside; a few were arrested and hanged. Others caught the imagination of a people infuriated by the humiliation of defeat and a corrupt government.

But Henry VI was incapable of exercising effective authority and unable to control an aristocracy whose chief function was to make war. It was said that the realm of England was out of all good governance, for the King was simple and led by covetous counsel.

May 1450 witnessed the outbreak of what became known as Jack Cade's Rebellion, a well-planned and organized movement that posed a serious threat to the government. It was orchestrated by intelligent men who were aware of the violent public feeling against the corrupt officials of the royal household and the magnates of the court faction who had abused their power. Many Kentishmen armed themselves and marched toward London. One of their leaders, Jack Cade, had published a manifesto listing a catalogue of grievances against the government, and incited the people by publicly declaring that the Queen meant to avenge her lover Suffolk by razing to the ground the houses of peasants and farmers in Kent.

The King and the court were at Leicester, where Parliament was in session. Henry VI was fortunate in having his lords to hand, and had no difficulty in raising a large army, which marched at once on the capital, with himself riding at its head.

Henry believed that York was the prime mover behind Cade's Rebellion and had incited it from his safe base in Dublin. He was convinced that the rebels' intention was to make York king. Yet there is no contemporary evidence that York was in any way connected to Cade's uprising.

Terrified for Henry's safety, Margaret had refused to leave his side and persuaded him to split his army in two: half remained with him at Blackheath, the rest marched on Sevenoaks, where a bloody skirmish took place and the rebels managed to overcome the royal forces.

When news of this disaster reached Blackheath, the King's soldiers mutinied, declaring themselves to be Cade's men, and ran riot through London, burning and looting the houses of those who supported the court faction and crying out that they would have the heads of the King's wicked counselors. At Margaret's urging, Henry fled to Greenwich. She wanted Lord Say, the unpopular Treasurer, to accompany them, but he refused, fearing that the rebels might pursue him and endanger the royal couple.

Henry's demoralized nobles attempted to muster the remainder of the royal army at Blackheath, but were alarmed when a man began shouting, "Destroy we these traitors about the King!" When other voices began clamoring for the blood of Lord Say and other members of the court party, the King ordered Say's arrest and imprisonment, for his own safety. On 25 June, Henry retreated with Margaret to Kenilworth, leaving a fearful and ineffectual Council to deal with the crisis. His retreat opened the way for Cade to march on London.

By now, the whole of southeast England was in a ferment. Men flocked to join Cade, confident he would lead them to victory. Yet they remained loyal to the King, believing he had been ill served and deceived by those whose heads the rebels meant to have. Royal government had virtually collapsed.

On 29 June, the rebel army occupied Blackheath. That day, in the chancel of Edington Church, Wiltshire, William Ayscough, Bishop of Salisbury, was preparing to celebrate Mass. A close friend of Suffolk, he had officiated at the marriage of the King and Queen, and it was he who had urged the King to avoid marital intercourse as much as possible. Yet he was a worldly bishop and a prominent member of the court faction who was so loathed that, as he turned to the altar, his congregation rose in fury and dragged him out to a nearby hill, where, in a frenzied attack, they hacked him to death.

On 2 July, Jack Cade occupied London and Lord Say was subjected to a mock trial and beheaded. Cade's men were out of control and causing mayhem in the city. He himself, puffed up with triumph, allowed them to ransack the house of a wealthy alderman, himself joining the looters. Most of his followers were appalled to witness this, and Cade's credibility melted away. When his remaining forces were engaged by soldiers from the Tower garrison, he withdrew to the Surrey shore.

Lord Scales, the governor of the Tower, ordered that the gates of London be locked. On the advice of the Queen and several bishops, he sent Cardinal Kempe to parley with Cade. The Cardinal was empowered, on behalf of the government, to promise him and his men pardons if they would lay down their arms and go home. Cade agreed, on condition that the demands in his manifesto be met. Kempe assured him they would be, promising that the King's commission would investigate all grievances.

Most of the rebels dispersed and went home, but Cade told the rest that their cause could not be considered as won until Parliament had agreed to their demands. He retreated to Rochester, then made an unsuccessful attempt to besiege Queenborough Castle on the Isle of Sheppey. On 10 July, he was publicly proclaimed a traitor and 1,000 marks (£64,450) were offered for his capture. He fled into Sussex but was captured at Heathfield. Mortally wounded, he was dragged off toward London, but died on the way, cheating the executioner.

Henry VI was bent on revenge. He and Margaret had returned to London on 10 July, after order had been restored by the Council. Henry presided over the trials of other rebels captured by the authorities in Kent and himself passed sentence of death on everyone. It was "a harvest of heads."[1] Eight were executed at Canterbury, twenty-six at Rochester, the King being present on each occasion.

The rebellion had achieved nothing. The court party remained supreme. However, what had been made strikingly manifest by Cade's uprising was Henry's inability to cope successfully with a crisis. A king was supposed to lead his armies, protect his people, and enforce justice, but Henry had fled, and in his absence the government of the realm had all but broken down. What had also been made alarmingly clear was how easy it had been for the insurgents to occupy the capital.

In France also, the situation was grave. July 1450 saw Somerset formally surrendering the city of Caen to the French. Most people in England considered this an unnecessary and dishonorable act, but Somerset was aware of the hopelessness of the English cause and returned to London.

York, like many others, concluded that the Duke's incompetence had led to the loss of much of Normandy, and wrote to the King demanding that his rival be arrested as a traitor. Henry reluctantly acceded to his "dear cousin's" request, and summoned Parliament, but Somerset, warned of what was afoot, pleaded his case with the Queen, who was sympathetic and promised she would not permit any charges to be laid against him. Henry bowed to her wishes and rewarded Somerset for his services in France, appointing him Constable of England and readmitting him to the Council, much to the fury of the people. Margaret's enemies promptly spread rumors that she was cuckolding the King with Somerset.

By the end of August, the last English garrisons in Normandy had surrendered to the French. The loss of Normandy signaled the end of English dominion in France, although English sovereigns would continue to style themselves as monarchs of France until 1802. It was regarded as an ignominious and humiliating defeat that had irredeemably tarnished the honor of England; and it had fatally undermined the credibility of a government whose policies had led to defeat. England's only remaining possessions in France were Calais and the duchy of Aquitaine. Aquitaine was of prime economic importance to England because of the wine trade centered upon Bordeaux, which had made many London merchants wealthy over the centuries.

News of Somerset's reception in England had angered York, who quickly made up his mind to return from Dublin to consolidate his own position and secure for himself the power and influence he had been denied for so long. He had received disturbing reports that the court party were plotting to indict him for treason and, without requesting permission from the King to leave his post, took ship for the Welsh coast and from there rode to Ludlow. Here he raised 4,000 men and marched toward London. His return created a sensation. Many welcomed him, and his ranks swelled with supporters; by the time he reached the capital, his army was said to be 50,000 strong. The court faction and the Queen viewed his return as a greater threat to their power than the loss of Normandy. To Margaret, he was the enemy, and she made it very clear that Somerset would continue to be preeminent in government, and that he enjoyed her favor and the King's.

The Council sent an armed force to arrest York, which he successfully evaded. He was widely hailed as the champion of good government, the man who would restore England's honor and rid the King of his corrupt advisers. He came with the purpose of reforming the government and gaining conciliar power for himself, though the Queen and many of the magnates believed he had designs on the throne.

On 29 September 1450, he arrived at Westminster and demanded an audience with the King. Henry had shut himself in his apartments, but York hammered on the door and insisted on being admitted, whereupon a petrified Henry "graciously" received him. York assured him of his loyalty but complained that justice was being subverted and urged him to implement certain reforms. He insisted that Henry dismiss his corrupt advisers and summon Parliament to deal with the abuses in government, and that he also make himself available to York for consultations on matters of state. Henry agreed to appoint a committee to consider York's suggestions, but he realized that his cousin had to be appeased if he was to remain loyal, so he admitted York to a newly constituted Council, with the rider that the Council would discuss York's proposals for reform and implement them as they saw fit. In other words, York would have a political voice at last, but no one would necessarily heed it.

On 6 November, Henry VI opened Parliament at Westminster. York had used his influence to get men of his own affinity elected, and they were the dominant party. The magnates brought with them such a massive armed presence that a clash between the followers of York and Somerset was expected daily. The Commons, who supported York, demanded, and got, an Act of Resumption providing for the return of all Crown lands alienated during the past twenty years and the establishment of a committee whose function was to oversee any royal grants proposed in the future. They also secured a promise from the King that efforts would be made to restore law and order in the shires.

In Parliament, York publicly criticized the government's policy of ignoring the demands of the people and taxing them heavily while rewarding royal favorites.

His influence prevailed even over the Queen's. On 1 December, Somerset was impeached by Parliament and condemned to imprisonment in the Tower of London, where he was taken that day. York was making plans to snare other members of the court party, but the King and Queen refused to accept the judgment of Parliament and Margaret ordered Somerset's release only hours later. York's supporters were incensed. A thousand of them marched on Somerset's house at Blackfriars, accompanied by a mob of angry citizens intent on killing him. They dragged him to a waiting barge, but the Earl of Devon, at York's request, calmed them. When Somerset returned home, he found that his house had been stripped of all his possessions. But he continued to ride high in royal favor and was soon afterward appointed chamberlain of the royal household and captain of Calais.

At the Feast of the Epiphany in 1451, the King and Queen took their places at table, only to be informed by the Steward of the Household that there was nothing to eat, as local tradesmen had refused to deliver any more on credit.

6

"In the hands of a woman"

✳

BY MAY 1451, THE COURT PARTY HAD REGAINED ITS SUPREMacy, despite the worsening situation in France, where the French were making serious inroads in Gascony and Aquitaine. But the mood of the times was made apparent when Thomas Young, a member of York's council, persuaded the Commons to submit a petition to the King requesting that, because he had no offspring, York should be named heir apparent for the security of the kingdom. His proposal provoked an uproar among the Lords and incurred Henry's displeasure. Young was clapped in the Tower.

On 30 June 1451, the French occupied Bordeaux, the capital of Aquitaine. The fall of Bayonne followed a few weeks later and, on 23 August, the duchy of Aquitaine itself surrendered to Charles VII. There was great shock and dismay in England, especially among the merchant community, who were concerned about the future of the lucrative wine trade.

The kingdom was in a state of high tension, characterized by intermittent outbreaks of rioting. By the autumn of 1451, it was obvious that Henry VI had no intention of implementing any plans for government reform. France was all but lost, his government in England was corrupt, local government and justice were subverted, and disorder and anarchy prevalent throughout the realm, yet Henry seemed unaware of the seriousness of the situation. Crucially, the pressing question of the succession had not been addressed.

Rumors of an imminent armed conflict between the opposing factions were rife.

By 1452, Margaret and Somerset had managed to convince Henry that York was plotting a coup to seize the crown. York's agents were putting it about that the King was fitter for a cloister than a throne and had effectively deposed himself by leaving the affairs of his kingdom in the hands of a woman who merely used his name to conceal her usurpation, since, according to law, a queen consort had no power. That there was truth in this propaganda is revealed by a study of the Queen's Wardrobe Book for 1452–3, in which the extent of her influence over the government is to be seen by the number of grants made "by the advice of the council of the Queen."

Anticipating that York was planning a confrontation, Margaret acted. When the Earl of Douglas visited the court that winter, she eagerly sought his friendship, knowing he could command substantial military support for her in Scotland. Douglas understood the Queen's concerns and promised he would bring an army to Henry's aid if the King was unable to prevail against York.

In enlisting the aid of Douglas, Margaret showed herself completely out of touch with English prejudices. She was unable to perceive that, while she saw the Scots as a much-needed ally, her husband's subjects regarded them as traditional enemies whose military presence on English soil had for centuries been feared and resisted. It was perhaps fortunate for her that Douglas was murdered not long after his return to Scotland.

Margaret's spies had informed her that York was mustering an armed force, and she urged Henry to do likewise. When he refused, she asked him what would become of her if he was killed. Reluctantly, he agreed to issue commissions of array for the raising of a royal army.

York now marched on London, aiming to take the capital. He sent heralds ahead, requesting that the citizens allow his troops peaceful passage. The Londoners' response was to man their defenses. They knew only too well that supporting York would be construed by the government as treason.

On 16 February, the King, the Queen, and the whole court left London with the royal army and marched toward Coventry, hoping to intercept York. But he managed to evade them and press on toward the capital. Henry forbade the Lord Mayor to allow York to enter the city and sent his forces to shadow the Duke. Neither side was keen to fight. York believed his show of force would be interpreted as an act of treason, and was relieved when, on the morning of 2 March, the Queen sent the bishops of Ely and Winchester and the earls of Salisbury and Warwick to negotiate a peaceful settlement. They commanded York, in the King's name, to return to his allegiance. He said he would willingly do so if Somerset was punished for his crimes against the state; he also demanded to be acknowledged as the King's heir.

Back in the royal camp, the two bishops asked Cardinal Kempe to keep the Queen occupied while they spoke with the King. In her absence, they urged Henry to agree to York's demands. At length, he gave his consent and ordered that a warrant for Somerset's arrest be drawn up. No one was to tell the Queen what was afoot. The deputation returned to York and told him that the King would agree to his demands on condition that he dismiss his army forthwith. Believing he had scored a victory, York ordered his men to disband.

The next morning, Somerset was arrested in the Queen's tent. As he was marched away, she exploded in fury and ordered the guards to let him go, then hastened to Henry's tent with Somerset in tow. When York arrived to make his peace with the King, he was dismayed to find Somerset and the Queen there, but resolutely knelt before Henry and presented him with a list of charges against Somerset.

It dawned on him that he had interrupted a furious quarrel between the King and Queen, which was immediately resumed in his presence. Margaret loudly demanded his arrest, but Henry refused to order it, although he agreed that Somerset should remain at liberty.

York was forced to travel with the court to London, riding ahead as if he were a prisoner. He was made to swear a solemn public oath in St. Paul's Cathedral that he had never rebelled against the King and would not rebel against him in the future. Then he was allowed to retire to Ludlow; that he had not been imprisoned or executed was due to the fact that the court party dared not risk the consequences of proceeding against the hero of the common people, and also to the fact that the Council had just received reports that York's ten-year-old heir, Edward, Earl of March, had mustered an army of 11,000 men and was advancing on London.

On 12 August, in the spirit of reconciliation, Henry visited York at Ludlow Castle while on his annual royal progress, during which Margaret visited Alice Chaucer at Wingfield Manor. But the court party had no intention of extending the hand of friendship to the Duke; instead, they excluded him from the Council. Humiliated and disgraced, he was once again left in political isolation, and for the next year or so, the court party, led by Somerset with the backing of Cardinal Kempe, who became Archbishop of Canterbury in 1453, was once again supreme.

From 1452, Margaret courted popularity with the people, believing that the best way to earn it was by reconquering Aquitaine. In March 1452, the King received a letter from the citizens of Bordeaux, begging for deliverance from their French conquerors. But there was no money to finance an armed expedition. Margaret wrote, explaining the problem, to Philip of Burgundy, who responded warmly and sent a large sum of money to finance an army and a fleet of ships. The King could now dispatch John Talbot, Earl of Shrewsbury, to France with a small but efficient force of 3,000 men. On 17 October, Talbot marched on Bordeaux, whose citizens took heart and evicted the French garrison, and the city was restored to English hands. The good news lightened the mood in England. Other towns in Aquitaine speedily expelled the French and welcomed Talbot with rejoicing. It seemed that the tide of war was turning.

Campaigning ceased in the winter, and the King's thoughts turned to his half-brothers, Edmund and Jasper Tudor, who were now in their early twenties and very dear to him, being members of his personal entourage. On 23 November, Henry raised them to the peerage, creating Edmund Earl of Richmond in Yorkshire, and Jasper Earl of Pembroke. The Tudor brothers were now accorded precedence over all other Englishmen below the rank of duke.

The King and Queen spent an extravagant Christmas at Greenwich with great revelry and disguisings. Then they returned to London where, on 5 January 1453, at a magnificent ceremony in the Tower of London, Henry invested his half-brothers with the trappings of their earldoms, giving them rich gowns of velvet and cloth of gold, furs, saddles, and fine caparisons for their horses. On the 20th, the new earls were summoned to Parliament for the first time. They would henceforth be given a voice in government and admitted to the King's Council. They remained utterly loyal to Henry VI and supported him against York.

7

"A sudden and thoughtless fright"

✳

Early in 1453, the heroic Talbot swept through the region around Bordeaux, recapturing town after town. These successes, the first the English had achieved in thirty years, gave rise to optimism back home. But when, in the spring, Talbot wrote asking the Queen to send reinforcements, Parliament hesitated and made excuses, leaving him fuming in frustration at what he saw as unnecessary prevarication.

In February, Margaret was distressed to receive news of the death of her mother, Isabella of Lorraine, after a long and painful illness, and donned dark blue, the color of royal mourning.

When Parliament met at Reading on 6 March, it had been purged of York's supporters. The Tudor brothers were present, taking their seats as the premier earls of England. Parliament voted the King and his immediate dependents a reasonable income, and generous provision was made for the Queen, who was granted new lands to augment her dower.

Fearing that York would rise again in rebellion, Parliament authorized the King to raise 20,000 archers at the expense of the shires and boroughs, if they were required for the defense of the realm.

On 24 March, her betrothal with John de la Pole having been annulled, Margaret Beaufort was given into the custody of Edmund and Jasper Tudor as their ward. Henry VI had decided that she should marry Edmund.

In the spring, the Tudor brothers accompanied the Queen on a progress through the Midlands, visiting the Pastons at Norwich and Alice Chaucer at Wallingford. At New Year, Margaret had sent an offering of a gold tablet encrusted with jewels to the shrine of Our Lady of Walsingham, who was famed for granting the prayers of those who desired children, and she now made a pilgrimage there.

At Hitchin, on her way south, Margaret was approached by Cecily Neville, Duchess of York, who was distressed by the King's coldness toward her husband. Margaret was evidently touched by her "immeasurable sorrow"—which Cecily feared would "diminish my days," as she wrote afterward to Margaret—and received her into her "most worthy and most high presence," "benignly" hearing her pleas for her husband, who was suffering "infinite sorrow" and whose "unrest of heart"[1] stemmed from his estrangement from the King. If Margaret did undertake to intercede for York to the King, she evidently failed to do so, or was unsuccessful, and after their meeting Cecily contracted a painful illness that prevented her from pursuing the matter.

In April, Margaret became joyfully aware that, after eight years of marriage, she was at long last pregnant. She did not break the news to Henry herself, but asked his chamberlain, Richard Tunstall, to convey "the first comfortable relation and notice that our most dearly beloved wife the Queen was with child, to our most singular consolation and to all true liege people's great joy and comfort," as the King later recorded. He was so delighted that he rewarded Tunstall with an annuity of 40 marks (£25,070).[2] He then commissioned his jeweler, John Wynne of London, to make a jeweled hip belt, or "demicent," for his "most dear and most entirely beloved wife, the Queen." It cost £200 (£192,870).

Hearing the news, and being somewhat recovered, Duchess Cecily wrote to the Queen, beseeching her, in the name of God and "that blessed Lady to whom you late prayed, by whose mediation it pleased our Lord to fulfill your right honorable body of the most precious, most joyful and most comfortable earthly treasure that might come unto this land and to the people thereof, the which I beseech His abundant grace to prosper in you and at such as it pleaseth Him to bring into this world with all honor, gracious speed and felicity . . ." Eventually, she came to the point, and begged Margaret "to be a tender and gracious mean unto our sovereign lord for the favor and benevolence of his hand to be showed unto my lord and husband."³ But, whatever Margaret's response, York remained in political isolation.

That summer, there was unrest and disorder throughout the kingdom, and Talbot was beset on every side by the French in Aquitaine. Parliament had not voted him the reinforcements he so badly needed, and Charles VII had taken advantage of this and invaded Aquitaine. By the middle of June, the French had advanced as far as Castillon, whose inhabitants sent a desperate plea for help to Talbot. His instinct counseled caution, but his knightly principles would not allow him to abandon those in distress, and in July he occupied Castillon. Soon afterward he received false intelligence that the French were withdrawing. On 17 July, he led his men out of the town and gave chase, but the enemy suddenly turned and confronted him, using their new artillery to devastating effect and pushing the English back to the banks of the River Dordogne, where Talbot was cut to pieces with a battle-axe. Learning of his death, his army quickly surrendered.

The English had lost their best commander, the only man who could have stemmed the tide of the French advance on Bordeaux. News of the disaster prompted a frantic Margaret hastily to summon Parliament, which now acted—too late. At the King's request, it voted enough money to finance 20,000 archers who were to be dispatched with all speed to Aquitaine in the hope of saving Bordeaux. But corrupt bureaucracy and local inefficiency stood in the way and not a single soldier enlisted. On 19 October 1453, Charles VII entered Bordeaux in triumph, and graciously permitted the English garrison to sail for home unmolested. Thus ended 300 years of English rule in Aquitaine—and the Hundred Years War, which had dragged on intermittently since 1337. Of England's former possessions in France, only Calais remained.

Henry's subjects blamed him for this crushing defeat, believing that had he shown something of the martial spirit of his father, France might not have been lost. Now England stood humiliated and disgraced. No one was more incensed than York, who had striven so hard and invested so much money to maintain Henry V's conquests.

Henry VI had been under severe strain. On 15 August, while dining at his hunting lodge at Clarendon in Wiltshire, he complained of feeling unnaturally sleepy. The next morning, he appeared to have completely lost his senses: his head was lolling, and he was unable to move or communicate with anyone. He had taken a "sudden and thoughtless fright"[4] that utterly baffled his contemporaries.

The Queen and the Council became increasingly alarmed, especially when Henry's condition showed no signs of improvement as days, and then weeks, passed. Margaret took him back to Westminster and made every effort to conceal his incapacity from his subjects, fearing that York would try to seize power. At seven months pregnant, she found herself responsible for the government of England. To begin with, she intended to remain with Henry at Westminster, but it soon became clear that his illness could be concealed only by removing him to Windsor.

By now, "a disease and disorder of such a sort" had so overcome the King "that he lost his wits and memory for a time, and nearly all his body was so uncoordinated and out of control that he could neither walk nor hold his head up, nor easily move from where he sat."[5] Henry later said he had been totally unaware of what was going on around him, and that all his senses were in a state of prolonged suspension. He was struck dumb, spending his days in a chair. It has been suggested that he was suffering from catatonic schizophrenia—complete mental withdrawal from normal life—or that he had fallen into a depressive stupor. Henry's contemporaries had one word for it: madness.

The Council summoned three physicians and two surgeons, but medieval doctors understood very little about mental illness. Madness was believed to result from an excess of black bile, one of the four humors that were thought to govern the functioning of the body, an imbalance of which led to illness. Mad people who were not violent were usually left at liberty within the community, often the butt of cruel taunts or ridicule; violent patients were locked up. Legally, the King had custody of all mad persons. Now he was one himself.

His doctors tried bleeding, head purges, ointments, syrup cordials, suppositories, gargles, laxatives, baths, special waters, electuaries (medicinal powders mixed with honey or syrup), and cautery. They even removed the King's hemorrhoids. None of these sometimes painful processes had any effect. But there was every hope, the doctors assured the Queen and Council, of his recovery. In case he was possessed by devils, priests were called in to exorcise any evil spirits that might have taken possession of the royal mind, to no avail.

All treatments having failed, the Council authorized the King's doctors to bleed him as often as they thought necessary to let the evil humors out of his body and apply various head poultices or any other remedy that seemed appropriate. Margaret herself sent to the Archbishop of Canterbury for holy water, but that had no effect either.

Politically, Henry's illness was calamitous. It deprived the realm of its head of state, however ineffectual. It brought the Queen, with her poor understanding of English politics, prejudices, and customs, to the forefront of power. It removed the last check on the rapaciousness of the court party. It plunged England into a national crisis at a time when the political situation could not have been much worse.

On 10 September, weighed down with anxiety, Margaret came to London, where she was received by the Lord Mayor and his brethren. They escorted her to the Palace of Westminster, where her child was to be born, and she sat enthroned in the great hall for her ceremonial leave-taking of the court prior to her withdrawal into seclusion to await the birth. Somerset was to run the kingdom in her absence. Prayers were offered up for the Queen's safe delivery and, following continental custom, a traverse, or heavy curtain, was drawn across the door to her suite, blocking the entrance until she left to be churched and purified after the birth. No men were allowed to pass beyond her outer chamber for the duration of her confinement; her women were to fill the places of her household officers.

Her Wardrobe Book records that money was kept in her bedchamber so that she could make offerings during services conducted by her chaplain in the oratory beyond the screen, although there was an altar in the bedchamber, too. Two cradles were made ready for the infant, a large cradle of state and a smaller one painted with an image of St. Edward the Confessor, the King's favorite saint.

At ten o'clock on the morning of 13 October 1453, Margaret produced the long-awaited Lancastrian heir, a healthy boy whom she named after St. Edward the Confessor, on whose feast day the child had been born, and after Edward III and the Black Prince, both of whom epitomized the heroic ideals of knighthood. The infant prince was styled Duke of Cornwall from birth.

Letters conveying the glad tidings were sent to all parts of the kingdom. One was displayed in the nave of Canterbury Cathedral, and in churches all over the land the *Te Deum* was sung. Church bells rang out the joyful news, and there was general rejoicing. But at Windsor, the Prince's father was still in a stupor, and did not even know he had a son.

The birth of an heir resolved the long-standing problem of the succession and put paid to any hopes York had entertained of being named heir presumptive. Overnight, his status had been diminished, as had that of his rival, Somerset, who had himself expected to be acknowledged as the King's successor.

On the day after his birth, the Prince was baptized by William Wayneflete, Bishop of Winchester, in a splendid ceremony in Westminster Abbey. The Queen chose as sponsors Somerset, the Archbishop of Canterbury, and Anne, Duchess of Buckingham, a granddaughter of John of Gaunt. Wrapped in a linen robe and ermine mantle, Prince Edward was carried in a procession led by monks carrying lighted tapers to a font swathed in twenty yards of russet cloth of gold. The Queen had paid £554:16s.8d. (£535,230) for this and the embroidered chrisom cloth in which the child was wrapped after the ceremony, when he was admitted to the Order of the Garter. The King, of course, did not attend the christening; nor was the Queen present, for she could not appear in public until she had been churched. However, she paid for a new stained-glass window in the Chapel of St. Mary le Pew in Westminster Abbey to commemorate the christening; it showed her and the King kneeling before the Virgin, and was embellished with the royal arms decorated with flowers.

8

"An infirmity of mind"

※

IT WAS CLEAR THAT THE KING WAS NOT GOING TO MAKE A QUICK recovery, and that the Queen and her advisers could not conceal his illness indefinitely. Margaret considered the possibility of Henry abdicating in favor of his son, perhaps anticipating that, even if he did recover, he would not be able to cope with the stresses of kingship. But there were other considerations: with the infant Prince elevated to the throne, Margaret could look forward to fifteen years in power as regent. However, when she sounded out the lords of the Council, they were unenthusiastic, for most expected Henry to recover.

They now had to address the urgent problem of how England was to be governed during the King's incapacity. Arrangements must be made for some kind of regency. Fortuitously, the birth of a son to the monarch necessitated the summoning of a great council of magnates, so that the Prince could be formally acknowledged as heir apparent. On 24 October, Somerset, in the Queen's name (for she was still in seclusion), summoned the lords. The omission of York's name from the list drew angry protests, and Somerset was obliged to invite him after all. When York finally arrived, he wasted no time in whipping up support against Somerset and the court party.

Among those who backed him were the influential Richard Neville, Earl of Warwick, one of the richest and most powerful noblemen in England, and his father, Richard Neville, Earl of Salisbury, whose sister Cecily was York's Duchess. This formidable alliance posed the greatest threat so far to the House of Lancaster and made York a force to be reckoned with. Looking back on that fateful friendship, Philippe de Commines, the French chronicler, believed it would have been better for the Queen if she "had acted more prudently in endeavoring to have adjusted the dispute" between the Nevilles and Somerset "than to have said, 'I am of Somerset's party. I will maintain it.'"

Warwick was the archetypal English magnate, whose chief motivation was the enrichment and aggrandizement of himself and his family. He was power-hungry, acquisitive, and arrogant, yet he had great abilities, being a man of considerable courage and a renowned naval commander. He could be ruthless and unscrupulous, and was capable of resorting to violence when he considered it expedient. He was a clever propagandist, forceful, manipulative, full of energy and tenacity. He used his wealth to buy the support and friendship of influential men and thus built up his own power, affinity, and military strength.

Warwick's personality was far more charismatic than York's. People might sympathize with York's grievances, but their imagination was stirred by Warwick, who came to enjoy greater influence with all ranks of society because he had the common touch, coupled with lavish, open-handed hospitality. By 1453, he owned land in eighteen counties and more than a score of magnificent castles. His territorial influence stretched from Cornwall to the mighty lordship of Castle Barnard in Yorkshire, while the greatest concentration of his lands lay in the west Midlands and south Wales. From these properties Warwick drew a huge income and could call upon formidable reserves of fighting men. The splendor and extravagance of his household was renowned, while his huge army of retainers and men of his affinity displayed on their livery of bright scarlet surcoats his personal badge of a white, muzzled bear and a ragged staff, a device inherited from the earls of Warwick.

With Warwick as an ally, York was in a strong position.

When the great council assembled, York argued that the Queen's child could not be recognized as the heir to England unless he was first acknowledged by the King and then presented by him to the nobility as his heir, according to ancient custom. A delegation of twelve lords, spiritual and temporal, therefore took the Prince to visit his father at Windsor in the hope that the sight of him would rouse Henry from his stupor. But he remained impervious to their attempts to make him acknowledge and bless the baby.

Until the King had acknowledged his son, Parliament could not pass legislation confirming the child's right to the succession or make provision for him as heir. This situation only served to fuel the rumors that flourished during the winter of 1453-4, that the Prince was a bastard, that he was not the King's son, and possibly not even the Queen's. It was alleged that he was either a changeling, smuggled into Margaret's bed after her own child had died, or the result of an affair between Margaret and Somerset. This was believable, given that the Queen had not conceived once during the first seven years of her marriage. Warwick went so far as publicly to refer to the Prince as the offspring of adultery or fraud in front of a packed assembly of the magnates at Paul's Cross in London. The King, he said, had not acknowledged him as his son and never would. Margaret never forgave Warwick for this insult. The rumors were also given credibility by people who were unaware of the King's condition, placing their own interpretation on why he had not recognized the child as his heir.

On 18 November, Margaret was churched at Westminster, wearing a gown of russet cloth of gold trimmed with 540 sables, which the King had given her months before specifically for the occasion. She was attended by the duchesses of York, Bedford, Somerset, Exeter, and Suffolk, eight countesses, and seven baronesses.

She returned with great determination to the political scene. The birth of a son had consolidated her power and her standing in the kingdom. She was confident that the King would eventually acknowledge the Prince. As mother of the heir apparent, she was resolved to dominate the government and rule with the support of the court party. Motherhood had transformed her into a tigress, fiercely protective of her son's rights, which she meant to safeguard by any means in her power. Her greatest ambition was to crush York, whom she regarded as the chief threat to her husband's throne and her son's succession. From now on, the conflict between Lancaster and York became a contest for political supremacy between York and Margaret, who was to prove the backbone of the Lancastrian cause.

York was poised for a return to the center stage of politics and courting support for a bid to become regent during the King's illness. The King's Tudor half-brothers, anxious to protect their own interests, and concerned about the extent of the court party's influence over Henry, supported York, while the court party seized every opportunity of advancing the claim of the Queen to be regent, though Margaret's sex was against her since most of the magnates found the prospect of petticoat government repugnant and improper.

By January 1454, York had won the support of several influential magnates. Alarmed, the court party made a final attempt to rouse the monarch. On 19 January, the Prince was again taken to Windsor. When he arrived, "the Duke of Buckingham took him in his arms and presented him to the King in goodly wise, beseeching the King to bless him; and the King gave no manner answer. Nevertheless, the Duke abode still with the Prince by the King, and when he could no manner answer have, the Queen came in and took the Prince in her arms and presented him in like form as the Duke had done, desiring that he should bless it, but all their labor was in vain, for they departed thence without any answer or countenance, saying only that once he looked on the Prince and cast down his eyen again, without any more."[1]

That month, the Queen, "being a manly woman, using to rule and not be ruled," made a determined bid for the regency, doubtless remembering how effectively her mother and grandmother had acted as regents in their day. But no English queen had held the office since Eleanor of Provence in the thirteenth century. Nevertheless, Margaret "made a bill of five articles, desiring those articles to be granted: the first is that she desireth to have the whole rule of this land; the second is that she may make the Chancellor, the Treasurer, the Privy Seal and all other officers of this land; the third is that she may give all the bishoprics of this land and all other benefices belonging to the King's gift; the fourth is that she may have sufficient livelihood assigned her for the King, the Prince and herself. But as for the fifth article," the writer did not know what it contained.[2]

Margaret was well aware that many magnates were reluctant to associate themselves with York in case it appeared that they were in treasonable opposition to the King. She tried to capitalize on this, cultivating the support of York's enemies, but her arrogant attempt to assume sovereign power and exercise the royal prerogative had offended and alienated many of them; nor did the common people wish to be ruled by their haughty, unpopular French Queen, and they made this very clear. Many lords who might not otherwise have done so now began to support York's bid for the regency.

In London, the political atmosphere was tense. Somerset and several other lords were preparing to attend Parliament at the head of their armies of retainers. Warwick sent 1,000 armed men ahead into London to ensure his safety; then, at the head of another private army, he escorted York into the City.

When Parliament assembled on 14 February, so few lords turned up that fines were imposed on the absentees for nonattendance. Undoubtedly, some had been intimidated, while others had preferred to remain neutral. The Prince was granted an allowance of 2,000 marks (£1,306,650), but some of York's supporters attempted to raise the sensitive question of his paternity. However, the Lords refused to listen and confirmed the infant's title and status as heir apparent. Along with the other magnates, York was required to acknowledge him as heir to the throne, but did so with ill-concealed chagrin. Some members of the court party were so concerned about his true intentions that they submitted to the Lords a bill providing for the safeguarding of the King and the Prince. On 15 March 1454, Edward was formally created Prince of Wales and Earl of Chester, and made a Knight of the Garter; in June, he was invested as Prince of Wales at Windsor.

The death in March of Cardinal Kempe, one of the mainstays of the court party, made the election of a regent even more pressing, since his successor to the See of Canterbury could only be chosen by the authority of the King. York now had the backing of a substantial number of peers who were anxious to prevent the Queen from seizing power.

Before reaching a decision, the lords of the Council made one further visit to the King to see if he showed any signs of recovery, but there were none. They "perceived that, if the King did not recover, England would soon be ruined under the government of the Duke of Somerset, so the noblemen of the kingdom sent for the Duke of York."[3]

On 27 March, Parliament nominated York as protector of the realm and provided that if the King did not recover sufficiently to reassume control of the government, the office of protector should devolve upon

Prince Edward when he attained his majority. As this would not happen for at least fourteen years, the lords had demonstrated singular confidence in York by entrusting to him the governance of the realm for so long.

Almost the first thing York did was depose Somerset from all his offices and order his arrest. Somerset was in the Queen's apartments when the guards came to take him to the Tower, and this time Margaret was powerless to save him. But she defiantly visited him in prison and assured him of her continuing favor. She also drew up a protest against York being named protector and demanded that Parliament name her regent, but was ignored.

On 3 April, York was appointed protector in a short, formal ceremony during which he reaffirmed the oath of allegiance he had made to Henry VI at the latter's coronation and signed the deed that named him protector. This provided that, should he break his oath, he would be dismissed from office. On the 10th, he appointed his ally Salisbury Chancellor of England. Margaret "greatly loathed them both."[4]

York ordered her to remove to Windsor to be with her husband, making it clear that her influence was to be confined solely to the domestic sphere; she was effectively under house arrest and not allowed to leave Windsor. She must have felt frustrated about this, and at being denied the regency, yet she made no attempt to undermine York's rule, even though she feared that the magnates had chosen him as protector because they were aiming to make him King; she was still convinced that he would make a bid for the crown.

York proved a conscientious and able protector. He made a vigorous effort to restore good government and carried out the duties of his office efficiently and with integrity. He behaved toward his opponents with moderation, trying to work with them in council for the benefit of the realm. He was ably supported by Salisbury and Warwick, making a formidable triumvirate who represented between them the larger part of the landed wealth and territorial influence of the aristocracy. York worked to consolidate his position by promoting men of his affinity to high office and appointed his kinsman Thomas Bourchier Archbishop of Canterbury.

He tried to sort out the Crown's finances. In November, he had the Council draw up ordinances for the reduction and reform of the King's household, in the interests of economy and cost efficiency. Even Henry's half-brothers found their establishments reduced. These household reforms were aimed primarily at the Queen, being an attempt to deprive her of the means with which to reward her favorites if she returned to power. Her household was reduced to 120 persons, and the Prince of Wales's to 38, which gave her further reason to hate York.

Despite his efforts, York failed to win over a majority of the peers. Some were suspicious of his motives and unwilling to trust him, and many still resented his manner.

In December 1454, Margaret took her husband to Greenwich. There, on Christmas Day, just as York was making headway with the task of reforming the administration, the King emerged from his stupor after sixteen and a half months. As soon as he could speak, he ordered that a Mass of thanksgiving be celebrated in St. George's Chapel and asked that prayers be offered night and day for his complete recovery.

The following afternoon, "the Queen came to him and brought my lord Prince with her. And then he asked what the Prince's name was, and the Queen told him 'Edward,' and then he held up his hands and thanked God therefor. And he said he never knew till that time, nor wist what was said to him, nor wit not where he had to be whilst he had been sick, till now. And he asked who were the godfathers, and the Queen told him, and he was well pleased. And she told him that the Cardinal was dead, and he said that he never knew of it till then."[5]

According to the Milanese ambassador, writing in 1461, Henry said that the Prince "must be the son of the Holy Spirit," which prompted ribald comments from York's followers (and some modern biographers). Yet there is no doubt that Henry unhesitatingly accepted Edward as his own child, having known of the Queen's pregnancy for some time before his illness. He would prove a consistently kind and loving father.

"Blessed be God," wrote Edmund Clere, an esquire of the King's household, to John Paston on 9 January 1455, "the King is well-amended and hath been since Christmas." The Bishop of Winchester and the Prior of St. John's, Clerkenwell, had seen him two days earlier, "and he spoke to them as well as he ever did, and when they came out they wept for joy. And he says that he is in charity with all the world, and he would that all the lords were so. And now he says Matins and Evensong, and hears his Mass very devoutly."[6]

Nevertheless, the *Croyland Chronicle* and other sources make it clear that Henry never fully recovered. In 1461, Croyland wrote: "The King, for many years, suffered an infirmity of mind; this mental weakness lasted for a long time." Margaret placed her faith in alchemy, through which it was believed basic substances could be transformed into efficacious medicine. Her physician served with Sir John Fortescue, her chancellor, on an alchemy commission in 1457, while others in the Queen's circle debated how alchemical means might help the King.

Henry's illness changed him. He became more unworldly and introspective, and turned excessively to religion for consolation. His instability left him at the mercy of his domineering wife and factious nobles.

9

"Wars of the Roses"

✳

Y ORK'S PROTECTORATE HAD NOT LASTED LONG ENOUGH FOR his reforms of the Council and the royal household to be of any lasting value. On 9 February 1455, the King appeared unexpectedly in Parliament, to the astonishment of all present, thanked the members for their loyalty and concern, and dismissed York from the office of protector. He then dissolved Parliament amid cheers from Lancastrian supporters.

As soon as York had stepped down, there was a Lancastrian backlash against his followers. Salisbury was dismissed, and the chancellorship went to Archbishop Bourchier, who was careful to remain neutral, although he later came to support the Yorkists. The Queen's favorite, James Butler, Earl of Wiltshire, was made Treasurer. Margaret, who had visited Somerset in the Tower and assured him of her continuing favor, insisted that the King release him, and the offices York had taken from him be immediately restored. "Once more, the Duke of Somerset became head of the government under the King, although in the past he had almost ruined England with his misrule."[1] Back at court and restored to his former eminence, Somerset plotted with the Queen to destroy York.

On hearing the news of Somerset's release, York retired in disgust to his northern stronghold, Sandal Castle, near Wakefield, Yorkshire, knowing that he had again been cast into the political wilderness and that

Somerset meant to have his revenge on him. But he and his allies had no intention of remaining out in the cold, and began discussing how best to deal with the situation.

By March 1455, many Lancastrian lords had been reinstated in their former positions of honor, a policy seemingly calculated to provoke York. The Queen had recently cultivated the support of the Earl of Northumberland and Lord Clifford, both committed Lancastrians. Neither had any reason to love York, for he was the ally of their greatest enemies, the Nevilles. Margaret was also rousing aristocratic support for the House of Lancaster in Wales and the West Country, well aware that York enjoyed considerable influence in the Welsh Marches, where lay the estates of Warwick, Sir William Herbert, and the Duke of Buckingham. Buckingham was staunchly loyal to the King, but what of the others? Margaret did her best to ensure the continuing loyalty of Jasper Tudor, Earl of Pembroke, and even set out to woo Herbert, who was of York's affinity. He was not a man to be trusted, and for the next few years, York and the Queen would compete for his loyalty.

Soon after Easter, another dispute arose between York and Somerset, who "was plotting the destruction of York. He offered advice to the King, saying that the Duke of York wished to depose the King and rule England himself—which was manifestly false."[2] Urged on by Warwick, York and Salisbury raised an army, mustering men from the North at Middleham Castle and Sandal Castle. Early in May, Warwick began assembling a large force at Warwick Castle. York, Salisbury, and Warwick all wrote to the King protesting their loyalty. Their letters were intercepted by the court faction and never reached him.

Early in May, the Queen and Somerset summoned a large number of loyal magnates to a great council at Leicester. The main agenda was to protect the King from his enemies. York, Salisbury, and Warwick were not invited, so there was little doubt who these enemies were. Margaret and Somerset persuaded Henry that York meant to seize his throne, and Henry issued a summons requiring him, Salisbury, and Warwick to present themselves before the council on 21 May. To York, this sounded ominously like a repeat performance of what had happened to the Duke of Gloucester in 1447, and he resolved to preempt Somerset and strike first.

A colorful legend, enshrined in Shakespeare's *Henry VI, Part 2*, relates how the Wars of the Roses broke out in the gardens of the Inns of Temple in London. York and Somerset were walking there and fell into an argument, in the course of which Somerset plucked a red rose from a nearby bush and said, "Let all of my party wear this flower!" York, not to be outdone, picked a white rose to be the emblem of his party.

There is no truth in the legend. York was in the North in May 1455, when the incident is said to have taken place, and there is no evidence that the red rose was used as a badge by the House of Lancaster at this date. Nevertheless, red and white roses have been grown in the Temple Gardens since the sixteenth century to commemorate the event.

The white rose was one of the badges of the House of York, although York's personal badge was the falcon and fetterlock. Many modern historians claim that the Lancastrian red rose symbol was invented as propaganda by Henry VII, but there is evidence that the red rose symbol dates from the period 1461–83, for a Yorkist genealogy drawn up during this period (now in the British Library) shows a bush bearing both red and white roses. The term "Wars of the Roses" was coined by Sir Walter Scott in his novel *Anne of Geierstein,* published in 1829, but the concept originated in fifteenth-century propaganda and was well established by Tudor times. In 1486, the Croyland chronicler wrote of the red rose defeating the white at Bosworth in 1485, while Vergil wrote that "the white rose was the emblem of one family, and the red of the other." Recently, it has been fashionable to refer to the conflict as "the Cousins' Wars," but there is no evidence that this term was used by contemporaries. Modern historians date the outbreak of the Wars of the Roses to May 1455, when the first pitched battle took place.

Disobeying the royal summons, York mobilized his army and marched south to London, probably intending to intercept the King before he left for Leicester. In the middle of May, Warwick led his forces across the heart of England, linking up with York and Salisbury on Ermine Street, the old Roman road. York's chief objectives were the annihilation of Somerset, the dispersal of the court party, and his own restoration to the Council, which would bring with it control of the King and the government. When Somerset heard of York's approach, he warned the King that he had come to usurp the throne. Henry authorized him to raise a small force.

On the way south, York tried to win more aristocratic support for his cause, but with little success. His advance at the head of an army looked very much like rebellion, even treason, in view of his public oath that he would never again take up arms against his sovereign.

On 20 May, at Royston, Hertfordshire, he issued a manifesto declaring to the people that he and his allies meant no harm to the King and were marching south "only to keep ourselves out of the danger whereunto our enemies have not ceased to study, labor and compass to bring us." A copy was sent to the King with a letter in which York and his allies begged him not to believe the accusations made against them by their enemies, but again both documents were intercepted, this time by Somerset himself, who destroyed them.

On 21 May, at Ware, the Yorkists learned that the King and his army were approaching. The Queen was not with them, having taken the Prince of Wales to Greenwich. Henry arrived at St. Albans early on 22 May. York's forces lay to the east of the town; his Northerners were regarded as savages in the South and enjoyed a fearsome reputation as ferocious fighters and rapacious looters. The King ordered that his standard be raised in the marketplace, donned armor, and mounted his warhorse, then remained under his banner for the duration of the battle.

"The fighting was furious,"[3] but it was all over within half an hour. Warwick's soldiers scythed mercilessly through the Lancastrian ranks, leaving "the whole street full of dead corpses."[4] As it became clear that the Yorkists had won, the King's army fled, abandoning Henry with arrows raining down about him. Wounded in the neck and bleeding profusely, he was urged by his remaining nobles to take shelter. "All who were on the side of the Duke of Somerset were killed, wounded, or, at the least, despoiled."[5] Somerset himself was among the fallen.

Now that the court faction had lost its chief mainstay, York was poised to crush it. He took control of the King, who was found in the house of a tanner, having his wound tended. When the Yorkist lords came before Henry, they fell on their knees "and besought him for grace and forgiveness of that they had done in his presence, and besought him to take them as his true liegemen, saying that they never intended hurt to his own person."[6] When Henry heard them declare themselves to be his "humble servants, he was greatly cheered."[7]

The fact that a battle had taken place at all shocked many, even the participants, and provoked the Yorkists into offering extravagant justification of their actions in which they attempted to shift the blame onto Somerset and the court party and thus avoid accusations of treason. Yet they had taken up arms against their anointed King, and this was enough, in the opinion of many, to brand them traitors.

Neither side had wanted an armed conflict; Henry, in particular, and most of his lords were determined that it should not occur again. But the divisions between Lancastrians and Yorkists were now so profound that it would need a committed effort on both sides to preserve the King's peace.

10

"By fair means or foul"

※

On 23 May, York escorted Henry back to London. Two days later, the King went in procession to St. Paul's Cathedral, wearing his crown, to reassure the people that his authority remained unchallenged.

News of the court party's defeat and the death of Somerset had quickly reached the Queen at Greenwich, causing her deep distress, as did the knowledge that York was now chief adviser to the King in Somerset's place. She sought safety in the Tower of London with her infant son.

York was immediately appointed Constable of England, an office Somerset had held, and was already filling the late Duke's other posts with men of his own choosing. Buckingham, Wiltshire, Pembroke, and other lords made peace with him and did their best to reconcile the two sides, but some members of the court party were more hostile than ever toward York and looked to the Queen for leadership. Accordingly, York forbade Margaret to enter London. By the beginning of July, he had established himself as the effective ruler of England, yet his continuing lack of aristocratic support led him to rely heavily on the Nevilles and pursue a policy of conciliation. He ruled as before, with wisdom and moderation. On 9 July, Parliament, summoned by the Duke in the King's name, met at Westminster in the presence of Henry VI, and York ensured the passing of an Act that justified his recent uprising on the grounds that "the government, as it was managed by the Queen, the Duke of

Somerset, and their friends, had been of late a great tyranny and injustice to the people."[1]

York sent Henry, Margaret, and Prince Edward to the Queen's castle at Hertford. Shortly afterward Margaret took the Prince to Greenwich. That autumn, she asked to be entrusted with the care of her husband, whom York allowed to join her at Windsor. This suggests that the King had suffered another mental breakdown. But Margaret had no intention of being relegated to the role of nurse—she meant to regain power for herself and her supporters and put an end to York's ambitions. In the wake of St. Albans, many of her household had deserted her, but now, by letters and messages, she was secretly cultivating support for her cause. Those who offered their allegiance included Henry Beaufort, the new Duke of Somerset, his brother Edmund, Owen Tudor and his sons, the Lord Chief Justice Sir John Fortescue, and the earls of Northumberland and Wiltshire.

In October 1455, Edmund Tudor, Earl of Richmond, married Margaret Beaufort. He was twenty-five, she was twelve, a strong-minded child who would grow up to be a formidable woman, renowned for her piety, her charities, and her unwavering devotion to the House of Lancaster. She was intelligent, serious, and high-minded, and her impeccable Lancastrian credentials, her great inheritance, and the fact that she was Somerset's niece made her a fitting match for the King's half-brother. By this marriage, Henry VI hoped to build up a core of committed family support for the Crown; for Richmond, it meant rapid social advancement.

In November, Parliament was recalled, and York was again appointed protector. He continued to act with moderation, insisting that everything he did be subject to approval by the Council and that the government of England should be reserved to the Council. He formulated a radical program of reforms aimed at the royal finances and the resumption of Crown lands.

As before, York enjoyed substantial support from the Commons, although the magnates were less enthusiastic about his reforms, many remaining suspicious of his true intentions. Because of this, they were particularly at pains to safeguard the rights of the Prince of Wales. Parliament settled 10,000 marks (£6,916,790) a year on the Prince until he reached the age of eight, when the sum would increase to 16,000 marks (£11 million) annually, payable until his thirteenth birthday. In February 1456, a London apprentice was hanged, drawn, and quartered for asserting that Prince Edward was not the Queen's son.

That month, Henry VI appeared in Parliament, reasserted his authority, and revoked York's appointment as protector. Anxious to avoid a rift, he insisted that his cousin retain his place on the Council. Both sides cooperated in Council and Parliament over the next few months. An uneasy peace would prevail for the next two years.

London was no longer sympathetic toward the House of Lancaster; its merchants had had enough of the King's misrule and the Queen's interference with their traditional privileges and had come out strongly in support of York. Margaret hated the Londoners as much as they did her. When a riot erupted, she ignored the fact that the City lay within the Lord Mayor's jurisdiction, and sent in troops under Buckingham and Exeter, who were armed with a royal commission authorizing them to try the ringleaders. The citizens were incensed at this violation of their rights and forcibly prevented the dukes from setting up their court. Bitter criticisms were leveled at the Queen, who had dared to challenge London's fiercely protected privileges.

In the spring of 1456, Margaret left the capital with the Prince for a progress in the Midlands. In April and May, she stayed at Tutbury and Chester, then took up residence at Kenilworth Castle, all the time canvassing support against the Yorkists and taking delivery of twenty-six cannon. Henry remained at Sheen with Pembroke, on whom he had come to rely heavily. At York's behest, he appointed Warwick captain of Calais. The court party had tried to secure the post for young Somerset, but York preempted them.

Securing Calais, "Christendom's finest captaincy,"[2] was a great achievement. Its captain, or governor, was the King's representative in the town and enjoyed considerable authority. The captaincy was the most important military command in the King's gift, and of such strategic importance that one might wonder why Henry agreed to bestow it on Warwick. Calais, in the years to come, would provide the Yorkists with an overseas base and a substantial garrison, whose loyalties were first and foremost to Warwick. It was excellently placed for invading England or policing the Channel. The Earl relocated there with his family.

He had made a brilliant marriage with the beautiful, pious Anne, daughter and heiress of Richard de Beauchamp, Earl of Warwick, through whom he had inherited his earldom, but it had produced only two girls, Isabel, born on 5 December 1451, and Anne, born on 11 June 1456. Anne, "this most noble princess, was born in the castle of Warwick, and in Our Lady's church there [the collegiate church of St. Mary in Warwick], with great solemnity, was she christened." She and Isabel were "born of the royal blood of divers realms, lineally descended from princes, kings, emperors and many glorious saints,"[3] but they were not destined to inherit Warwick's estates, for they were entailed in the male line.

We know very little about their childhood, but they had grown up in Warwick Castle, which the Nevilles had transformed into a mighty stronghold with two massive defensive towers, Caesar's Tower and Guy's Tower, and at the far end of the vast bailey, the old keep on its original mound. Within the bailey were situated the thirteenth-century great hall, the chapel, dating from 1119 (both rebuilt in the seventeenth century), private apartments, and barracks. Now the girls would spend the next few years in Calais.

After Warwick had left court, York rode north to Sandal Castle and Henry VI set out on his summer progress. He and Margaret were reunited at Chester. In August they began a leisurely tour of the Midlands, arriving at Coventry at the beginning of September. Entering through the Bablake Gate, they were accorded a warm welcome, with lavish pageants mounted in their honor, in which Margaret was lauded as "Empress, Queen, princess excellent, in one person all three,"[4] and as the mother of England's heir and an equal partner with her husband in governing the realm. One pageant showed St. Margaret slaying a dragon. Another had St. Edward the Confessor calling the Prince "my ghostly child, whom I love principally."[5] It was carefully orchestrated propaganda, paving the way for Margaret to take on the regency should Henry become ill again.

Margaret had no intention of allowing Henry to return to London, which was hostile to her, and persuaded him to establish his court in the Midlands, the Lancastrian heartlands. For a time, Coventry, the fourth-largest and most prosperous town in England, became the seat of government and the premier residence of the sovereign. Here, Margaret created a center of patronage, surrounding herself with artists, musicians, and scholars in an attempt to re-create the splendors of the courts of the South. She encouraged industry and founded schools and hospitals. The citizens of Coventry, proud to be so honored, were generous with gifts; on one occasion the mayor presented the Queen with oranges especially imported from Italy. The city came to be known as the Queen's safe harbor.

Although Coventry Castle was the King's official residence, he preferred to stay in a nearby priory, while the Queen often lodged at the house of Richard Woods, a rich merchant. The royal couple may also have stayed at the thirteenth-century manor of Cheylesmore, once owned by the Black Prince. The great Coventry Tapestry in St. Mary's Guildhall in Coventry, which dates from around 1500, depicts Henry VI and Margaret of Anjou and their court, although they bear a strong resemblance to Henry VII and Elizabeth of York, who were King and Queen when it was made, and wear sixteenth-century dress.

Moving the seat of government caused administrative problems, since most of the great departments of state were based in London, but it served Margaret's purpose. On 24 September, her chancellor, Laurence Booth, was entrusted by the King with the Privy Seal, thus allowing Margaret complete power over the machinery of government. She immediately replaced most of York's officers with men of her own choosing. "Almost all the affairs of the realm were conducted according to the Queen's will, by fair means or foul."[6]

That summer, York waited to see what her next move would be, "and she waited on him."[7] In London, ballads were pinned to church doors, savagely attacking the government. The City witnessed riots and violence, particularly against Italian merchants who had been given preferential treatment and privileges by the court party. Trade suffered, there was a further deterioration of law and order in the shires, and the south coast was raided by the French.

York realized that he had a new rival in the young Duke of Somerset, who was much favored by the Queen and being groomed to fill his father's shoes. Margaret was also cultivating the support of members of the royal household and soliciting the favor of the people by parading her son in public wherever she went. She again began intriguing with England's enemies, the Scots. Rumor had it that she had offered them the counties of Northumberland, Cumberland, and Durham in return for aid against York and his allies, and while that may have been unfounded, many people believed it. Her negotiations with the Scots dragged on fruitlessly for two years; in 1457, she tried to arrange marriages for Somerset and his brother with two Scottish princesses, but without success. Her efforts to build up her party, to the exclusion of all else, took precedence over the government of the country, which suffered accordingly. But, as a foreign queen, perceived as a Frenchwoman, she faced significant challenges in rallying the English nobles and people to her side. Anti-French sentiment was strong in England, fueled by decades of warfare with France, and many viewed her with suspicion and hostility.

Her sex also provoked opposition. The notion of a woman wielding such influence and involving herself in military operations was deeply unsettling to many in the male-dominated society of the age; such prejudice was still lively in the age of Shakespeare, who portrayed Margaret as a ruthless adulteress—the "she-wolf of France, but worse than wolves of France, whose tongue more poisons than the adder's tooth." Nevertheless, Margaret remained resilient and determined to marshal all the resources at her disposal in the interests of saving the House of Lancaster from those she perceived as its enemies.

Edmund Tudor, Earl of Richmond, had been protecting King Henry's interests in Wales, where, for generations, the Tudors had been sworn enemies with York's forebears, the Mortimers, because of territorial rivalries. Nevertheless, Richmond had given his support to York because he believed that the Duke's reforms could only benefit the King. But York's affinity in south Wales had recently taken steps to reassert his authority there. In the spring of 1456, the Queen had ordered Richmond to move against them. Initially, he enjoyed some success, restoring royal authority in Carmarthen. But York, as constable of Carmarthen Castle, resented Richmond's occupying the fortress. That summer, his adherent, Sir William Herbert, marched on Carmarthen, seized it, and took Richmond prisoner.

At the time, however, the King had good reason to be grateful to York, for in August the Scots had invaded England and burned twenty villages, but had been routed by the Duke. Soon afterward, Henry sent for York and Warwick to join him on his progress, and received them most graciously, "though the Queen loathed them both."[8]

The King and Queen summoned a great council of nobles to meet at Coventry. All the Yorkist lords were invited, but, mistrustful of Margaret, they presented themselves in council then withdrew and left Coventry without delay, "in right good conceit with the King, but not in great conceit with the Queen."[9] York went to Ludlow, Salisbury to Middleham, and Warwick to Calais.

Margaret persuaded Henry to dismiss York's partisans from office and replace them with men of her own party. Archbishop Bourchier lost the chancellorship, which was given to William Wayneflete, Bishop of Winchester. These changes must have angered the Yorkists and aroused their anxieties, though the Queen as yet had made no move against them. At her behest, Henry VI summoned Parliament to meet at Coventry, so that the measures planned by her party could be implemented.

That autumn, Richmond was released from captivity but remained at Carmarthen Castle. He died there of bubonic plague on 1 November, aged just twenty-six.

Pembroke was at court when he learned of his brother's death and immediately left for Wales to set his affairs in order. He was an honorable man, one of the King's most trusted counselors, and he had come to realize he could no longer support York and remain loyal to Henry. He therefore dissociated himself from the Duke and dedicated his life to upholding the authority of the House of Lancaster in Wales.

His first concern was the fate of Richmond's thirteen-year-old widow. Margaret Beaufort was six months pregnant, and Pembroke offered her a safe refuge at Pembroke Castle. There, on 28 January 1457, she gave birth to a son, Henry, who was styled Earl of Richmond from birth. Bearing a child at such a tender age damaged her to the extent that she would never bear another.

No one could have predicted that Henry Tudor, this obscure scion of the royal house, would one day become the founder monarch of the Tudor dynasty. He was a sickly babe and survived only because of Margaret's diligent care. For the first five years of his life, he lived at Pembroke Castle with his devoted mother and his uncle.

II

"A great and strong labor'd woman"

※

Disorder in England was escalating. The great magnates had now taken to paying pirates to plunder foreign shipping. In London, there were further riots. Yet still the court remained in the Midlands. In January, Margaret ordered a vast stock of arms and ammunition to be delivered to Kenilworth Castle. The royal household now had sixteen sheriffs in its pay, men with considerable influence in the shires; in return they were expected to favor those who supported the Queen's party. Other sheriffs found themselves faced with demands for money in a kind of royal protection racket.

That January, Henry granted Margaret the right to oversee the Prince's council. To emphasize her new status, she insisted on being escorted by the mayor of Coventry bearing his mace whenever she left the city, as if she were king, outraging the city fathers to the extent that she felt obliged to reduce the vast retinue that attended her to one more fitting for a queen.

In the early months of 1457, her agents were busy hunting for Sir William Herbert, who had spent the winter harrying the countryside of southeast Wales and undermining the King's authority. When he was finally captured, she ordered his imprisonment in the Tower of London. She would have had him and York executed, for she believed that Herbert had been acting on York's orders, although there was no proof of this. Buckingham, ever the peacemaker, dissuaded her from proceeding against York, who was sent back to Dublin to resume his duties as lieutenant of Ireland.

In March 1457, Herbert and his accomplices stood trial at Hereford in the presence of the King and Queen. Although all were found guilty and sentenced to be attainted for treason, Herbert received a royal pardon, which prompted him to turn his coat, and for a time he and his brother Richard offered their loyalty to the Queen. His position was not easy, for most of his neighbors in southeast Wales were Yorkists, but he managed to balance the interests of all the parties, retaining Margaret's friendship and trust as well as that of his former allies.

Rumors were still circulating about the Prince's paternity. In March, London's Court of Common Council warned the guilds not to meddle in the affairs of the King, Queen, or Prince, but to hold their tongues and not speak any unseemly, scandalous, or disgraceful words at their peril.

At Pentecost, the King and Queen observed an age-old custom by wearing their crowns in an elaborate ceremony in Coventry. In May, Margaret watched Coventry's famous cycle of Corpus Christi plays, apart from *The Last Judgment*, which could not be staged because the evening was too dark. That night, she stayed in the house of a member of the Grocers' Company.

August found her negotiating a new peace treaty with France, so that she could call on her uncle, Charles VII, for military aid if necessary. As her go-between, she used Maurice Dolcereau, the secretary of her former admirer, Pierre de Brézé (now Grand Seneschal of Anjou, Poitou, and Normandy), to carry highly sensitive communications to Richard de Beauchamp, Bishop of Salisbury, England's ambassador in France.

But that month, Brézé himself landed a French fleet on the Kent coast, plundering and burning Sandwich. Afterward, the victorious French played tennis in the smoking ruins of the town, before being driven away by Sir Thomas Kyriell. The raid unnerved the English, who were alarmed at the government's inability to prevent it, and the Queen was the target of furious criticism. She tried to pin the blame on Exeter, the Lord High Admiral, but no one was fooled, and the Yorkists immediately spread word that Margaret had actually invited Brézé to raid the coast in order to discredit Warwick, who should have been patrolling the Channel. No one thought to criticize Warwick, who had not lifted a finger against the

French, and had indeed decided not to intercept them, knowing that anything they might do would stir up feeling against the Lancastrians.

This fresh wave of criticism targeting Margaret fueled the rumors about the paternity of the Prince of Wales, which (according to Chastellain) named the late Duke of Somerset or the Queen's current favorite, Wiltshire, as his father and branded him a "false heir" born in "false wedlock." One rumor had it that the Queen "sustained not a little slander and obloquy of the common people, saying that he was not the natural son of King Henry, but changed in the cradle."[1] A Norfolk man, John Wood, made allegations "against the King's person, and against the persons and honor of Queen Margaret and Prince Edward,"[2] necessitating an inquiry by a royal commission.

Margaret incurred more vilification in September when she defied the King over the appointment of a new bishop of Durham. She wanted her chancellor, Laurence Booth, to have the see, but the King had nominated another candidate. Margaret secretly put pressure on the Pope, and Booth was elected on 15 September.

The raid on Sandwich had shown that it was impossible for the administration to function effectively away from London, and reluctantly the Queen agreed to return south to Westminster. At Michaelmas 1457, the court left Coventry.

Even with Warwick in Calais and York in Dublin, Margaret did not feel safe. It was imperative that she could call upon an armed force if either of them threatened her, yet such was the reputation of the government that she doubted she could raise enough men. Therefore, she introduced conscription, a measure hitherto employed by the kings of France. In December, she dispatched commissions of array to every shire, empowering the sheriffs to demand that, when she gave the command, every village, township, and hamlet was to provide the King with a number of able-bodied men and archers at its own expense, to defend the realm against the Yorkists.

Henry was determined to foster peace between the opposing factions. In January 1458, he commanded that the magnates attend a peace conference at Westminster. That month, he lost one of his most staunch supporters when Thomas Courtenay, Earl of Devon, died at Abingdon Abbey, "poisoned, as men said, and being there at that time with Queen

Margaret." It was asserted that the Prior administered the poison on her orders,[3] although it is highly unlikely that she would have murdered her ally; moreover, Devon's son remained a stout Lancastrian.

The conference lasted for two months, but achieved only superficial success and resulted in a public display of amity. On Lady Day, the Feast of the Annunciation, there was staged a ceremony that became known as the "Loveday." The King, followed by the Queen and York, walking hand in hand, and the leaders of both factions, went in procession through the streets of London to a service of reconciliation at St. Paul's Cathedral. They showed loving faces to each other, to convince the watching crowds of their sincerity.

Henry VI and Archbishop Bourchier had labored to bring about this reconciliation. In fact, Henry had commanded it "at the oft-repeated request and insistence of the Queen, whose heartfelt wish was for us to do this. She has been, and still is, desirous of the said unity, love and accord, and wishes for it as strongly as she possibly can."[4] Henry was overjoyed that his initiative had produced such a visible result. "Rejoice, England, in concord and unity!" exclaimed a popular ballad commemorating the occasion,[5] and his subjects were only too glad to do so, hoping that this was a lasting reconciliation. But Robert Fabyan, the Tudor chronicler, was nearer the truth when he referred to the event as "this dissimulated Loveday," because lining the streets had been the retainers and supporters of the rival parties, many heavily armed, and most regarding each other with ill-concealed animosity.

Three days later, Henry and Margaret made a state entry into London and took up residence in the Bishop's Palace by St. Paul's. York returned to Ludlow, Salisbury to Middleham, and Warwick to Calais. At Whitsun, there were jousts before the Queen at the Tower of London, with Somerset and Anthony Widville, the heir to Lord Rivers, leading the challengers. The King, happily believing that his factious nobles were at peace, kept Easter alone at St. Albans Abbey. He was becoming more absorbed in his devotions and his foundations, retreating from political life, and leaving most executive decisions to the Queen.

Warwick now began courting the friendship of Philip of Burgundy, for the English merchants were anxious to preserve the important trade links between England and Burgundy. By the summer of 1458, he had reached an understanding with Philip and dispatched Sir John Wenlock to him to negotiate on the King's behalf—without consulting Henry or Margaret—a marriage between the Prince of Wales and a Burgundian princess. Afterward, Wenlock went to France on Margaret's behalf to open negotiations with Charles VII for the Prince's marriage to a French princess. These negotiations were complicated and drawn out, but they had the advantage of keeping both France and Burgundy well disposed toward England for the time being.

Warwick had been engaging in acts of piracy, once notoriously ordering his ships to plunder the fleet of the German merchants of the Hanseatic city of Lübeck. This attack violated a truce between the Hanseatic League and the English government, and the Germans protested strongly to Henry VI about Warwick's behavior. The Queen, who wished to oust the Earl from the captaincy of Calais, now saw her chance to get rid of him. She summoned him to London and ordered him to explain his actions before the Council.

Warwick arrived in London at the head of 600 armed and liveried retainers. Undeterred, Margaret demanded of the Council that he stand trial. Warwick publicly protested that the interrogation he had been made to undergo had been unduly rigorous, and that he believed there was a plot to discredit him. The Queen, he complained, had been acting insincerely on the Loveday, and had no regard for the glory of England's achievement on the high seas.

The next day, incited by Warwick's protests, his supporters ran riot, demonstrating against Margaret and the authorities. The Attorney General was murdered. Margaret commanded that pikemen be sent to the City to restore order, and those aldermen and citizens who had taken part in the riot were thrown into jail. Thanks to the dilatoriness of the Council, her attempt to eliminate Warwick failed.

In the autumn, he again visited the court at Westminster. As he was passing through the royal kitchens, one of the King's scullions nearly impaled him on a spit. It was an accident, but Warwick chose to believe that Margaret had ordered the scullion to murder him. A fight broke out between his followers and the royal servants who had rushed to defend the scullion. During the scuffle Warwick was set upon by the royal guard, though his men soon gained the upper hand, and the unfortunate scullion was seized by them and hauled before the Queen. Margaret knew that if she defended the man, Warwick would accuse her of murder, so she ordered his execution. However, he was allowed to escape, while she announced defiantly that the fight had been caused by Warwick's supporters at his instigation. According to Fabyan, she persuaded the Council to draw up an order for the Earl's arrest and committal to the Tower.

As soon as he heard of this, Warwick sped to the safety of Calais. In November, the Queen and Council, incensed at his escape, demanded that he surrender his post to Somerset. At this, Warwick returned to London and stood defiantly before the Council, stating that Parliament had appointed him to his post, and therefore Parliament was the only authority that could revoke the appointment. Tempers were running high and, as he left the council chamber, he was attacked by retainers of Somerset and Wiltshire and only narrowly escaped. This time his claim that the Queen had tried to have him killed was perhaps justified.

Warwick knew it was not safe for him to remain in England and, after a hurried consultation with his father, Salisbury, he returned to Calais, where he defiantly continued his attacks on the Lübeck fleet. It was probably this that drove the conciliatory Buckingham off the political fence and firmly into the camp of the Queen's party.

It now seemed that a new confrontation between Lancastrians and Yorkists was inevitable. Margaret knew she had to take decisive action. "The Queen," wrote a Paston correspondent, "is a great and strong labor'd woman, for she spareth no pain to sue her things to an intent and conclusion to her power." Her supporters knew she would do her utmost to destroy the Yorkists. She and her allies caused the Duke "to stink in the King's nostrils even unto death, as they insisted that he was endeavoring to gain the kingdom into his own hands."[6]

It was obvious to everyone that Henry VI was no longer capable of leading an initiative against his enemies. The Queen's party needed a more inspiring figurehead, and who better than the appealing figure of the five-year-old Prince, a symbol of hope for the future? Margaret even sounded out some of the lords about persuading Henry to abdicate in favor of his son, but Henry flatly refused. So, late in 1458, she set about raising support by taking her son on progress in Cheshire and Lancashire, cultivating support among the nobility and gentry and recruiting men. Having adopted Edward III's swan badge for the Prince, she made him bestow a livery of swans to all the county gentlemen, trusting that they would remain loyal to him. Aware that she was "defamed and slandered" by rumors that "he that was called Prince was not her son, but a bastard gotten in adultery, [and] dreading that he should not succeed his father," she "allied unto her all the knights and squires of Cheshire and held open household among them."[7]

The Queen spent the early months of 1459 at Coventry. In the spring, Sir William Herbert urged her to take the field with her Cheshire levies before the Yorkists had time to unite in arms. Margaret saw the sense in this, and the Council approved it. In April, she persuaded the King to issue writs commanding all his loyal magnates to meet with him at Leicester on 10 May with as large an armed force as possible. She also ordered that new commissions of array be issued throughout the realm, conscripting young men from every town, village, and hamlet. York responded by issuing a manifesto condemning conscription, asserting that this French innovation was unwelcome to all Englishmen.

Somerset and other nobles began to muster their private armies, and the city of Coventry sent the Queen forty able men at its own expense. In May, Pembroke was allocated a tower at Westminster as his London headquarters, so that he could be at hand to defend the palace if it was attacked. Soon afterward, the King and Queen took the Prince on a progress through Warwickshire, Staffordshire, and Cheshire in an attempt to rally further support.

York and Salisbury were also preparing for war, resorting to the kind of propaganda that had proved successful on previous occasions. Early in 1459, seditious bills and mocking verses against the Queen's government proliferated in London. Once again, the Prince's paternity was questioned, and Margaret was accused of ruling like a tyrant through extortion and corrupt practices. This propaganda hit home, especially among the merchant community, who were making highly vocal protests against Lancastrian misrule and were already inclined to support York, even though Lancastrian counterpropaganda claimed that people were being deceived and blinded by subtle and covert malice.

Favoring the Duke was one thing, but rising in arms on his behalf might be construed as treason. York did not find it easy to enlist volunteers. He could, however, call upon his vast following of tenants and retainers, as could Salisbury, and in the spring the two lords summoned their affinities. However, with York at Ludlow and Salisbury at Middleham, they faced the problem of joining forces before the Lancastrian army, concentrated in the Midlands, could intercept them.

The fact that the Yorkists were arming at all, even in self-defense, was interpreted by the Queen as treason. She "believed for certain that there was a malignant enterprise whereby the Duke of York might attain the sovereignty."[8] In June, "the King held a great council at Coventry, which was attended by the Queen and the Prince. Despite being summoned to attend, the Archbishop of Canterbury, the Duke of York, and other lords were absent."[9] York and Salisbury had instead sent an urgent message to Warwick, warning him that the Queen intended their ruin and begging him to come to their aid.

Warwick speedily raised 200 men-at-arms and 400 archers. Leaving his uncle, William Neville, Lord Fauconberg, in charge of the Calais garrison, he crossed with his troops to England and advanced on London. On 21 September, he entered the City unopposed, then pressed on toward Warwick Castle, where his allies had planned to rendezvous. Their plan was to go together to the King at Kenilworth at the head of their combined armies and lay their grievances before him.

To avoid the royal armies, Warwick diverted west toward Ludlow, where York's contingent waited. On the way, he was warned that the Queen and Somerset had sent a sizeable force to intercept him. Just in time, he managed to avoid it. Salisbury, meanwhile, had left Middleham with a considerable following and made for Ludlow. No longer did the Yorkist lords entertain ideas of an appeal to the King. Their objective now was to combine their forces and march on London.

Margaret was recruiting in Cheshire when she learned of Salisbury's advance, and she and her commanders decided to intercept him as he marched through Staffordshire. She issued a summons to Lord Stanley and other local magnates, commanding them to muster their retainers at once and join the King; then she hastened to Eccleshall Castle, where Henry joined her. She persuaded him to send a great force of Cheshiremen, nominally under the command of the Prince of Wales, but actually led by Lords Audley and Dudley, to apprehend Salisbury before he linked up with York. The main body of the royal army was to remain at Eccleshall with the Queen, and Audley was to bring Salisbury to her, alive or dead.

"A great and strong labor'd woman" 189

On 23 September 1459, warned that his route was blocked by Audley's men, Salisbury drew up his troops in battle order on Blore Heath. When Audley's army approached, "Salisbury entered into negotiations with them, asking that they might permit his passage. When they refused to allow this, the Earl engaged in battle with them."[10] After a fierce and bloody struggle, Audley's line broke and his men fled. During the rout, he and many of his captains were brutally slain.

Salisbury had scored a victory. Local legend had it that the Queen and the Prince watched the fighting from the tower of Mucklestone Church, their presence being commemorated by a modern stained-glass window, while in the churchyard stands an ancient anvil from a forge where Margaret was said to have had her horse's shoes reversed so that she could escape pursuit after Audley's defeat. However, it is unlikely that Margaret was in Mucklestone at all that day, for the village was behind the Yorkist lines; she was probably awaiting news at Eccleshall Castle, ten miles away. After the battle the remnants of Audley's army fled there. Henry VI was shocked to learn of the defeat and the death of his commander, and was roused to anger against the Yorkists.

Salisbury wanted to press on to join York, but was aware that the Queen's force was only ten miles away. It was now nearing night, and very dark. The Earl cunningly entrusted his cannon to an Augustinian friar, who agreed to fire them off intermittently throughout the night, leading the Lancastrians to believe that the Yorkists were still encamped on Blore Heath. They did not discover the truth until the next morning, when the King and Queen rode over at the head of their army, determined to surprise Salisbury's force. The only thing they found was the deserted camp, the frightened friar, and the battlefield strewn with corpses. All they could do was order the capture of the Yorkist cannon. Salisbury, meanwhile, had gone to Market Drayton, where he received a congratulatory message from the perfidious Lord Stanley, who promised he would secretly continue to support the Yorkists. The Queen had been angered by Stanley's failure to arrive on the battlefield with reinforcements, and had him impeached in Parliament for it, but her anger was short-lived, and she afterward pardoned him.

Salisbury arrived safely at Ludlow, followed soon after by Warwick. York had heard that the royal army, reportedly 30,000 strong, was advancing rapidly toward them. The Queen was bent on routing the Yorkists and taking them prisoner, and her recruits were ready to fight "for the love they bare to the King, but more for the fear they had of the Queen, whose countenance was so fearful and whose look was so terrible that to all men against whom she took displeasure, her frowning was their undoing and her indignation their death."[11]

The Yorkists led their army of 25,000 men out of Ludlow, and marched toward Worcester, making for London, but the royal forces blocked their way on the road between Kidderminster and Worcester. While the royal troops were getting into battle order, with the King's standard displayed to proclaim his presence, York ordered a retreat to Worcester, having no desire to engage in battle with an army under the direct command of his sovereign. In Worcester Cathedral, the Yorkist lords publicly swore an oath to render obedience and respect to the King. This promise was enshrined on vellum and given to a deputation of clergy headed by the Prior of Worcester to take to the King, although Henry, persuaded by the Queen, ignored it.

When the King pursued him to Worcester, York moved on to Tewkesbury. Henry sent the Bishop of Salisbury after him, offering the Yorkist lords a pardon if they submitted, but they knew that would put an end to all they had fought for, and Warwick publicly declined the offer. As the King advanced on Tewkesbury, York crossed the River Severn, making for Ludlow, anxious to protect his Marcher lordships from being sacked by the royal forces.

At Ludlow, the Yorkist army camped south of the town, near Ludford Bridge. On the evening of 10 October, the King's army finally arrived, pitched its tents, and prepared for battle.

York and his allies had no desire to engage in a war with the King; their chief intent was to negotiate. They wrote to Henry, suing for peace and protesting their loyalty to the Crown, but they also referred to "the great and lamentable complaints of your true, poor subjects, of robberies, ravishments, extortions, oppressions, riots, unlawful assemblies, wrongful imprisonments, universally throughout every part of your realm. Your said true subjects suffer such wrongs without remedy." As for themselves, "our lordships and tenants been of high violence robbed and spoiled." The letter was intercepted by servants of the Queen, who forged a reply saying that King Henry would meet his enemies in the field.

The King, wishing to avoid further bloodshed, had sent a herald to the Yorkists to proclaim a free pardon to anyone, except Salisbury, who would return to their allegiance within six days. Henry had between 40,000 and 60,000 men as well as a considerable number of magnates. The Yorkists had a smaller force of 20,000 to 30,000, some inadequately armed. York had expected to be joined by Sir William Herbert, but the Queen had persuaded Herbert to support the King.

Many of the Duke's men were overawed at the sight of the royal standard fluttering at the other side of the bridge and began to have second thoughts about where their loyalties lay. Some laid down their arms and raced to join the King's army. York resorted to desperate measures to raise the spirits of his remaining troops, even announcing that he had just received news of the King's death. But the Queen took care to ensure that Henry was highly visible to all, and York's ploy was soon seen for what it was, losing him credibility with many of his men.

Buckingham persuaded the King to repeat his offer of a pardon, but as it was being proclaimed at the town gates, the Yorkist lords gave the signal for their guns to be fired at the royal lines. Even as the reports sounded, there were mass desertions from the Yorkist ranks, which led to panic among those remaining, many of whom ran away.

The situation was now hopeless for the Yorkists. At midnight on 12 October, York, Salisbury, and Warwick abandoned their forces and fled, which contemporaries viewed as a cowardly and dishonorable act. The Lancastrians streamed across the bridge and occupied Ludlow, arresting many of York's chief supporters and pillaging the town, drinking, and raping women. Powerless to stop them from sacking Ludlow Castle, the Duchess of York left the stronghold and stood bravely by the Market Cross, holding the hands of her two youngest sons, George and Richard, and her daughter Margaret. She was placed under house arrest in the charge of her sister, the Duchess of Buckingham.

12

"A dolt and a fool"

✺

Henry and Margaret returned in triumph to Coventry, where they disbanded their army, then rode to Worcester, hoping that the Yorkists were finished.

York fled to Ireland, where he was received like a second Messiah. His son, Edward, Earl of March, crossed to Calais with Salisbury and Warwick. They plundered the countryside round about and seized or harried merchant ships. They placed restrictions on English ships coming to Calais and disseminated virulent propaganda claiming they were victims of the King's evil counselors.

With her enemies out of the way, "the Queen and those of her affinity ruled the realm as her liked, gathering riches innumerable. The officers of the realm, especially Wiltshire, Treasurer of England, for to enrich himself, peeled the poor people and disinherited rightful heirs, and did many wrongs. In this time the realm of England was out of all good governance, for the King was simple and led by covetous counsel and owed more than he was worth. For these misgovernances, the hearts of the people were turned away from them that had the governance of the land, and their blessings were turned to cursing."[1] Yorkist propaganda claimed that Margaret had persuaded the King to appeal secretly to Charles VII for military aid against York; as Brézé's agent Dolcereau had been with her during the recent campaign, this was probably true, and she was using Brézé as a go-between in the negotiations.

* * *

On 20 November, Parliament, summoned at short notice, assembled at Coventry. Because it was packed with the Queen's supporters, it became known as "the Parliament of Devils." As York had not submitted to the King, Margaret commanded Parliament to arraign him and his associates on a charge of high treason. A Bill of Attainder was drawn up that same day, in which York, Salisbury, Warwick, Edward of March, and others were declared guilty of high treason and sentenced to forfeiture of their lives, estates, titles, honors, and chattels. Should any of them return to England they would face arrest and execution unless the King pardoned them. Duchess Cecily was brought into Parliament and made to witness her husband's humiliation.

The confiscated estates, comprising a vast amount of landed wealth, were then distributed by the King and Queen among their supporters, a generous share going to Owen Tudor and his son Jaspar, Earl of Pembroke, who afterward returned to Wales to stamp out Yorkist resistance there and prevent York from returning via the principality to England. Somerset was appointed captain of Calais in place of Warwick—a title he would hold in name only, as Warwick was still in possession of the town. Wiltshire became lieutenant of Ireland, but York was already in control there and the Irish parliament was resolved to protect him, passing legislation to provide that anyone seeking his death or inciting rebellion against him would be deemed guilty of high treason. When Wiltshire sent a messenger to Dublin with a royal writ for the Duke's arrest, the hapless emissary was immediately charged with treason, brought to trial before York, and sentenced to be hanged, drawn, and quartered.

In Parliament, the magnates were obliged to swear a new oath of allegiance to Henry VI, which had been altered to include vows of fidelity to "the most high and benign Princess Margaret, the Queen, our sovereign lady, and of her most high and noble estate, she being your [Majesty's] wife," and to the Prince of Wales.[2] Parliament also assigned all revenues from the city of Coventry to the Queen, to be used for the benefit of the Prince, although she took this to include financing her war against the Yorkists. After Parliament's business was concluded she remained in Coventry for the winter.

* * *

Somerset was determined to drive Warwick from Calais and establish himself as its captain. Margaret urged him to act, and he took ship with an army of retainers and attempted to land at Calais. But the garrison remained loyal to Warwick, and the gates of the town were firmly shut to him. To make matters worse, Burgundy was showing friendship to the Yorkist lords.

In November, Somerset mustered an army of a thousand men and crossed the Channel again. This time he succeeded in capturing Guînes Castle, an English stronghold, from which he was able to wage petty warfare on Warwick in Calais.

The Queen began raising reinforcements for him, but it was now winter and the campaigning season was over. Nor were there sufficient funds to finance a new enterprise. On 21 December, the government issued new commissions of array, but the mood of the people was ugly, and the loyalties of many were with the Yorkists. The Queen feared that York might take advantage of this to press his claim to the throne, since he now had nothing to lose by doing so.

In January 1460, Richard Widville, Lord Rivers; his wife, Jacquetta; and their son Anthony Widville were lodging at Sandwich, where Rivers was assembling a fleet for the invasion of Calais. But before dawn on 15 January, Sir John Dynham, acting on orders from Warwick, landed without warning and occupied Sandwich, capturing Rivers and Jacquetta as they lay in bed; they also captured Anthony Widville as he came rushing to his father's aid, and 300 of Rivers's men. All were hauled off to Calais.

When the Widvilles arrived, the Yorkist lords prevented them from entering the town until evening because they did not want them to excite the sympathies of the inhabitants. They held them in captivity until 28 January, when they were brought before Warwick, Salisbury, and March. Salisbury turned on Rivers, "calling him knave's son, that he should be so rude to call him and these other lords traitors, for they shall be found the King's true liege men, when he [Rivers] should be found a traitor. And my lord of Warwick rated him and said that his father was but a squire and made by marriage, and that it was not his part to have such language of lords being of the King's blood. And my lord of March rated him in like wise."[3]

The capture of Rivers caused Margaret great distress, and the government, believing that his abduction heralded a Yorkist invasion, stepped up its efforts to raise an army. This was timely, as York and his allies were determined to launch one final, decisive offensive against the court party. Warwick visited York in Ireland, where they formulated plans for a two-pronged invasion of England. York was to land in the North, and the other Yorkist lords in Kent. The Council soon discovered what was afoot. In May, Exeter sailed from Sandwich with fifteen ships and 1,500 men to intercept Warwick, but his men were openly voicing Yorkist sympathies, so he put in at Dartmouth and dismissed most of them. The Channel was now Warwick's.

After Warwick's return from Ireland in June, Yorkist supporters gathered in Calais, although York himself remained in Ireland. Warwick raised funds for the invasion, and he and the other Yorkist lords also mounted an extensive propaganda campaign through their friends in England. A manifesto outlining their grievances and their intentions, drawn up in Ireland, was widely distributed. In it they asserted that the King was still led by evil counselors and had put himself above the law and banished justice from the realm. They alleged that the King had promised all the men of Cheshire and Lancashire who fought for him that they would be allowed to steal what they liked and wreak havoc in the South, thus fueling the southern prejudice against Northerners. So successful was this libel that proclamations were hastily issued in the names of the Queen and the Prince of Wales denying that the King had ever made such promises.

The Council had decided to appoint Kenilworth as Henry's chief military base, and he rode there to see new fortifications being erected. He also sent for all the guns and armaments in the Tower of London, which filled forty carts. On 11 June, a royal proclamation was issued, asserting that the King had consented freely to the Yorkists' attainders and commanded all men to obey the royal summons to array.

The royal family were at Coventry. Edward, now six, had recently been "committed to the rule and teaching of men," his governess, Lady Lovell, having been dismissed in March because he was too old for "the governance of women."[4] But it was Margaret who remained the dominant influence in his life and instilled in him her own ideals and prejudices.

The court remained at Coventry until late June 1460, when Warwick, Salisbury, and March landed at Sandwich with 2,000 men and received a warm welcome from the people. Margaret had sent ships to Calais to prevent them from leaving harbor, but her sailors had mutinied and the Yorkist ships had passed unmolested.

On landing at Sandwich, Warwick sent messengers to the other Cinque Ports, asking for assistance in the form of armed men and stressing that he came to remove the evil counselors about the King. Archbishop Bourchier, who had hitherto acted as mediator between the opposing sides, had become sickened by the Queen's misrule and urged the men of Kent to rally to Warwick's banner, which they did in large numbers.

Canterbury afforded the invaders a warm welcome. After Warwick, Salisbury, and March had offered at the shrine of Becket and received the blessing of the Archbishop, who agreed to ride with them, they pressed on toward London, recruiting as they went. In their train was the Papal legate, Francesco dei Coppini, Bishop of Terni. The previous spring, Coppini had been sent to England by Pope Pius II to effect a reconciliation between the rival factions, but the Queen had not been interested in his offer to mediate, guessing that his sympathies lay with the Yorkists, but that was only because the Lancastrians had rebuffed him. The legate dearly wanted a cardinal's hat and was hoping that this mission would be a means to obtaining one. He had with him Papal bulls stating that the Pope had excommunicated all who had opposed York. His open support of the Yorkists swayed the opinions of several English bishops, who felt they should follow the Pope's lead.

When news of the invasion reached London, the Mayor, aldermen, and Court of Common Council dispatched a messenger to warn the Yorkist lords that they would not be allowed to enter the capital. Warwick, however, had many supporters in London and through their influence the Lord Mayor was persuaded to rescind his order. On 2 July, the gates of London were thrown open and the Yorkist lords rode into the city with a vast army of around 40,000 men. Hordes of Londoners surged forward in welcome. On 3 July, the Yorkist earls addressed the Convocation of Canterbury in St. Paul's Cathedral, emphasizing the misrule of the Queen's party. They swore an oath on the Cross of Canterbury that they intended nothing contrary to the estate of King Henry, declaring that they wished only to lay their case before him in person and protest their innocence, and were prepared to die for their cause. But Coppini, in a letter to Pius II, wrote that, despite the strictures of the Holy Church and his own role as an angel of peace, Warwick, Salisbury, and March appeared ready to resort to armed force rather than peaceful negotiations in order to have their way.

The Yorkists were indeed determined that this time they would gain control of the King and oust the court party for good. Warwick called Henry "a dolt and a fool," and all but accused Margaret of adultery, telling Coppini that the kingdom was "in the hands of his wife and those who defiled the King's bedchamber," whereupon Coppini concluded that Margaret was plotting to make Henry abdicate in favor of their son, whom he assumed to be a bastard. Warwick declared, "The Duke of York would now be on the throne if there were any regard for justice. We shall drive our foes from the King's side and ourselves govern the kingdom. The King will retain only the bare name of sovereign."[5]

On 5 July, Lord Fauconberg left London at the head of 10,000 men for the North. The Lancastrians were still anticipating that York would invade from Ireland and were reluctant to move south to defend London, in case he raised Wales and the North behind them. Warwick and March soon followed Fauconberg north, leaving Salisbury in London to lay siege to the Tower and hold the capital.

The King's commanders urged him to seek refuge in the Isle of Ely in the then almost impenetrable Fens, but the Yorkists learned of this plan and moved their army to Ware, ready to intercept the royal forces. But Henry had ignored his captains' advice and remained in Coventry, where the Queen had gathered a large army; he now planned to march on Northampton. Bidding farewell, he kissed the Prince and commanded Margaret, for her safety, not to join him unless he sent her a secret token known only to themselves. When the army left, Margaret rode with her son to Eccleshall Castle to await events. One unsubstantiated tale has her watching the ensuing battle with her son from the top of a bell tower.

Lancastrians and Yorkists engaged in battle on 10 July in a meadow outside Northampton. The Yorkists successfully breached the Lancastrian entrenchment and won a resounding victory that left 300 to 400 dead on the field. Buckingham, one of the mainstays of the King's cause, was among them. He was succeeded as 2nd Duke of Buckingham by his grandson, seven-year-old Henry Stafford.

Henry VI was captured and confined to his tent. Knowing that the day was theirs, Warwick, March, and Fauconberg found him there alone. They kneeled and craved his forgiveness for having taken up arms against him, stressing that their only motive had been the desire to establish a stable and just government, and assuring him of their continuing loyalty. Then March, who had not yet sworn fealty to his sovereign, did him homage. For all their subservience, however, the Yorkist lords now had the King in their custody. Later that day, they conducted him in procession to Northampton. Meanwhile, Wiltshire and many other prominent Lancastrians had gone into hiding. Some Lancastrian prisoners taken in the battle, including Lords Hungerford and Lovell, gave their captors the slip and rode to join the Queen, but others transferred their loyalties to the Yorkists.

Margaret had been waiting anxiously for news at Eccleshall Castle. When it came, it could not have been worse: the battle lost, many of her supporters dead or fled, and the King in the hands of the Yorkists, who were now in control. However, with the Queen and her son still at large, they would have no scope for complacency.

Margaret fled with the Prince and five attendants via Leicester and Tutbury into Wales, heading north for Chester Castle. But near Malpas Castle, she encountered a gang of men led by one of her son's former servants, John Cleger, who robbed her of her treasure and jewelry, and threatened to kill her and the Prince, at which point some of her attendants deserted her. As Cleger was rifling through her baggage, she and Edward managed to escape with the help of her four remaining attendants and a courageous fourteen-year-old boy, John Coombe of Amesbury, with whom she and the Prince rode pillion across the mountains of Wales to Pembroke at Harlech Castle. There she "had many great gifts and was greatly comforted, for she had need thereof,"[6] though Pembroke was aware that he would not be able to shelter her for long.

He had taken York's castle of Denbigh and suggested that she move there. Letting it be known that she had gone to France to raise troops, she left Harlech by stealth "for she durst abide in no place but in private" because "counterfeit tokens were sent unto her, as though they had come from her most dread lord the King, but it was not of his sending, but forged things, for they that brought the tokens were of the King's house, and bade her beware that she gave no credence thereto, for the lords would fain [have] had her unto London, for they knew well that all the workings that were done grew by her, for she was more wittier than the King."[7]

At Denbigh, Margaret was joined by Exeter and other prominent Lancastrians. On their advice, she wrote to Somerset, Devon, and other faithful adherents, asking them to raise an army in the North and wait for her at Hull. On 9 August, Pembroke was ordered by the Yorkist council to surrender Denbigh. He refused, continuing to recruit Welshmen for the Queen and the Prince. As a result, York never regained his former supremacy in Wales.

On 16 July, the King, escorted by the Yorkist earls, entered London with a great retinue and was lodged in the Bishop's Palace, while Londoners "gave Almighty God great thanks and praise" for the Yorkist victory.

13

"Madam, your war is done"

✳

THE MILANESE AMBASSADOR BELIEVED THAT YORK'S AFFINITY would attempt to put his son March on the throne and pass over King Henry and Prince Edward, "as they are already beginning to say that he is not the King's son. Similarly, the Queen also runs great danger." In retaliation, Margaret determined to take decisive action. In her husband's absence, she would lead the Lancastrian opposition.

Leaving Denbigh, she sailed north and all around the Scottish coast to Berwick, intending to seek aid from Scotland, where James II, whose mother was Joan Beaufort, had been a friend to the Lancastrians. But he had just been blown up by an exploding cannon while besieging Yorkist sympathizers at Roxburgh. Fortunately, his support for the House of Lancaster was shared by his widow, Mary of Guelders, and the Bishop of St. Andrews, who jointly headed the regency council that was ruling on behalf of the eight-year-old James III.

Advised of Margaret's coming, the Dowager Queen Mary sent an envoy, Duncan Dundas, to escort her to Dumfries, where she and her son were warmly received. They were lodged at nearby Lincluden Abbey as Mary's guests and royally entertained by Provost James Lindsay.

From Lincluden, Margaret wrote to Henry, informing him of their safe arrival, and to Mary of Guelders, begging for assistance against her enemies. Mary responded sympathetically and visited Lincluden with the young King to comfort Margaret and reassure her that help would be forthcoming. The two Queens stayed at the abbey for twelve days, discussing what form that help would take. At length, Mary agreed to provide men and money for a campaign against the Yorkists, on condition that Margaret surrender the town of Berwick to the Scots. For centuries, Berwick had been fought over by the English and the Scots and had changed hands a dozen times. Margaret readily agreed. She had no understanding of the horror with which her husband's subjects would view her raising a Scottish army against them and bargaining away this most fought-over border town to their enemy. Mary ordered the earls of Douglas and Angus to muster their retainers and accompany Margaret into England. Such was Margaret's courage that these hardened warlords came to respect her.

While preparations for war were under way, Mary invited Margaret to remain in Scotland, where she stayed at Falkland Palace and other royal residences until she was ready to march into England.

York was now convinced that the only way to establish firm government and hold on to power was to assert his right to the crown. The issue of dynastic right had become the subject of public discussion and speculation. By 1460, after suffering years of misrule, people were beginning to question the right of the House of Lancaster to occupy the throne and showing signs of taking the claim of York seriously.

York was descended from Edward III's second son through two females, Philippa of Clarence and Anne Mortimer, which made him Edward III's heir general. Henry VI, descended in the male line from Edward's fourth son, was his heir male. In the fifteenth century, the law of primogeniture was not strictly defined. The Lancastrian Lord Chief Justice, Sir John Fortescue, had declared that a woman was not fit to rule or transmit a claim, and that Adam was superior to Eve because he was able to teach her the moral virtues of prudence, courage, and temperance, while man was to woman as the soul to the body. But when it came to the question of who should have the crown of England, Fortescue played it safe and suggested that the Pope should be asked to decide the issue.

York was not concerned with legal niceties. His patience was at an end. His ineffective cousin must stand aside for one who was determined and able to restore good government and rid the realm of corrupt advisers—and that man was Richard Plantagenet himself. In September 1460, he returned from Ireland and marched to Hereford. His Duchess had been freed from house arrest after the Battle of Northampton and had been living at Baynard's Castle by the Thames with her younger children. Now, summoned by York, she traveled to meet him at Hereford. He had timed his return so that he would be in London when Parliament met in early October. He made no attempt to conceal the fact that he had come to assert his claim to the throne and proceeded to the capital with as much state and ceremony as if he were king already. At Abingdon, he summoned trumpeters and issued them with banners displaying the royal arms of England undifferenced—the sovereign's arms. And thus he came to London.

Parliament assembled in Westminster Hall on 7 October 1460. The King attended the opening ceremony but thereafter remained in the Queen's apartments. On 10 October, people were astonished to see York riding into London at the head of a great retinue, preceded by his trumpeters, and with his sword of state borne upright before him. His arrogant and dignified bearing proclaimed his intentions, and it was noted that he acted more like a king than a duke.

Dismounting at the door of Westminster Hall, he strode through the assembled throng to the dais at the far end, on which stood the empty throne beneath a canopy of estate. After bowing to the Lords, he placed his hand firmly upon it, symbolically demonstrating that it was his by right. Lords and Commons alike surged forward and watched incredulously as he turned to face them, expecting cheers of acclamation. Instead, there was a shocked silence.

Furious, he moved away from the throne and announced that he was claiming the realm of England as the heir of King Richard II and meant to be crowned on All Hallows Day, 1 November. The Archbishop of Canterbury suggested he obtain an audience with the King to discuss his claim, but this angered York. "I know of no one in the realm who would not more fitly come to me than I to him," he declared.

Nevertheless, he marched off to the royal apartments, intent on seeing the King. Thrusting aside the guards, he burst in. Henry faced him calmly but stood by his right to occupy the throne of his forefathers.

The reaction of most lords to York's astonishing act was one of profound dismay. How could they be expected to uphold his claim when they had taken an oath of allegiance to Henry VI? That Henry should have inspired such loyalty after decades of misrule is testimony to the mystical power of the institution of monarchy and the esteem in which Henry was held for his personal virtues. Equally remarkable was the King's failure to capitalize on that loyalty.

Even Warwick, Salisbury, and March were shocked by York's behavior. They had supported his calls for reform and his attempts to gain power for himself, but they now felt he had gone too far, and without even consulting them. Nor did they feel able to support his claim because—in common with most magnates—they saw no reason why Henry VI, England's acknowledged and anointed King for the past thirty-eight years, should be deposed.

Although it was made clear to York that the nobility stood by their oaths of allegiance to Henry VI, he was determined to force the issue. On 16 October, sitting on the throne in Westminster Hall, he formally claimed the crown of England by right of inheritance and submitted to the Lords in Parliament a genealogy showing his descent from Henry III. They made their disapproval plain, asking him why he had not put forward his claim before. He answered, "Though right for a time may rest and be put to silence, yet it rotteth not, nor shall it perish."[1]

The next day, when they respectfully asked the King for his views, he instructed them to draw up a list of objections to York's claim. They laid the matter before the justices, the serjeants-at-law, and the royal attorneys, but all were extremely reluctant to express an opinion, saying it was not within their competence to do so, but was a matter for the King and York to determine between them. In fact, it was such a high matter that it was above the law and beyond their learning, and they referred it back to a higher legal authority—the Lords in Parliament.

There followed much debate and poring over genealogies, statutes, and precedents.

At length, the Lords grudgingly concluded that York did indeed have a better right to the crown than Henry VI, but, by a majority of five, they decided that a change of dynasty was unthinkable at this stage. Parliament resolved that Henry should enjoy the throne of England as long as he lived; Prince Edward should be disinherited, and York proclaimed heir apparent.

On 24 October, an "Act of Accord" was drawn up, enshrining the new order of succession in law. Four days later, King Henry, under pressure from the few magnates who were present in Parliament (the rest having deemed it politic to stay away) agreed to its terms, and the Act became law. Henry immediately sent a message to the Queen, commanding her to bring the Prince to London and warning that if she failed to do so, she would be denounced as a rebel.

Parliament reversed the attainders against York and his followers. On 31 October, it was announced that the King and York were reconciled. The next day, in St. Paul's Cathedral, Henry wore his crown and led a procession of lords as an outward sign of concord. On 8 November, York was proclaimed heir apparent and protector of England. The Lords swore allegiance to him as the King's successor, and he swore fealty to Henry VI, saying he would abide by all the compacts that had been agreed.

Now that the dynastic issue had been raised, the Wars of the Roses changed course. No longer were they primarily a struggle for supremacy between York and the Queen's party; they had become a contest for the throne itself.

York now ruled England in the name of the King. He might have thought himself in an invincible position, but once again he was mistaken.

The Act of Accord provoked a furious political storm. In November 1460, an outraged Margaret wrote to the Lord Mayor of London deploring York's extreme malice in trying to seize her husband's throne and assuring him that there was no basis to Yorkist propaganda alleging that she intended to march on the City with an army of foreigners disposed to rob and despoil the people, and that they would find her "such lady as of reason ye shall be largely content."[2] This was barefaced lying, given her pact with the Scots. And she had been intending to seek further military aid in France.

She wrote to the Common Council of the City of London, requesting monetary and military aid, but was ignored. York, however, was granted a loan of 500 marks (£310,910) to finance his campaign. He also controlled the royal arsenal of weapons in the Tower, and commandeered several guns to take north with him. He and Salisbury rode out of London on 9 December, cheered on by crowds lining the streets and leaving Warwick to maintain order in the capital. They marched north via Nottingham, recruiting on the way, but Lancastrian scouts were able to report that York's army was vastly inferior to their own.

On 21 December, York arrived at Sandal Castle and set his men to digging trenches and positioning their guns at strategic points on the walls, intending to put himself in a good defensive position should the Lancastrians attack. While he waited for March to arrive with reinforcements, he settled down with his men to celebrate Christmas.

Somerset and Northumberland would have liked to lay siege to Sandal Castle, but, lacking the necessary resources, they decided that York must be lured out to fight before March appeared. By the end of December, the Duke was in an increasingly precarious situation. The Lancastrian army numbered at least 18,000 men, far more than he had.

At Christmas, Somerset rode over to parley with York, and agreed a truce until after Epiphany on 6 January. The Lancastrian commanders, however, had no intention of keeping it. Three days running, they dispatched a herald with instructions to provoke York into taking the offensive. On 29 December, they disguised 400 men as Yorkist reinforcements, and sent them to join the garrison at Sandal. The deception worked.

York left the safety of Sandal Castle on 30 December. He had no idea that the enemy was near at hand in such strength, waiting to ambush him and his soldiers. Nor had he listened to the repeated advice of his captains to await reinforcements. Unsuspecting, he and Salisbury rode across the drawbridge at the head of their men and cantered down the hill to Wakefield Green. With them rode York's seventeen-year-old son, Edmund, Earl of Rutland. The waiting Lancastrian center charged to meet them and there was a tremendous clash between the two armies, with the Yorkists fighting fiercely, believing they had the upper hand. But Somerset and Clifford sent Wiltshire to take Sandal Castle, blocking York's line of retreat. Suddenly, York found himself surrounded on three sides and hopelessly outnumbered. Many of his men were slaughtered, while he was pulled from his mount and killed in the midst of the fighting.

Benet stated that about a thousand men were killed in the Battle of Wakefield. As York's son Rutland left the field, accompanied by his tutor,

Lord Clifford drove his dagger into his heart, shouting, "By God's blood, thy father slew mine! So will I slay the accursed blood of York!" Salisbury was captured and taken to Pontefract Castle, where he was held prisoner. He bribed his jailer to set him free, but the local people, who hated him, dragged him out and chopped off his head. His death left his son Warwick the richest magnate in the realm, for he inherited his father's vast concentration of lands and power in the North, along with the earldom of Salisbury and the castles of Middleham and Sheriff Hutton. Warwick now owned twice as much land as any English subject had ever owned before him, which made him an enemy to be truly feared.

After the battle, Lancastrian soldiers retrieved York's body, propped it up against an ant-heap, and crowned it with a garland of reeds. They made a mockery of bowing to it, crying, "Hail, king without a kingdom!" Clifford ordered that the corpse be decapitated and had the heads of York and Rutland impaled on lances; a paper crown was placed on York's head. His kinsfolk never forgave Clifford for this and vowed that they would not rest until the two men had been avenged.

Hall and Holinshed would incorrectly assert that Clifford took the heads to the city of York and presented them to the Queen, saying, "Madam, your war is done. Here is your king's ransom." She supposedly laughed and slapped York's face, then ordered that the heads be placed on pikes above the Micklegate Bar, the royal entrance to the city, and that two empty pikes be placed next to them, ready for the heads of March and Warwick. The heads of York, Salisbury, and Rutland were indeed exhibited above the Micklegate Bar, their bodies having been quietly buried at Pontefract, but despite assertions by Waurin and other foreign chroniclers that Margaret was at Wakefield when the battle was fought, she was still in Edinburgh.

Few magnates mourned York's death. He had not inspired affection among his peers, but the common people, whose champion he had professed to be, grieved for his passing. He was succeeded as Duke by his son March, who now became, at the age of eighteen, the premier English magnate. Henry VI, however, refused to acknowledge his right to succeed his father or bear the title Earl of Chester, as he was entitled to do as heir to the throne under the terms of the Act of Accord.

14

"Captain Margaret"

※

MARCH WAS CELEBRATING CHRISTMAS AT SHREWSBURY when he received news of the deaths of his father and brother. Stricken with grief, he was determined to avenge them and enforce his claim to the throne. Speedily, he raised an army in the Welsh Marches, mustering his men at Wigmore and Ludlow. With him were Sir William Herbert and other men of York's local affinity.

On 5 January 1461, the two Queens, Margaret and Mary, reached a formal agreement whereby Margaret undertook to cede Berwick to the Scots in return for troops and the marriage of Prince Edward to Mary's daughter, Margaret Stewart. Henry had tried to stop her, but she had constrained him to agree. Brézé wrote to Charles VII: "If those with her knew of her intention and what she has done, they would join themselves with the other party and put her to death."[1]

When Margaret received news of the victory at Wakefield, she marched south at the head of her Scottish recruits, riding a silver jennet and clad ostentatiously in mourning robes given her by Queen Mary—a black gown and a black bonnet with a silver plume. Her intent was to consolidate the advantage gained at Wakefield and eliminate Warwick and March, and to rendezvous with her main force, which was waiting for her near Hull. She cannot have been pleased to receive Coppini, who had been sent by Warwick to warn her not to rejoice in her triumph, for the people were incensed against her, and to advise her to make peace.

Her army was reinforced on the way by hordes of men from the northern shires. What Mary had been unable to provide was sufficient money to pay the troops, and as Margaret was without funds herself, she was obliged to promise them unlimited plunder once they were south of the Trent. Word of this spread and, anticipating growing rich on the spoils of war, many Northerners came to swell her army. Meanwhile, Somerset and Devon were moving up from the southwest toward York with a great company of soldiers. On 12 January, Lord Neville's troops, growing restive at Hull, surged into Beverley and inflicted savage brutalities upon the citizens, a foretaste of what the South could expect.

By 20 January, the Queen's forces, which now numbered about 20,000, had joined up with the main Lancastrian army at York. The raising of such a fighting force so late in the year, when the campaigning season had finished, is testimony to her tenacity and fierce determination to protect her son's interests.

In York, a large gathering of Lancastrian nobles immediately confirmed the agreement between Margaret and Mary of Guelders and pledged themselves to persuade Henry VI to consent to it. News of this concord had been conveyed to Charles VII, Scotland's ally, who was greatly pleased, and when Margaret appealed to him through Brézé's agent Dolcereau for military aid, he ordered that all the harbors of Normandy be opened to her and her friends, should they have need of them. Believing that Charles would come to her aid himself, if need be, Margaret was ready to march south.

The Queen was advised by her lords "to march with all possible strength to London."[2] On 20 January, the Lancastrian army, under the command of Somerset and Northumberland and now 30,000 to 40,000 strong, began advancing toward the capital. Its advance soon encompassed a line thirty miles wide.

Once it had crossed the Trent, the northern soldiers began robbing, raping, torturing, burning, and looting at will, "laying waste all the towns and villages that stood along their way."[3] Croyland described how they rode "like a whirlwind from the north" and "overran the whole of England with the impulse of their fury," committing many unspeakable crimes, "murdering anyone, including clergy, who resisted, and robbing the rest, even digging up valuables whose whereabouts they discovered by threats of death." They sacked abbeys and priories, burned villages, barns, and manor houses after carrying off their treasures, and stole cattle and provisions. Many fled south from the wrath of the Northerners, carrying with them dreadful tales of atrocities. Croyland recorded the terror of the monks of his abbey and their neighbors in nearby villages, who brought their valuables to the Abbot for safekeeping, much to the dismay of the brethren. Mercifully, the Queen's soldiers passed them by at a distance of six miles. "Blessed be God, who did not give us for a prey unto their teeth," he wrote. Because of the hardships of campaigning in winter, it is likely that many soldiers were foraging for food, but their seizure of it meant starvation for country communities, as supplies were usually running low by that time of year.

The Yorkists were busily spreading propaganda against the Lancastrians, warning what the Northerners in the Queen's army would do if they were victorious and proclaiming that she had licensed her soldiers to plunder the South: houses would be sacked and burned, women raped, lands ravaged, and citizens murdered. This appeal to the prejudices of the Southerners, who regarded Northerners as a race of uncivilized savages (and not without justification on this occasion), met with marked success, bringing in recruits eager to defend their own, in unprecedented numbers.

In a unanimous decision, the Council voted Warwick 2,000 marks (£1,106,350) for the defense of the realm. Throughout January and early February, a nervous government issued streams of commissions of array and warrants for the arrest of dissidents and persons uttering false tidings, holding unlawful assemblies, or hindering those trying lawfully to defend the King. On 17 January, the Council ordered the town dignitaries of Stamford in Lincolnshire to put its defenses in order, anticipating that Margaret would march that way as she advanced south down the Great North Road via Lincoln, Peterborough, and Royston. On 23 January, it was rumored in London that the Queen's supporters and their retinues would arrive within three weeks.

On 5 February, the Council ordered Sir William Bourchier and others to raise the Essex lieges and march with them to the King. The ports of Norfolk were told not to permit the shipment of provisions to the Lancastrian army. Castles were garrisoned, curfews imposed.

Meanwhile, Pembroke and Wiltshire, who had raised an army of Welsh soldiers and French, Breton, and Irish mercenaries, were planning to march east from Wales to link up with the Queen's main force. But March had summoned the levies of eight counties to meet him at Hereford, and was himself planning to march on London, intent on avenging the deaths of his father and brother. Warwick, who had been joined by Fauconberg, was holding the capital, and March meant to link up with him before the Queen reached the city or intercept her on the way.

When he learned that Pembroke's army was making for the Midlands, he swung round and marched west to dispose of this new threat before advancing on London. Early on Candlemas Day, 2 February 1461, he and his army came to Mortimer's Cross, a hamlet in Marcher territory. That morning, a strange sight was seen in the sky above the astonished Yorkists: three suns appeared on the firmament and suddenly merged as one. It was a rare phenomenon called a parhelion, or mock sun, which occurs when light is refracted through ice crystals. Such things were, of course, not understood in the fifteenth century, and the Yorkist soldiers wondered what it portended, some crying out in fright. But March proclaimed it an omen of victory foretelling the joyful reunion of the three sons (suns) of York—himself and his brothers, George and Richard. At his words the entire Yorkist army sank to its knees in prayer, overawed by the vision. In time, he would incorporate those three suns into his personal badge, "The Sun in Splendor."

The Battle of Mortimer's Cross was one of the bloodiest engagements of the Wars of the Roses. The Yorkists quickly overcame the Lancastrians, inflicting heavy casualties. Realizing that the day was lost, Pembroke fled the field, leaving his men—and his father, Owen Tudor—to the Yorkists, who proceeded to butcher them. Four thousand men are said to have been slaughtered.

On 3 February, Owen Tudor and other Lancastrian captains were taken to the marketplace in Hereford to be executed. It is likely that March ordered the sentence on Tudor, Henry VI's stepfather, to avenge the death of his own father. Until the collar of his red velvet doublet was torn from his shoulders, Tudor did not believe he would be beheaded. As realization struck, he commented, "That head shall lie on the stock that was wont to lie on Queen Katherine's lap." Then, "trusting that he should not be beheaded till he saw the axe and the block," he "full meekly took his death."[4] His head was displayed "upon the highest step of the market cross, and a mad woman combed his hair and washed away the blood off his face" before lighting over a hundred candles and setting them about him. His body was buried in the church of the Greyfriars at Hereford, which has long since disappeared, and Welsh bards wrote a number of poignant laments in his honor.

Wiltshire and Pembroke had gone into hiding. Three weeks after the battle, Pembroke fled abroad. For more than two decades, he would be a fugitive, moving between France, Scotland, Wales, and northern England, ever constant in the cause of Lancaster.

As the Queen's army advanced through the east Midlands, the men of the South and East Anglia hastened to arms. Reports of atrocities had caused many towns to switch sides, including Coventry, which had hitherto been Lancastrian in sympathy. Meanwhile, bands of Welsh soldiers, escaping after Mortimer's Cross, were hastening to join the Queen.

Warwick had dallied in London when he should have been raising an army in the Midlands to counteract the threat posed by Margaret's advancing forces. Instead, he waited until she had reached Hertfordshire before he began recruiting in London, Kent, and the eastern and southern counties. On 12 February, the Council commissioned March, still making his way to the capital, to array the lieges of the West to march with him against the Lancastrians.

On that day, King Henry rode out of London to Barnet, followed by Warwick with a great army and ordnance, making for Ware. Four days later, the Queen's host reached Luton. Warwick had laid an ambush south of the town, but it was seen and Margaret was warned, so she ordered her army to swing west and take the Dunstable road instead of that to St. Albans. Meanwhile, some of her unruly troops were ravaging the countryside between Hitchin and Buntingford.

A detachment of Warwick's army under the command of a local butcher was waiting for the Queen at Dunstable, but fared badly in the ensuing skirmish, losing 200 men before being driven out of the town. The butcher, overcome with shame at his defeat, promptly committed suicide. The royal army then proceeded down Watling Street toward St. Albans.

On 17 February, King Henry rode into St. Albans to rendezvous with Warwick, who was waiting to confront the Queen's advance guard. Warwick had a large army and a detachment of 500 Burgundian soldiers, who were preparing to shoot flaming arrows and had rudimentary handguns that fired lead pellets.

Contemporary chroniclers estimated—doubtless with some exaggeration—that the Queen had 80,000 men, of whom only 24,000 were Southerners. They wore Prince Edward's livery, in whose name they fought. Sir John Grey commanded the cavalry. Food was in short supply, and by the time it reached St. Albans, the Lancastrian army was already disintegrating. Having got their booty from plundering, many of the Queen's Northerners had deserted and gone home.

Warwick believed Margaret to be nine miles off when she took him by surprise, entering St. Albans, not as expected from the Verulamium end, but from the northwest. Despite heavy casualties from enemy arrows, her army succeeded in driving Warwick's archers out of the town. As the Lancastrian vanguard advanced, the Yorkists fired their cannon, but with little success because falling snow had damped down the powder. Some of the handguns exploded or backfired, causing severe injuries to their owners; eighteen were burned to death by their own fire.

Somerset followed with the main battle of the royal army but found it difficult to breach the Yorkist position. Warwick might have won the day had it not been for the treachery of Sir Henry Lovelace, who held back his troops until he saw the tide turning in favor of the Lancastrians, then deserted to them. The gap he left in the Yorkist lines was soon targeted by the enemy commanders, who launched a charge of mounted knights, which shattered the Yorkist front.

The Lancastrians had scored a decisive victory. Awaiting the outcome with her son in Lord Clifford's tent, Margaret would have been triumphant to learn that Warwick had sounded the retreat and withdrawn the remnants of his army in an orderly manner from the field. Marching west through the night with a force of 4,000 men, aiming to link up with March, he left behind him a battlefield strewn with between 2,000 and 4,000 dead. Sir John Grey, the husband of Elizabeth Widville, was among them.

Henry VI was found seated under an oak tree, smiling at the discomfiture of the Yorkists. He was escorted to the tent of Lord Clifford to be reunited with the Queen and Prince Edward. He rejoiced to see them after so many months apart and embraced and kissed them, thanking God for bringing them back to him.

On 18 February, at Dunstable, at the Queen's request, the seven-year-old Prince, wearing a soldier's brigandine of purple velvet, received his father's blessing and was knighted by him, after which thirty others were dubbed knight by young Edward himself. He was described as having excellent natural qualities that were being cultivated by the anxious care of his mother. Margaret had cultivated fierceness in him, too.

Lord Bonville and Sir Thomas Kyriell, whom Warwick had appointed to keep watch on the King, were brought before Henry to be sentenced. He had promised to show them mercy, and they expected to be dealt with leniently, for they had behaved honorably toward him. But the Queen had appointed the Prince president of the court, and asked him, "Fair son, what death shall these two knights die?" There was a shocked hush as the child answered, "Let them have their heads taken off." A shocked Kyriell cried, "May God destroy those who taught thee this manner of speech!"[5]

The executions aroused fury among the Yorkists. Both men had been acting under orders and had taken no part in the fighting. Kyriell, however, had only recently gone over to the Yorkists and was regarded by the Queen as a traitor, which was enough to secure his fate. The bloodshed did not end there, for several other prisoners were executed on Margaret's orders.

The King and Queen gave thanks for their victory at the abbey of St. Albans. In the porch, they were received by Abbot Whethamstede and his monks with triumphal hymns, then processed into the church for the service. Afterward, they stayed in the abbey's guesthouse.

News of Warwick's defeat reached London on 18 February. The Venetian ambassador reported that the citizens "dreaded the menace of the Queen and the Duke of Somerset, forasmuch as the Queen with her council had granted and given leave to the Northmen for to spoil and rob the City."

A wave of fear swept London and streets emptied as merchants locked up their shops and people barricaded themselves inside their houses. The Lord Mayor arranged for the city militia to patrol the walls, himself accompanying them. London had for years now been sympathetic to the Yorkist cause, and the reported atrocities of the Lancastrian army disposed the citizens even more stoutly in its favor.

On 19 February, it was reported in London that March was in the Cotswolds. Warwick had ridden there at speed and met up with him. March apologized for having no money, but his men were more concerned about protecting their homes and families from the Queen's army than about being paid, and Warwick told him to be of good cheer, for the commons of England were on his side. They formulated a plan to race for London and have March proclaimed king before the Lancastrians got there, both aware that this offered their only hope of victory.

Meanwhile, Margaret's victorious Northerners were enthusiastically pillaging and plundering St. Albans and the countryside round about, leaving a trail of destruction. The Abbot persuaded Henry to issue a proclamation forbidding such behavior, but no one took any notice, saying they had the Queen's sanction, and that their plunder was remuneration for their services. Margaret tried to stop them, promising pardons to all those who had committed crimes, but they paid her no heed. Their violence was visible proof that Yorkist propaganda had not exaggerated, and it was so savage that it horrified the Abbot, who charitably concluded that these Northerners had been brutalized by poverty and deeply resented the prosperity of the Southerners. The King insisted that the Queen order them at least to spare the abbey from further harm, and she seems to have met with some success.

The royal army was now running desperately short of food, so the Queen sent her chaplain to the Lord Mayor of London with a peremptory demand for bread, victuals, and money. The frightened Mayor hastily arranged for a number of carts to be laden with meat, fish, other foodstuffs, and coin, but the Londoners, emboldened by news that March and Warwick were marching on the City, seized the carts and locked the city gates, mounting a guard so that no one could get in or out. They distributed the food among themselves and stole the money.

When Margaret heard, she was so furious that she allowed her soldiery to plunder and lay waste the countryside. Had she regrouped her army and marched on London, she might have emerged victorious, but she and Henry were fearful of further alienating the Londoners by unleashing their uncontrollable troops on the City, and their captains may have advised them to wait and intercept the Yorkists as they marched on London. Whatever the reason, Margaret hesitated—and, as Lord Rivers soon afterward declared to the Milanese ambassador, the Lancastrian cause was "lost irredeemably."

After learning of the royal victory at St. Albans, the Lord Mayor of London had sent the duchesses of Bedford and Buckingham and Lady Scales to Henry and Margaret to offer his obedience in return for an assurance that London "would not be plundered or suffer violence."[6] On 20 February, Margaret sent the three ladies back to him. They "reported that the King and Queen had no mind to pillage the chief city of their realm, and so they promised. But at the same time, they did not mean that they would not punish the evil-doers."[7]

The city fathers sent the noblewomen back to the King and Queen, hoping to come to an arrangement whereby Henry and Margaret might enter the capital, provided that it did not suffer plunder, punishment, or violence. But the Londoners had heard too many reports of the atrocities committed by Margaret's troops; they were also heartily sick of Lancastrian misgovernment and their French Queen. It was an abuse, wrote an anonymous Londoner, "for a woman of a land to be a regent; Queen Margaret, I mean, that ever meant to govern all England with might and power, and to destroy the right was her intent, wherefore she hath a fall, to her great languour. And now she né wrought so that she might attain, though all England were brought to confusion, she and her wicked affinity certain[ly] intend utterly to destroy this region."

The citizens prevaricated and dithered: should they admit the Queen? News of the plundering of St. Albans was the deciding factor. The Lord Mayor and a few aldermen were now virtually the only people in London who supported Margaret, and they were overridden by the angry citizens, who were fearful for their homes, womenfolk, and possessions. The City's gates were closed. It was a blow to the Queen's hopes.

Around 21 February, Margaret divided her army; the main body retired to Dunstable with her, while a detachment of the best troops was sent to Barnet, where it halted. Feelings were running high among the soldiers, who were unpaid and underfed. Many were on the brink of mutiny, and Margaret knew she had to find food and money imminently or risk disaster. Moving to Barnet, she wrote two letters to the citizens of London, warning that March had "feigned a title to my lord's crown and royal estate" and praying them "in our most hearty and desirous wise" that they would "diligently intend to the surety of my lord's royal person, so that through the malice of his said enemy he be no more troubled, vexed or jeopardized." She assured the Londoners that rumors that she was bringing "an unseen power of strangers, disposed to rob and despoil you of your goods and property," had been put about by her enemies. "We desire that you know for certain that none of you shall be robbed, despoiled or wronged by any person."[8] Her commanders warned her not to proceed farther south, but to return north and avoid forcing the issue with the Londoners, but the Northerners, seeing their prospects of pillaging the capital and its environs receding, erupted in fury. Hundreds deserted. However, since the victory at St. Albans had led to new recruits joining the Lancastrian forces, the army was kept more or less up to strength.

Margaret sent back the deputation of ladies to negotiate the terms of London's surrender, ordering the citizens to proclaim March a traitor and assuring them of an amnesty. They did not trust her, and with good cause, for her next move was to order 400 of her elite troops to march on Aldgate, where they demanded admittance to the City in the King's name. But the Mayor, thoroughly cowed by the people, refused them. Another troop of the Queen's soldiers reached Westminster, but were roughly dealt with by indignant citizens, who drove them back with threats.

"Captain Margaret" (as her enemies were now mockingly calling her) soon realized that an attempt on London was impossible and ordered a retreat to Dunstable, hoping to allay the fears of the citizens. That gave March the chance to advance on the capital unhindered. He sent ahead a messenger to proclaim that although the Lancastrians had given their soldiers license to rob, he had forbidden his own troops to do so. The citizens, eager to demonstrate their support of the Yorkists, collected the princely sum of £100 (£85,100), which was sent to help finance his campaign.

15

"Great slaughter"

✳

On 27 February, at the head of 20,000 knights and 30,000 foot soldiers, March rode through the gates of London and took possession of the City. Even at eighteen, he cut an impressive figure. The Londoners welcomed him with rapturous acclaim as the man who would save them from the Lancastrian menace. At his side rode Warwick, and there were fervent cheers for him too, for he had long been a favorite with the Londoners.

March did not claim to have taken up arms to remove Henry VI from the influence of evil counselors. People were acknowledging that the endemic disorder was directly attributable to Henry's weak government, and March's intention was to remove him from power and make himself King. This was imperative for, despite his warm welcome in London, he was not in a strong position, being technically an attainted traitor, and lacking funds and the support of a majority of the magnates, who had not forgotten or forgiven his father's poor attempt to take the throne.

On 1 March, to test the mood of the people, the Lord Chancellor, George Neville, addressed a crowd of citizens who were mingling with the Yorkist army in St. John's Fields, declaring that Edward, Earl of March, was the rightful King of England and that Henry of Lancaster was a usurper. When the Bishop asked the Londoners for their opinion, they shouted, "Yea! Yea! King Edward!" and clapped their hands, while the soldiers drummed on their armor.

Two days later, the Archbishop of Canterbury and other lords spiritual and temporal held a council at Baynard's Castle, at which all the magnates there present agreed that March should be offered the throne. The next day, Warwick led a deputation of lords and commons to Baynard's Castle and presented a petition begging him to accept the crown and royal dignity of England, while outside a crowd of Londoners was shouting, "King Edward! God save King Edward!" and begging him to avenge them on King Henry and Queen Margaret. March graciously acceded to the lords' petition and was proclaimed King Edward IV.

London's leading citizens were summoned to St. Paul's, where they enthusiastically acclaimed their new sovereign. In the cathedral, Edward IV made a thanksgiving offering to God, and then went in procession to Westminster Hall, where he took the oath required of a new monarch. Afterward, attired in royal robes and a cap of estate, he was enthroned upon the King's Bench, to the cheers of the assembled lords, who then escorted him past ecstatic crowds to Westminster Abbey, where the Abbot presented him with the crown and scepter of St. Edward the Confessor. He made more offerings at the Confessor's shrine before returning to the choir and mounting the coronation chair, which had been hastily placed there. He addressed the congregation, asserting his right to the crown, declaring that Henry VI had forfeited his right to the throne by failing to honor the Act of Accord and allowing his wife to take up arms against the true heirs.

When he had finished speaking, the lords asked the people if they would have him for their King, at which they cried that they indeed took him for their lawful King. The magnates knelt one by one before him and paid homage, and afterward the abbey was filled with the glorious sound of a *Te Deum*.

Later that day, Edward's councillors made plans for his formal coronation, but he vowed that he would not be crowned until Henry VI and Margaret of Anjou had been taken and executed or driven into exile.

Edward IV's accession was hailed by his supporters and propagandists as the restoration of the true Plantagenet line. It was hoped that God would now look benevolently upon the kingdom and allow peace and good government to be restored. "King Henry and his wife were overthrown and lost that crown which Henry IV had violently usurped and taken from King Richard II. Men say that ill-gotten goods cannot last."[1]

* * *

But the deposed King and Queen were still at large, and in command of a sizeable army. No one believed that the conflict would end here. Edward, it was said, feared Margaret more as a fugitive and in want of the absolute necessities of life than he did all the princes of the House of Lancaster combined. On 5 March, the Milanese ambassador heard a rumor that Henry VI, learning of Edward's accession, had abdicated in favor of his son. Queen Margaret, went the story, was so angry that she "gave the King poison. At least he will know how to die, if he is incapable of doing anything else!" Although the rumor had no foundation in fact, it is testimony that the Queen's reputation was such that people believed her capable of the deed.

Shocked and despondent, Henry, Margaret, their son, and the entire Lancastrian army retreated north, effectively surrendering the military initiative to the Yorkists. They marched to the city of York, their men pillaging as they went, leaving havoc and misery behind them. With his forces camped outside the city walls, Henry sent letters to his loyal lieges, enumerating March's misdeeds and commanding them to raise their affinities and attend him in arms with all speed. The Queen also called upon all true subjects of King Henry to rally to his standard and appealed to Mary of Guelders for reinforcements. Mary responded with a small force of men. Some chroniclers claimed that, within days, Margaret had increased the size of her army to 60,000 men, but the figure is likely to have been nearer 30,000. Her generals, Somerset, Northumberland, and Clifford, began planning a decisive campaign, and persuaded Henry and Margaret to remain in York while they rode to face the enemy.

Edward knew that if he did not deal decisively with the Lancastrians, he would never be secure on his throne. Henry had to be overthrown in fact as well as in name. On 6 March, having rewarded Warwick for his inestimable service by appointing him Great Chamberlain of England, captain of Dover, and Lord Warden of the Cinque Ports, and confirming him as captain of Calais, Edward sent him north to muster support for the Yorkists in his territories in the Midlands. On 13 March, Edward marched out of London with a great host whose ranks were swelled by new recruits as he advanced north, rumors of the brutality of the Lancastrian army having impelled many to join him. By 27 March, he was at

Pontefract, "collecting men in thousands," according to the Milanese ambassador. "Some say that the Queen is exceedingly prudent, and by remaining on the defensive, as they say she is well content to do, she will bring things into subjection and will tear into pieces those attacks of the people."

Edward was now closing in on the Lancastrian army, which was blocking the road to York. Between them the two armies had between 60,000 and 100,000 men, yet sources differ as to whether the armies were of equal strength.

At dawn on Palm Sunday, 29 March 1461, both armies awoke in the midst of a snowstorm. They faced each other across what would soon be known as the "Bloody Meadow." The Battle of Towton, the largest, longest battle of the Wars of the Roses, took place during a thick blizzard that continued all day. For ten hours, in one of the most terrible and bloody struggles in English history, Lancastrians and Yorkists were locked in a vicious mêlée in driving snow and bitter winds. Edward, remembering the fate of his father and brother, was bent on revenge. He commanded that no quarter be given nor any prisoners taken; even the common foot soldiers were not to be spared. When his men appeared to be flagging he dismounted in the thick of the fighting and rallied them, crying that he intended to live or die with them that day.

"There was great slaughter that day at Towton, and for a long time no one could see which side could gain the victory, so furious was the fighting."[2] The snow was red with blood. It was not clear who was winning until dusk fell, when at last the Lancastrians were driven back to the western side of the meadow. At this point, a strong force sent by the Duke of Norfolk attacked the Lancastrian left flank. Realizing then that the day was lost and that they would all be dead men unless they got away, the Lancastrians fled the field. As their forces broke, the Yorkist cavalrymen raced to the horse park behind their own lines and mounted their steeds to give chase, butchering every man they caught.

The Yorkists had scored a decisive and overwhelming victory. King Edward surmised that about 20,000 had been killed; his heralds, after surveying the carnage, estimated 28,000, a figure given by several contemporary chroniclers. The real figure, taking account of those who perished in the rout, was probably nearer 40,000. The slaughter of Towton broke the power of the great families of the North, and the Lancastrians lost some of their best captains, including the Earl of Northumberland.

Savagery on such a scale was thought shocking, even in that warlike age, and the Milanese ambassador observed, "Anyone who reflects at all upon the wretchedness of the Queen and the ruins of those killed, and considers the ferocity of that country and the state of mind of the victors, should indeed, it seems to me, pray to God for the dead, and not less for the living."

16

"Traitors and rebels"

✴

WHEN HENRY AND MARGARET WERE TOLD OF THE TERRIBLE Lancastrian defeat, and that their army had been virtually annihilated, they packed up everything they could carry, gathered their train, and fled from York. Racing north through the Forest of Galtres, Margaret vowed that she would one day be revenged on the House of York. Edward IV might have scored a resounding victory, but she, Henry, and their son could still be a focus for resistance to Yorkist rule.

On the morning after the battle, King Edward rode in triumph to York, where he received a warm welcome, but when he saw the rotting heads of his father, his brother, and his uncle of Salisbury above the Micklegate Bar, he vowed that the Lancastrians would taste his vengeance and that those responsible for the deaths of his kinsfolk would be relentlessly sought out and slaughtered. His first order was that the heads be taken down and decently interred at Pontefract with the bodies.

He told his lords that he would never rest until he had killed or captured King Henry and his wife, or driven them from the country, as he had sworn to do.

Many Lancastrians went into exile or changed sides, believing that, in granting Edward so decisive a victory, God had declared His pleasure. Those who regarded him as a usurper were now in a minority, yet although he was in control of most of England, the Lancastrians still held the border counties in the North and several strategic castles in Wales.

Lord Rivers was one of those who acknowledged him as the rightful King, whereupon Edward forgave his past support of the Lancastrians and pardoned him and his son Anthony Widville, who had both fought for Henry VI at Towton. By March 1463, the two men had been admitted to the royal Council.

After celebrating Easter in York, Edward marched north in pursuit of Henry and Margaret, who were making for Scotland with Somerset, Exeter, and a clever Oxford lawyer, Dr. John Morton. By 7 April, the fleeing Lancastrians had reached Newcastle; whence they pressed north to Alnwick. From there, Margaret sent an urgent message to the Bishop of St. Andrews, the Scottish regent, begging him to issue safe-conducts so that they could cross the border into Scotland. At Wark Castle, they were besieged by a Yorkist force led by Sir Robert Ogle. Retainers of their late ally Northumberland relieved the siege, enabling the royal party to escape through a little postern gate at the back of the castle and proceed in haste to Berwick. Here, while awaiting word from Scotland, they enjoyed a few days of rest; Margaret even went hunting and shot a buck.

In Scotland, Mary of Guelders found herself in a difficult position. Burgundy, her uncle, was hoping to secure an alliance with Edward IV, but a show of friendship by his niece to Edward's enemies might scupper negotiations. Warwick, aware of the Queen Regent's dilemma, persuaded her to agree that the Scots would not offer military support to the Lancastrians. But he could not stop them from granting asylum to the dispossessed royal family. The safe-conduct was issued and Henry, Margaret, the Prince, and 6,000 followers crossed the border into Galloway. Henry sought refuge in the convent of the Greyfriars at Kirkcudbright, while Margaret and her son traveled on to the Scottish court at Linlithgow Palace, where Mary accorded them a sympathetic welcome and ordered that apartments be prepared for them. Margaret stayed there for a time, then at Dresdner, Dumfries, and Lanark, before the Bishop of St. Andrews arranged in July for her to move to more convenient lodgings in Lincluden Abbey near Edinburgh. She later stayed at the house of the Blackfriars in the Cowgate.

The Yorkists had pursued their quarry almost to Scotland, but now returned south, much dispirited. At Newcastle, Edward IV ordered the execution of Wiltshire, whose head was displayed on London Bridge. Margaret was distressed when told, for she had loved him greatly.

Because the North of England was still strongly Lancastrian, Edward dared not penetrate beyond Newcastle. The North would remain disaffected for some time to come, with Margaret fueling hatred of the Yorkists by disseminating propaganda and appealing to the loyalties of local landowners. On 18 April, the Milanese ambassador had prophesied: "If the King and Queen of England, with the other fugitives, are not taken, it seems certain that in time fresh disturbances will arise." He also predicted that "before long, grievances and recrimination will break out between King Edward and the Earl of Warwick. King Henry and the Queen will be victorious."[1]

Margaret managed to persuade the reluctant Scottish government to conclude a treaty providing for the marriage of Prince Edward to James III's sister Margaret Stewart. In return, Henry would surrender Berwick, as already promised, and when he was restored to his throne, he would grant the Scots lands in England and make the Bishop of St. Andrews Archbishop of Canterbury. England would then enter into a tripartite alliance with Scotland and France, her traditional enemies. For the Scots, this was a deal-breaker.

When Edward IV learned of this new concord, he issued a proclamation, publishing its terms in full and accusing Margaret of "exciting and provoking the greatest and largest cruelty against our subjects, unto the execution of her insatiable malice toward them." He wrote an angry letter to King James, saying: "Whereas ye took and received our traitors and rebels, we require and exhort you to deliver [them] unto us without delay." The regents, in James's name, refused; they would not break such an advantageous alliance, nor jeopardize the Princess Margaret's marriage.

Although Queen Mary took Prince Edward into her household to learn the knightly graces, Margaret found herself in desperate financial straits. Having pawned her plate to raise funds for a fresh onslaught upon the Yorkists, she had to resort to borrowing money from Mary. Between May and July, Mary loaned her a total of £200 (£170,210), but Margaret had no means of paying it back. Soon she was in want of the very necessities of life.

On 25 April, in the name of Henry VI, Margaret formally ceded Berwick to the Scots, infuriating the English and giving the Yorkists an excellent propaganda weapon. The loss of the last English-owned fortified border town deprived Edward of an invaluable bridgehead for invading Scotland, weakened his diplomatic bargaining position, and gave the French a potential advantage. Worst of all, in Scottish hands, Berwick became a springboard for Lancastrian raids into Northumberland.

After signing the treaty, Margaret appears to have spent some time at Dunfermline Palace. Tradition has it that she introduced fine needlework to the women of the town.

Edward had returned to London, where he received a hero's welcome as the man who had saved the City from the brutality of the Northerners. That summer, he issued a stream of commissions of array, testimony to his fear that a Lancastrian counterattack was imminent.

In June, accompanied by her son, Margaret led an army of Scotsmen into England, aiming to take Carlisle, which she had promised to the Scots. She laid siege to the town and burned its suburbs, but was driven back by Warwick's brother, John Neville, Lord Montagu, who had been sent to guard the northern border from attack.

Henry VI now joined Margaret and, undaunted, they led their forces farther south, making for Durham. Edward commanded the Archbishop of York to muster his tenants and join a force led by Lords Fauconberg and Montagu. When, on 26 June, the Lancastrian standards were raised at Ryton and Brancepeth, the levies raised by the Archbishop, which were now under the command of Warwick himself, repelled the Lancastrians, who retreated north two days later.

Thanks to Warwick's presence in the region, the Yorkists had gained a foothold in the North and were gradually overcoming Lancastrian resistance. On 31 July, Edward appointed Warwick warden of the East and West Marches and instructed him to bring the North to the King's allegiance or reduce it to submission. A month later, it was reported in Milan that Warwick had prevented the Lancastrians from invading Northumberland.

17

"The handsomest prince my eyes ever beheld"

✸

ON 28 JUNE 1461, THE MORNING OF HIS CORONATION DAY, Edward IV issued a proclamation promising his subjects good and just government, and condemning the evils of Lancastrian rule. He was crowned in Westminster Abbey amid great splendor, to rapturous public acclaim. "I am unable to declare how well the commons love and adore him, as if he were their god," wrote a London merchant. "The entire kingdom keeps holiday for the event, which seems a boon from above. Thus far he appears to be a just prince, and to mean to mend and organize matters otherwise than has been done hitherto."

Unlike Henry VI, Edward was a splendid figure of a king. He was "very tall of personage, exceeding the stature almost of all others, of comely visage, pleasant look, broad breasted."[1] In 1789, when his skeleton was found by workmen repaving the choir in St. George's Chapel, Windsor, it was discovered to be more than six foot three inches long, and still had wisps of golden-brown hair adhering to the skull. The head and shoulders portrait of him in the Royal Collection is a copy by a Flemish artist of an original believed to have been painted before 1472 and shows a strongly built man with a marked resemblance to Henry VIII, Edward's grandson.

Commines, who saw Edward in 1470, called him "the handsomest prince my eyes ever beheld." In November 1461 the Speaker of the Commons, addressing the King in Parliament, referred to "the beauty of personage that it hath pleased Almighty God to send you." The chronicler Olivier de la Marche stated that Edward "was a handsome prince and had style, and truly he seemed a person well worthy to be king." By the standards of his day, Edward was remarkably clean, having his head, legs, and feet washed every Saturday night, sometimes more often. He was lean, energetic, and active.

Edward was aware of the effect his good looks had on people, and enjoyed showing off, wearing magnificent, daringly cut clothes that revealed his fine physique. Chroniclers were scandalized by the dress of his courtiers, especially the short doublets of the men, which were worn over tight hose that revealed the outlines of their genitals. The extravagant headdresses of the noble ladies, steeple-shaped hennins and precarious affairs of wire and gauze known as "butterflies," also drew adverse comments from the moralists, who saw in them the lure of the Devil.

In 1461, Coppini described Edward as "young, prudent and magnanimous." The King deployed his "invincible courage,"[2] determination, and resourcefulness to advantage, and was pragmatic, generous, witty, and ruthless when necessary. Dominic Mancini, who visited England in the 1480s, described him as gentle and cheerful by nature. The common touch came naturally to him. "He was easy of access to his friends, even the least notable. He was so genial in his greeting that if he saw a newcomer bewildered at his royal magnificence, he would give him courage to speak by laying a kindly hand upon his shoulder." Yet "should he assume an angry countenance, he could be very terrible to beholders"[3] and as terrifying as his grandson, Henry VIII.

In adversity, Edward was "nothing abashed"; in times of peace he showed himself "just and merciful."[4] He was pious and intelligent, but no intellectual, yet he was a noted collector of richly illustrated manuscripts and books. He was deeply immersed in the Arthurian legends and the cult of St. George, both of which underpinned English court culture, and he was interested in the history of ancient Rome. When his collection became too unwieldy to transport on his travels, he deposited it at Windsor, where it became the basis of the present Royal Library. Despite his preference for illuminated manuscripts, he became a patron of William Caxton, the first English printer. He was fluent in Latin and French, and wrote a fine italic hand, rare in a medieval English sovereign. He was fascinated by the contemporary science of alchemy, through which it was believed that base metal could be turned into gold.

In his tastes Edward followed the dictates of the court of Burgundy, which at that time led the rest of Europe in style, culture, manners, and etiquette. "In those days," remembered Croyland, "you would have seen a royal court worthy of a leading kingdom, full of riches and men from every nation." Such magnificence had not been seen at court since the time of Richard II. Scholars and men of learning were warmly welcomed. Elaborate codes of courtesy and etiquette were followed meticulously, these being considered the outward manifestations of an ordered society.

Edward spent lavishly on clothing, jewels, and plate, and indulged his passion for building. He improved and beautified many of his palaces, notably Greenwich, Westminster, Windsor, and Eltham. One of his favorite palaces was that in the Tower of London, where he spent more time than any sovereign before him. He made extravagant improvements, patronizing architects, stonemasons, sculptors, glaziers, silversmiths, goldsmiths, jewelers, and merchants dealing in luxury goods such as tapestries and fabrics. Walls were hung with rich cloth of Arras, tables set with fine napery and gold, silver, and gilt plate, chairs and cushions upholstered in velvet and damask, and beds covered with sheets of fine holland cloth and counterpanes of crimson damask or cloth of gold trimmed with ermine. Today, St. George's Chapel, Windsor, and the great hall at Eltham Palace in Kent bear witness to the largely vanished splendors of his reign.

Once firmly established on the throne, Edward gave himself up to the pursuit of pleasure. He was extravagant, dissolute, and "accustomed to more luxuries and pleasures than any prince of his day," and enjoyed "dances, hunting, hawking and banqueting."[5] He was a good dancer, excelled at sports, and preferred to indulge in his pleasures than attend to matters of state. Almost the only person of whom he went in awe was his formidable mother, Duchess Cecily, who could "rule the King as she pleases."[6]

Edward's chief vice was his sensuality, and his debaucheries were soon notorious. "This prince was thought to have indulged his passions and desires too intemperately."[7] Philippe de Commines observed: "He thought of nothing but upon women, and on that more than reason would; and on hunting, and on the comfort of his person." "Given to bodily lust," he "would use himself more familiarly among private persons than the honor of his majesty required."[8] "He was of youth greatly given to fleshly wantonness, for no woman was there anywhere whom he set his eye upon but he would importunately pursue his appetite and have her."[9]

Mancini too thought Edward "licentious in the extreme. Moreover, it was said that he had been most insolent to numerous women after he had seduced them, for as soon as he grew weary of dalliance, he abandoned the ladies, much against their will, to the other courtiers. He pursued with no discrimination the married and unmarried, the noble and lowly. However, he took none by force. He overcame all by money and promises, and having conquered them, he dismissed them."

Later, it would be said that his sexual excesses in youth had permanently undermined his health and constitution. Few of his intrigues lasted for long, but none of his mistresses was allowed to interfere in politics. The names of two are known: Elizabeth Lucy, a married woman who had an affair with Edward early in his reign and bore him a son, Arthur Plantagenet, and possibly a daughter; and Elizabeth Shore, commonly miscalled Jane, who was his lover in the latter years of his life.

It was not just his good looks that made Edward IV a popular king. He excelled Henry VI in nearly every way, especially as a statesman and a general. He was a firm and resolute ruler, shrewd and astute, and had real ability and business acumen. He was successful in his determination to restore the authority of the monarchy and make it an institution to inspire reverence and respect. At nineteen, he was already the veteran of several important battles and the victor of two decisive ones. In the field he was vigorous and valiant, "earnest and horrible to the enemy, and fortunate in all his wars,"[10] even though he hated war for its own sake and tried to avoid it whenever possible. Unlike his predecessors, he had no ambitions to conquer France.

Next to the King, the greatest man in England was Warwick, Edward's mainstay and foremost supporter. Now thirty-three, Warwick virtually controlled the government for the first three years of Edward's reign, carried along on a tide of public popularity. He was so well loved that whenever he showed himself in public, accompanied by his customary train of 600 liveried retainers, crowds would run to greet him, crying, "Warwick! Warwick!" "Warwick seems to me everything in this kingdom," commented the Milanese ambassador. Edward made the Earl his chief adviser and allowed him to control foreign policy. He was content for him to share the burdens of state while he himself enjoyed the more pleasurable aspects of kingship.

Yet, while Edward relied on Warwick in many ways, he would not be ruled by him. This was not apparent to everyone, even Warwick himself, who certainly overestimated his influence over the King, nor was it obvious to most foreign observers, who tended to exaggerate his role. One citizen of Calais wrote to the King of France: "They tell me that they have but two rulers in England: Monsieur de Warwick, and another whose name I have forgotten."

Warwick bestrode the North. His aim was to establish the Nevilles as the leading power in the realm and dominate the other magnates, many of whom were jealous of his power and wealth. Yet his influence with the King was such that no one dared criticize him.

Also prominent among the royal councillors was thirty-year-old Sir William Hastings, Edward's close friend and confidant, who controlled the area around Leicester—previously Lancastrian in sympathy—with unprecedented authority. Hastings came from a family of Yorkshire gentry who had loyally served the House of York through four generations. He had risen to power when, in youth, he was placed in the household of the Duke of York. In 1461, he had fought for Edward at Towton and been rewarded for his loyalty with a knighthood, vast lands, a seat on the royal Council, the office of King's Chamberlain, and a barony. Sir William Herbert was appointed governor of south Wales, where his word was law; Thomas Mowbray, Duke of Norfolk, and John de la Pole, Duke of Suffolk (who was married to the King's sister Elizabeth), controlled East Anglia, while the new Earl of Devon and Humphrey Stafford held sway in the West Country.

The influential Londoners had long since given their allegiance to the Yorkist cause, and the King formulated his policies to their advantage.

His mercantile enterprises enabled a sense of affinity to develop between him and the London merchants. Despite the unpopular forced loans which were demanded of them from time to time, and the liberties taken by the King with their wives and daughters, they prospered, and gave thanks for his virtues.

18

"I will either conquer or be conquered"

✴

ONCE BERWICK WAS THEIRS, THE SCOTS SAW NO FURTHER ADvantage to be gained from the Lancastrian exiles, and lost interest in their cause, while Queen Mary was finding it expensive to support them. By the summer of 1461, it was obvious to Margaret that the Scots were unlikely to offer her any more financial aid. All she could expect was the goodwill of individuals such as the Earl of Angus, who offered her men in return for the promise of a dukedom in England. Her best hope now, she realized, lay in appealing to Charles VII for assistance.

In July, she dispatched Somerset and Pierre de Brézé to the French court to ask for men, ships, and a loan to enable the Lancastrians to conquer the Channel Islands and so create a bridgehead to England. With French help, the Lancastrians occupied Jersey that year, though it was later recaptured by the Yorkists.

Invoking foreign aid from England's traditional enemies might have been the only realistic option open to Margaret, but it made her cause doubly unpopular in England and provided the Yorkists with splendid propaganda opportunities. Her actions changed the course of the Wars of the Roses, which now became dependent on the tortuous diplomacy and shifting alliances of European politics, while her involvement of foreign princes in the conflict enabled them to destabilize England by playing off one faction against the other there and inciting rebellion.

On 22 July 1461, Charles VII died and was succeeded by his son,

Louis XI. This was bad news for Margaret, because Louis hated his mother's family, the House of Anjou, and immediately demonstrated this by imprisoning Margaret's envoys. It also suited him to see England riven by divisions. He had hitherto been friendly toward the Yorkists, and news of his accession was greeted with some relief at Edward IV's court as fears of a French invasion receded. But this euphoria was short-lived. In the 1460s, international politics were dominated by rivalry between France and Burgundy; both sought the friendship of England, but France, although more powerful, was England's traditional enemy, while the Low Countries, ruled by Burgundy, were the chief market for English wool.

Louis's main ambition was to conquer Burgundy and Brittany, and absorb them into the kingdom of France. He resented and feared the power of Burgundy and was determined to prevent Edward IV from forming a defensive alliance with Duke Philip. Louis would come to be known as the "Universal Spider" because his web of political intrigue encompassed the whole of Europe.

Edward IV was in a strong position. He was a bachelor, free to make a marriage alliance with either France or Burgundy. It was just a question of waiting to see who could offer the most advantageous terms.

On 30 August, Somerset and Brézé wrote to inform Margaret that they had been summoned to see King Louis. "Madam, fear not, but be of good comfort, and beware ye venture not your person nor my lord the Prince by sea till ye have other word from us, [unless] your person cannot be secure where you are and extreme necessity drive you from there. And, for God's sake, give the same advice to the King."

To their surprise, the envoys found Louis prepared to be very friendly toward them and their mistress, for it suited his purpose to see England divided by civil war. He had decided on pursuing an aggressive policy against Burgundy and did not want Edward IV to unite with Philip against him. He told the envoys that he would support Margaret in her attempts to subvert the North of England. This was good news indeed, and Margaret began hoping to meet with Louis and conclude a formal alliance.

Edward's spies had intercepted one of the envoys' letters, which proved that Margaret was intriguing with the French. From now on, he had to live with the ever-present fear of invasion. Believing that it would target the North, he sent Warwick to capture Alnwick Castle, seat of the Earl of Northumberland. In September, Warwick took Alnwick, and Bamburgh Castle. The chief strongholds of the North were now in Yorkist hands.

Edward entrusted the task of crushing the Lancastrians in Wales to Lord Ferrers and Sir William Herbert, who had been created Lord Herbert in July. Their first objective was to take Pembroke Castle, which surrendered on 30 September. When Herbert took possession, he found four-year-old Henry Tudor living in the castle with his mother, Margaret Beaufort, and her second husband. An erudite, pious, and virtuous woman of strong character, Margaret had prudently married a loyal Yorkist, Sir Henry Stafford, the Duke of Buckingham's brother. Previously, Edward IV had shown himself hostile toward her, but this new marriage changed things, and she was now treated with the deference due to one of royal blood.

Herbert bought Henry's wardship for £1,000 (£851,040) and removed him from his mother's care, taking him into his own household. Although a rough and often violent man, he proved a kindly guardian, providing the boy with an excellent education. Henry's tutor, Andreas Scotus, observed that he had never seen a child so quick in learning. A marriage was planned between Henry and Herbert's daughter Maud, but Henry saw little of his mother during the next nine years, when he lived at Raglan Castle. It was Edward IV's intention that Herbert should replace Pembroke, who had fled to Scotland, as the King's representative in south Wales—no easy job, for there were many there who lamented the departure of Pembroke and resented the presence of Herbert.

In the first Parliament of Edward's reign, which met in November 1461 at Westminster, the King raised his brothers to the peerage, creating George Duke of Clarence and Richard Duke of Gloucester. Around 1465, when he was thirteen, Richard was sent to receive a knightly education with other noble boys in Warwick's household, which was based chiefly at Middleham Castle in Yorkshire, one of the great Neville strongholds. Here, his companions may have included Warwick's daughters, Isabel and Anne, and the Earl's ward, Francis Lovell, who would remain a lifelong friend. At Middleham, Richard learned the arts of warfare and the skills required of a nobleman, as well as receiving some rudimentary training in law. He remained in Warwick's household until 1470, when he reached eighteen.

Parliament passed Acts of Attainder against 150 Lancastrians, including "the usurper" Henry VI, Margaret, "late called Queen of England," eight-year-old Prince Edward (who was referred to as her son, not Henry's), Somerset, Exeter, Wiltshire, Northumberland, Fortescue, and several others.[1] Many were dead, but their relatives were dispossessed of their property. All were declared traitors. The confiscation of so many estates enabled Edward to reward his supporters handsomely, and there followed a large-scale redistribution of lands, titles, and offices among the Yorkist hierarchy. The duchy of Lancaster was declared forfeit to the Crown, in whose hands it has remained ever since, and all true subjects were forbidden, on pain of death, to communicate with the former King and Queen.

Parliament also deprived Henry Tudor of his earldom of Richmond, which was given to the King's brother Clarence. Exeter fled into exile on the Continent. Other Lancastrian supporters chose to remain in England and work for the restoration of Henry VI. Early in 1462, John de Vere, 12th Earl of Oxford, was in communication with the exiled royal family in Scotland. He was one of Margaret's chief agents in England and the head of a group of conspirators who were planning a Lancastrian invasion and the overthrow of Edward IV. Unfortunately for him, his courier was a Yorkist double agent, who took his letters straight to the King. In February, Oxford was convicted of treason and sentenced to a traitor's death. Edward IV permitted his son John to inherit the earldom and married him to Warwick's sister to keep him loyal, but the younger John de Vere remained a staunch Lancastrian to the end of his days.

Margaret's expectations of King Louis were high, especially after she learned that he had been actively involved in Oxford's conspiracy. She was appalled, therefore, to hear from her agents in France that Somerset had been boasting to Louis about the mutual love between her and himself. When he returned to Scotland, she made her displeasure evident and relations between them were strained for a time. She was also disappointed that her envoys had failed to obtain anything other than verbal support from Louis. Nevertheless, Edward IV believed that Somerset's arrival in Scotland presaged a Lancastrian invasion and decided to take preventive action by putting diplomatic pressure on Mary of Guelders to abandon the exiles. He even offered to marry her, though Mary was noncommittal and the plan was dropped.

In May, to show Mary of Guelders that Edward meant business, Warwick led an army across the border and seized a Scottish castle. The ploy worked. Later that month, Mary signed a truce, which Warwick hoped would lead to a more permanent peace that would effectively close Scotland to the Lancastrians.

Margaret knew she must meet Louis face-to-face and solicit his help. Early in April, leaving Henry at Kirkcudbright, she embarked on a French ship, taking with her the Prince and Sir John Fortescue. On Good Friday, 16 April, they landed in Brittany, where she was warmly welcomed by Duke Francis II, grandson of Joan of Navarre, who presented her with 12,000 crowns (£1:9 million). Awaiting her was Pembroke, who had learned of her coming and ridden to join her. Duke Francis told her that King Louis was away in the South of France, so she traveled on to Angers, where, in May, she was reunited with her father, King René. Still impoverished, René had had to borrow 8,000 florins (£128,600) to entertain her sumptuously. He was unable to offer her any help, for his slender resources were eaten up by a costly, unnecessary war with Aragon. After a fortnight, Margaret bade him farewell and set off to find Louis.

Having trailed the French court for several weeks, she caught up with it at Amboise. When she was admitted to the King's presence, she stunned onlookers by prostrating herself at his feet in tears and begging him to help her husband regain his throne. Louis appeared unmoved. By showing himself uninterested, he meant to force the Queen to an arrangement favorable to his own ends. "I assure you," he wrote to one of his ministers, "I foresee good winnings."[2]

Under pressure from his mother, Marie of Anjou, and King René, he granted Margaret another interview and told her that if she would agree to surrender Calais to him, he would lend her 20,000 livres (£16,931,170) to finance an invasion of England. But Margaret demurred, saying she dared not alienate the English further by surrendering Calais. Louis conceded the point, and in June, as a favor to her, he released Pierre de Brézé from prison. On 13 June, when he saw Margaret again and offered her, in return for Calais, 2,000 men under Brézé, 20,000 livres in cash, and the authority to muster men in Normandy, she capitulated—an act the English would see as treason. On 28 June, at Chinon, on Henry VI's behalf, she signed a treaty of peace with France, providing for a hundred-year truce and barring all Englishmen from entering France unless they were certified true subjects of King Henry. Both sides agreed not to enter into alliances with each other's enemies or rebellious subjects. That day, Louis handed over the 20,000 livres and Margaret formally undertook to surrender Calais within a year or pay him twice that sum. She was fêted by Louis as an honored guest and stood sponsor with him to the son of the Duke of Orléans.

She traveled to Rouen to recruit men, while Louis sent ships to harry the English coast and Brézé raised a force of soldiers and mercenaries. Margaret reminded her captains of her previous successes against her enemies: "I have often broken their battle line. I have mowed down ranks far more stubborn than theirs are now. You who once followed a peasant girl now follow a queen. I will either conquer or be conquered with you." All "marveled at such boldness in a woman, at a man's courage in a woman's breast, and at her reasonable arguments. They said that the spirit of the Maid was renewed in the Queen."[3]

When news of the treaty reached England, Margaret was castigated as a traitor for promising Calais to the French, and King Edward dispatched seventy ships to harry the French coast and intercept any fleet that might be sailing to Scotland or England.

Margaret's supporters were also anticipating a Lancastrian invasion from France. In October, Sir Richard Tunstall, a champion of the Queen, seized Bamburgh Castle. On the 19th, Margaret, her son, Brézé, and 2,000 French troops sailed from Normandy in a dozen ships and made for the coast of Northumberland. After the Yorkist garrison at Tynemouth prevented them from landing by firing cannon at them, their ships were scattered in a violent storm, and some were lost. Yet as soon as the sea was calm again, they sailed farther up the coast and landed at Bamburgh. But when they were warned that Warwick was approaching with an army of 40,000, most of the mercenaries abandoned Margaret and fled to the ships for safety, leaving her, Brézé, and the Prince standing disconsolately on the shore, watching their fleet retreating out to sea. Eventually, they found a fisherman who agreed to take them farther along the coast, but another storm blew up and his boat broke apart on the rocks at Bamburgh. They barely escaped with their lives, and their provisions, baggage, and weapons were washed overboard.

Margaret expected loyal Lancastrians to rally to her at Bamburgh, but those who might have joined her were dismayed to find she had brought no armed force with her, and deemed it safer to stay away. Undaunted, she reinforced the garrison at Bamburgh with French troops who had sailed up the coast and rejoined her, then marched on to Dunstanburgh Castle and took it, and proceeded from there to Alnwick Castle, to which her remaining soldiers laid siege. Lacking provisions, the fortress capitulated. Soon afterward, Warkworth Castle also fell to the Lancastrians. With these strongholds in her hands, Margaret was in virtual possession of Northumberland, but very few Englishmen had joined her cause, and many local people resented the French garrisons. Having ordered that each castle be stocked with sufficient provisions to withstand a siege, Margaret progressed north to Berwick, where she found Henry VI, Somerset, Exeter, Pembroke, and Morton waiting for her.

Mary of Guelders was not pleased to be asked for yet more aid, and gave only a pittance to finance further action. Leaving the Prince at Berwick, Henry and Margaret left to invade England, accompanied only by their retinue and Margaret's 800 remaining men.

On 30 October, news of the invasion reached London by fast courier. This new threat stretched Edward's resources, and he was obliged to levy heavy taxes and borrow money from London merchants to meet the costs of raising an army. He sent Warwick north to lay siege to Berwick, then, in November, marched north to confront the invaders, accompanied by thirty-one peers, a record for the period. This turnout reflected the view expressed in a contemporary ballad that it was "a right great perversion for a woman of a land to be a regent—Queen Margaret, that ever has meant to govern all England with might and power; and to destroy the right line was her intent."

News of the King's coming soon reached Margaret, who placed Somerset in command of the garrison at Bamburgh. Her soldiers, meanwhile, had descended on the priories at Hexham and Durham and demanded funds for her use. When Edward IV arrived in Durham, he was confronted by an angry prior demanding repayment of 400 marks (£221,270) that Margaret had forced him to lend her, while the Prior of Hexham was writing to anyone who might be sympathetic, complaining about the money she had made him give her through dread and fear.

On 13 November, having realized that her small force was nowhere near equal to the advancing Yorkist host, Margaret fled with Henry VI, Brézé, and over 400 soldiers from Bamburgh, and put to sea in a small caravel, with as much luggage as it would hold, hoping that a French ship would rescue them. As they neared Holy Island, a storm blew up that so terrified Margaret that she took a fishing boat back, which was as well, as the caravel sank and all the goods were lost. Four hundred of her men were left stranded on Holy Island and obliged to surrender to local Yorkists. Some were taken prisoner and others, not so lucky, were put to the sword as an example to would-be traitors. When Edward learned of Margaret's flight, he resolved to pursue her but was struck down by a virulent attack of measles and confined to bed at Durham.

Meanwhile, Warwick had captured Warkworth Castle and made it his headquarters. He laid siege to Bamburgh, where the Lancastrian garrison under Somerset held out for as long as possible, while Warwick sent messages promising him a generous pension if he would surrender. In return, Somerset demanded that the lords with him be restored to their estates, and the lives of the garrison be spared. Warwick agreed, and on Christmas Eve, Somerset gave up the keys of the castle.

Somerset's desertion of the Lancastrians may have been prompted by the desire for personal gain or by rivalry with Brézé for the Queen's favor; relations between himself and Margaret had been strained of late. He now formally pledged his allegiance to Edward IV and rode to assist Warwick at the siege of Alnwick. Edward had for some time cherished notions of winning over Somerset and had been prepared to be more than conciliatory, knowing that the defection of one of their staunchest adherents would be a sickening blow to his enemies.

Parliament, at the King's wish, reversed the attainder on Somerset, restoring his titles and estates. Edward himself cultivated Somerset's friendship and accorded him a place of honor at court, hunting and feasting with him and taking him with him on his travels around the kingdom. Tournaments were held in his honor. It seemed as if Edward had succeeded in making the Duke forget those he had betrayed.

By 6 January 1463, Alnwick and Dunstanburgh had surrendered to the Yorkists, and Pembroke, unwilling to reach any compromise with Edward IV, had returned to Scotland. The surrender of the Northumbrian castles effectively ended the campaign, and the King withdrew his army south, ordering Warwick to guard the border. "King Edward now possessed the whole of England."[4]

19

"Dire vicissitude"

✷

MARGARET TOOK REFUGE IN SCOTLAND. EDWARD, DETERmined to prevent her from obtaining any further support from the French, sent an embassy to negotiate a treaty of friendship with Louis. When Margaret heard, she resolved to sabotage any pact between them, and to persuade the French King to provide further aid for her own cause.

Her French and Scottish mercenaries had followed her to Scotland, where they regrouped. Just before Lent, with herself and Brézé at their head, they crossed the River Tweed into Northumberland and retook Bamburgh, Dunstanburgh, and Alnwick. Margaret, Henry VI, and Brézé made Bamburgh their headquarters. With the Northumbrian fortresses restored to her, Margaret was nominally in command of much of the North, although the local people were less than enthusiastic in their support, being sickened by constant strife and warfare. Moreover, the benefits of two years of Edward's rule were beginning to manifest themselves.

In London, the government and citizens were horrified at the swift success of the Lancastrian invasion, and the King sent Warwick north again, commanding that the rebels Henry and Margaret should not be allowed to escape by sea.

Early in June, fearing that Louis was going over to the Yorkists, Margaret appealed to Philip of Burgundy for aid. She had learned that a peace conference between England, France, and Burgundy was to take place on 24 June at Saint-Omer and was worried that Burgundy would sign a concord with England and France that would leave her politically isolated. On the day the conference began, Philip sent her a token gift of 1,000 crowns (£160,750), which greatly encouraged her; she did not realize that it was a sop to keep her quiet—and away from Saint-Omer.

During the conference, Edward and Louis, through their envoys, concluded a truce and agreed not to succor each other's enemies, which effectively closed France to the Lancastrian exiles. Margaret was now desperate to cross the Channel and see Philip face-to-face, to preempt him from entering into any agreement with France or England. Although they had never been friends, he was now her last hope.

Warwick was hoping to consolidate the new amity between Edward and Louis by negotiating his master's marriage to a French princess. Louis's daughter Anne was just an infant, so he offered instead Bona of Savoy, who was rising fourteen and the sister of his Queen, Charlotte of Savoy. Fearing that such an alliance posed a threat to Burgundy, Philip countered the offer by offering Edward one of his nieces. Edward did not respond to either proposal, though he was more inclined toward friendship with France.

In June, Lord Montagu repelled a Lancastrian attack on Newcastle, and ships from France, laden with supplies for Margaret, were intercepted by sailors loyal to King Edward. At that time, the Lancastrians, led by Margaret, were besieging Norham Castle, which stood on the banks of the Tweed and was owned by the Bishop of Durham. They were assisted by the Scots, who stood to gain more advantage from the capture of the castle than the Lancastrians would, but Margaret needed Scottish aid and had no choice but to be accommodating. The siege lasted eighteen days, until Warwick arrived and, with the help of Montagu, put both Scots and Lancastrians to flight.

Hotly pursued by their enemies, Margaret and her men fell back on Bamburgh.

It was during their flight that one of the most famous and romanticized episodes of the Wars of the Roses took place. Many modern historians dismiss the story as mere legend, but later that year Margaret herself related in detail what had happened to the Duchess of Bourbon in the presence of Burgundy's official chronicler, Georges Chastellain.

The story is also recounted by Waurin, who wrote that "after hiding some of her best rings in her clothes, she and her son mounted ponies and set off with guides, riding only by night until they came to a very large and dense forest. Here, they were ambushed by thieves and murderers, but a great argument broke out over who was to have Margaret's rings and jewels. While it pleased God that these murderers should be quarrelling with each other, the Queen, taking her son in her arms, hid in the forest. Finally, overcome by hardship, she had no choice but to entrust her child to another brigand whom she encountered in the woods, saying to him, 'Save your King's son!' Through this man, she and her son escaped and got away."

Margaret went into more detail, as reported by Chastellain, relating how she and her son had become separated from the others when suddenly a gang of robbers sprang out from nearby bushes and "dragged her with brutal violence and furious menaces before their leader." He grabbed her by her robe, wielding a drawn sword as if he would cut her throat, and threatened her with indignities and tortures, "whereupon she threw herself on her knees with clasped hands, weeping and crying aloud for mercy, and implored them by every consideration, human or divine, and for the honor of nobility, of royalty and, above all, for the sake of womanhood, to have pity on her and not to mangle or disfigure her unfortunate body, so as to prevent it being recognized after death."

"For although I have had the ill-luck to fall into your hands, I am the daughter and wife of a king and was in past time recognized by yourselves as your Queen," she said. "Wherefore, if you now stain your hands with my blood, your cruelty will be held in abhorrence by all men in all ages."

Clasping her son, she continued: "If it is gold you seek, I can give you none, for others before you have taken all I had. But if you have a heart which can be touched with pity, if you once had a mother who stooped over your cradle, I entrust this child to you. He is the son of your rightful King, heir to the crown of England. In saving him, you will save your soul and your country. I place him under your protection." She begged him, "by the passion of our Lord and Savior Jesus Christ, to have pity on her and do what he could to assist her to make her escape."

Her words wrought a curious change in the robber. He fell on his knees before her, told her he was known as Black Jack, and swore "that he would die a thousand deaths and endure all the tortures that could be inflicted on him, rather than abandon, much less betray, the noble child."

"Madam, mount behind me," he bade her, "and my lord the Prince in front, and I will save you or die, seeing that death is more likely to come to me than not."

That night, he led them by a secret route through Hexham Forest. To the terrified Margaret, every tree looked like a man with a drawn sword. But at length they came to a well-hidden cave beside a stream in Dipton Woods, which is still known as Queen's Cave. Here, they sheltered for two days while Black Jack located Brézé and his squire Barville. On bidding farewell to him and pardoning him for the offenses he had committed, Margaret said, "Of all I have lost, I regret nothing so much as the power of recompensing such virtue." She and Brézé rode to Carlisle and thence across the Scottish border to Kirkcudbright. She told her squire that it had not been for herself that she feared, but for her son.[1]

While she was at Kirkcudbright, an English spy called Cork devised a plan to kidnap her and take her to Edward IV. He paid his men well, and one night they laid hands on Brézé and Barville and forced them into a small rowing boat, where they were bound and gagged. After that, it was an easy matter to capture the unguarded Margaret and her son, drag them on board, and put to sea. There they remained all night, but in the light of dawn, Margaret recognized Brézé and surreptitiously helped to loosen his bonds. Once free, he knocked Cork senseless and seized the oars. For some hours, the boat was tossed in the choppy waters of the Solway Firth before being beached at Kirkcudbright Bay, a wild and desolate place. Brézé carried Margaret ashore and laid her on the sand to recuperate, while Barville followed with the Prince in his arms. When they had recovered, they walked to a nearby hamlet and begged shelter. Brézé sent Barville to Edinburgh—a hundred miles away—to enlist the help of Queen Mary. He returned with a message that Mary would see Margaret, but only in private, and that the betrothal between the Prince and Margaret Stewart had been broken at Burgundy's request.

Perplexed and angry, Margaret made her way to Edinburgh but could not prevail upon the embarrassed Scottish government to change its mind. All Mary would do was help her to return to her friends in Northumberland.

Margaret was now in desperate straits. Making her way back with Brézé toward Bamburgh, she met up with her husband and son, but their food supplies quickly ran out and they "were reduced to such abject misery and destitution that for five days they had but one herring between the three and no more bread than would have sufficed a day's nourishment." At a Mass in honor of her patron saint, St. Margaret, on 20 July, Margaret could not find one "black penny" for the offering, but had to borrow a groat from a Scottish archer.[2]

Meanwhile the activities of the Lancastrians in the North had rebounded on Somerset, who had not been involved. Many at court could not forget that he had supported the Lancastrians. In late July, the King sent him away for his own safety, apparently to one of the royal castles in Wales.

In July 1463, Margaret learned that Warwick was marching north with a great host. Knowing she had no hope of holding out against him, she decided to make a personal plea to Burgundy for help. Brézé later told Chastellain that she was destitute. Even though he himself was in extreme poverty, he had been funding her and the Prince and it had cost him 50,000 crowns (£8 million), all he had. "It was a piteous thing [he said] to see this mighty princess in such dire vicissitude and, after a narrow escape from the most extreme perils, dying almost of hunger and fatigue, [and now] constrained to give herself up to [Burgundy] who, of all the world, was the most exasperated against her. Yet she was full of hope that she should be able to obtain grace if she might be permitted to enter his presence, and that her high and noble courage in her calamities would move him to pity—perhaps to succor her."

After bidding farewell to Henry VI at Bamburgh, and promising that she would be back in the spring with a new army, she sailed across the North Sea with Brézé, Exeter, Fortescue, Morton, and 200 men in four fishing vessels, while Henry made his way to Berwick. Margaret would never see him again.

On 31 July, after enduring twelve hours of violent gales, Margaret's boats were obliged to dock at Sluys in the duchy of Burgundy because they were too damaged to sail farther. Accompanied by just Brézé and seven female attendants, she had no money, no jewels or royal robes, no change of clothing, and no possessions of value to pledge—they had been sold to finance her military ventures. "Formerly one of the most splendid women in the world," all she had to wear was a red gown, cut to the knee like a peasant's. Her women were as poorly attired as she was, and she was totally dependent on Brézé for money and food. "It was a thing piteous to see, truly, this high princess so cast down and laid low in such great danger, dying of hunger and hardship."[3]

Margaret was trusting in a safe-conduct issued by Philip years before to guarantee her safe passage through his territories, but her welcome in Sluys was frosty. The people were loyal to their Duke; remembering that this woman had been his mortal enemy in the days of her prosperity, they made many savage comments on her misfortunes. Yet still she was resolved to see Philip and sabotage the peace conference at Saint-Omer.

She wasted no time in sending a messenger to request an audience, saying she came "in humility and poverty to seek of his greatness a refuge for herself and her child in her distress, which she trusted he was too proud not to deny her."[4] Philip showed himself sympathetic, but he was anxious to conclude the treaty of friendship with Edward IV and so preserve the trade links between England and Burgundy. He did not want Margaret embarrassing him in front of the English envoys, so he played for time, pleading that his lodgings were "too small to receive a princess of her quality, and that he could not permit her to undertake the fatigue of a journey to him; that it was the etiquette for him to visit her, and that he certainly should have done so but for the accident of his sickness." He was clearly hoping that she would go away. When it became plain that she was bent on seeing him, he sent to say he had gone on pilgrimage to Our Lady of Boulogne and, as English-owned Calais was nearby, it was too dangerous for her to join him. Margaret told his messenger, "On departing from the place where I had the grief of leaving my lord and husband, he charged me not to allow any earthly consideration to prevent me from coming to his fair cousin of Burgundy to explain to him the multitude of malicious reports that have been made to him of us by our enemies. I will go in quest of him whether it imperil me or not, for I regard it a matter of duty. Were my cousin of Burgundy to go to the end of the world, I would follow him, begging my bread along the way until I have found him."⁵

The messenger hurried back to Philip and told him that nothing on earth could deflect Margaret from her purpose and "see him she would." Philip said he would see her if he had to, at Boulogne, doubtless hoping that the English might capture her on the way. Then his chivalry and famed courtesy prevailed, and he sent a message informing her that he would meet her at Saint-Pol. By the time he got there, the English envoys would have departed.

Leaving her son at Bruges, and traveling with Brézé and three women, Margaret proceeded toward Lille in a covered cart drawn by four mares, "dressed like a village woman in the garb of a chambermaid." At Lille, she was welcomed by Burgundy's son and heir, Charles, Count of Charolais, who enjoyed defying his father and paid her all the honors due to a queen of England. He gave her money and urged her to scupper the peace talks between England and France.

Margaret set off for Boulogne. At Béthune in northern France, the English rode out of Calais in force, hoping to capture her, but an escort of archers sent by Burgundy fortuitously arrived and drove them off. Margaret arrived at Saint-Pol on 31 August, where Philip came to see her on 2 September. He arrived in magnificent array, and though she had come in a canvas wagon, attended only by three women, yet "she deported herself with no less dignity than when she swayed the scepter in London and exercised in her single person the whole of the regal authority there."⁶ Informed that the Duke was entering the town, she came out into the street to greet him. They kissed, she curtseyed, and he bowed low.

Their differences were glossed over by pleasantries. Philip told Margaret she was welcome in Burgundy and, weeping, said he was sorry for her misfortunes. "It was remarked that the Duke typified all that is majestic in man" and the Queen "would have served as the exemplification of the same in woman." She poured out her woes to him, saying she was entirely at his mercy, "a poor outcast queen reduced to the condition of a chambermaid." He gave her fair words, but did not commit himself, saying only that in his dealings with Edward IV, he would have an eye to her interests, but would not do anything to her prejudice at the peace conference at Saint-Omer. Margaret thanked him, saying she blessed the hour she had set out to meet him.

She wept when he left Saint-Pol the next day, but soon afterward he sent her 2,000 gold crowns (£31,500) and a rich diamond, 100 crowns (£16,000) for Brézé, and 100 crowns each for her ladies. She declared that meeting with him "was the best exploit she had achieved since her reverse of fortune"; and she would tell the citizens of Bruges that she had found him "the best among the good and the gentlest," a man "of better sense than anyone on Earth."[7]

Philip had summoned his sister Agnes, Duchess of Bourbon, and her daughter Marie, who was married to Margaret's brother John of Calabria, to act as companions for her. There were great celebrations at Saint-Pol in honor of their coming, and a warm friendship flowered among the women. Margaret recounted in detail to the Duchess the sufferings she had endured and told her that no parallel to her adventures could be found in books. The Duchess listened with interest. "Why, Margaret," she declared, "I have never heard nor read of a noblewoman so blameless who has suffered so; a princess who, without having committed notorious crimes, has been reduced so low as not to possess a foot of land or a house, nor yet money of silver or copper, unless borrowed, to purchase the common necessities of life." If a book were to be written on the troubles of royal ladies, she added, Margaret would be found to excel them all in calamity.[8]

Henry had written from Bamburgh, urging Margaret to make new approaches to France, Burgundy, and Brittany, so that she could send him cannon and food and dispatch an army under Pembroke to Wales. But Margaret was in no position to help.

At five o'clock in the morning of 3 September, she said goodbye to the Duchess of Bourbon and left for Bruges, escorted by several lords and a force of Burgundian archers. At Bruges, she received a royal welcome and the people came running to see her, bearing gifts of wine. She was overjoyed to be reunited there with her son. Soon, the Count of Charolais arrived. At a banquet given in her honor, she indicated that he should use the finger bowl set before herself and the Prince. But he, following the example of his father, who always insisted on paying due reverence to crowned heads, absolutely refused, saying that the son of a duke ought not to wash with the son of a king. The Burgundian court, where great attention was paid to matters of etiquette, was abuzz with consternation in case some offense had been given, and messengers were even sent to the Duke to ask his advice on the question of precedence. He agreed that Charles had acted properly and preserved the honor of Burgundy.

In Bruges, Margaret met the chronicler Georges Chastellain and, at his request, sat with him and recounted her adventures, which he related in detail in his chronicle. He was fascinated by her, his imagination was stirred by her beauty and her misfortunes, and he was sad to see her "distraught with grief." She wept bitterly, "oft-times wringing her hands from excess of sorrow," making him cry himself. He was grieved to hear her say she had several times thought of killing herself, "but happily the fear of God, and His restraining grace, had preserved her from so deadly a sin."

Margaret's image features five times in Chastellain's chronicle. He portrayed her as "the most doleful and discomforted Queen of England." In his treatise, *The Temple of the Ruin of Certain Noble Unfortunates,* he showed her and himself passing the tomb of Boccaccio, with Margaret begging the great writer to awaken and write down an account of her calamities. He was portrayed as rising from the dead and—through fifty chapters—offering consolation by recounting to her the misfortunes of other princes, including her father and Charles VII, showing her "that there is nothing more propitious than, in true faith, to have recourse to God and to put all things in His hands."

Relieved that his unwanted guest was finally leaving Burgundy, Philip ordered his treasurer to send Margaret 12,000 crowns (£2:5 million). When the treasurer tried to extort some of the money, Margaret complained to the Duke, who ordered the man's execution, but it was thanks to her intervention that he was spared.[9]

Margaret traveled to Nancy to see her father, King René. Realizing the hopelessness of her cause and knowing it would be dangerous for her to return to Scotland, he persuaded her to remain in France for the present, assigned her 2,000 livres (£1,693,120) in rents, and lent her his castle of Koeur-la-Petite, which lay near Saint Michiel-en-Barin in the duchy of Bar, 150 miles east of Paris. There she was conducted by an escort provided by Burgundy. In the summer of 1467, someone—it is not known who—paid for Koeur to be refurbished and for sixteen large windows to be installed in its great hall. The exterior masonry was repaired and the moat stocked with fresh fish.

At Koeur, and later at Louppy-le-Château, Margaret set up a small court of exiles, which included Sir John Fortescue, Dr. John Morton, and George Ashby, her Clerk of the Signet, who dedicated to her son his poem "The Active Policy of Princes." René allocated her 6,000 crowns (£965,000) a year, but this did not cover her expenses and for most of her seven-year exile she lived on or near the breadline. "We beeth all in great poverty," reported Sir John Fortescue, "but yet the Queen sustaineth us in meat and drink, so as we be not in extreme necessity." Margaret's straitened circumstances impelled her to pay long visits to various relatives, including her brother John of Calabria, and her aunt the Dowager Queen Marie of France, at Amboise. Occasionally, she went to Paris to try to revive King Louis's interest in her cause, but in vain. She also attempted to enlist the support of the Emperor Frederick III, the King of Portugal, and Charles of Charolais, but met with no better success.

When Louis urged her to make suit against her sister, Yolande, for the right to succeed to their mother's estates, the two women quarreled bitterly, and Margaret left Louppy and took up residence at Angers.

All her hopes for the future rested on her ten-year-old son. She was now able to devote some time to his education, and appointed Fortescue his chief tutor. Fortescue wrote a treatise on the laws of England, *De Laudibus legum Angliae*, for the boy, and schooled him well, probably with the help of George Ashby. Edward flourished under his guidance and doubtless benefited from a more settled existence. His mother taught him courtesy and social skills, and he received the customary military training considered appropriate for a boy of his rank from the men of her household. He "applied himself wholly to feats of arms [and] practiced also sometimes with the pike and sometimes with the sword."[10]

Early in December 1463, King Edward's prolonged negotiations with the Scots bore fruit in the form of a truce, with James III undertaking not to give any further help to the Lancastrians. This caused the Scots no heart-searching, for they believed that Henry VI's cause was irrevocably lost. On 8 December, Henry left Scotland with his small court and again took up residence at Bamburgh Castle, where for the next few months he would rule what remained of his kingdom—the Northumbrian castles. Margaret frequently corresponded with him and strove to organize the delivery of arms and military supplies to Bamburgh. Meanwhile, Edward had put in place a coast guard to prevent her from invading England.

Increasingly, Somerset's frustration had mounted at Edward's failure to pay him the pension promised a year earlier. He may also have felt guilty about abandoning Henry VI. In December 1463, he deserted Edward and rode north to Newcastle, having sent ahead to instruct his men there to open the gates. In an inn near Durham, he was recognized and, being awakened in the dead of night by footsteps outside his room, was obliged to escape through the window wearing only his shirt and no shoes. The Yorkist garrison at Newcastle had already learned of his coming and put his retainers to flight, so he was therefore obliged to leave England and make his way to Margaret's court at Koeur, where he begged her forgiveness for his disloyalty. Glad to have him at her side once more, she readily made her peace with him.

Edward was bitterly wounded by Somerset's defection. In Wales, Pembroke was doing his best to rouse the people in support of Henry VI, and during the early months of 1464, the deposed King's supporters were very active in the North, stirring the commons to rebellion. Henry himself rode south as far as Lancashire to raise support, and soon his followers had sufficient strength to launch successful raids against the castles at Bywell, Langley, and Hexham. There were minor risings in support of Henry elsewhere, but Edward suppressed them all with ruthless thoroughness.

Margaret was trying to interest the Duke of Brittany in supporting the Lancastrian cause. Pembroke persuaded him to give ships and men for an invasion of Wales, and was allowed to gather a fleet at Saint-Malo, whence he sailed in March. But news of the suppression of the Lancastrian risings in England made him turn back, and the projected invasion was abandoned. Somerset had returned to England, but a brief, fierce battle on Hedgeley Moor, Northumberland, on 25 April saw his forces scattered by an army under Lord Montagu. Afterward, a fifteen-year truce between England and Scotland was agreed at York. Meanwhile, Somerset and his remaining companions had rejoined Henry VI in Tynedale, where they sat fast, planning their next strategy. Within three weeks, Somerset had regrouped his army and recruited more men. He marched south, determined to restore Henry VI, who was then staying at Bywell Castle. But Montagu, advancing to meet this new threat, had possibly as many as eight times more men.

The two armies came face-to-face on 15 May 1464 at Hexham, south of the River Tyne. When Montagu's men charged headlong into their ranks, Somerset's men panicked and fell into disarray. He himself was captured, and his army annihilated, effectively crushing Lancastrian resistance in the North for good. Immediately after the battle, in accordance with the King's wishes, Montagu ordered the executions of Somerset and other captured peers. The Duke was beheaded and his body interred in Hexham Abbey. He had never married, and left only a bastard son, Charles Somerset, who became the ancestor of the dukes of Beaufort.

After Hexham, Yorkist soldiers were sent to Bywell Castle to capture Henry VI, but a messenger bringing news of the Lancastrian defeat got there first. Henry made such a precipitate departure that he left behind his helmet, surmounted with a crown, his sword, his cap of estate, his armor, and other valuables. He remained a fugitive for over a year, hiding in safe houses in Lancashire, Yorkshire, and the Lake District, his only companion being his chamberlain, Sir Richard Tunstall.

In gratitude for his victories, Edward created Montagu Earl of Northumberland and granted him most of the ancestral lands of the Percies. Alnwick Castle fell to the Nevilles soon afterward and the capitulation of Dunstanburgh and Bamburgh followed in late May. The fall of Bamburgh deprived the Lancastrians of their last power base in the North. There now remained just one bastion of resistance, Harlech Castle in northwest Wales, which had been providing safe asylum for Lancastrian refugees since 1461. "This castle is so strong that men said that it was impossible to get it," wrote "Gregory." In the autumn of 1464, Edward IV charged Lord Herbert to take it for the Yorkists. He began a prolonged siege, but still the Lancastrians held out behind Harlech's forbidding walls, confident that Pembroke would come to their relief. But he was in the North of England, and would soon go abroad to canvass the support of the princes of Europe.

PART FOUR

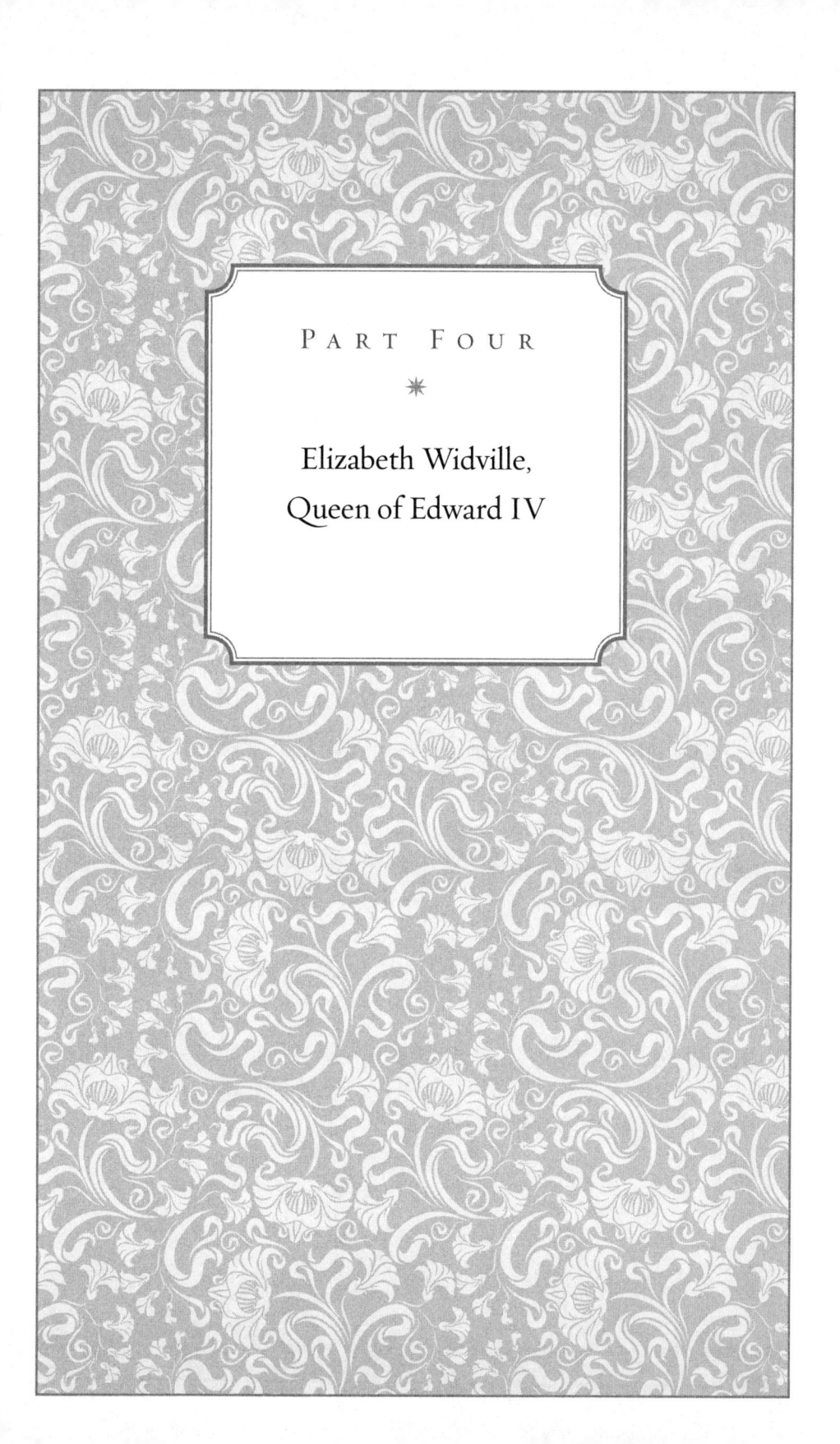

✶

Elizabeth Widville,
Queen of Edward IV

I

"Now take heed what love may do"

✳

By 1464, Edward's subjects were concerned that he had been "so long without any wife and afeared that he had not been chaste in his living." His lords had "moved him and exhorted him in God's name to marry and live under the law of God and church, [saying] they would send overseas to find a queen of good birth."[1] For almost a year now, Warwick had been negotiating with Louis XI for a marriage between the King and Bona of Savoy. Warwick believed that a firm alliance between England and France, sealed by a royal marriage, was the only way to prevent the slippery Louis from showing friendship toward the Lancastrians.

During the summer, Edward's envoy, Lord Wenlock, had visited Louis at Hesdin and been presented to a splendidly attired Bona, with whom he was very impressed. Louis offered Wenlock a huge reward if he could persuade Edward to agree to the marriage, and Warwick added his own pleas, wishing to preempt any prospect of an alliance with Burgundy, who had shown no inclination to honor and reward him as Louis had. Warwick was in thrall to Louis, who had flattered and beguiled him, calling him "cousin" and promising to make him a sovereign prince with his own European duchy. Warwick was due to go to Saint-Omer in October for another peace conference and hoped to conclude the marriage negotiations then.

Burgundy, naturally, did not favor such an alliance; he wanted Edward to join him in a defensive pact against France, which would also boost trade between the duchy and England. Edward was inclined to favor Burgundy, but he was currently striving to negotiate the lifting of Burgundian restrictions on English imports and was playing for time, knowing that his marriage was a powerful bargaining counter.

"Now take heed what love may do!" wrote "Gregory," "for love will not cast no fault nor peril in nothing." It rarely figured in the unions of kings. All was well between Edward and Warwick until 1464, when Edward married an impoverished Lancastrian widow, Elizabeth Widville, Lady Grey, who was twenty-seven, four years his senior. She was of medium height with a good figure, and very beautiful, having long gilt-blond hair and an alluring smile. But she was also a Lancastrian widow whose mother's first husband had been Henry V's brother John, Duke of Bedford, which firmly placed Elizabeth in the wrong camp as far as the Yorkists were concerned.

The Widvilles were said to have been descended from a Norman called William de Widville who married a Saxon woman called Emma. Their name is usually spelled Woodville now, but that is a rare form in contemporary documents; on Elizabeth's tomb, and on a receipt of 1491 signed by her, now in the National Archives, it is spelled Widville. This old-established Northamptonshire family had lived at Grafton since the twelfth century. In 1370, they had purchased the Mote, a house east of Maidstone, Kent, not far from Ightham Mote, where Elizabeth's great-aunt Joan Widville and her husband, Sir William Haute, now lived.

Elizabeth's grandfather Richard Widville, chamberlain to John, Duke of Bedford, distinguished himself fighting for Henry V in France, and his services were rewarded with lands, lucrative offices, a knighthood, and a seat on Henry VI's Council. His son, Sir Richard Widville, born around 1405 and said to be "the handsomest knight in England,"[2] was given his own command in France in 1429 and was also made chamberlain to Bedford.

In 1436, Sir Richard took the enormous liberty of secretly marrying Jacquetta of Luxembourg, Bedford's widow. Aged twenty and "an exceedingly handsome gentlewoman,"[3] she was the daughter of Peter, Count of Luxembourg (in Burgundy), Count of Saint-Pol (in France),

Church roof boss depicting Joan of Navarre

Joan's father, Charles II, "the Bad," King of Navarre

Joan of Navarre with her first husband, John IV, Duke of Brittany, and their children

Henry IV

Called Henry IV

The coronation of Joan of Navarre

Pevensey Castle, where Joan was imprisoned for witchcraft

Leeds Castle, owned by several medieval queens of England

Tomb of Henry IV and Joan of Navarre, Canterbury Cathedral

Tomb effigies of Charles VI, King of France, and his wife, Isabeau of Bavaria, parents of Katherine of Valois

Henry V

The marriage of Henry V and Katherine of Valois

The birth of Henry VI

Henry V, statue in York Minster
showing him with long hair

Bermondsey Abbey, where Katherine of Valois died

Katherine of Valois, funeral effigy, Westminster Abbey

The tomb of Katherine of Valois, Westminster Abbey

René of Anjou, father of Margaret of Anjou

Margaret of Anjou: medal by Pietro da Milano

Henry VI

The ruins of Titchfield Abbey, where Henry VI married Margaret of Anjou

The marriage of Henry VI and Margaret of Anjou

Margaret of Anjou: drawing of lost window in the Church of the Cordeliers, Angers

John Talbot, Earl of Shrewsbury, presenting the Talbot Shrewsbury Book to Henry VI and Margaret of Anjou

The prayer roll of Margaret of Anjou

The château of Amboise, where Margaret of Anjou was reconciled to Warwick, and Anne Neville married Edward of Lancaster

Margaret of Anjou, from the Roll of the Fraternity of Our Lady, of the Skinners Company of London

The marriage of Edward IV and Elizabeth Widville (Bibliothèque Nationale, Paris, MS. Français 85, folio 215)

Edward IV

Elizabeth Widville

Elizabeth Widville, from the guild book of the London Skinners' Fraternity, of the Assumption of the Virgin

Frontispiece of the Luton Guild Book showing the Holy Trinity, the founders of the Guild, and Edward IV and Elizabeth Widville

Edward IV and Elizabeth Widville, detail of the Royal Window in Canterbury Cathedral

Anne Neville and her two husbands, Edward of Lancaster, Prince of Wales, and Richard III

Edward of Middleham, Prince of Wales

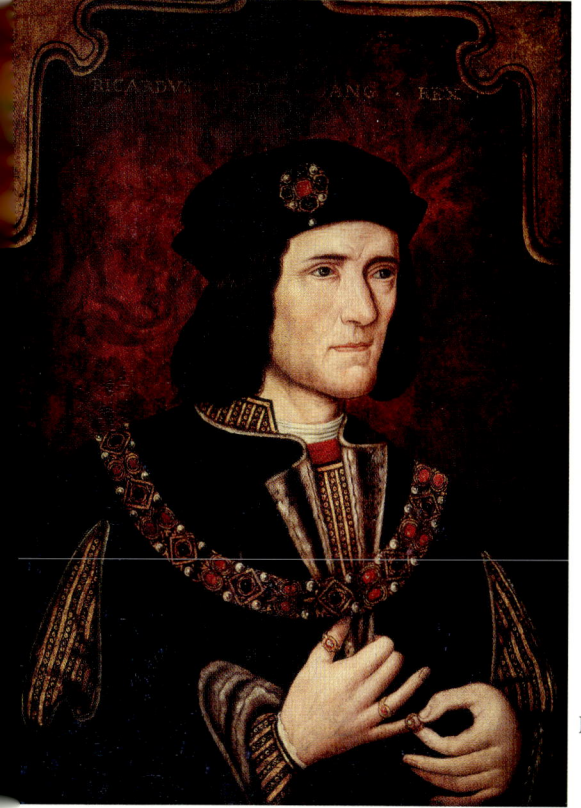

Anne Neville, Richard III, and their son, Edward of Middleham (from the Rous Roll, British Library, Additional MS. 48976 ff.62–65)

Richard III

Elizabeth of York

Henricus VII

Henry VII

The tomb of Edward IV and Elizabeth Widville in St George's Chapel, Windsor

and Constable of France. Peter was a descendant of Charlemagne; his family was said to be descended from Melusine, a water nymph or witch of the Rhine, from whom, legend had it, the Plantagenet dynasty was also descended.

In 1436, Jacquetta was a desirable rich widow, having inherited all her childless husband's estates. Her marriage to Sir Richard Widville caused a huge scandal. Her brother refused to have anything further to do with her, and (according to the chronicler Monstrelet) she and Widville "could never visit the continent or [he] would have slain them both." In England they were fined £1,000 (£927,330) for marrying without the King's consent, but Jacquetta still remained Duchess of Bedford and ranked as first lady in the realm until Margaret of Anjou married Henry VI in 1445. In 1448, Widville was created Baron Rivers.

He and Jacquetta were renowned as the handsomest couple in England. They had sixteen children, eight boys and eight girls. The date of Elizabeth's birth is often given as 1437, based on the date 1463 on a later portrait, which gives her age as twenty-six that year. But she would not have been painted as Queen in 1463, the year before she married Edward IV, while an earlier version of the portrait in Queens' College, Cambridge, is dated 1465, so the other inscription cannot be correct. She is unlikely to have been the eldest child, since her sister, also Jacquetta, was married by 1450. Given that the youngest age at which the Church permitted a wife to cohabit with her husband was twelve, the fact that a suitor was enamored of Elizabeth's "womanhood" (see below) in 1451, and she had her first son around 1455, Elizabeth was probably born around or before c.1439.

Under Henry VI, Lord Rivers allied himself with Suffolk and the Beauforts, and he also had connections with the influential Bourchier and Ferrers families. He and his eldest son, Anthony, were cultivated men of many talents and "very great valor."[4] To contemporaries, Rivers was the very mirror of Chaucer's "parfait, gentil knight"—brave, chivalrous, cultivated, elegant, charming, devout, and well educated, and his feats in the jousting lists were renowned. Deeply religious, he wore a hair shirt beneath his rich robes. He "was always considered a kind, serious and just man, and one tested by every vicissitude of life. Whatever his prosperity, he had injured nobody, though benefitting many."[5] He traveled in Italy and made pilgrimages to Rome and the shrine of St. James at Compostela, and it was his unfulfilled life's ambition to go on a crusade against the Infidel. Such was his reputation that Pope Sixtus IV appointed him Defender and Director of Papal Causes in England. Widville was also an able military commander and diplomat. Jacquetta was close to Margaret of Anjou, who gave her gifts of jewels; her sister Isabella had married Margaret's uncle Charles, Count of Maine.

Around 1451, Elizabeth acquired a suitor, Sir Hugh Johns, who served in the Duke of York's retinue. York himself informed her in a letter that "our right hearty and well-beloved knight, for the great womanhood and gentleness approved and known in your person, you his heart wholly have, whereof we are right well pleased." He hoped that she would look favorably upon Johns's suit, "wherein ye shall do not only to our pleasure, but (we doubt not) to your own great weal and worship in time to come; certifying that if ye fulfill our intent in this matter, we will and shall be to him and to you such a lord as shall be to your great profit and honor."[6]

Sir Hugh Johns was probably more than twenty years Elizabeth's senior. He had once gone crusading in Byzantium and been knighted in the Church of the Holy Sepulchre in Jerusalem; and he had served under the Duke of Somerset in France. Great lords like York did not expect their wishes to be flouted, but when Elizabeth discovered that Johns was poor, she turned him down. York tried to persuade her to change her mind, as did Warwick, but she refused.

Before January 1455, when her jointure was assigned, she married a well-born Lancastrian knight, Sir John Grey of Groby (pronounced Grooby). Born around 1432, John was heir to Sir Edward Grey, a younger son of Lord Grey de Ruthin, and Elizabeth, heiress of Reginald, Lord Ferrers of Groby, whose barony had passed to Sir Edward in 1445. Lord Grey gave the newlywed couple, in trust, the manors of Newbottle, Brington, and Woodham Ferrers, which provided an annual income of 100 marks (£69,170). Elizabeth went to live with John at the family seat, thirteenth-century Groby Manor (now called Groby Hall), near Leicester, which was originally built around a quadrangle near the mound of a ruinous castle; the brick frontage that survives today dates from the late fifteenth century. The couple may also have spent time at Bradgate Park, which was part of the manor of Groby, or at Astley Manor in north Warwickshire.

They had two sons, Thomas in *c.*1455 and Richard about a year later. When the Wars of the Roses broke out, Sir John Grey was given command of Henry VI's cavalry, but was killed in 1461, leading the last Lancastrian charge against the Yorkists at the Battle of Towton. Fortunately, he escaped attainder and his lands were not confiscated; his elder son inherited the manor of Bradgate in Leicestershire. But his widow was not left comfortably off. Elizabeth Widville should have received as dower the three manors granted by Lord Ferrers, but they were claimed by her mother-in-law, who was now married to Sir John Bourchier, son of the Earl of Essex, so an impoverished Elizabeth was obliged to return to live with her parents at Grafton. Nevertheless, she remained friendly with the Bourchiers, and several members of the family would later serve in her household.

On 13 April 1464, Elizabeth entered an agreement with her Leicestershire neighbor William, Lord Hastings, which provided for the marriage of her eldest son (or the younger, if he died) to Hastings's daughter, if one was born to him in the next five years; failing that, the bride would be a daughter of his sister Anne, who had married into the Ferrers family. Hastings, who was close to the King and highly influential, undertook to help Elizabeth recover her dower lands, and it was agreed that, if they succeeded, they would share the rents from them until Thomas Grey reached the age of twelve. Hastings was to pay Elizabeth 500 marks (£371,260) for the marriage, but if it did not take place, she was to pay him half that sum. The agreement was of mixed advantage to Elizabeth, but she may have felt it worth the financial risk to secure such a powerful ally. Yet soon she was to have no further need of financial help, for her claim was resolved on 26 May 1464, after two of the three trustees who administered the disputed manors ruled that the income should go to Elizabeth. And greater things were to come.

2

"Governed by lust"

✴

It is not known for certain when Edward IV first became attracted to Elizabeth Widville. According to Sir Thomas More, Elizabeth first met Edward in 1461 when she presented a petition to the Lord Chancellor for the restoration of her dower, although it is more likely that someone influential presented the petition on her behalf. Sir Thomas More also stated that Elizabeth waylaid Edward in Whittlebury Forest, Northamptonshire, kneeling with a child on either side beneath an oak tree, and begged to restore to her the lands her late husband had assigned her for her jointure. A big oak tree at Yardley Gobion is still known as the Queen's Oak, and the tale went that she made her appeal so enchantingly that Edward was overcome with desire for her "mournful beauty."[1] Hall placed the meeting in Wychwood Forest, Oxfordshire. This romantic tale is unsubstantiated by contemporary evidence, although Elizabeth had submitted a petition to Edward in May 1461, which chimes with the Milanese ambassador claiming in 1464 that the King had "long loved" her. He may have become enamored of her before he pardoned her father and brother after Towton, for Waurin claimed that Sir Richard Widville owed his pardon to the King's love for his daughter, in which case, Edward's interest could have been kindled while Sir John Grey was alive.

Whatever the circumstances, Edward "first fell in love with her beauty of person and charm of manner."[2] Elizabeth "found such grace in the

King's eyes that he not only favored her suit, but much fantasized her person. For she was a woman of such beauty and favor, with her sober demeanor, lovely looking and feminine smiling, neither too wanton nor too humble. Her tongue was so eloquent, and her wit was pregnant." She was "moderate of stature, well made and very wise." In no time at all, "she allured and made subject to her the heart of so great a king."[3]

Elizabeth was the first English queen of whom panel portraits survive, although they are all later copies of a lost original of *c.*1464 (possibly by John Stratford). These, and representations of her in stained glass, show a poised, elegant, blond woman with the shaven forehead fashionable at that time and facial features that would be considered striking in any age.

The most famous portrait of Elizabeth is the late-sixteenth/early-seventeenth-century wooden panel in Queens' College, Cambridge (Margaret of Anjou's foundation, which Elizabeth refounded). The college owns four other versions, one a three-quarter length painted by Thomas Hudson in 1766, and there are two in the Royal Collection (one dating from *c.*1513–30, but heavily overpainted, the other from the late sixteenth century) and others in the Ashmolean Museum, Dunham Massey, Minster House at Ripon, and several private collections.

Elizabeth appears with Edward IV and their children in the Great North Window ("the Royal Window") of Canterbury Cathedral, in the northwest transept, above the site of St. Thomas Becket's martyrdom. Crafted probably by the King's glazier William Neve around 1479–82, and gifted by Edward IV, it was badly damaged by the Puritans in 1642, and the faces of the King and Queen are the only surviving originals; they are almost certainly portraits, and Elizabeth's is striking in its beauty; the broom-cod device of the Widvilles features in the glass. She also appears in a set of windows depicting the royal family in St. Giles's Church, once part of Little Malvern Priory, Worcestershire. They were donated in 1480–2 by John Alcock, tutor to Edward V; those portraying Edward IV and Richard, Duke of York, are lost, and Elizabeth Widville's head is missing.

Small corbel heads flanking the gateway to Abingdon Abbey are thought to represent Edward and Elizabeth. They appear enthroned in a manuscript of Anthony Widville's *Dictes and Sayings of the Philosophers,* now in Lambeth Palace Library, in which Elizabeth is shown crowned with her fair hair loose. She is also depicted in a manuscript called *Chroniques de Angleterre*,[4] which shows her crowned with her hair falling to her knees, garbed in a gown of cloth of gold, ermine, and blue satin. An illuminated manuscript in Canterbury Cathedral Library shows Lord Rivers introducing Caxton to Edward IV, Elizabeth Widville, and their eldest son. She appears in the guild book of the Skinners' Company in London (of which she was a member), a manuscript in Liverpool Cathedral, and the Luton guild book of *c.*1472, now in private ownership.

For years, rumors about Edward's courtship persisted. According to one account, "after the King had well considered all the lineaments of her body and the wise and womanly demeanor that he saw in her," he urged Elizabeth to become his mistress. But she replied that "as she was unfitted for the honor to be his wife, then for her own honesty she was too good to be his concubine." Her refusal ignited such "a hot burning fire" in Edward that he resolved to marry her.[5] After pursuing so many women, he realized that none were of "such constant womanhood" and "stable mind" as Elizabeth.[6]

An Italian poet,[7] writing before 1468, gave more details, asserting that when Elizabeth refused to submit to Edward's advances, he threatened to rape her, whereupon she seized a dagger and tried to kill herself, crying that "she knew herself unworthy to be a queen, but valued her honor more than to be a concubine"—or, according to the Milanese ambassador, *she* threatened Edward with the dagger. Death, she cried, would be preferable to living in "eternal filth and squalor" when his "vain pleasures were soon over." Appalled, the King offered her marriage.

Mancini gave yet another version of the dagger story, stating that when Edward "placed a dagger at her throat to force her to submit to his passion, she remained unperturbed and determined to die rather than live unchastely with the King. Whereupon Edward coveted her much the more and judged the lady worthy to be a royal spouse who could not be overcome in her constancy, even by an infatuated king." When he realized "he could not corrupt her virtue by gifts or menaces," his lust deepened into love. Fabyan asserted that Duchess Jacquetta had cast a spell on the King.

Caspar Weinreich, the Danzig chronicler, claimed that the King fell in love with Elizabeth "when he dined with her frequently," which may be nearer the truth, while Polydore Vergil was probably correct in saying that Edward was led into wedlock "by blind affection and not by the rule of reason." John Hardyng too wrote that Edward had been "led rather by blind Cupid than by any reason." There can be no doubt that it was a love match. "Prompted by the ardor of youth and relying entirely on his own choice," Edward secretly married her "without consulting the nobles of the kingdom."[8]

The fact that Edward married Elizabeth in secret shows that he knew he was making an unsuitable match and throwing away the major political advantages to be obtained from taking a foreign princess to wife. He must have been aware that no king since the Norman Conquest of 1066 had married a commoner, and of course he knew that Warwick was negotiating a marriage with Bona of Savoy. But these things evidently counted for very little against his passion for Elizabeth. "Governed by lust,"[9] he took the impulsive decision to marry her and make her the first native-born queen of England since the Conquest.

The date of the wedding is often given as 1 May 1464, in accordance with Gregory's Chronicle and that once attributed to John Warkworth, but it does not fit comfortably with other evidence. Fabrian's account stated that in the spring, Edward was on his way north to suppress a rising in favor of Henry VI. On the way, he stayed at Stony Stratford, whence—on the pretext of going hunting—he rode to Lord Rivers's manor at Grafton. Here, early in the morning of 1 May, "in most secret manner," he married Elizabeth. The ceremony perhaps took place in the Hermitage, a chantry chapel of the Widvilles tucked away in the woods near the manor house; excavations on the site in 1964–5 uncovered the remains of a pillared cloister, the chapel itself, several other buildings, and tiles bearing the white rose of York and the Widville arms. (The Hermitage was demolished after the Dissolution of the Monasteries in the 1530s.) The only witnesses were the priest, the Duchess of Bedford, two gentlemen, and a young man who helped the priest to sing.[10] The priest was John Eborall, Vicar of Paulerspury, near Grafton. He was said to have been buried "before the altar at the church of the Minoresses at London Bridge."[11]

Afterward, Edward and his bride went to bed to consummate their marriage, "and so tarried there upon three or four hours."[12] A contemporary French chronicler, du Clercq, was one of several foreigners to imply that this was not the first time they had slept together, and Louis XI told the Milanese ambassador that Elizabeth had already borne Edward two children, although no English chronicler mentions that. Edward rode back to Stony Stratford, "as if he had been hunting, and then returned at night," when Elizabeth was again smuggled into his bedchamber by her mother. He stayed for four days and Elizabeth "nightly to his bed was brought, in so secret manner that almost none but her mother was of counsel. And so this marriage was a season kept secret."[13]

But was it? The date, 1 May, fits into Edward's itinerary, but almost certainly the wedding did not take place until around late August 1464. Not only did negotiations for Edward's marriage to Bona of Savoy continue throughout the summer, at his behest, but it is hardly likely that Elizabeth would have needed to secure Hastings as an ally in April if her marriage to the King had been imminent. Edward was away in the North from 7 May until late August. Absence may have made his heart grow fonder, and it is likely that the romance flowered on his return and that his decision to marry Elizabeth was an impulsive one, taken in the heat of the moment. It may be that accounts of the wedding are correct in essence, but misdated.

On 4 September, a great council of the magnates assembled at Reading. That week, Warwick put pressure on the King to conclude the marriage alliance with France, until he received "sure knowledge by the letters of his friends that the King had got him a wife privily, and he was so earnestly moved with it that he thought best that the King should be deposed from the crown as one not worthy of such a kingly office."[14]

On 14 September, with "a right merry" countenance,[15] Edward shocked his councillors, announcing that he was married already. The magnates were stunned, and horrified when they learned the identity of their new Queen. They could not hide their disapproval. Lord Wenlock informed the Burgundian ambassador that the King's announcement had been the cause of "great displeasure to many great lords, and especially to the larger part of all his Council, and greatly offended the people of England." The nobility took the marriage amiss because Edward "had with such immoderate haste promoted a person sprung from a comparatively humble lineage to share the throne with him."[16] "She was not his match, however good and fair she might be, and he must know well that she was no wife for a prince such as himself, for she was not the daughter of a duke or earl, but her mother had married a simple knight, so that though she was the child of a duchess and a niece of the Count of Saint-Pol, still she was no wife for a prince such as himself."[17]

In an age in which kings married foreign princesses for political advantage, marrying for love was regarded as akin to insanity, and choosing the widow of a man who had fought for the King's enemies was even worse. Most peers regarded the Widvilles as upstarts, and it was seen as scandalous that Edward had set aside every notion of duty and obligation to marry for love, and beneath him, into the bargain. It was not that long since he had abused Elizabeth's father for being too lowly in rank to presume to marry her mother. In choosing Elizabeth, he showed appalling political judgment and irresponsibility. He gained no financial or political advantage, and threw away any opportunity of making an important foreign alliance.

"The great part of the lords and the people in general" were shocked.[18] "Not only did he alienate the nobles," wrote Mancini, "but he offended most bitterly" his mother and brothers. The Duchess of York violently disapproved. She had never remarried, and carried herself as if she were a queen, styling herself in letters "the rightful inheritor's wife of the realm of England, the King's mother, Duchess of York." Until now, she could "rule the King as she pleases."[19] She was mortified therefore at having acquired a commoner as a daughter-in-law. Nineteen years later, Mancini claimed that she "fell into such a frenzy that she offered to submit to a public inquiry, asserting that Edward was not the offspring of her husband, but was conceived in adultery, and therefore in no wise worthy of the honor of kingship." It would be unwise to read too much into her words, as they were uttered in anger.

According to More, Cecily also objected to Edward marrying a widow, telling him that was reason enough "to refrain you from her marriage, since it is an unfitting thing, and a very blemish and higher disparagement to the sacred majesty of a prince, to be defouled with bigamy in his first marriage." Although Elizabeth's former husband was dead, remarriage carried some stigma in fifteenth-century society, even though the Church did not frown on it. As Caspar Weinreich understood it, "the coronation in England demands that a king should marry a virgin, legitimately born and not a widow—yet the King took this one against the will of all his lords." Clarence was in no doubt, declaring that his brother, "who ought to have married a virgin wife, had married a widow in violation of established custom."[20] No one had complained about Henry IV marrying a widow, but Joan of Navarre had been of royal birth.

Edward defended his wife to his mother, saying, "She is indeed a widow and hath children; and, by God's blessed Lady, I, who am but a bachelor, have some too, and so each has proof that neither of us is likely to be barren. Madame my mother, I pray you be content."[21]

As time passed, Cecily evidently thawed toward her daughter-in-law, to the extent of guiding her in the early years of her queenship.

According to Mancini, the King's brothers, Clarence and Gloucester, were "sorely displeased at the marriage," especially Clarence, the heir presumptive, who "vented his wrath more conspicuously by his bitter and public denunciation of Elizabeth's obscure family." Gloucester, "being better at concealing his thoughts," kept quiet. Some lords declared they "would not stoop to show regal honor in accordance with her exalted rank," and many members of the King's household were "bitterly offended" by his choice of bride. Die-hard Yorkists expressed anger that he had married a woman whose father, brother, and husband had fought for Henry VI. And Isabella of Castile, one of the princesses mooted as a bride for Edward, was greatly put out and declared she was "turned in her heart" against England for the unkindness of the King in refusing her and marrying "a widow of England."[22]

The person who was offended most by the marriage was Warwick. He rightly saw it as an affront to France—and to himself. He had been negotiating for a French bride, and now he had been made to look a fool. He and other magnates were furious that Edward had taken such a momentous step without consulting them and at having been presented with a fait accompli. Louis XI, on being informed of the marriage, expressed the hope that it would provoke Warwick to mount a rebellion against Edward.

But Warwick had no intention of overthrowing the King. He was Edward's chief counselor and the most powerful man in the realm. As soon as he found out what Edward had done, he had written to several of his friends abroad. One letter survives, to King Louis, informing him that

Warwick and Edward were on bad terms. But Louis soon heard that the rift had been patched over. However angry Warwick might have been, he still had hopes of concluding a treaty of friendship between Edward and Louis. He made his peace with the King and amity was restored, at least on the surface, although the friendship never recovered from the blow dealt it by Edward's marriage, which signaled Edward's determination to act independently of Warwick and form his own policies. It "kindled after much unkindness between the King and the Earl, and much heart burning was ever after between the Earl and the Queen's blood so long as he lived."[23]

If there was anger at court about the King's marriage, it was not manifested in East Anglia. On 22 September, Sir John Howard reported to Sir Richard Widville that he had been riding around the region to spread the news and "to feel how the people of the country were disposed; and in good faith, they are disposed in the best wise, and glad thereof; also I have been with many divers estates [ranks] to feel their hearts, and I found them all right well disposed, save one." He did not record the name of the dissenter.[24] Howard was sympathetic to the new Queen and at Christmas that year gave her a courser named Lyard Lewes.

On Michaelmas Day, 29 September, Elizabeth Widville was escorted into Reading Abbey by Clarence and Warwick and presented to the magnates and the people as their sovereign lady and Queen. The assembly knelt and honored her, and a week of celebrations followed.

3

"The Rivers run so high"

※

Edward and Elizabeth presided over what was described in 1466 by a Bohemian visitor, Gabriel Tetzel, as "the most splendid court that could be found in all Christendom." It presented "no other appearance than such as fully befits a most mighty kingdom filled with riches."[1] Court etiquette was highly formal and a strict code of courtesy prevailed. On state occasions, and at the Christmas and Easter courts, the King and Queen always appeared wearing their crowns.

In 1464, the rambling old Palace of Westminster was much in need of upgrading, and after his marriage, Edward set about creating new royal lodgings, including separate ranges of private apartments for himself and Elizabeth. The creation of a new "Queen's side," which was begun in 1464, may have come about because the King's mother was living at court and appropriate accommodation was needed for both ladies. Elizabeth used Joan of Navarre's tower for official business.

Mancini called her "an undistinguished woman promoted to exalted rank." Aware of what people thought of her, she was careful to emphasize her new royal status. She adopted as her device the gillyflower, a symbol of the Virgin Mary's purity and motherhood. In a pageant staged at Coventry in 1474, it was claimed that she was descended from the Magi.[2] She insisted on the most elaborate ceremonial whenever she appeared in public. Even her mother and her brother Anthony had to kneel when addressing her.

Sir Francis Bacon, writing in the early seventeenth century, had no doubt that Elizabeth was "a busy and negotiating woman." It was unwise to cross her or infringe her rights, as can be seen from a stiff letter she sent to Sir William Stonor (now in the National Archives):

> Whereas we understand, by report made unto us at this time, that you have taken upon you now of late to make mischief within our forest and chase of Barnwood and there, in contempt of us, uncourteously to hunt and slay our deer, to our great marvel and displeasure, we will you wit [know] that we intend to sue such remedy therein as shall accord with my lord's laws. In the mean season, we will that you spare of hunting within our said forest, as you will answer at your peril.

In December 1464, before he took his new Queen to Eltham for Christmas, Edward summoned his Council to Westminster to settle her dower, and granted her 4,000 marks (£2,970,090) yearly from confiscated Lancastrian estates, less than that granted to Margaret of Anjou. He also gave her the palaces of Sheen and Greenwich, and, in 1467, the ruinous Ormond Place, a London town house in Knightrider Street (now Giltspur Street) just beyond the City wall, near Smithfield, once the property of the earls of Ormond. It was demolished in the 1590s.

Like her husband, Elizabeth followed the lavish courtly fashions set by Burgundy, and the expenses of her chamber, wardrobe, and stable for the Christmas of 1464 alone totaled £400 (£456,940), yet she managed her dower well and her household was not as extravagantly wasteful as Margaret of Anjou's, being better administered. She lived within her means, her expenditure amounting to about half of Margaret's, while spending lavishly on clothes—£1,000 (£1,142,340) in one year, for example—and maintaining the magnificence expected of her.

Edward IV chose to advance his legion of in-laws by securing for them the best matches the aristocracy could offer. In a deliberate effort to counterbalance the power of the Nevilles, he built up the power of the Widvilles, bestowing on them titles and offices, "to the exaltation of the Queen and the displeasure of the whole realm."[3] Not since the aggrandizement of the relatives of Henry III's unpopular consort, Eleanor of

Provence, in the thirteenth century had the English court witnessed such large-scale promotion of a queen's relatives. Elizabeth's influence must have been instrumental in bringing about this remarkable advancement of her family.

While some nobles were eager to mate with the Widvilles, seeing such marriages as a means to advancement and royal favor, others—especially Warwick, who could hardly contain his "secret displeasure"[4]—were scandalized and resentful, for the Widvilles "were advanced beyond those who excelled them in breeding and wisdom."[5] They regarded the family as too low-born for such honors and influence, which was then considered the privilege of the nobility, not upwardly mobile parvenus.

Edward's policy led to the creation of a powerful new faction at court that quickly came to rival the influence of the Nevilles. Overnight, Lord Rivers found himself one of the most important men at court. His younger sons, Lionel and Edward, were respectively made Bishop of Salisbury and Lord High Admiral. The first of a succession of brilliant Widville marriage alliances was concluded in September 1464, when the Queen's sister Margaret was betrothed to Thomas, Lord Maltravers, son and heir of the Earl of Arundel. In January 1465, Elizabeth's nineteen-year-old brother, John, made—according to an outraged contemporary—a "diabolical marriage" with the Dowager Duchess of Norfolk, "a slip of a girl about eighty."[6] (In fact she was sixty-seven.)

Most of Elizabeth's sisters made brilliant marriages. Around February 1466, the King arranged for Katherine to marry eleven-year-old Henry Stafford, Duke of Buckingham. He had been six when Edward IV succeeded, but his loyalties, instilled by his mother, who had been a Beaufort, had remained with the House of Lancaster. In 1464, Elizabeth Widville was granted his wardship, which outraged this proud child who "loathed" the Widvilles.[7] He grew up in the Queen's household with his brother, Humphrey. She received £500 (£505,340) per annum from the King for their keep, and engaged a scholar to teach them grammar, installing him in a house in Smithfield. Buckingham was "forced" to marry Katherine Widville and despised his bride, "whom he scorned to wed on account of her humble origin."[8] Years later, he complained he had been disparaged by the union. But he had no choice in the matter.

The marriages of the Queen's other sisters followed. Anne married William, Viscount Bourchier, the King's cousin; Eleanor married Lord

Grey de Ruthin, whose father had recently been created Earl of Kent in place of the deceased Fauconberg; Mary married William, son and heir of Lord Herbert, the King bestowing upon the bridegroom the barony of Dunster, which Warwick himself had claimed as heir to the Montagus; Jacquetta married Lord Strange; and Martha married Sir John Bromley. The Queen's Haute cousins, the four sons of her great-aunt Joan Widville and Sir William Haute, were given minor court posts, and their sister Alice married Sir John Fogge, Treasurer of the Household.

Most nobles dared not risk the King's displeasure by refusing to allow the Widvilles to mate with their children; indeed, they were obliged to turn down other offers, which removed most of the eligible heirs to the peerage from the marriage market, and this angered Warwick because he had two daughters as yet unspoken for. Earlier in 1464, he had met with the King's brothers and proposed that they marry Isabel and Anne. But Edward had angrily forbidden it. It may have been to mollify Warwick that he promoted his brother George Neville to the archbishopric of York in September.

The Widvilles were actively hostile to the Nevilles, whose power over the King they resented. Warwick, in turn, was determined never to play a subordinate role to the Widvilles, while they were opposed to the French alliance he so desired and supported the King's attempts to forge a friendship with Burgundy. This led inevitably to a further rift between Edward and Warwick and created dangerous tensions at court.

At Whitsun 1466, Edward created his wife's father Earl Rivers, "to the honor of the Queen and the displeasure of the whole kingdom."[9] In March, he had appointed him Treasurer of England, thereby offending Warwick, whose uncle Walter Blount, Lord Mountjoy, had been asked to resign to make way for Rivers. It seemed unjust, for Blount had given diligent service. Matters were made worse in October 1466, when the Queen's eldest son, Thomas Grey, was married to Anne Holland, daughter of the Duke of Exeter by the King's sister Anne Plantagenet. This marriage infuriated Warwick more than any of the others, because the King had paid the Duchess of Exeter 4,000 marks (£2,627,760) to break a previous alliance between Anne Holland and Warwick's nephew. (Grey would be created Marquess of Dorset in 1475.) It seemed that the Queen had deliberately set out to slight Warwick.

Elizabeth further offended him when she placed his great-niece, Anne, daughter of Sir William Stonor by Anne Neville, the daughter of Lord Montagu, in a great household, possibly that of the King's sister Elizabeth of York, Duchess of Suffolk. The Stonors were unhappy about it and young Anne begged to be allowed to go home. Aware that Elizabeth was offended, her parents would not allow it. "Daughter," her mother wrote, "ye wot well ye are there as it pleased the Queen to put you." Anne could come home, "provided that my husband or I may have writing from the Queen with her own hand, or else he nor I neither dare nor will take upon us to receive you, seeing the Queen's displeasure afore."[10]

Elizabeth's high-handedness toward Warwick's connections helped to kindle "the spark of envy which, by continuance, grew to so great a blaze and flame of fire that it flamed not only through all England, but also into Flanders and France."[11]

The mass advancement of the Queen's family drew adverse comment everywhere. Not only the nobles complained, but also the common people, whose sense of fitness was outraged. Even Edward's court jester dared to joke, in his presence, that "the Rivers run so high that it is impossible to get through them!" Yet, as time passed, people would begin to realize the advantages of mating with the Widvilles. "Marry right nigh to the Queen's blood so that you can get your land again,"[12] Sir John Paston's mother urged in 1478.

Warwick could no longer consolidate the proposed French alliance with a marriage treaty, but Louis did not let that prevent him from continuing to negotiate with the Earl to bring their two countries closer together. Edward had recently made friendly approaches to Burgundy and Brittany, and Louis had no intention of letting these escalate into alliances. Warwick continued to put pressure on Edward to agree to what both he and Louis wanted, yet Edward refused to commit himself. In January 1465, he sent envoys to Duke Philip to inform him that Queen Elizabeth would be crowned on the Sunday before Pentecost and inviting him to send someone to represent him. Philip's son Charolais informed Edward that the Queen's coronation "would be attended by her kindred"[13] of the House of Luxembourg. Now that she was Queen, her mother's relatives had ceased ostracizing her.

In April, at Sheen, Elizabeth's brother Anthony—now Lord Scales by virtue of his marriage to Elizabeth, heiress to the barony—approached her, as he recalled, and spoke to her on his knees, his bonnet in his hand. Then her ladies tied around his thigh a collar of gold and pearls adorned with an enameled flower symbolizing chivalrous endeavor, and dropped into his bonnet a scroll of parchment tied with gold ribbon challenging him to a tournament in their honor. He turned to his sister and thanked her humbly for the honor she had done him, then took the parchment to the King, who gave permission for the tournament to take place the following October. This was typical of the chivalric conceits much beloved at court.

On 24 May, Elizabeth came from Eltham to Blackheath ahead of her state entry into London, wearing a tunic of gold and blue stripes beneath a blue satin ermine-trimmed surcoat with long sleeves encrusted with tiny pearls. On her head was a steeple headdress embroidered with fleurs-de-lis and encircled by a diadem of pearls, beneath which her gilt-blond hair hung loose to her knees. The authorities had outlaid 200 marks (£134,280) on decorations, and when Lord Mayor Thomas Cook and his brethren received the Queen at Shooter's Hill, they presented her with a gift of 1,000 marks (£671,390). They escorted her across London Bridge, which was newly repainted and festooned with decorations of colored and gilded paper and buckram, and so into the City, where forty-five loads of sand had been spread on the streets. There were pageants—one featuring St. Elizabeth, another a man dressed as St. Paul, a play on "Saint-Pol," in tribute to the Queen's maternal ancestry—and singing children. Six ballads (which do not survive) were illuminated for presentation to Elizabeth.

The city fathers accompanied her to the Tower, where she was to stay that night. Edward awaited her there, and that evening he created forty Knights of the Bath in her honor. Among them were the Duke of Buckingham, the Earl of Oxford, Lord Hastings, her brothers Richard and John Widville, and the Lord Mayor.

The next day, clad in white cloth of gold with her hair loose beneath a gold, bejeweled circlet, Elizabeth went in procession through London to Westminster, attended by the new Knights of the Bath, bishops, lords, and dignitaries. She rode in a horse litter slung between poles and drawn by six white ponies, the poles being carried by four noblemen on each side. Choristers and members of the Company of Parish Clerks and boy choristers sang to her as she passed.

The next day was Whitsunday, 26 May, Elizabeth's coronation day. She wore a coronal on her head, satin robes, and a purple surcoat and mantle trimmed with ermine and laden with many gold jewels and precious stones purchased by the King from foreign merchants for the crowning of "our most dear wife, the Queen." Walking beneath a canopy carried by the barons of the Cinque Ports, she went in procession to Westminster Abbey, escorted by the archbishops of Canterbury and York. Her train was borne by Anne Neville, Duchess of Buckingham, the King's aunt, and immediately behind came his sisters Elizabeth and Margaret, with Duchess Jacquetta, followed by twenty-seven peeresses and twelve ladies. The King's mother did not attend the coronation. Clarence led the cavalcade, ahead of the officers of state.

Elizabeth was crowned by Archbishop Bourchier. Her mother, standing by, reverently helped to support the heavy crown on her head. The Bishop of Rochester celebrated Mass. After the ceremony, the new Queen was borne to Westminster Hall in a litter drawn by two horses, a chestnut and a white. A London silkwoman had provided fabric for the litter and a pillion saddle, while a Florentine merchant had supplied cloth of gold.

At the coronation banquet that followed, the King sat at the high table with the Bishop of Rochester at his right hand and the young Duke of Buckingham at his left. Elizabeth sat apart and was served by the highest lords in the land. Edward had borrowed £20 (£20,660) from Sir John Howard for the plate she used. Fifty-one dishes were served; between courses, the hundred minstrels brought by various nobles joined forces with the King's minstrels to play for the Queen. The nobility and their ladies were present, as was Elizabeth's uncle, her mother's younger brother Jacques of Luxembourg, Seigneur de Richebourg, who had brought a retinue of a hundred persons to London, while Philip of Burgundy had sent representatives. To mark her coronation, Edward gave Elizabeth a golden goblet and basin costing £108 (£111,560) and two lengths of cloth of gold costing £80 (£82,630).

A great tournament was held on 27 May, in which the flower of Burgundian chivalry took part and Thomas, Lord Stanley, carried the honors of the day and won the prize, a ruby ring. Warwick was not present, having been sent with Lord Hastings on an embassy to Burgundy. Thanks to Edward's procrastination and determination to befriend Philip, the Earl's hopes of a French alliance were fading fast, and by the end of that year, England's relations with France would be very strained indeed.

Elizabeth confounded her critics and adapted to her role with grace and dignity, demonstrating that she could fulfill her royal duties as well as any born princess and use her influence in beneficial ways. She was pious and charitable; in 1471, the Provost of Eton left orders that her generosity be commemorated on his tomb. It was at Elizabeth's wish that the King founded a fraternity at Leadenhall in London; she herself planned to found a college near the Tower, but her plans never came to fruition.

The records of London's Mercers' and Merchant Adventurers' companies show that Elizabeth exercised considerable influence with the King, for on Lord Hastings's advice, they paid her to act as an intermediary for them with the King in a customs dispute, which she did successfully. She and her son Dorset interceded with Edward when the Merchant Adventurers were accused of false accounting. They knew that appealing to her—"in whom we trust in God to have help and comfort"—would secure favor from the King, at the instance of the Queen, even if it came at a substantial price. But Elizabeth was not just on the make. She understood the need for good relations between Crown and City, and she once soothed Edward's fury when fighting broke out between the Londoners and royal servants.

Elizabeth enjoyed the King's absolute trust, and by turning an unseeing eye to his many infidelities, she retained his respect and affection. She was very influential behind the scenes—and it was this that Warwick and others continued to resent, along with the power enjoyed by her kinsmen. The Queen was seen as grasping and interfering, and responsible for the promotion of her relations and their undue influence on Edward. The Duke of Milan was informed that, "since her coronation, she has brought things to such a pass that they have the entire government of this realm, to such an extent that the rest of the lords about the government were one with the Earl of Warwick, who has always been great, and deservedly so." Twenty years later, the Widvilles were still "detested by the nobles because they, who were ignoble or newly made, were advanced beyond those who excelled them in breeding and wisdom."[14] Yet they were not without virtues or political strengths, even if they were rapacious. They were loyal to Edward IV and served him well, and they did not dominate in his counsels to the exclusion of all others, for Warwick, Lord Hastings, and John Howard remained highly influential in Edward's inner circle of advisers.

4

"Very great division"

✳

SOME STILL CHERISHED HOPES OF A LANCASTRIAN RESTORAtion. Several of Henry VI's supporters had joined Queen Margaret at Koeur. Late in 1464, the Earl of Ormond had traveled to Portugal to see if King John II, a descendant of John of Gaunt, would be interested in helping Henry VI to regain his throne. Soon Ormond informed Margaret that John would be pleased to assist, but these proved to be empty words. King René's subjects in Bar constantly urged him to give more succor to his daughter, and ballads were written about her plight, but René was too impoverished himself to offer Margaret more than the 6,000 crowns (£965,000) a year he had already assigned to her.

She still had friends in England and had been gratified to hear from them of Warwick's displeasure at King Edward's marriage. Early in 1465, she again appealed to Louis for aid. "The Queen has written to the King here that she is advised that King Edward and the Earl of Warwick have come to very great division and war together. She begs the King here to be pleased to give her help, or at least allow her to receive assistance from the lords of this kingdom who are willing to afford this, and if he will not take any one of those course, she writes that she will take the best course that she can."[1]

"Look how proudly she writes!" commented Louis,[2] amused—or perhaps riled—at the imperious tone of her letter. But he would not help her; he even took Brézé from her, summoning him to do military service in the war against Burgundy. Margaret never saw Brézé again, for in 1465 he was killed fighting for Louis at the Battle of Montlhéry and she lost her finest champion.

By July 1465, Henry VI had spent a year moving from safe house to safe house in the North, relying on the loyalty of Lancastrian partisans for shelter and protection from the Yorkist agents who were looking for him. That month, he and Tunstall were guests of Sir Richard Tempest at Waddington Hall in Lancashire. Tempest considered himself honored to be able to shelter the man he regarded as his rightful sovereign, but because his brother John lived nearby and was not sympathetic to the Lancastrian cause, it was decided that the King's true identity should remain a secret—easily accomplished, for John Tempest had never seen the King. But another guest in the house, a Benedictine monk, recognized Henry and had no compunction about doing what he felt to be his duty. He informed John Tempest that his brother's guest was in fact the deposed King.

John rode with a handful of men to Waddington Hall, where he challenged Henry to reveal his true identity. A brief but violent struggle followed in which Tunstall broke John Tempest's arm. He then grabbed Henry by the hand and made for nearby Clitheroe Forest. But John's men overtook them. They were caught as they were attempting to ford the River Ribble near Bungerly Hippingstones.

Edward IV was on pilgrimage with the Queen to the shrine of St. Thomas Becket at Canterbury when he was informed of Henry's capture. He had the news proclaimed and ordered that a service of thanksgiving be held in the cathedral.

Henry was brought south under guard to Islington, and there delivered to Warwick, who was waiting to escort him into London. On 24 July, the deposed King rode into the capital on a small horse, without spurs, with his legs ignominiously bound with leather thongs to his stirrups, a rope round his body lashing him to the saddle, and a straw hat on his head. In Cheapside, Cornhill, and Newgate, crowds gathered to see him, shouting derisory remarks and pelting him with rubbish and stones. One called Queen Margaret a ribald creature, shameless with her body. At length, the mournful procession arrived at the Tower, where Henry was confined.

Loyal Yorkists were appointed his jailers and allocated £3 (£3,100) a week for his maintenance. Lancastrian chroniclers alleged that he was not well treated during his imprisonment, but although he may not have been kept very clean, his keepers were fairly accommodating, for the King had ordered them to treat him with humanity and respect: Henry was allowed the services of a chaplain who came to say the holy offices each day for him, and permitted to receive visitors. Edward even sent him wine from his own cellar. Henry spent much of his time reading or at prayer, but there were occasions when the reality of his defeat and imprisonment hit him, and he would gasp with shame or burst into tears and lament his lot, asking what sin he had committed to deserve to be locked up. Otherwise, he bore his confinement with fortitude and patience.

The news of her husband's capture reached Margaret in August. It came as a terrible blow that wrecked her hopes of a Lancastrian restoration, for even if she persuaded France or Burgundy to finance an invasion force, Edward was holding Henry hostage for her good behavior in a virtually impregnable prison, and she could not risk his life.

On 28 September 1465, George Neville was enthroned as Archbishop in York Minster, and there was a lavish feast afterward at Cawood Castle, his episcopal residence in Yorkshire. The Nevilles were out in force, among them Warwick's daughters Isabel and Anne; Richard, Duke of Gloucester, now nearly thirteen, sat with them at the feast. But the failure of the King and Queen to attend the ceremony gave rise to speculation about deteriorating relations between Edward and Warwick. "The rift between them grew greater and greater."[3] The chief reason for Warwick's alienation was not so much the Widville marriage as disagreement over foreign policy. He still had high hopes for King Louis, but Edward was unwavering in his determination to befriend Burgundy, and constantly thwarted Warwick's ambitions. Early in 1466, Philip's ambassadors arrived to discuss a marriage between Edward's sister Margaret and Charles, Count of Charolais.

In January 1466, Elizabeth Widville retired to her chamber at Westminster to await the birth of her first child. Archbishop Bourchier and nine other bishops were summoned to the Palace of Westminster, to be ready and waiting to baptize the infant as soon as it was born.

The birth of a son and heir to assure the continuance and future prosperity of his dynasty was of paramount importance to Edward IV. His physicians had assured him that "the Queen was conceived with a prince, and especially one named Master Dominic [Sirego], by whose counsel great provision was ordained for the christening of the said Prince." Prior to the seventeenth century, custom forbade male physicians to attend pregnant women unless there was an emergency, but Dr. Sirego was determined to "be the first that should bring tidings to the King of the birth of the Prince," for messengers bringing such glad tidings often received "great thanks and reward." Midwives delivered babies, and only women were allowed into the birth chamber, but when the Queen went into labor on 11 February, Dr. Sirego managed to gain entry to the antechamber to the room where she travailed. Hearing a baby cry, he called out, asking "what the Queen had," at which one of her ladies called back, "Whatsoever the Queen's Grace hath here within, sure it is that a fool standeth there without!" The baby was a girl, and the doctor made a hasty departure, avoiding seeing the King.[4]

Edward rewarded his wife with a jewel costing £125 (£126,330) to mark the birth of "our most dear daughter," who was baptized Elizabeth by her kinsman George Neville, Archbishop of York, "with most solemnity" in a new font set up in St. Stephen's Chapel in Westminster Palace, just as if she had been the desired prince. By tradition, the King and Queen did not attend the christening, but Edward made it the occasion for a show of solidarity, even though the players were privately at odds or disapproved of his marriage. The Princess's sponsors were her grandmothers, the duchesses of York and Bedford, and Warwick. Walter Blount, Lord Mountjoy, Treasurer of England, received 1,000 marks (£656,940) for his diligence at the baptism, then was promptly told to resign his office to the Queen's father, Lord Rivers.

The Princess was assigned a stately household under the charge of a lady mistress, or governess, Margaret, Lady Berners, who received a salary of £100 (£101,070). Under her were a nurse, a wet nurse—for queens did not suckle their children—pages of the chamber, and rockers to lull the Princess to sleep in her cradle.

In late March, Elizabeth was churched at a magnificent service in

Westminster Abbey. "The Queen left her childbed that morning and went to church in stately order, accompanied by many priests [going ahead] bearing relics and by many scholars singing and carrying lights. There followed a great company of ladies and maidens, then came a great company of trumpeters, pipers and players of stringed instruments. The King's choir followed, forty-two of them, who sang excellently. Then came twenty-four heralds and pursuivants, followed by sixty earls and knights. At last came the Queen, escorted by two dukes. Above her was a canopy. Behind her were her mother and maidens and ladies to the number of sixty. Then the Queen heard the singing of an office."

After the service of purification that marked her return to society after her confinement, "she returned to the palace in procession, as before. Then all who had joined the procession remained to dine." Custom decreed that it was not proper for the King to attend his wife's churching, but so many guests were present that they "filled four great rooms" of an "unbelievably costly apartment" hung with colorful tapestries.

Elizabeth might have been deemed an unsuitable bride for the King, but she was determined that no one should remember it, and the etiquette that surrounded her on this occasion was rigorous. "The Queen sat alone at table on a costly golden chair. The Queen's mother and the King's sister [Anne, Duchess of Exeter] had to stand some distance away. When the Queen spoke with [them], they knelt down before her until she had drunk water. Not until the first dish was set before the Queen could [they] be seated. The ladies and maidens and all who served the Queen at table were of noble birth, and had to kneel so long as the Queen was eating; the meal lasted for three hours. The food served to the Queen, the Queen's mother, the King's sister and others was most costly. Everyone was silent and not a word was spoken." Afterward, doubtless to everyone's relief, there was dancing, with the ladies curtseying elegantly to the silent Queen.

This account of the day was written by Gabriel Tetzel, a chronicler in the train of Leo, Lord of Rozmital, the Queen of Bohemia's brother, one of the guests. Rozmital dined at the King's table with Warwick, who was representing his sovereign. Rozmital's attendants, including Tetzel, were allowed to stand in the corner of the Queen's room and watch her eat. "The courtly reverence paid to the Queen was such as I have never seen elsewhere."

To foreign visitors, Warwick appeared as powerful as ever. They were amazed at his wealth and influence, and even more at his lavish, now legendary hospitality. Acting as host to the Lord of Rozmital and his suite, he served them a banquet with sixty courses. On 15 April, on Edward's orders, he was in Calais to meet Charolais and discuss the proposed Burgundian alliance. The meeting was hardly a success, for Warwick did not hide his hostility to the plan and made it clear that he was determined to conclude an alliance with France, come what may.

Soon afterward Warwick and Louis met at Calais and signed a two-year truce, under which Louis again promised not to support Margaret, and Edward undertook not to help Burgundy or Brittany against the French. Louis also agreed to find a French husband for Margaret of York and provide her with a dowry. Edward had sanctioned the truce as a sop to Warwick but had no intention of keeping to its terms and, indeed, broke them shortly afterward by sending a safe-conduct to the Duke of Brittany's envoys, enabling them to come to England. Edward was determined to assert his own authority in this matter: the English might resent Burgundy, but they loathed the French, having never forgiven or forgotten the humiliations they had suffered at their hands at the end of the Hundred Years War. In October 1466, Edward and Philip of Burgundy agreed to sign a secret treaty of friendship.

Anticipating that an Anglo-Burgundian alliance was imminent, Queen Margaret guessed how disillusioned and frustrated Warwick was feeling. She knew that Louis too had wanted friendship with the English. If the Earl could be persuaded to abandon his Yorkist affinities and throw in his lot with the Lancastrians, Louis might consider funding a Lancastrian invasion of England. He had great respect for Warwick, who was the one man who might make a success of the venture.

Swallowing her pride, for Warwick had been one of her greatest enemies, Margaret sent a messenger secretly into England to sound him out. But near Harlech, he was apprehended by Herbert's men, who searched him and found Margaret's letter. He was sent to London under armed escort, where, under torture, he revealed that she had indeed sought a rapprochement with Warwick. Edward himself questioned Warwick about it, but the Earl denied that he had ever had any dealings with "the foreign woman."

Margaret's hopes were disappointed, but she knew it would not be long now before her son was old enough to take up the banner of Lancaster on his own behalf; he was eager to do so, having recently recovered from an illness so serious that his mother had gone on a pilgrimage to the shrine of St. Nicholas at Nancy to render thanks for his restoration to health.

Prince Edward had grown up surrounded by intrigue and the horrors of war, and he had been exposed to Margaret's passions and prejudices from an early age; thus was his character shaped. The Milanese ambassador in France reported that the boy, "though only thirteen years of age, talks of nothing else but cutting off heads or making war, as if he had everything in his hands or was the god of battle."

In the eighteenth century, the Abbé Prévost claimed that in 1467, Margaret visited England in secret, disguised as a priest in the train of a great churchman and peer of France, Antoine du Bec-Crespin, Archbishop of Narbonne, Brézé's brother-in-law, and that she approached one of Henry's keepers in the Tower and prevailed on him to arrange a meeting between them. William of Worcester reported that several members of the embassy were apprehended for carrying letters from Margaret, but it seems highly unlikely that she would have run the risk of coming to England, where she could have been condemned as a traitor.

5

"Secret displeasure"

✶

EARLY IN 1467, THWARTED OF VARIOUS MARRIAGE ALLIANCES he had been considering for his daughters, Warwick began seriously to pursue the plan that would outshine them all. Isabel would marry Clarence, and Anne, Gloucester. According to Strickland, a Flemish chronicler, Majerres, claimed that, when Gloucester was growing up in Warwick's household, he nurtured a strong affection for Anne. In August 1469, when Anne was thirteen, the Milanese ambassador in London heard an unfounded rumor that they were actually married.

Burgundy had offered Clarence the hand of his granddaughter, Charolais's heiress, Mary, but Edward IV was not enthusiastic because Mary would one day inherit Burgundy and her husband would become its sovereign duke. Edward did not want Clarence gaining such power on the Continent, nor did he want him embroiled in European politics, fearing that it would bode ill for England. Edward did not trust him.

George Plantagenet, Duke of Clarence, was now seventeen, a tall, blond, handsome youth who carried himself like the king he wished to be. Witty and charming when he chose, he was unstable, impressionable, changeable, and easily led. His jealousy of his brother had long been apparent and was now eating at him, for he was intensely ambitious. Although he had been generously endowed by Edward with lands, chiefly in the West Country, and had a great household of his own staffed by 300 servants and maintained at a cost of £4,000 (£4,042,700) a year, he was dissatisfied, for it was power he craved, and Edward had so far denied him that, being aware of his weaknesses.

When Warwick put it to him that he should marry Isabel, Clarence was quick to realize the benefits of such a union. But he was unable to keep the plan a secret, as Warwick had enjoined, and word of the matter soon reached the King, causing him to be greatly perturbed. He did not want his brothers allied to Warwick, who had more than enough power as it was without extending his influence through marriage with the royal house. Besides, Edward saw this as a plot to counterbalance the power of the Widvilles. He did not want his brothers squabbling over the Neville girls' inheritance in the event of Warwick's death. Even though these marriages would bring that inheritance to the House of York, Warwick might intrigue against Edward to make one of his daughters queen, or incite his brothers to treason.

Edward summoned Clarence and Gloucester and demanded to know the truth. Clarence said he knew nothing about such a marriage, although he thought it would not be a bad match. At this, the King angrily sent them from his presence, firmly forbidding Clarence to contemplate a union with Isabel. Consequently, there was "secret displeasure" between Edward and Warwick, and the King suspected that the Earl and Clarence might defy him and go ahead with the marriage anyway. He therefore instructed his agents in Rome to do all in their power to prevent the Pope from issuing a dispensation, which was necessary as the parties were within the forbidden degrees of consanguinity.

Years of stress had taken their toll on Margaret. Over the years, she had made many bargains with God and innumerable vows to the Church, which she now lacked the energy to keep, for her health was not good. In 1467, at her petition, an understanding Pope Paul II gave her permission to choose a priest to grant her absolution, as she had been "constrained by many sufferings and tribulations" and it was impossible for her to fulfill her vows "on account of her weak health; for example, the observance of which vows very often involves fasting four or five times a week and several pilgrimages to divers places unsafe for her without manifest bodily peril, wherefore because she is deprived of her movable goods, she cannot conveniently fulfill." Instead of fasting and going on pilgrimage, she was to "commute into other works of piety all her vows, past and future, which she is unable conveniently to observe."[1]

In June 1467, Philip of Burgundy's natural son, Antoine, Bastard of Burgundy, arrived in England, ostensibly to meet Anthony Widville, Lord Scales, in the lists, both being renowned throughout Europe as unparalleled jousters. But he really came to discuss the proposed Anglo-Burgundian alliance and the proposed marriage between Charolais and Margaret of York. "If this takes place," commented the Milanese ambassador in France, "they [the French] have talked of treating with the Earl of Warwick to restore King Henry in England, and the ambassador of the old Queen of England is already here."

An English alliance with Burgundy would have released Louis from his undertaking not to aid the Lancastrians, and he was aware that a Lancastrian invasion would prevent Edward from joining Burgundy in a war against France. He was still toying with the idea of approaching Warwick when, in February 1467, Margaret of Anjou's brother, John of Calabria, begged him not to do so, saying that Warwick had always been her enemy and the cause of Henry VI's fall from power. "His Majesty would do better to help his sister to recover her kingdom than to favor the Earl of Warwick." Louis asked what security the Lancastrians could give: would they offer the Prince as hostage? But neither Calabria nor Margaret was prepared to agree to such terms.[2]

Louis ignored Calabria's advice and went on scheming to bring Warwick and Margaret together. The major obstacle to a rapprochement would be persuading both parties to be reconciled. Margaret had regretted her earlier abortive approach to Warwick because she could not suppress her bitterness toward him or forget that he was her husband's archenemy and a traitor of the worst kind. Warwick, in turn, held Margaret responsible for the deaths of his father, brother, uncle, and cousin. It was not going to be easy for Louis to bring them together, especially since Margaret was now declaring that she wanted nothing to do with Warwick. Louis, however, was not a man to give up easily.

* * *

On 3 June, Archbishop Neville, the Lord Chancellor, pleaded illness and did not appear in Parliament. The "illness" seems to have stemmed from his displeasure at the warm welcome and lavish entertainments laid on for the Bastard of Burgundy. Edward did not trust George Neville, and with good reason, for he had just discovered that the Archbishop—without asking his permission, as was customary—was putting pressure on the Pope to grant a dispensation for his niece Isabel to marry Clarence—and bestow a cardinal's hat on himself.

A week later, the ailing Philip of Burgundy died, and was succeeded by his son, who became known as Charles the Bold. Thanks to Edward's diplomacy, the terms of his proposed alliance with Burgundy were so advantageous to England that even Warwick had no choice but to agree to it. Privately, he was still calculating how best to sabotage the alliance and persuade Edward to turn to Louis instead for friendship. That June, he met with the French King at Rouen to discuss this, but on his return, he found that his brother had been dismissed from the chancellorship and replaced with Robert Stillington, Bishop of Bath and Wells. It was as if Edward, who was now cold in his manner toward Warwick and his family, was demonstrating to the Nevilles that he was capable of curbing their power and ambitions.

Warwick burned with resentment. He "took on as many knights, squires and gentlemen as he could to swell his forces, [while] the King did all he could to reduce the Earl's power. They never again found pleasure in each other's company."[3] Once, when Warwick saw the King at Westminster and asked if he would receive Louis's envoys to discuss an alliance, Edward refused to acknowledge his presence and Warwick stalked out, furious. The next day he brought the French ambassadors before the King, the Queen and her relatives being present. Again, Edward ignored Warwick, greatly offending the Frenchmen. As they left with him in his barge, Warwick cried, "Have you not seen what traitors there are about the King's person?" One of the envoys tried to calm him down, but Warwick retorted, "Know that those very traitors were the men that had my brother displaced from the office of Chancellor!" It was plain to him that the Widvilles now had the upper hand and that Edward sided with them against him. Croyland states that he had continued to show himself friendly to the Queen and her kindred until he found that, contrary to his wishes, they were using their utmost endeavors to promote the Burgundian alliance, which was concluded in November that year. Desired not only by the King and the Widvilles, but also by the London merchants who would profit by it, the treaty was made in the interests of the nation's prosperity and appealed to patriotic sentiment, which was against friendship with France.

Warwick felt he now had no choice but to throw in his lot with Louis. He was not prepared to play a subordinate role to the Widvilles, and from now on would rarely attend the court if the Queen's kindred were present.

On 11 August 1467, at Windsor Castle, Elizabeth bore another daughter, Mary, who had fair hair and blue eyes. Elizabeth's mother, the Duchess of Bedford, had come to court to assist at the lying-in. The new baby was baptized at Westminster in the presence of the French ambassador, Archbishop Bourchier being one of the sponsors.

Elizabeth was granted £400 (£384,590) annually for the expenses of her two daughters until they married, and in October, Mary was sent to Greenwich Palace to be brought up with her sister Elizabeth under the care of Lady Berners. Elizabeth designated Sheen Palace as a nursery for her children. Nearby was the Carthusian priory known as the Charterhouse, which had been founded by Henry V and was well patronized by royalty; Elizabeth had Papal permission to visit and was now its patron. In 1472, she and Edward would there be granted a share in the universal pardoning of the sins of all who had donated money for its buildings to be restored.

The King kept Christmas at Coventry, where it was noted that, "for six days, the Duke of Clarence behaved in a friendly way."[4] Soon after Epiphany, Archbishop Neville persuaded Warwick to attend a council at Coventry, where he and the King were ostensibly reconciled.[5] But nothing had changed. In February 1468, Edward and Charles signed the treaty providing for the latter's marriage to Margaret of York. It dashed the hopes of Louis XI and Warwick, and Warwick resolved to undermine it. He urged Edward to abandon Burgundy, and when Edward made it clear that was out of the question, he sent his retainers to incite the London merchants, warning them that they would not profit from the alliance.

Many believed his propaganda; some planned an attack on Flemish merchants living in Southwark, but the authorities prevented them, narrowly averting a bloodbath. Undeterred, in the spring, Edward IV concluded an alliance with Brittany, another thorn in Louis's side.

In the reign of Henry VIII, it was alleged that in February 1468, Elizabeth Widville had stolen Edward IV's signet ring and given the order for the execution of Thomas FitzGerald, Earl of Desmond, the King's Lieutenant in Ireland. This was in revenge for his making disparaging remarks to Edward IV about his choice of bride and telling him he should have wed a foreign princess. It was also asserted that Elizabeth persuaded Edward to appoint the infamous John Tiptoft, Earl of Worcester, "the Butcher of England," as lieutenant in Desmond's place, as Tiptoft had promised to avenge the slight. On 14 February 1468, Worcester had Desmond executed at Drogheda. In fact, Desmond had been attainted for treason in a Parliament held at Drogheda, for championing the Irish against the Crown's unpopular policies and exactions, although it has been suggested that the charges were trumped up by Worcester.

But Worcester was said to have exceeded his brief by murdering two of the Earl's young sons, a deed attested to in the Register of the Mayors of Dublin: "This year, the Earl of Desmond and his two sons were executed by the Earl of Worcester at Drogheda," with the younger asking the executioner to take care as he had a boil on his neck.[6] The names of five of Desmond's sons are known, but none can be identified with the sons who were supposedly executed.

The Queen's role in the affair was first publicly referred to in a petition supposedly submitted in 1538 by James FitzJohn, Desmond's grandson, to the Privy Council. The text appears in the Calendar of Carew Manuscripts, yet no source is given for it and the original cannot be traced today, which has led some to suggest that it was a fabrication. A corroborating account appears in the Book of Howth, also dating from the Tudor period, but there are obvious errors in it. Given the unreliable evidence, the Tudor accounts should be discounted.

6

"A most deadly hatred"

✴

LANCASTRIAN PARTISANS WERE STILL WORKING SECRETLY TO restore Henry VI, despite the harsh penalties lying in wait for those who were caught. At Whitsuntide, "a certain Cornelius, a shoemaker serving Robert Whittingham, who was with Queen Margaret, was captured secretly bringing divers letters into England from Queen Margaret's party, [and] was tortured until he confessed. He then accused many of the receipt of letters from Queen Margaret."[1] Another Lancastrian agent, one Hawkins, was also tortured. The two men were then tried by Chief Justice Markham, a just and fair man who refused to admit the Crown's evidence as it had been obtained under torture. Lord Rivers suggested to the King that Markham be removed from his office, to which Edward agreed. The unfortunate Cornelius was again put to the question, having his flesh torn from his body with red-hot pincers, but died without having disclosed any further names of those with whom Margaret had corresponded.

The government was hunting down anyone suspected of being a Lancastrian adherent, and many arrests were made. Several lords whose families had supported Henry VI came under suspicion, and the Earl of Devon's brother, Henry Courtenay, was apprehended, along with Thomas, son of Lord Hungerford, and John de Vere, Earl of Oxford. All were suspected of organizing a new conspiracy to restore Henry VI, but as there was very little evidence, Oxford was released, although the rest were detained.

The year 1468 witnessed the fall of Alderman Sir Thomas Cook, which illustrated just how powerful the Widvilles had become. Cook was a rich London merchant and former Lord Mayor, an articulate, clever man who was respected by his colleagues and favored by the King. The Widvilles suspected him of harboring Lancastrian sympathies, for the agent Hawkins had spoken his name under torture, claiming he had tried to borrow money on Margaret's behalf from him. Cook had refused, but that did not save him from the Widvilles' displeasure or the trap they set for him.

In Cook's house hung a beautiful tapestry depicting the siege of Jerusalem, much admired by the Duchess of Bedford, who demanded that Cook sell it to her at a price far less than the £800 (£735,800) he had paid for it. He declined, and the Widvilles retaliated by accusing him of secretly working for the Lancastrians, reiterating what Hawkins had said. Rivers sent men to sack Cook's houses in London and the country and seize his goods, including the tapestry. Then, as Constable of England, he convicted Cook of misprision of treason for not having disclosed his dealings with Margaret's agent, and the Council agreed that he should be fined the huge sum of £8,000 (£7,358,010), which impoverished him. Elizabeth Widville claimed an ancient privilege called Queen's Gold, which entitled her to claim a further 800 marks (£478,270) from the convicted man's estate. No payment of Queen's Gold is recorded, but Cook was obliged to give "many good gifts" to Elizabeth's lawyer before she would remit the fine.[2] After this harsh treatment, he did defect to the Lancastrians and, far from being ruined, he "builded and purchased as he did before."[3]

On 3 July 1468, Margaret of York was married to Charles the Bold at Damme in Flanders. "At this marriage the Earl of Warwick conceived great indignation, it being much against his will that the views of Burgundy should in any way be promoted by means of an alliance with England. The fact is that he pursued that man [Burgundy] with a most deadly hatred."[4] Five days after the wedding, Edmund Beaufort, brother of the late Duke and self-styled Duke of Somerset, who had been a fugitive in Bruges, left the city before the new Duchess of Burgundy arrived and traveled to Queen Margaret at Bar.

Warwick could not conceal his anger at the marriage, which "was really the cause of the dissensions between the King and the Earl, and not the marriage of the King with Queen Elizabeth. Indeed, it is the fact that the Earl continued to show favor to all the Queen's kindred, until he found that her relatives and connections, contrary to his wishes, were using their utmost endeavors to promote the other marriage and were favoring other designs to which he was strongly opposed."[5]

Louis XI, meanwhile, was determined to undermine Edward's new alliance by aiding the Lancastrians, and had provided Pembroke with money, ships, and men. He took Margaret under his wing and welcomed her supporters to his court, and both he and she alerted her friends in England to be ready to fight for her. In October, Louis would declare that he meant "to help the old Queen of England and favor her in that enterprise as much as possible."[6]

Early in July, Pembroke landed in Wales, near Harlech, and marched east, inciting rebellion against the Yorkists. Lord Herbert retaliated by launching a new onslaught on Harlech Castle, which he had been besieging for four years without success. Pembroke, meanwhile, was sweeping all before him and holding many sessions of assizes, all in Henry VI's name. News of his astonishing success spread rapidly to France, and Margaret resolved to go to Paris to ask Louis to send reinforcements to aid him. Her elation was premature. On 14 August, Harlech finally surrendered to Herbert and the last bastion of the Lancastrians fell into Yorkist hands.

Pembroke was devastated by the fall of Harlech. He marched on Denbigh, burned the town, and occupied the castle, but was pursued and driven out by Herbert and his brother Sir Richard. He was then obliged to dismiss his men and go into hiding, disguising himself as a peasant, and made his way to the coast, where he boarded a ship bound for Brittany. On 8 September, a grateful Edward IV bestowed his earldom of Pembroke on Herbert, "for that nobleman, at this period, had great weight in the counsels of the King and Queen, his eldest son having married one of the Queen's sisters."[7]

Jasper Tudor was not the only man infuriated at Herbert's promotion.

Warwick resented the new Earl's prominence at court and was jealous of the high favor shown him by the King. Pembroke's links with the Widvilles alone were enough to damn him in Warwick's eyes, but so also were his plans to take possession of lands confiscated from the Percies and Tudors and now held by Warwick and Clarence, in order to provide handsome dowries for his daughters and increase his influence by allying himself to other great magnates. Warwick feared that Edward would agree to Herbert's schemes, given the bad feeling between himself and the King, and the Widvilles' apparent determination to slight him. The rivalry between Warwick and Herbert grew daily, and may have been the final straw that prompted Warwick's defection from the King.

Between autumn 1468 and spring 1469, "many rumored tales ran in the City of conflict atween the Earl of Warwick and the Queen's blood, the which Earl was ever had in great favor of the commons of this land," who were also hostile to the Widvilles and frequently complained about "the great rule which the Lord Rivers and his blood bare that time within the realm."[8] Warwick made no secret of his grievances, complaining that the King took more account of upstart gentlemen than of the ancient houses of nobility. He could not stomach seeing Rivers wielding power.

Warwick was still in touch with King Louis through his agent, William Moneypenny, but he was alarmed by Edward's growing hostility to France, which had recently prompted Parliament to vote £62,000 (£57,024,570) for an invasion of that kingdom. That was the last thing Warwick wanted, and all his hopes now rested on Louis. He must have been aware that Louis was intriguing to reconcile him to Queen Margaret and was considering whether or not to throw in his lot with the Lancastrians. What Warwick really wanted, however, was to be in control of King Edward and rule through him.

Warwick knew that Clarence was also highly dissatisfied with his lot, being jealous of his brother and frustrated because Edward would not allow him any position of influence. Edward had been very generous to Clarence, but the latter was jealous and hungry for power. Both men were angry with him for forbidding Clarence's marriage to Isabel Neville, and Clarence hated the Widvilles, believing it was they who were preventing him from enjoying his supposed rights as the King's brother.

Warwick renewed his efforts to obtain a Papal dispensation for Isabel's marriage to Clarence, but came up against a reluctant Pope, who had already assured Edward's envoys that it would not be granted. Undeterred, Warwick began to negotiate a price. Sulking on his estates in the North, he refused to obey two summonses to court. The King, alarmed, strengthened England's defenses. Then Archbishop Neville stepped in and persuaded Warwick that he should make his peace with the Widvilles. A superficial ceremony of reconciliation between Warwick and the King and Rivers followed, but changed nothing.

Warwick formed an alliance with Clarence. Throughout the winter and the spring of 1469, they plotted how they might undermine Edward's authority. Sir John Conyers, Warwick's cousin by marriage and one of his most loyal adherents, was ready to take up arms on his behalf, but Warwick preferred to wait until he was in a position to ensure the success of any uprising against the King.

Warwick was more popular than Edward and he exploited that by fueling public discontent in his own territories. Hitherto, Edward had depended on the Nevilles to hold the North safely for him, but Warwick's disaffection undermined that security. It was easy for the Earl to resurrect the slumbering grievances of the Northerners, and not long before the North became a hotbed of anti-Yorkist feeling, so much so that England seemed to be on the brink of another civil war.

Edward's position might have been more secure had he had a son to succeed him, but on 20 March 1469, at Westminster, the Queen gave birth to "a very handsome daughter" called Cecily. The King and his lords "rejoiced exceedingly, though they would have preferred a son,"[9] especially now, when Edward's throne was under threat. His lack of a male heir was becoming a matter of concern to everyone.

By the spring of 1469, Warwick was secretly in league with Louis XI, who had promised to give him the principalities of Holland and Zeeland if he could bring about the overthrow of King Edward. Warwick may not have intended to go so far, but he was scheming actively to curb Edward's autonomy and become once more the power behind the throne. Clarence, however, enthusiastically supported Louis's plan, for his main objective was the crown. He attempted to undermine Edward by spreading an unfounded rumor that the King was not the son of Richard, Duke of York, but the bastard son of Duchess Cecily by an archer of Calais, whom Commines later called Blaybourne. The tale quickly gained currency and was gleefully repeated by both Louis XI and Charles of Burgundy; in the next reign, it would be raked up again.

That spring, Warwick and his family returned to Calais. From there, he masterminded a full-scale revolt against the King, to be led by Sir John Conyers. It was arranged that Warwick's kinsmen (including his brother George, Archbishop of York) and their allies would raise their tenantry and affinities to crush the Widvilles, restore Neville influence at court, and seize control of the King. Around 28 May, they answered the call to arms, rioting and inciting the people to rebellion.

Edward did nothing until 18 June, when he began recruiting men and recalled Warwick to England, commanding him to raise a force to march against the northern rebels, but Warwick summoned his servants and well-wishers to arm themselves, secretly intending to join those rebels. The King grew suspicious and issued an order prohibiting his subjects from forming assemblies unless he himself authorized them to do so.

In late June, Edward stayed at Croyland Abbey in Lincolnshire, then joined Elizabeth at Fotheringhay Castle, where they stayed for a week until 5 July, when he rode to Stamford and she returned to London. At Stamford and Newark, the King wrote to the mayors of various towns, commanding them to furnish him with troops of soldiers arrayed for war. But "the common people came to him more slowly than he had anticipated,"[10] and in insufficient numbers; judging by alarming reports from the North, he had one man to every three rebels. Knowing he could not hope to prevail, he reluctantly marched his army south to Nottingham, there to summon and await reinforcements from the West.

Warwick had finally secured a dispensation from the Pope for the marriage of Isabel to Clarence. In early July, despite his mother trying to dissuade him, Clarence sailed to Calais with Warwick, Archbishop Neville, and the Earl of Oxford. There, they were "solemnly received and joyously entertained"[11] by the Countess of Warwick and her two daughters. On 11 July, in defiance of the King, Clarence and Isabel were married at the Church of Our Lady in the castle of Calais, with Archbishop

Neville officiating, "in the presence of the Countess of Warwick and her daughter Anne."[12] There were "very few guests and the celebrations only lasted two days, for Clarence was married on a Tuesday, and on the following Sunday he returned to England."[13]

From Calais, the next day, Warwick issued a manifesto proclaiming that he and Archbishop Neville had been urged by the King's true subjects to save him from the rule and guiding of certain seditious persons. He went on to list all-too-familiar grievances, such as poor government, inordinate taxes, and the corruption of justice, and promised the people that he would petition the King to remove his evil counselors, the Widvilles and William Herbert, Earl of Pembroke, cut taxation, and pay heed in the future to the true lords of his blood, meaning Warwick and Clarence. If the King did not meet these demands, he would deserve to be deposed. The manifesto ended with a plea for armed support from all true subjects of the King and a promise that Warwick would be in Canterbury in three days. Already, his agents were in Kent enlisting men.

Soon afterward, Sir John Conyers marched south through Yorkshire at the head of 20,000 supporters. He was calling himself "Robin of Redesdale," a persona based on Robin Hood, the people's hero. Reports of his advance caused panic in the South.

After Warwick had failed to obey his summons, Edward ordered the Widvilles to seek refuge in strongholds in East Anglia and Wales, but Rivers and his son Sir John Widville, who had been lodging in Pembroke's castle at Chepstow, joined him on his march north to intercept the rebels. In Yorkshire, Northumberland forced Redesdale's men to disperse, but they merely crossed the border into Lancashire and regrouped.

On 16 July, later than planned, Warwick and Archbishop Neville returned to England unopposed and received a heartening welcome in Kent. At Canterbury, crowds of armed men flocked to join them, and the common people hailed Warwick as their deliverer. On 18 July, he marched on London at the head of a substantial army, and the Lord Mayor permitted him to pass through the city on his way north, believing he was taking reinforcements to the King. Crowds cheered him as he went.

Pembroke, meanwhile, was hastening to join Edward with his Welsh reinforcements. He set up camp near Edgcote Hill, six miles northeast of Banbury. The next day, he sighted Robin of Redesdale's northern army, which caught him unprepared. The Battle of Edgcote took place on

26 July 1469. Pembroke found it impossible to maintain a continuous battle line, but he nevertheless led a ferocious charge and forced the rebels to fall back. Victory was almost within the Yorkists' grasp when Warwick's advance guard came thundering downhill behind them. Terror-stricken, Pembroke's Welshmen fled the field. The Nevilles and their rebels had scored a resounding victory. Pembroke was taken prisoner, and Rivers and Sir John Widville went into hiding. Conyers and his Northerners returned home.

After the battle, Warwick had no compunction in condemning Pembroke and his brother as traitors and ordering their executions. He had no legal justification for this, since neither Herbert nor his confederates had committed treason against their lawful sovereign. But Pembroke's "crime" was having "great weight in the counsels of the King and Queen, his eldest son having married one of the Queen's sisters."[14]

People were shocked. Pembroke had been one of the chief mainstays of Edward IV's throne. The loss of his powerful guardian left young Henry Tudor without a protector, but the widowed Countess of Pembroke took him to live with her at Weobley in Herefordshire. His mother, Margaret Beaufort, tried at this time to regain custody of him, but without success.

At Olney, near Coventry, Edward learned of Pembroke's crushing defeat, news that prompted many of the nobles with him to desert, leaving him isolated and vulnerable. Only Gloucester and Hastings remained with him, having stayed loyal throughout the rebellion. Archbishop Neville soon found out that the King was at Olney, and, on Warwick's advice, rode with a few horsemen to seize him. He greeted Edward courteously but told him he must rise and go to meet with Warwick. On 2 August, the King was brought before Warwick and Clarence at Coventry and greeted them amiably, making no protest against the way he had been treated. Warwick seemed not to know what to do with him. He had no royal authority himself, and he and Clarence were not in a strong enough position to indict and execute Edward without fear of reprisals, nor had they gathered enough support to depose him and set Clarence on the throne in his place. Moreover, by deferring to their captive as King, they had placed themselves in an invidious position, for it was treason to imprison an anointed sovereign—and without the King at the helm much of the business of government must be held in suspension.

Warwick and Clarence tried to resolve their dilemma by placing Edward in honorable confinement in Caesar's Tower in Warwick Castle and attempting to rule England in his name. But his subjects remained staunchly loyal, and the magnates were determined to curb Warwick's power rather than help to expand it. Without their support, the Earl found that ruling England was impossible. There was a general feeling that, this time, he had gone too far.

Edward was acting like a well-behaved puppet, doing as he was told, signing everything Warwick put before him, and comporting himself with unfailing courtesy and good humor. He knew that Warwick could not hope to keep him under restraint. Fearing a rescue attempt, the Earl had the King moved at the dead of night to Middleham Castle in Yorkshire.

At the time of Edgcote, Elizabeth Widville was visiting Norwich with her daughters. Entering by the Westwyk Gate, they had been received with pageants, banners, songs, and ceremony, and were lodged in the house of the Friars Preachers. There they received the dreadful news that Warwick had not only emerged victorious at Edgcote, but had taken the King prisoner, and that Lord Rivers and John Widville had been apprehended in the Forest of Dean. In Coventry, both were condemned to death and were beheaded on 12 August at Gosford Green outside the city walls. Rivers's body was carried to Kent and buried in All Saints' Church in Maidstone, where an indent remains to show where his brass lay.

Appalled, Elizabeth hurried south with her children to join her widowed mother in London, vowing vengeance on those who had perpetrated the deed. Then she learned that Warwick had had the Duchess of Bedford arrested and charged with witchcraft. Perhaps capitalizing on Jacquetta's alleged descent from the witch Melusine, he had apparently paid one Thomas Wake of Northamptonshire and a parish clerk to give evidence that she had made obscene leaden or wax images of Edward IV and her daughter and practiced her black arts to bring about their marriage. It was also alleged that she had cast another image to cause Warwick's death. Realizing that there was a political agenda behind this, the Duchess sought the protection of the Lord Mayor and aldermen of London. The Mayor, remembering how she had tried to save London from the savagery of Queen Margaret's northern army in 1461, forcefully interceded on her behalf with the Council.

A formal investigation proved that the evidence against Jacquetta was deeply suspect. Public support was with her, and when it came to testifying against her, the bribed witnesses would not take the oath in court, so the prosecution's case collapsed and was dismissed. Jacquetta was freed. In February 1470, having affirmed that she had always believed in God, she would be officially declared innocent of all slanders by Edward IV. This unpleasant episode, and Rivers's execution, showed how far Edward's enemies were prepared to go to bring down the Widvilles.

7

"The marriage of the Queen of England and the Earl of Warwick"

With her husband a captive, the Queen sought refuge in the royal apartments of the Tower of London. Warwick left her there unmolested, insisting only that she kept "scant state."[1] By the end of August, however, his authority was crumbling and the government was beginning to descend into anarchy. The people were angry with him for imprisoning the King. In London, mobs were gathering, threatening violence, while Clarence and Archbishop Neville vainly strove to maintain a semblance of normality at Westminster. Warwick himself issued proclamations in the King's name demanding civil obedience, but the people ignored them. The situation was spiraling out of control.

At that moment, Warwick's cousin, Humphrey Neville of Brancepeth, who had fought for the Lancastrians at Hexham, raised Henry VI's standard and incited his northern compatriots to rebellion. Multitudes responded. Warwick hastened north with an army to suppress it but was unable to make any headway because his men threatened to desert unless they were assured of Edward IV's health and safety. Nor would the magnates support Warwick. He had no choice but to invoke Edward's authority, and Archbishop Neville asked the King if, in return for a degree of liberty, he would support Warwick against the rebels. Edward declared himself willing to cooperate, telling the Archbishop that he harbored no ill will against the Nevilles. He was taken to York, where his entry to the city was marked by fanfares and ceremony. Crowds turned out to cheer him, and lords thronged round him, eager to renew their vows of homage. When, at Warwick's request, he summoned his lieges to arms, such was his authority that there was an enthusiastic response. The royal army, commanded by Warwick, then marched north and effortlessly crushed the rebellion. Humphrey Neville himself was beheaded at York in the presence of the King.

It was clear to Warwick and Clarence that their victory had been a hollow one that gained them nothing. Now they had to ensure that they were not charged with treason, for there was no way of holding Edward. Early in October, with Warwick's blessing, Edward rode out of York toward London and freedom. He arrived in triumph and received a tumultuous reception from the citizens. Immediately, he set to work to reestablish his authority, adopting a conciliatory policy to bring those who had deserted him back to their allegiance.

When Warwick and Clarence arrived at Westminster in December, the King staged a public ceremony of reconciliation. John Paston reported that he had "good language of the lords of Clarence and Warwick, saying they be his best friends; but his household men have other language, so what shall hastily fall I cannot say." Soon afterward, Warwick and Clarence returned north, where they remained for the rest of the winter. By the spring of 1470, the King had regained control of the government and denounced them as traitors, prompting them to flee abroad.

Quick to take advantage of the political confusion in England, Louis XI had made public his intention of allying himself to the House of Lancaster. In December, in response to his invitation, Margaret left Bar and traveled to Tours with her son to see him. At the French court, she had an emotional reunion with her father, her brother John, her sister Yolande, and Ferry de Vaudémont. Louis himself extended a warm welcome to her, assuring her that the restoration of Henry VI was now one of his prime concerns.

News of events in France prompted unfounded rumors in England that Margaret was at Harfleur with an invasion fleet, ready to set sail. In fact, she was still at Tours, discussing strategies with Louis and her relatives. Presently, she wrote to her supporters in England, warning them to be ready to rise against the Yorkists, for the time was fast approaching when King Henry would come into his own once more.

By February 1470, Warwick was again plotting with Clarence, both resolving that this time they would not be satisfied with anything less than the deposition of the King and the elevation of Clarence to the throne. Warwick must have known that Clarence was unstable and could not be counted upon to restore him to his former power, but the only alternative was Henry VI, and Warwick still had no wish to ally himself with Margaret, even if she was willing, for she was unlikely to allow him his former dominance at court once her husband had been restored.

Warwick's strategy was to instigate another rebellion against the King. While Edward was preoccupied with suppressing it, he would enlist the help of King Louis to depose him. He was hoping for an armed confrontation in which the King would be defeated and overthrown, or even killed.

No sooner was the plan conceived than Warwick began to put it into action, using all the resources at his disposal and his old tactic of exploiting the grievances of the commons to incite a popular rising. The commons responded avidly to his propaganda, as did gentlemen with Lancastrian sympathies who heartily resented the Yorkist King and his onerous taxes. With Warwick's encouragement, these men and their tenantry rose with the aim of restoring Henry VI.

Edward raised an army, displaying no trace of the lethargy that had proved so damaging before Edgcote. Few joined the rebels; even the supporters of Warwick and Clarence stayed away. Edward confronted the rebels in a field at Empingham, striking so swiftly that Warwick and Clarence had no time to bring reinforcements. When Edward marshaled the full force of his artillery against the rebels, the casualties were so many that large numbers panicked and fled, some throwing off their surcoats as they ran, which led to the battle being named "Losecoat Field." When the King arrived in Grantham, the captured rebel leaders were brought before him and publicly confessed their faults, revealing that Warwick and Clarence had initiated the rising. On 13 March, Edward issued an urgent summons to both men to present themselves before him in humble wise to answer grave charges of treason. They ignored his order and proceeded to orchestrate another rebellion in Yorkshire.

The King rode north in pursuit, worried that Northumberland would desert him for his brother. On 25 March, he deprived Montagu of his earldom and restored it to young Henry Percy, a move that found favor with the Northerners and was intended to counterbalance the power of the Nevilles, the Percies' greatest rivals in the region. The King created John Neville Marquess of Montagu to compensate him for the loss of the earldom, but failed to endow him with any lands, leaving him unable to support the dignities of his new rank. Angrily he complained that Edward had given him "a magpie's nest," and even the creation of his son, George, as Duke of Bedford did not mollify him.

Edward had made a grave misjudgment, but matters were seemingly put right when he offered the hand of the four-year-old Princess Elizabeth to young Bedford, knowing that if anything should happen to him, Montagu would then ensure that Elizabeth's right to succeed him would be upheld. Edward was determined at all costs to prevent Clarence from being crowned, and knew he could rely on Montagu's self-interest, for what man could resist the prospect of his son becoming a king?

On 24 March 1470, Edward issued a proclamation denouncing Warwick and Clarence as "great rebels" and putting a price on their heads. He issued a further summons ordering them to appear before him by 28 March at the latest or be dealt with as traitors. On the 27th, he left York with his host to hunt them down, marching south via Nottingham and Coventry.

Warwick and Clarence fled to Warwick Castle, collected the Countess of Warwick and Anne Neville, and raced for Southampton, whence they could escape to Calais to raise support. But the King had anticipated their arrival and sent ahead Anthony Widville, now Lord Rivers, and John Howard, who captured all Warwick's ships. Warwick and Clarence were forced to continue to Exeter by land, where, on 18 March, they were reunited with Clarence's wife, Isabel, then nine months pregnant. On 3 April, they commandeered a ship and put to sea. Eleven days later, the King reached Exeter to find them beyond his reach.

Meanwhile, Warwick had appeared before Calais, which was under the command of Lord Wenlock. He had received orders from the King not to allow Warwick to land and fired cannon at his ship, which had to remain at anchor off Calais. On 16 April, Isabel went into labor. Despite Warwick's entreaties, Wenlock would still not let them land; even when her pains grew severe and complications arose, he remained obdurate, though he did send two flagons of wine for her. Fortunately, her mother was able to assist her during a very difficult delivery, but she could not save the baby, who died immediately after birth. The tiny corpse was taken ashore at Calais and buried there, and Warwick then sailed on toward Honfleur, harrying and capturing Breton and Burgundian merchant ships as he went.

His timely arrival in France gave Louis the opportunity to implement the plans he had been devising. When Warwick and Clarence anchored off Honfleur on 1 May, they were formally welcomed by Louis's representatives, the Admiral of France and the Archbishop of Narbonne, who had been commanded to tell Warwick that their master would do everything in his power to help him recover England, either by negotiating an alliance with the Lancastrians, or by any other means Warwick might suggest. Either would suit Louis's purpose of driving a wedge between England and Burgundy, but he wanted the decision to attempt a Lancastrian restoration to be Warwick's.

Warwick installed his womenfolk in abbeys near the banks of the River Seine. Louis was hoping to bring about a reconciliation and alliance between him and Queen Margaret that would lead to the restoration of Henry VI. He invited Margaret and Warwick to visit him at Angers. The Milanese ambassador in France reported: "The Earl of Warwick does not want to be here when the Queen arrives, but wishes to allow his Majesty to shape matters a little with her and move her to agree to an alliance between the Prince her son and a daughter of Warwick." After some persuasion, however, he agreed to meet Louis, who promised to see him separately and to act as mediator.

On 8 June 1470, Queen Elizabeth and her two eldest daughters joined King Edward at Canterbury for a great celebration of the feast of Pentecost. Prior John Oxney and his monks received them at the great door of the abbey of St. Augustine, and a service of thanksgiving followed. Elizabeth's brother Earl Rivers arrived the next day with other distinguished guests, and on Sunday the royal family went in procession to High Mass. Monday was spent at the abbey, then the Queen traveled back to London and Edward journeyed east to inspect the fortifications at Dover and Sandwich before rejoining her.

That same day, King Louis graciously received Warwick and his family at the château of Amboise on the Loire, with Clarence present. Knowing himself to be in a desperate situation, Warwick had persuaded himself that the only way out was to abandon his plan to put Clarence on the throne and ally himself to the Lancastrians. He therefore indicated that he was willing to link his fortunes with those of Henry VI and Margaret of Anjou, and was ready to fight for them. Louis promised to press Margaret to pardon him and guarantee him a prominent role in the government of England, should their plans come to fruition. He was very persuasive, and Warwick allowed himself to be convinced.

The King promised a fleet of ships, men, and money for the enterprise, on condition that, as soon as victory was his, Warwick would undertake to bind England in a treaty of peace with France and aid Louis in his proposed offensive against Burgundy. Warwick was willing to agree, especially when Louis suggested that the alliance with Margaret be sealed by the marriage of his daughter Anne to Edward of Lancaster.

Louis wrote to Margaret, proposing that she sign a thirty-year truce between France and the House of Lancaster in return for his promise to help Henry VI recover his kingdom. She readily consented, and as a compliment to his new allies, Louis chose Prince Edward as a godfather to his newborn son, the Dauphin Charles (the future Charles VIII).

When Margaret and her son arrived at Amboise on 29 June, Louis and Queen Charlotte received them "in a very friendly and honorable manner." Louis spent "every day in long discussions to induce her to make the alliance with Warwick and to let the Prince her son go with the Earl to the enterprise of England."[2] He told her that, with his help, the Lancastrians had a good chance of overthrowing Edward IV, but that this could only be achieved with the assistance of Warwick, and he urged her seriously to consider allying herself with the Earl since he was the only man who could win England for her.

Margaret was horrified—and furious. When she could speak, she launched a tirade of arguments as to why such an alliance was impossible. "The Queen has shown herself very hard and difficult, and although his Majesty offers her many assurances, it seems that on no account whatever will she agree to send her son with Warwick, as she mistrusts him."[3]

Louis waited until the storm had passed, then told Margaret bluntly that her objections might be valid, but if she was to regain her husband's throne, she should put her personal feelings aside and be pragmatic. If she refused, he could not support her. But she was immovable, saying that "King Henry, she and her son had certain friends which they might lose by this mean, and that might do them more harm than the [good] that the Earl might bring. Wherefore she besought the King that it would please him to leave off." Warwick, she cried, "had pierced her heart with wounds that could never be healed; they would bleed till the Day of Judgment, when she would appeal to the justice of God for vengeance against him. His pride and insolence had first broken the peace of England and stirred up those fatal wars which had desolated the realm. Through him, she and her son had been attainted, proscribed and driven out to beg their bread in foreign lands, and not only had he injured her as a queen, but he had dared to defame her reputation as a woman by divers false and malicious slanders, as if she had been false to her royal lord the King—which things she could never forgive."[4]

Louis persevered, and Sir John Fortescue added his own pleas, believing this concord to be the only way of restoring Henry VI. Eventually, Margaret allowed Louis to overrule her objections and consented to grant Warwick an audience, saying she would let him have her final decision after the interview. She would not agree in any circumstances to the Prince accompanying him to England, despite Louis's arguments that his presence would inspire the people to rise in favor of Lancaster. She feared to expose the boy to the risks of such an expedition, but Louis was relentless in insisting that he should go. Again, Margaret stated she would defer any decision on the matter until she had seen Warwick.

On 15 July, the court moved to Angers, where the Countess of Warwick and her daughter Anne were formally presented to Margaret. Later that day, when Louis told the Queen that Warwick was ready to agree to a marriage between Anne and Prince Edward, she exploded in rage.

"What!" she cried. "Will he indeed give his daughter to my son, whom he has so often branded as the offspring of adultery or fraud?" And she "would not in any wise consent thereunto. She said that she saw never honor ne profit for her, ne for her son," and "alleged that, if she would, she should find a more profitable advantage with the King of England. And indeed, she showed unto the King of France a letter which she said was sent to her out of England last week, by the which was offered to her son my lady the Princess [Elizabeth]."[5]

Edward IV had broken Elizabeth's betrothal to George Neville after his father had gone over to Warwick. Marrying her to Edward of Lancaster would have been one way to prevent the latter from wedding Anne Neville and might have averted a further war between Lancaster and York. No doubt Margaret envisaged her son being acknowledged as Edward IV's heir and perhaps ascending the throne on the King's death. But Queen Elizabeth was expecting another child that might be a son, and there is no other evidence that Edward IV offered the Princess to Margaret at this time; the letter may have been a forgery intended to extract better terms from Warwick.

Louis reported everything Margaret had said to Warwick so that the latter could marshal his arguments. On the evening of 22 July, the Earl was ushered by the King into the frigid presence of the Queen and abased himself on his knees, "addressing her in the most moving words he could devise, begging forgiveness for all the wrongs he had done her, and humbly beseeching her to pardon and restore him to her favor."[6] He conceded "that by his conduct King Henry and she were put out of the realm of England," but said he had believed they "had enterprised the destruction of him and his friends in body and in goods, which he had never deserved. He told her he had been the means of upsetting King Edward and unsettling his realm" and promised that he would in the future "be as much his foe as he had formerly been his friend and maker."[7] He now offered himself as a true friend and subject of King Henry.

Margaret "scarcely vouchsafed him any answer and kept him on his knees a full quarter of an hour."[8] Seeing that matters were not going as he had planned, Louis stepped in and offered personally to guarantee the Earl's fidelity. Margaret demanded that Warwick publicly withdraw his slanderous remarks concerning the paternity of her son, which he assured her he would do, not only in France, but also in England, when he had conquered it for her. At length, after much persuasion, the Queen was "induced to consent to all that his Majesty desires both as regards a reconciliation with Warwick and the marriage alliance," and "graciously forgave" Warwick.[9]

Louis then brought in the Earl of Oxford, who received a much warmer reception. Margaret forgave him also, saying that his pardon was easy to purchase, for she knew well that he and his friends had suffered much for King Henry's quarrels.

Over the next three days, Louis, Margaret, and Warwick negotiated terms, aided by King René's advisers. Commines thought the proposed marriage of Prince Edward and Anne Neville "strange. Warwick had defeated and ruined the Prince's father, and now he made him marry his daughter." After prolonged discussions, Margaret finally agreed to the marriage, although she would not allow it to take place until Warwick had proved his loyalty by taking the field against King Edward, and it should not be consummated until England was conquered. The Prince was to stay in France while the Earl invaded England, and Anne Neville "was to remain in the hands and keeping of Queen Margaret."[10] "If matters go prosperously, then the Prince will go back immediately."[11]

Louis undertook to provide money, soldiers, and a fleet of ships. All the parties were aware that Henry VI would never be fit to rule by himself, so Margaret agreed that, when he took possession of England, Warwick would be named regent and governor. Should Henry die before the Prince attained his majority, Warwick would become the boy's guardian. If Edward died without issue, the kingdom would pass to Clarence and his heirs. It was also agreed that Exeter, Somerset, and all who had been exiled or dispossessed in Henry's cause could return to England and recover their property. Finally, England would join France in an offensive alliance against Burgundy. The alliance between Warwick and Margaret astonished contemporaries.

On 25 July 1470, Prince Edward was betrothed to Anne Neville in Angers Cathedral in the presence of King Louis, King René, Queen Margaret, the Duke and Duchess of Clarence, and the Earl and Countess of Warwick. "Today," observed Louis, "we have made the marriage of the Queen of England and the Earl of Warwick."

Nothing is recorded of the feelings of the young couple. The chronicler John Rous, a chantry priest of Guy's Cliffe near Warwick who revered the Nevilles, called Anne Neville "the most noble lady and princess, born of the royal blood of divers realms, lineally descending from princes, kings, emperors and many glorious saints." This paragon now had to do reverence to a formidable future mother-in-law who had made it quite clear that she did not want her for her son but had only agreed to their marriage as a means of restoring the House of Lancaster to the throne. Nor was her sixteen-year-old bridegroom the most prepossessing of young men, having a notorious penchant for war and violence and harboring all the grudges of his mother and her desire for revenge on their enemies.

Anne and Edward could not yet be married because they were cousins in the second degree, being great-grandchildren of John of Gaunt, and a Papal dispensation had to be obtained. It was vital that the Pope be made to see the urgency of the matter, but to speed up the process took money. Louis had therefore procured a loan from a merchant in Tours to pay whatever bribes were needful, then dispatched his envoys to the Vatican. After the betrothal ceremony, Anne was committed to the safekeeping of Margaret. Over the coming weeks, Louis paid for her plate and her pleasures.

Clarence, no fool, had soon realized that he was to play never a part at all in the French plan save that of supporting Warwick, and that his father-in-law was less interested in making him king than in serving his own interests. He had refused to attend the betrothal and was now sulking in Normandy, furious that Warwick had abandoned him without a qualm and was now promoting the claims of Lancaster; and it was for this that Clarence had betrayed his brother, slandered his mother, and risked his own life and his fortune.

Margaret had kept her part of the bargain; now it was up to Warwick to fulfill his. On 30 July, in Angers Cathedral, he publicly swore an oath on a fragment of the True Cross to keep faith with King Henry, Queen Margaret, and Prince Edward, and to uphold the right of the House of Lancaster to the throne. Margaret, in turn, swore to treat him as a true, faithful subject and never to reproach him for his past misdeeds.

It had been agreed by the allies that Warwick and Jasper Tudor (who had recently arrived in France), would lead the invasion force, and that Margaret and her son would follow them to England when it was safe to do so. Warwick was to target the southeast coast, while Jasper would lead an assault on Wales, where he could count on the support of many loyal Lancastrians. Warwick had sent word of his coming to his affinity in

Yorkshire and they were arming themselves, while Margaret had written to her supporters in England, bidding them be ready to rise when Warwick came.

On 31 July, Margaret, the Prince, and Anne Neville left Angers for Amboise. Warwick then set off for the coast to prepare for the invasion. Margaret joined him at Harfleur to help him recruit men. Clarence arrived, having swallowed his grievances for the time being, and he and Warwick issued a manifesto addressed to the commons of England, which was dispatched across the Channel and posted on church doors in London and elsewhere. It referred in harsh terms to Edward IV's misrule and the oppression and injustice that had resulted from it, and ended with a promise from Warwick that he would redeem forever the kingdom from thraldom to other nations.

Meanwhile, Edward IV was raising men for the defense of the South. Early in August, the Milanese ambassador reported that an invasion was expected at any time. Warwick was anxious to see his daughter married to Prince Edward before he left for England, but the dispensation did not arrive in time, so he had to content himself with Louis's promise that Anne would be treated as if she were royalty and married as soon as it came.

8

"Forsaken of all her friends"

✳

At the beginning of August, Lord FitzHugh, Warwick's brother-in-law, staged a sham rebellion in Yorkshire as a trick to lure the King away from London. It worked, and Edward summoned his levies. Before he left the capital, he installed his pregnant Queen in the Tower of London, where she occupied luxuriously appointed chambers, one of which was prepared for her confinement, and arranged for them to be "well-victualled and fortified."[1]

By the middle of August, Edward was in Yorkshire, commanding his lieges to attend him to vanquish the traitors in his realm. Yet there was now no one to vanquish, for at news of his advance, FitzHugh had fled north to seek asylum in Scotland.

The real danger was approaching from the south. On 9 September, Warwick and Clarence and a fleet of sixty ships carrying their invasion force sailed from Normandy. Their company included Jasper Tudor, Oxford, and Thomas Neville, Bastard of Fauconberg. Edward IV had deployed a royal fleet to prevent Warwick from landing, but a storm had scattered it, leaving the coast unguarded. On 13 September, when Edward was still in Yorkshire, the Earl's fleet put in at Dartmouth and Plymouth.

Warwick was still popular in England and "found infinite numbers to take his part."[2] In Exeter, he issued a proclamation declaring that his invasion was authorized "by the assent of the most noble princess, Margaret, Queen of England, and the right high and mighty Prince Edward," her son. It called upon all true subjects of Henry VI, "the very true and undoubted King of England," to take up arms against the usurper Edward, whose misgovernment was dwelled upon in some detail. The proclamation also prohibited members of the invasion force from pillaging and raping. No one wanted a repeat of the atrocities of 1461.

Jasper Tudor left for Wales to recruit more men, while Warwick marched north. From all over England, Lancastrian supporters came rallying to his banner, and many deserted the King's army to join him. On 29 September, Edward IV learned of Warwick's advance. He also heard that Montagu was coming to his aid with a large force, and galloped south to meet him. But at Doncaster, he received news that Montagu had gone over to Henry. His desertion was a terrible blow, for Edward had relied on him to hold the North secure while he dealt with Warwick.

By now, Edward's men were deserting in large numbers, and his force had been reduced to a mere 2,000 soldiers. Realizing that his authority was rapidly crumbling, he had no choice but to flee. Accompanied by Hastings, Gloucester, Rivers, and those troops who remained loyal, he raced for the coast and, on 2 October, took ship from Bishop's (King's) Lynn in Norfolk to seek asylum with his ally, Charles of Burgundy.

On 1 October, the news of Edward's flight was cried in London. At eight months pregnant, Queen Elizabeth no longer felt safe in the Tower, and that night, with her daughters and her mother, she sought refuge in Westminster Abbey, which had afforded sanctuary to criminals and debtors since Saxon times. The great, grim cruciform stronghold of the sanctuary building had been built by Edward the Confessor in the eleventh century. Two stories high, it stood apart from the abbey on the site now occupied by Westminster Guildhall, and was demolished with great difficulty in 1750.

When Elizabeth arrived, eight months pregnant, desperate, bereft of comfort, and, according to Warkworth, "in great penury and forsaken of all her friends," Abbot Thomas Milling received her kindly and would not hear of her lodging with the common rabble in the sanctuary building, placing at her disposal the three best rooms in Cheyneygates, his house within the abbey precincts, and providing for her comfort. Despite wartime bombing, parts of medieval Cheyneygates survive today, notably two splendid rooms over the entrance to the cloisters, and (now part of the Deanery) the sumptuous Jerusalem Chamber, the Abbot's principal apartment, then hung with rich tapestries, which served as Elizabeth's great chamber. She also had the use of the Abbot's great hall with its minstrels' gallery, a privy chamber, which was probably used as a bedchamber, and the courtyard.

Law and order had broken down in London, which seethed with unrest as felons left sanctuary to infest the streets, prisons were broken open, and mobs looted and rioted unchecked—all in the name of Warwick. The Queen, alarmed, sent Abbot Milling to entreat the Lord Mayor and aldermen not to resist Warwick's forces or do anything to provoke him, lest his men forced their way into the abbey and killed her. She urged them to take command of the Tower of London and secure the city against the approaching army. The Mayor himself knew it would be folly to resist such a large force, and that he and his fellows would be better advised to come to terms with Warwick and entreat him to spare the city from the more violent members of his affinity.

Warwick sent his representative, Sir Geoffrey Gate, ahead into London to receive its submission and free Henry VI. On 3 October, the constable of the Tower surrendered the fortress to Gate, who asked the Bishop of Winchester to liberate the King. Henry emerged "as a man amazed, utterly dulled with troubles and adversities." He "was not worshipfully arrayed as a prince, and not so cleanly kept as should seem such a prince."[3] Gate arranged for him to be moved to the sumptuous rooms prepared for Queen Elizabeth's confinement.

Two days later, Archbishop Neville marched into London at the head of a strong force and took control of the Tower. The next day, Warwick and Clarence rode in triumphal procession into the city and made straight for the Tower, where they kneeled before Henry VI and greeted him as their lawful King. Warwick ordered that he be clothed in a new robe of blue velvet, then escorted him in procession into London, passing along Cheapside to the Bishop's Palace by St. Paul's, where Henry was to lodge temporarily. Here, the lords sat him on a throne and placed the crown on his head. Warwick paid him "great reverence, and so he was restored to the crown again, whereof all his good lovers were full glad."[4] Historians refer to Henry VI's restoration as "the Readeption."

It was noted that Henry sat on his throne as limp and helpless as a sack of wool, "mute as a crowned calf,"[5] probably bewildered by this new turn of events. "He was a mere shadow and pretense,"[6] a puppet worked by Warwick, who, as the King's Lieutenant, was now the real ruler of England.

That day, Edward IV's ignominious flight from England was announced to the people from Paul's Cross and he was declared deposed. On 13 October, Warwick had King Henry attired in his crown and King Edward's robes of state and paraded through the streets of London to St. Paul's Cathedral, himself bearing the King's train. Crowds gathered, rejoicing, crying out, "God save King Henry!" After a service of thanksgiving, Henry took up residence at Westminster.

On learning of Henry VI's restoration, Louis ordered that a *Te Deum* be sung in Notre-Dame and that the event be marked by a three-day holiday and festival. He commanded the chief dignitaries of Paris to prepare an honorable welcome for Queen Margaret, the Prince of Wales, the Countess of Warwick, and her daughters, who would be arriving very soon, en route for England. Margaret, Edward, and Anne Neville had been staying as guests of King René. In October, Jasper Tudor arrived in Hereford, where his nephew Henry Tudor was living with Lady Herbert's niece and her husband, Sir Richard Corbet. Corbet handed over the boy, now thirteen, to his uncle, who took him to London to be presented to Henry VI. Jasper was now styling himself Earl of Pembroke, although the attainder against him had not been reversed. He tried to have the earldom of Richmond restored to Henry Tudor, but was unsuccessful because it was still held by Clarence.

By November 1470, Warwick "had all England at his leading and was feared and respected through many lands."[7] He was again Great Chamberlain of England and captain of Calais. Clarence had been appointed Lieutenant of Ireland and given a place on the Council. Yet Warwick's situation was not as strong as it seemed. Many die-hard Lancastrians regarded him as a traitor who had brought about the ruin of the House of Lancaster. Nor could he count on the loyalties of those Yorkists who had previously supported him, for many felt he had gone too far in deposing King Edward. The only persons on whom he could rely were his Neville adherents and those Lancastrian nobles who had benefited from the Readeption. The rest of the nobility merely paid lip service to Warwick's government. It was only among the commons that Warwick was popular.

There was no guarantee that Margaret would allow him to remain in power once she returned to England, especially as the Prince was now seventeen, older than Henry VI had been when he attained his majority. Warwick knew that the success of his régime depended on cooperation between himself, the unstable and increasingly dissatisfied Clarence, and the Lancastrian and Yorkist magnates—and that the prospect of that was remote.

Warwick had little reason to love Elizabeth Widville, but he did not persecute women. In fact, he issued a proclamation forbidding his followers to befoul churches and sanctuaries in London and elsewhere, on pain of death. Yet the Queen evidently felt it was safer to stay in sanctuary with her daughters, with the situation so volatile and uncertain. But she was in "deep trouble and heaviness," lacking even "such things as mean men's wives have in superfluity."[8] A London butcher, John Gould, came to her rescue, loyally donating "half a beef and two muttons weekly" for her household. A kindly fishmonger provided victuals for Fridays and fast days. As the Queen neared her confinement, Elizabeth Greystoke, Lady Scrope, was appointed by Henry VI's Council to wait on her and paid £10 (£9,100) for her services. Marjory Cobb, who had delivered Princess Cecily, was brought in as midwife, and Elizabeth's own physician, Dr. Sirego, was permitted to attend her. (These details were recorded in a letter written by Edward IV to the Lord Privy Seal in 1473.)

On 2 November, in the Abbot's House, she "was delivered of a son, in very poor estate."[9] She named him Edward. It seemed ironic that the long-awaited heir had been born during his father's exile, yet the Yorkists derived some hope and consolation from it. King Henry's adherents, however, thought the birth of the child of no importance. Baby Edward was baptized by Prior John Estney in the Abbot's House "with no more ceremony than if he had been a poor man's son."[10] The Abbot and Prior were godfathers, and Lady Scrope godmother. Four-year-old Princess Elizabeth held the chrisom, the robe put on a child after baptism to symbolize its purification from sin.

The Queen was aware that her son might be seen as a threat to the new régime. She knew that "the security of her person rested solely on the great franchise of that holy place." But Warwick left them alone, and she "sustained" her ordeal "with all manner of patience belonging to any creature, and as constantly as ever was seen by any person of such high estate to endure." Yet "what pain had she, what labor and anguish did she [suffer]? To hear of her weeping it was great pity," and "when she remembered the King, she was woe."[11]

Warwick too realized that the birth of a Yorkist heir might prove a focus for rebellion and would inspire Edward to greater efforts to recover his kingdom. He decided that it was time for Queen Margaret to bring the Prince of Wales and his future bride to England, reasoning that a prince nearly grown to manhood would have more popular appeal than one in swaddling bands. He persuaded Henry VI to agree and wrote to Queen Margaret, urging her to return at once.

Henry presided in person over the Parliament that met at Westminster on 26 November and confirmed his right to be King of England, vesting the succession in the Prince of Wales and his heirs and, failing them, the Duke of Clarence and his heirs. "King Edward was disinherited with all his children, and proclaimed throughout the city as usurper of the crown. Gloucester, his younger brother, was pronounced a traitor, and both were attainted."[12] All attainders passed since 1461 on Lancastrian nobles were reversed. Jasper Tudor was formally restored to the earldom of Pembroke and given back his property as well as being handsomely rewarded by the King with other estates, including Herbert's lands in South Wales and the Marches. Parliament recognized Warwick as protector of the realm and of the King, acknowledged Clarence as his associate, and dismantled much of the machinery of Yorkist government.

9

"My cousin of York, you are very welcome"

✳

MARGARET, PRINCE EDWARD, THE COUNTESS OF WARWICK, and her daughters had remained at the French court at King Louis's expense. Margaret was wary of returning to England, believing it was still an unsafe place for the Prince, yet she was inclined to agree with Warwick that the birth of a son to Elizabeth Widville posed a threat to Henry VI, and reluctantly began making plans to leave France.

On 3 December, Louis XI formally repudiated his treaty of friendship with Burgundy, declaring it void by virtue of Charles's alliance with Edward IV. This would mean war between Louis and his powerful vassal, which was what he had intended all along. Aiming to crush Burgundy with England's help, he ordered his army to advance into Burgundian territory. Only then did he send his ambassador to discuss what form England's aid would take, presenting Warwick with a fait accompli.

Before the French ambassadors left, they had an audience with the Prince of Wales, who agreed to make war on Burgundy until every last part of the Duke's territories was conquered, and to persuade his father the King to ratify this undertaking. In England, the ambassadors began pressing Warwick to fulfill his part of the agreement with Louis, but they met great difficulty in convincing the English magnates and merchants that an alliance with France would be more advantageous than that which Edward IV had already made with Burgundy. The last thing the London merchants wanted at this time was an alliance with France. Nor did the common people, for the treaty with Burgundy had brought new prosperity to England and safeguarded the lucrative market for her goods. If Warwick honored his agreement with Louis, he would not be seen to be upholding the interests of the English people.

Charles the Bold had shown himself cordial to the restored Henry VI, but he was now reconsidering his position and wondering if it would be more profitable to support the Yorkists, who had always shown themselves friendly toward him.

The Pope had still not granted a dispensation for the marriage of Prince Edward and Anne Neville, and an impatient Louis had sent the Grand Vicar of Bayeux to procure one from the Latin Patriarch of Jerusalem, since Margaret's father still claimed to be King of Jerusalem. This arrived early in December, whereupon the King moved to Amboise for the wedding. On 13 December, the young couple were married by the Grand Vicar of Bayeux in a sumptuous ceremony in the palace chapel, which was attended by a host of members of the royal houses of France and Anjou, as well as the Countess of Warwick and Clarence.

There is good reason to believe that Queen Margaret had forbidden her son to consummate the marriage. Should Warwick be toppled, Anne would no longer be a fit wife for the heir to Lancaster, and if the union had not been consummated, an annulment could easily be obtained, leaving the Prince free to marry a more suitable bride. In 1472, Anne would be described by Croyland as a "maiden" or "damsel," terms normally used to describe an unmarried virgin.

Reports received by Louis from his ambassadors in London convinced him and Margaret that it was now safe for her to return to England. On the day after the wedding, with the Prince and Princess of Wales and the Countess of Warwick, she left Amboise, escorted by a guard of honor. They made a ceremonial entry into Paris, being received outside the city gates by the chief officers of the university, the Parliament, and the Châtelet, as well as the civic authorities, all wearing their finest robes. They conducted the Queen and her party into a city made festive with tapestries and painted cloths hanging from windows and balconies, its streets thronged with cheering citizens. In England, King Henry was instructing his Exchequer to pay £2,000 (£1,820,490) to enable Warwick to cross to France with an army of ships and men "for the bringing home of our most dear and entirely beloved wife, the Queen, and our son, the Prince."

Margaret remained in Paris over Christmas and was preparing to leave for England when she learned that Burgundy and Edward IV had met near Saint-Omer. Although unnerved, she was reassured by reports from the French ambassadors in London that the political situation there was stable and that it would still be safe for her and her son to return. She therefore traveled to Rouen to await the arrival of Warwick, who was to escort her to England. There, on King Louis's orders, she received a rapturous welcome.

Warwick never came. Short of funds, he had spent the money granted for his journey on more urgent things, and could not now afford to go to France to collect the Queen. Unaware of this, Margaret refused to consider leaving until Warwick had shown up at a French port. While she waited at Rouen, he waited for her at Dover, confident that she would have sailed without him. Soon, pressing matters of state obliged him to return to London.

At length, Margaret had to accept that Warwick was not coming, and proceeded with the Prince, Anne Neville, and the Countess of Warwick to Dieppe, to avoid further delay. When the masters of her ships warned her that the January weather was unfavorable, she refused to listen. Three times her fleet put to sea, and each time it was hurled back upon the coast of Normandy by rough winds and storm-tossed waves. Some ships were badly damaged and had to be repaired, and the more superstitious among the Queen's men said that the tempest had been conjured up by sorcerers employed by the Yorkists; others perceived the hand of God at work. It would be some time before the weather broke, and Margaret had no choice but to wait, fuming in frustration.

Back in England, Warwick was desperately trying to consolidate his position. Parliament would agree only to a ten-year truce with France, not a formal alliance, and—knowing the temper of the people—it would not sanction a declaration of war on Burgundy. Warwick, however, assured Louis's envoys that England would help their master, that he had already begun recruiting an army and would send it to France as soon as possible. In February, on his instructions, the garrison at Calais prepared to attack Burgundy's lands, driving him to ally himself with Edward IV. Furious about Warwick dragging England into a war against Burgundy without Parliament's consent, for it would be highly injurious to the City's economic prosperity, the London merchants refused to lend any more money to the Readeption government. Knowing that the deposition of Henry VI would deprive Louis of his principal ally and remove the threat of war, Burgundy agreed to help Edward IV recover his kingdom and gave him 50,000 crowns (£8 million).

By late February, with the help of his sister Margaret, Duchess of Burgundy, Edward had raised an army of Englishmen and Flemish mercenaries. He had also obtained, through the good offices of the Hanseatic League, a fleet of ships that were waiting in Flushing harbor for his order to sail. But Edward, like Margaret, was obliged to wait for a break in the weather.

In England, his invasion was expected and commissions of array had been sent to Wales and the Marches. Parliament granted the Prince of Wales the power to array men for the defense of the realm, and commissions were sent out in his name, threatening those who did not comply with a traitor's death. Montagu was mustering an army at Pontefract; Oxford was guarding the coast of East Anglia; Pembroke was preparing to defend Wales; Clarence was in Bristol, ready to defend the West Country; and the Bastard of Fauconberg had been placed in command of the royal fleet, which was stationed on alert in the English Channel.

But Warwick's authority was crumbling, especially in London. He had alienated not only the middle and lower classes, but also the lords, who increasingly resented his self-aggrandizement. Neither Lancastrians nor Yorkists trusted him, and his legendary popularity was fast fading. Neville supremacy in the North had declined since Percy's restoration to the earldom of Northumberland and the removal of Montagu from that sphere of influence. Percy now held sway in the North, and Warwick knew for a certainty that he would not support him.

On 14 March, Edward landed at Ravenspur in Yorkshire—at the same spot where Henry of Bolingbroke had landed seventy-two years earlier, and a long way from the South, where most of his support was concentrated. He had with him his brother Gloucester and Earl Rivers.

To show his men that he had no intention of retreating, Edward ordered his ship to be burned. The East Riding of Yorkshire rose up in arms against him, yet he managed to convince the leaders that he had come to claim only his duchy of York, and they let him continue on his way to the city. He met with no opposition, but did not attract much support, for few believed he stood much chance of victory.

Warwick responded to the news of Edward's coming with a summons to all loyal Englishmen to take up arms, but some Lancastrian nobles disobeyed it, preferring to await Queen Margaret's arrival. Nevertheless, Warwick managed to raise a sizeable army and marched north, leaving Archbishop Neville responsible for the safekeeping of King Henry and the capital.

When Edward arrived before the walls of York, the city magistrates at first refused him entry. But he again pleaded that he was but a simple duke, come only to claim his rightful inheritance. The city fathers were further convinced of his good intentions when "afore all the people, he cried, 'À King Harry! À King Harry!,'"[1] and stuck an ostrich feather, the badge of the Prince of Wales, in his hat. On 18 March, he was allowed to ride into York with a few companions, leaving his army encamped outside the city walls. He then swore a solemn oath before the citizens that he had no intention of reclaiming the throne.

Warwick was marching on Coventry to join up with Oxford and Clarence. The combined strength of Edward's enemies presented a formidable challenge, but he was equal to it. He left York on 19 March and began recruiting men, then made for Nottingham, where he abandoned his pretense of having come to claim only the duchy of York and issued proclamations using the royal style. The townsfolk, seeing him astride his horse, smiling, confident, and handsome, came swarming to his standard. He was now approaching the territory of his Yorkist supporters, and many knights and magnates joined him. With an army now numbering over 2,000 and swelling daily, he next advanced to Leicester, where he was joined by nearly 3,000 of Hastings's men, and on toward Coventry. There, Warwick withdrew his troops inside the walls to await the arrival of Oxford and Clarence with reinforcements.

* * *

Margaret had received alarming reports that Edward IV was planning to invade England. Years of being a fugitive and an exile had taught her caution, and she decided to delay her departure from France to wait upon events. When Louis suggested that when his ambassadors returned from England, she should use their ships, she was too fearful and declined the offer. Soon afterward, Sir John Langstrother sailed his own ship over to France to collect her, having been sent by Warwick with £2,000 (£1,820,490) toward her expenses. On 24 March, with grave misgivings, Margaret sailed from Harfleur, accompanied by the Prince and Princess of Wales, Fortescue, Wenlock, Morton, and 3,000 French knights and squires. The Countess of Warwick boarded a different ship, which landed ahead of the Queen's fleet at Portsmouth. Knowing that Margaret was planning to land on the southwest coast, the Countess boarded a ship bound for Weymouth, but a fierce storm blew up and tossed it back to Southampton. With the turbulent weather showing no sign of abating, she decided to travel overland to join the Queen. On 28 March, the Milanese ambassador reported that Margaret was now believed to be on her way to England.

The next day, Edward arrived before Coventry and shouted out his defiance of Warwick, calling upon him either to come forth in peace and receive a pardon, or to come out and fight. Looking out upon Edward's sizeable host, Warwick was well aware that if he agreed to decide their quarrel by recourse to arms, the day might go against him. Moreover, many men in his army were averse to confronting the King in the field. since he had never yet lost a battle.

For three days running, Edward sent heralds bearing formal challenges to Warwick, but, receiving no reply, he withdrew and seized Warwick Castle. There, he had himself formally proclaimed King. Clarence chose this moment to make public his intention of returning to his allegiance to his brother.

Both Burgundy and the Duchess of York had put pressure on Clarence to make peace with Edward; Gloucester had paid a secret visit to his brother and persuaded him to submit to the King. Clarence had needed little persuading. His patience had run out when, on 23 March, Warwick had forced him to surrender some of his property to Queen Margaret and Prince Edward, despite agreements made with them and Warwick that he could retain all his possessions until duly recompensed. Clarence was well aware that Warwick's position was becoming precarious and that it would be wise to dissociate himself from him.

On 3 April, Clarence led his army of 12,000 men into the King's camp at Banbury and knelt in submission. Edward forgave him and promised to restore all his estates. The royal brothers then rode to Warwick, where they issued a final challenge to the Earl at Coventry. Appalled by Clarence's defection and the size of the forces ranged against him, Warwick was still looking for the arrival of fresh reinforcements and would not consider confronting Edward until these had come.

Having learned that the Queen was sailing for the West Country, Somerset and other lords left London, recruiting as many men as possible to receive her. In fact, Margaret had been delayed by a contrary wind and was still waiting to put to sea.

Both Edward and Warwick knew that whoever could secure London stood a good chance of gaining a decisive victory. The race for the capital began. As Edward neared London, his army growing all the time, Warwick sent letters to the City authorities and Archbishop Neville, ordering them to bar the gates until he himself arrived with his army "utterly to destroy Edward and his men." The Archbishop summoned to St. Paul's lords who were loyal to Henry VI and Warwick, and some 6,000 to 7,000 gathered there. He had King Henry mount a horse and ride through the City to St. Paul's, hoping to encourage the citizens to stand by him. Yet Henry VI, slouched on his horse, wearing an old blue gown that had seen better days, and regarding the people with sad, tired eyes, was hardly a sight to inspire confidence. He lost many supporters, and won few.

From Dunstable, on 9 April, Edward sent "very comfortable messages to his Queen, his true lords and his servants and supporters in London. Wherefore, they considered as secretly as possible how he might be received and welcomed there."[2]

On 10 April, "the rulers of the city were in council, and had set men at all the gates and wards." Seeing that the power of Henry VI and his adherents was so feeble, they "could find no courage" to support them. "Rather the opposite obtained, as they well saw that Henry's forces could not resist the King, who was approaching the city. The Mayor and the aldermen determined to keep the city for [him and] to open it to him at his coming, so they sent to him that they would be guided at his pleasure."[3] Many of the Lancastrian lords had left London to meet up with Queen Margaret, and there remained no one powerful enough to hold the City against Edward or to resist the Lord Mayor's decision to open the gates to him.

Archbishop Neville, fearful for his own skin, also sent a message to the King, desiring to be admitted to his good grace and promising in return to look to his well-being and security, to which Edward agreed. The Archbishop kept his promise, undertaking to deliver Henry VI into Edward's hands. That night, the Tower of London fell to the King.

At noon the next day, King Edward and his brothers marched into London, which joyfully opened its gates to him. The Mayor and chief citizens welcomed him warmly and the crowds lining the streets yelled their appreciation. Edward went immediately to St. Paul's Cathedral to hear the Archbishop of Canterbury give thanks for his restoration and declare King Henry deposed. Then he entered the Bishop's Palace, where Archbishop Neville presented him to Henry VI. Henry embraced him, saying, "My cousin of York, you are very welcome. I know that in your hands my life will not be in danger." Edward promised that Henry had nothing to fear, but ordered his immediate transfer to the Tower.

The King had already sent a deputation to Westminster Abbey to escort the Queen and her children from sanctuary to the Palace of Westminster. He made his way to Westminster Abbey, where Archbishop Bourchier set the crown on his head to show the people that he was formally restored to the throne, after which he knelt and gave thanks to God, St. Peter, and St. Edward the Confessor.

Having ordered his army of 7,000 to hold London against Warwick, he processed from the Abbey to the Palace of Westminster, where Queen Elizabeth and their children awaited him, having just emerged from sanctuary. There followed an emotional reunion, which proved almost too much for Elizabeth, and a weeping Edward had to comfort her, for she had been deeply affected by her long ordeal in sanctuary. "Ne'theless, she had brought into the world, to the King's greatest joy, a fair son, a prince, wherewith she presented her husband at his coming, to his heart's singular comfort and gladness, and to all them that truly loved him."[4] A contemporary poem celebrated this touching reunion:

> *The King comforted the Queen and other ladies eke [also],*
> *His sweet babes full tenderly he did kiss;*
> *The young Prince he beheld, and in his arms did bear;*
> *Thus his bale [anguish] turned him to bliss.*
> *After sorrow, joy, the course of the world is.*
> *The sight of his babes released part of his woe;*
> *Thus the will of God in everything is do.*[5]

Cradling his heir, Edward expressed his "greatest joy" and "his heart's singular comfort and gladness," calling him "God's precious sending and gift, and our most desired treasure."[6] In October 1472, William Allington, Speaker of the House of Commons, would speak of "the great joy and surety of this land in the birth of a prince," and commended Elizabeth for her "womanly behavior and great constancy when [Edward] was beyond sea." "O Queen Elizabeth, O blessed creature, O glorious God, what pain had she!"[7]

In July 1471, the King appointed Abbot Milling chancellor to Prince Edward in reward for his kindness to the Queen and her children while they were in sanctuary, and in 1474 he made him Bishop of Hereford. Milling also received £520 (£540,140) from the King, the Queen, and Prince Edward toward roofing the nave of Westminster Abbey. In return for his "true heart," Butcher Gould was given permission to load his ship at any port and trade freely with her for a year. Dr. Sirego was paid £40 (£36,250) for attending the Queen's confinement, and Mother Cobb received a pension of £12 (£10,880) for her services. In 1479, in thanksgiving for the safe delivery of the Prince, Elizabeth Widville secured a royal charter endowing the foundation of a chantry chapel in Westminster Abbey dedicated to St. Erasmus, the protector of women in childbirth. The King gave lands in Worcestershire, so that Mass could be sung there daily for the good estate of himself and the Queen.

10

"The last hope of thy race"

※

On the night of 11 April, Edward returned to London with Elizabeth and their children. They stayed at Baynard's Castle, the London residence of Duchess Cecily. In the evening, the King and Queen attended divine service, and the next day, the royal family kept Good Friday with all solemnity. Then the Queen, her children, her mother, and the Duchess of York, accompanied by Earl Rivers and the Archbishop of Canterbury, moved to the royal palace in the Tower of London for safety.

Edward had stayed in London long enough for his captains to recruit and muster reinforcements. On the afternoon of 13 April, taking King Henry with him, as well as his brothers Clarence and Gloucester, he led his forces ten miles north to Barnet, where he would meet his enemy.

That evening, as the armies prepared to do battle, the fleet carrying Margaret, Prince Edward, Anne Neville, and a great company landed at Weymouth. They had endured the most appalling voyage, having been at sea for several days "for lack of good winds and because of great tempests." Yet Margaret remained undaunted, determined to raise the southwest. This was no vain hope, for many of her chief adherents held lands there and exercised political influence, among them Somerset, Exeter, and Devon—and Clarence, of whose defection she knew nothing.

Margaret did not know that the Readeption government was already discredited, due to Warwick's unpopular foreign policy, and that she had arrived too late to undo the damage. Nor did she know that Henry VI had again been overthrown by Edward IV. "I trow," wrote a Paston correspondent, on learning of the Queen's arrival, "that tomorrow, or else the next day, King Edward will depart from hence [toward her] to drive her out again."

Early on Easter Sunday, at Barnet, Edward fell on his knees before his army and "committed his cause to Almighty God." He knew he was outnumbered, for Warwick had the larger army, but he "advanced banners, blew the trumpets and set upon [Warwick's forces]. With the faithful and mighty assistance of his supporters, [he] vigorously, manfully and valiantly assailed his enemies in the center and strongest part of their army, and with great violence."[1]

Hard-pressed in the thick of the mêlée, Warwick failed to rally his men. He could not halt the surge of terrified soldiers fleeing the field. Realizing that the day was lost, he too decided on flight, and made his way on foot toward Wrotham Wood, where his horse was tethered. The King, knowing that victory was his, had sent a messenger cantering across the field to shout out the order that Warwick's life was to be spared, but a group of Yorkist soldiers, having seen the Earl making his escape, bore down on him and killed him, stripping his body of its armor and leaving it lying there naked. As news of his death spread, the remnants of his army lost heart and fled.

So fell the mighty Kingmaker, who had overplayed his hand once too often; his lust for power had outweighed his defects as a military commander, and he was felled by the forces of the man he had helped to set on the throne. He had made and unmade kings, yet his death on the battlefield sealed the fate of the very dynasty he was trying to restore.

Men had come running into London, crying that Edward and his brothers had been routed and slaughtered. No one knew if it was true until the King's messenger came riding at speed into the City, triumphantly waving one of his gauntlets as a sure token of his victory before taking it to Queen Elizabeth. That afternoon, the King himself entered London with Clarence and Gloucester and a great retinue of magnates, and was welcomed "with much joy and gladness."[2] By evening Henry VI was once more a prisoner in the Tower, where four days later he was joined by the perfidious Archbishop Neville.

The bodies of Warwick and Montagu were brought back to London on Easter Monday and displayed naked, except for loincloths, in a single open coffin at St. Paul's Cathedral, so that people would not believe seditious tales claiming that Warwick still lived. The bodies were buried at Bisham Priory.

Despite the rejoicing in London, Edward IV knew that the struggle was not yet over, and that he must recruit more men, for he had yet to deal with the threat posed by Queen Margaret in the West.

The Countess of Warwick had been traveling toward Dorset, hoping to meet up with Queen Margaret and her troops. On the way, she learned of her husband's death. Fearing that King Edward's vengeance would fall upon her, she fled through the New Forest and sought sanctuary at Beaulieu Abbey.

On Easter Monday, Margaret and her company reached Cerne Abbey in Dorset, where they stayed in the guesthouse for ten days. There, they were joined by Pembroke, Devon, Somerset, and his younger brother John. When they broke the news of Warwick's defeat and death at Barnet, Margaret "fell to the ground. Her heart was pierced with sorrow, her speech was in a manner gone; all her spirits were tormented with melancholy." When she could speak, she "reviled the calamitous times in which she lived and reproached herself for all her painful labors, now turned to her own misery, and declared she desired rather to die than live longer in this state of infelicity."[3]

Thinking that all was lost, her chief concern was the Prince's safety, and she "passionately implored" her supporters to do all in their power to ensure it. In her opinion, no good could come of a further armed confrontation with King Edward, therefore it would be best if she and the Prince returned to France, "there to tarry until it pleased God to send her better luck."[4] But the lords prevailed on her to stay and persevere. Warwick's defeat had been a setback, but they were confident that many Englishmen remained eager to fight for Lancaster. Many considered her "prospects favorable, because it is reckoned she ought to have many lords in her favor who intended to resist her because they were enemies of Warwick."[5] She and the Earl had at best been reluctant allies, forced out of necessity to make a pact, but if her army triumphed, the House of Lancaster would be able to reign unhampered by the problem of Warwick. Nevertheless, she informed King Louis that, contrary to what he might have heard, the Earl was still alive, but was in hiding, nursing a wound, while the Prince was in London with a great following of men. Clearly, she did not want Louis to think she was fighting for a lost cause.

Margaret and Prince Edward sent out summonses to their supporters. Over the next few days, more Lancastrian peers and their companies arrived at Cerne, their appearance reviving Margaret's spirits. Soon, she recovered her former energy and began to feel optimistic about the outcome of her enterprise. And still they kept coming, men from Dorset, Somerset, and Wiltshire, to join her ever-increasing army.

Pembroke was dispatched to Wales to recruit men there, and it was agreed that the Queen would march west and link up with him.

Edward IV was in London when he received news of the Queen's landing. "Worn down by many different blows," he had had little time in which to "refresh himself. No sooner was he done with one battle in the East, than he was faced with another in the western part of England, and had to prepare himself to fight at full strength." He had dismissed his army after Barnet and now had to send "to all parts to get him fresh men." But he was eager to confront his enemies. He issued a proclamation against Margaret and her supporters, branding them traitors and reminding the people that God had vindicated his right to the throne by giving him the victory at Barnet and "in divers battles against our great adversary Harry and his adherents."[6] Speed, he realized, was crucial to his success. Having ordered the repair of the royal ordnance, he rode to Windsor to gather an army with Lord Hastings's help.

On 23 April, Edward celebrated the feast of St. George with his Knights of the Garter at Windsor Castle. The next day, accompanied by his brothers and Lord Hastings, he led a great host westward in pursuit of Queen Margaret, hoping to overtake her before she crossed the River Severn and joined forces with Jasper Tudor in Wales. Margaret intended to cross the Severn at Gloucester, and although she and her captains took precautions to conceal their movements, Edward's scouts managed to shadow them for most of the time. To put her pursuers off the scent, her own scouts were ordered to move east, as if her army meant to march on London, but the King's outriders soon discovered the Queen's true intentions. Thereafter, the Lancastrians "knew well that the King ever approached toward them, near and near, ever ready, in good array," which made them panicky and all the more eager to press on to Wales. Nevertheless, their ranks were still swelled daily, for "there were many in the West who favored King Henry's cause."[7] Marching at great speed, Edward drove his soldiers on mercilessly, not even permitting them to stop to eat or forage for food.

Margaret marched west to Exeter, where her appearance, and that of the Prince and his Princess, inspired many men of Devon and Cornwall to come flocking to them. Then it was on to Taunton, Glastonbury, and Wells, where the Lancastrian army arrived on 27 April and sacked the Bishop's palace. The lords advised the Queen to pause awhile to allow more men to muster. Although she was anxious to press on, she agreed.

Two days later, Edward arrived at Cirencester, where he learned that Margaret was on her way north to Bath. Discounting reports that she would be advancing on Cirencester, the King moved south, hoping to intercept her at Malmesbury. Informed that she was in Bath, he went after her there, but when he arrived on 1 May, he found that she had gone west to Bristol and was planning to meet him in the field at nearby Chipping Sodbury.

In Bristol, Margaret received a warm welcome and was given ordnance, provisions, and money. She took fresh courage at this, and rested awhile at Berkeley Castle, having left her vanguard at Chipping Sodbury to put the King off her trail. When Edward arrived there, his scouts found no trace of the Lancastrian army.

On 2 May, Margaret left Berkeley Castle and marched through the night to Gloucester, where she planned to cross the Severn. Once she had joined forces with Pembroke, Edward would stand little chance of prevailing against their combined strength. Tradition has it that Margaret stayed at Owlpen Manor on the way to Gloucester. The Prince had sent from Weymouth to John Daunt, the owner, asking him to raise men and money.

Determined to overtake the Lancastrian army before it could cross the river, Edward commanded Gloucester's governor to close his gates to the Lancastrians. His messenger circumvented the Queen's army by taking a different route and reached the city first. Edward, meanwhile, had drawn up his army in battle array and begun a thirty-mile march through the Cotswolds to Cheltenham.

When Margaret and her army reached Gloucester and demanded admission, the gates remained closed, and she had no alternative but to cross the River Portway and make for Tewkesbury, ten miles to the north. There they could cross the Severn into Wales. At four o'clock in the afternoon of 3 May, they arrived at Tewkesbury, utterly weary after the long march; some had collapsed with heat and fatigue. Margaret herself was exhausted, and it was decided that everyone should have a much-needed rest. The Queen, the Princess of Wales, the Countess of Devon, and other ladies-in-waiting all retired for the night to nearby Gupshill Manor, a house built in 1430 in the shadow of Gupshill Castle; it survives as an inn.

When Edward arrived in Cheltenham, he was informed that the Lancastrians were making for Tewkesbury. He ordered his men to rest for a while, then pressed on to Tredington, three miles from Tewkesbury, where he set up camp for the night. Like the Lancastrians, his men were so footsore and thirsty that they could have marched no farther.

At dawn, the Lancastrian army, apprised of his position, began preparing for battle. Somerset, as commander in chief, drew up his men in a strong position on a hill rising from a field at the southern end of Tewkesbury, with the town and abbey at their backs, although his captains and the Queen expressed concern that all around them were foul lanes and deep dykes. Today, the place is still known as Margaret's Camp.

Later that morning, the King's army caught up with the Lancastrians at Tewkesbury, taking up battle stations 400 to 600 yards south of the enemy.

Queen Margaret and the Prince of Wales rode through the Lancastrian ranks, speaking words of encouragement to their soldiers and promising them fame, glory, and great rewards if they fought well. Margaret then left the field and returned to Gupshill Manor, leaving Somerset in command. She and Anne Neville, with Margaret's trusty lady-in-waiting, Katherine Vaux, remained there to wait for news.

It had been decided that Prince Edward, seeing active service for the first time, was to lead the center, under the tutelage of Lord Wenlock, a seasoned soldier. Somerset chose to lead the right wing and gave Devon command of the left. On the Yorkist side, the King commanded the center, Gloucester the left wing, and Hastings the right. Thomas Grey, Marquess of Dorset, Elizabeth Widville's son by her first husband, led the rear guard.

The Lancastrian army numbered around 5,000 to 6,000 men, the Yorkists around 3,500 to 5,000. The King had more aristocratic support than Somerset, and consequently more professional troops with better arms and equipment. Seizing an advantage, Gloucester led his men in a vicious onslaught on the Lancastrian center. Prince Edward resisted valiantly, but his line broke and his men scrambled off in a full-scale retreat. King Edward surged forward and there followed a desperate rout in which the Lancastrians fled the field, hotly pursued by Yorkists out for their blood. Many were cut down as they ran, while others sought refuge in Tewkesbury Abbey, little realizing that it did not enjoy the privilege of sanctuary. Hundreds tried to escape by crossing the River Severn but perished by drowning or at the hands of their pursuers. Many more were trapped and slaughtered, but the worst carnage was to be seen on the battlefield, which is still called the "Bloody Meadow."

During the rout, Yorkist soldiers forced their way into Tewkesbury Abbey and ran riot, looting and vandalizing its sacred buildings. Anyone who resisted was dealt with savagely, and Lancastrian soldiers who had sought refuge were brutally dispatched, their blood desecrating the sanctified ground. There survives in the sacristy today a wooden door covered with plates of armor stripped from Lancastrian casualties or prisoners, and perforated with gunshot or arrow holes.

King Edward had won "a famous victory,"[8] having inflicted a devastating and decisive defeat on the Lancastrians, 2,000 of whom were killed in the battle. Among the dead was Prince Edward of Lancaster. Commines and most other contemporary writers stated that he died in the field, crying "for succor to his brother-in-law, Clarence."[9] But a French source dating from 1473 hinted that Edward was killed after the battle, and Croyland, writing in 1486 after Edward IV and his brothers were dead, claimed that he died "either on the field, or after the battle, by the avenging hands of certain persons." *The Great Chronicle of London* and the sixteenth-century historians Vergil, More, and Hall all implicated Gloucester in his death, stating that the Prince was taken during the rout and brought before King Edward when the battle had ended. The King received him graciously and asked him to explain why he had taken up arms against him. The youth retorted defiantly, "I came to recover my father's heritage. My father has been miserably oppressed, and the crown usurped." This made Edward angry, and with "a look of indignation" he slapped the Prince across the mouth with his gauntlet. At that moment Clarence, Gloucester, and Hastings raised their swords and cut the youth down.

The tale may not have been an invention. In the confusion following the battle, it would not have been difficult to make it appear that the Prince had fallen in the field. Edward had good reason to want the Lancastrian heir dead, and Croyland was perhaps hinting that there was more to his death than other reports had made clear.

With Prince Edward died the hopes of the House of Lancaster. His remains were interred with other corpses in Tewkesbury Abbey with only "maimed rites." A modern diamond of brass directly beneath the church tower and a vaulted roof emblazoned with gilded suns in splendor (placed there to commemorate the Yorkist victory) marks his resting place, and bears the Latin inscription:

> *Here lies Edward, Prince of Wales,*
> *cruelly slain while a youth.*
> *Anno Domini 1471.*
> *Alas, the savagery of men,*
> *Thou art the sole light of thy mother,*
> *the last hope of thy race.*

II

"He has, in short, chosen to crush the seed"

✳

WHILE THE BATTLE OF TEWKESBURY RAGED, QUEEN MARGAret and Anne Neville had remained at Gupshill Manor, anxiously awaiting news. When a messenger brought them the dreadful tidings of the Lancastrian defeat, the Queen determined on flight, but was so overcome by the realization of the disaster that had overtaken her and anxiety as to the fate of her son, of whom there was no news as yet, that she fainted and had to be carried out by her ladies to a waiting litter. She and her party then traveled to a house called Payne's Place in the village of Bushley, where a loyal family was willing to hide them for the night. The house survives, in private ownership; a room on the first floor, overlooking Tewkesbury Abbey and the battlefield, is still called the Queen's Room.

Somerset and other Lancastrian leaders, including Sir John Fortescue and Dr. John Morton, had sought sanctuary in Tewkesbury Abbey, but were dragged out by the King's men. Some were killed on the spot, others left to await judgment, while the rest, including Fortescue and Morton, remained prisoners for a time.

On 6 May, Somerset and twelve others were brought before a military tribunal presided over by Gloucester, as Constable of England, and condemned to immediate execution as traitors and rebels. Somerset was beheaded in the marketplace at Tewkesbury and buried in the abbey. On his death, Margaret Beaufort became the senior representative of the Beaufort family.

The Battle of Tewkesbury was the last battle of the wars between Lancaster and York and effectively ended Lancastrian resistance for good. Henry VI was now a prisoner, his only son was dead, his wife was in hiding, and the last male heir of the Beauforts—whom Henry might conceivably have chosen to succeed him—had perished. No one yet regarded Henry Tudor, a fourteen-year-old fugitive, as the hope of the House of Lancaster. Even Margaret Beaufort had abandoned the Lancastrian cause and declared her loyalty to Edward IV. "In every part of England, it appeared to every man that the said party was extinct and repressed for ever, without any hope of again quickening."[1]

On 5 May, the King rode in triumph to Worcester, having been informed that Margaret could not be found and had probably fled after the battle. In fact, she and Anne Neville had made their way in secret to Birtsmorton Court, a fourteenth-century moated and fortified manor house in Little Malvern in Worcestershire, where Margaret was accommodated in a chamber that still exists. Evidently she felt it was not safe to remain there, for she soon moved with her party to Little Malvern Priory, "a poor religious place" founded in 1171 and situated in woodland beneath Hereford Beacon. There "she hid herself for the surety of her person."[2]

Pembroke had been at Chepstow with Henry Tudor when he learned of the Lancastrian defeat, and was now doing his best to maintain his hold over south Wales. On Edward's orders, Roger Vaughan of Tretower tried to trap him there, but was unsuccessful, and it was Pembroke who captured Vaughan and had him beheaded. Some said that this was in revenge for Vaughan having urged Edward to order the execution of Pembroke's father, Owen Tudor, in 1461. The Earl then fled west to Pembroke Castle, where he was besieged by Yorkist partisans, but rescued a week later.

On 7 May, Sir William Stanley and his men discovered Queen Margaret and Anne Neville at Little Malvern Priory and took them into custody to await the King's orders. Stanley informed the Queen, none too gently, of her son's death. She collapsed on hearing this bitter news and had to be dragged almost senseless from the priory by his soldiers. Anne Neville was doubtless grieved too, having been widowed at fourteen so soon after losing her father, although we know nothing of her feelings for her husband. Even so, she was in a frightening situation.

On 11 May, the two women were brought before the King at Coventry. Margaret was deeply distressed, calling down curses on Edward's head and screaming abuse at him, until he seriously considered ordering her execution. But he relented: knights did not behave thus to women, and this woman was distracted by grief. When she had calmed down, he informed her that she would be dealt with honorably and with respect, to which she meekly replied that she placed herself at his commandment.

On 14 May, Edward left Coventry for London with Margaret in his train in the custody of Sir William Stanley, having pardoned Anne Neville and placed her in the charge of her brother-in-law Clarence, who arranged for her to enter his household and made her a ward of her older sister, the Duchess Isabel. Her name does not appear among those of the prisoners who rode with Edward to London.

While these events were taking place, "the frenzy of the King's enemies was in no way quelled, and their numbers increased in spite of the fact that King Edward's double victory seemed to all a clear sign of the justice of his cause. Incited by the few men who remained of those who had been with the Earl of Warwick, such men assembled under the command of Thomas, Bastard of Fauconberg."[3] Fauconberg was Warwick's cousin and had managed to retain control of his ships. When he landed in Kent and began to incite rebellion, men came flocking to him, marching on London. On 8 May, Fauconberg demanded that the Lord Mayor open the gates to him, but the Londoners had already learned of the King's victory at Tewkesbury and were not going to be bullied. When Edward IV heard of Fauconberg's rising, he sent commissions of array out to many shires and within days "there came to him men to the number of 30,000."[4]

On 13 May, the Bastard appeared before London on the Surrey shore of the Thames and announced his intention of taking the city and freeing Henry VI from the Tower. The Lord Mayor and aldermen refused him entry, declaring that they were holding the capital for King Edward. Fauconberg then marched to Kingston and crossed the Thames there, lined his guns up along the shore, and fired upon the Tower. The city fathers began building barricades and "moved the King in all possible haste to approach and come to the City, to the defense of the Queen, then being in the Tower of London [with] my lord Prince and my ladies his daughters, all likely to stand in the greatest jeopardy that ever was."[5] Lord Rivers was in command of the Tower, and ably defended the city against its attackers, ordering an intense bombardment of Fauconberg's position by the cannon on the Tower walls and beating off the rebel assault.

The following day, Fauconberg made a futile attempt to burn London Bridge, but was driven back by cannon-fire. Meanwhile, 3,000 of his men had burst into the city and were rampaging through the streets, firing guns and arrows indiscriminately and setting fire to Aldgate and Bishopsgate. At that point, the Earl of Essex arrived to reinforce the city levies and sent them against the rebels, just as Rivers was sallying forth from the Tower with 4,500 men. Fierce fighting ensued, but gradually the rebels were forced back to the banks of the Thames. On 15 May, they retreated to Blackheath, but when they learned that the King was advancing at the head of 30,000 men, they dispersed. Gloucester, riding ahead of the King's main force, received Fauconberg's submission. Nothing now stood in the way of Edward's triumphal return to London.

On Tuesday 21 May, accompanied by almost the entire peerage of England, Edward IV rode into the capital. The Londoners cheered exuberantly and cried out blessings upon him. He had emerged victorious after a brilliant campaign, during the course of which he had eliminated his greatest enemies. His success had been due not only to his speed, tenacity, and daring, but also to his outstanding abilities as a general and his deployment of men of caliber in positions of command.

Commines believed there were three chief reasons for Edward's rapturous reception in London: the birth of the Prince, "the great debts" the King owed in the City and could now settle, and "the ladies of quality and rich citizens' wives, with whom he had formerly intrigued" and who had "forced their husbands and relations to declare themselves on his side."

But if there was triumph in London that day, there was also the personification of tragedy, for at the rear of the King's procession "was borne a carriage"[6] flanked by soldiers, in which sat Queen Margaret, exposed to the derision and taunts of the crowds and tasting the bitter dregs of humiliation and grief. As she passed, bystanders flung mud and stones at her, yelling abuse. At the end of the day, Gloucester escorted her to the Tower and entrusted her to the charge of the Constable, Lord Dudley. During her captivity, the King paid daily expenses for her maintenance and for the attendants she was permitted to have with her.

Even with Prince Edward dead, Edward IV was aware that while the deposed King lived, there would always be the risk of further risings and military confrontations. "And in the same night that King Edward came to London, King Henry, being in ward in prison in the Tower of London, was put to death, between eleven and twelve of the clock, being then at the Tower the Duke of Gloucester."[7] Tradition has it that Henry's murderer came upon him as he knelt at prayer in his chamber in the Wakefield Tower.

The official account of his death in the *Arrivall* stated that Henry reacted to news of the death of his son, the capture of his wife, and the bitter certainty that his cause was "utterly despaired of" with "so great despite, ire and indignation that, of pure displeasure and melancholy he died." Few believed this. The Milanese ambassador in Paris believed that King Edward had "caused King Henry to be secretly assassinated in the Tower. He has, in short, chosen to crush the seed."

Richard of Gloucester was then eighteen. He may not personally have struck the blow that killed Henry, but had probably been sent to the Tower by the King to convey the order and ensure that the deed was done. Commines asserted that he "killed poor King Henry with his own hand, or else caused him to be killed in his presence." By the sixteenth century, it was generally believed that "Gloucester killed him with a sword."[8] Yet any order for the murder of Henry VI (if murder it was) can only have come from the King. It is inconceivable that Gloucester would have acted alone in such a matter. Alternatively, it is possible that he just happened to be at the Tower after delivering Margaret into captivity.

Richard had been born on 2 October 1452 at Fotheringhay Castle. John Rous's hostile account of his life describes him as coming into the world after two years in his mother's womb, with teeth, long hair to his shoulders, a humped back, and his right shoulder higher than his left. More repeats these details, adding cautiously that "either men of hatred report the truth, or else nature changed her course in his beginning."

"Richard liveth yet," recorded the anonymous annalist in the chronicle of William of Worcester, with apparent surprise. However, the boy survived the perils of early childhood and spent his younger years in the company of his older brother George in the care of their mother at Fotheringhay. He was nine when he was created Duke of Gloucester.

In the 1460s, Edward IV did little more for him, heaping honors instead upon George. But it was Gloucester who stayed loyal to the King when Warwick and Clarence turned traitor in 1468–9. Gloucester was then appointed Lord High Admiral of England, Chief Justice of the Welsh Marches, and Chief Constable of England. In 1470, he replaced the disgraced Warwick as Chief Steward and Chamberlain of South Wales, becoming the King's chief representative in the principality. Later that year, he accompanied Edward IV into exile, and after Edward's restoration in 1471, was rewarded for his loyalty with yet more offices, replacing Warwick as Great Chamberlain of England.

Richard's childhood and formative years were overshadowed by war, treachery, and violent death. When he was eight, his father and his brother Edmund were killed in battle. He grew to maturity in an uncertain, insecure world, and twice suffered exile. He saw his brother the King betrayed by their brother Clarence, and by Warwick, who had been as a father to Richard. Small wonder if, by the age of eighteen, he had become hardened to the realities of political expediency.

Gloucester first saw battle at Barnet in 1471, where he acquitted himself well leading the vanguard of the royal forces, showing considerable ability in warfare whilst in the thick of the fighting. He also fought brilliantly at Tewkesbury, for which he received yet more lands by way of reward.

It was after Tewkesbury that his ruthlessness first became apparent, when, as Constable of England, he tried and sentenced to death Somerset and other prominent Lancastrians, including one in holy orders who was entitled to immunity from the death penalty. Whether or not Gloucester struck the fatal blow that killed Henry VI, he had been shown that it was prudent, even necessary, to eliminate the threat posed by the continued existence of a deposed king, and that the end—peace and strong government—justified the means.

Gloucester strove all his adult life to win popularity. He had a quick, alert, and "overweening" mind; he was courageous and daring, and had "a sharp wit [and] courage high and fierce."[9] Nicholas von Poppelau, a Silesian knight who met him in 1484, said he had "a great heart." Able, hardworking, and conscientious, he had the Plantagenet charisma, which inspired loyalty. He was a typical late-medieval magnate: acquisitive, ambitious for wealth and power, brave, tough, and energetic. He took a keen interest in warfare and loved hunting and hawking. He owned several devotional books, including a copy of John Wycliffe's English translation of the New Testament (now in the New York Public Library), which had been banned in England as heretical; it bears his signature. He also owned the works of Chaucer and books on heraldry, war, and the art of government.

Gloucester acknowledged two bastards, who were probably born before 1472. One was John of Pontefract (or John of Gloucester), who was knighted in 1483 and still underage in 1485 when his father appointed him captain of Calais. The other was Katherine, who was generously dowered by Richard when she married William Herbert, Earl of Huntingdon, in 1484. A mysterious Richard Plantagenet of Eastwell in Kent is sometimes said to have been a bastard son of Richard's, although that cannot be proved, and there may have been four others, including one Stephen Hawes, but the evidence for these is unreliable.

In 1911, when Henry VI's body was exhumed and examined, it was seen that he had died of the effects of a severe blow to the head. The bones of the skull were "much broken" and "to one of the pieces of skull there was still attached some of the hair, which was brown in color, save in one place, where it was much darker and apparently matted with blood."[10]

Croyland was in no doubt as to the cause of death. "I shall pass over the discovery of the lifeless body of King Henry in the Tower of London. May God have mercy upon, and grant sufficient time for repentance to, him, whoever he may be, who dared to lay sacrilegious hands on the Lord's Anointed! Let the doer merit the title of tyrant, and the victim be called a glorious martyr."

On 22 May, Henry's corpse was laid in a coffin and carried through the streets of London to St. Paul's, where it lay in state for several days. "And his face was open that every man might see him, and in his lying he bled on the pavement there; and afterward at the Blackfriars was brought, and there he bled new and fresh."[11] The people murmured at this and "the common fame then went that the Duke of Gloucester was not all guiltless" of Henry's death.[12]

Margaret's reaction to the news of her husband's death is not recorded (one unsubstantiated account claimed that she howled so loudly that she could be heard in the streets surrounding the Tower), but she did make a determined attempt to gain custody of his body, which was denied her. Before long, she received a letter from her grief-stricken father, King René: "My child, may God help thee with His counsels! For rarely is the aid of man tendered in such reverse of fortune." René himself had suffered a triple bereavement the previous year when his son John of Calabria, his bastard daughter Blanche, and his son-in-law Ferry de Vaudémont had all died within weeks of each other. "When you can spare a thought from your own sufferings," he wrote to Margaret, "think of mine. They are great, my daughter, yet would I console thee."

Henry VI's funeral service was conducted at the monastery of the Blackfriars, after which his body was carried to Chertsey Abbey in Surrey, where it was honorably interred in the Lady Chapel. In 1484, Richard III ordered his reburial in St. George's Chapel, Windsor.

His reign had been one of the most catastrophic in England's history, yet after his death tales of his piety and holy life spread quickly. Within weeks, pilgrims were hastening from all over the kingdom to pray at his tomb, many from the North of England, where Lancastrian sympathies were still strong. Soon, Henry was venerated as a saint, and many miracles were said to have taken place at his tomb, most of them cures for the sick. People forgot that Henry had failed them in nearly every way that mattered—as king, as warlord, and as the fount of justice—and remembered only his virtuous life and the fact that he had bequeathed to them two enduring monuments to his piety and love of learning—Eton College and King's College, Cambridge.

12

"More like a death than a life"

※

Following the Lancastrian defeat at Tewkesbury, Pembroke fled into exile, taking Henry Tudor with him. Still styling himself Earl of Richmond, Henry spent his youth in penury at the court of Brittany. Both he and Pembroke remained stoutly loyal to the House of Lancaster, and Henry was regarded by some as its natural heir; indeed, he was the only viable Lancastrian claimant. He always deferred to his mother, Margaret Beaufort, as the heiress of the House of Lancaster, but neither of them ever contemplated her actually ruling because she was a woman. All her ambitions were for her son, but clearly Edward IV did not perceive Henry as much of a threat, since he made only sporadic attempts to capture him. It would be many years before Henry's claim was taken seriously by a Yorkist king.

Queen Margaret did not remain long in the Tower. Elizabeth Widville pleaded with the King to mitigate the severity of her imprisonment, and he took pity on Margaret, permitting her to reside in the London house of Lord Audley, appointing fifteen well-born male and female attendants to serve her, among them the faithful Katherine Vaux. Soon, she was moved to Windsor Castle, where she remained under house arrest until January 1472, when she was moved to Wallingford, near Ewelme, both residences of Alice Chaucer, Duchess of Suffolk. This was also at the behest of Queen Elizabeth, who showed herself impressively charitable to her husband's enemy, for Alice was one of Margaret's closest friends and had been in possession of Wallingford Castle for many years. The King appointed her Margaret's guardian and assigned her 8 marks (£4,690) a week for her expenses and adequate daily allowances for her and her attendants. Margaret may have spent time at Ewelme, Alice's preferred residence.

It was probably a peaceful existence for some months—until 1473, when a French fleet commanded by the Earl of Oxford threatened England's shores, and Edward sent Margaret back to the Tower. From Easter, Lord Dudley, the Constable, received £5 (£5,180) daily for her food, and the King sent money for woolen cloth and velvet for new gowns. Dudley's son William, Dean of the Chapel Royal, was paid to wait on Margaret.

Margaret would have been saddened by news of the death of the Duchess Alice in May or June 1475. In July, the King granted her permission to join the Skinners' fraternity of Corpus Christi as "the Queen Margaret, sometime wife and spouse to King Harry the Sixth."[1] Elizabeth Widville was also a member. The guild book of the London Skinners' Company, dating from 1475, shows Margaret kneeling in prayer before the Virgin, dressed as a widow in a nunlike robe of blue—the color of royal mourning—with a white wimple and an ermine-trimmed black cloak. The lady kneeling behind may be Katherine Vaux, who was also admitted to the fraternity.

That year, Edward sent Sir Thomas Montgomery and Dr. John Morton to France to discuss the price of Margaret's release. On 29 August, the King himself met with Louis at Picquigny and signed a peace treaty that provided for the French King to ransom her for 50,000 crowns (£8:5 million), in return for her surrendering all her rights in England to him. The first 10,000 crowns (£1:7 million) were to be paid when Margaret was formally handed over, and the rest would be paid in installments. On 2 October, Margaret formally renounced her consort's crown and her dower, assigning all her possessions in England to Edward. In November, Thomas Thwaites, her custodian, was ordered to deliver her to Sir Thomas Montgomery, who was to escort her to King Louis.

Margaret returned to France on 13 November 1475, attended by three ladies and seven gentlemen. "She was sent home with as much misery and sorrow as she was received with pomp and triumph. Which mutation and change of the better for the worse could not but nettle her and sting her with pensiveness."[2] Her party traveled from London to Sandwich, where they took ship for Calais. In January 1476, Montgomery traveled with her to Rouen. There she was received by Jean de Hazes, captain of Rouen, and Jean Raguier, receiver of Normandy, and the first payment of her ransom was entrusted to Montgomery.

Louis was demanding compensation for his efforts to restore the House of Lancaster to the throne. On 29 January 1476, at Rouen, Margaret renounced to him all her rights inherited from her mother in the duchy of Lorraine and those she would inherit from her father in Anjou, Bar, and Provence, signing herself, "I, Margaret, formerly married in the kingdom of England."

Only then was she allowed to journey on to Anjou, having been told that she was now free to go wherever she wished. King René settled on her a modest pension and placed at her disposal the castle of Reculée near Angers, where he had created a beautiful garden and a sculpture gallery.

Before she arrived, however, she had to pass through villages inhabited by English families who had been unable to afford to return to England when the French reclaimed Normandy. These people hated Margaret, seeing her as the architect of their misfortunes, and they stormed one house where she was staying, intent on killing her. Her escort drew their swords and managed to repel the onslaught, then stood guard over the house until reinforcements could be summoned to spirit Margaret away to Rouen. From there, she took a different route to Angers, where she set up her modest household. Katherine Vaux was with her, and she had a pack of hunting dogs, so she could enjoy the pleasures of the chase.

But it was otherwise a sad, dismal existence. "And where, in the beginning of time, she lived like a queen, in the middle she ruled like an empress, toward the end she was vexed with trouble, never quiet nor in peace, and in her very extreme age she passed her days in France, more like a death than a life, languishing and mourning in continual sorrow, not so much for herself and her husband, but for the loss of Prince Edward, her son."[3]

In 1479, nearing fifty, she entertained a party of exiled Lancastrian lords, who were saddened to find her looking so changed. The Comte de Villeneuve, King René's early-nineteenth-century biographer, was descended from men who served René, whose written testimony formed the basis of his book. One of his ancestors saw Margaret at this time and recorded that "the once peerless [Queen] had become a horror to look upon. Grief had turned the whole volume of her blood to water; her once superb eyes were swollen and red with weeping, and her skin covered with blotches like leprosy."[4] It might have been eczema.

When King René died, "very old and very sad,"[5] on 10 July 1480 at Aix-en-Provence, Margaret's pension ceased, leaving her in very reduced circumstances. He had left her 1,000 gold crowns (£171,000) and an annuity of 2,000 livres (£1,920,670), but despite his deathbed plea to King Louis to take care of Margaret, Louis took both when he sequestered René's hands. On 1 August, Margaret wrote to Monsieur du Bouchage, one of his former councillors, at the French court: "I commend myself unto you as much as I can. The King [Louis] has made known to the town of Angers that the King of Sicily, Monseigneur my father, is gone to God. I am writing to him that it may please him to take my poor case, in the matter of what can and should belong to me, into his hands, to do with it according to his good will and pleasure, and still keep me in his good grace and love, in which I pray you to be good enough to maintain me always."[6]

We do not know what efforts Bouchage made on Margaret's behalf, but Louis insisted that she reconfirm her renunciation of 1476, and obtained her consent to his pressing her sister, Yolande, to cede to him her rights in Bar. Only then did he grant Margaret a meager pension of 6,000 livres tournois (£1 million), but the first payment was not made until 12 February 1481. In the meantime, she was penniless, in such straits that she could no longer afford to live at Reculée, and moved to Saumur, but was soon obliged to accept the charity of one of her father's courtiers, Francis de Vignolles, Lord of Morains, to whom René had entrusted her care. He offered her hospitality at his bijou château standing on a rock at Dampierre, near Saumur, which had been built in 1460-2. Margaret lived out her days there in great poverty, attended to the end by Katherine Vaux.

The unspecified illness that carried her off at the age of fifty-two was of short duration. On 2 August 1482, she made her will, declaring that she was "sane in understanding, but weak and infirm in body." She asked that her body be "interred in holy ground, according to the goodwill and pleasure" of King Louis, "and if it pleases him, I elect and choose to be buried in the cathedral church of St. Maurice at Angers." She left everything—all her rights and possessions—to Louis. "My wish is that, if it please the lord King, the small amount of property which God and he have given to me be employed in burying me and in paying my debts. And in case that my goods are not sufficient for this, as I believe will be the case, I beg the said lord King of his favor to pay them for me, for in him is my sole hope and trust." Ten days later, Louis wrote to Jeanne Chabot, Madame de Montsoreau, demanding that she send Margaret's dogs to him. "She has made me her heir, and this is all I shall get; also it is what I love best. I pray you not to keep any back, for you would cause me a terribly great displeasure."[7]

Margaret died on 25 August 1482 at Dampierre. Four days later, her body was taken from Saumur to the collegiate church of Saint-Laud in Angers, then carried the next day to Saint-Maurice. In the procession walked members of the secular colleges of Angers, the four mendicant orders, and the nuns of Saint-Aubin. On 26 August, as she had requested in her will, Margaret was buried next to the tomb of her parents in Angers Cathedral. She has no memorial or epitaph because the tomb was destroyed, and her bones exhumed and scattered, during the French Revolution. In 1895, there was no trace of them when her father's tomb was opened and his crowned remains were seen. A stained-glass window in the cathedral, modern statues in Angers, and one with her son in the Jardin du Luxembourg, Paris, commemorate her.

Jean Vignolles acted as Margaret's executor and informed King Louis of her death. Louis consented to her goods being sold to meet the funeral expenses and the wages of her servants, and agreed that the rest could go to the cathedral, which received 75 ells of "blue golden cloth" and a casket full of holy relics.[8] In England, in St. Paul's Cathedral, a Requiem Mass was sung for the repose of Margaret's soul.

In 1485, in the first Parliament of his reign, Henry VII had Margaret's attainder reversed and it was acknowledged that Henry VI had been the rightful King of England.

Margaret had attracted criticism in her day because she had challenged the expected role of a woman. Commines wrote that she "would have done much better if she had acted as a judge or mediator between the two parties, instead of saying, 'I will support this party,' for there were many battles as a result, and in the end almost everyone on both sides was killed." Hall called Margaret "a cankered crocodile and subtle serpent," while for Shakespeare she was "a foul withered witch" and a "hateful, withered hag." Later writers sometimes portrayed her as a tragic heroine, for example, in Michael Drayton's "Miseries of Queen Margaret" (1627) and "England's Heroical Epistles" (1598). In 1737, Michael Baudier wrote *An History of the Memorable and Extraordinary Calamities of Margaret of Anjou, Queen of England,* a romance translated from a French manuscript. A few years later, the Abbé Prévost authored an imaginative two-volume work, *Histoire de Marguerite d'Anjou,* which owed more to fiction than fact. In 1820, an opera, *Margherita d'Anjou,* was composed by Giacomo Meyerbeer.

It was Shakespeare's portrayal of Margaret that endured, to her lasting infamy. He invented the epithet "She-Wolf of France" for her and depicted her as a scheming and vindictive adulteress and virago who waged war in the most unwomanly way. The epithet stuck until the eighteenth century, when England was at war with France and the poet Thomas Gray applied it to Edward II's Queen, Isabella.

Margaret's vigorous support of her husband and her son must have seemed her only option, and totally justified, at the time, even if she did make some disastrous decisions. One can only admire her strength and tenacity, her loyalty and steadfastness, and pity her too because she strove in vain on behalf of her husband and son, and ended up alone and impoverished.

13

"Privy pleasures"

※

Now finally established on his throne, Edward settled down to rule England firmly and well. Having seen the splendors of Bruges during his exile, he was even more determined to emulate the Burgundian court, and its influence was at its greatest during this latter part of his reign. In 1472, he had the *Black Book* drawn up, the first set of ordinances to regulate English court ceremonial and etiquette, and in them the influence of Burgundy was manifest. Edward's purpose was to create a display of magnificence, as Burgundian custom dictated. From now on, there would be two households at court: abovestairs, the Lord Chamberlain's department, or "the King's house of magnificence"; and belowstairs, the Lord Steward's department, the "house of providence." Edward was determined to impress with the outer trappings of majesty, and observers were struck by his extravagance, his luxurious chambers hung with rich tapestries, the ostentatious clothes he wore, the costly jewels, and the sumptuousness of his table.

Gone, however, was the glorious youth of Edward's earlier years. At thirty, he was losing his handsome looks and, by 1475, "a little inclining to corpulence."[1] He "was most immoderate with food and drink. It was his habit to take an emetic for the pleasure of gorging his stomach again. For this reason, he had grown fat in the loins, whereas previously he had not only been tall but rather lean and very active."[2]

Despite his overindulgent habits, Edward did not lose his grip on affairs of state. "This Prince, although he was thought to have indulged his passions and desires too intemperately, was still a most devout Catholic, a most unsparing enemy to all heretics, and a most loving encourager of wise and learned men, and of the clergy. Men of every rank and condition wondered that a man of such corpulence, and so fond of boon companionship, vanities, debauchery, extravagance and sensual enjoyments should have had a memory so retentive in all respects."[3]

Edward kept three mistresses during these later years. According to More, two were "greater personages" than the third, and "content to be nameless, but the merriest was Shore's wife, in whom the King therefore took special pleasure, for many he had, but her he loved, whose favor she never abused."

Elizabeth Shore, who is sometimes incorrectly called Jane, was born around 1450 and was the daughter of John Lambert, a prosperous London mercer. She was married "'ere she were well ripe" to a goldsmith, "an honest citizen, young and godly and of good substance," called William Shore, but "she not very fervently loved" her husband, who was "frigid and impotent" in bed.[4] By 1476, she was the King's mistress.

More knew Elizabeth Shore at the end of her long life and left a description of her, saying "proper she was, and fair," and diminutive in stature. "Yet men delighted not so much in her beauty as in her pleasant behavior, for a proper wit had she, and could both read and write. She was merry in company, ready and quick of answer, neither mute nor full of babble. She never abused to any man's hurt, but to many a man's comfort and relief. Where the King took displeasure, she would mitigate and appease his mind. Where men were out of favor, she would bring them into his grace." She was, "of all women, the one the Queen most hated," for she was the one "whom the King her husband most loved."[5] Elizabeth Shore had no political influence, but one suspects that she was the kind of woman to whom powerful men could unburden themselves.

Edward had "many promoters and companions of his vices, the most important and especial [being] the relatives of the Queen, her two sons" and Lord Rivers.[6] An erudite scholar, Rivers was popular with the people, although Dorset and Grey had "earned the hatred of the populace on account of their morals, but mostly because of a certain inherent jealousy which arises between those who are equal by birth when there has been a change in their station."[7]

Rivers patronized William Caxton, who set up the first English printing press at Westminster in 1476. Caxton would print three devotional works that Rivers had translated, including *The Dictes and Sayings of the Philosophers,* the first book ever printed in England. Edward IV was also Caxton's patron and took the royal family to visit his shop by Westminster Abbey.

William, Lord Hastings, Edward's Chamberlain and loyal friend, "was also the accomplice and partner of his privy pleasures."[8] His contemporaries, with whom he was exceedingly popular, praised his loyalty, his upright character, his sense of honor and duty, his liberality, his many charities and benefactions, and his patronage of the arts. His closeness to the King gave him greater influence than many of higher rank. This, and his participation in Edward's debaucheries, earned him the jealousy and hatred of the Queen and her faction, which was exacerbated in 1482 by a dispute over the governorship of Calais. Hastings was appointed to the post by the King in preference to Earl Rivers. A piqued Rivers accused Hastings of intriguing to sell Calais to the French, and Hastings retaliated by leveling the same accusation at Rivers. He then, to his dismay, discovered the extent of the power of the Widvilles, who managed to have his informers against them executed for treason, conspiracy, and sedition. He succeeded in convincing the King of his own innocence, but from that time he "maintained a deadly feud" with Dorset and remained on bad terms with the Queen.[9]

Hastings was also a bitter rival of Lord Dorset, for they were continually trying to steal women from each other. They were also rivals for the favors of Elizabeth Shore.

On 26 June 1471, the King's heir was created Prince of Wales and Earl of Chester. The Widvilles were riding high, and that was the way they intended things to continue. From the first, the Prince's household was in their control. That June, the Queen appointed Elizabeth, Lady Darcy, lady mistress of his nursery, with responsibility for a large staff of attendants. Lady Darcy was married to Richard Haute, a cousin of the Queen; in 1473, his father would be appointed one of the Prince's councillors and controller of his household. In June 1471, Avice Welles, a widow, was given the post of nurse to young Edward.

On 3 July, the King commanded his chief magnates to swear an oath of allegiance to the Prince as his undoubted son and heir. Forty-seven lords gave their oath, foremost among them the dukes of Clarence, Gloucester, and Buckingham. Five days later, the King appointed a council that would be responsible for the administration of his son's household and estates until he reached the age of fourteen, his expected majority. Its members comprised the Queen, Clarence, Gloucester, and several bishops.

Sir Thomas Vaughan was made the Prince's chamberlain; on ceremonial occasions, his duty was to walk behind the King, carrying the child in his arms. Vaughan would remain with Edward for most of his life, offering him dedicated service, and it appears that his charge became very close to him. The Queen's brother Lionel Widville was appointed Edward's chaplain.

Queen Elizabeth had some intellectual influence on her children, especially her daughters. Princess Elizabeth's signature bears a strong resemblance to her mother's, suggesting that the Queen took an active role in her education. She was a patron of education and poor scholars. When Andrew Docket approached her in 1465, she refounded Margaret of Anjou's college at Cambridge; its name was changed from Queen's to Queens' College, and her arms replaced Margaret's on its seal. In 1475, she gave the college its first statutes. With her brother Rivers, Elizabeth was a bountiful patroness to Eton College.

Queen Elizabeth also patronized Caxton, who dedicated *The Knight of the Tower* to her in 1483. She commissioned him to print *The History of Jason* as a present for Prince Edward; it was translated from a French romance written in 1460 by Raoul le Fèvre, chaplain to Philip the Good. She also owned Caxton's *Receil of the Histories of Troy*.

Books were luxury items, often bequeathed in wills, and Elizabeth owned or commissioned several, notably a French prose *Romance of the Saint Graal* (which she purchased for £10 [£11,420] soon after marrying the King), Walter Map's *De Nugis Curialium,* and an illuminated book of devotions, *The Hours of the Guardian Angel*, dedicated to a queen called Elizabeth; it was once thought that this book was presented to Elizabeth of York, but it has been dated on artistic style to 1475–83.

In September 1471, the King and Queen went with a great retinue to Canterbury. "Never were so many people seen heretofore on pilgrimage, men say."[10] They kept the Christmas of 1471 in great state at Westminster, with a disguising—an entertainment in which the performers would hide their identities—and a great banquet for the Lord Mayor of London. They usually followed the custom of wearing their crowns, which was traditionally observed at the great festivals of Easter, Whitsuntide, and Christmas. Elizabeth did not wear hers on Twelfth Night because she was five months pregnant, but she went in procession with the King to Mass, and watched a disguising. On 10 April 1472, she would bear a fourth daughter, Margaret, at Windsor Castle.

PART FIVE

✴

Anne Neville,
Queen of Richard III

I

"Violent dissensions"

✳

IN 1471, GLOUCESTER SET HIS SIGHTS ON MARRYING ANNE NEVille. She and her sister, Isabel, were not co-heiresses to Warwick's vast estates because they were entailed on the male line; the late Kingmaker's heir was his six-year-old nephew, George Neville, son of his deceased brother, Montagu. Nevertheless, the girls would in time inherit their mother's considerable dower lands. Edward IV, however, had seized control of the Warwick inheritance, depriving the Dowager Countess of her dower. He had given many of her lands and offices to Clarence, in right of his wife, Isabel, and some to Gloucester. Neither the King nor his brothers heeded the vociferously voiced complaints of the Countess of Warwick.

Anne was fifteen. Since Edward of Lancaster's death she had been living in Clarence's great London house, the Erber, on Dowgate near the Thames (on the site of the present Cannon Street station). "In presence she was seemly, amiable and beauteous, and in conditions full commendable and right virtuous and, according to the interpretation of Anne her name, full gracious," wrote Rous, who revered Anne as Warwick's daughter. There are sketches of her in heraldic robes in the Rous Roll and the Beauchamp pedigree, also by John Rous; the former depicts a slender woman with long fair hair. Anne also appears in an armorial drawing in a contemporary manuscript in the collection of the Duke of

Buccleuch. Sadly, the stained glass depicting her in the church at Skipton-in-Craven is lost.

Clarence, who had received the lion's share of the Countess of Warwick's lands, felt he should have all, and was furious when, around Michaelmas, Gloucester "sought to make Anne his wife" and claim half of them. "This decision did not suit the plans of the Duke of Clarence, since he feared a division of the Earl's property, which he wished to come to himself alone in right of his wife, and not be obliged to share it with any other person."[1]

Neither brother took into account Anne's right, as a widow, to take charge of her own affairs, or her opinion as to whom she wished to marry, although she probably welcomed the prospect of marriage to a powerful prince who had the means to restore her rightful inheritance and rescue her from her subjugated existence. But Clarence was so fiercely determined to prevent her from marrying Gloucester, or anyone else, that he "caused the damsel to be concealed in order that it might not be known by his brother where she was. Still, however, Gloucester was so much the more astute that he discovered the young lady in the City of London, disguised in the habit of a cook-maid." Immediately, "he had her moved into sanctuary" at St. Martin le Grand, a religious house near Newgate. Given that Anne was the Duchess Isabel's ward, this constituted abduction, even if Anne had been complicit. "In consequence of this, violent dissensions arose between the brothers."[2] An angry Clarence demanded that Anne be returned to his house, but Gloucester placed her under the protection of her uncle, the Archbishop of York, who allowed her to visit Queen Margaret, who was then in the Tower.

"At last, their most loving brother the King agreed to act as mediator."[3] In February 1472, at Sheen, Edward entreated "my lord of Clarence for my lord of Gloucester and, as it is said, he answereth that he [Gloucester] will have my lady his sister-in-law, but they shall part no livelihood."[4] Gloucester refused to agree to such a condition, proof that he was motivated by the desire for Anne's inheritance rather than the young lady herself. Both brothers pleaded their cases before the Council and, through the intervention of the King, "the whole misunderstanding was set to rest, through the mediation of arbitrators."[5] A private war had only just been averted.

A seething Clarence had to agree to the carving up of the Countess of Warwick's estates, even though he himself received the greater share of them and, on 25 March, was created Earl of Warwick and Salisbury in right of his wife. Edward decreed that he should have the lands in the Midlands, even though the widowed Countess held some of them in her own right. The King ignored her desperate pleas from sanctuary at Beaulieu, and proceeded as if she did not exist. Gloucester was to have the estates in Yorkshire, Northumberland, and Cumberland, where he would inherit the loyalty and service of those who had served the Nevilles. It was a great landed inheritance.

Given her later treatment of her mother, which is described below, Anne may have colluded in depriving her mother of her rights; she would benefit, after all.

Gloucester was then nineteen. Unlike Edward IV and Clarence, he resembled his father; like him, he was "of low stature."[6] A Scots envoy who saw him in 1484 noted he had "such a small body." That same year, Nicholas von Poppelau described him as lean, with "delicate arms and legs," while Rous wrote of "his little body and feeble strength" and his "delicate arms and limbs." After his remains were found under a car park in Leicester in 2012, it was found that he had been five feet eight inches tall—actually, an average height for a man at that time.

Polydore Vergil, whose description was said to be based on the testimony of those who had known Gloucester, later claimed that he was "deformed." Before his skeleton was uncovered in 2012, when it became clear that he had scoliosis, the question of his deformity long puzzled historians. The Elizabethan antiquarian John Stow told Sir George Buck "he had spoken with old and grave men who had often seen [him], and they had affirmed he was not deformed, but of person and bodily shape comely enough." However, York Civic Records record that, during a fight in 1491, a schoolmaster called John Payntour called him a "Crouchback," the first use of a nickname that stuck. Richard was well-known in York. Perhaps Payntour was merely being provocative, but it is possible that he had seen him and knew there was no longer any need for tact.

John Rous, writing before 1490, stated that Richard had "unequal" shoulders, "the right higher and the left lower," and a humped back. According to Vergil and More, the left shoulder was "higher than the right." By then, it was believed that Richard had been "ill featured of limbs" and "crook-backed." To contemporary eyes, physical deformity was the outward manifestation of evil character. Portraits of Richard, held to have been painted with the aim of flattering him, were altered in Tudor times to show a deformity, but that is not evident in the earliest representation of him, the line drawing by John Rous in the first York Roll. His portraits show a serious-looking man with a jutting chin, prominent nose, thin lips, and long dark, or dark blond, hair. The recent reconstruction of his face, based on scans of his skull, was partly conjectural, as no soft tissue survived.

By 16 February 1472, Gloucester and Anne were betrothed. That day, "the King, the Queen, my lords of Clarence and Gloucester went to Sheen to pardon, men say not all in charity. What will fall men cannot say."[7] But the outcome was a settlement between the King's brothers.

Gloucester was anxious for the marriage to go forward, but a Papal dispensation was necessary because of the various degrees of consanguinity and affinity that existed as impediments. The couple were first cousins once removed and thus related in the second degree; they were also second cousins in the third degree and third cousins in the fourth degree. Another impediment arose from their being brother- and sister-in-law, on the grounds that it effectively made them brother and sister and placed them in the first degree of affinity. That would not have been the case had there been no close blood ties between the families of the couple, but in this case there plainly were.

The Church forbade marriages between third cousins related by blood or marriage. Without a dispensation—which would have been problematic for those within the first three degrees—such a union would have been invalid. Despite claims by some modern historians that Gloucester never obtained a dispensation, it has now been established that he did petition the Vatican: "Richard, Duke of Gloucester, layman of the diocese of Lincoln, and Anne Neville, woman of the diocese of York, wish to contract marriage between them, but as they are related in the third and fourth degrees of affinity, they request a dispensation."[8]

A dispensation was granted by the Pope himself on 22 April 1472, permitting the parties to marry within the third and fourth degrees of kinship, which covered two of the cousinly relationships, but not the more serious impediments of kinship in the first and second degrees. When the marriage contract was drawn up, the King had ruled that, in the absence of a dispensation, were the marriage to be annulled on the grounds of consanguinity, Anne's share of the Neville estates would revert to Gloucester. The Act of Parliament of 1474 (see below) in which this provision was enshrined, referred to the possibility of the couple needing a second ceremony because of the irregular nature of their union. It is hard to believe that Gloucester and Anne were unaware of the undispensed impediments to their union. Possibly they intended to seek a further dispensation, but never did; maybe Gloucester feared that the Pope would turn down the request. What is clear is that most of their contemporaries were unaware of the illegality of their union. None of Gloucester's enemies would ever seek to make capital out of that.

The wedding went ahead; it was solemnized after 16 February, and probably took place after Easter, which fell on 7 April, given that marriages were not solemnized in Lent. Anne was first referred to as Duchess of Gloucester in the autumn of 1472. It is not known where the ceremony took place; traditionally, Westminster Abbey or St. Stephen's Chapel in the Palace of Westminster have been suggested as the venue. In the absence of a second dispensation—and there is no evidence that one was ever granted—the marriage was invalid, and the legitimacy of any child born to the couple would always be open to challenge.

The marriage brought Gloucester a mighty power base in the North that would give him great territorial and political advantages and the loyalty of the Neville affinity, which would counterbalance any remaining Lancastrian affinity in the region. After the wedding, he probably took Anne north to Middleham Castle, the massive eleventh-century stronghold on high ground overlooking the River Ure in Yorkshire, which had been much enlarged by the Nevilles, to whom it had passed by marriage in 1260. This was Anne's home territory; Gloucester was more closely associated with Barnard Castle in County Durham.

Although primarily built for defense, Middleham was palatial. It boasted luxurious private apartments with fireplaces and communal latrines; there was a chapel, and plenty of accommodation for the many scores of retainers a royal duke needed in his retinue. Gloucester is not known to have made any improvements to the castle, and probably there was no need, since the Nevilles had made it a magnificent residence. It is now a ruin, but enough remains to give a good impression of the splendor that once earned it the name "the Windsor of the North."

The couple divided their time between Middleham and Barnard Castle; when visiting York, where they sometimes kept Easter, Christmas, and the feast of Corpus Christi—they were enrolled in the Corpus Christi guild in 1477—they may have stayed at Sheriff Hutton Castle, another Neville stronghold, which had been granted to Gloucester in 1471. They jointly owned a manuscript of *The Book of Ghostly Grace* by St. Mechtilde of Hackeborn, suggesting a shared piety; Anne inscribed it "Anne Warrewyk," below which Richard signed himself "R. Gloucestr." Anne may have given him his Book of Hours. After his death, it became the property of Margaret Beaufort, who was almost certainly responsible for deleting his name from the text and on the end page. It is now in Lambeth Palace Library.

In February 1476, Anne was admitted to the consorority of St. Cuthbert at Durham Priory (later the Cathedral) by the Prior and chapter of Durham, who wished to repay her "for the devotion of the mind and the completeness of the sincere affection which she has for them and for their monastery, which they know from experience, by admitting her to their spiritual sisterhood and granting her special participation in all Masses, vigils, fasts, prayers, and good works in the monastery of Durham and its dependent cells, in perpetuity, with prayers for her, just as for their other spiritual brethren and sisters, for all time after her death, once they have certain knowledge thereof."[9] Such a privilege was conferred only on those who had demonstrated a special devotion to St. Cuthbert.

That year, Anne apparently acted for Gloucester during his absence from Middleham, according to a message she sent to York via one of his councillors. In 1477, the couple founded a chantry at Queens' College, Cambridge. We know little about their personal life. The Milanese ambassador in Paris reported in 1474 that Clarence had asserted that

Gloucester had married Anne "by force," although he may have been referring to the Duke's tactics in securing his bride, rather than his constraining her to wed him. In the seventeenth century, Richard's apologist, George Buck, would claim that he had had no part in killing Anne's first husband, but had respected her as his mother's kinswoman and loved her "very affectionately, though secretly." It's possible—as many historical novelists have imagined—that he had come to have feelings for her when he was growing up in her father's household, although she had been only twelve when he left it. Rous claimed that they were "unhappily married," but at Christmas 1476, in London, Gloucester bought furs and silk for his "most dear consort," and he referred to her as his "most dearly beloved consort" in estate accounts.

Anne largely vanishes from the historical record in the first decade after her marriage. Her movements are rarely recorded. There is no mention of her at any of the state occasions Gloucester attended, or of his making any provision for a dower or jointure for her. However, he appropriated the lordships of Glamorgan and Abergavenny, which should have been held by George Neville, and kept them in Anne's name, so their revenues may have been used to support her.

Gloucester apparently had a mistress, for his bastard son, John of Gloucester, was conceived possibly in 1473 or 1474. In March 1474, he granted "my beloved gentlewoman," Alice Burgh, an annuity of £20 (£20,770) for life from issues from Middleham "for certain special causes and considerations." Possibly she was John's mother. Richard had a long association with Alice, who came from Knaresborough and whose sister Isabel was wet nurse to Edward of Middleham, Richard and Anne's son. He was "born in the castle of Middleham,"[10] probably early in 1476, as Rous states he was seven and a half in August 1483, while the chronicle of Tewkesbury Abbey stated in c.1478 that Anne "bore a son named— at the castle of Middleham in the year of Our Lord 1476." The first mention of Edward was in a deed issued by his father on 1 April 1477 to Queens' College, where he was styled Earl of Salisbury and called the couple's "first-begotten son."[11] The Prince's Tower at Middleham has traditionally been identified as the place of Edward's birth. A survey conducted in 1538 describes it as "the Round Tower," but mentions a first-floor nursery next to it, so there may be some basis for the tradition.

It is often said that there were no more children, but there was just possibly a second son who died young, which might be inferred from the wording of the grant to Queens' College, and by Richard referring in 1483 to Edward as "our dearest first-born son,"[12] suggesting that there was perhaps a younger son who died before 1484, when *The Great Chronicle of London* referred to Edward as "the only son." Had Edward been the only son, his father would surely have called him simply "our dearest son," unless, of course, he was hoping for other sons. But in the Tewkesbury Chronicle, the name George was later inserted into the gap left in the passage recording Edward's birth. Was this the name of a second son, confused by the monkish scribe with the first?

Anne's health may have been delicate, or she perhaps suffered from low fertility, like her mother, who had borne just two girls. Her evident absence from the great ceremonies at Fotheringhay in the summer of 1476 (which are described below) may indicate that she took some time to recover from giving birth, or that she was concerned for her baby's health. Edward seems to have been frail, as he rarely left Middleham. His wet nurse was Isabel Burgh, and he was later cared for by Jane Collins. Anne Idley, the mistress of his nursery, was the widow of Peter Idley, who had written a book of improving verses called "Instructions to his Son," which may have recommended Anne Idley to the Duchess. Edward was later tutored by a Master Richard Bernall.

2

"The world seemeth queasy"

✳

I N OCTOBER 1472, EDWARD IV WELCOMED TO WINDSOR LOUIS, Lord of Gruthuyse and governor of Holland, who had offered him shelter and hospitality in Bruges during his exile. When he brought Gruthuyse to visit the Queen, she was playing at "marteaux" (marbles) and "closheys" (ninepins) with Princess Elizabeth and her ladies, "which sight was full pleasant."

The following evening, after the King had dined with his guest, "the Queen did ordain a grand banquet in her own apartments, at which King Edward, her eldest daughter, the Duchess of Exeter, the Lady Rivers and the Lord of Gruthuyse all sat with her at one mess [course]; and at another table sat the Duke of Buckingham, my lady his wife, my Lord Hastings," and other nobles. After the dancing, the ladies accompanied the King and Queen when they paid their guest the honor of conducting him to the sumptuous apartments that Elizabeth had had made ready for him: three chambers hung with white silk and linen cloth and laid with carpets—a sign of wealth, as carpets were costly and usually draped across tables to preserve them. A bed had been prepared with a counterpane of cloth of gold furred with ermine, a tester and canopy of shining cloth of gold, and curtains of white sarcenet.

Baths had been prepared for the guests, "and when they had been in their baths for as long as was their pleasure, they had green ginger, divers syrups, comfits and hippocras, served by the order of the Queen."[1] The feasting continued for a fortnight, then the court moved to Westminster. Edward and Elizabeth wore their crowns when the King created Gruthuyse Earl of Winchester in Parliament, and the Duke of Clarence carried his train.

After their guest had gone home, the King opened Parliament. Afterward, he returned to the White Hall in the Palace of Westminster, where the Queen, wearing her crown, joined him, the Prince being carried by Sir Thomas Vaughan. Then the royal party processed into Westminster Abbey, where they made offerings at the shrine of St. Edward the Confessor.

Princess Margaret died, aged eight months, on 11 December 1472, and was buried in Westminster Abbey in an altar tomb of gray marble by St. Edward's shrine. Her tomb brass and inscription have long vanished, but the Latin epitaph read: "Nobility and beauty, grace and tender youth are all hidden here in this chest of death."

Gloucester and Clarence were still warring over the division of the Warwick lands. On 2 April 1473, a Paston correspondent reported: "The world seemeth queasy, for all the persons about the King's person have sent for their armor on account of the quarrel regarding the inheritance of Anne."

The Countess of Warwick had remained in sanctuary at Beaulieu Abbey since Warwick's death, sending urgent petitions for the restoration of her lands to the King, the Queen, the Duchess of York, and even Princess Elizabeth—all to no avail. Gloucester and Clarence evidently saw her persistence as a threat, for if she remarried, her husband might demand the restoration of her lands. The King was soon to sanction the division of the Warwick estates between his brothers as if the Countess were dead. Gloucester determined to install her at Middleham, under his "protection." On 13 June 1473, the Paston Letters recorded that "the Countess is now out of Beaulieu sanctuary, and Sir James Tyrell conveyeth her northward, men say by the King's assent." Rous later stated that the Countess had fled to Gloucester "as her chief refuge," only to find herself "locked up for the duration of his life." Certainly, she did not appear in public after this time. He also wrote that Anne chose to collude in the treatment of her mother, stating that she was kept in confinement at Middleham "with the greatest strictures" at her daughter's direction.

Clarence and Gloucester finally came to an agreement and in June 1474, an Act of Parliament broke the entail, settled all the Warwick estates on them in right of their spouses, disinherited George Neville, and deemed the Dowager Countess to be legally dead. The Act took no account of the principles of established law, and we might wonder how matters stood at Middleham between Anne and her mother.

Parliament further confirmed that Gloucester could retain Anne's share of the Warwick inheritance if their marriage was annulled, but not if he remarried. He could keep them even if Anne divorced him, as long as "he did his best to be reconciled and remarried to her."[2]

There was cause for rejoicing when the Queen bore a second son, Richard, on 17 August 1473 at the Dominican Friary in Shrewsbury. In May 1474, he was created Duke of York in honor of the grandfather whose name he bore, thus instituting the tradition whereby, to this day, the second son of the monarch bears the title.

In 1473, when he was three, the Prince of Wales's household was established at Ludlow Castle, where he was to reside as nominal president of the Council of Wales and the Marches. That autumn, the Queen took him there with his household, which was under the governance of Lord Rivers, who was also appointed the Prince's governor, a post that made him effective ruler of Wales. Rivers was also preferred to the Prince's newly formed Council, commissioned in the names of the child and his mother to govern and restore order to the Welsh Marches on behalf of the King. Edward's half-brother, Sir Richard Grey, was also on his Council, as was Sir Richard Haute. The Council was nominally accountable to the Prince, but the man with real power was its Lord President, John Alcock, Bishop of Worcester (later Bishop of Ely), who had been assigned responsibility for the Prince's education and tutored him personally. Vaughan, now treasurer, continued to care for the child's daily needs. Young Edward "was brought up virtuously by virtuous men" and showed himself "remarkably gifted, and very well advanced in learning for his years."

Elizabeth Widville's influence was clear from the first. "Everyone as he was nearest of kin unto the Queen, so was planted next about the Prince, whereby her blood might of youth be rooted in the Prince's favor."[3] She was a member of young Edward's Council, which acted only "with the advice and express consent of the Queen." She also had responsibility for nominating the officers who served her son. This domination of the heir and his Council by the Widvilles was intended to secure the family's continuing power in the next reign.

For the next ten years, the Prince lived at Ludlow, and "devoted himself to horses and dogs and other useful exercises."[4] The castle was his chief residence, but he spent time also at the manor of Tickenhill at Bewdley, which his father had had prepared as a kind of holiday retreat for him. The boy was brought to court on special occasions, and his mother visited him.

Young Edward was exceptionally lucky in his governor and uncle, who was as powerful a figure in the Welsh Marches as Gloucester was in the North, and also "a kindly, serious and just man, and one tested by every vicissitude of life. Whatever his prosperity, he had injured nobody, though benefiting many, and therefore he had entrusted to him the care and direction of the King's son."[5]

But Rivers was first and foremost a Widville, loyal to his sister and her faction, and his appointment as governor of the Prince, together with the careful selection of the members of the Council of the Marches, meant that young Edward would grow to maturity firmly under Widville control, influenced by his mother's supporters throughout his formative years.

In October 1474, under the terms of a treaty signed in Edinburgh, Cecily of York, aged five, was betrothed to the future James IV, King of Scots, then only two years old, in the interests of peace. Edward had tried to avoid war with France, but now that he was more secure on his throne, he decided to press his claim to the French throne and prepared to invade. He did not want Scotland, France's ancient ally, to cause trouble, so Cecily's betrothal was arranged to preempt that.

In 1475, Edward made his will, naming his "most entirely beloved wife, Elizabeth the Queen" as the first of ten executors. He appointed the

Prince of Wales Keeper of the Realm during his coming absence in France. The Queen was granted £2,200 (£2,274,570) yearly for the maintenance of her eldest son while he lived at court. The Prince made a state entry into London on 12 May, and was knighted by his father on Whitsunday at Westminster.

That summer, having invaded France, bent on conquest, Edward found himself abandoned by his allies Burgundy and Brittany, and settled instead for coming to terms with King Louis, who had dangled the carrot of a lavish pension. On 29 August, the two kings met on a bridge at Picquigny and parleyed through a wooden trellis. The result was the Treaty of Picquigny, which sealed a peace between England and France. One of its provisions was the betrothal of the Princess Elizabeth to the Dauphin Charles. Louis promised to dower Elizabeth with rents to the annual value of £60,000 (£62 million) for her maintenance in a manner befitting the future Queen of France; this was fifteen times the dower settled on Elizabeth Widville. It was agreed that the Princess would go to France when she was twelve. If she died before the wedding, her sister Mary was to take her place.

This was an achievement for Edward, for no English princess since the Conquest had ever become queen of France. The King and Queen were deeply committed to this marriage, and Elizabeth Widville's pride was so inflated that she wrote repeatedly to King Louis to know when she should send him "her Dauphiness."[6] On 2 November, she bore another princess, called Anne, at Westminster.

In July 1476, the King took his family to Fotheringhay in Northamptonshire. For over a century, the castle had been one of the chief seats of the House of York. Richard of Gloucester had been born there, and Fotheringhay was Edward IV's favorite residence outside London. He had enlarged the castle, building beautiful lodgings for himself and his Queen, creating a palace with a double moat and a towering gatehouse.

The royal family had returned to Fotheringhay to give their dead fitting burial. Clad in deep mourning, they attended somber ceremonies on 29–30 July, when the bodies of Richard, Duke of York, and Edmund, Earl of Rutland, were brought from their humble resting place in the church of the Mendicant friars at Pontefract and reinterred with all due honors in the collegiate church at Fotheringhay.

On 29 July, the King and Queen and their family stood at the entrance to the churchyard, waiting to receive the cortège. Clarence, Dorset, Rivers, Hastings, and other noblemen were present. Gloucester, with other lords and officers of arms, all in black, followed York's funeral chariot, which was drawn by six horses, wearing black caparisons with the arms of England. An effigy of the late Duke in an ermine-furred mantle and cap of maintenance, covered with a cloth of gold, lay on his coffin on a bier blazing with candles and guarded by an angel of silver bearing a crown of gold, to signify that he had been the rightful King of England.

When the procession drew to a standstill, the King made an obeisance to his father's coffin, laying his hand on it, and kissed it, weeping. Then the processions of prelates and peers advanced into the church, where two hearses were waiting, one for the body of the Duke, the other for that of Rutland. Masses were sung and the King's chamberlain, on his behalf, laid seven palls of cloth of gold on the coffins.

The next day, there were three funeral Masses. After the King and Queen had offered at the altar, the bodies of York and Rutland were interred in the church, where tombs were later built to their memory. Afterward, the royal family distributed alms among the 5,000 people who had gathered outside. It was said that 20,000 were present at the feast that followed, which was served partly in the castle and partly in the King's tents and pavilions.

The year ended in tragedy. The Duchess of Clarence's first child had died at birth, but in 1473 she had borne a daughter, Margaret, and in 1475 a son, Edward, who was styled Earl of Warwick in right of his mother. A fourth child, Richard, arrived in October 1476 in the infirmary at Tewkesbury Abbey in Gloucestershire, but Isabel never recovered from the birth and was taken home to Warwick Castle to die. She lingered until 21 December, and her infant son followed her to the grave on 1 January. She was buried in Tewkesbury Abbey.

That winter, Edward opened negotiations for the marriage of the Prince of Wales to the Infanta Isabella, heiress of the Spanish sovereigns, Ferdinand, King of Aragon, and Isabella, Queen of Castile, whose marriage had unified Spain. Two years later, when a male heir to Spain was born, these negotiations foundered, and a daughter of the Holy Roman Emperor Frederick III was then sought for young Edward. However, "the chief difficulty" in regard to arranging a marriage for him was proving to be the huge amount of money the King wanted.

Around March 1477, Elizabeth gave birth to a third son, George. In 1478, he was designated Duke of Bedford, the title of which the hapless George Neville had been deprived, although there is no record of any formal creation. That year, the Queen, her daughter Elizabeth, and her sister-in-law the Duchess of Suffolk, were made Ladies of the Order of the Garter, and participated in the traditional three-day Garter celebrations at Windsor. On St. George's Day, they rode at the head of a company of ladies to St. George's Chapel to hear Mass, all wearing a livery of mulberry red embroidered with Garters. Stalls were not allocated to Ladies of the Garter, so they watched the service from the rood loft. Afterward, they observed the annual Garter feast from the gallery above St. George's Hall, where Edward IV sat enthroned in solitary state at the high table.

3

"A rondolet of Malmsey"

※

THE OUTWARD DISPLAYS OF UNITY BY THE YORKIST FAMILY masked deep divisions. Clarence was still burning with resentment because Gloucester had received so much of the Warwick inheritance and now held sway in the North, where once the Nevilles had ruled, whereas he himself was barred from power by the King, who would not even let him go to Ireland to fulfill his duties as Lord Lieutenant. At court, the Widvilles dominated.

Early in 1477, Charles the Bold had been killed at the Battle of Nancy, leaving his duchy in the hands of his only legitimate child, Mary of Burgundy. The dukes of Burgundy were descended from Charles V of France and had constantly striven for independence from the French Crown. Now Louis XI promptly declared the duchy extinct, claiming that it properly belonged to France.

Charles's widow, Margaret of York, began scheming to marry her stepdaughter Mary to her brother Clarence, who leaped at the idea, seeing himself gaining a great European fiefdom. However, that would seriously have prejudiced England's recent alliance with France, and given the untrustworthy Clarence a rival power base on the continent, with all the riches of Burgundy at his disposal as well as control over the North Sea coast. Edward IV feared that Clarence might deploy these resources to challenge his throne, and threw every impediment in the way, which "increased Clarence's displeasure" still further. Edward was aware that

Mary of Burgundy had a claim to the English throne through her grandmother Isabella of Portugal, a granddaughter of John of Gaunt. He did not want Clarence entertaining dreams of becoming King. A popular prophecy then in circulation foretold that "G" should follow "E" to the throne, which greatly troubled Edward. From that time, the brothers "each began to look upon the other with no very fraternal eyes."[1]

When Louis XI invaded Burgundy and seized it, Clarence retaliated by striking at Edward through the Queen. Elizabeth had in her service a woman called Ankarette Twynho, a respectable widow who had previously served the Duchess of Clarence. In April 1477, without a warrant, a hundred of Clarence's retainers dragged Ankarette from her home, seized her valuables, and imprisoned her at Warwick. Three days later, she was brought before the justices at Warwick Guildhall and accused of having administered poison to the Duchess, and of helping the Queen to bewitch her sister-in-law and bring about her death. The jury, intimidated by Clarence, duly found the hapless Ankarette guilty, and she was taken that same day to the public gallows and hanged, pitifully protesting her innocence. With her suffered John Thoresby of Warwick for allegedly poisoning the Duchess's baby.

The allegations made by Clarence against Ankarette Twynho were so patently fabricated, and so touched the Queen's reputation and honor, that retribution was inevitable. Furthermore, Clarence had debased royal justice by unlawfully arresting and murdering his victims.

The Widvilles had never had any reason to love Clarence. He had denounced the King's marriage and been responsible with Warwick for the executions of the Queen's father and brother in 1469. It was hardly surprising that the Widvilles now leveled a countercharge of sorcery against the Duke, and that the King decided to deal decisively with him.

Early in May, Edward IV ordered the arrest of Dr. John Stacey, an Oxford clerk and astronomer of sinister reputation. After lengthy questioning and torture, Stacey revealed that Thomas Burdett, a member of Clarence's household, had asked him to cast the horoscopes of the King and the Prince of Wales, with a view to predicting when they might die. Evidently the forecast was unsatisfactory, as before long the two men were allegedly molding leaden images of Edward and his son in order to bring about their deaths by black magic. The implication was that Clarence was the prime mover in the plot, but the King did not yet go so far as to arrest him. Stacey and Burdett were arraigned and condemned as a warning to him, and were executed on 20 May. Clarence protested their innocence before the Council, but was ignored, and the Council declared that the evidence against Ankarette Twynho would be reexamined.

Clarence now began publicly to denounce the King as a bastard and a necromancer, and allege that his marriage to Elizabeth Widville was null and void because tradition forbade kings of England to marry widows. He then incited a minor rebellion in the eastern counties against the King, while rumor had it in Europe that he was plotting with Louis XI to help Margaret of Anjou invade England. There was probably no truth in it, but it did not help matters. Finally, Clarence attacked the Queen, openly accusing her of having murdered his Duchess by poison and sorcery, and pointedly refusing to eat or drink anything at court.

The King, with astonishing forbearance, turned a blind eye. Few took Clarence seriously, for he had very little real power. But when Edward moved to Windsor in June, Clarence went beyond the point of no return. Storming into the council chamber at Westminster, he insultingly denounced the King's justice and the sentences on Stacey and Burdett, and had their written declarations of innocence read aloud by a priest who was with him.

The King's patience gave way. Honor demanded that Clarence be punished for this crowning act of lèse-majesté. He summoned him to Westminster and accused him of going above the law, of conduct derogatory to the laws of the realm, and of usurping the royal prerogative by acting as if he were King. Clarence could not deny his guilt, and on 10 June, he was incarcerated in the Tower of London, charged with committing acts violating the laws of the realm. He languished in his prison, traditionally in the Bowyer Tower, until in November, Edward made up his mind to try him publicly for his offenses. Parliament was then summoned, chiefly for this purpose.

These dark days were enlivened by another splendid royal occasion. On 15 January 1478, the King's second son, Richard, Duke of York, aged four, was married to the flame-haired, six-year-old Anne Mowbray, Duchess of Norfolk in her own right since the death in 1476 of her father, John Mowbray, 4th and last Duke of Norfolk in the Mowbray line.

Through this marriage, Edward secured for his son the rich Norfolk estates. The wedding took place in St. Stephen's Chapel in the Palace of Westminster. This beautiful gothic chapel, built in the late thirteenth century in emulation of St. Louis IX's Sainte-Chapelle in Paris, had a vaulted ceiling of sky blue with numerous gold stars. For this occasion, the chapel walls, adorned with murals of angels, kings, and religious scenes in vivid scarlet, green, and blue, had been hung with azure cloth embroidered with gold fleurs-de-lis.

The Queen escorted her son to the marble altar, where he waited with the bride's mother, Elizabeth Talbot, Dowager Duchess of Norfolk. Then Lord Rivers and the King's nephew John de la Pole, Earl of Lincoln, led in the bride. Apart from Clarence, the entire royal family was present, as well as foreign ambassadors, lords, ladies, knights, squires, and guards and servants in the mulberry and blue livery of the House of York. The King and Queen watched from beneath a cloth-of-gold canopy as the Papal dispensation permitting this marriage of cousins was read out. Then the King gave Anne Mowbray away, and the marriage service commenced.

Afterward Gloucester showered gold and silver coins upon the crowds outside, as spices and wine were served to the wedding party. There were jousts and a lavish banquet in the Painted Chamber, at which the little bride was named "Princess of the Feast."

On 8 February 1478, Parliament passed an Act of Attainder against Clarence, condemning him for having "falsely and traitorously intended and purposed firmly the extreme destruction and disinheriting of the King and his issue" and spreading "the falsest and most unnatural-colored pretense that man might imagine, that the King our sovereign lord was a bastard and not begotten to reign upon us."[2]

The King himself sat in judgment on his brother. Clarence's protests were in vain. Edward meant to have a conviction for high treason and did not give the Duke an opportunity to defend himself. It was widely believed at the time that the Queen and her faction had been the prime movers in the matter. In 1483, Mancini heard that Elizabeth's brother Edward Widville and her sons Dorset and Grey had been instrumental in securing Clarence's conviction. She "remembered the insults to her family and the calumnies with which she was reproached, namely that she was not the legitimate wife of the King. Thus she concluded that her offspring by the King would never come to the throne unless the Duke of Clarence were removed, and of this she easily persuaded the King. The Queen's alarm was intensified by the comeliness of the Duke of Clarence, which would make him appear worthy of the crown."[3] Elizabeth's fear of Clarence was, it seems, greater than the King's, and this has led some writers to conclude that he knew something about her past that she did not want revealed. That is pure supposition. If Clarence had really known any secrets about her that could be used to his advantage, he would surely not have hesitated to make them public by now. Yet the Widville presence in this Parliament was "easily the most powerful faction." Clarence's attainder deprived him of his life, titles, and estates, and the rights of himself and his heirs to the succession.

When it came to it, Edward IV was reluctant to put his own brother to death and refused for over a week to give his assent to Clarence's execution. But the Commons were clamoring for justice to take its course, and the Speaker came to the Bar of the Lords, requesting that what was to be done should be done at once. The King had no alternative but to accede to their demands. At the request of the Duchess Cecily, the sentence usually meted out to traitors—hanging, drawing, and quartering—was commuted to beheading or, according to the French chronicler Molinet, any other method preferred by Clarence. The Duchess also begged that the execution take place in private, to avoid further scandal.

On 18 February 1478, Clarence was put to death in the Tower. According to *The Great Chronicle of London,* he "made his end in a rondolet of Malmsey" (Madeira wine). Being drowned in wine was an unusual method of execution, but Molinet asserted that Clarence had once suggested it jokingly to the King, adding that he had expressed the wish to die in this manner. Many contemporary chroniclers, including Commines, Mancini, and the Frenchmen Jean de Roye and Olivier de la Marche, corroborated the story; only Croyland was noncommittal, saying: "The execution, whatever its nature may have been, took place in the Tower of London." A portrait of Clarence's daughter, Margaret, painted around 1530, shows her wearing a miniature wine-cask on a bracelet at her wrist—a poignant memento of her father's fate.

Clarence was buried beside his wife in Tewkesbury Abbey (a skull and a few bones displayed in a wall niche in a vault, reputedly theirs, are now known not to have belonged to either of them). He was given a noble funeral, and a beautiful tomb, surmounted by effigies of the Duke and Duchess, was raised in their memory, but has long since disappeared.

Clarence's attainder prevented his orphaned children from inheriting his titles and estates, which had reverted to the Crown. Warwick, however, held his earldom in right of his mother, and the King allowed him a portion of her estates. The Queen's eldest son, Lord Dorset, bought his wardship and marriage, and he and his sister Margaret were sent to Sheen to be brought up with Edward IV's children.

Gloucester was "so overcome with grief for his brother that he could not dissimulate so well, but he was overheard to say that he would one day avenge his brother's death."[4] Yet he lifted not a finger to save him. He may even have acquiesced in his brother's fall, for there is some evidence that he was involved in the proceedings against Clarence and benefited more than anyone else from his fall. Clarence's attainder left Gloucester next in line to the throne after the King's sons. Even before his death, Gloucester had requested his share of the Warwick inheritance. On 5 February, his son, Edward of Middleham, was created Earl of Salisbury, and on 21 February, Gloucester himself was given Clarence's office of Great Chamberlain of England. "Some wise men" were of the opinion that he was not displeased by Clarence's fall.[5] That he was affected by it, however, is attested to by a letter he sent much later to James FitzGerald, Earl of Desmond, in which he recalled he had had to keep his inward feelings hidden.

"Thenceforth, Richard came very rarely to court."[6] From 1472, he governed England north of the River Trent on behalf of the King. His power in that region was almost absolute, and the success of his administration was due in no small part to the loyalty of his followers and deputies, and his marriage to the Neville heiress: as Anne's husband, he was seen as successor to that great northern family. Thanks to his strong, stable government, which brought peace to the region and eliminated much of its lawlessness, many Lancastrian loyalties were transferred to the House of York. Gloucester now enjoyed unprecedented power, greater than any other magnate to date, reflecting Edward's complete trust in his integrity.

In the South, and at court, Gloucester was a comparative stranger. Here, the Widvilles dominated. Mancini was amazed at the power of the Queen, who had "attracted to her party many strangers, and introduced them to court, so that they alone should manage the public and private business of the Crown, give or sell offices, and finally rule the very King himself." There was rank corruption in high places, and the Widvilles were at the very center of it. Edward showed special favor to his wife's sons, Dorset and Grey, and her brother Rivers.

He did not perceive that his policy of entrusting the upbringing of his heir to the Widvilles was at variance with his making an overmighty subject of Gloucester, their enemy, whose hatred and fear of them was probably what caused him to visit the court only rarely. "He kept himself within his own lands and set out to acquire the loyalty of his people through favors and justice. The good reputation of his private life and public activities powerfully attracted the esteem of strangers. By these arts, Richard acquired the favor of the people, and avoided the jealousy of the Queen, from whom he lived far separated."[7] Probably he feared her influence, given what had befallen Clarence, while her later actions show that she, in turn, distrusted and feared him.

Some modern writers have linked the subsequent brief imprisonment of Robert Stillington, Bishop of Bath and Wells, with the fall of Clarence. Stillington, a brilliant intellectual, had been Chancellor of England from 1467 to 1473 and enjoyed the favor of Edward IV. But at some point in the week between 27 February and 5 March 1478, he was arrested on a charge of violating his oath of fidelity by uttering words prejudicial to the King. What he said is not recorded, nor is there any evidence that this was connected with Clarence. It is possible that Clarence had allied himself with Stillington; his West Country estates bordered upon Stillington's diocese. It has been suggested that the Bishop had helped to spread Clarence's slanders about the King's bastardy and his marriage, but if his offense had been treasonable, or if he had posed any real danger to the King's security or the royal succession, he would surely have suffered a greater punishment. Instead, he was released on 20 June on payment of a fine, and later given several respectable positions at court.

4

"An unknown disease"

✳

IN MARCH 1479, TWO-YEAR-OLD GEORGE, DUKE OF BEDFORD, died at Windsor Castle—possibly of the plague that visited England that year—and was buried in St. George's Chapel. The loss of her youngest son must have been hard for the Queen, who was pregnant again. On 14 August 1479, she gave birth to her sixth daughter, Katherine, at Eltham Palace.

St. George's Day was celebrated with great pomp. The Queen wore her robes as chief Lady Companion of the Order of the Garter, and the Garter was bestowed on the Princesses Mary and Cecily. That year, the King and Queen made a pilgrimage to the shrine of St. Frideswide in Oxford with the duchesses of Bedford and Suffolk. As they entered the town, crowds carrying torches ran beside their chariot. They were received at the university with a welcome address by Lionel Widville, who had just been appointed its chancellor. The royal party left after dinner the next day.

That year, the Duchess of York, now sixty-five, enrolled herself as a Benedictine oblate and retired to her castle at Berkhamsted to pursue a life of religious devotion. As an oblate, she wore sober secular robes and embraced the spirit of the Benedictine vow in her life in the world, dedicating herself to the service of God. Daily she observed the canonical hours, prayed, and read the Scriptures, leaving just a little time for enjoying wine and recreation with her ladies.

On 10 November 1480, Elizabeth Widville gave birth to her tenth and last child at Eltham Palace. It was another girl, who was called Bridget, an unusual choice of name that had no royal precedent but was perhaps chosen by Duchess Cecily, who cherished a special devotion to St. Bridget of Sweden, foundress of the Bridgettine order. Choosing the name of a saint who left the royal court of Sweden to found a monastic order suggests that the King and Queen decided from the first that they would devote this daughter to God. It was not unusual for wealthy medieval parents to do so, as a gesture of thanksgiving, or to lay up treasure for themselves in Heaven.

In November 1481, Anne Mowbray died at Greenwich Palace, aged eight, and was buried with great pomp in the Chapel of St. Erasmus, Elizabeth Widville's own foundation in Westminster Abbey. When this chapel was demolished in the early sixteenth century to make way for the Henry VII Chapel, Anne's remains were moved to the Minoresses' convent at Aldgate. Workmen excavating the site in 1964 found her lead coffin, buried eleven feet deep. She was still wrapped in a shroud and red hair adhered to her skull. Her remains were examined by medical experts and then reburied near her original resting place in Westminster Abbey.

Edward IV had envisaged a string of marriage alliances for his heir and his five "fine looking and most delightful, beautiful girls."[1] Elizabeth was to marry the Dauphin, the most prestigious match of them all. In 1481, Edward reached an agreement with Duke Francis of Brittany that Prince Edward should marry Anne, the Duke's four-year-old heiress. Mary was betrothed to the future King Frederick I of Denmark, and James III of Scots began pressing Edward IV to send Cecily to Scotland to be betrothed to his son. Anne had been betrothed to Philip of Austria in 1480. Among the husbands proposed for Katherine were the heir to the Spanish throne, and the Earl of Ormond. Through the unions of his daughters, Edward envisioned English influence extending through France, Scotland, Denmark, Burgundy, the Empire, and Spain—and beyond.

Tragedy intervened to prevent the fruition of one of these alliances when, on 23 May 1482, the Princess Mary died at Greenwich, aged just fifteen. She was buried in St. George's Chapel, Windsor, where she was laid to rest beside her brother George, the Prince of Wales being present as chief mourner.

Possibly King Louis had never had any real intention of allowing

Princess Elizabeth's marriage to the Dauphin to go ahead, but when Mary of Burgundy died in March 1482 after a fall from her horse, her Flemish subjects, who did not want to be ruled by her husband, Maximilian of Austria, made overtures to Louis, who seized his advantage. On 23 December 1482, the Treaty of Arras was concluded between Louis IX and the Flemings, providing for the marriage of the Dauphin to three-year-old Margaret of Austria, Maximilian's daughter. The treaty left Edward IV's foreign policy in shreds, and his daughter was to suffer the humiliation of being publicly jilted.

Unsuspecting, "King Edward kept the feast of the Nativity at his palace at Westminster, frequently appearing clad in a great variety of most costly garments." His "most elegant figure overshadowed everyone else" as he "stood before the onlookers like some new and extraordinary spectacle. In those days you would have seen a royal court worthy of a most mighty kingdom, filled with riches and men from almost every nation, and, surpassing all else, those beautiful and most delightful children, the issue of his marriage with Queen Elizabeth," among them his daughters, five "most beauteous maidens."[2] Twelve-year-old Prince Edward had come up from Ludlow and appeared in a dazzling outfit of white cloth of gold, while the Queen and Princess Elizabeth had received fifteen yards of green taffeta silk cloth of gold.

The fair-haired Prince Edward took after his father in character. Mancini, who may have seen the Prince and certainly spoke with those who knew him, wrote: "In word and deed he gave so many proofs of his liberal education, of polite, nay, rather scholarly attainments far beyond his age. He had such dignity in his whole person, and in his face such charm that however much they might gaze, he never wearied the eyes of beholders." He had been "brought up virtuously by virtuous men," and was "remarkably gifted and well-advanced in learning for his twelve years."[3] The Prince was very much his mother's child and under the influence of her faction, to which he naturally inclined.

The news that the Princess Elizabeth had been jilted reached England in January, and Edward IV's fury knew no bounds. He summoned Parliament and demanded that England make war on France.

He never carried out his threat. On 9 April 1483, after a short illness lasting five days, he died at Westminster, aged just forty-one. He was "neither worn out with old age, nor seized with any known kind of malady";

he just "took to his bed on the feast of Easter"[4] and succumbed to "an unknown disease."[5] Mancini says he had caught a chill at the end of March while out in a small boat fishing at Windsor. "Being a tall and very fat man, he let the damp cold chill his vitals and contracted a sickness from which he never recovered." The royal physicians could do nothing for him. Edward then suffered an apoplexy and "perceived his natural strength so sore enfeebled that he despaired all recovery" and summoned the Queen and his magnates to his bedchamber. He commanded Hastings and Dorset to make peace with each other, at which the two lords were outwardly reconciled. Hastings and the Queen put on a similar charade for the King's benefit, but "there still survived a latent jealousy."[6]

It is not known whether Elizabeth was present when Edward "rendered his spirit to his Creator at the Palace of Westminster,"[7] nor did anyone record how deeply she mourned him. Her actions after his death, as will be seen, show that she was not prostrated by grief, yet she would soon find that the loss of her husband, the man who had advanced and protected her, would prove cataclysmic.

Edward IV died rich, powerful, and esteemed throughout Christendom as a strong ruler, but he had failed to unify the rival factions in his kingdom and created two mighty power centers in his realm, the Widvilles and Gloucester, who were in opposition to each other. Even as Edward's body was being prepared for its lying-in-state at Westminster, it was dawning upon many that a new era of uncertainty had arrived, and that the next weeks would prove crucial.

Edward was succeeded by his twelve-year-old son, now Edward V, who was proclaimed King on 11 April. A new bidding prayer, to be read in churches at the beginning of the new reign, enjoined all to pray for "our dread King Edward V, the lady Queen Elizabeth his mother [and] all the royal offspring."[8] In Edward IV's only surviving will, dated 1475, he entrusted the care of his son to "our dearest wife the Queen," although she was not named among the chief executors. She was to have any household goods she desired and authority to dispose of the rest and her daughters' dowries, which they were to have if they were governed and ruled by her in their choice of husbands. No provision was made for a minority.

5

"Demanding rather than supplicating"

✳

When Edward IV died, "the Queen, with her second son, the Duke of York, and the rest of her family were in London, where was also the chamberlain, Hastings, with the bishops of York and Ely, friends of the King."[1] The Widvilles were then in a strong position. They controlled the young King, the court, the Council, the Tower of London, the fleet, the royal children, and the royal treasure, "the weight of which was said to be immense"; it "was kept in the hands of the Queen and her people" at the Tower.[2] In March, the office of deputy constable of the Tower of London had been transferred from Rivers to Dorset, who was now in effective control of both the late King's treasure and the royal ordnance held at the fortress. Mancini wrote of the hatred in which Rivers, Dorset, and Sir Richard Grey were held by the populace "on account of their morals, but mostly because of a certain inherent jealousy." They still "had to endure the imputation of causing the death of the Duke of Clarence."[3]

On his deathbed, Edward IV must either have drawn up a new will, or added a codicil to the first, as attested to by the fact that the executors who met after the King's death were not those listed in the 1475 will, the Queen being the most notable omission. Rous states that Gloucester was named protector of the realm by this deathbed "ordinance," and Mancini "heard men say that in the same will [Edward IV] appointed as protector of his children and realm his brother, Richard, Duke of Gloucester." Clearly, Edward's councillors were aware of his dying wishes.

Apparently, Edward intended that Gloucester should govern the kingdom while the King was a minor and have care and control of the royal children. Rivers, it seems, was to be removed from his office of governor, and the Queen was apparently given no power at all. What probably prompted the late King's change of heart was his realization of the need to mitigate the rapaciousness and unpopularity of the Widvilles.

They had no intention of allowing Gloucester to seize power; they clearly foresaw the continuance and flowering of their supremacy under Edward V. The late King's councillors were with the Queen at Westminster, and she and Dorset called a council meeting, as if she were regent. There were heated discussions and arguments, while Elizabeth "most beneficently tried to extinguish every mark of murmur and disturbance."[4] Soon it became clear that the councillors were divided into three camps: the Queen's party, which was the largest and included her kinsmen and most of the bishops, notably Thomas Rotherham, now Archbishop of York; the smaller anti-Widville faction led by Lord Hastings with the support of Lord Stanley; and a group including the Archbishop of Canterbury and John Russell, Bishop of Lincoln, who would not commit themselves either way. No one declared openly for Gloucester. The only common cause between these factions was loyalty to the son of Edward IV.

Hastings was under no illusions. The Widvilles' hostility toward him and the older nobility was palpable, and "he feared that if supreme power fell into the hands of those of the Queen's blood, they would most bitterly revenge themselves on himself for the injuries which they claimed he had done to them."[5] Hastings, in turn, "was hostile to the entire kin of the Queen, on account of the Marquess of Dorset,"[6] for their bitter rivalry had been exacerbated by Hastings making Elizabeth Shore his mistress as soon as Edward IV was dead. He and others now declared "that the guardianship of so youthful a person [as Edward V], until he should reach the years of maturity, ought to be utterly forbidden to his uncles and brothers by the mother's side."[7]

The Widvilles were seeking a legal means to prevent Gloucester from becoming protector. They had discovered that, according to precedent, the office was purely an interim one, its purpose being to ensure the security and protection of the realm until the sovereign was safely crowned, at which time it would lapse. In 1429, during the minority of Henry VI,

Humphrey, Duke of Gloucester, had relinquished his office of lord protector as soon as the young King (then aged seven) had sworn to protect and defend the Church and his realm at his coronation.

The Widvilles urged that Edward V be crowned immediately, intent on thwarting Gloucester's claim to be protector. The Parliament that would be called in Edward V's name after his crowning would have the authority finally to determine who should wield power during his minority. The young King, having been under the influence of his mother's faction from infancy, was unlikely to be well disposed toward anyone who opposed them, and if the precedent set by Henry VI was followed, he would come of age in three and a half years' time, so his wishes would be influential.

The Queen demanded that Edward V be brought to London at once, accompanied by an army of soldiers, but Hastings, who foresaw trouble and bloodshed, exploded with anger and threatened to retire to Calais—of which he was captain—unless a smaller escort was provided. His threat was implicit: it was in Calais that Warwick had plotted against Edward IV in 1470, and Hastings made it quite clear that he would not scruple to move likewise against the Widvilles. Hard words followed, but it was the Queen who backed down, agreeing to limit the King's escort to 2,000 men. Hastings signified his approval, and Dorset wrote at once to Rivers and "to the young King Edward, that he should reach the capital three days before the date appointed" for the coronation.[8]

At the time of Edward IV's death, Gloucester was 240 miles away at Middleham Castle. Hastings, as Lord Chamberlain, wrote to him with the sad tidings and informed him that the late King, on his deathbed, had "committed to him only [his] wife, children, goods and all that ever he had." He apparently warned the Duke that the Queen's party meant to oust him from power, and urged him "to hasten to the capital with a strong force and avenge the insult done him by his enemies. He might easily obtain his revenge if, before reaching the City, he took the young King Edward under his protection and authority, while seizing, before they were alive to the danger, those of the King's followers who were not in agreement with this policy."[9]

Croyland implies that Hastings also confided his fears in a letter to

Henry Stafford, 2nd Duke of Buckingham, one of the most important noblemen in England. The Staffords were known to their contemporaries as hard-dealing men. They had been loyal to the House of Lancaster during the Wars of the Roses. Young Buckingham was fabulously wealthy, owning lands, manors, and castles in twenty-two counties, and himself had a claim to be in the line of succession to the throne by virtue of his descent from Thomas of Woodstock, the youngest son of Edward III. In 1474, in recognition of this, he had been granted the right to display a coat of arms similar to that of the King. The deaths of Henry VI and his heir had put an end to his hopes for the overthrow of the House of York, yet enabled him to claim the lands of his Bohun ancestors, which had been in the hands of Henry VI. But Edward IV had seized all Henry VI's estates and possessions, and thereafter Buckingham harbored a grudge against him for depriving him of what he considered to be rightfully his. It was probably because of this, and his ill-concealed resentment of the Widvilles, that Buckingham had not gained much advancement at court under Edward IV. But now, in writing to Buckingham, Hastings had good reason to believe he would secure an ally.

Hastings's news alarmed Gloucester, who feared that if he did not act urgently and decisively, he would be ousted from power by the Widvilles. His very life might even be in danger, bearing in mind what had happened to Clarence. He was also aware that his office of protector-designate would lapse with the coronation, and he could perhaps foresee a Widville-dominated Council ruling through an acquiescent king hostile to himself. In such circumstances, it was unlikely that he would be allowed to retain his power and vast lands in the North. Everything he held dear was at stake. It was imperative that he act to overthrow the Widvilles and seize the reins of government himself.

Immediately, he took Hastings's advice and decided to ride south and meet up with Buckingham. With Gloucester, Hastings, and Buckingham allied in a coalition to bring down the Widvilles, the stage was set for a fatal power struggle. Mancini believed that from the moment he learned of Edward IV's death, Gloucester was plotting to seize the throne himself, and Croyland was of the opinion that he plotted it before he left the North.

To show that his intentions were honorable, the Duke immediately wrote "the most pleasant letter to console the Queen; he promised to come and offer submission, fealty, and all that was due from him to his lord and king, Edward V,"[10] and professed his willingness to take on the office of protector entrusted to him by his brother.[11] His "loving" letter promised Elizabeth "seas and mountains,"[12] but evidently did not allay her fears, or divert her and her faction from their determination to bar him from power.

Gloucester also sent a formal letter to the Council, declaring that he had been loyal to his brother Edward, and would, if permitted, be loyal to his brother's son and all his brother's issue, even female, "if perchance (which God forbid) the youth should die. He would expose his life to every danger that the children might endure in their father's realm. He asked the councillors to take his desserts into consideration when disposing of the government, to which he was entitled by law and his brother's ordinance."[13] In fact, Edward IV had had no legal right to name Gloucester as protector; a dead king's wishes held no force in law. Only Parliament had the right to decide who should govern the realm during a royal minority.

Wearing deepest black, Gloucester left Middleham around 20 April and rode south. Two days earlier, after lying in state at Westminster, Edward IV's body had been conveyed up the Thames to Windsor and there buried in St. George's Chapel. By custom, the Queen was not present.

Although Gloucester had not yet been confirmed as lord protector and had no legal mandate, he was determined to seize the young King as he was escorted to London by his uncle Earl Rivers, his half-brother Sir Richard Grey, Sir Thomas Vaughan, and Sir Richard Haute.

On 21 April, Buckingham was at Brecon on the Welsh Marches when he received Gloucester's letter, in which the Duke complained "of the insult done to him by the ignoble family of the Queen. Buckingham, since he was of the highest nobility, was disposed to sympathize, because he had his own reason for detesting the Queen's kin."[14] It was his burning desire to see the Widvilles crushed, and his hope that, once in power, Gloucester would grant him the Bohun inheritance, that made him decide to ally himself with the Duke.

In London, "on completion of the royal obsequies, and while many peers of the realm were collecting in the City, a Council assembled,"[15] summoned by the Queen and Dorset in the King's name. This was a lawful assembly of magnates, instituted because there had to be some form of administration until Edward V was crowned. Nevertheless, many were uneasy about its convening, and were not reassured when Dorset commanded its members to gather in the Queen's presence as if she were already regent.

The Council met around 20 April. "The most urgent desire of all present was that the Prince should succeed his father in all his glory."[16] Dorset urged that he be crowned as planned on 4 May, but some councillors raised objections, guessing the motive for such haste, and Mancini says there were those, foremost among them Hastings, who "said that everything ought not thus to be hurried through; rather they should await the young King's uncle." To this Dorset "is said to have replied, 'We are so important that even without the King's uncle we can make and enforce our decisions.'" This arrogant remark provoked a heated debate over who should govern the country, which lasted for several days.

The Widvilles believed they had the Council in their pocket, but it soon became obvious that they did not have a sufficiently large majority to persuade the councillors to name the Queen regent. Yet they were still a political force to be reckoned with, even though they had many enemies opposing them, chiefly Hastings, who had insulted them in the council chamber by insisting that the base blood of the Queen's kindred unfitted them for the task of governing the realm. There were rumors that the Widvilles were plotting to seize power, which only further inflamed the people's hatred toward them. "The more prudent [councillors] were of the opinion that the guardianship of so youthful a person [as the King] ought to be utterly forbidden to his uncles and brothers of the mother's side."[17]

Hastings proposed that the Duke of Gloucester should govern because Edward IV had wished it. The Council considered this, discussing what powers Gloucester might enjoy as protector, a subject on which opinions were divided. Dorset envisaged Gloucester as a figurehead presiding over the Council, but other councillors argued that the King's will had conferred upon him sovereign power. If he were to be appointed protector now, he would expect to have his powers extended beyond the coronation, until the King gained his majority. This might not be for very long, for Edward IV had only intended the Council of the Marches to act on his son's behalf until the boy reached fourteen. Henry VI had declared himself of age at sixteen, but there were no set rules as to when a minor achieved majority, and Edward IV may have expected his son to attain his on his fourteenth birthday in November 1484, eighteen months hence.

The Widvilles did not want Gloucester exercising sovereign power as protector, even for a short time, and proposed "that the government should be carried on by many persons, among whom the Duke should be accounted the chief. By this means the Duke would be given due honor and the royal authority greater security, because it had been found that no regent ever laid down his office save reluctantly and from armed compulsion, whence civil wars had often arisen. Moreover, if the entire form were committed to one man, he might easily usurp the sovereignty. All who favored the Queen's family voted for this proposal, as they were afraid that if Richard took unto himself the crown, or even governed alone, they, who bore the blame for Clarence's death, would suffer death or at least be ejected from their high estate."[18] It had already occurred to the Widvilles that Gloucester might try to usurp the throne.

While the Council was debating these proposals, Gloucester's letters arrived. The one to the Council was publicly circulated by his supporters, on his instructions, and "had a great effect on the minds of the people who, as they had previously favored the Duke in their hearts from a belief in his probity, now began to support him openly and aloud, so that it was commonly said by all that the Duke deserved the government. However, the Council voted in a majority for the alternative policy and fixed a day for the coronation," 4 May.[19] Mancini felt that the councillors had deliberately flouted Edward IV's wishes; but they had acted with wisdom and moderation, curbing the ambitions of the Widvilles while according Gloucester not supreme power, but the leadership of the Council and a say in the government.

On 29 April, with his forces bolstered by those of his ally, Buckingham, Gloucester intercepted the King's party at Stony Stratford.

Rivers and the rest had no idea they were walking into a trap. The next day at dawn, after sharing a convivial meal with them, Gloucester suddenly seized Rivers, Grey, Vaughan, and Haute, who were conveyed north to prison at Sheriff Hutton Castle and Pontefract Castle. It was clear that this was the prelude to the overthrow of Widville rule. The lack of any outcry in response to Gloucester's coup shows that he and his allies had calculated correctly that hatred of the Queen's faction was widespread and deeply rooted. Many nobles approved of his decisiveness.

Gloucester "did not omit or refuse to pay every mark of respect to the King his nephew, in the way of uncovering his head, bending the knee, or other posture required of a subject."[20] Buckingham also paid homage to Edward on his knees, and the boy "received them in very joyous and amiable manner."[21]

The two dukes "exhibited a mournful countenance, while expressing profound grief at the death of the King's father, whose demise they imputed to his ministers, since they were accounted the servants and companions of his vices and had ruined his health."[22] This was a direct thrust at the Widvilles. Therefore, the Duke continued, these ministers should be removed from the King. Gloucester accused the Widvilles of conspiring his own death and of preparing ambushes in the capital and on the road. He said it was common knowledge that they had attempted to deprive him of the office of regent conferred on him by his brother. He said that he himself, whom the King's father had approved, could better discharge the duties of government, not only because of his experience of affairs but also on account of his popularity. He would neglect nothing pertaining to the duty of a loyal subject and diligent protector. He added that he had been forced, for his own safety's sake, to arrest Lord Rivers.

Young Edward was skeptical and declared that he had great confidence in the peers of the realm and the Queen. On hearing the Queen's name, Buckingham retorted that it was not the business of women but of men to govern kingdoms, and if the King cherished any confidence in her, he had better relinquish it. "Let him place all his hope in his barons, who excelled in power and nobility." Edward had no choice but to "surrender himself to the care of his uncle, which was inevitable, for although the dukes cajoled him by moderation, yet they clearly showed that they were demanding rather than supplicating."[23]

6

"The present danger"

※

THE QUEEN RECEIVED A TERRIBLE SHOCK WHEN NEWS OF Gloucester's coup reached London "a little before midnight" on 30 April. "The unexpectedness of the event horrified everyone."[1] Elizabeth was appalled by the sudden realization that, after nearly twenty years, her family's power and influence were at an end, and that her feared enemy was in control of her son.

She had no cause to expect any kindness or clemency from Gloucester, especially after doing her best to prevent him becoming protector. Her very life might be in danger. There was no time to lose. With the aid of Dorset, she "began collecting an army to defend themselves and set free the young King from the clutches of the dukes. But when they had exhorted certain nobles and others, to take up arms, they perceived that men's minds were not only irresolute, but altogether hostile to themselves. Some even said openly that it was more just and profitable that the youthful sovereign should be with his paternal uncle than with his maternal uncles and uterine brothers."[2]

"Fearing the sequel of this business," Elizabeth decided there was only one course of action open to her—one she had taken before in a crisis. That same night, she resolved to take sanctuary at Westminster, "to the intent she might deliver her other children from the present danger." In the early hours of 1 May, "in great fright and heaviness, bewailing her child's ruin, her friends' mischance and her own infortune, she got herself with all haste possible, with her daughters and her younger son, out of the palace of Westminster" and fled into sanctuary at Westminster Abbey.[3]

She and her children were received in the College Hall by John Esteney, Abbot of Westminster, and "registered as sanctuary persons."[4] He took them all under his protection, and did not demur at Elizabeth "lodging herself in the Abbot's palace,"[5] Cheyneygates, where she had stayed in 1470-1. She was joined there by Lionel Widville and Dorset, who escaped from sanctuary some weeks later and went into hiding.

Convinced that Gloucester intended harm to them all, Elizabeth was in a state of near collapse. She had fled the palace precipitately, leaving orders for her belongings to be conveyed across to the abbey after her. When Thomas Rotherham, Archbishop of York, arrived at the sanctuary before dawn, bringing the great seal of England to the Queen, he found "much heaviness, rumble, haste and busyness" surrounding her, for "the carriage and conveyance of her stuff" was already in hand. The Archbishop, who owed his advancement to the Queen, was astounded to see "chests, coffers, packs, fardels, trussed all on men's backs, no man unoccupied, some loading, some coming, some going, some discharging, some coming for more, some carrying more than they ought the wrong way, and some breaking down the walls to bring in the next way." Amid all the flurry, "the Queen sat alone, a-low on the rushes, all desolate and dismayed. The Archbishop comforted [her] in the best manner he could, showing her that he trusted the matter was nothing so sore as she took it for," saying he had been reassured by a message sent to him by Lord Hastings.

"Ah, woe worth him," the Queen cried, "for he is one of those that laboureth to destroy me and my blood."

"Madam," Rotherham replied, "be ye of good cheer, for I assure you, if they crown any other king than your son, we shall on the morrow crown his brother whom you have here with you." Then he delivered up to her the great seal, "which, as that noble prince your husband delivered unto me, so here I deliver it unto you, to the use and behoof of your son."

When he left at dawn and returned to York Place, his London residence, he saw through "his chamber window all the Thames full of boats of the Duke of Gloucester's servants, watching that no man should go into sanctuary, nor none pass unsearched."[6] Elizabeth would soon realize that she was now a virtual prisoner, unable to leave the abbey.

As the momentous news of Gloucester's coup spread, there was "great commotion and murmur, as well in other places as in the City, the people diversely divining upon this dealing."[7] Some lords "collected their forces at Westminster in the Queen's name, and others at London under the shadow of Lord Hastings."[8] Many citizens donned armor, and crowds gathered in the streets, speculating on what would happen next. There became "current in the capital a sinister rumor that the Duke had brought his nephew, not under his care, but into his power, so as to gain the crown for himself."[9]

The Council met at Westminster to discuss the situation. On being summoned to attend, Archbishop Rotherham had second thoughts about having precipitately surrendered the great seal to the Queen "without especial commandment of the King, [and he] secretly sent for the Seal again, and brought it with him after the customable manner."[10] Gloucester would reprimand him for having given it to the Queen and dismiss him from his office as chancellor, which was given to John Russell, Bishop of Lincoln, on 10 May.

Gloucester's letters were "read aloud in the council chamber." Hastings addressed the councillors, saying he was assured that the Duke was "fastly faithful to his prince" and that he had arrested Rivers and the rest only to ensure his own safety, for he was certain they had planned to murder him. He would make sure that his prisoners received impartial justice when he arrived in London, and he implored the lords not to take up arms on Edward V's behalf. The councillors were "somewhat appeased" by this and they "all praised the Duke of Gloucester for his dutifulness toward his nephews and for his intention to punish their enemies."[11] More believed that Hastings's reassurances did much to discredit the Widville faction on the Council.

On 4 May, Gloucester, clad in black, rode into London with the young King, who was wearing royal mourning of blue velvet for his father. People noted with approval that the Duke showed him much respect and honor. But he and Buckingham "were seeking at every turn to arouse hatred against the Queen's kin, and to estrange public opinion from her relatives," and "they took especial pains to do so the day they entered the City. For ahead of the procession they sent four wagons loaded with weapons bearing the devices of the Queen's brothers and sons, besides criers to make generally known that these arms had been collected by the Duke's enemies so as to attack and slay [him]."[12] The weapons had, in fact, been stored against war with the Scots.

Everyone, says Croyland, "was looking forward to the peace and prosperity of the kingdom," and Lord Hastings "was overjoyed at this new world, saying that nothing more had happened than the transfer of the rule of the kingdom from two of the Queen's relatives to two more powerful factions of the King's, without any slaughter." It now seemed that the Queen's flight into sanctuary had been too precipitate. Gloucester was named protector and saw to it that the laws of the realm were enforced in Edward V's name; coins were struck bearing the boy's image and royal honors paid to him. The Council refused to proceed against Rivers, Grey, and the rest because Gloucester had not—at the time—had the authority to arrest them; nevertheless, they remained in prison. A new date, 24 June, was set for the coronation. But the Council had made it clear that the office of protector would still lapse then, and Gloucester knew that the days of his power might be numbered.

The atmosphere in sanctuary was heavy with grief and fear, nonetheless. Although Elizabeth and her children were housed in some luxury, they were dependent on the Abbot for their security and, before long, for the very necessities of life. For on 7 May, Edward IV's executors declined to administer his will, on the grounds that while the Queen held his daughters in sanctuary, his bequests to them could not be carried out. Accordingly, the Archbishop of Canterbury placed the late King's goods under sequestration. The Queen and her children were rendered penniless. When the Abbot tried to assure her that Gloucester had no ill intentions toward her, she retorted, "As far as ye think I fear too much, be you well aware that you fear far too little."

She clearly felt exposed and vulnerable. Although sanctuaries were regarded as holy places that were to be treated with reverence, there were notorious examples of their being breached. But the sanctuary at

Westminster had long enjoyed the patronage and protection of English kings, who regarded it as an outward symbol of royal power and mercy.

The Council felt it was not suitable for the King to stay at the Palace of Westminster because of its proximity to the sanctuary where his mother and siblings lay. Instead, it was decided, at Buckingham's suggestion, that he should lodge in the palace of the Tower of London, where monarchs traditionally stayed before their coronations. The Tower had not yet acquired the sinister reputation it was to gain under the Tudors; it had been one of Edward IV's favorite residences and would have held happy associations for Edward V. But the Tower was also a strong and secure fortress.

By May, the Council was becoming uneasy about Elizabeth Widville's continued sojourn in sanctuary and the imprisonment of her kinsmen, and concerns were expressed that "the Protector did not, with a sufficient degree of considerateness, take fitting care for the preservation of the dignity and safety of the Queen."[13] Gloucester responded by appointing a committee of lords, headed by Buckingham and the Archbishop of Canterbury, to negotiate Elizabeth's voluntary withdrawal with her children from sanctuary. The committee assured her of their safety, but their efforts were doomed to failure; indeed, they had provoked a barrage of scorn, tears, and indignation. Early in June, the Council tried again to persuade the Queen to leave sanctuary and go into honorable retirement, but again she refused.

It was in Gloucester's interests for her to leave sanctuary. Her presence there was an embarrassment and a constant reproach, its implication being that her life and her children's lives, despite all assurances to the contrary, were in danger while he was in power, which was damaging to his reputation. He encouraged the lords to visit her in sanctuary, and many called to pay their respects. Yet it soon became apparent that he was taking every opportunity to incite hatred against her and to influence public opinion against the Widvilles, portraying them as aggressors. Almost his first act as protector was to seize the estates of Rivers, Grey, Dorset, and other members of the family, as if they had been forfeited by Act of Attainder. Such seizure was illegal, as was the redistribution of those lands among Gloucester's supporters, and news of it would surely have strengthened Elizabeth's resolve not to leave sanctuary.

There were Widville sympathizers on the Council, which showed

Gloucester that he could never enjoy complete security as protector. His office, moreover, must be surrendered in little more than a month, and while there was every expectation that he would head the regency council that would supersede it, his survival would be in jeopardy once the young King attained his majority. Edward's loyalties were to his mother and his Widville relatives and he would surely seek to restore them to power, releasing those whom Gloucester had imprisoned, whose first thought would be to exact vengeance under the benevolent eye of a young king already hostile to his uncle. Gloucester could not expect any favors at the hands of Edward V, or mercy at the hands of the Queen. Mancini says he made no secret of his fears of the Widvilles, proclaiming "that he was harassed by the ignoble family of the Queen and the affronts of Edward [IV]'s relatives by marriage."

On 10 June, he sent a letter asking the civic council of York to muster troops to march on London against "the Queen, her blood, adherents and affinity, which have intended and daily doth intend to murder and utterly destroy us and our cousin, the Duke of Buckingham, and the old royal blood of this realm; and, as is now openly known, by their subtle and damnable ways forecasted the same and also the final destruction and disinheriting of you and all other inheritors." It did not matter that the Queen was in sanctuary, powerless, and her kinsmen were scattered, either in prison or in hiding; Gloucester merely wished to bolster his power with military force.

On 5 June, he moved from Baynard's Castle, where he had been staying, to Crosby Place in Bishopsgate, a magnificent house he had leased in 1476 from the widow of Sir John Crosby, a prosperous grocer who had built it in 1466 on the site of a Roman villa. The Elizabethan antiquarian John Stow described Crosby Place as a "great house of stone and timber, very large and beautiful, and the highest at that time in London." It was built round a courtyard and had a solar, a great chamber, a chapel, a garden, and a superb great hall with an oriel window, a marble floor, and a vaulted ceiling thirty-eight feet high, decorated in red and gold. Behind the house there were gardens. (The great hall survived the fire that destroyed the rest of the house in the late seventeenth century, and in 1908 was moved to Chelsea, where it still stands today, in private ownership.)

Later that day, Gloucester welcomed his wife, Anne, to Crosby Place;

she had traveled to London from Yorkshire, leaving their son at Middleham, and had been royally received in York by the Mayor and aldermen. One of the first things Anne did when she reached London was send a box of wafers to her friend, the Duchess of Norfolk. "At about this time, Gloucester gave orders that the son of the Duke of Clarence," the eight-year-old Earl of Warwick, "should come to the City, and commanded that the lad should be kept in confinement in the household of his wife, the child's maternal aunt."[14]

Preparations for the coronation were well advanced, and time was running out for Gloucester; his bid to remain in power afterward might fail in Parliament. If he had not thought before of trying to seize the throne from Edward V, he certainly did so now. Knowing it was not enough to have control of the King, he "resolved to get into his power the Duke of York, for Gloucester foresaw that the Duke of York would by legal right succeed to the throne if his brother were removed. To carry through his plan," he brought forward the date of the coronation by two days, to 22 June.[15] He had an excellent pretext for removing York from sanctuary, for the boy's absence from his brother's coronation would have been a political embarrassment.

On 11 June, Gloucester wrote further letters appealing for aid to the Earl of Northumberland and other northern magnates. He also had warrants forwarded to Sheriff Hutton for the executions of Rivers, Grey, Vaughan, and Haute, which he had had drawn up in defiance of the Council.

He had lavishly rewarded Buckingham for his support, appointing him Constable of England, Chief Justice, and Lord Chamberlain of Wales for life. Buckingham could now exercise almost sovereign power in Wales, where he replaced Rivers on the Council of the Marches. Buckingham's influence was vast, and he "was always at hand ready to assist Gloucester with his advice and resources."[16] There are indications that Gloucester had already promised to restore to Buckingham the Bohun inheritance and had agreed to marry his son to Buckingham's daughter.

Hastings, resentful that Buckingham had usurped his prominence on the Council, and mistrusting Gloucester's intentions, now switched sides to the Queen, although his prime loyalty was to Edward V. He was said to be in secret communication with Elizabeth. But on 13 June, Gloucester found out that Hastings had confided his concerns about the protector's true ambitions to Archbishop Rotherham, John Morton, now Bishop of Ely, and Lord Stanley. He responded with a preemptive strike.

That morning, he summoned Hastings and others to a council meeting in the Tower, and there—in a dramatic scene later immortalized by Shakespeare—accused him of treason and had him summarily executed, "without judgment or justice."

Stanley, Morton, and Rotherham were arrested, but spared execution and sent to Wales to be imprisoned in various strongholds.

With "the three strongest supporters of the new King removed, and all the rest of his faithful subjects fearing the like treatment—the two dukes did thenceforth just as they pleased."[17]

7

"Seditious and disgraceful proceedings"

✸

AROUND THIS TIME, GLOUCESTER "LEARNED FROM HIS SPIES that the Marquess [of Dorset] had left the sanctuary and, supposing that he was hiding in the same neighborhood, he sought for him, after the manner of huntsmen, by a very close encirclement, but he was never found."[1] There can be little doubt that Dorset's flight was prompted by news of Hastings's end. He fled to France, probably taking his share of Edward IV's treasure with him, as Gloucester tried, and failed, to find it.

In sanctuary, the Queen must have heard about Elizabeth Shore being made by Gloucester to do public penance on 15 June at St. Paul's for her harlotry, clad only in a sheet, before being committed to Ludgate Prison. In fact, Mistress Shore had been arrested for being the go-between for her lover Hastings and the Queen, and her public punishment was probably intended to discredit them both and give weight to Gloucester's summary sentence on Hastings.

Ominously, "after Hastings was removed, all the attendants who had waited upon the King were debarred access to him."[2] Edward V was now a virtual prisoner. Dr. John Argentine, "the last of his attendants whose services the King enjoyed, reported that the young King, like a victim prepared for sacrifice, sought remission of his sins by daily confession and penance, because he believed that death was facing him."[3]

On 16 June, when a wary and nervous Council met at the Tower, Gloucester "submitted how improper it seemed that the King should be crowned in the absence of his brother, who, on account of his nearness of kin and his station, ought to play an important part in the ceremony."[4] He continued: "What a sight it shall be to see the King crowned if, while that the solemnity of triumphant pomp is in doing, his mother, brother and sisters remain in sanctuary."[5] He argued that, since the Duke of York "was held by his mother against his will in sanctuary, he should be liberated, because the Sanctuary had been founded by their ancestors as a place of refuge, not of detention, and this boy wanted to be with his brother."[6] He spoke scathingly of the Queen's malice and how she was trying to discredit the Council; he said it was bad for York to have no one of his own age to play with and to be "in the company of old and ancient persons" and proposed that Cardinal Bourchier convey a command to the Queen to release her son. When the octogenarian prelate refused to sanction the boy's removal from sanctuary by force, fearing that reasonable persuasion might fail because of "the mother's dread and fear," Buckingham retorted that the Queen's behavior was not prompted by fear but by "womanly frowardness. I never before heard of sanctuary children." A child had no need of sanctuary and therefore no right to it, he argued. The Council agreed to Gloucester's demand, whereupon "he surrounded the Sanctuary with troops."[7]

York had been brought up at court by the Queen his mother. Molinet says he was "joyous and witty, nimble, and ever ready for dances and games." Such a lively child would probably have welcomed being released from the restrictions of life in sanctuary. But York was only nine years old, too young to understand what his liberation might mean.

Gloucester and his entourage of magnates, prelates, and soldiers "came with a great multitude to Westminster" that same day, "armed with swords and staves." On arrival, he "compelled the Lord Archbishop of Canterbury, with many others, to enter the Sanctuary in order to appeal to the good feelings of the Queen and prompt her to allow her son to come forth and proceed to the Tower, that he might comfort the King his brother."[8]

The Cardinal and Lord Howard confronted the Queen in the Abbot's House, informing her that Gloucester desired to take her son under his protection. They begged her to agree, to avoid a scandal, and promised that York would be safe and well looked after. When Elizabeth expressed fears for his safety, Howard asked her why her sons should be in any danger. She was at a loss for an answer, and Bourchier indicated firmly to Howard that he should say no more. They tried to reassure her. "Suspecting no guile," Bourchier persuaded her to surrender her son, "seeking as much to prevent a violation of the sanctuary as to mitigate by his good services the fierce resolve of the Duke."[9] No one doubted that Gloucester would employ force to remove York, if need be: the soldiers outside bore testimony to that. But Bourchier promised the Queen that the Duke "thought or intended none harm."[10]

"When the Queen saw herself besieged and preparation for violence, she surrendered her son, trusting in the word of the Cardinal of Canterbury that the boy should be restored after the coronation."[11] Although Vergil asserted that the innocent child was pulled out of his mother's arms, Croyland stated that the Queen "assented with many thanks to this proposal," while *The Great Chronicle of London* claimed that she did so "because of the trust [she] had in the Archbishop, who thought and planned no harm. She handed over to them the Duke of York."

The lords took him to the Palace of Westminster, where Gloucester received him "with many loving words,"[12] and thence by boat to the Tower, where he was reunited with his brother. The two Princes were "seen shooting and playing in the garden of the Tower by sundry times"[13]—but not for long. Soon, "all the attendants who had waited upon the King were debarred access to him."[14] After this, he and his brother were "holden more straight,"[15] and "withdrawn into the inner apartments of the Tower proper, and day by day began to be seen more rarely behind the bars and windows, till at length they ceased to appear altogether."[16]

This happened between mid-June and 6 July, when Mancini was recalled from England. His account suggests that the Princes had been moved to the White Tower—the "Tower proper"—and his mention of bars indicates that they were securely held as prisoners of state. He saw "many men burst forth into tears and lamentations when mention was made of [Edward V] after his removal from men's sight; and already there was a suspicion that he had been done away with."

Mancini's evidence is corroborated by Croyland, who stated that the Princes were "holden more straight, and there was privy talk that the Lord Protector should be king." After 8 June, no more grants were made in the name of Edward V. Gloucester postponed the coronation indefinitely, although preparations were still going ahead. Indeed, from the day York was removed from sanctuary, Gloucester and Buckingham "no longer acted in secret but openly manifested their intentions,"[17] which boded no good for Elizabeth and her children. Gloucester was clearly determined to prevent a Widville-dominated king from reigning.

When news that a large armed force had been summoned from the North reached London, there was great alarm, especially since Gloucester already had a considerable military presence, wearing his livery, in the City. The mood of the capital was so tense that the Lord Mayor organized a watch in the interests of keeping the peace.

Sunday 22 June, should have been Edward V's coronation day. Instead, Londoners attending a sermon at Paul's Cross in London heard his claim to the throne impugned. The preacher was Dr. Ralph Shaa, the Mayor's brother, and he took his text from the Apocrypha: "But the multiplying brood of the ungodly shall not thrive, nor take deep rooting from bastard slips, nor lay any fast foundations."

Gloucester had "so corrupted" Dr. Shaa and other "preachers of the divine Word that in their sermons"—that at Paul's Cross was not the only one of its kind delivered that day—"they did not blush to say, in the face of decency and all religion, that the progeny of King Edward should be instantly eradicated, for neither had he been a legitimate king, nor could his issue be so. Edward IV, said they, was conceived in adultery, and in every way was unlike the late Duke of York; but Richard, Duke of Gloucester, who altogether resembled his father, was to come to the throne as the legitimate successor."[18] At this point Gloucester was meant to appear with Buckingham and other lords in a nearby gallery but he mistimed his entrance and the dramatic gesture fell flat. Dr. Shaa praised the Duke's virtues and stressed that by character and descent he was legally entitled to the throne, but his speech met with scant approval from the citizens, whose initial liking for Gloucester had dissolved in the wake of Hastings's execution, the canceled coronation, and the armed threat from the North.

Allegations of bastardy were common propaganda tools in the fifteenth century. Warwick and Clarence had called Edward IV a bastard for their own political purposes, but without substantiating their claims by evidence. Few believed the allegations of Dr. Shaa and others, but this was scant comfort to the Duchess of York, who, "being falsely accused of adultery, complained afterward in sundry places to right many noble men, whereof some yet live, of that great injury which her son Richard had done her."[19] Possibly her complaints carried some weight, for the allegations were suddenly dropped.

Shortly afterward, however, Gloucester ordered the preaching of further sermons in which it was alleged that Edward IV's marriage to Elizabeth Widville was invalid because he had at the time been "contracted to another wife," rendering their children bastards and incapable of inheriting the throne.[20]

Commines claimed that on 8 June, Bishop Stillington had "discovered to the Duke of Gloucester" and the Council that, before Edward IV married Elizabeth Widville in 1464, he "had been formerly in love with a beautiful young lady and had promised her marriage, on condition that he might lie with her. The lady consented and, as the Bishop affirmed, he married them when nobody was present but they two and himself. His fortune depending on the court, he did not discover it, and persuaded the lady likewise to conceal it, which she did, and the matter remained a secret."

Any bishop or cleric worth his salt would have known that a ceremony of marriage conducted without any witnesses present was invalid, but even if Stillington had officiated, it seems strange that, in the wake of the scandal over the Widville marriage, it had taken him nearly twenty years to speak out, because the existence of a previous secret marriage rendered the second union bigamous, with serious implications for the legitimacy of the children born of it. Shillington had sworn allegiance to the Prince of Wales as Edward IV's undoubted heir in 1472, a peculiar thing to do if he knew the boy was illegitimate. But Commines was the only chronicler to state that Stillington officiated at the marriage; English sources do not mention him.

The lady Edward was said to have married was Eleanor Butler, daughter of the great John Talbot, Earl of Shrewsbury. Around 1449–50, she had married Thomas Butler, heir to Ralph Butler, Lord Sudeley, but had been left a childless widow by 1461, with a legal dispute on her hands. Sudeley had transferred two manors to his son on his marriage, but had failed to obtain the King's license to do so beforehand and the manors had been confiscated. Shortly after being widowed, Eleanor is said to have petitioned Edward IV for their restoration, which was granted her in 1461. This is the only contemporary record of any dealings between her and the King.

Eleanor died in 1468 and was buried in the church of the Carmelite friars in Norwich. In the seventeenth century, Sir George Buck stated that Eleanor had retired to a convent at Norwich shortly after giving birth to a child by the King, but there is no contemporary evidence for this. The child, said to have been known at first as Giles Gurney and later as Edward de Wigmore, was supposed to have been the great-grandfather of Richard de Wigmore, secretary to Elizabeth I's chief minister, Lord Burleigh. Buck also says that Lady Eleanor's family persuaded Stillington to go to Gloucester with the truth.

But was it the truth? For centuries writers have argued the pros and cons of the matter, and still cannot reach agreement. The overwhelming consideration must be that public acceptance of the invalidity of Edward V's claim to the throne was highly advantageous to Gloucester, who had everything to gain from it. Furthermore, these revelations were made at a most convenient time—if they were made at all—and they were never legally tested. Indeed, as several writers have pointed out, their very timeliness undermines their credibility.

Although Commines stated that Edward "stood married and troth-plight" to the lady, more English sources mention only a precontract, a mutual promise to wed; once cemented by sexual intercourse, it became as binding in the eyes of the Church as a marriage. In the fourteenth century, the Church had reluctantly allowed that such clandestine marriages—with no calling of banns or blessing by a priest at the church door—were valid. By 1330, canon law recognized that an existing precontract with one partner was a bar to marriage with another and sufficient to bastardize any children of a subsequent marriage. In practice, many couples considered themselves married on the basis of a precontract alone, but there is no good evidence that Edward IV made any promises to Eleanor Butler or considered himself precontracted to her.

Significantly, neither Eleanor Butler nor her powerful family ever joined the chorus of protest when the news broke that the King—allegedly her husband—had married Elizabeth Widville, who was of lower rank than herself; nor did her family ever speak up in her favor when the alleged precontract was made public. In 1464, people were not afraid to protest against the Wytheville marriage, so there is no reason why she and her kin would not have done so. Moreover, as a notably pious lady, she surely would not have allowed the continuance of a situation in which her husband was putting his immortal soul at risk.

If Elizabeth Widville had married Edward IV in good faith, not knowing that he was already precontracted to another lady, her marriage could have been regularized and her children declared legitimate after Eleanor Butler's death in 1468; then the legitimacy of her sons, who were born later, would never have been in doubt. And it is inconceivable that Edward IV, who lived in an age in which lawful title to the crown was often bloodily disputed, would knowingly have made a bigamous marriage, or would not have taken steps to ensure that his heirs' legitimacy could never be challenged.

Given Edward IV's reputation with women, the precontract tale may have sounded convincing. The sudden emergence of this information, however, is not only suspicious, but also astonishing. Many regarded it merely as an excuse for his seizing the throne—"the color for this act of usurpation," as the Croyland chronicler scathingly put it—and what More called a "convenient pretext"; and it is obvious that many continued to regard Edward IV's children as the rightful heirs of the House of York. Croyland insisted that the whole precontract story was false: "There was not a person but what knew very well who was the sole mover of such seditious and disgraceful proceedings." Mancini did not believe it either. Of course, both Edward IV and Eleanor Butler were dead, and could neither confirm nor deny the allegations.

Gloucester's informant was said to have produced "instruments, authentic doctors, proctors and notaries of the law" as well as the "depositions of divers witnesses," none of which survives or was publicly produced at the time. If this evidence had been as compelling as Gloucester claimed, it is odd that he did not refer it to an ecclesiastical court, for no secular court—not even Parliament—had jurisdiction over such cases. Probably he realized that the story would not stand up.

For Elizabeth, worse was to come. On 25 June, her brother Rivers, her son Grey, Vaughan, and Haute were beheaded at Pontefract Castle on the patently false charge that they had plotted the death of the protector. They had been condemned without any form of trial—another act of tyranny. Their executions prompted a rising in Kent by Elizabeth's outraged kinsmen, the Hautes, and although it proved abortive, it was sufficient to prove to Gloucester that the Widvilles were still a force to be reckoned with.

8

"God save King Richard!"

※

On 25 June 1483, at the Guildhall, in the presence of the lords who had been summoned for Parliament, the Lord Mayor, and the citizens of London, Buckingham presented Gloucester with a written address on parchment, in which it was asserted that the sons of King Edward were bastards. The petition (and a subsequent Act of Parliament) stated that the late King's marriage to Elizabeth Widville was invalid on three counts: firstly, because it had been made without the assent of the lords of the land and as a result of sorcery practiced by Elizabeth and her mother; secondly, because it had been made secretly, without banns, and not openly in the face of the Church; and thirdly, because "at the time of contract of the said pretenced marriage, and before and long time after, King Edward was married and troth-plight to one Dame Eleanor Butler. Which premises being true, as in very truth they be true, it appeareth and followeth evidently that King Edward and Elizabeth lived together sinfully and damnably in adultery against the laws of God and His Church, and all the issues and children of the said King Edward been bastards and unable to claim anything by inheritance, by the law and custom of England."[1]

At this, "a low whispering broke out, as of a swarm of bees." As next in the line of succession, and the only "certain and uncorrupted blood of Richard, Duke of York"—Clarence's heir, Warwick, being barred because of his father's attainder—Gloucester was "entreated" to accept the crown.[2]

The lords, who had been ordered to bring only small escorts to London, found themselves intimidated by the presence of "unheard of terrible numbers" (estimated at 6,000 by Mancini) of Gloucester's and Buckingham's armed retainers in the City, and they and the commons unanimously signaled their approval. Some may have regarded a grown man with a proven record of service in government and in battle as preferable to a child king. Even so, unsupported allegations about Edward V's legitimacy and an address made before an assembly of nobles were no substitute for a ruling by an ecclesiastical court and constituted a very shaky foundation on which to base a claim to the throne. All the same, the next day, at Baynard's Castle, Gloucester was again entreated to bow to the lords' petition. With a show of reluctance he agreed and was proclaimed King Richard III.

It is not known whether Anne Neville was present, yet she may have come to Baynard's Castle with Richard. Having been deprived of the prospect of a crown by the death of her Lancastrian prince, she must surely have reflected on this latest turn of the wheel of Fortune that had made her a Yorkist queen.

Contemporaries found it shocking that, whereas previous kings—Edward II, Richard II, and Henry VI—had been deposed because of their bad government, Edward V had not been given a chance to prove his ability, while the speed of Gloucester's coup and his ascent to the throne strongly suggested that he had all along meant to oust his nephew. Moreover, Edward had been deposed, and he and his siblings branded bastards, on highly dubious grounds. These rapidly unfolding events must have horrified Elizabeth Widville—and now the man she feared most would be King, and she and her children were all at his mercy.

The coronation of Richard III and Anne Neville was set for 6 July and "hasty provision" was made for it.[3] On 1 July, the army Richard had summoned from the North, 6,000 strong, arrived at the gates of London. "He himself went out to meet the soldiers before they entered the City" and they were "stationed at suitable points" along the streets, where they stayed after the coronation, because the King "was afraid lest any uproar should be fomented against him."[4]

On 3 July, Richard gave Anne a "special gift" of twenty-four yards of purple cloth of gold embellished with garters and roses, and seven yards of purple velvet.[5] The next day, the royal barge carried them from Westminster to the Tower, where they took up residence in the royal apartments. There were none of the usual pageants and security was tight, and that same day, a proclamation ordered the imposing of a 10 P.M. curfew for the next three nights and forbade the citizens of London to carry arms. Visitors to the City had to stay in officially approved lodgings.

On 5 July, the King donned Anne's gifts of a gown of blue cloth of gold and a mantle of purple trimmed with 3,000 ermine tails. She was dressed in "a kirtle of white cloth of gold and a mantle with a train of the same" furred with ermine and miniver, with her hair loose, in token of the symbolic virginity of a queen. On her head was a gold circlet encrusted with pearls and gemstones.

Then they left the Tower, Richard on horseback and Anne in a litter of white damask and cloth of gold, preceded by her chamberlain and followed by seven ladies on horses saddled in crimson velvet and five henchmen in crimson satin and blue velvet. They passed "through the midst of the City, attended by the entire nobility and a display of royal honors," and rode in state to the Palace of Westminster. Four thousand "gentlemen of the north" followed in the procession. The King, "with bared head, greeted all onlookers, and himself received their acclamations."[6] But the mood of the public was resentful, even hostile, for all that many were carried away by the holiday atmosphere of the occasion. Nevertheless, this was to be one of the most splendid of all English medieval coronations, and the best attended, as almost the entire peerage had come to London for the Parliament which had been postponed.

On the morning of 6 July, Queen Anne gave her husband an embroidered gown of purple cloth of gold lined with white damask, made to her order by Piers Curteys, Keeper of the Wardrobe, and embroidered with garters and roses—"the gift of our sovereign lady the Queen."[7] She herself had donned a mantle and robe made from fifty-six yards of crimson or purple velvet and trimmed with miniver, with laces made of sixteen yards of purple silk and Venetian gold thread. She wore her hair loose about her shoulders with a jeweled circlet of gold on her head. She appears thus attired in the Rous Roll.

Richard and Anne came out of the White Hall into Westminster Hall and went directly to the King's Bench, where they sat awhile, for it was the seat of regal authority. Then, preceded by the nobility of England, they processed barefoot along a striped cloth that stretched to St. Edward's shrine in Westminster Abbey. The barons of the Cinque Ports bore a canopy over Richard's head, and the Duke of Norfolk, officiating as Earl Marshal and High Steward, carried the crown. Buckingham, who had devised the ceremonial, carried Richard's train, Suffolk carried the scepter, his son the Earl of Lincoln the orb, and the Earl of Surrey the sword of state. Richard was supported by Bishop Stillington.

Thanks to accounts preserved in the Harleian manuscripts, Grafton, and other sources, we have a detailed account of the coronation of an English medieval consort. "Our sovereign lady the Queen" followed the King into the abbey, "over her head a canopy, and at every corner a bell of gold; and on her head a circlet of gold with many precious stones set therein; and on every side of the Queen went a bishop. Earls and barons preceded her; the Earl of Huntingdon bore her scepter, Viscount Lisle the rod with the dove, and the Earl of Wiltshire her crown." Her train was carried by Margaret Beaufort, and her twenty noble ladies were led by the duchesses of Suffolk and Norfolk. Significantly, perhaps, the King's mother, the Duchess of York, did not attend the coronation. The Duchess of Buckingham was also absent, by order of her husband, who did not want to parade his Widville wife for all to see.

"So they went from St. Edward's shrine to the seats of state by the altar, and when the King and Queen were seated, there came forth their Highnesses' priests and clerks, singing most delectably Latin and prick-song, full royally." At the most sacred moment of the ceremony, Richard and Anne "put off their robes and stood all naked from their waists upward, till the Bishop had anointed them." In fact, Anne was only required to unlace her surcoat to the waist.

As the King and Queen were robed in cloth of gold, a *Te Deum* was sung "with great royalty," after which Archbishop Bourchier, "albeit unwillingly, anointed and crowned [Richard] King of England."[8] Then Anne "was anointed and crowned queen,"[9] after which Richard's sister, the Duchess of Suffolk, led her to her throne; before being seated, she curtseyed to her husband.

"The homage was paid at that part of the Mass called the Offertory, during which time the Queen sat with the bishops and peeresses. The bishops of Exeter and Norwich stood on each side of her; the Countess of Richmond was on her left hand and the Duchess of Norfolk knelt behind her with the other ladies. Then the King and Queen came down to the High Altar and kneeled, and the Cardinal turned with the Holy Sacrament in his hand and parted [the wafer] between them both, and thus they received the good Lord."[10] After that, they made offerings at the Confessor's shrine, at which the King offered up his crown and regalia. Then he and Anne donned purple velvet robes of state, with one of Anne's gentlewomen assisting her. When they returned to the altar, Imperial crowns—circlets with arches enclosing caps of maintenance—were placed on their heads.

Anne had more than fulfilled her father's ambitions for her. This "most noble lady and princess" had been "marvelously conveyed by all the corners and parts of the wheel of Fortune and eftsoons exalted again to the most high throne and honor over all other ladies of this noble realm, anointed and crowned queen of England."[11]

The procession re-formed and left the abbey at four o'clock. The King preceded the Queen, who had her scepter in her right hand and the rod with the dove in her left. They returned to Westminster Hall and mounted the steps to the marble table on the high dais, then, leaving their robes of estate there, they retired for a short while, returning soon afterward for the coronation banquet, which lasted five and a half hours. "The King sat at the middle of the table, the Queen at the left hand, and on each side of her stood a countess holding a cloth when she listed to drink."[12] Sir Robert Dymock, the King's Champion, wearing white armor, rode a horse caparisoned in white and scarlet into the hall and flung down his white gauntlet, challenging any man to dispute the King's title. No one did, and many shouted, "King Richard! God save King Richard!"

Then the banquet was served. Richard's plates were of gold, Anne's of gilt, and everyone else had silver. It was noticed that the Archbishop did not attend. Among the seventy-five dishes served were wildfowl, pheasant, cygnet, goose, lamb, boar, rabbit, chicken, suckling pig, venison, pigeon, capon, cygnet, heron, peacock, lamprey, pike, porpoise, bream, salmon, trout, carp, crayfish, cod, sturgeon, dates, prunes, oranges, and gilded strawberries, many flavored with expensive spices or Madeira sugar. As the evening drew to a close, "the Lord Mayor served the King and Queen with hippocras, wafers and sweet wine, and by that time it was dark night, and anon the King and Queen rose up and went to their chambers," to a fanfare of trumpets and clarions.[13]

In the Abbot's House, Elizabeth Widville must have heard the three Westminster sanctuary bells, which were customarily rung when a monarch was crowned—and she may have heard the crowds outside, and even the music in the abbey.

9

"Assemblies and confederacies"

※

A DAY OR SO AFTER THE CORONATION RICHARD AND ANNE went to Greenwich Palace. There, on 13 July, the King heaped more honors on Buckingham, who was given wider powers to ensure his continuing support. Richard also issued a provisional grant naming the Duke rightful heir to the disputed Bohun inheritance, this grant to be confirmed by Parliament, which would reverse a former grant assigning some of the Bohun estates to Elizabeth Widville. On 15 July, Buckingham was appointed Lord High Constable of England.

On 19 July, the court moved to Windsor. The northern troops were sent home, and the King began organizing his Council; he appointed his son lieutenant of Ireland, and planned a progress through his kingdom. It was to be an exercise in public relations, with Richard exerting himself to charm and win over his new subjects—especially the Northerners— with liberality and accessible justice. On 20 July, he left Windsor, leaving Anne behind; it had been arranged that she would join him later.

Richard had need of Buckingham's support, for already there were reports of agitation and confederacies in the South and West in favor of liberating Edward V. Richard's actions during the weeks leading up to his accession had incurred public opprobrium and dismay, and there is every reason to suppose that, like the chroniclers of the time, many of his subjects regarded him as a usurper, a tyrant, and a hypocrite. His seizure of the crown had been achieved at the cost of his popularity in the South, where people did not approve of the manner in which he had mounted the throne or believe his claim to be lawful.

The only informed account of what happened next comes from Croyland, who stated that, while the coronation and progress "were taking place, King Edward IV's two sons were in the Tower of London under special guard. In order to release them from such captivity, people in the vicinity of London, throughout the counties of Kent, Essex, Sussex, Hampshire, Dorset, Devonshire, Somerset, Wiltshire and Berkshire, as well as some others of the southern counties of the kingdom," being determined "to avenge their grievances" and free them, began to "murmur greatly and to form assemblies and confederacies, many of which worked in secret, others openly, with this aim." The conspirators appear to have been disaffected Yorkists, loyal to the blood of Edward IV, as well as Lancastrian dissidents and the Widville faction: the Queen's brothers, Lionel, Edward, and Richard, were all involved. Some of the plotters appealed to Buckingham to join them, but he refused.

Few details of these conspiracies are known. John Stow wrote in 1580 of a plot in July 1483 to secure the release of Edward V from the Tower by diverting his jailers with a blaze, but there is no other evidence for it. "There was also a report that it had been recommended by those men who had taken refuge in the sanctuaries that some of the King's daughters should leave Westminster, and go in disguise to parts beyond the sea, in order that, if any fatal mishap should befall the male children of the King [Edward IV] in the Tower, the kingdom might still, in consequence of the safety of the daughters, someday fall again into the hands of the rightful heirs."[1]

There can be little doubt that Elizabeth Widville herself was involved: her cooperation would have been vital to such a plan, for her daughters could not have left sanctuary without her collusion. She had good reason to resort to desperate measures. Already her brother and one of her sons had been executed without trial. Her royal sons had disappeared into the Tower, and she was probably so fearful for their safety that she was prepared to risk the perils attendant on her daughters escaping abroad in order to ensure the survival of Edward IV's line.

The "Sanctuary plot," as it was called, took Richard by surprise when his spies reported it to him at Minster Lovell in late July. It caused him the deepest concern and anxiety. He ordered that the Abbey be placed under siege, whereupon "the noble church of Westminster assumed the appearance of a castle and fortress, while men of the greatest austerity were appointed by King Richard to act as the keepers thereof; the captain and head of these was one John Nesfield, Esquire, who set a watch upon all the inlets and outlets of the monastery. Not one of the persons there shut up could go forth, and no one could enter, without his permission."[2]

Nesfield was also responsible for guarding the Queen and her children while they were in sanctuary. A soldier who was first mentioned in 1470, when Edward IV appointed him "riding forester of the forest of Galtres" in Yorkshire, he had hunted down Lancastrian adherents. In 1480, he had served in Calais, where he helped to recapture an English ship that had been seized by the French. He was now a staunch supporter of Richard III and ensured that his men-at-arms kept strict guard over the Queen and her daughters. He was "a man of the greatest austerities."[3]

The conspiracies were so vigorously suppressed that most of the evidence documenting them is missing, yet the fact that they had occurred at all probably convinced Richard that he would never be secure on his throne while his nephews lived.

There are many theories as to what became of the Princes in the Tower; the evidence is laid out in my books *Richard III and the Princes in the Tower* and *Elizabeth of York: The First Tudor Queen*. It overwhelmingly points to their having been murdered on Richard's orders; he had the most compelling motive and the best opportunity. The evidence also strongly suggests that, on the night of 3 September 1483, the Princes were suffocated by assassins hired by one of his trusted retainers, Sir James Tyrell.

Buckingham was with Richard at Gloucester until 2 August, but this would be the last time they saw each other, for dissension had sprung up between them. Vergil claimed that Richard had refused to grant Buckingham the Bohun inheritance, but he had made a provisional grant of it, so this cannot have been the reason for Buckingham's sudden disaffection. More was probably nearer the truth when he conjectured that when the King confided to him that he had ordered the killing of the Princes,

Buckingham felt that things had gone too far and did not want to be a party to infanticide. Only something as cataclysmic could have provoked him to abandon the man to whom he owed his vast wealth and political influence.

Buckingham left the progress at Gloucester, pleading pressing business on his Brecon estates. On his way there, he considered how best to remove this "unnatural uncle and bloody butcher from his royal seat and princely dignity."[4]

Richard arrived at Warwick Castle on 8 August. Queen Anne had already arrived with young Warwick, having traveled north in great state from Windsor, attended by bishops and nobles. She had also brought with her a Spanish envoy, Graufidius de Sasiola, who had been sent to England by Ferdinand and Isabella. Anne was with Richard when Sasiola proposed a marriage between Edward of Middleham and a Spanish infanta. Richard was already preparing his seven-year-old son for kingship, having placed him in nominal control of his northern estates and presented him with a copy of Vegetius's *De Re Militari* on the art of war, which bears the boy's coat of arms. Young Edward also owned a book of hours covered in black satin, and a psalter, and in 1483 he made offerings at five abbeys in Yorkshire, including Fountains and Jervaulx.

In the town of Warwick, there were five days of ceremonies, and a visit to see John Rous at Guy's Cliffe, where he presented to Anne his "Roll of the Earl of Warwick." The King and Queen then moved on to Coventry (where he paid a London mercer for goods delivered to Anne), then to Leicester and Nottingham, where, on 24 August, Richard created his heir Prince of Wales. On 23 August, John Kendall, the King's secretary, informed York Civic Council that Richard and Anne were in good health.

After visiting Doncaster, the royal couple arrived at Pontefract on 27 August. There, they were reunited with Prince Edward, who had traveled by chariot from Middleham, in slow stages. The journey of fifty-eight miles had taken eight days, at a time when a horse-drawn vehicle could cover twelve miles a day. This, and the fact that Edward had not been taken south for the coronation or his investiture, suggests that he was delicate or sickly.

In late August, crowds were out in force to see the King and Queen make their ceremonial entry into York. Their reception was not entirely spontaneous because a week beforehand, at Richard's command, John

Kendall had written to the city fathers commanding them "to receive his Highness and the Queen as laudably as your wisdoms can imagine. Many southern lords and men of worship are with them and will greatly mark you receiving their Graces." They should be "worshipfully received with pageants" and other celebrations—guaranteed crowd-pullers. The civic authorities had risen magnificently to the occasion. The Mayor and aldermen greeted the King and Queen at Breckles Mill outside the city, and escorted them through the Micklegate Bar and the great crowds assembled along Micklegate. Three lavish pageants were mounted in their honor, and the Mayor gave a welcoming speech and presented Richard with 100 marks (£48,490) in a golden cup; Anne received £100 (£74,610) in gold on a piece of plate—a substantially larger gift, in acknowledgment of the esteem in which the Nevilles were held in the North. The King and Queen processed to York Minster, where the *Te Deum* was sung, then took up residence in the Archbishop's palace.

On 7 September, the famous Creed Play of the guild of Corpus Christi was performed before the King and Queen in the Guildhall. The next day, the feast of the Nativity of the Virgin Mary, the royal couple wore their crowns in procession through York, Anne leading Prince Edward by the hand into York Minster, he "having on his head a demi-crown." After a Mass that seemed to onlookers like a second coronation, the King knighted him, along with Warwick and his own bastard, John of Gloucester. Then the procession re-formed and made its way to the Archbishop's palace opposite, where young Edward was invested as Prince of Wales in a ceremony designed to show the Northerners and the Neville affinity that a king with Neville blood would one day succeed to the throne. It was "a day of great state for York, there being three princes wearing crowns, to the great honor, joy and congratulation of the inhabitants, as in a show of rejoicing, they extolled King Richard above the skies."[5]

At the end of September, the court returned to Pontefract Castle, and Queen Anne left for Middleham with the Prince of Wales and Warwick, leaving Richard to continue with his progress alone.

Buckingham had arrived at his castle at Brecknock by the middle of August. There, John Morton, Bishop of Ely, was under house arrest. It was apparently during conversations with the formidable Bishop—a dedicated Lancastrian who was Margaret Beaufort's chaplain but had nevertheless served Edward IV devotedly and been present at his deathbed—that Buckingham decided to rise in rebellion against the King.

Some writers have suggested that Buckingham's initial plan was to seize power for himself. Vergil later claimed that, having "suddenly remembered" that he himself was descended from Edward III, he had met Margaret Beaufort on the road to Brecon, and realized that her claim was far superior, although none of this sounds very likely, and Buckingham did not at any time press his own claim. It is clear that Morton initially urged the restoration of Edward V, for on 24 September Buckingham wrote appealing for support from Henry Tudor in the "liberation" of the Princes. Just then, "a rumor was spread that the sons of King Edward had died a violent death, but it was uncertain how."[6]

The rumor proliferated and irrevocably damaged the King's reputation. Fabyan recorded it being said in London that he had put to death the children of King Edward, "and thereby lost the hearts of the people, whereupon many gentlemen intended his destruction." Within weeks, it was widely accepted that he had had the Princes murdered in the Tower. This was hardly surprising, since no one had seen them since early July. Evidence that the rumors were believed is to be found in the commonplace book of a London merchant, for the year 1482-3: "This year the sons of King Edward were put to silence." Fabyan says it was soon "the common fame" that King Richard had killed his nephews. The rumors were taken as fact as far away as Danzig, as Caspar Weinreich's contemporary chronicle recorded that year: "Later this summer, Richard, the King's brother, had himself put in power and crowned King of England; and he had his brother's children killed." Certainly Buckingham, who may have had good cause, took the rumors seriously.

Ruthlessness in war and politics was tolerated: child murder was a step too far. The Tudor royal historian, Bernard André, wrote that, in the wake of the rumors, "the entire land was convulsed with sobbing and anguish. The nobles of the kingdom, fearful of their lives, wondered what might be done against the danger. Faithful to the tyrant in word, they remained distant in heart." We must allow for a degree of exaggeration from a partisan observer, but this was written less than twenty years later, when many people would have remembered the events of 1483.

Public conviction that Richard had murdered his nephews cost him the brief popularity fueled by the progress. It also lost him much support among the Yorkist old guard who had served Edward IV and prompted more people to join those who were already conspiring against him. Alive, the Princes had represented a potential threat to Richard's security; dead, they were a very real danger.

Buckingham and his associates assumed that they were dead, which was a reasonable conclusion, given the rumors and how ruthlessly Richard had eliminated everyone else who had stood in the way of his ambitions. The Duke and his fellow conspirators had been joined by a large number of alienated Yorkists. They now realized that they had to find someone to replace the usurper, and Buckingham and Morton began seriously to consider the claim of Henry Tudor. This was perhaps Morton's doing. He seems to have worked covertly to bring together the Lancastrian party, the Widvilles, the Yorkist dissidents—and Margaret Beaufort.

Margaret was prominent at Richard III's court, but she remained a devout Lancastrian at heart. She was a formidable woman of strong character and steely resolve, and she leaped at this opportunity to place her son, Henry Tudor, on the throne.

Vergil asserted that, while Morton and Buckingham were plotting at Brecknock, a new conspiracy was brewing in London between Margaret Beaufort and Elizabeth Widville. But possibly Margaret was already in league with Buckingham, and in contact with him through the good offices of Morton; her chaplain Christopher Urswick; and her servant Reginald Bray. And "she, being a wise woman, after the slaughter of King Edward's children was known, began to hope well of her son's fortune."[7] According to Vergil, it was Margaret who first conceived the momentous idea of uniting the rival houses of Lancaster and York through a marriage between her son and Elizabeth of York, who was now, in the eyes of many, the rightful Queen. Elizabeth was then seventeen years old and in sanctuary with her mother and sisters.

The success of the plan depended, of course, on the Princes being dead. Clearly, Buckingham, Margaret Beaufort, and Henry Tudor all believed that they were, probably with good reason. There have been theories that any one of them could have arranged their murder. But while a handful of contemporary writers suggested that Buckingham was involved, no one—not even Margaret of Burgundy, his mortal enemy—ever accused Henry Tudor or Margaret Beaufort of the deed.

Enlisting Buckingham to her son's cause was a great coup for Margaret. All that was needed now was to win over Elizabeth Widville. But first, Elizabeth had to be told about the tragic fate of her sons.

10

"The rightful inheritor"

Dr. Lewis Caerleon, a Welshman, was Margaret Beaufort's physician, and because he was very experienced, she often spoke freely, lamenting her adversity. During one of their talks, she asked him to put the conspirators' plan to the Queen Dowager, who also consulted him. She told him the time had come for Elizabeth of York to be given in marriage to her son Henry and urged him to deal secretly with the Queen in the matter. In September 1483, Dr. Caerleon braved Nesfield's soldiers and visited Elizabeth Widville in sanctuary, ostensibly in his official capacity. There he broke the dread news that her sons had been murdered.

The impact must have been dreadful. She "fell in a swoon and lay lifeless a good while. After coming to herself, she wept, she cried aloud, and with lamentable shrieks made all the house ring. She struck her breast, tore and pulled out her hair and, overcome with dolour, prayed also for her own death, calling by name now and then among her most dear children, and condemning herself for a mad woman for that, being deceived by false promises, she had delivered her younger son out of sanctuary, to be murdered by his enemy. After long lamentation, she kneeled down and cried to God to take vengeance, who, she said, she nothing doubted would remember it."[1]

Learning that the Princes had been killed was devastating enough, but not knowing exactly what had happened to them, or being able to lay them decently to rest, would have caused unbearable anguish. Their mother would always be imagining dreadful scenarios—and there was room for doubt, even hope.

To mitigate the dreadful tidings and bring the Queen over to the side of Margaret Beaufort and Buckingham, Dr. Caerleon came to the real point of his visit, reminding her that her daughter Elizabeth was now the rightful inheritor of the realm and that she could still become the mother of a monarch. If she would agree and find means to marry her daughter to Henry Tudor, there was no doubt that the usurper would soon be shortly deposed, and her heir restored to her right.

At this point Henry Tudor was not much of a catch. He was a landless exile without a title. But Elizabeth saw in him her only hope of revenge on the man she believed had killed her sons and brought her to her present sorry condition, and readily gave her consent. She commanded Caerleon to return to Margaret and tell her that she would do her best to persuade all the late King Edward's friends to support Henry, if he would swear an oath to marry her daughter after he had taken the realm. Her agreement to the scheme to bring down Richard III—which was not without considerable risk—is proof that she truly believed her sons had been murdered.

Plans for the rebellion were made over the next two or three weeks. Margaret Beaufort sent her chaplain Richard Fox to Brittany with the news that Elizabeth Widville had agreed to acknowledge Henry as King if he married her daughter. On Morton's advice, Buckingham sent word to Henry, "inviting him to hasten into the kingdom of England as fast as he could reach the shore, to marry Elizabeth; and with her, at the same time, take possession of the whole kingdom." He informed Henry that his supporters would rise on 18 October, and that he himself would raise the men of Wales. A proclamation was then made to the confederacies that Buckingham "had repented of his former conduct and would be the chief mover"[2] in the planned risings.

Henry Tudor entered enthusiastically into the conspiracy. Anne of Brittany might have brought him a duchy, but Elizabeth of York could just bring him a kingdom. Word of the proposed marriage spread rapidly and won the conspirators the loyalty of Yorkists—among them many former members of Edward IV's household—who had been outraged at

Richard's disinheriting of the late King's children and the likely murders of his sons.

On 3 October, Henry's fleet sailed from Brittany, but a storm drove his ships back and kept them in port. The rebels were supposed to rise on 18 October and there were to be six separate insurrections. In Kent, the Hautes were to march from Ightham Mote; Exeter was to be roused by Dorset, Sir Thomas St. Leger (the husband of Richard III's sister Anne), and members of the Lancastrian Courtenay family, earls of Devon; Lionel Widville was to organize a rising in Salisbury; Buckingham would have an army standing at battle alert, with the aim of raising Brecon and south Wales. There were planned risings in Guildford and Newbury. The Queen's younger brothers, Sir Edward and Sir Richard Widville, were involved. But the various groups were poorly coordinated and on 10 October, the Hautes orchestrated premature risings at Maidstone and Ightham Mote, only to be repelled by John Howard, now created Duke of Norfolk.

Already, though, "the whole design of this plot had, by means of spies, become perfectly well known to King Richard, who, as ever, did not act sleepily, but swiftly, and with the greatest vigilance." On 15 October, Richard had Buckingham proclaimed a rebel and offered free pardons to all who surrendered. He "contrived that, throughout Wales, armed men should be set in readiness around the Duke as soon as ever he had set a foot from his home."[3]

Unsuspecting, Buckingham left Brecon on 18 October, as planned, and advanced through the Wye Valley, making for Hereford. But storms and flooding wrecked his plans, his army deserted him, and he was forced to flee into Shropshire, where he sought shelter in the cottage of a poor retainer, who betrayed him for a handsome reward. Under arrest, he was led to the city of Salisbury, where the King had come with a very large army. On 2 November, regardless of the fact that it was All Souls' Day, Richard had him beheaded in the marketplace.

On 31 October, unaware that the rebellion had collapsed, Henry again set sail from Brittany, but was blown off course by foul weather. He was at anchor off Plymouth harbor when news of Buckingham's death and the flight of his supporters reached him. Realizing his cause was hopeless, he put out to sea and fled back to Brittany.

The rebellion had nevertheless demonstrated that Henry was a serious contender for the crown. On Christmas Day, determined to establish his importance in the eyes of the world at large, he went to Vannes Cathedral and, in the presence of 500 disaffected Yorkists, promised on oath that, as soon as he was King of England, he would marry Elizabeth of York and unite the rival Houses of Lancaster and York. Afterward his supporters swore to be loyal to each other, then knelt before Henry, paying him homage as if he had been already crowned King. They all swore they would one day return to England and overthrow the tyrant Richard.

This oath, optimistic though it was, was a brilliant masterstroke because it united both Lancastrian and Yorkist supporters. Until now, few had taken Henry's claim to be the Lancastrian claimant seriously, but his vow to wed Elizabeth of York was a deciding factor for many.

Queen Anne, having heard the news about Buckingham's rebellion, had left the Prince of Wales at Middleham and traveled south to London to be with Richard, who granted her some of the money confiscated from those attainted for treason. They kept Christmas together in ceremonious splendor, and purchased new clothes and gifts costing £1,200 (£895,280).

Elizabeth Widville must have endured a mournful Christmas, compared with the splendid celebrations of the previous year, and in January 1484, she suffered more bitter humiliation when Richard's first Parliament passed an Act entitled *Titulus Regius*, which confirmed the King's title to the throne and set forth the grounds of his claim. It declared how, thanks to "the ungracious pretended marriage" of Edward IV, "the order of all politic rule was perverted," and went on to state: "We consider how the pretended marriage between King Edward and Elizabeth Grey was made of great presumption, without the knowledge and assent of the lords of this land, and also by sorcery and witchcraft committed by the said Elizabeth and her mother, Jacquetta, Duchess of Bedford, as the common opinion of the people and the public voice and fame is throughout all this land, and as the case shall require, shall be proved sufficiently in time and place convenient." In other words, this was all hearsay and yet to be proved. "And here also we consider how that the said pretended marriage was made privily and secretly, without edition of banns, in a private chamber [which was untrue], a profane place, and not openly in the face of the Church after the law of God's Church, but contrary thereto and the laudable custom of the Church of England. And how also that at the time of the contract of the said pretended marriage, and before and long after, King Edward was and stood troth-plight to one Dame Eleanor Butler, daughter of the old Earl of Shrewsbury, with whom King Edward had made a precontract of matrimony long time before he made the said pretended marriage with Elizabeth Grey. Which premises being true, as in very truth they been true, it appeareth and followeth evidently that King Edward and Elizabeth lived together sinfully and damnably in adultery, against the law of God and His Church. Also it followeth that all th'issue and children of the said King Edward been bastards and unable to inherit or to claim any thing by inheritance."[4]

Croyland protested that Parliament, being a lay court, had no jurisdiction to pronounce on the validity of the King's marriage, but "it presumed to do so, and did do so, because of the great fear [of Richard] that had struck the hearts of even the most resolute." Nor had those who drafted the Act included any details of the Butler precontract, which seems a significant omission.

Parliament also passed Acts of Attainder against 100 people, including Henry Tudor and Buckingham; this represented a quarter of all attainders passed in fifty years. Yet Richard made no move against Elizabeth Widville and her kinsmen; in fact, he offered clemency to Dorset, Morton, and Richard Widville. Suspecting a trap, they stayed in Brittany, having fled there to join Henry Tudor.

The King was remarkably lenient with Margaret Beaufort, despite her having treasonably conspired against him; she was lucky to escape being attainted by Parliament. He contented himself with giving her estates to her husband, depriving her of her title, and ordering Lord Stanley—who claimed he had known nothing of her subversive activities—to keep his wife a virtual prisoner "in some secret place," apart from her household.

II

"On the word of a king"

✱

THE FAILURE OF BUCKINGHAM'S REBELLION HAD EXTINguished Elizabeth Widville's hopes, leaving her isolated and demoralized. She had been shut away from the world for nine months and must have found it tedious in the extreme. She was now penniless, for Parliament had just enacted a statute confiscating her property. Yet she undoubtedly regarded her sanctuary as a place of safety and showed no sign of leaving it. This caused embarrassment to the King, who was determined to gain custody of Elizabeth of York and arrange a marriage for her, putting her beyond the reach of Henry Tudor. He could not continue to allow the Queen Dowager and her daughters to go on hiding in sanctuary, as if they were in danger from him; it did not do his tarnished reputation any good. By now, the rumors that were proving so damaging were widespread: Early in 1484, the Chancellor of France had publicly accused him of "murdering with impunity" his nephews, and Commines records that Louis XI believed Richard to be "extremely cruel and evil" on account of his having had "the two sons of his brother put to death." Commines himself held that the King had "barbarously murdered his two nephews." In December 1483, Mancini (who had been recalled to France in July) had written that Richard had "destroyed his brother's children." But if Richard could secure the persons of his nieces, he could show the world he had no evil intent toward them.

He sent "grave men promising mountains" to Elizabeth Widville to persuade her to leave sanctuary with her daughters. Vergil wrote that they prejudiced their arguments at the outset by referring to "the slaughter of her sons," after which she would not be comforted; but this seems unlikely, as it implies an admission by Richard's emissaries that he had murdered the Princes. Croyland stated that they used "frequent entreaties and threats" and "strongly solicited" Elizabeth to comply with the King's wishes, while Rous says she was "harassed by repeated intercessions and dire threats."

It had become alarmingly clear that the sanctuary could no longer be regarded as a place of refuge, and that Richard might use force to remove the girls if she resisted him. But Elizabeth seized her advantage and insisted that he swear a solemn public oath to protect and care for her daughters. He agreed, which shows how anxious he was to bring the girls under his control and be seen to have reached an understanding with their mother, to whom he now offered a pension of 700 marks (£381,170), which she accepted. Agreement was reached on all these matters by the end of February, and on 1 March, the King summoned the estates to Westminster and, in their presence, placed his hand on sacred relics of the Holy Evangelists and swore an oath (which he afterward put in writing):

> I, Richard, by the grace of God, King of England, in the presence of you my lords spiritual and temporal, and you, Mayor and aldermen of my City of London, promise and swear on the word of a king, and upon these holy evangelies [Gospels] of God, by me personally touched, that if the daughters of Dame Elizabeth Grey, late calling herself Queen of England, that is, Elizabeth, Cecily, Anne, Katherine and Bridget, will come unto me out of the sanctuary of Westminster, and be guided, ruled and demeaned after me, then I shall see that they shall be in surety of their lives, and also not suffer any manner hurt in their body by any manner [of] person or persons to them, or any of them in their bodies and persons by way of ravishment or defouling contrary to their wills, not them or any of them imprison within the Tower of London or other prison; but that I shall put them in honest places of good name and fame, and them honestly and courteously shall see to be founden and entreated, and to have all things requisite and necessary for their exhibitions [display] and findings [maintenances] as my kinswomen; and that

I shall marry such of them as now be marriable to gentlemen born, and every of them give in marriage lands and tenements by the yearly value of 200 marks [£108,910] for term of their lives, and in like wise to the other daughters when they come to lawful age of marriage if they live. And such gentlemen as shall hap to marry with them I shall straitly charge from time to time lovingly to love and entreat them, as wives and my kinswomen, as they will avoid and eschew my displeasure. And moreover, I promise to them that if any surmise or evil report be made to me of them by any person or persons, that I shall not give thereunto faith ne credence, nor therefore put them to any manner punishment, before that they or any of them so accused may be at their lawful defense and answer. In witness whereof to this writing of my oath and promise aforesaid in your said presences made, I have set my sign manual the first day of March, the first year of my reign.

This oath undoubtedly reflected stipulations made by Elizabeth Widville, and it shows that she was suspicious of Richard's motives. While he may have offended his sister-in-law by calling her "Dame Elizabeth Grey," he had publicly guaranteed the safety and welfare of her daughters. His oath reflected widespread concerns that he had done away with her sons, for whose safety, as opposed to that of her daughters, he gave no reassurances. This strongly suggests that they were dead, while his specific mention of the Tower may be significant.

Richard had also promised Elizabeth that he would pardon Dorset if he returned to his allegiance, abandoned Henry Tudor, and came home to England. Elizabeth wrote to Dorset, urging him to agree and promising that Richard would treat him well. She also ordered him to break off negotiations for the marriage between Elizabeth of York and Henry Tudor. Dorset secretly left Henry's court but was intercepted by his spies and warned not to go back to England. He complied, but for a long time afterward Henry Tudor would not trust him.

On the same day that Richard swore his oath, Elizabeth sent her daughters to him at Westminster. It must have been a hard thing to do. Hall castigated her for surrendering them to her enemy: "Putting in oblivion the murder of her innocent children, the infamy and dishonor spoken of the King her husband, the living in adultery laid to her charge, the bastardizing of her daughters, forgetting also the faithful prayers and open oath made to the Countess of Richmond, mother of the Earl Henry, blinded by avaricious affection and seduced by flattering words, [she] delivered into King Richard's hands her five daughters as lambs once again committed to the custody of the ravenous wolf."

Modern revisionist historians argue that Elizabeth would never have agreed to place her daughters into the care and control of the man who had murdered her sons. But that is exactly what she did do, believing that he had not only done away with the Princes, and knowing that he had also murdered another of her sons, Sir Richard Grey, who had been executed without justification or a proper trial. Yet what choice had she really had? Richard was thirty-one and might be in power for a long time. She could not stay in sanctuary forever, especially in the face of his guarantees; her continuing presence was compromising the Abbot's standing with his monarch, and she had already been dependent on his kindness and charity for nearly a year. Furthermore, the abbey was still under siege on her account. If she refused to let her daughters leave, then Richard might well remove them, as he had done young York, and on the same pretext. Her capitulation does not mean she did not believe the King had murdered the Princes; it shows that she was a realist and a pragmatist.

Vergil stated that "King Richard received all his brother's daughters out of sanctuary into the court." He caused them "to be conveyed into his palace with solemn receiving; as though, with his new, familiar, loving entertainment they should forget, and in their minds obliterate, the old committed injury and late perpetrated tyranny."[1] They were "very honorably entertained and with all princely kindness."[2] Even so, it may have been a bitter experience for them to return to the place where, just a year before, they had been honored as royal princesses. Possibly resentment against their uncle, and anxiety about their mother, warred with pleasure and relief at being out of sanctuary and able to enjoy worldly pleasures and freedoms again in luxurious surroundings.

Foreign visitors to Richard III's court were awed by its splendor. It exceeded his brother's in magnificence, for he was well aware of the political value of impressive ceremonial. He lived in ostentatious luxury and dressed himself in sumptuous imported Italian velvets, cloth of gold, silks, and satins, many embroidered and furred with ermine. His preferred colors were crimson, purple, and dark blue.

Richard was a generous patron of the arts and learning. He was interested in architecture and Rous praised his achievements as a builder. He made improvements to many royal residences, including Nottingham Castle and Warwick Castle, where he built the Bear and Clarence towers in 1478, although his great keep, the "Tower House," was left unfinished at his death. These works may have been undertaken at Anne's behest; Rous noted that she took a particular interest in the town of Warwick, her birthplace.

Richard established collegiate churches at Barnard Castle, Middleham, and Durham for the spiritual weal of himself and Anne. In 1484, he founded the College of Arms in London. William Caxton had earlier dedicated his book *The Order of Chivalry* to him.

Musicians from all over Europe came to Richard in search of preferment, for his cultural and musical interests were well-known. The court of Edward IV had been famed for its music, and Richard built on that reputation, patronizing the composers William Pasche and Gilbert Banastre, and taking a special interest in the choir of the Chapel Royal. Queen Anne had her own minstrels as well. Scholars sought the King's patronage. He was a notable patron of the universities of Oxford and Cambridge, and of King's College, Cambridge. He was interested in the study of politics and employed as his personal chaplain the humanist John Droget.

Anne enjoyed books. She may have collaborated with her mother in commissioning the manuscript known as *The Pageants of Richard Beauchamp, Earl of Warwick*, which commemorated the deeds of her renowned maternal grandfather, and was written around 1483. The images of Joan of Navarre and Katherine of Valois that appear in it may have been based on Anne herself; certainly the costumes in which they are depicted are the fashions of her day. *The Rous Roll*, written by John Rous, ends with Anne being crowned Queen.

The late King's daughters would have been placed in the Queen's household; as unmarried girls of royal birth, it was the only suitable place for them in a court populated mainly by men.

* * *

There is confusion over what happened to Elizabeth Widville. Clearly, she did not leave sanctuary with her daughters, for the King authorized payment of her pension via John Nesfield, the man he had placed in charge of security at the abbey and whose duty it was to attend upon the former Queen. But by the summer of 1484, Nesfield was serving as a naval captain, fighting the French, and Elizabeth Widville had apparently emerged from sanctuary at last.

Where she went is uncertain. It is unlikely, given the bad feeling between her and the King, that she went to court, and Croyland says that "the Lady Elizabeth [of York] was, with her four younger sisters, sent by her mother to attend the Queen at court" the following Christmas, from which we can infer that they were then living with her elsewhere. It may be that the girls accompanied the King and Queen to Nottingham in March and returned to London at the end of July, and that they joined their mother then. Elizabeth's properties had been confiscated by Parliament, so the King must have provided them with accommodation. Both he and Parliament had stipulated her pension of 700 marks (£381,170) was to be paid not to her, but to John Nesfield, who was to continue as the former Queen's "attendant," or rather, custodian, and historian David Baldwin has offered the compelling theory that she was sent to live in his charge, perhaps at Heytesbury, a manor near Devizes, Wiltshire, which he had been granted on 5 April by Richard III, possibly for the purpose of accommodating her.

At Heytesbury, Elizabeth would have resided at East Court, a medieval manor house dating from the fourteenth century. It was rebuilt in the sixteenth century and may have occupied the site of Heytesbury House, home of the poet Siegfried Sassoon, which still stands and probably incorporates some fragments of the medieval building.

Maybe it was Nesfield who made certain that Elizabeth Widville sent messages to Dorset in Brittany, urging him to abandon Henry Tudor and put an end to any idea of a marriage between Henry and her daughter Elizabeth. Her decision struck a blow to Henry's hopes and provoked consternation and censure among his supporters, but it had been both wise and necessary. In January, Parliament had attainted Henry Tudor as a traitor, which meant that if he ever returned to England, he would be arrested and summarily executed. Elizabeth must have realized that anyone supporting a marriage between him and her daughter could be deemed guilty of misprision of treason.

It has been suggested by several historians that, in 1484, Elizabeth's daughters were sent to live at Sheriff Hutton Castle in Yorkshire, in the care of John de la Pole, Earl of Lincoln, who had recently been appointed King's Lieutenant in the North and presided over the Council of the North, set up by Edward IV in 1472. Richard III had established a royal household for him and young Warwick at Sheriff Hutton in September 1483. Certainly, Elizabeth of York was staying there in the summer of 1485. But because she and her sisters were sent by their mother to court at Christmas 1484, and there is no record of Elizabeth Widville living at Sheriff Hutton, it is more likely that they were then living with her, probably at Heytesbury. Moreover, there is no record of the younger daughters ever being at Sheriff Hutton, and Elizabeth, now eighteen, was too old to be one of the children referred to in the ordinances for the household there.

12

"An incestuous passion"

※

THAT SPRING, THE PEERS MET AT WESTMINSTER AT THE SPEcial command of the King and took a new oath of adherence to Prince Edward, Richard's only son, as his heir. In March, Richard and Anne left London for Nottingham. They spent a few days in Cambridge, where Anne endowed Queens' College with substantial rents. Richard undertook to bestow lands and cash on the college in return for the recognition of Anne as its foundress and patron, which was agreed, and an annual Mass for them both was instituted. On 15 March, they lodged at the Bishop of Lincoln's palace at Buckden, and in April, the court moved to Nottingham Castle.

Here "it was fully seen how vain are the thoughts of a man who desires to establish his interests without the aid of God." For at Eastertide, the Prince of Wales, "this only son of his, in whom all the hopes of the royal succession, fortified by so many oaths, were centered, was seized with an illness of but short duration and died at Middleham Castle."[1] Dr. Saxon Barton suggested in the 1930s that the illness could have been appendicitis because the Prince suffered violent stomach pains, though no contemporary source for this is cited. Whatever the cause, the child, aged perhaps just seven or eight, suffered what Rous called "an unhappy death."

The news was cataclysmic for Richard and Anne. "You might have seen his father and mother in a state almost bordering upon madness by reason of their sudden grief."[2] Not only had they lost their only child, and had no time to get to him before he died, but Richard had also lost his heir, which left his realm vulnerable to a disputed succession in the event of his early death. It undermined his throne and prompted some nobles to reflect on whether the hand of God was evident in this latest circumstance, a consideration that persuaded some to transfer their loyalty to Henry Tudor. The Prince's death also undermined Queen Anne's position, since she was apparently unable to give Richard more children and was no longer of use to him.

Richard was devastated. Forever after he would refer to Nottingham as his "Castle of Care." We do not know if he saw the loss of his son as a divine judgment on him for murdering the Princes, but that was how the majority of his subjects viewed it, with the tragedy provoking a fresh crop of rumors about the Princes in the Tower. "After Easter," there was "much whispering among the people that the King had the childer of King Edward put to death," with a good deal of speculation as to how.[3] Hearing of Prince Edward's death, "Englishmen declared that the imprecations of the agonized mother [Elizabeth Widville] had been heard."[4] This latest wave of widespread rumors lost Richard III "the hearts of the people" once and for all. The Milanese ambassador wrote in 1496 that his subjects abandoned him, "taking the other side because he put to death his nephews, to whom the kingdom belonged."

Public feeling against Richard was not limited just to the populace; Croyland stated that he "fell in great hatred of the more part of the nobles of his realm, insomuch as such as before loved and praised him now murmured and grudged against him." Many crossed to Henry Tudor in Brittany, for the death of Edward of Middleham had strengthened Elizabeth of York's position as the rightful Yorkist heir.

Richard and Anne left Nottingham for York at the end of April. On 5 May, they were at Middleham, probably for the burial of their son in the collegiate church of St. Mary and St. Alkelda. Some still believe that Edward of Middleham was buried in Sheriff Hutton Church, where a tomb bearing the damaged alabaster effigy of a boy stands beneath a window containing fragments of fifteenth-century glass showing the Yorkist emblem of the sun in splendor, but the effigy dates from the first half of the fifteenth century and probably commemorates a member of the Neville family, perhaps either Ralph or Robert Neville, sons of the Earl of Salisbury, who had died in infancy in 1440 and 1446, respectively. Anne remained at Middleham while Richard spent the next months moving around his realm.

In 1484, Richard tried to have Henry Tudor extradited from Brittany, but Henry received a warning from Bishop Morton and fled to France, where he was warmly welcomed by the regent Anne de Beaujeu, who was happy to add to Richard III's many problems and prevent him from pursuing an aggressive policy toward her country. With French backing, Henry posed a dangerous threat to Richard's future security.

Thwarted of his prey, Richard "took all necessary precautions for the defense of his party."[5] He strengthened England's defenses, issued proclamations branding Henry a traitor, put his commissioners of array on special alert, and made friendly overtures to foreign princes, hoping to prevent them from giving aid to his enemy. The French, in turn, encouraged Henry Tudor to expedite plans for an invasion of England, realizing that Richard might at any time marry Elizabeth of York to someone else, in consequence of which Henry's cause would be irretrievably lost.

On 9 November, the King and Queen returned to London, to be welcomed by the Mayor and aldermen, who escorted them to the priory of Blackfriars. It was clear that Anne, now twenty-eight, was a sick woman. In September 1483, Thomas Langton, Bishop of St. David's, had said of Richard that "his sensuality appears to be increasing," but Anne was no longer able to satisfy those needs and there was no hope of her giving Richard the son he needed. The next heir, but for his father's attainder, would have been young Warwick, but Richard was evidently considering another nephew, John de la Pole, Earl of Lincoln, whom he made lieutenant of Ireland in Prince Edward's place, and to whom he granted the revenues of Cornwall, the earldom customarily granted to the heir to the throne. But he did not have Lincoln proclaimed his heir, probably because he was hoping to have another son of his own.

In 1484, Elizabeth of York was eighteen. In looks, she resembled her mother, but her long red-gold hair was inherited from her Plantagenet forebears. Of medium height, she had "large breasts," according to a

Portuguese ambassador, and portraits of her show that she must have been very comely. She was intelligent, pious, and literate; could speak French and a little Spanish; delighted in music, card games, books, and gardens; and was renowned for her skill at embroidery. Commines records a rumor circulating in 1484 that Richard had considered marrying her to Bishop Stillington's bastard son, but such a marriage would not have been in keeping with the terms of the King's undertaking to Elizabeth Widville.

In December, "the Lady Elizabeth was, with her four younger sisters, sent by her mother to attend the Queen at court at the Christmas festivals kept with great state in Westminster Hall. They were received with all honorable courtesy by Queen Anne, especially the Lady Elizabeth, who was ranked familiarly in the Queen's favor, who treated her as a sister. But neither the society that she loved, nor all the pomp and festivity of royalty, could heal the wound in the Queen's breast for the loss of her son."[6] By Christmas 1484, she was ailing, and her death was anticipated. Nevertheless, she played her part in the festivities.

"The feast of the Nativity was kept with due solemnity at the Palace of Westminster" and the King and Queen appeared wearing their crowns on the feast of the Epiphany, 6 January. Croyland wrote: "There may be many other things that are not written in this book and of which it is shameful to speak, but let it not go unsaid that during this Christmas festival, immoderate and unseemly stress was laid upon dancing and festivity, and vain changes of apparel of similar color and shape being presented to Queen Anne and the Lady Elizabeth, the eldest daughter of the late King, a thing that caused the people to murmur and the nobles and prelates greatly to wonder thereat, while it was said by many that the King was bent either on the anticipated death of the Queen taking place, or else by means of a divorce, for which he supposed he had quite sufficient grounds, on contracting a marriage with the said Elizabeth. For it appeared that in no other way could his kingly power be established, or the hopes of his rival being put an end to." Croyland, perhaps a royal councillor, was doubtless privy to discussions about an annulment. He made it clear that there were more reasons for conjecture than just the similar gowns given by Richard to his wife and niece, while his statement that Richard supposed he had sufficient grounds for divorce shows that the matter had already been discussed, perhaps in Council. Richard doubtless knew that his marriage was invalid and that he had a good case for an annulment.

One modern historian has asserted that it is ridiculous to suppose that he gave identical outfits to the Queen and his niece, or to infer anything amiss about it, and suggested that Anne herself had given Elizabeth the same attire as a mark of favor or affection. But Croyland clearly stated that the clothes were presented to them both. And it is small wonder that people were scandalized by the King's bastardized niece appearing dressed as a queen. The fifteenth century was an age of strict sumptuary laws reserving the right to wear luxurious materials to the upper ranks of society; an Act prohibiting everyone but the King's family from wearing purple, silk, and cloth of gold had been passed only two years earlier. The Queen's clothes were expected, by law and tradition, to be more sumptuous than those of women of lower rank, so the sight of Elizabeth "arrayed like a second queen" in robes to which she had no right would inevitably have prompted comment. It is hardly credible that Anne would have suggested out of kindness that her niece wear the same clothes as herself. Born into the higher nobility, she would have known that there would be an adverse reaction, and Elizabeth was under her protection, the Queen being the moral guardian of the unmarried girls in her retinue. It could only have been King Richard, eager to discountenance Henry Tudor, who ordered that Elizabeth appear dressed as a queen; and in that he showed scant regard for her reputation—or his ailing wife.

But this was not the only cause for gossip and speculation. In the wake of that Christmas court, "the King's determination to marry his niece reached the ears of his people, who wanted no such thing."[7] Many found the notion of an uncle marrying his niece shocking. In the North, the Neville affinity were outraged; their loyalty was to Anne, and only given to Richard because he was her husband. They would not countenance his setting her aside.

The plan was damned as ill-judged and inept. Richard surely knew it would be controversial, but there were compelling reasons for pressing ahead with it. Since many recognized Elizabeth as the legitimate, rightful heiress of the House of York, marriage to her could cement Richard's title and hopefully render it unassailable; it would crush Henry Tudor's pretensions once and for all, and hopefully silence the rumors about the Princes. It would stabilize Richard's tenure of the throne and enlist the troublesome Widvilles on the side of the Crown. A union with the popular Princess would also help to restore Richard's damaged reputation and win over the loyalty of disaffected Yorkists. He desperately needed a son to succeed him, and Elizabeth, born of fruitful stock, was likely to provide one.

It may be that Richard was personally attracted to Elizabeth. Aside from Croyland's hints, the King's most trusted advisers, Sir Richard Ratcliffe and Sir William Catesby, were to warn him that people would believe he was pursuing this marriage to "gratify an incestuous passion for his niece."[8] They appear to have had a clearer view of what was morally permissible or practically workable than Richard seems to have had, and if he had wanted merely to put Elizabeth beyond Henry Tudor's reach, any bridegroom would have sufficed—it did not have to be himself.

His plan was fraught with difficulties. Elizabeth's bastardization was the grounds of Richard's title to the throne. Either he was being ruthlessly pragmatic, or at heart he knew that she was indeed the lawfully born heiress of the House of York. If she could supply all that was wanting in Henry Tudor's title, she could also supply all that was lacking in Richard's, although that would have raised awkward issues, for his marriage to her would be seen by many as a tacit admission that her brothers were not only legitimate but also dead. Declaring her and her sisters legitimate would have been tantamount to proclaiming that Edward V was not only the rightful King, but that he and his brother Richard were dead, which would have raised yet more contentious questions and given rise to further damaging rumors; it would also have made Richard King only in Elizabeth's right. Yet it is hard to see how he could have married her without legitimizing her, for kings did not marry bastards.

Queen Anne was not a serious obstacle to Richard's plans. Their marriage was not valid anyway and the law would allow him to keep her lands if either of them remarried.

The major obstacle was that marriage between an uncle and niece was frowned upon by the Church and forbidden by canon law, as it was within the third degree of consanguinity. Dispensations for unions within these prohibited degrees could, for "great and pressing" reasons, be granted by the Pope. For example, in 1528, wishing to marry the sister of his former mistress, Henry VIII obtained a dispensation that would have allowed him to marry within the first degree, which meant that he could have wed his mother or daughter; however, since the Pope had not annulled his marriage to Katherine of Aragon, and never would, such a dispensation was irrelevant. In 1496, Ferdinand II, King of Naples, was granted a dispensation to marry his aunt Juana of Aragon and in 1582, Ferdinand II, Archduke of Austria, was permitted to wed his niece Anne Gonzaga. Otherwise, examples of uncle-niece marriages are rare. That Richard risked a moral backlash shows how eager he must have been to marry Elizabeth.

Whatever his motivation, he moved quickly, for Henry Tudor's prospects were looking decidedly brighter. Over Christmas, Richard had received news from his spies abroad that his adversary would, without question, invade England the following summer. Moreover, the French were determined to annex Brittany by forcing a marriage between its duchess and Charles VIII. Fearing that Richard would support Brittany's independence, they were ready to offer Henry support, which made him an even greater threat to Richard.

It seems likely that Elizabeth Widville had known of Richard's intentions before Christmas, when she sent her younger daughters to court to "color" their elder sister's appearance there. Stuart and Georgian historians asserted that the proposed marriage was Elizabeth's idea, but there is no evidence for it. Richard's apologists have claimed that she would never have consented to her daughter marrying the man she believed had killed her sons; and whether he had murdered the Princes or not, he had executed without trial Sir Richard Grey. Those who believe Richard innocent of the Princes' death often overlook the fact that Elizabeth Widville schemed to marry Elizabeth to Henry Tudor, the man whom some still account the real murderer.

Following her usual pragmatic instincts, and having abandoned her hopes of Henry Tudor, Elizabeth undoubtedly saw great advantages in her daughter marrying the King. Elizabeth of York would be accorded her rightful rank and dignity and her mother could expect to be restored to power and influence.

Elizabeth of York herself may initially have thought of her uncle with revulsion, for later chroniclers testified to her devotion to her brothers. But she was ambitious, like her mother, and she had been twice thwarted of her chance of a crown. Now the prospect of queenship was opening up once again, and it seems that she embraced it. With no guarantee that

Henry Tudor would ever successfully claim her, she must have known that she would be more safe and secure as Richard's Queen than in the limbo she now inhabited. She may have been living in dread of an unworthy marriage being arranged for her, and in fear for her own and her family's future. Pragmatism, necessity, and ambition had overcome her mother's scruples in regard to Richard, but in her case, there was probably a more altruistic reason for pursuing a marriage with him. Probably she was resolved to consent to the marriage for love of her mother and sisters, sacrificing herself to ensure their futures and prevent their situation from becoming any worse. Her becoming Queen would restore their lost prestige, and she would be in a position to use her influence on their behalf, particularly in regard to finding husbands for her sisters. The advantages of such a marriage were sufficiently powerful considerations to outweigh any revulsion or fears that she might have felt, and Elizabeth of York probably saw it as the only way of ensuring her own and her family's future security.

13

"A burden to her husband"

✳

"In the course of a few days after Epiphany, the Queen fell extremely sick, and her illness was supposed to have increased still more and more, because the King entirely shunned her bed, declaring that it was by the advice of his physicians that he did so. Why enlarge?"

It has been inferred from this passage by Croyland that Anne's doctors believed her illness to be contagious, hence the long-held theory that she was suffering from tuberculosis. It can spread rapidly through the lungs and used to be called galloping consumption. Yet Anne may have had cancer or some other illness, to which grief over her son's death may have undermined her resistance. Richard might have believed her contagious, "completely spurning his consort's bed." But Croyland's cynical aside suggests either that he did not believe Richard's excuse for shunning her bed, or that he thought the King was glad to have such an excuse.

Hall asserted that Anne, "understanding that she was a burden to her husband, for grief soon became a burden to herself and wasted away." It may be that Anne knew that she could no longer bear children, and that this was why Richard did not visit her bed. Their six-month separation the previous year may have been due to her need to grieve at Middleham, where her son had spent much of his short life, yet it is odd that a king who needed an heir would have been content with being so long apart from his wife. Yet there had been other separations before that.

Both Croyland and Hall agreed that Anne's condition was exacerbated by Richard's neglect and callousness, and that he made it quite plain that she was of no further use to him, and that he was just waiting for her to die. Hall added that, even though he knew she was dying, he "daily quarrelled" with her and complained of her being barren. Vergil stated that after abstaining from her bed, the King unburdened himself to Archbishop Rotherham about Anne's "unfruitfulness," appearing most distressed about it, and probably paving the way for an annulment if death did not intervene quickly enough. Rotherham was sympathetic, but tactlessly spread the word that the Queen "would suddenly depart from this world."

According to Vergil and More, Richard was also broadcasting the Queen's imminent demise and spreading rumors calculated to reach her ears, so that she would be frightened to death. In February 1485, as she was dressing, one of her ladies told her there was a rumor in the court that she had died. "Supposing that her days were at an end," Anne hastened straight to her husband, with her hair unbound, and, weeping lamentably, "demanded of him what cause there was why he should determine her death." He soothed her, kissing and comforting her, and bidding her, "Be of good cheer, for in sooth ye have no other cause." Vergil was writing much later, but his story is corroborated by Hall and by Croyland's assertion that Richard used psychological means to hasten Anne's death, and it is in keeping with other evidence. It also, intriguingly, shows that the Queen thought her husband capable of murder. She probably knew that Richard was waiting for her to die so that he could marry again and have more children. She may also have been aware of his intentions regarding Elizabeth of York.

According to Richard's Jacobean apologist, George Buck, "When the days of February were gone, the Lady Elizabeth, being very desirous to be married and growing impatient of delays, wrote a letter to John Howard, Duke of Norfolk, intimating first that he was the one in whom she most affied [trusted], because she knew the King her father much loved him, and that he was a very faithful servant unto him and to the King his brother, then reigning, and very loving and serviceable to King Edward's children. She prayed him, as before, to be a mediator for her in the cause of the marriage to the King who, as she wrote, was her only joy and maker in this world, and that she was his in heart and in thought, in body and in all. And then she intimated that the better part of February was past, and that she feared the Queen would never die. And all these be her own words, written with her own hand, and this is the sum of her letter, whereof I have seen the autograph or original draft under her own hand."

The letter no longer survives. Buck stated he had seen it in the Earl of Arundel's cabinet among precious jewels. Arundel was descended from Norfolk, and he was Buck's patron, to whom Buck dedicated his history of Richard III. Several historians have dismissed the letter as an invention, but it is hardly likely that Buck would have made up something so open to disproof by Arundel. Moreover, the contents of the letter are corroborated to a degree by Croyland. Only Tudor sources stress Elizabeth's aversion to the idea of marriage with Richard III. There is no reason, therefore, to dismiss this letter as an invention; on the contrary, it has all the hallmarks of authenticity.

Buck observed that "by this letter, it may be observed that this young lady was inexpert in worldly affairs." But her mother was not, and the letter may well have been a diplomatic ploy to bring Richard to the point and discover his true intentions, which he may have been reluctant to declare while his wife lived. It could even have been dictated by Elizabeth Widville, in which case her daughter had perhaps returned to Heytesbury after Christmas, which would explain why she was writing to Norfolk rather than approaching him personally. It is unlikely she would have sent such a letter without her mother's knowledge and approval.

Queen Anne lingered into the early spring of 1485, attended by many physicians, but they could do nothing to save her. On the morning of 16 March 1485, this "lady of gracious fame"[1] died during a great eclipse of the sun, a circumstance that people saw as ominous and portentous. Nine days later, on the Feast of the Annunciation, she was buried in Westminster Abbey "with no less honor than befitted the interment of a queen,"[2] "by the south door that leads into St. Edward's Chapel"[3] in front of the sedilia by the ancient tomb of Sebert, King of the East Saxons. Croyland recorded that Richard wept openly at the funeral. It was not a costly one, no provision was made for a tomb—events would ensure that Richard had no time to commission one—and the site of her grave is lost. Anne is commemorated only by a small bronze wall plaque by Sebastian Comper, with a quote from John Rous, and an armorial shield, both erected in 1960 on the wall by Sebert's tomb.

Afterword:

"Without any worldly pomp"

✷

RICHARD'S REACTION TO ANNE'S DEATH IS NOT RECORDED. A fortnight before, the Exchequer had made payments in his name for "the household of our most dear wife the Queen."[1] In the week preceding her passing, he had spent much of his time hunting. Agostino Barbarigo, the Doge of Venice, hearing of the loss of Richard's "beloved" Anne, wrote to him: "Your consort led so religious and catholic a life, and was so adorned with goodness, prudence, and excellent morality as to leave a name immortal." He exhorted him to "bear the disaster calmly and resign yourself to the divine will."

Vergil asserted that as soon as he was "loosed from the bond of matrimony," Richard began to "cast an eye upon Elizabeth, his niece, and to desire her in marriage. Because the young lady herself, and all others, did abhor the wickedness so detestable, he determined therefore to do everything by leisure." But London was once more vocal with rumors, and it was clear that public opinion was against such a marriage, while Richard's enemies had been spreading sedition. The *Acts of Court of the Mercers Company* record that, in the days immediately following Anne's death, there was "much simple communication among the people by evil-disposed persons, contrived and sown to very great displeasure of the King, showing how that the Queen, as by consent and will of the King, was poisoned, to the intent that he might then marry and have to wife Lady Elizabeth, eldest daughter of his brother."

According to *The Great Chronicle of London,* there was "much whispering among the people that the King had poisoned the Queen his wife and intended with a license purchased to have married the eldest daughter of King Edward." Even the King's northern stalwarts, "in whom he placed great reliance," willingly imputed "to him the death of the Queen," and there was much "whispering of poison" among them. Given his previous notoriety, people had no difficulty in believing that Richard had murdered his wife.

John Rous, who devotedly chronicled all the deeds of the Neville family, had no time for Richard after Anne's death, describing him only as her "unhappy husband," where once he had extolled him. Rous believed the rumors. "Lady Anne, his queen, he poisoned," he wrote. "Some said he had her killed," wrote Commines. Vergil claimed that the King "desired the death of his wife Anne, which in any way he decided to accelerate. But the Queen, whether she was despatched by sorrowfulness or poison, died." Hall, years later, stated: "Some think she went her own pace to the grave, while others suspect a grain was given her to quicken her in her journey to her long home."

Richard was swift to deny the rumors, and that he intended to marry Elizabeth of York. Within six days of Anne's passing, "the King's purpose and intention being mentioned to some who were opposed thereto, [he] was obliged, having called a council together, to excuse himself with many words, and to assert that such a thing had never once entered his mind. There were some persons, however, present at that same Council, who very well knew the contrary. Those who were most strongly against the marriage" were Sir Richard Ratcliffe and Sir William Catesby, "two men whose views even the King himself seldom dared oppose. By these persons the King was told to his face that if he did not abandon his intended purpose, and deny it by public declaration before the Mayor and commons of the City of London, opposition would not be offered to him merely by the warnings of the voice; for all the people of the North, in whom he placed the greatest reliance, would rise in rebellion and impute to him the death of the Queen, in order that he might, to the extreme abhorrence of the Almighty, gratify an incestuous passion for his niece." This was the motive imputed to Richard by Tudor chroniclers such as Hall, who stated that Richard "compassed by all the means and ways that he could invent how carnally to know his own niece under the pretense of a cloaked matrimony." To give weight to their protests, Ratcliffe and Catesby "brought to him more than twelve doctors of divinity who had sat on the case of a marriage of an uncle and niece and had declared that the kindred was too near for the Pope's bull to sanction."[2]

These were powerful arguments against the match, but "it was supposed by many" that Ratcliffe, Catesby, and others nursed darker, more self-interested concerns, and that they "threw so many impediments in the way for fear lest, if the said Elizabeth should attain the rank of queen, it might at some time be in her power to avenge upon them the death of her uncle, Earl Anthony [Rivers], and her brother, Richard [Grey]." Ratcliffe, moreover, had supervised the executions of Rivers and Grey. There is no evidence that Elizabeth of York had it in her to be vengeful, but she was a Widville, so it is credible that Ratcliffe and Catesby believed they had reason to fear that she might seek to avenge her kinsmen's deaths or would be persuaded to it by her mother. Some of Richard's northern councillors had received Widville lands and were worried that they might lose them if a queen of Widville stock married the King. But Vergil, writing much later, deemed it politic to state that Elizabeth of York had more pressing concerns. "The young lady herself, and all others, did abhor this wickedness so detestable. To such a marriage the girl had a singular aversion," and the councillors now began decrying the match because "the maiden herself opposed the wicked act."

Richard followed the advice of his councillors. Two weeks after Anne's death, "a little before Easter, in the great hall of St. John's [Hospital at Clerkenwell] and before the Mayor and citizens of London, the King totally repudiated the whole idea in a loud, clear voice." The *Acts of Court of the Mercers Company* record that he "showed his grief and displeasure and said it never came in his thought or mind to marry in such manner-wise, nor willing nor glad of the death of his queen, but as sorry and in heart as heavy as man might be." He ended by commanding his subjects to cease all discussion of the matter on pain of his displeasure and indignation. Letters reiterating his public denial were sent to major towns and cities such as York and Southampton. His statement was seen as a public humiliation; "people thought it was more because of his advisers' wishes than his own."[3]

Richard still urgently needed to beget an heir to his throne; he could not afford to observe a decent period of mourning for Anne. On 22 March

1485, he sent Sir Edward Brampton to Portugal to negotiate two marriages: one for himself with the Infanta Joana, daughter of Alfonso V, King of Portugal, and the other for Elizabeth of York with the future King Manuel I. Nothing came of either proposal.

Richard had lost popular support. He "was never quiet in his mind, never thought himself secure, his hand ever on his dagger," and "he took ill rest at night."[4]

Charles VIII recognized Henry Tudor as King of England and gave him money, ships, and French troops for an invasion. Many Englishmen hastened to France to join him. Others were preparing to support him. On 1 August, his invasion fleet set sail from Harfleur in Normandy. Edward Widville was in his army. After landing at Milford Haven, he moved eastward, as Richard marched to confront him. Their armies met in Leicestershire, near Market Bosworth, on 22 August. The Battle of Bosworth lasted two hours, with an estimated 20,000 men engaging in combat, the majority fighting in the royal forces. It was a savage battle. Henry did not engage in the fighting, but remained under his standard behind the lines, leaving the experienced Earl of Oxford to command his vanguard. Margaret Beaufort's husband Lord Stanley positioned himself to the north with his forces, waiting to see which way the battle was going before joining it.

When the King's side appeared to be losing the day, Richard gathered a small band of loyal followers and made one final, desperate charge, bearing down on the red dragon banner of Henry Tudor. He cut down the standard-bearer, and was about to swoop on Henry himself, but Lord Stanley came racing to Henry's aid, which decisively turned the tide of the battle, and the victory was Henry's.

Croyland recorded that it was during the fighting, and not in the act of flight, that Richard fell, "like a brave and most valiant prince." Rous was moved to write: "Let me say the truth to his credit, that he bore himself like a noble soldier and honorably defended himself to his last breath, shouting again and again that he was betrayed, and crying, 'Treason! Treason! Treason!'" Even Vergil wrote admiringly that King Richard was killed "fighting manfully in the thickest press of his enemies."

"Providence," declared Croyland, "gave a glorious victory to the Earl of Richmond."

With Richard III's death, 331 years of Plantagenet rule had come to an end. The Tudor age had begun, and the new King, Henry VII, began to be praised by all, as if he had been an angel sent down from Heaven to bring peace. "The children of King Edward," commented Croyland, had been "avenged" at last; "in this battle: the boar's tusks quailed, and, to avenge the white, the red rose bloomed."

Within hours of his victory at Bosworth, even before departing from Leicester, the new King sent men to Sheriff Hutton to escort Elizabeth of York to her mother.

Apartments had been made ready for them at Margaret Beaufort's residence, Coldharbour, which lay just outside London's walls; and it was there that they were reunited. Elizabeth Widville had been staying at Sheen when Bosworth was fought, but had immediately hastened to the capital.

Henry VII made a triumphal entry into London on 3 September. After giving thanks at St. Paul's Cathedral for his victory and his crown, he summoned his first Privy Council and declared his intention of marrying Elizabeth of York. But there were two obstacles to be overcome. Parliament had to repeal the Act *Titulus Regius* to declare her legitimate and restore her royal status, and a dispensation for the marriage had to be obtained, for Henry and Elizabeth were related in the fourth degree of kinship. Legislation and dispensations took time, but the delay suited Henry well, for he did not want it to be thought that he owed his crown to his Queen.

A "device" for a joint coronation was drawn up, but Henry could not afford to defer his crowning until he was married, while a joint ceremony with Elizabeth might have sent out the message that they were equal sovereigns. Elizabeth was not even present at the solemnities in Westminster Abbey on 30 October.

Parliament then proceeded to repeal *Titulus Regius,* effectively proclaiming Elizabeth Widville's marriage lawful and her children legitimate. "The King ordaineth that Elizabeth, late wife to Edward IV, late

King of England, have and enjoy from henceforth all such estate, dignity, and preeminence and name as she should or might have had if no Act of Parliament had been made against her in the time of Richard III."[5] From now on, she would not be known, humiliatingly, as Dame Elizabeth Grey, but as Elizabeth, Queen Dowager of England.

Parliament also repealed Richard III's Act confiscating her property. It was not all immediately returned to her, but she was allowed her widow's jointure. Henry VII granted her an income of £400 (£381,320) per annum from more than seventy manors, the rights to feed pigs in Savernake Forest and dredge for mussels at Tilbury, as well as other privileges normally enjoyed by a queen dowager. In March 1486, she would receive a grant of the substantial part of her dower lands, and in April a separate grant for the remainder, "in full satisfaction of her dower."[6]

Henry commanded that *Titulus Regius* be deleted from the Statute Books. He was sensitive about marrying a princess whose legitimacy had been called into question, and it was essential that the Act that impugned her legitimacy be eradicated. The Parliament Roll of 1484 was suppressed and all official documents referring to the Act, as well as those depriving Elizabeth Widville of her dower, were burned. By royal command, anyone having in their possession a copy of it was required to relinquish it to the Lord Chancellor by Easter 1486 on pain of imprisonment and a fine, "so that all things said and remembered in the said Act may be for ever out of remembrance and forgot."

The text of the Act appeared in the *Croyland Chronicle,* which was completed in the spring of 1486. Soon afterward, the original, and nearly every copy, was destroyed. Thus, when Tudor historians came to write their versions of recent events, they had no access to this valuable source. Vergil, Henry VII's official historian, tried to deny that the legitimacy of Edward IV's children had ever been called into question, and that the precontract story was the product of rumor and had never been used by Richard III to justify his usurpation.

This censoring of history meant that Eleanor Butler's name disappeared from the records for more than a hundred and thirty years. Not until the early seventeenth century did Sir George Buck unearth the only surviving copy of the *Croyland Chronicle* and the contents of *Titulus Regius* were revealed in print.

Afterword: "Without any worldly pomp"

* * *

Late in 1485 King Henry rewarded those who had supported him: Morton was appointed Lord Chancellor of England; Stanley was created Earl of Derby; Jasper Tudor received the dukedom of Bedford and married Buckingham's widow, Katherine Widville. Dorset, Sir Edward, and Richard Widville were all restored to their lands and honors.

On 18 January 1486, Henry VII married Elizabeth of York at Westminster, either in the Abbey or in St. Stephen's Chapel. Much was made of this union of the white rose of York and the red rose of Lancaster, which was seen as symbolizing the end of the conflict between the two royal houses. "By reason of which marriage, peace was thought to descend out of Heaven into England, considering that the lines of Lancaster and York were now brought into one knot and connexed together, of whose two bodies one heir might succeed, which after their time should peaceably rule and enjoy the whole monarchy and realm of England."[7]

Elizabeth of York proved a model Queen, gentle, pious, fruitful, and charitable. In the past, historians tended to compare her favorably to Margaret of Anjou, yet today, in the wake of a feminist revolution, it is the proactive Margaret, vigorously fighting her husband's cause, who earns our admiration, rather than the passive Elizabeth. Unlike Margaret, Elizabeth never identified herself with factions at court; unlike her mother, she did not promote a horde of ambitious relatives. She was not as politically inclined as Elizabeth Widville, and she never enjoyed anything approaching her mother's influence. If she had been strongly identified with the Widville faction prior to her marriage, that was all at an end, for her mother's family were never allowed much influence by Henry VII, who clearly preferred to emphasize Elizabeth's paternal descent.

Henry had to maintain not only his wife but also her mother—effectively, he was supporting two Queens, which placed an unusual strain on his finances, as a new queen was usually assigned the dower of her predecessor. As has been noted, Henry had granted other lands to Elizabeth Widville.

* * *

In the spring of 1486 Henry VII felt it politic to go on a progress to Lincolnshire and Yorkshire to be seen by his northern subjects. Elizabeth, who was pregnant, stayed behind at the palace of Placentia at Greenwich with her mother. At the end of August, the King and Queen traveled to Winchester, where, early in the morning of 20 September, the Queen bore a son. Henry named him Arthur after the hero-king of legend, in order to underline his much-vaunted (but mythical) descent from King Arthur and his dynasty's links with the ancient rulers of Britain.

On 24 September, Arthur was borne to his christening in Winchester Cathedral. Elizabeth Widville and other members of the Widville family were assigned prominent roles. Her daughter Cecily carried the Prince to church, where Elizabeth was awaiting her grandson's coming, for she was to stand godmother to him. After his baptism, she bore him to the high altar, as the choir sang *Veni Creator Spiritus* and the *Te Deum*. She laid him on the altar and Peter Courtenay, Bishop of Exeter, confirmed him. After he was taken back behind the curtain to be dressed, wine and spices were served to the godparents, who presented many costly gifts to the child. Elizabeth Widville's was a "a rich cup of gold, covered, which was borne by Sir Davy Owen," the King's bastard uncle.[8]

Now that Elizabeth of York was the mother of a prince, plans were made for her crowning. Her Widville relations were held in high favor by the King. On 19 November, Thomas Grey was confirmed as Marquess of Dorset and granted an annuity; Sir Richard Widville received a similar reward in January, and his brother Edward was made a Knight of the Garter. The court kept Christmas at Greenwich. Although Elizabeth Widville seems to have accompanied the Queen back to London from Winchester, she is not recorded at this Christmas court.

Again, Elizabeth of York's coronation had to be deferred, for in January the King received news that a pretender to his throne, one Lambert Simnel, had appeared in Ireland, claiming to be the Earl of Warwick and to have escaped from the Tower, where Henry had had Warwick imprisoned. Later it emerged that Simnel was the bastard son of an Oxford organ-maker. He was said to have been coached in his role by an ambitious priest, Richard Symonds, who had apparently had a dream that he would be tutor to a king, although it is likelier that he was acting on behalf of more powerful Yorkist interests.

Many were taken in by Simnel: the boy was well spoken, handsome, and gracious, and he spoke accurately and convincingly of his past, as if he really were Warwick, and scathingly of the "Welsh milksop" who had seized his crown. It is likely that the driving force behind the Simnel plot was the Earl of Lincoln, the hope of those who still wanted a Yorkist king on the throne; and that it was he who had secretly had Simnel groomed as a pretender to mask his own intention of seizing the crown. Lincoln's ambitions had been overthrown by the victory of Henry VII, and although he had offered Henry his allegiance, and been outwardly reconciled to the new régime, he had never enjoyed the same income and honors that had been his under King Richard.

On 10 July 1486, Elizabeth Widville took a forty-year lease on Cheyneygates, the Abbot's House at Westminster Abbey; after her previous sojourns there, while in sanctuary, it may have represented a refuge from a court where she may have felt increasingly unwelcome—and it was conveniently situated for worship at the Abbey and for visiting the Palace of Westminster. But she was not to enjoy it for long.

That same month, in negotiating a truce with Scotland, Henry VII suggested that she marry the widowed James III of Scotland, even though she was nearing fifty (James was thirty-four) and highly unlikely to bear him children. If she married abroad, Henry would have been relieved of the burden of providing for her, but the plan was complicated by the fact that two of her daughters had been proposed as brides for the Scots King's eldest son, James, and his second son, Alexander Stewart, Earl of Ross, and there ensued some discussion about proposing one of her younger girls, Anne or Bridget, for the King instead. Negotiations dragged on until, abruptly, they were halted by James III's assassination in June 1488.

Long before then, Elizabeth Widville was out of the running. On 2 February 1487, the Council met at Sheen to discuss the threat from Simnel. Among other matters, it was resolved that the Queen Dowager "should lose and forfeit all her lands and possessions" because she had imperiled Henry's cause when she made "peace with King Richard [and] voluntarily submitted herself and her daughters to [his] hands—whereat there was much wondering," and that, by leaving sanctuary, she had "broken her promise to those (mainly of the nobility) who had, at her own most urgent entreaty, forsaken their own English property and fled to Henry in Brittany, the latter having pledged himself to marry her elder daughter, Elizabeth."[9] She "was deprived of the income from her estates so that she should offer an example to others to keep faith. Through her double dealings, it was likely to have followed that the marriage [of her daughter] could not take place, nor might the noblemen who, at her request, took King Henry's part return without danger to their lives."[10]

It is hardly surprising that there was "much wondering," for Elizabeth had left sanctuary three years before, and Henry had made no move against her for eighteen months: indeed, up to now he had behaved toward her with courtesy and respect and had chosen her as a sponsor for Prince Arthur.

Not until the early seventeenth century was it asserted by Sir Francis Bacon that Henry distrusted his mother-in-law and banished her to Bermondsey Abbey because she had been the prime mover behind the Simnel conspiracy. "It cannot be but that some great person that knew [Warwick] particularly and familiarly had a hand in the business. That which is most probable, out of precedent and subsequent acts, is that it was the Queen Dowager from whom this action had the principal source and motion. For certain it is she was a busy negotiating woman, and in her withdrawing chamber had the fortunate conspiracy for the King against King Richard III been hatched, which the King knew and remembered perhaps but too well." As she had plotted on Henry's behalf, the theory went, so she might decide to plot against him. Apparently, she had anticipated that her daughter would enjoy more influence as Queen—the kind of influence she herself had enjoyed in her day—but it had quickly become clear that Elizabeth of York was to be allowed no real power at all. Because of this, the Queen Dowager "was at this time extremely discontent with the King, thinking her daughter not advanced, but depressed." And "none could hold the book so well to prompt and instruct this stage play as she could." Thanks to Bacon, there has been speculation ever since that Elizabeth Widville was behind the Simnel plot.

Yet it is inconceivable that she would have intrigued against Henry to the detriment and ruin of her own daughter and grandson, and there is no other evidence that she did. She had actively worked for Elizabeth's marriage to the King. If her daughter had little power as Queen, she would have even less if Henry were deposed and Lincoln became King. Even if the Queen Dowager really believed Simnel to be Warwick, which is highly unlikely, she would almost certainly not have lent her support to the son of Clarence, in whose ruin she and her party had probably been complicit, or promoted the interests of Warwick above those of her own grandson. The fact that Henry imprisoned her son Dorset in the Tower until the threat from Simnel and his supporters had been successfully dealt with appears to support Bacon's assertions, but Sir Edward Widville was to fight for the King against Simnel's forces.

Henry VII took all Elizabeth's property into his hands, and on 20 February, Parliament declared her estates forfeit and granted her in exchange a pension of 400 marks (£238,980), which Henry paid in annual installments to "our right dear and right well-beloved Queen Elizabeth, late wife unto the noble Prince of famous memory, King Edward, and mother unto our dearest wife the Queen." This was 300 marks fewer than Richard III had assigned Elizabeth in 1484.

Later that spring, warrants were issued to officers of the Royal Exchequer to pay all issues from the confiscated estates to Elizabeth of York. Probably Henry's true objective in depriving his mother-in-law of her lands was to dower his financially embarrassed wife.

Around 12 February 1487, Elizabeth Widville retired to St. Savior's Abbey at Bermondsey. Founded in the fourteenth century, this Benedictine house had long been favored by royal ladies. It had elegant gardens and commanded a site on the Surrey shore of the Thames, opposite the Tower of London. Originally a priory, it had been founded in the eleventh century on the site of what had been a Saxon monastery and, later, a royal manor recorded in Domesday Book. From the twelfth century, it had enjoyed the patronage of royalty, and in 1399 it had become an abbey. This was where Katherine of Valois had died fifty years before Elizabeth arrived. The present Abbot, John Marlow, had been among the clergy who officiated at the obsequies of Edward IV.

It has been suggested that Elizabeth retreated to Bermondsey at her own request, possibly because of ill health or because she did not wish to marry King James, but subsequent events would suggest otherwise. It could not have been because she wanted to retire from the world to lead a life of piety, because Bermondsey was a house of monks, and her marriage to James was still being mooted nine months later. And if she had gone willingly to Bermondsey, why had she taken a forty-year lease on Cheyneygates less than a year earlier?

At Bermondsey, Elizabeth was registered as a boarder, which entitled her to free board and lodging in an old range of apartments formerly used by the earls of Gloucester, early benefactors of the monastery, whose line had died out in the fourteenth century. These rooms seem not to have offered luxurious, or even comfortable, accommodation. In the fifteenth century, Bermondsey was still a large and important religious house, but it was not an ideal retreat. It had been poorly run and allowed to fall into neglect—its history is a long catalogue of debt and mismanagement—and it was located in a damp and unhealthy situation. If Elizabeth Widville retired there solely on account of her failing health, it was a strange choice. For Henry VII, though, it provided a solution to the problem of maintaining his mother-in-law, for a condition of the original royal grant of the land stipulated that the monks must always keep a residence for the use of the monarch. Thus, Henry could send the Queen Dowager there at no cost to himself.

Bacon claimed that Elizabeth Widville was now so tainted with treason "that it was almost thought dangerous to visit her, or even see her." Hall asserted that she now lived "a wretched and miserable life" at Bermondsey. Yet in no sense was she a prisoner. Henry VII continued to refer to her in letters and grants as his "right dear mother, Queen Elizabeth" or "our right well beloved Queen Elizabeth, mother of our dear wife the Queen." After her retirement, she went to court occasionally and was visited by her daughters at the abbey. Over the years, she was given various grants by the Exchequer, such as payments for Christmas sundries and wines. The King gave her sums of money from time to time, and they exchanged gifts—in 1488 he rewarded her for sending him a tun of wine, and in 1490 he gave her 50 marks (£30,920) "against the feast of Christmas."[11] This all suggests cordiality rather than antagonism. In November 1487, Henry again put Elizabeth forward as a bride for James III, which he is hardly likely to have done if he believed she had been plotting treason and saw her as a threat to him—or if she had retired to Bermondsey because of ill health.

Elizabeth's wishes for the disposition of her youngest daughter,

Bridget, were honored by the King. Between 1486, when Bridget was considered as a potential bride for James III, and 1492, when she is recorded as coming from Dartford to Windsor, Bridget was sent to the Dominican priory at Dartford, Kent, to join the sisters of the Order of St. Augustine, a house of enclosed nuns. Dartford was the only Dominican nunnery in England, and the seventh-richest convent in the land at the time of the dissolution of the monasteries in the 1530s. It was famous as a center for prayer, spirituality, and education, and had enjoyed royal patronage since its foundation by Edward III in 1349.

Bridget had been destined for the religious life from birth, so possibly she was sent to Dartford soon after her mother had retired to Bermondsey, when she was six. Initially, like other children of noble families, she would have lived in the priory as a boarder before entering the novitiate. The earliest date she could have taken her final vows was November 1493, for girls had to be thirteen to become professed Dominican nuns. Candidates had to be highly educated, and to that end Bridget would have been tutored well in the priory's school and become familiar with the holy texts in its library. On entry to the order, she donned the requisite white tunic and scapular, the black mantle and veil, and embraced a strict régime of prayer and contemplation.

On 25 November 1487, Elizabeth of York was crowned. Elizabeth Widville was not present in Westminster Abbey to see her daughter's triumph (although, as her biographer Arlene Okerlund suggests, she perhaps saw the river pageant from Bermondsey), nor were Elizabeth's younger sisters; but Dorset was there, having been allowed out of the Tower for the occasion.

The Queen Dowager was at court at Christmas, which was kept at Greenwich. The King presided over the customary feast in the great hall of the palace, while the Queen dined with her mother and Margaret Beaufort in her chamber. Her sister Cecily, with her new husband, John, Viscount Welles, joined the festivities.

In November 1489, Elizabeth Widville came to court to support her daughter during her second confinement. A few days after the Queen had taken to her chamber an exception was made to the strict protocol prohibiting men from admittance. In the interests of good diplomatic relations, the two Queens privately received the new French ambassador, their cousin, Francis, Sieur de Luxembourg, Viscount of Geneva. Two other men were allowed to be present, Elizabeth of York's chamberlain and Garter King-at-Arms, and Margaret Beaufort was also in attendance. Elizabeth Widville deputized with her for the Queen at another reception for the ambassadors.

On 28 June 1491, at Greenwich Palace, Elizabeth of York bore a second son, called Henry after his father, and perhaps after Henry VI, whom the King hoped to have canonized. The child was red-haired and sturdy, a true Plantagenet who much resembled his grandfather, Edward IV. As Henry VIII, he was to become the most famous of Elizabeth Widville's grandchildren.

On 8 June 1492, Elizabeth died at Bermondsey Abbey. She must have been unwell since at least 10 April, when she had made her will. Elizabeth of York could not be with her at the end, for she was in the ninth month of her pregnancy and had been obliged to take to her chamber at Sheen, knowing that her mother was very ill. But her sisters and Dorset were present, with Grace, a bastard daughter of Edward IV.

The dying Queen "desired on her deathbed that, as soon as she should be deceased, she should in all goodly haste, without any worldly pomp, by water be conveyed to Windsor, and there to be buried in the same vault that her husband was buried in, according to the will of my said lord and mine, without pompous interring or costly expenses."[12]

In her short will, witnessed by Abbot John and Benedict Cun, "doctor of physick," the Queen Dowager, "being of sound mind, seeing the world so transitory and no creature certain when they shall depart from hence, having Almighty God fresh in mind, in whom is all mercy and grace," bequeathed her soul "into His hands, beseeching Him of the same mercy to accept it graciously, and Our Blessed Lady, Queen of Comfort, and the whole company of Heaven to be good means for me." She lamented: "Where I have no worldly goods to do the Queen's Grace, my dearest daughter, a pleasure with, neither to reward any of my children, according to my heart and mind, I beseech Almighty God to bless her Grace, with all her noble issue, and with as good heart and mind as is to me possible, I give her Grace my blessing, and all the aforesaid my children . . . And I beseech my said dearest daughter, the Queen's Grace, and my son, Thomas, Marquess Dorset, to put their good wills and help for the performance of this my testament," to ensure that her last requests were carried out and her "small stuff and goods" be sold to pay her debts "for the health of my soul," or divided among her relatives. Her possessions were few; she left no money or estates.

Elizabeth's wishes in regard to her interment were respected. Her body was wrapped in fifty folds of wax canvas and, on the evening of Whitsunday, 10 June, it was conveyed by barge to Windsor, attended only by her executors—her chaplain, the Prior of the Charterhouse at Sheen, a Mr. Haute, a clerk called Dr. Brent, and Mistress Grace. The coffin was placed on a hearse "such as they use for the common people, with wooden candlesticks about it and a black pall of cloth of gold on it [with] four candlesticks of silver gilt." It was borne "privily through the little park and conveyed into the castle without ringing of any bells or receiving of the Dean and canons, but only by the Prior of the Charterhouse of Sheen and her chaplain. And so, privily, about nine of the clock in the night, she was buried" in Edward IV's tomb in St. George's Chapel, Windsor, "without any solemn dirge or the ringing of any bell, or Mass done for her."

On the Tuesday following, Elizabeth's younger daughters, Anne, Katherine, and Bridget, attended by Lady Dorset and other ladies, arrived by barge at Windsor for the Requiem Mass, Bridget having traveled from Dartford Priory. Later, they were joined by several relatives, including Dorset, the late Queen's brother-in-law, the Earl of Essex, and her son-in-law, John, Viscount Welles. Her daughter Cecily was not present, possibly because she was ill or pregnant, so the Princess Anne was chief mourner, deputizing for Queen Elizabeth.

The mourners attended the ceremonies in St. George's Chapel that evening, when the dirge was begun, and the next night. There were murmurs that the obsequies were conducted cheaply and shabbily, because the only others present were the Garter officers, servants, and the Poor Knights of St. George—"a dozen divers old men holding old torches and torched ends," who came "in return for their dinner, for charity"; but they had been performed as Elizabeth Widville had directed.

"The next morning, one of the canons sang Our Lady's Mass, at which Lord Dorset offered a piece of gold, kneeling down at the hearse head.

The ladies came not to the Requiem, and the lords sat about in the choir. The officers of arm, there being present, went before the Lady Anne, which offered the Mass penny at the head of the Queen" on Elizabeth of York's behalf. And the Viscount Welles took his wife's offering, and Dame Catherine Grey bore the Lady Anne's train; every one of the late Queen's daughters offered, followed by everyone else present. Dorset paid the cost of the funeral.

On 2 July, Elizabeth of York bore a second daughter, who was baptized Elizabeth in honor of her late grandmother.

The Chapter Records of St. George's Chapel, Windsor, record that in 1789, workmen restoring the choir accidentally broke into Edward IV's tomb. The canons entered the vault containing the coffins of the King and Elizabeth Widville; hers, much decayed, was lying on top of his, and her skeleton was seen; the coffin ornaments were missing, as the vault had been plundered by Parliamentarians in the 1650s. Edward's skeleton was lying in a viscous liquid with no smell or taste.

The canons also discovered a small "secret" vault next to the tomb, which contained the bodies of two children. It was assumed that they were those of Edward and Elizabeth's children Mary and George, and their names were added to the inscription on the restored tomb. But in 1810, when Cardinal Wolsey's tomb house was excavated to construct a burial vault for George III and his family, the coffin of George, clearly labeled "*serenissimus princeps Georgius filius tercius Christianissimi principis Edvardi iiij,*" was found, and next to it one that was almost certainly Mary's, as a contemporary account of her funeral states she was buried beside her brother. In 1813, both were moved into their parents' vault. Unfortunately, on neither of the occasions when Edward IV's vault was opened were the two coffins of the unidentified children opened, sketched (as other parts of the vault were), or even described.

It has been suggested that they could have been the Princes in the Tower, perhaps secretly laid to rest with their parents by a guilty Richard III, but until further investigations are made—and the Sovereign's permission would be required for that—there is too little evidence to say whose remains they are. No other royal children are recorded as having been buried, with graves unaccounted for, in St. George's Chapel prior to 1789.

A clue to the mystery may lie in Westminster Abbey. During the Reformation, the sarcophagus of Edward and Elizabeth's infant daughter Margaret was moved from the steps of St. Edward the Confessor's shrine to the side of his chapel. A history in the abbey's library records that, when the sarcophagus was opened later, it was found to be empty, so it is possible that the body was removed to Windsor at the time the tomb was relocated. As to who the other child might be, that remains a mystery.

Epilogue

✳

IN THIS BOOK, AND THE THREE BOOKS PRECEDING IT, I HAVE told the story of England's medieval queens from the time of the Norman Conquest to the fall of the Plantagenet dynasty, looking at the lives and historical significance of twenty queens. I have numbered the Empress Maud among them because, although she was never crowned or styled Queen of England, she was chosen as such and, for a very brief time, wielded sovereign power.

The experiences of all these women were very different. Some, namely Matilda of Flanders, Eleanor of Aquitaine, Eleanor of Provence, Eleanor of Castile, Isabella of France, and Margaret of Anjou, exercised real power. Margaret and Isabella raised and led armies, as did Matilda of Boulogne. Others conformed to the traditional role of the good queen: they were virtuous, pious, fruitful, charitable, and true helpmeets to their husbands. Notable examples are Matilda of Scotland, Margaret of France, and Philippa of Hainault. Some queens fulfilled their dynastic duty by bearing many children: Matilda of Flanders, Eleanor of Castile, and Philippa of Hainault all had large families. Those who were childless, like Adeliza of Louvain, Berengaria of Navarre, Isabella of Valois, and Joan of Navarre, made little impact on English history. Margaret of Anjou's apparent barrenness in the eight years before she bore a son was a factor in the lead-up to the Wars of the Roses.

Before 1464, English kings took brides from the royal houses of Europe. Nine of the nineteen consorts came from what is now France, three from the Iberian Peninsula, three from the Low Countries, one from Scotland, and one from the Holy Roman Empire. These marriages were all made for political advantage, to forge political alliances or bring about a peace, and the queens were expected to bolster those alliances by maintaining friendly networks and relations with their own families. But in 1464, Edward IV broke the mold—and caused a scandal—by marrying Elizabeth Widville, a commoner, for love, while his brother Richard III took a bride, Anne Neville, from the English nobility, a match that, by contract, was politically advantageous.

Foreign queens were not always popular. Some, such as Isabella of Angoulême and Eleanor of Provence, brought to England hordes of relatives all hungry for rich pickings, much to the disgust of the English. Edward IV's policy of advancing Elizabeth Widville's many kinsfolk earned him—and them—similar criticism. Eleanor of Castile was hated for her rapacity. Several queens were seen as extravagant, notably Eleanor of Provence, Eleanor of Castile, Isabella of France, Philippa of Hainault, and Joan of Navarre, although in reality some found it hard to live within their means. Philippa, however, was much loved by her husband's subjects for her intercessions and her promotion of trade; Matilda of Scotland was loved for her piety and her beneficial foundations, while Eleanor of Aquitaine, in widowhood, acquired the reputation of a wise and compassionate stateswoman.

Some queens committed transgressions. William the Conqueror publicly castigated Matilda of Flanders for supporting their son Robert, who had risen against him. Henry II kept Eleanor of Aquitaine in prison or under house arrest for sixteen years because she, like Matilda, took the part of their sons, who were, not unreasonably, demanding a greater share of power; and she compounded that by trying to enlist the aid of the French King. Isabella of Angoulême plotted to assassinate the King of France and had to hide in a convent for the rest of her days. Isabella of France, provoked beyond endurance, invaded England with her lover, Roger Mortimer, and deposed her husband, Edward II, then proceeded to rule in the name of her son, losing popularity because of her greed and because she outraged the English by making a shameful peace with the Scots. Later, she would be accused—probably falsely—of complicity in the supposed murder of Edward II, and would become known as the "She-Wolf of France."

Medieval queens were meant to embody contemporary ideals of beauty. Chroniclers almost routinely described them as "fair," which in some cases must have been flattery, yet it is clear that a few were truly beautiful, such as Eleanor of Aquitaine, Isabella of France, and Elizabeth Widville.

Queens did not usually meet their future husbands until shortly before the wedding. Some married very young: Isabella of Valois was not quite seven when Richard II wed her in 1396. Several royal brides were barely twelve, the age at which the Church permitted a wife to start cohabiting with her husband. Love was a duty laid upon women, expected to come after marriage. Several queens found love in their political marriages, for example, Matilda of Flanders, Matilda of Boulogne, Eleanor of Provence, Eleanor of Castile, Margaret of France, Philippa of Hainault, Anne of Bohemia, and Elizabeth Widville—although not all these marriages ended happily. The marriage of Henry II and Eleanor of Aquitaine was quite clearly as founded upon lust as it was on territorial gain. Matilda of Scotland, Adeliza of Louvain, Eleanor of Aquitaine, Isabella of Angoulême, and Elizabeth Widville had to endure their husbands' infidelities. The Empress Maud and her husband, Geoffrey of Anjou, hated each other.

English queenship did not change markedly over the four centuries covered by this series of books. It is hard to generalize because so much depended on the character of each queen and the power they were able to exercise. As with monarchs who ruled on a personal level, personality was everything. All queens led public lives and were at the heart of the political and cultural world of their day. Many exercised what we now call "soft power," that is, they used their influence in private, making it difficult to quantify and analyze. Others wielded power openly. Some had little influence. Not until the sixteenth century would the medieval ideal of queenship be overturned in England.

Appendix Notes on Some of the Chief Sources

The London Chronicles

The so-called London Chronicles provide us with an observant and detailed record of events in the late fifteenth century. The first is that chronicle known as B. L. Cotton MS. Vitellius AXVI, written during the early years of Henry VII's reign and published by C. L. Kingsford as *Chronicles of London* in 1905. A fragment from the commonplace books of a London merchant was discovered in the College of Arms in 1980, and published as *Historical Notes of a London Citizen, 1483–1488* in 1981. The other London Chronicles were written, at least in part, by Robert Fabyan (d.1513), a wealthy London clothier and alderman of the City of London. He made a compilation of several London chronicles (the originals of which are now lost) which is known as *The Great Chronicle of London* and is in the Guildhall Library. Despite being pro-Lancastrian in sympathy, this is a major source for the period, for all its errors and confused chronology. It is an eyewitness account, clearly based on firsthand knowledge of some of the events described and reflecting the public opinion of its day.

Fabyan also wrote *The Book of the Concordance of Histories,* a history of England from the Conquest to his own time, which was printed in 1516 as *The New Chronicles of England and France.* It was based in part on Fabyan's own diaries but is not as comprehensive as *The Great Chronicle of London.*

Jean de Waurin

Jean de Waurin's *Ancient Chronicles of England* covers the period 688 to 1471. He lived from *c.*1400 to 1471. He was the bastard son of a Burgundian nobleman, a soldier during the Hundred Years War, a diplomat, and a partisan of the House of York. He knew some of the political players about whom he wrote (notably Anthony Widville) and witnessed some events firsthand. While extensive and detailed, his work has an Anglo-Burgundian bias and is not always accurate.

Philippe de Commines

The chief foreign source for the Yorkist period is the *Mémoires* of Philippe de Commines, a French politician and diplomat who moved in the highest circles of the courts of France and Burgundy. He compiled his memoirs after his retirement in 1490, and they cover the period 1464-98. After 1480, however, Commines no longer enjoyed the confidence of those who ruled France, but he had met Edward IV and later knew Henry Tudor during his exile. There are obvious flaws in his work, yet he did record the gossip then circulating on the Continent and may well have had access to more reliable sources of information for the later period.

The *Arrivall*

The History of the Arrival of Edward IV in England, and the Final Recovery of his Kingdoms is a contemporary chronicle describing the events of 1471. The author served the King, but his name is unknown; his work has a strong Yorkist bias. He was writing soon after the events he describes and witnessed some of them himself. He also obtained information from the people involved. His history is therefore deemed the best source for this period.

The Croyland Chronicle

Another major source for the period is the second continuation of the *Croyland Chronicle*. The magnificent abbey of Croyland (now spelled Crowland) in Lincolnshire was the most important and wealthiest religious foundation in the East of England, and its mitred Abbot ranked with the bishops. Royal visitors to the abbey in the late fifteenth century included Henry VI, Edward IV, and Richard III when he was Duke of Gloucester.

Several chronicles detailing the history of England and of the abbey were written at Croyland. Those prior to 1117 are spurious, but the three anonymously written continuations, spanning the periods 1144–1469, 1459–86, and 1485–6, are genuine.

The author of the second continuation (1459–86) states that it was written in the ten days ending on 30 April 1486. His work is without doubt the best source for the period. Where verifiable, it is highly accurate, and its author was clearly a man who could write authoritatively and from personal knowledge of many of the events he describes. He withheld information that was politically sensitive, and his silence on certain subjects sometimes speaks volumes. Much of what he wrote can be substantiated by other writers, such as Dominic Mancini, Polydore Vergil, and Thomas More, who never read his manuscript.

The author of the *Croyland Chronicle* did not approve of Richard III, yet he declared his intention of writing his history "in as unprejudiced a manner as we possibly can," stating that he was presenting the reader with "a truthful recital of the facts without hatred or favor." He was a surprisingly objective, if ironic, observer for his time.

But who was he? He described himself as a doctor of canon law and a member of the royal Council. He was a cultivated man and well acquainted with the workings of Council, Parliament, Convocation, and Chancery. There is good reason to identify him with John Russell, Bishop of Lincoln (1480–94), Keeper of the Privy Seal (1474–83), and Lord Chancellor of England (1483–5). Croyland Abbey lay within Russell's diocese, and the third continuation of its chronicle records his monthlong visit there in April 1486, when the second continuation was written. Russell could well have dictated his history to a member of his retinue of twenty persons or to a monk living in the abbey. Yet some believe that the author was Henry Sharp, Head of the Exchequer.

The second continuation was suppressed by Henry VII, who also ordered the destruction of all copies of the Act of Settlement known as *Titulus Regius* (1484), which set forth Richard III's title to the throne: the text of the Act was incorporated in the *Croyland Chronicle*. A few copies survived, having been hidden, but the second continuation was not used as a historical source until 1619.

John Rous

John Rous (1411–92) was a Warwickshire chantry priest and antiquarian, and the author of *Historia rerum Angliae* and the York Roll, known as *The Rous Roll*, which he himself may have illustrated. He was clearly not an eyewitness to most of the events he describes, and not averse to recording gossip as fact. Rous was first and foremost a chronicler of the Beauchamp and Neville earls of Warwick, to whom he was devoted. In 1483–5, he compiled the York Roll, an illustrated history of these families, which is now in the British Library.

Rous's writings show with striking clarity how the accession of Henry VII in 1485 affected his view of recent events. In the York Roll, Richard III appears in this as the husband of Anne Neville and is referred to as "a mighty prince and especial good lord; . . . a most virtuous prince."

Rous made two copies of the York Roll; he could not retrieve the first after Richard III's death at Bosworth, so he altered his own Latin copy (now in the College of Arms, London), mutilating it wherever a picture of Richard appeared. His laudatory description of him was deleted and in its place were just the words *"infelix maritus"*—the "unhappy spouse"—of Anne Neville.

Rous also wrote a history of England dedicated to Henry VII, which was completed in 1490; in it, he portrays Richard III as a deformed monster and tyrant, likening him to the Antichrist. It has been suggested, however, that Rous's hostility toward Richard derived not so much from his desire to win the favor of Henry VII as from his conviction that Richard had murdered Anne Neville, whom he revered as the daughter of Warwick the Kingmaker.

Dominic Mancini

Mancini was an Italian monk who lived in France and died after 1494. He visited England in 1482 in the train of the French ambassador, having been instructed to report back to the Archbishop of Vienne on English affairs. He remained in London until July 1483, leaving England the week after Richard III's coronation.

Mancini's book, *De Occupatione Regni Anglie per Riccardum Tercium libellus* (*The Occupation of Richard III*), which he completed on 1 December 1483, was an official report on recent events in England. His stated intention was "to put in writing by what machinations Richard III attained the high degree of kingship," and he fulfilled this in a vivid and objective manner. It is Mancini's objectivity that makes his book an invaluable source because he had no reason to write anything hostile to Richard III. He confined himself only to facts and avoided falling into the habit affected by so many contemporary writers, that of using them to illustrate a lesson in morality.

Mancini's account is corroborated by other sources, notably the *Croyland Chronicle* and the later histories of Polydore Vergil and Sir Thomas More, none of whom had access to Mancini's book. Indeed, it was lost for centuries; no one knew of its existence until 1934, when it was discovered by Professor C. A. J. Armstrong in the archives of the Bibliothèque Municipale at Lille, and subsequently published.

Mancini was reluctant to name his sources, but his account suggests that he had contacts at court, some of whom were apparently hostile to Richard III.

The only source mentioned by name is Dr. John Argentine, physician to Edward V, who could speak Italian. Mancini could also have made use of Italians living in London, in particular Pietro Carmeliano, a court poet to both Edward IV and Henry VII.

There are flaws in Mancini's book, of which he himself was aware, stating his reluctance to commit his account to paper as he did not know the names of some of those mentioned or their motives. He admitted that his account was incomplete in details. He lacked an understanding of the English language and a knowledge of English geography, and he paid little regard to chronology, although, in fairness to him, this was a period when recording dates was not considered of prime importance by historians. Nor is there in his book any physical description of Richard III—perhaps we should assume he never saw him. This, and the fact that the latter part of the account is less detailed, suggests that Mancini was no longer able to make use of some of his former court informants.

The Song of Lady Bessy

A near-contemporary metrical chronicle, "The Song of Lady Bessy," describes Elizabeth of York's involvement in the momentous events of 1485. Although the earliest surviving text dates from c. 1600, the song was written in Henry VII's reign, probably before 1500, and perhaps disseminated as popular propaganda against Richard III.

It was probably composed by Lord Stanley's squire, or agent, Humphrey Brereton, who himself features in it and was the person best placed to recount the events the ballad describes. Opinions vary as to its historical accuracy. A few parts are demonstrably inventions. The inaccuracies probably arise from the author exaggerating his own role. He invented speeches for his characters, which was standard practice in historical writing in this period. Lord Stanley's role in this episode may also have been overstated, for the poem was probably written under his auspices, and with the benefit of hindsight—and with a good dollop of poetic license.

There is no way of proving if the substance of the poem is based on fact, as other sources are silent on Elizabeth of York's role in the events it describes. Yet the minute and exact details suggest a close acquaintance with real people and events, and some historians have concluded that there is a great deal of truth in the poem.

There can be little doubt that Brereton was privy to much that was going on in Lord Stanley's life at that time, and the details he gives suggest that the song is firsthand evidence of Elizabeth's involvement in the conspiracy to put Henry Tudor on the throne.

Polydore Vergil

The chief narrative source dating from the early Tudor period is the *Anglica Historia* of Polydore Vergil. Vergil, a cleric from Urbino, Italy, came to England around 1501 and stayed. He was a renowned Renaissance scholar and humanist, and a friend of Desiderius Erasmus and Thomas More. He quickly attracted the attention of Henry VII, who made use of his talents and rewarded him with benefices. After the accession of Henry VIII, however, Vergil made an enemy of Cardinal Wolsey and fell from favor. He left England in 1551 and died in Italy in 1555.

In 1507, Henry VII commissioned Vergil to write an official history of England. Vergil spent six years doing research and wrote the first draft in c.1512–14. It took him a further nineteen years to complete all twenty-six books in the *Anglica Historia*. The finished work, dedicated to Henry VIII, was published in 1534 in Basel.

A skillful historian and writer, Vergil followed the Renaissance tradition of using history to teach a moral lesson, from which the reader might benefit. He could be maddeningly vague at times, and selective about what he included, yet he was no sycophant. He was critical of Henry VII in parts, and raised a storm by his rejection of the time-honored notion that the Arthurian legends were based on fact. Thus, he was no mere propagandist, but an objective writer who drew his own conclusions.

Vergil seldom cited his sources, but Henry VII gave him unrestricted access to official records and himself imparted details of his exile and his early years as King. Other contemporaries passed on their recollections of previous reigns. Vergil claimed to have consulted a great number of chronicles and other documents; in 1574 it was alleged by John Caius of Cambridge that he had destroyed cartloads of ancient manuscripts so as to ensure that the flaws in his history would not be detected. Vergil himself wrote that he could find very few written sources for the period after 1450.

There is no proof that he ever saw the *Croyland Chronicle,* which had been suppressed long before his time, but the two histories do often corroborate each other. Vergil's account also substantiates in many respects that of Sir Thomas More (see below), but is less detailed. Vergil never saw Mancini's history, yet again the two accounts often agree.

Sir Thomas More

The first—and the most controversial—biography of Richard III was written by Sir Thomas More. Entitled "The History of King Richard III," it was written around 1514–18 and revised in the late 1520s. More's account is rich in compelling, authentic, eyewitness detail—which in itself argues its reliability—and shows familiarity with the workings of the royal household. Approximately one-third of it contains eloquent speeches invented by More for his characters, but based on authentic source material.

More's history has its obvious flaws: some names and dates are incorrect or missing, and parts may well be based on inaccurate sources or—as More admits—are the result of "divining upon conjectures." Nevertheless, it has been verified in so many respects, and by so many other sources—such as Mancini and Croyland, who were not known to More, and Vergil, who was—that there is little reason to doubt its overall authenticity.

Sir Thomas More was a lawyer, a humanist scholar, and a politician, a man whose reputation for integrity and scholarship was famous throughout Christendom. He served for a short time as Henry VIII's Lord Chancellor before resigning because his conscience would not allow him to condone Henry's break with Rome. He was executed for his defiance in 1535 and later made a saint by the Roman Catholic Church.

More brought to his history of Richard III the benefit of his fine legal mind and his intellectual judgment. There is little doubt that he went to great trouble to find out the truth about the Princes in the Tower, whose fate was the central theme of his book. Roger Ascham, the great Elizabethan scholar, described it as a model of historical writing.

It was never More's intention to write propaganda for the Tudors, although many have accused him of doing so. He was no yes-man: in 1504 he had risked a charge of high treason when he opposed the King in Parliament. Henry VII realized that Thomas could not pay the fine his offense merited, so he imprisoned and fined his father, Judge Sir John More. Nor was More any sycophant to Henry VIII, who for many years valued his opinion because he knew it was an honest one.

More's work was never intended for publication but was written purely for private intellectual recreation. He did not finish it. It may be that he was persuaded by someone influential to abandon it because of content that could have proved embarrassing to those of Richard's contemporaries who were still alive, or their descendants. Alternatively, More may simply have lost interest in the project or lacked the time in which to complete it.

His work has value because it was relatively objective. He had no motive for lying. He used a wide variety of sources and obtained firsthand information from those courtiers and others who had been alive in Richard III's time.

Other Tudor Chroniclers

Later Tudor chroniclers such as Edward Hall and Raphael Holinshed all relied on Vergil and More. But in 1611, the antiquary John Speed discovered a draft of the suppressed Act *Titulus Regius,* which outlined the grounds on which Richard III had claimed the throne. Speed printed the original draft of the Act that year, and six years later Sir William Cornwallis published *The Encomium of Richard III,* which was in effect a defense of Richard against the charge that he had murdered the Princes.

Sir George Buck

Cornwallis's theme was taken up even more enthusiastically in 1619 by Sir George Buck, who was described by the historian William Camden as "a man of distinguished learning." Buck was of an old Yorkist family, the great-grandson of John Buck, a member of Richard III's household who was executed after having supported Richard at Bosworth. He had risen to prominence at the court of Elizabeth I, and became Master of the Revels to James I, licensing several of Shakespeare's plays in this capacity. Tragically he went insane in 1621 and died the next year.

Buck's *The History of King Richard the Third* was written in 1619. It was a vast work, carefully researched from early manuscripts preserved in the Tower of London, Sir Robert Cotton's library (which contained an original copy of the *Croyland Chronicle*), the College of Arms, and the private papers of Thomas Howard, Earl of Arundel, to whom the work was dedicated.

Buck's aim in writing his book was to proclaim Richard III's innocence of the crimes laid at his door by earlier writers. He was not entirely impartial—his family had supported Richard and he felt this needed justification. He claimed that More's biography was too full of errors to be reliable. Many people found Buck's portrayal attractive and credible, and it was at this point that the controversy over Richard III that persists to this day began in earnest.

Buck's holograph MS. (Cotton MS. Tiberius E.X 238)—"corrected and amended on every page"—was damaged in the Cottonian fire; only fragments remain in the British Library. Another version of the first two books of the manuscript is British Library Egerton MS. 2216-2220, but this is a copy. Buck's nephew, another George Buck, printed an abridged and censored version of the work in 1646, the only version available until 1979, when A. N. Kincaid published his splendid edition of the original text, which revealed several convincing details and exposed the deficiencies in the 1646 edition.

Sir Francis Bacon

The History of Henry VII by Sir Francis Bacon (1561–1626) was published in 1622. This erudite work by the famous lawyer, statesman, and Lord Chancellor was for centuries the standard biography of Henry, well researched, objective, and advanced for its time. Placed as he was, Bacon had access to official records, some no longer extant, and his work has value for this alone.

Select Bibliography

✷

Primary Sources

The Rolls Series [referred to below], comprises *Chronicles and Memorials of Great Britain and Ireland during the Middle Ages,* published by H.M. Stationery Office, London, under the direction of the Master of the Rolls.

Account Book of the Receiver General of Queen Elizabeth (Miscellaneous Books, Exchequer records, The National Archives)
Acts of Court of the Mercers Company, 1453–1537 (ed. L. Lyell and F. D. Watney, Cambridge, 1936)
Adam of Usk: *Chronicon* (ed. E. M. Thompson, London, 1876)
Additional MSS (The British Library)
André, Bernard: *Hymi Christiani Bernardae Andreae poetae Regii* (Paris, 1517)
—"Vita Henrici VII" (in *Memorials of King Henry VII*)
The Antiquarian Repertory: A Miscellany, intended to Preserve and Illustrate Several Valuable remains of Old Times (4 vols, ed. F. Grose and T. Astle, London, 1775–84, 1808)
Archaeologia, or Miscellaneous Tracts relating to Antiquity (102 vols, various editors, The Society of Antiquaries of London, 1773–1969)
Arundel MSS

The Babees' Book: Medieval Manners for the Young (tr. Edith Rickert and L. J. Naylor, Cambridge, Ontario, 2000)
Bacon, Sir Francis: *The History of the Reign of Henry VII* (London, 1622; ed. J. R.

Lumby, Cambridge, 1881; ed. F. Levy, Indianapolis, 1972; ed. Brian Vickers, Cambridge, 1998)

Baker, Richard: *A Chronicle of the Kings of England from the Time of the Romans' Government unto the Death of King James* (London, 1643)

Balliol College Oxford MS. 354

Battle Abbey MS. 937 (Huntington Library, California)

The Beaufort Hours (B.L. Royal MSS 2A XVIII)

Benet, John: *John Benet's Chronicle for the years 1400 to 1462* (ed. G. L. Harriss and M. A. Harriss, Cambridge, 2009)

Bibliothèque d'Angers, MS. 656

Blacman, John: *Collectarium mansuetudinum et bonarum morum Regis Henrici VI* (ed. and tr. M. R. James, Cambridge, 1919)

Bodleian MSS (Bodleian Library, Oxford)

The Book of the Fraternity of Corpus Christi (Guildhall Library, London)

The Book of Noblesse (ed. J. G. Nichols, 1860)

Bouchart, Alain: *Grandes Chroniques de Bretagne* (3 vols, ed. Marie-Louise Auger, Gustave Jenneau, and Bernard Guenée, Paris, 1986)

The Breknoke Computus (Dugdale Society)

British Library Harleian Manuscript 433 (4 vols, ed. Rosemary Horrox and P. W. Hammond, Upminster and London, 1979–83)

The Brut, or the Chronicles of England (2 vols, ed. F. Brie, Early English Texts Society, London, 1906, 1908)

Buck, Sir George: *The History of the Life and Reign of Richard III* (B.L. Cotton MS. Tiberius, E.X; 5 vols, ed. George Buck, nephew of the author, London, 1646; reprinted in *A Complete History of England*, Vol. V, ed. White Kennett, London, 1719; ed. as *The History of King Richard the Third by Sir George Buck, Master of the Revels* by A. N. Kincaid, Stroud, 1979; revised 1982)

Bulletin du Comité Historique des Monuments Écrits de l'Histoire de France (Vol. 4, Paris, 1853)

"Bull of Pope Innocent II on the Marriage of Henry VII with Elizabeth of York" (1486; ed. J. Payne Collier, *Camden Miscellany* 1, 1847)

Calendar of Charter Rolls preserved in the Public Record Office (6 vols, London, 1903)

Calendar of Close Rolls: Edward IV (www.british-history.ac.uk)

Calendar of Documents relating to Scotland (5 vols, ed. Joseph Bain, Edinburgh, 1881–8)

Calendar of Durham Cathedral Archives (https://reed.dur.ac.uk)

Calendar of Entries in the Papal Registers relating to Great Britain and Ireland (ed. W. H. Bliss, 1893; London, 1960)

Calendar of Letters, Despatches and State Papers relating to Negotiations between

Select Bibliography

England and Spain, preserved in the Archives at Simancas and Elsewhere (17 vols, ed. G. A. Bergenroth, P. de Goyangos, Garrett Mattingley, R. Tyler et al., H.M.S.O., London, 1862–1965)

Calendar of Patent Rolls: Edward IV: 1461–1467 (H.M.S.O., London, 1897)

Calendar of Patent Rolls: Edward IV: 1467–1477 (H.M.S.O., London, 1899)

Calendar of Patent Rolls: Edward IV, Edward V, Richard III: 1476–1485 (H.M.S.O., London, 1901)

Calendar of Patent Rolls: Henry VII: 1485–1509 (2 vols, H.M.S.O., London, 1914–16)

Calendar of Patent Rolls preserved in the Public Record Office (London, 1906)

Calendar of State Papers and Manuscripts existing in the Archives and Collections of Milan, Vol. I, 1385–1618 (ed. Allen B. Hinds, London, 1912)

Calendar of State Papers and Manuscripts relating to English Affairs preserved in the Archives of Venice and in the other Libraries of Northern Italy (7 vols, ed. L. Rawdon-Brown, Cavendish Bentinck et al., H.M.S.O., London, 1864–1947)

Calendars of Charter Rolls (The National Archives)

Calendars of Close Rolls (The National Archives)

Calendars of Patent Rolls (The National Archives)

Camden, William: *Britannia* (London, 1588, 1607)

Capgrave, John: *The Book of the Illustrious Henries* (ed. and tr. F. C. Hingeston, London, 1858)

—*The Chronicle of England* (ed. F. C. Hingeston, London, 1858)

Catalogue of Romances in the Department of Manuscripts in the British Museum (ed. J. A. Herbert, London, 1883–1910)

The Cely Letters, 1472–1488 (ed. Alison Hanham, Early English Texts Society, Oxford, 1975)

The Cely Papers (ed. H. E. Malden, London, 1900)

Chamber Receipts (E.101) (The National Archives)

Chapter Records XXIII to XXVI (The Chapter Library, St. George's Chapel, Windsor; Chapel Archives and Chapter Library at www.stgeorges-windsor.org/archives)

Chastellain, Georges: *Oeuvres de Georges Chastellain* (ed. M. Le Baron Kervyn de Lettenhove, Brussels, 1863–5)

Christ Church Oxford MSS

Chronicle of the Grey Friars of London (ed. J. Nichols, Camden Society, 1852)

Chronicle of London, 1089–1483 (ed. Sir Harris Nicolas, The Society of Antiquaries of London, 1827)

Chronicle of the Rebellion in Lincolnshire, 1470 (ed. J. G. Nichols, Camden Society, London, 1847)

Chronicle of Saint-Denis (Bibliothèque Sainte-Geneviève)

Chronicles of London (ed. C. L. Kingsford, Oxford, 1905)
Chronicles of Lorraine (Bibliothèque Nationale, Paris)
Chronicles of the Wars of the Roses (ed. Elizabeth Hallam, London, 1988)
Chronicles of the White Rose of York (ed. J. O. Halliwell, Camden Society, 1839)
Clercq, J. du: *Memoires sur le Regne de Philippe le Bon, Duc de Bourgogne* (4 vols, ed. M. le Baron de Reiffenberg, Brussels, 1935-6)
Coke, Sir Edward: *The First Part of the Institutes of the Laws of England* (London, 1628)
A Collection of Ordinances and Regulations for the Government of the Royal Household made in divers reigns from King Edward III to King William and Queen Mary (Society of Antiquaries of London, 1790)
A Collection of Wills of the Kings and Queens of England from William the Conqueror to Henry VII (ed. J. Nichols, Society of Antiquaries of London, 1780)
"Collections of a Yorkist Partisan" (in *English Historical Literature of the Fifteenth Century*, ed. C. L. Kingsford, Oxford, 1913)
College of Arms MSS (The College of Arms, London)
Commines, Philippe de: *Mémoires* (3 vols, ed. J. Calmette and G. Durville, Paris, 1924-5; ed. M. Jones, London, 1972)
Concilia Magnae Brittaniae et Hiberniae (4 vols, ed. David Wilkins, London, 1737)
Cornazzano, Antonio: *The 'De Mulieribus Admirandis' of Antonio Cornazzano* (ed. Conor Fahy, no provenance, 1960)
The Coronation of Elizabeth Wydeville, Queen consort of Edward IV, on May 26th, 1465: A Contemporary Account Now First Set Forth from a XV Century Manuscript (ed. G. Smith, London, 1935)
The Coronation of Richard III (ed. Anne F. Sutton and P. W. Hammond, Stroud, 1983)
Cotton MSS (The British Library)
The Coventry Leet Book or Mayor's Register Containing the records of the city Court Leet or View of frankpledge, AD 1420–1555 with divers other matters (London, 1907)
The Croyland Chronicle Continuation, 1459–1486 (ed. N. Pronay and J. Cox, Stroud, 1986; ed. W. Fulman as *Historiae Croylandensis continuato in rerum Anglicarum Scriptores veterum*, Oxford, 1684; Ingulph's *Chronicle of the Abbey of Croyland* contains the third continuation, *Historiae Croylandensis*, of which the original no longer exists; ed. and tr. H. T. Riley, London, 1854)

Davies' Chronicle: An English Chronicle of the Reigns of Richard II, Henry IV, Henry V and Henry VI (ed. J. S. Davies, London, 1856)

Dépêches des Ambassadeurs Milanais en France sous Louis XI et Francois Sforza (2 vols, ed. B. de Mandrot, Paris, 1916-19)
Dugdale, William: *Monasticon Anglicanum* (3 vols, London, 1693)

Egerton MSS (The British Library)
Elmham, Thomas: *Gesta Henrici Quinti* (ed. J. A. Giles, London, 1846)
—"Liber metricus de Henrico Quinto" (in *Memorials of Henry V*)
English Coronation Records (ed. Leopold G. W. Legg, Westminster, 1901)
English Historical Documents, Vol. 4, 1327–1485 (ed. A. R. Myers, London, 1969)
English Historical Literature in the Fifteenth Century (ed. C. L. Kingsford, Oxford, 1913)
Excerpta Historica (ed. S. Bentley and Sir Harris Nicolas, London, 1831)
Exchequer Records: Exchequer of Receipt: Warrants for Issues (E.404) (The National Archives)
Exchequer Records: Issue Rolls (E.403) (The National Archives)
Exchequer Records: King's Remembrancer, Accounts Various (E.101) (The National Archives)
Exchequer Records: King's Treasurer's Accounts (E.404) (The National Archives)
Exeter College MSS (University of Oxford)
Extracts from the Municipal Records of the City of York during the Reigns of Edward IV, Edward V and Richard III (ed. R. Davies, London, 1843)

Fabyan, Robert: *The Concordance of Histories: The New Chronicles of England and France* (London, 1516; ed. H. Ellis, London, 1811)
Facsimiles of National Manuscripts from William the Conqueror to Queen Anne (ed. Henry James, Southampton, 1865)
Fèvre, J. le: *Chronique de Jean Le Fèvre, seigneur de Saint-Remy* (2 vols, ed. F. Morand, Paris, 1876-81)
The First English Life of Henry V (ed. C. L. Kingsford, Oxford, 1911)
Foedera, Conventiones, Et . . . Acta Publica inter Reges Angliae (ed. Thomas Rymer, London, 1704-17)
Forojuliensis, Titus Livius: *Vita Henrici Quinti* (ed. T. Hearne, Oxford, 1716)
Fortescue, Sir John: *The Works of Sir John Fortescue, collected by Thomas, Lord Clermont* (2 vols, London, 1869)
"Fragment of an Old English Chronicle of the Affairs of King Edward IV" (ed. Thomas Hearne in *Thomae Sprotti Chronica*, Oxford, 1719)
Froissart, Jean (c.1337-c.1405): *Chronicles of England, France and Spain* (25 vols, ed. Kervyn de Lettenhove, Brussels, 1867-77; ed. J. Jolliffe, London, 1967)

Gascoigne, Thomas: *Loci e Libro Veritatum* (Lincoln College, Oxford)
Gesta Henrici Quinti: The Deeds of Henry V (ed. B. Williams, English Historical Society, 1850; ed. F. Taylor and tr. J. S. Roskell, Oxford, 1975)
"Giles' Chronicle," or *Incertie scriptoris chronicon Angliae de Regnis Henrici IV, Henrici V et Henrici VI* (ed. J. A. Giles, London, 1848)
Grafton, Richard: *The Chronicle of John Hardyng, together with the Continuation by Richard Grafton* (ed. H. Ellis, Society of Antiquaries of London, 1812)
—*Grafton's Chronicle, or History of England* (London, 1569; 2 vols, ed. H. Ellis, London, 1809)
The Great Chronicle of London (ed. A. H. Thomas and I. D. Thornley, London, 1938; reprinted Stroud, 1983)
Gregory, William: *Gregory's Chronicle, or the Historical Collections of a Citizen of London in the Fifteenth Century* (ed. J. Gairdner, Camden Society, 1876)
Gruel, Guillaume: *Chronique d'Artur de Richemont* (ed. Le Vavasseur, Paris, 1890)
Guildhall MSS (Guildhall Library, London)

Hall, Edward: *The Union of the Two Noble and Illustrious Families of Lancaster and York* (London, 1550; ed. H. Ellis, London, 1809)
Hardying, John: *The Chronicle of John Hardying* (ed. H. Ellis, Society of Antiquaries of London, London, 1812)
Harleian MSS (The British Library)
Hastings MSS (Historical Manuscripts Commission)
Historians of Scotland (4 vols, ed. W. F. Skene, Edinburgh, 1871–2)
Historical Poems of the 14th and 15th Centuries (ed. R. H. Robbins, New York, 1959)
History of the Arrival of Edward IV in England, and the Final Recovery of his Kingdoms from Henry VI, A.D. MCCCCLXXI (ed. J. Bruce, Camden Society, 1838)
Holinshed, Raphael: *Chronicles of England, Scotland and Ireland* (6 vols, ed. H. Ellis, London, 1807–8, republished 1976)
Household Books of John Howard, Duke of Norfolk, temp. 1481–90 (ed. John Payne Collier, Roxburgh Club, London, 1844)
The Household of Edward IV: The Black Book and the Ordinance of 1478 (ed. A. R. Myers, Manchester, 1959)

Illustrations of Ancient State and Chivalry from Manuscripts Preserved in the Ashmolean Museum (ed. W. H. Black, Roxburgh Club, London, 1840)
Ingulph: *The Chronicle of the Abbey of Croyland* (ed. H. T. Riley, London, 1854)
Intimate Letters of England's Queens (ed. M. Sanders, London, 1957)
Issues of the Exchequer, from King Henry III to King Henry VI (ed. F. Devon, London, 1837)

Select Bibliography

Jean le Bel: *Chronique de Jean le Bel (1400–62)* (2 vols, ed. J. Viard and E. Deprez, Paris, 1904–5)

John of Fordun: *Chronicle of the Scottish Nation* (Edinburgh, 1872)

Journal des États Généraux de France tenus à Tours en 1484 (ed. J. Masselin and A. Bernier, Paris, 1835)

Keepe, Henry: *Monumenta Westmonasteriensia* (London, 1683)

Kings' Letters: From the Days of Alfred to the Accession of the Tudors (ed. Robert Steele, London, 1903)

King's MSS (The British Library)

Lambeth MSS (Lambeth Palace, London)

Lansdowne MSS (The British Library)

Latin MSS (John Rylands Library)

Legeaud MSS (Bibliothèque Nationale, Paris)

Leland, John: *Antiquarii de Rebus Britannicis Collectanea* (6 vols, ed. T. Hearne, Chetham Society, Oxford, 1770–4)

—*The Itinerary of John Leland in or about the years 1535–1543* (5 vols, ed. Lucy Toulin Smith, London, 1906–10)

Letters of the Kings of England (2 vols, ed. J. O. Halliwell-Phillipps, London, 1846–8)

The Letters of Margaret of Anjou (ed. Helen Maurer and B. M. Cron, Woodbridge, 2019)

Letters of Medieval Women (ed. Anne Crawford, Stroud, 2002)

Letters and Papers illustrative of the Reigns of Richard III and Henry VII (2 vols, ed. J. Gairdner, Rolls Series, London, 1861–3)

Letters and Papers illustrative of the Wars of the English in France during the Reign of Henry VI (3 vols, ed. J. Stevenson, Rolls Series, London, 1861–4)

Letters of Queen Margaret of Anjou and Bishop Beckington and others (ed. C. Munro, Camden Society, 1863)

Letters of the Queens of England, 1100–1546 (ed. Anne Crawford, Stroud, 1994)

Letters of Royal and Illustrious Ladies of Great Britain (3 vols, ed. Mary Anne Everett Wood, London, 1846)

Lettres de Rois, Reines et Autres Personnages de Cours de France et d'Angleterre (2 vols, ed. J. J. Champollion-Figeac, Paris, 1839–47)

Lettres et mandements de Jean V, Duc de Bretagne (7 vols, ed. René Blanchard, Nantes, 1890)

A London Chronicle in the Time of Henry VII and Henry VIII (ed. C. Hopper, Camden Society, 1839)

Lydgate, John: *Troy Book* (London, 1513)

Mancini, Dominic: *De Occupatione Regni Anglie per Riccardum Tercium libellus (The Occupation of Richard III)* (ed. and tr. C. A. J. Armstrong, Oxford, 1936; reprinted Oxford, 1969, and Stroud, 1984)

Manners and Household Expenses of the 13th and 15th Centuries (Roxburgh Club, London, 1841)

Manners and Meals in Olden Time (ed. F. J. Furnivall, Early English Texts Society, 32, 1868)

Marche, Olivier de la: *Memoires d'Olivier de la Marche* (ed. H. Beaune and J. d'Arbaumont, Paris, 1883)

Materials for a History of the Reign of Henry VII (2 vols, ed. William Campbell, Rolls Series, 1873–7)

Medieval Age: Specimens of European Poetry from the 9th to the 15th Century (ed. Angel Flores, 1963)

Memoranda Rolls (The National Archives)

Memorials of Henry V (ed. C. A. Cole, Rolls Series, London, 1858)

Memorials of King Henry VII (ed. J. Gairdner, Rolls Series, London, 1858; published as *The Life of Henry VII*, tr. and intro. by Daniel Hobbins, New York, 2011)

Miscellanea Genealogica et Heraldica (ed. W. Bruce Bannerman, London, 1912)

Miscellaneous Books (E.36) (The National Archives)

Molinet, Jean: *Chroniques des Ducs de Bourgogne, 1476–1506* (5 vols, ed. J. A. Buchon, Paris, 1827–8)

—*Chroniques de Jean Molinet, 1476–1506* (3 vols, ed. J. Doutrepont and O. Jodogne, Academie Royale de Belgique, Brussels, 1935–7)

Monstrelet, Enguerran de: *Chroniques d'Enguerran de Monstrelet* (ed. L. Douet d'Arcq, Paris, 1857–62)

More, Sir Thomas: "The History of King Richard III" (in *The Complete Works of Sir Thomas More*, Vol. 2, ed. R. S. Sylvester et al., Yale, 1963; London, 1979)

Munimenta Gildhallae Londoniensis (4 vols, ed. H. T. Riley, Rolls Series, London, 1859–62)

The Narrative of the Marriage of Richard, Duke of York with Anne of Norfolk, 1477 (ed. W. G. Searle, Cambridge, 1867)

"Narratives of the Arrival of Louis of Bruges, Lord of Gruthuyse" (ed. Sir Frederic Madden, *Archaeologia*, Vol. 26, 1836)

Original Letters illustrative of English History (11 vols, ed. H. Ellis, London, 1824–46)

Original Letters, written during the reigns of Henry VI, Edward IV, and Richard III, by various persons of rank or consequence: containing many curious anecdotes, relative to that period of our history (5 vols, ed. Sir John Fenn, 1789–1823)

Select Bibliography

Oudin, Guillaume: *Extrait d'un manuscrit de Messire Guillaume Oudin, prestre sacristin de l'abaye de Nostre Dame du Ronceray, depuis l'année 1447 jusqu'en l'an 1499* (MS. 0976 [0858], Municipal Library of Angers)

A Parisian Journal, 1405–1449 (ed. Janet Shirley, Oxford, 1968)
The Paston Letters (6 vols, ed. J. Gairdner, London, 1904)
Paston Letters and Papers of the Fifteenth Century (2 vols, ed. Norman Davis, Oxford, 1971, 1976)
Pepys, Samuel: *Diary* (8 vols, ed. H. B. Wheatley, London, 1926)
The Pipe Rolls (The National Archives)
Pius II, Pope: *The Commentaries of Pius II* (tr. Florence Alden Gragg, ed. Leona C. Gabel, Northampton, Massachusetts, 1957)
Political Poems and Songs relating to English History (1327–1483) (2 vols, ed. T. Wright, Rolls Series, London, 1859–61)
The Private Lives of the Tudor Monarchs (ed. Christopher Falkus, London, 1974)
Privy Purse Expenses of Elizabeth of York, Queen of Henry VII, with a Memoir of Elizabeth of York (ed. J. P. Collier, Camden Miscellany, 1, 1847)
Proceedings and Ordinances of the Privy Council of England, 1386–1542 (7 vols, ed. Sir Nicholas Harris Nicolas, London, 1834–37)

Rawlinson MSS (The Bodleian Library, Oxford)
Records of the Keeper of the Privy Seal: Edward III to Henry VIII (PSO 1) (The National Archives)
Records of the Lord Chamberlain (LC) (The National Archives)
Records of the Skinners of London: Edward I to James I (ed. J. J. Lambert, London, 1933)
Recueil des actes de Jean IV, Duc de Bretagne (3 vols, ed. Michael C. E. Jones, Brest, 1980
Registrum Abbatiae Johannis Whethamstede, Abbatis Monasterii Sancta Albani (2 vols, ed. H. T. Riley, Rolls Series, London, 1872–3)
Registrum Thome Bourgchier, Cantuariensis Archiepiscopi, A.D. 1454–1486 (ed. F. R. H. DuBoulay, Canterbury and York Society, Liverpool, 1957)
The Reign of Henry VII from Contemporary Sources (3 vols, ed. A. F. Pollard, London, 1913–4; reprinted New York, 1967)
Rotuli Parliamentorum (The Rolls of Parliament) (7 vols, ed. J. Strachey, Records Commissioners, 1767–1832)
Rous, John: *Historia rerum Angliae* (ed. T. Hearne, Oxford, 1716)
—*The Rous Roll* (ed. C. R. Ross and W. Courthope, Stroud, 1980)
Royal and Historical Letters during the Reign of Henry IV, 1399–1404 (2 vols, ed. F. C. Hingeston, London, 1860)
Royal MSS (The British Library)

Roye, Jean de: *Journal de Jean de Roye connu sous le nom Chronique Scandaleuse, 1460–1483* (2 vols, ed. B. de Mandrot, Paris, 1894–6)
Rudborne, Thomas: "Historia Major" (in Wharton: *Anglia Sacra*)
Rymer, Thomas: *Foedera* (London, 1704–35; ed. T. Hardy et al., Records Commission, 1816–69)

Saint-Paul, Jean de: *Chronique de Bretagne* (ed. Arthur de la Borderie, Nantes, 1881)
Secular Lyrics of the XIVth and XVth Centuries (ed. Rossell Hope Robbins, Oxford, 1964)
Selden MSS (Bodleian Library, Oxford)
Six Town Chronicles of England (ed. R. Flenley, Oxford, 1911)
"The Song of the Lady Bessy" (in *English Historical Literature of the Fifteenth Century*, ed. C. L. Kingsford, Oxford, 1913)
Special Collections (S.C.) (The National Archives)
Speed, John: *The History of Great Britain* (London, 1611)
Statutes of the Realm, 1101–1713 (11 vols, Records Commissioners, London, 1810–28)
The Stonor Letters and Papers, 1290–1483 (2 vols, ed. C. L. Kingsford, Camden Society, 1919)
Stow, John: *The Annals of England* (London, 1592; ed. C. L. Kingsford, 2 vols, Oxford, 1908)
—*The Survey of London* (London, 1598; 2 vols, ed. C. L. Kingsford, Oxford, 1908; ed. H. B. Wheatley, London, 1987)
Strecche, John: "The Chronicle of John Strecche for the Reign of Henry V" (ed. F. Taylor, *Bulletin of the John Rylands Library*, 16, 1932)

Thomas of Burton, Abbot of Meaux: *Chronica monasterii de Melsa* (ed. E. A. Bond, Rolls Series, 1866–8)
Three Chronicles of the Reign of Edward IV (ed. Keith Dockray, Stroud, 1988)
Three Fifteenth-Century Chronicles with Historical Memoranda by John Stowe (ed. J. Gairdner, London, 1880)

Vergil, Polydore: *Anglica Historia* (Basel, 1555; ed. and tr. D. Hay as *The Anglica Historia of Polydore Vergil, A.D. 1475–1573*, Camden Series, 1950)
—*Three Books of Polydore Vergil's English History* (ed. H. Ellis, Camden Society, 1844)
Vita et Gesta Henrici Quinti (ed. T. Hearne, Oxford, 1727)
The Voice of the Middle Ages in Personal Letters, 1100–1500 (ed. Catherine Moriarty, London, 1989)

Wace, Robert (*c.*1110–after 1174): *Roman de Brut* (ed. and tr. Judith Weiss, Exeter, 2002)
—*Roman de Rou et des Ducs de Normandie* (tr. Alexander Malet, London, 1860)
Walsingham, Thomas: *Chronicon Angliae* (ed. E. M. Thompson, Rolls Series, London, 1874)
—*Gesta abbatum monasterii S. Albani* (3 vols, ed. H. T. Riley, Rolls Series, London, 1867–9)
—*Historia Anglicana, De Tempore Regis Henrici, Post Conquestum Quarti* (2 vols, ed. H. T. Riley, Rolls Series, London, 1863–4)
Wardrobe and Household Accounts (The National Archives)
Warkworth, John: *A Chronicle of the First Thirteen Years of the Reign of King Edward the Fourth* (ed. J. O. Halliwell, Camden Society, 1839)
Warrants for Issues (Exchequer Records, The National Archives)
Waurin, Jean de: *Anchiennes Chroniques d'Engleterre* (3 vols, ed. Mlle. E. Dupont, Paris, 1858–63)
Weever, John: *Ancient Funeral Monuments within the United Monarchies of Great Britain, Northern Ireland and the Islands Adjacent* (London, 1631)
Weinreich, Caspar: *Caspar Weinreichs's Danziger Chronik, ein Beitrag zur Geschichte Danzigs, der Lande Preussen und Polen, des Hansabundes und der Nordischen Reiche* (ed. Theodor Hirsch and F. A. Vossberg, Berlin, 1855; reprinted 1973)
Westminster Abbey Muniments
William of Worcester: "Annales rerum Anglicarum" (in *Liber Niger Scaccarii*, 2 vols, ed. T. Hearne, Oxford, 1728; also in *Letters and Papers illustrative of the Wars of the English in France during the Reign of Henry VI*)
—*Itinerarium* (ed. J. Nasmith, Cambridge, 1778)
Writs of the Privy Seal (Chancery Records, Warrants for the Great Seal, Series 1, The National Archives)

York Civic Records, Vols I and II (ed. Angelo Raine, Yorkshire Archeological Society, Record Series CIII, 1939–41)

Secondary Sources

Abbot, Jacob: *Margaret of Anjou* (New York, 2010)
Abernethy, Susan: Joan of Navarre, Queen of England (https://thefreelance historywriter.com, 2021)
Adair, John: *The Royal Palaces of Britain* (London, 1981)
Alberge, Dalya: "Found in a Castle Vault, the Scraps of Lace That Show Lingerie Was All the Rage 500 Years Ago" (*Daily Mail*, 17 July 2012)

Select Bibliography

Alderman, Clifford Lindsay: *Blood Red the Roses: The Wars of the Roses* (New York, 1971)
Anglo, Sidney: "The Court Festivals of Henry VII" (*Bulletin of the John Rylands Library*, 43, 1960–1)
Arman, Joanna: *Margaret of Anjou, She-Wolf of France, Twice Queen of England* (Stroud, 2023)
Armstrong, C. A. J.: "The Piety of Cecily, Duchess of York" (in *For Hilaire Belloc*, ed. D. Woodruffe, 1942)
Ashdown, Dulcie M.: *Ladies in Waiting* (London, 1976)
—*Princess of Wales* (London, 1979)
—*Royal Weddings* (London, 1981)
Ashdown-Hill, John: *Eleanor, the Secret Queen* (Stroud, 2009)
—"The Fate of Edward IV's Uncrowned Queen, the Lady Eleanor Talbot, Lady Butler" (*The Ricardian*, 2, 1997)
—*The Last Days of Richard III* (Stroud, 2010)
—*Richard III's "Beloved Cousyn": John Howard and the House of York* (Stroud, 2009)
Ashley, Mike: *British Monarchs* (London, 1998)
Aslet, Clive: *The Story of Greenwich* (London, 1999)

Backhouse, Janet: *The Illuminated Page: Ten Centuries of Manuscript Painting in the British Library* (London, 1997)
Bagley, J. J.: *Margaret of Anjou, Queen of England* (London, 1948)
Baldwin, David: *Elizabeth Woodville: Mother of the Princes in the Tower* (Stroud, 2002)
—"Elizabeth Woodville" (in *The Women of the Cousins' War*, by Philippa Gregory, David Baldwin, and Michael Jones, London, 2011)
—*The Lost Prince: The Survival of Richard of York* (Stroud, 2007)
Barber, Richard: *Magnificence and Princely Splendor in the Middle Ages* (Woodbridge, 2020)
Baudier, Michael: *An History of the Memorable and Extraordinary Calamities of Margaret of Anjou, Queen of England* (London, 1737)
Baxter, Ron: *The Royal Abbey of Reading* (Woodbridge, 2016)
Beattie, Andrew: *Following in the Footsteps of the Princes in the Tower* (Barnsley, 2019)
Beauclerk-Dewar, Peter, and Powell, Roger: *Right Royal Bastards: The Fruits of Passion* (Burke's Peerage, 2006)
Beckington, T.: *Memorials of the Reign of Henry VI* (2 vols, London, 1872)
Bell, Mrs. Arthur G.: *The Royal Manor of Richmond* (London, 1907)
Bennett, H. S.: *The Pastons and Their England* (Cambridge, 1968)
Bennett, Michael: *The Battle of Bosworth* (Stroud, 1985, 2008)

Select Bibliography

Bicheno, Hugh: *Battle Royal: The Wars of Lancaster and York, 1440–1462* (London, 2015)

Black, Edward: *Royal Brides: Queens of England in the Middle Ages* (Lewes, 1987)

Bradley, E. T., and Bradley, M. C.: *Westminster Abbey* (London, 1953)

Bramley, Peter: *The Companion and Guide to the Wars of the Roses* (Stroud, 2007)

Brand, Emily: *Royal Weddings* (Oxford, 2011)

Brewer, Clifford: *The Death of Kings: A Medical History of the Kings and Queens of England* (London, 2000)

Brindle, Stephen, and Kerr, Brian: *Windsor Revealed: New Light on the History of the Castle* (London, 1997)

Brook, R.: *The Story of Eltham Palace* (London, 1960)

Brooke-Little, J. P.: *Boutell's Heraldry* (London, 1973)

Brown, Geoff: *The Ends of Kings: An Illustrated Guide to the Death and Burial Places of English Monarchs* (Stroud, 2008)

Burke, John, and Bernard, John: *The Royal Families of England Scotland and Wales, with Their Descendants etc.* (2 vols, London, 1848 and 1851)

Burke's Guide to the Royal Family (Burke's Peerage, 1973)

Cannon, John, and Griffiths, Ralph: *The Oxford Illustrated History of the British Monarchy* (Oxford, 1988)

Cannon, John, and Hargreaves, Anne: *The Kings and Queens of Britain* (Oxford, 2001)

Carleton-Williams, E.: *My Lord of Bedford* (London, 1963)

Carson, Annette: *Richard III: The Maligned King* (Stroud, 2008)

Carter, Alicia: *The Women of the Wars of the Roses* (self-published, 2013)

Castor, Helen: *She Wolves: The Women Who Ruled England Before Elizabeth* (London, 2010)

Cheetham, Anthony: *The Life and Times of Richard III* (London, 1972)

—*The Wars of the Roses* (London, 2000)

Chrimes, S. B.: *Henry VII* (London, 1972)

—*Lancastrians, Yorkists and Henry VII* (London, 1964)

Christie, M. E.: *Henry VI* (London, 1922)

Clarke, Edward T.: *Bermondsey: Its Historic Memories and Associations* (London, 1902)

Clarke, Peter D.: "English Royal Marriages and the Papal Penitentiary in the Fifteenth Century" (*English Historical Review*, 120, 2005)

Clive, Mary: *This Sun of York: A Biography of Edward IV* (London, 1973)

Cloake, John: *Palaces and Parks of Richmond and Kew* (Chichester, 1995)

—*Richmond Palace: Its History and Its Plan* (Richmond Local History Society, 2001)

Cole, Hubert: *The Wars of the Roses* (London, 1973)

Cole, Teresa: *Henry V* (Stroud, 2015)

The Complete Peerage (13 vols, ed. V. Gibbs, H. A. Doubleday, D. Warrand, Thomas, Lord Howard de Walden, and G. H. White, 1910–59)

Connolly, Sharon Bennett: *Heroines of the Medieval World* (Stroud, 2017)

Cook, Petronelle: *Consorts of England: The Power Behind the Throne* (New York, 1993)

Cooke, Sir Robert: *The Palace of Westminster* (London, 1987)

Cooper, C. H.: *Memoir of Margaret, Countess of Richmond and Derby* (London, 1874)

Corbett, Chris: *Marguerite: A Biography of Margaret of Anjou* (York, 2002)

Coss, Peter: *The Lady in Medieval England* (Stroud, 1998)

Costain, T. B.: *The Last Plantagenets* (London, 1962)

Cracknell, Eleanor (Assistant Archivist): *The Princes in the Tower?* (Chapel Archives and Chapter Library, 2012, www.stgeorges-windsor.org)

Crawford, Anne: "The King's Burden? The Consequences of Royal Marriage in Fifteenth-Century England" (in *Patronage, the Crown and the Provinces in Later Medieval England,* ed. Ralph A. Griffiths, Gloucester, 1981)

—"The Piety of Late-Medieval English Queens" (in *The Church in Pre-Reformation Society,* ed. C. M. Barron and C. Harper-Bill, Woodbridge, 1985)

—"The Queen's Council in the Middle Ages" (*English Historical Review,* 116, 469, 2001)

—*The Yorkists: The History of a Dynasty* (London, 2007)

Crofton, Ian: *The Kings and Queens of England* (London, 2006)

Cron, B. M.: "The 'Champchevrier Portrait': A Cautionary Tale" (*The Ricardian,* 12, 154, 2001)

—*Margaret of Anjou and the Men Around Her* (Bath, 2021)

Crosland, Margaret: *The Mysterious Mistress: The Life and Legend of Jane Shore* (Stroud, 2006)

Crull, John: *The Antiquities of St. Peter's* (London, 1711)

The Cultural Patronage of Medieval Women (ed. J. H. McCash, Georgia, 1996)

Cunningham, Sean: *Henry VII* (London, 2007)

—*Richard III: A Royal Enigma* (The National Archives, 2003)

Dart, John: *Westmonasterium, or The History and Antiquities of the Abbey Church of Westminster* (2 vols, London, 1723)

Davenport, Mila: *The Book of Costume* (1948)

Davey, Richard: *The Pageant of London* (2 vols, London, 1906)

Davies, Katharine: *The First Queen Elizabeth* (London, 1937)

Dean, Christie: *On the Trail of the Yorks* (Stroud, 2016)

—*The World of Richard III* (Stroud, 2015)
De-la-Noy, Michael: *Windsor Castle, Past and Present* (London, 1990)
The Dictionary of National Biography (22 vols, ed. Sir Leslie Stephen and Sir Sidney Lee, 1885–1901; Oxford, 1998)
Dockray, Keith: *Edward IV* (Stroud, 2015)
—*Henry V* (Stroud, 2004)
—*Henry VI, Margaret of Anjou and the Wars of the Roses: A Source Book* (Stroud, 2000)
—*Richard III: Myth and Reality* (Bangor, 1992)
—*Richard III: A Source Book* (Stroud, 1997)
Dodson, Aidan: *The Royal Tombs of Great Britain: An Illustrated History* (London, 2004)
Dowle, Margaret: *The King's Mother: Memoir of Margaret Beaufort, Countess of Richmond and Derby* (London, 1899)
Dowsing, James: *Forgotten Tudor Palaces in the London Area* (London, undated)
Draper, P.: *The House of Stanley* (Ormskirk, 1864)
Drayton, Michael: *England's Heroical Epistles* and "Miseries of Queen Margaret" (in *The Works of Michael Drayton*, 5 vols, ed. J. William Hebel, K. Tillotson, and B. H. Newdigate, Oxford, 1931–41)
Duffy, Mark: *Royal Tombs of Medieval England* (Stroud, 2003)
Dunbar, Janet: *A Prospect of Richmond* (1966)
Dunn, Diana: "Margaret of Anjou: Chivalry and the Order of the Garter" (in *St. George's Chapel, Windsor, in the Late Middle Ages,* ed. Colin Richmond and Eileen Scarff, Windsor, 2001)

Earenfight, Christina: *Queenship in Medieval Europe* (London, 2013)
Earle, Peter: *The Life and Times of Henry V* (London, 1972)
Edwards, J. G.: "The 'Second' Continuation of the Crowland Chronicle" (*Bulletin of the Institute of Historical Research*, 39, 1966)
Edwards, Rhoda: *The Itinerary of King Richard III, 1483–1485* (London, 1983)
Eltham Palace (ed. Kate Jeffrey, London, 1999)
England in the Fifteenth Century (ed. D. Williams, Woodbridge, 1987)
Erlanger, Philippe: *Margaret of Anjou, Queen of England* (France, 1932; England, 1970)
Evans, H. T.: *Wales and the Wars of the Roses* (Stroud, 1998)
Evans, Michael: *The Death of Kings: Royal Deaths in Medieval England* (London, 2003)

Fahy, C.: "The Marriage of Edward IV and Elizabeth Woodville: A New Italian Source" (*English Historical Review*, 76, 1961)
Falkus, Gila: *The Life and Times of Edward IV* (London, 1981)

Field, John: *Kingdom, Power and Glory: A Historical Guide to Westminster Abbey* (London, 1996)
Finch, Barbara Clay: *Lives of the Princesses of Wales* (3 vols, London, 1883)
Fisher, Deborah: *Henry V: A History of His Most Important Places and Events* (Barnsley, 2022)
Fletcher, Benton: *Royal Homes Near London* (London, 1930)
"Friaries: The Dominican Nuns of Dartford" (in *A History of the County of Kent: Volume 2*, ed. William Page, Victoria County Histories, 1926)
Fryer, M. B., Bousfield, A., and Toffoli, G.: *Lives of the Princesses of Wales* (1983)
Fuller, Thomas: *History of the Worthies of England* (1662)
The Funeral Effigies of Westminster Abbey (ed. Anthony Harvey and Richard Mortimer, Woodbridge, 1994)

Gairdner, James: *Henry VII* (London, 1889)
—*The Life and Reign of Richard III* (Cambridge, 1898)
Gasquet, F. A.: *The Religious Life of Henry VI* (1923)
Gill, Louise: *Richard III and Buckingham's Rebellion* (Stroud, 1999)
Gillingham, John: *The Wars of the Roses* (London, 1981)
Given-Wilson, Chris: *Henry IV* (Yale, 2016)
Given-Wilson, Chris, and Curteis, A.: *The Royal Bastards of Medieval England* (London, 1984)
Glasheen, Joan: *The Secret People of the Palaces* (London, 1998)
Goodall, John: *The English Castle* (Yale and London, 2011)
—*Pevensey Castle* (London, 1999)
Goodman, Anthony: *The Wars of the Roses: Military Activity and English Society, 1452–1497* (London, 1981)
—*The Wars of the Roses: The Soldiers' Experience* (Stroud, 2005)
Gothic: Art for England 1400–1547 (ed. Richard Marks and Paul Williamson, Victoria and Albert Museum, London, 2003)
Gough, Richard: *Sepulchral Monuments in Great Britain* (2 vols, London, 1796)
Green, Mary Anne Everett: *The Lives of the Princesses of England* (6 vols, London, 1849–55)
Green, V. H. H.: *The Later Plantagenets* (London, 1955)
Gregory, Philippa, Baldwin, David, and Jones, Michael: *The Women of the Cousins' War* (New York, 2011)
Griffiths, Ralph A.: "Queen Katherine of Valois and a Missing Statute of the Realm" (*Law Quarterly Review*, 93, 1977)
—*The Reign of King Henry VI* (London, 1981)
Griffiths, Ralph A., and Thomas, Roger S.: *The Making of the Tudor Dynasty* (Stroud, 1993)

Gristwood, Sarah: *Blood Sisters: The Hidden Lives of the Women Behind the Wars of the Roses* (London, 2012)

Halsted, Caroline Amelia: *Life of Margaret Beaufort, Countess of Richmond and Derby, Mother of Henry the Seventh* (London, 1839)
Hamilton, Jeffrey: *The Plantagenets: History of a Dynasty* (London, 2010)
Hammond, Peter: *The Children of Richard III* (York, 2018)
—*Her Majesty's Royal Palace and Fortress of the Tower of London* (London, 1987)
Hammond, Peter, and Sutton, Anne F.: *Richard III: The Road to Bosworth Field* (London, 1985)
Hancock, Peter A.: *Richard III and the Murder in the Tower* (Stroud, 2009)
Hand, G.: "The King's Widow and the King's Widows" (*Law Quarterly Review*, 93, 1977)
The Handbook of British Chronology (ed. Sir F. Maurice Powicke and E. B. Fryde, Royal Historical Society, 1961)
Hanham, Alison: *Richard III and the Early Historians* (Oxford, 1975)
—"Sir George Buck and Princess Elizabeth's Letter: A Problem in Detection" (*The Ricardian*, 7, 1987)
Harris, Barbara J.: *English Aristocratic Women, 1450–1550* (Oxford, 2002)
Harrod, H.: "Queen Elizabeth Woodville's visit to Norwich in 1469" (*Norfolk Archeology*, 5, 1859)
Harvey, John: *The Plantagenets* (London, 1948)
Hassall, W. O.: *Who's Who in History, Vol. 1: British Isles, 55 B.C. to 1485* (Oxford, 1960)
Haswell, Jock: *The Ardent Queen: Margaret of Anjou and the Lancastrian Heritage* (London, 1976)
Hedley, Olwen: *Royal Palaces* (London, 1972)
Henry, David: *An Historical Account of the Curiosities of London* (3 vols, London, 1753)
Hepburn, Frederick: *Portraits of the Later Plantagenets* (Woodbridge, 1986)
Hibbert, Christopher: *Agincourt* (London, 1964)
—*The Court at Windsor* (London, 1964)
—*The Tower of London* (London, 1971)
Hichens, Mark: *Wives of the Kings of England, from Normans to Stuarts* (Brighton, 2008)
Hicks, Michael: *Anne Neville, Queen to Richard III* (Stroud, 2006)
—*Edward V: The Prince in the Tower* (Stroud, 2003)
—*False, Fleeting, Perjur'd Clarence: George, Duke of Clarence, 1449–78* (Gloucester, 1980)
—*The Family of Richard III* (Stroud, 2015)

—"King of Morals or Incestuous Hypocrite?" (*BBC History Magazine's Richard III*, 2015)
—*Richard III* (London, 1991; revised Stroud, 2000)
Higginbotham, Susan: *Margaret of Anjou's Last Days: Her Dogs and Her Burial* (www.susanhigginbotham.com)
—*The Woodvilles: The Wars of the Roses and England's Most Infamous Family* (Stroud, 2013)
Hilliam, David: *Crown, Orb and Scepter: The True Stories of English Coronations* (Stroud, 2001)
—*Kings, Queens, Bones and Bastards* (Stroud, 1998)
Hilton, Lisa: "Medieval Queens" (in *Royal Women*, BBC History Magazine special, Bristol, 2015)
—*Queens Consort: England's Medieval Queens* (London, 2008)
Hinde, Thomas: *Hinde's Courtiers: 900 Years of English Court Life* (London, 1986)
Hipshon, David: *Richard III and the Death of Chivalry* (Stroud, 2009)
A History of Fotheringhay (ed. S. J. Hunt, Peterborough, 1999)
The History of the King's Works, Volume II: The Middle Ages (ed. H. M. Colvin, London, 1963)
Hodder, Sarah J.: *The Queen's Sisters: The Lives of the Sisters of Elizabeth Woodville* (Alresford, 2020)
—*The Woodville Women* (Barnsley, 2022)
Hollman, Gemma: *Royal Witches: From Joan of Navarre to Elizabeth Woodville* (Cheltenham, 2019)
Hookham, M. A.: *The Life and Times of Margaret of Anjou* (1872)
Horrox, Rosemary: "The History of King Richard III (1619) by Sir George Buck, Master of the Revels" (*English Historical Review*, 97, 382, January 1982)
Horspool, David: *Richard III: A Ruler and His Reputation* (London, 2015)
A House of Kings: The History of Westminster Abbey (ed. Edward Carpenter, London, 1966)
The Houses of Parliament: History, Art, Architecture (ed. Iain Ross, London, 2000)
Howard, Philip: *The Royal Palaces* (1970)
Hughes, Jonathan: *Arthurian Myths and Alchemy: The Kingship of Edward IV* (Stroud, 2002)
Hutchison, H. F.: *Henry V* (London, 1967)

Impey, Edward, and Parnell, Geoffrey: *The Tower of London: The Official Illustrated History* (London, 2000)

Jacob, E. F.: *The Fifteenth Century, 1399–1485* (Oxford, 1961)
James, Jeffrey: *Edward IV: Glorious Son of York* (Stroud, 2015)

Jenkins, Elizabeth: *The Princes in the Tower* (London, 1978)
Jenkyns, Richard: *Westminster Abbey* (London, 2004)
Jenner, Heather: *Royal Wives* (London, 1967)
Joelson, Annette: *Heirs to the Throne* (London, 1966)
Jones, Christopher: *The Great Palace: The Story of Parliament* (London, 1983)
Jones, Dan: *The Hollow Crown: The Wars of the Roses and the Rise of the Tudors* (London, 2014)
Jones, Michael K., and Underwood, M. G.: *The King's Mother: Lady Margaret Beaufort, Countess of Richmond and Derby* (Cambridge, 1992)
—*Psychology of a Battle: Bosworth, 1485* (Stroud, 2002)
Jones, Nigel: *Tower: An Epic History of the Tower of London* (London, 2011)
Jones, T. Artemus: "Owen Tudor's Marriage" (*Bulletin of the Board of Celtic Studies*, 11, 1943)

Kelly, H. A.: "Canonical Implications of Richard III's Plan to Marry His Niece" (*Traditio*, 23, 1967)
Kendall, Paul: *Wars of the Roses* (Barnsley, 2023)
Kendall, Paul Murray: *Richard the Third* (London, 1955)
—*Warwick the Kingmaker* (London, 1957)
—*The Yorkist Age: Daily Life During the Wars of the Roses* (1962)
Kenyon, John R.: *Middleham Castle* (London, 2015)
Kincaid, A. N.: "Buck and the Elizabeth of York Letter: A Reply to Dr. Hanham" (*The Ricardian*, 8, 1988)
Kings and Queens of England (ed. Antonia Fraser, London, 1975)
Kirby, J. L.: *Henry IV of England* (London, 1970)

Labarge, Margaret Wade: *Henry V: The Cautious Conqueror* (London, 1975)
—*Women in Medieval Life* (London, 1986)
Lamb, V. B.: *The Betrayal of Richard III* (London, 1959; revised, with notes and an introduction by P. W. Hammond, Stroud, 1990)
Lander, J. R.: *Conflict and Stability in Fifteenth-Century England* (London, 1969)
—"Henry VI and the Duke of York's Second Protectorate, 1455–1456" (*Bulletin of the John Rylands Library*, 43, 1960)
—"Marriage and Politics in the Fifteenth Century: The Nevilles and the Wydevilles (*Bulletin of the Institute of Historical Research*, 36, 1963)
—*The Wars of the Roses* (London, 1965; Stroud, 1990)
Lane, H. M.: *The Royal Daughters of England* (2 vols, London, 1910)
Lawrance, Hannah: *Historical Memoirs of the Queens of England, from the Commencement of the Twelfth to the Close of the Fifteenth Century* (London, 1840)
Laynesmith, J. J.: *Cecily, Duchess of York* (London, 2017)
—*The Last Medieval Queens: English Queenship, 1445–1503* (Oxford, 2004)

Leary, Francis: *The Golden Longing* (London, 1959)

Lee, Patricia-Ann: "Reflections of Power: Margaret of Anjou and the Dark Side of Queenship" (*Renaissance Quarterly*, 39, 1986)

Lee, Paul: *Nunneries, Learning and Spirituality in Late Medieval English Life: The Dominican Priory of Dartford* (York, 2001)

Leeds Castle (London, 1976, 1989, 1994)

Lenz-Harvey, Nancy: *Elizabeth of York, Tudor Queen* (London, 1973)

Lewis, Matthew: *Richard, Duke of York: King by Right* (Stroud, 2016)

Leyser, Henrietta: *Medieval Women* (London, 1995)

License, Amy: *Anne Neville: Richard III's Tragic Queen* (Stroud, 2013)

—*Cecily Neville, Mother of Kings* (Stroud, 2014)

—*Edward IV and Elizabeth Woodville: A True Romance* (Stroud, 2016)

—*Elizabeth of York: The Forgotten Tudor Queen* (Stroud, 2013)

—*Henry VI and Margaret of Anjou: A Marriage of Unequals* (Barnsley, 2018)

—*The Lost Kings: Lancaster, York and Tudor* (Stroud, 2017)

—*Red Roses: Blanche of Lancaster to Margaret Beaufort* (Stroud, 2016)

—*Royal Babies: A History, 1066–2013* (Stroud, 2013)

Lindsay, Philip: *King Henry V: A Chronicle* (London, 1934)

Llywelyn, John F. M.: *The Chapels in the Tower of London* (St. Ives, 1987)

Loades, David: *The Kings and Queens of England: The Biography* (Stroud, 2013)

Lockyer, R.: *Henry VII* (London, 1968; revised 1983)

Lofts, Norah: *Queens of Britain* (London, 1977)

Louda, J., and MacLagan, M.: *Lines of Succession: Heraldry of the Royal Families of Europe* (London, 1981)

Lowe, D. E.: "Patronage and Politics: Edward IV, the Wydevilles and the Council of the Prince of Wales, 1471-83" (*Bulletin of the Board of Celtic Studies*, 29, 1981)

Lyte, Henry Churchill Maxwell: *A History of the University of Oxford from the Earliest Times to the Year 1530* (London, 1886)

Macalpine, Joan: *The Shadow of the Tower: Henry VII and His England* (London, 1971)

MacGibbon, David: *Elizabeth Woodville (1437–1492): Her Life and Times* (London, 1938)

Mackie, J. D.: *The Earlier Tudors, 1485–1558* (Oxford, 1952; revised 1966)

MacNalty, Arthur Salusbury: *The Princes in the Tower and Other Royal Mysteries* (London, 1955)

Markham, C. R.: *Richard III: His Life and Character* (1906)

Marsden, Jonathan, and Winterbottom, Matthew: *Windsor Castle* (London, 2008)

Marshal, E.: *The Early History of Woodstock Manor* (1873)

Maurer, Helen E.: *Margaret of Anjou: Queenship and Power in Late Medieval England* (Woodbridge, 2003)

McFarlane, K. B.: "The Lancastrian Kings, 1399–1461" (*Cambridge Medieval History,* 8, 1936)

McIntosh, Marjorie Keniston: *Autonomy and Community: The Royal Manor of Havering, 1200 to 1500* (Cambridge, 1986)

McKelvey, Elaine Clark Beuchner: Thomas Stanley, First Earl of Derby, 1435–1504 (unpublished PhD thesis, Pennsylvania State University, 1966)

McKendrick, Scot, and Doyle, Kathleen: *Royal Illuminated Manuscripts, from King Athelstan to Henry VIII* (The British Library, London, 2011)

McKendrick, Scot, Lowden, John, Doyle, Kathleen, et al.: *Royal Manuscripts: The Genius of Illumination* (The British Library, London, 2011)

McSheffrey, Shannon: "Sanctuary and the Legal Topography of Pre-Reformation London" (*Law and History Review,* 27, 2009)

Medieval Mothering (ed. John Carmi Parsons and Bonnie Wheeler, New York and London, 1996)

Medieval Queenship (ed. John Carmi Parsons, Stroud, 1993, 2008)

Mitchell, Dorothy: *Richard III and York* (York, 1983)

Mitchell, J. Allen: "Queen Katherine and the Secret of Lydgate's *The Temple of Glass*" (*Medium Aevum,* 77, 2008)

Mortimer, Ian: *The Fears of Henry IV: The Life of England's Self-Made King* (London, 2007)

Mowat, A. J.: "Robert Stillington" (*The Ricardian,* 4, 1976)

Myers, A. R.: "The Captivity of a Royal Witch: The Household Accounts of Queen Joan of Navarre, 1419–21" (*Bulletin of the John Rylands Library,* 24 and 26, 1940)

—*Crown, Household and Parliament in Fifteenth-Century England* (London, 1985)

—"The Household Accounts of Queen Margaret of Anjou, 1452–3" (*Bulletin of the John Rylands Library,* 40, 1957–8)

—*The Household of Edward IV* (1959)

—"The Household of Queen Elizabeth Woodville, 1466–7" (*Bulletin of the John Rylands Library,* 50, 1967–8)

—"The Princes in the Tower" (*The History of the English Speaking Peoples,* vol. 2, 1970)

Norton, Elizabeth: *England's Queens: The Biography* (Stroud, 2011)

—*Margaret Beaufort, Mother of the Tudor Dynasty* (Stroud, 2010)

—*She Wolves: The Notorious Queens of England* (Stroud, 2008)

Norwich, John Julius: *Shakespeare's Kings* (London, 1999)

Okerlund, Arlene: *Elizabeth Wydeville: The Slandered Queen* (Stroud, 2005)
—*Elizabeth of York* (New York, 2009)
Ormrod, W. M.: *The Kings and Queens of England* (Stroud, 2001)
The Oxford Book of Royal Anecdotes (ed. Elizabeth Longford, Oxford, 1989)
The Oxford Dictionary of National Biography (www.oxforddnb.com)

Painter, G. D.: *William Caxton: A Quincentenary Biography of England's First Printer* (London, 1976)
Palmer, Alan: *Princes of Wales* (London, 1979)
Palmer, Alan and Veronica: *Royal England: A Historical Guide* (London, 1983)
Palmer, C. F. R.: "History of the Priory of Dartford in Kent" (*Archeological Journal*, 36, 1879)
Parrott, Kate: *Shakespeare's Queens (of England)* (Bloomington, 2007)
Parsons, John Carmi: "Mothers, Daughters, Marriage, Power: Some Plantagenet Evidence, 1150–1500" (in *Medieval Queenship*, ed. John Carmi Parsons, Stroud, 1993, 2008)
—"Ritual and Symbol in English Medieval Queenship to 1500" (in *Women and Sovereignty*, ed. Louise Olga Fredenburg, Edinburgh, 1992)
Patronage, the Crown and the Provinces in Later Medieval England (ed. Ralph A. Griffiths, Gloucester, 1981)
Penn, Thomas: *The Brothers York: An English Tragedy* (London, 2019)
—*Winter King: The Dawn of Tudor England* (London, 2011)
Pine, L. G.: *Princes of Wales* (1959)
The Plantagenet Encyclopedia (ed. Elizabeth Hallam, Twickenham, 1996)
Platt, Colin: *Medieval England: A Social History and Archeology from the Conquest to 1600 A.D.* (London, 1978)
Platts, Beryl: *A History of Greenwich* (London, 1973)
Pollard, A. J.: *Richard III and the Princes in the Tower* (Stroud, 1991)
—*The Wars of the Roses* (London, 1988)
Prevost, Abbé: *Histoire de Marguerite d'Anjou* (2 vols, Amsterdam, 1750)
Priestley, John: *Eltham Palace* (Chichester, 2008)
Pyne, W. H.: *The History of the Royal Residences* (3 vols, 1819)

Queens and Power in Medieval and Early Modern England (ed. C. Levin and R. Bucholz, Nebraska, 2009)

Ramsay, J. H.: *Lancaster and York* (2 vols, Oxford, 1892)
Rawcliffe, Carole: *The Staffords: Earls of Stafford and Dukes of Buckingham, 1394–1521* (Cambridge, 1978)
Reese, M. M.: *The Royal Office of Master of the Horse* (London, 1976)
Richard III: Crown and People (ed. J. Petre, London, 1985)

Richardson, Geoffrey: *The Popinjays* (Shipley, 2000)

Roberts, Marilyn: *Lady Anne Mowbray: The High and Excellent Princess* (Scunthorpe, 2013)

Robinson, John Martin: *Royal Palaces: Windsor Castle: A Short History* (London, 1996)

Rose, Alexander: *Kings in the North: The House of Percy in British History* (London, 2002)

Rose, Tessa: *The Coronation Ceremony of the Kings and Queens of England and the Crown Jewels* (London, 1992)

Ross, Charles: *Edward IV* (London, 1974)

—*Richard III* (Yale and London, 1981)

—*The Wars of the Roses: A Concise History* (London, 1976)

Routh, E. M. G.: *Lady Margaret: A Memoir of Lady Margaret Beaufort, Countess of Richmond and Derby, Mother of Henry VII* (Oxford, 1924)

Rowse, A. L.: *Bosworth Field and the Wars of the Roses* (London, 1966)

—*The Tower of London in the History of the Nation* (London, 1972)

—*Windsor Castle in the History of the Nation* (London, 1974)

Roy, J. J. S.: *Histoire de Marguerite d'Anjou* (Tours, 1872)

Royal Palaces of England (ed. R. S. Rait, London, 1911)

Royle, Trevor: *The Wars of the Roses: England's First Civil War* (London, 2009)

Rushforth, Gordon McNeill: *Medieval Christian Imagery as Illustrated by the Painted Windows of Great Malvern Priory Church, Worcestershire, Together with a Description and Explanation of All the Ancient Glass in the Church* (Oxford, 1936)

St. Aubyn, Giles: *The Year of Three Kings: 1483* (London, 1983)

Sandford, Francis: *A Genealogical History of the Kings and Queens of England and Monarchs of Great Britain, 1066–1677* (Savoy and London, 1677; continued by Samuel Stebbings, Newcombe, 1707)

Santiusti, David: *Edward IV and the Wars of the Roses* (Barnsley, 2010)

Saunders, Hilary St. George: *Westminster Hall* (London, 1951)

Sayles, G. O.: "The Royal Marriages Act 1428" (*Law Quarterly Review*, 94, 1978)

Scarr, M. M.: *Queens' College, Cambridge* (Cambridge, 1983)

Schofield, John: *Medieval London Houses* (Yale and London, 1995)

Scofield, Cora L.: "Elizabeth Wydeville in the Sanctuary at Westminster" (*English Historical Review*, 24, 1909)

—*The Life and Reign of Edward the Fourth* (2 vols, London, 1923; reprinted 1967)

Scott, A. F.: *Every One a Witness: The Plantagenet Age* (New York, 1976)

Searle, William George: *The History of the Queens' College of St. Margaret and St. Bernard in the University of Cambridge, Vol. 1* (Cambridge, 1867)

Seward, Desmond: *The Last White Rose: Dynasty, Rebellion and Treason: The Secret Wars Against the Tudors* (London, 2010)
—*Richard III: England's Black Legend* (London, 1982; revised 1997)
Simons, Eric N.: *The Reign of Edward IV* (London, 1966)
Skidmore, Chris: *Bosworth: The Birth of the Tudors* (London, 2013)
—*Richard III: Brother, Protector, King* (London, 2017)
Smith, Emily Tennyson (Bradley), and Micklethwaite, J. T.: *Annals of Westminster Abbey* (London, 1898)
Softly, Barbara: *The Queens of England* (London, 1976)
Souden, David: *The Royal Palaces of London* (London, 2008)
Stanley, Arthur Penrhyn: *Historical Memorials of Westminster Abbey* (London, 1867)
Starkey, David: *Crown and Country: A History of England Through Monarchy* (London, 2010)
—*Monarchy: From the Middle Ages to Modernity* (London, 2006)
Steane, John: *The Archeology of the Medieval English Monarchy* (London, 1993)
Story, R. L.: *The End of the House of Lancaster* (London, 1966)
Strickland, Agnes: *The Lives of the Queens of England* (8 vols, London, 1851; reprinted Bath, 1973)
Strong, Roy: *Coronation: A History of Kingship and the British Monarchy* (London, 2005)
—*Tudor and Jacobean Portraits* (2 vols, London, 1969)
Sutton, Anne, and Visser-Fuchs, Livia: "The Device of Queen Elizabeth Woodville: A Gillyflower or Pink" (*The Ricardian*, March 1997)
—*The Hours of Richard III* (Stroud, 1990)
—"A 'Most Benevolent Queen': Queen Elizabeth Woodville's Reputation, Her Piety and Her Books" (*The Ricardian*, 10, 1995)
—*The Reburial of Richard, Duke of York, 21–30 July 1476* (London, 1996)

Tanner, Lawrence E.: *The History and Treasures of Westminster Abbey* (London, 1953)
Taute, Anne, Brooke-Little, J., and Pottinger, D.: *Kings and Queens of England: A Genealogical Chart Showing Their Descent, Relationships and Coats of Arms* (1970; revised 1986)
Thomas, Melita: Did the Relationships Between the Medieval Queens of England and the City of London Impact National Politics? (MRes in Historical Research, Institute of Historical Research, University of London, 2020)
—*The House of Grey: Friends and Foes of Kings* (Stroud, 2019)
Thompson, C. J. S.: *The Witchery of Jane Shore* (London, 1933)
Thornley, I. D.: *England Under the Yorkists, 1460–1485* (London, 1920)

Select Bibliography

Thornton-Cook, E.: *Her Majesty: The Romance of the Queens of England* (New York, 1926)

—*Kings in the Making: The Princes of Wales* (London, 1931)

Tingle, Louise: *Chaucer's Queens* (London, 2020)

Tomaini, Thea: *The Corpse as Text: Disinterment and Antiquarian Inquiry, 1700–1900* (Woodbridge, 2017)

Trowles, Tony: *Treasures of Westminster Abbey* (London, 2008)

Tucker, M. J.: "Life at Henry VII's Court" (*History Today*, May 1969)

Tudor-Craig, Pamela: *Richard III* (National Portrait Gallery exhibition catalogue, 1973; revised 1977)

Turton, W. H.: *The Plantagenet Ancestry of Elizabeth of York* (London, 1928)

Vaughan, Richard: *Philip the Good* (London, 1970)

Villeneuve-Bargement, Louis François, Viscomte de: *History of René d'Anjou, King of Naples, Duke of Lorraine and Count of Provence* (3 vols, Paris, 1825)

Visser-Fuchs, Livia: "English Events in Caspar Weinreich's Danzig Chronicle, 1461–1495" (*The Ricardian*, 7, 1986)

Wadmore, J. F.: *Some Account of the Worshipful Company of Skinners of London, Being the Guild or Fraternity of Corpus Christi* (London, 1902)

Ward, Jennifer: *Women in England in the Middle Ages* (London, 2006)

The Wars of the Roses (ed. Antonia Fraser, London, 2000)

Warwick Castle (Birmingham, 2002)

Weaver, John: *Middleham Castle* (London, 1998)

Weightman, Christine: *Margaret of York, Duchess of Burgundy, 1446–1503* (Stroud, 1989)

Weir, Alison: Britain's Aristocratic Families, 1066–1603 (unpublished)

—*Britain's Royal Families: The Complete Genealogy* (London, 1989)

—*Elizabeth of York: The First Tudor Queen* (London, 2013)

—*Lancaster and York: The Wars of the Roses* (London, 1994)

—*Richard III and the Princes in the Tower* (London, 1992)

Westervelt, T.: The Woodvilles in the Second Reign of Edward IV, 1471-83 (unpublished MPhil dissertation, Cambridge, 1997)

Westminster Abbey: Official Guide (Norwich, 1966)

Wilkins, Christopher: *The Last Knight Errant: Sir Edward Woodville and the Age of Chivalry* (London, 2010)

Wilkinson, B.: *Constitutional History in England in the Fifteenth Century* (London, 1964)

—*The Later Middle Ages in England, 1216–1485* (London, 1969)

Wilkinson, James: *Henry VII's Lady Chapel* (London, 2007)

Wilkinson, James, and Knighton, C. S.: *Crown and Cloister: The Royal Story of Westminster Abbey* (London, 2010)

Wilkinson, Josephine: *The Princes in the Tower* (Stroud, 2013)

—*Richard, the Young King to Be* (Stroud, 2008)

Williams, Barrie: "The Portuguese Connection and the Significance of the 'Holy Princess'" (*The Ricardian,* March, 1983)

Williams, D. T.: *The Battle of Bosworth Field* (Leicester 1973, 1996)

Williams, E. Carleton: *My Lord of Bedford* (London, 1963)

Williams, Neville: *The Life and Times of Henry VII* (London, 1973)

Williamson, Audrey: *The Mystery of the Princes* (Gloucester, 1978)

Williamson, David: *The National Portrait Gallery History of the Kings and Queens of England* (London, 1998)

Wilson, Derek: *The Tower, 1078–1978* (1978)

Windsor Castle: A Thousand Years of a Royal Palace (ed. Stephen Brindle, London, 2018)

Women and Sovereignty (ed. Louise Olga Fradenburg, Edinburgh, 1992)

Wood, Charles T.: "The First Two Queens Elizabeth" (in *Women and Sovereignty,* ed. Louise Olga Fradenburg, Edinburgh, 1992)

Wood, Margaret: *The English Medieval House* (London, 1965, 1994)

Woodacre, Elena: *Joan of Navarre: Infanta, Duchess, Queen, Witch?* (Routledge, 2023)

Woolgar, C. M.: *The Great Household in Late Medieval England* (Yale and London, 1999)

Wylie, J. H.: *The History of England Under Henry IV* (4 vols, 1884–98)

Wylie, J. H., and Waugh, W. T.: *The Reign of Henry V* (3 vols, 1914–29)

"The Yorkist Age" (in *Proceedings of the 2011 Harlaxton Symposium,* ed. Hannes Kleineke and Christian Steer, Harlaxton Medieval Studies XXII, 2011)

Sources of Quotes in the Text

✷

Introduction

1 Froissart

PART ONE: JOAN OF NAVARRE, QUEEN OF HENRY IV

1 "Mutual affection and delight"

1 Saint-Paul 2 Ibid. 3 *Foedera* 4 Bouchart 5 Chronicle of Saint-Denis 6 Saint-Paul; Chronicle of Saint-Denis 7 *Recueil des actes de Jean IV* 8 Cotton MS. Julius 9 Bouchart

2 "This blessed sacrament of marriage"

1 *Calendar of Close Rolls* 2 *Foedera* 3 Saint-Paul 4 *Foedera* 5 Exchequer Records: Issue Rolls 6 *Facsimiles of National Manuscripts* 7 Exchequer Records: Issue Rolls 8 Cotton MS. Julius 9 Ibid.

3 "His beloved consort"

1 Adam of Usk 2 Cited Kingsford: *English Historical Literature in the Fifteenth Century* 3 *Foedera* 4 Stow: *The Survey of London*

4 "Cruelly tormented"

1 Capgrave 2 *Rotuli Parliamentorum* 3 Capgrave 4 *Lettres et mandements de Jean V; Foedera* 5 *Foedera* 6 Elmham 7 Adam of Usk 8 Walsingham

5 "A woman of great prudence and judgment"

1 Cited Myers: *Crown, Household and Parliament* 2 *Bulletin du Comité Historique des Monuments Écrits* 3 Walsingham 4 Elmham 5 *Letters of the Queens of England, 1100–1546*

PART TWO: KATHERINE OF VALOIS, QUEEN OF HENRY V

1 "Your fair and noble daughter"

1 Capgrave 2 Walsingham 3 *Rotuli Parliamentorum* 4 Harleian MSS

2 "Our dearest and best-beloved son"

1 *Chronicle of London, 1089–1483* 2 Cotton MS. Vespasian 3 Gruel 4 *Rotuli Parliamentorum* 5 Waurin 6 Monstrelet 7 Ibid.

3 "The superstitious deeds of necromancers"

1 *Foedera* 2 Calendars of Patent Rolls 3 *Concilia Magnae Brittaniae et Hiberniae* 4 *Chronicles of London; The Brut* 5 Walsingham 6 *Rotuli Parliamentorum* 7 *Foedera* 8 *Chronicle of London, 1089–1483* 9 Walsingham 10 Ibid.

4 "My dear Englishman"

1 Hall 2 Chastellain 3 Hall 4 Lydgate 5 Monstrelet; Capgrave; *The First English Life of Henry V* 6 Monstrelet 7 Ibid. 8 Ibid. 9 *A Parisian Journal, 1405–1449* 10 *Rotuli Parliamentorum* 11 *The Brut* 12 Monstrelet 13 Ibid. 14 *The Brut* 15 Ibid.

5 "His bed of pain"

1 *The First English Life of Henry V* 2 Monstrelet 3 Historians of Scotland 4 *Rotuli Parliamentorum* 5 Speed 6 *The First English Life of Henry V*

Sources of Quotes in the Text

6 "That godly, faithful, true Princess"

1 *Lettres et mandements de Jean V*   2 Weever   3 Harleian MSS   4 Vergil   5 *Rotuli Parliamentorum*   6 Speed   7 Selden MSS   8 Additional MSS; Harleian MSS   9 Cited Mitchell: "Queen Katherine and the Secret of Lydgate's *The Temple of Glass*"

7 "Following more her own appetite"

1 *Rotuli Parliamentorum*   2 Latin MSS   3 Evans: *Wales and the Wars of the Roses*   4 Sir John Wyn of Gwydir, cited Griffiths and Thomas   5 Vergil   6 *The Great Chronicle of London;* Hall   7 Vergil   8 Hall   9 *Proceedings and Ordinances of the Privy Council*   10 *Rotuli Parliamentorum*   11 *The Great Chronicle of London*

8 "I did kiss a queen"

1 Exchequer Records: Issue Rolls   2 Cotton MS. Tiberius   3 *Rotuli Parliamentorum*   4 William of Worcester   5 Stow: *The Survey of London*   6 National Archives   7 Gough

9 "A king greatly degenerated from his father"

1 *Proceedings and Ordinances of the Privy Council*   2 Cotton MSS   3 *Registrum Abbatiae Johannis Whethamstede*   4 Blacman   5 Bodleian MSS   6 Blacman   7 *The Great Chronicle of London*   8 Blacman   9 *Rotuli Parliamentorum*

PART THREE: MARGARET OF ANJOU, QUEEN OF HENRY VI

1 "The magnificent and very bright Margaret"

1 Chastellain   2 Warkworth   3 *Foedera*   4 *The Brut*

2 "A queen not worth ten marks"

1 *Foedera*   2 *Rotuli Parliamentorum*   3 Ibid.   4 The Breknoke Computus   5 *Calendar of State Papers: Milan*   6 Capgrave   7 *Calendar of State Papers: Milan*   8 Royal MSS   9 *Foedera*   10 Hall

3 "Of stomach and courage more like to a man"

1 Stow **2** *The Brut* **3** Fabyan **4** *The Brut* **5** Stow **6** *The Brut* **7** Ambassadors' report, Bibliothèque Nationale, Paris **8** *Calendar of State Papers: Milan* **9** Chastellain **10** Hall **11** *Secular Lyrics of the XIVth and XVth Centuries*

4 "The solicitation and exhortation of the Queen"

1 *The Letters of Margaret of Anjou* **2** Ibid. **3** Gascoigne **4** *A Collection of Wills of the Kings and Queens of England* **5** Waurin **6** Ibid. **7** Benet

5 "A harvest of heads"

1 *Gregory's Chronicle*

6 "In the hands of a woman"

(There are no source notes for this chapter.)

7 "A sudden and thoughtless fright"

1 Battle Abbey MS. 937 **2** *Rotuli Parliamentorum* **3** Battle Abbey MS. 937 **4** *The Paston Letters* **5** *Registrum Abbatiae Johannis Whethamstede*

8 "An infirmity of mind"

1 *The Paston Letters* **2** Ibid. **3** Benet **4** Ibid. **5** *The Paston Letters* **6** Ibid.

9 "Wars of the Roses"

1 Benet **2** Ibid. **3** Ibid. **4** *Registrum Abbatiae Johannis Whethamstede* **5** Benet **6** *The Stonor Letters and Papers* **7** Benet

10 "By fair means or foul"

1 *Rotuli Parliamentorum* **2** Commines **3** Rous **4** *The Coventry Leet Book* **5** Ibid. **6** Thomas Gascoigne, cited Wilkinson: *Constitutional History in England in the Fifteenth Century* **7** *The Paston Letters* **8** Benet **9** *The Paston Letters*

Sources of Quotes in the Text 505

11 "A great and strong labor'd woman"

1 Fabyan 2 Calendars of Patent Rolls 3 *Davies' Chronicle* 4 *Registrum Abbatiae Johannis Whethamstede* 5 Cotton MSS 6 *The Croyland Chronicle* 7 *Davies' Chronicle* 8 Vergil 9 Benet 10 Ibid. 11 Hall

12 "A dolt and a fool"

1 *Davies' Chronicle* 2 *Rotuli Parliamentorum* 3 *The Paston Letters* 4 Calendars of Patent Rolls 5 Pius II 6 *Gregory's Chronicle* 7 Ibid.

13 "Madam, your war is done"

1 Cited Gillingham 2 Harleian MSS

14 "Captain Margaret"

1 *The Letters of Margaret of Anjou* 2 William of Worcester 3 Benet 4 *Gregory's Chronicle* 5 Waurin 6 *Calendar of State Papers: Milan* 7 Ibid. 8 *Letters of the Queens of England, 1100–1546*

15 "Great slaughter"

1 Waurin 2 Ibid.

16 "Traitors and rebels"

1 *Calendar of State Papers: Milan*

17 "The handsomest prince my eyes ever beheld"

1 Vergil 2 Commines 3 Mancini 4 More 5 Commines 6 *The Paston Letters* 7 The *Croyland Chronicle* 8 More 9 Ibid. 10 Vergil

18 "I will either conquer or be conquered"

1 *Rotuli Parliamentorum* 2 Legeaud MSS 3 Lee: "Reflections of Power" 4 Warkworth

19 "Dire vicissitude"

1 Chastellain 2 Ibid. 3 Ibid. 4 Ibid. 5 Ibid. 6 Ibid. 7 Ibid.
8 Ibid. 9 Chronicles of Lorraine 10 Fortescue

PART FOUR: ELIZABETH WIDVILLE, QUEEN OF EDWARD IV

1 "Now take heed what love may do"

1 *Gregory's Chronicle* 2 Monstrelet 3 Ibid. 4 *Calendar of State Papers: Milan* 5 Mancini 6 Royal MSS; *Archaeologia*

2 "Governed by lust"

1 Hall; More 2 Mancini 3 Hall 4 Royal MSS 5 Hall 6 "Fragment of an Old English Chronicle" 7 Cornazzano 8 Croyland 9 Mancini 10 Fabyan 11 "Fragment of an Old English Chronicle" 12 Fabyan 13 Ibid. 14 Hardyng 15 Waurin 16 Croyland 17 Waurin 18 *Calendar of State Papers: Milan* 19 *The Paston Letters* 20 Mancini 21 More 22 *Letters and Papers illustrative of the Reigns of Richard III and Henry VII* 23 *The Great Chronicle of London* 24 *Manners and Household Expenses of the 13th and 15th Centuries*

3 "The Rivers run so high"

1 Croyland 2 *The Coventry Leet Book* 3 *Letters and Papers illustrative of the Reigns of Richard III and Henry VII* 4 Ibid. 5 Mancini 6 *Letters and Papers illustrative of the Reigns of Richard III and Henry VII* 7 Mancini 8 Ibid. 9 *Letters and Papers illustrative of the Reigns of Richard III and Henry VII* 10 *The Stonor Letters and Papers* 11 *The Great Chronicle of London* 12 *The Paston Letters* 13 Monstrelet 14 Mancini

4 "Very great division"

1 *Calendar of State Papers: Milan* 2 Ibid. 3 Warkworth 4 Additional MS. 198

5 "Secret displeasure"

1 *The Letters of Margaret of Anjou* 2 *Calendar of State Papers: Milan* 3 Warkworth 4 *Letters and Papers illustrative of the Reigns of Richard III and*

Henry VII **5** Ibid. **6** The Register of the Mayors of Dublin, from 1406 to 1622: Additional MS. 4791

6 "A most deadly hatred"

1 William of Worcester **2** *The Great Chronicle of London* **3** Fabyan **4** Croyland **5** Ibid. **6** *Calendar of State Papers: Milan* **7** Croyland **8** *The Great Chronicle of London* **9** *Calendar of State Papers: Milan* **10** Croyland **11** Hall **12** Ibid. **13** Waurin **14** *Rotuli Parliamentorum*

7 "The marriage of the Queen of England and the Earl of Warwick"

1 *Calendar of State Papers: Milan* **2** Ibid. **3** Ibid. **4** Harleian MSS **5** Ibid. **6** Chastellain **7** Harleian MSS **8** Ibid. **9** *Calendar of State Papers: Milan* **10** Harleian MSS **11** *Calendar of State Papers: Milan*

8 "Forsaken of all her friends"

1 Warkworth **2** Commines **3** Warkworth **4** Ibid. **5** Commines **6** *The Great Chronicle of London* **7** Rous **8** Warkworth **9** Commines **10** More **11** On the Recovery of the throne by Edward IV, Royal MSS; *Political Poems and Songs* **12** *The Great Chronicle of London*

9 "My cousin of York, you are very welcome"

1 Warkworth **2** *History of the Arrival of Edward IV in England* **3** Ibid. **4** Ibid. **5** *Political Poems and Songs* **6** *History of the Arrival of Edward IV in England* **7** On the Recovery of the throne by Edward IV, Royal MSS; *Political Poems and Songs*

10 "The last hope of thy race"

1 *History of the Arrival of Edward IV in England* **2** Ibid. **3** Hall **4** Ibid. **5** *Calendar of State Papers: Milan* **6** Croyland **7** Ibid. **8** Ibid. **9** *History of the Arrival of Edward IV in England*

11 "He has, in short, chosen to crush the seed"

1 *History of the Arrival of Edward IV in England* 2 Ibid. 3 Croyland 4 Warkworth 5 Waurin; *History of the Arrival of Edward IV in England* 6 Croyland 7 Warkworth 8 Vergil 9 *Archaeologia* 10 Warkworth 11 *The Great Chronicle of London* 12 Ibid.

12 "More like a death than a life"

1 Wadmore 2 Holinshed 3 Hall 4 Villeneuve-Bargement 5 Ibid. 6 *The Letters of Margaret of Anjou* 7 Ibid. 8 Bibliothèque d'Angers, MS. 656

13 "Privy pleasures"

1 Commines 2 Mancini 3 Croyland 4 More 5 Ibid. 6 Mancini 7 Ibid. 8 Ibid. 9 Ibid. 10 *The Paston Letters*

PART FIVE: ANNE NEVILLE, QUEEN OF RICHARD III

1 "Violent dissensions"

1 Croyland 2 Ibid. 3 Ibid. 4 *The Paston Letters* 5 Croyland 6 Buck 7 *The Paston Letters* 8 Clarke: "English Royal Marriages and the Papal Penitentiary" 9 Calendar of Durham Cathedral Archives 10 Rous 11 Searle 12 Harleian MSS

2 "The world seemeth queasy"

1 "Narratives of the Arrival of Louis of Bruges, Lord of Gruthuyse" 2 *Rotuli Parliamentorum* 3 More 4 Mancini 5 Ibid. 6 Commines

3 "A rondolet of Malmsey"

1 Croyland 2 *Rotuli Parliamentorum* 3 Mancini 4 Ibid. 5 More 6 Mancini 7 Ibid.

4 "An unknown disease"

1 Waurin 2 Croyland 3 Rous 4 Croyland 5 Vergil 6 Mancini 7 Croyland 8 Cotton MS. Cleopatra

Sources of Quotes in the Text

5 "Demanding rather than supplicating"

1 Mancini 2 Ibid. 3 Croyland 4 Ibid. 5 Ibid. 6 Mancini 7 Croyland 8 Mancini 9 Ibid. 10 Croyland 11 Mancini 12 Vergil 13 Mancini 14 Ibid. 15 Ibid. 16 Croyland 17 Mancini 18 Ibid. 19 Ibid. 20 Croyland 21 More 22 Mancini 23 Ibid.

6 "The present danger"

1 Mancini 2 Ibid. 3 More 4 Hall 5 More 6 Ibid. 7 Ibid. 8 Croyland 9 Mancini 10 More 11 Mancini 12 Ibid. 13 Croyland 14 Mancini 15 Ibid. 16 Ibid. 17 Ibid.

7 "Seditious and disgraceful proceedings"

1 Mancini 2 Ibid. 3 Ibid. 4 Ibid. 5 Vergil 6 Mancini 7 Ibid. 8 Croyland 9 Mancini 10 Croyland 11 Mancini 12 *The Stonor Letters and Papers* 13 Croyland 14 Mancini 15 Croyland 16 Mancini 17 Croyland 18 Mancini 19 Vergil 20 Mancini

8 "God save King Richard!"

1 Croyland 2 Ibid. 3 *The Great Chronicle of London* 4 Mancini 5 *Household Books of John Howard, Duke of Norfolk* 6 Mancini 7 *Household Books of John Howard, Duke of Norfolk* 8 Mancini 9 Rous 10 Harleian MSS 11 Rous 12 Harleian MSS 13 Ibid.; Grafton

9 "Assemblies and confederacies"

1 Croyland 2 Ibid. 3 Ibid. 4 More 5 Vergil 6 Croyland 7 Vergil

10 "The rightful inheritor"

1 Vergil 2 Croyland 3 Ibid. 4 Ibid.

11 "On the word of a king"

1 Hall 2 Buck

12 "An incestuous passion"

1 Croyland 2 Ibid. 3 *The Great Chronicle of London* 4 More 5 Croyland 6 Ibid. 7 Ibid. 8 Ibid.

13 "A burden to her husband"

1 *The Great Chronicle of London* 2 Croyland 3 *The Great Chronicle of London*

Afterword: "Without any worldly pomp"

1 Exchequer Records: Exchequer of Receipt: Warrants for Issues 2 Croyland 3 Ibid. 4 More 5 *Rotuli Parliamentorum* 6 Calendars of Close Rolls 7 Hall 8 Leland: *Antiquarii de Rebus Britannicis Collectanea* 9 Vergil 10 Hall 11 Calendars of Charter Rolls 12 Arundel MSS

Epilogue

(There are no source notes for this chapter.)

Index

Abergavenny, Wales, lordship of, 361
Abingdon, Oxon., 202
　Abbey, 183, 261
Accord, Act of, 1460, 204, 206, 218
Adam of Usk, 29, 32
Agenais, France, 44
Agincourt, Battle of, 1415, 86
Alcobaça, Pedro de (Peter de Offball), 58
Alençon, Normandy, 11, 47, 50
Alfonso of Aragon, Count of Provence, 109
Alfonso V, King of Portugal, 446
Agnes, Countess of Foix, 5
Alcock, John, Bishop of Rochester, Worcester and Ely, 261, 365
Aldrewick, Nicholas, 19, 27, 30
Alfonso of Aragon, Duke of Gandia, 109
Alfonso V, King of Portugal, 446
All Saints' Church, Maidstone, Kent, 298
Alnwick Castle, Northld., 234, 238–41, 252
Amboise, France, 250, 310, 318
　Château of, 305

Amiens, France, 64
André, Bernard, 416
Anglesey, Wales, 86–87
Angers, Anjou, 236, 250, 304, 306, 310, 344–46
　Cathedral, 308–9, 346
　Château of, 110
　Church of Saint-Laud, 346
　Cordeliers, Church of, 121
Angoumois, France, 44
Angus, Earl of (see Douglas, George)
Anjou, France, 109, 111–13, 125, 132–34, 138, 344
　Counts of, 107–8, 112, 120, 139
　House of, 233, 318
Anne de Beaujeu, Dr. of Louis XI, 433
Anne of Bohemia, Queen of England, 19, 30, 32, 463
Anne of Brittany, later Queen of France, 420
Anne of Burgundy, Duchess of Bedford, 53
Anne, Duchess of Buckingham, 160
Antoine, Bastard of Burgundy, 287

Aquitaine, Duchy of, 2, 44, 50, 60, 112, 148, 150, 153, 157
Aragon, Kingdom of, 236
Armagnac, Count of (see John IV)
Armagnacs, French political faction, 32-34, 52, 63
Arras, Bishop of (see Poré, Martin)
  Treaty of, 1435, 93
  Treaty of, 1482, 379
Arthur III, Duke of Brittany, 10, 14, 27, 33, 47, 49, 55, 61
Arthur, King, 66, 450
  Arthurian legends, 227, 472
Arthurton, George, 80
Arundel Castle, Sussex, 28
Arundel, Earls of (see FitzAlan)
Arundel, Thomas, Archbishop of Canterbury, 16, 20, 31-33
Ashby, George, 250
Ashmolean Museum, Oxford, 261
Astley, Joan, 70
Astley Manor. Co. Warwick, 258
Audley, Lord (see Tuchet, James)
Auxerre, France, 34
Avignon, France, 16
Ayscough, William, Bishop of Salisbury, 119, 121, 146

Bacon, Sir Francis, 269, 452-54
Baker, Richard, 136
Baldwin, David, 429
Bamburgh Castle, Northld., 234, 237-39, 241-42, 245, 248, 250-52
Banbury, Oxon., 296, 323
Bangor, Bishop of, 86
Barante, Amable Guillaume Prosper Brugière, Baron de, 112
Barbarigo, Agostino, Doge of Venice, 443
Barnabas, St., 67

Barnard Castle, Co. Durham, lordship, 162
  Castle, 359, 360
  Collegiate Church, 428
Barnet, Herts., 211, 215-16
  Battle of, 1471, 326-27, 329, 339
Barrow, William, Bishop of Carlisle, 89
Barton, Dr. Saxon, 431
Barville, squire, 244
Basin, Thomas, 120
Bath, Knights of the, 124, 273
Bath, Somerset, 102, 330
Battle, Abbot of, 99
Baugé, Battle of, 1421, 67
Bayeux, Grand Vicar of, 318
Baynard's Castle, London, 82, 202, 218, 326, 394, 406
Bayonne, France, 150
Beauchamp, Eleanor, Duchess of Somerset, 143
The Beauchamp Pageant, 20-21, 62, 70, 428
Beauchamp, Richard de, Bishop of Salisbury, 182
Beauchamp, Richard, 13th Earl of Warwick, 80, 177, 428
Beaufort, Dukes of, 28, 32-33, 82, 252
Beaufort, Edmund, 85
Beaufort, Edmund, Duke of Somerset, 92, 125, 131, 135-39
Beaufort, Edmund, "Duke of Somerset," 291
Beaufort, Eleanor, Countess of Wiltshire
Beaufort family, 28-30, 32-33, 136, 141, 257
Beaufort, Henry, Bishop of Lincoln and Winchester, Cardinal, 18-20, 48, 59, 66, 70, 77-79, 81, 90, 92, 107, 119, 123, 137
Beaufort, Henry, Duke of Somerset, 175

Index

Beaufort, Joan, Queen of Scots, 67, 81–82, 200
Beaufort, John, 18, 28
Beaufort, John, Duke of Somerset, 141
Beaufort, John, Earl of Somerset, 141
Beaufort, Margaret, later Countess of Richmond and Derby, 141–42, 155, 175, 180, 234, 297, 334–35, 342, 360, 408, 416–18, 420, 423, 455–56
Beaufort, Thomas, Duke of Exeter, 77
Beaulieu Abbey, Hants., 328, 364
Beaumont, Jeanne de, 5
Beaumont, John, Viscount, 135
Bec-Crespin, Antoine du, Archbishop of Narbonne, 283, 304
Becket, St. Thomas à, 35, 65, 127, 196, 278
Bedford, Beds.
   Duchess of (see Jacquetta of Luxembourg)
   Dukes of (see John of Lancaster, George of York)
Bedford Hours, 51
Bella Court, Greenwich, 137
Benedict XIII, Pope, 16, 82
Benedictine Order, 377, 453
Berkeley Castle, Gloucs., 330
Berkhamsted Castle, Herts., 40, 83, 377
Bermondsey Abbey, Surrey, 57, 99, 456
Bernall, Richard, 362
Berners, Margaret, Lady, 280, 288
Berry, Duke of (see John of Valois)
Berwick, Northld., 201–2, 207, 223–25, 232, 238, 245
Béthune, France, 247
Beverley, Yorks., 208
Bibliothèque Nationale, Paris, 120
Bigorre, France, 44

Birtsmorton Court, Little Malvern, Worcs., 335
Bisham Priory, Berks., 328
Bishop's Waltham Palace, Hants., 77
Blackheath, Kent, 20, 65, 75, 145–46, 273, 337
Black Jack, robber, 244
Black Prince (see Edward of Woodstock)
Blacman, John, 100–102, 121
Blanche of Brittany, 10, 18
Blanche of Lancaster, Duchess of Lancaster, 28
Blanche of Lancaster, Electress Palatine, 29
Blaybourne, archer, 295
Blore Heath, Battle of, 1459, 189
Blount, Walter, Lord Mountjoy, 271, 280
Boccaccio, Giovanni, 110, 249
Bodmin Moor, Cornwall, 18
Bohun, Eleanor de, Duchess of Gloucester, 28
Bohun family and estates, 28, 38–39, 395, 411, 413
Bohun, Humphrey de, Earl of Hereford, Essex, and Northampton, 28
Bohun, Mary de, Countess of Derby, 28–29, 38
Bona of Savoy, 242, 255, 263–64
Boniface IX, Pope, 16
Bonville, William, Lord, 213
Book of Howth, 289
Booth, Laurence, Archbishop of York, 129, 178, 183
Booth, William, Archbishop of York, 129
Bordeaux, Aquitaine, 24, 148, 150, 153, 155, 157
Bosworth, Battle of, 1485, 171, 446–47, 470

Index

Boteler, Dame Alice, 80, 83
Boulogne, France, 13, 74, 246–47
Bourbon, Duchess of (see Jeanne of Valois)
Bourchier family, 257, 259
Bourchier, Henry, 1st Earl of Essex, 259
Bourchier, Henry, 2nd Earl of Essex, 259
Bourchier, John, Lord Ferrers, 234, 258–59
Bourchier, Thomas, Bishop of Ely, Cardinal, Archbishop of Canterbury, 152, 166, 169, 180, 184, 196, 274, 279, 288, 324, 365, 381, 398–99, 396, 408, 415
Bourchier, Sir William, later Lord, 209, 270
Bourges, France, 62
  Archbishop of (see Boisratier, Guillaume de)
Bowet, Henry, Bishop of Bath and Wells, 16
Brampton, Sir Edward, 446
Brancepeth, Co. Durham, 225
Bray, Reginald, 417
Brecknock Castle, Wales, 415, 417
Brecon, Wales, 385, 414, 416, 421
  Charter of, 1409, 88
Brent, Dr, 457
Brest, Château of, Brittany, 11
Breteuil, Château of, Normandy, 5
Brétigny, Treaty of, 1360, 44
Brézé, Pierre de, Sieur de la Varenne, 111
Bridget of Sweden, St., 378
Bridgewater, Edward, 90
Bridport, Dorset, 19
Brington, Northants., 258
Bristol, Somerset, 320, 330
British Library, 45, 120, 171

Brittany, Duchy of, 3–6, 8, 10, 13, 15–18, 24–27, 31, 33, 36, 38, 49, 54, 56, 58, 60, 77–79, 99, 100, 233, 236, 248, 272, 282, 289, 292, 342, 367, 420–23, 429, 432–33, 437, 452
  Dukes of (see John IV, John V)
Brocart, Petronelle, 54
Bromley, Sir John, 271
Bruges, Burgundy, 292, 348, 363, 247–49
Buck, Sir George, 357, 402, 448
Buckden, Hunts., 431
  Bishop of Lincoln's Palace, 431
Buckingham, Dukes of (see Stafford, Humphrey; Stafford, Henry)
Bulgnéville, Battle of, 1431, 108
Bungerly Hippingstones, Lancs., 278
Buntingford, Herts., 211
Burdett, Thomas, 371
Burgh, Alice, 361
Burgh, Isabel, 362
Burgundians, French political faction, 32–34, 50, 108
Burgundy, Duchy of, 15, 26, 185, 228, 233, 241–42, 246–49, 255–56, 269, 271–72, 275, 278–79, 282, 284, 286–88, 304–5, 308, 317, 319–20, 348, 367, 370–71, 378
  Dukes of (see Philip the Bold, John the Fearless, Philip the Good, Charles the Bold)
Butler, Eleanor, 401–3, 405, 423
Butler, James, Earl of Wiltshire, 130, 169
Butler, Ralph, Lord Sudeley, 401
Butler, Thomas, 401
Byleigh, Abbot of, 24
Bywell Castle, Northld., 251–52
Byzantium, 258

Index

Cade, Jack, 145
   Rebellion, 1450, 145–46
Caen, Normandy, 147
Caerleon, Dr Lewis, 419–20
Calais, France, 4, 12, 27, 44 65, 74,
   126, 142, 148–49, 157, 176–77,
   180, 183–86, 188, 192–96, 219,
   230, 236–37, 246–47, 282,
   295–96, 303–4, 314, 320, 340,
   344, 350, 383, 413
Cambridge, Cambs., 431
   University of, 24, 102, 127, 257,
   261, 341, 351, 360, 428, 472
Camoys, Thomas, Lord, 17, 18, 59
Canterbury, Kent, 65, 75, 147, 160,
   165, 296, 304, 351
   Abbey of St. Augustine, 304
   Abbot of St. Augustine's, 99
   Blean Wood, 127
   Cathedral, 22, 35, 99, 127, 160, 196,
   261–62, 278
   Convocation of, 196
   Cross of, 197
   Prior of Christchurch, 99
Capet, House of, 27
Capgrave, John, 119
Capua, Palace of, Italy, 110
Carlisle, Cumb., 225, 244
   Bishop of (see Barrow, William)
Carmarthen Castle, Wales, 179–80
Castile, Kingdom of, 5, 28
Castillon, Aquitaine, 157
Catesby, Sir William, 436, 444–45
Catherine, St., 66
Catour, William, 134
Caxton, William, 227, 262, 350–51, 428
Cawood Castle, Yorks., 279
Cecily of York, Dr. of Edward IV, 366
Cerne Abbey, Dorset, 328
Chabot, Jeanne, Madame de
   Montsoreau, 346

Chalons, France, 113
Chamberlayne, Margaret, 118
Champagne, France, 60
Channel Islands, 232
Chapel Royal 343, 428
Charlemagne, Roman Emperor, 257
Charles the Bold, Count of Charolais,
   later Duke of Burgundy, 107, 287,
   291, 318, 370
Charles, Count of Maine, 258
Charles I, Count of Nevers, 111–12
Charles of Valois, Dauphin of France
   (see Charles VII)
Charles of Valois, Dauphin of France
   (see Charles VIII)
Charles V, King of France, 5, 44, 370
Charles VI, King of France, 3, 8–10, 12,
   18 27, 29, 32, 34, 40, 43–45, 50,
   52, 61, 64, 71, 95
Charles VII, King of France, 91–92,
   107–8, 111–12, 114, 132, 134,
   138, 140, 150, 157, 182, 185, 192,
   207–8, 232, 249
Charles VIII, King of France, 305, 437,
   446
Charles II, King of Navarre, 4
Charles of Valois, Duke of Orléans,
   45–46, 107, 117, 126, 128, 237
Charlotte of Savoy, Queen of France,
   242, 305
Charter Rolls, 121
Charterhouse, Sheen, 288
   Prior of, 457
Chastellain, Georges, 119, 243, 245, 249
Château Gaillard, Normandy, 58
Chaucer, Alice, Duchess of Suffolk,
   114, 117, 142–43, 153, 156, 342
Chaucer, Geoffrey, 38–39, 89, 114, 340
Chaucer, Thomas, 43
Cheapside, London, 20, 82, 124, 278,
   313

Chelsea, London, 394
Cheltenham, Gloucs., 331
Chepstow Castle, Wales, 296, 335
Cherbourg, Normandy, 117
Chertsey Abbey, Surrey, 79, 341
Chester, City of, 176-77
   Castle, 198
Cheylesmore Manor, Co. Warwick, 178
Chichele, Henry, Archbishop of Canterbury, 59, 63, 65-66, 70
Chinon, France, 237
Chipping Sodbury, Gloucs., 330
Cinque Ports, 196
   Barons of the, 65, 219, 274, 408
Cirencester, Gloucs., 25, 330
Clarence, Duke of (see Lionel of Antwerp, Thomas of Lancaster, Plantagenet, George)
Clarendon, Wilts., 157
Cleger, John, 198
Clercq, Jacques du, 264
Clere, Edmund, 167
Clifford, John, Lord, 170, 205-6, 212, 219
Clisson, Château de, Brittany, 10
Clisson, Oliver de, 7-11, 14
Cobb, Marjory, 315, 325
Cobham, Eleanor, Duchess of Gloucester, 79
Coke, Sir Edward, 89
Colchester, Essex
   Abbot of, 24
College of Arms, London, 428
Colles, Roger, 54, 56
Collins, Jane, 362
Commines, Philippe de, 100, 162, 226, 229, 295, 308, 332, 337-38, 346, 374, 401-2, 424, 434, 444
Comper, Sebastian, 442
Constance of Castile, Duchess of Lancaster, 28

Conwy Castle, Conwy, 30
Conyers, Sir John, 294-97
Cook, Sir Thomas, Lord Mayor of London, 273, 291
Coombe, John, 198
Coppini, Francesco dei, Bishop of Terni, 196-97, 207, 277
Corbeil, France, 63, 72
Corbet, Sir Richard, 314
Cork, spy, 244
Cornelius, shoemaker, 290
Cornwall, John, 27
Cosne, France, 72
Court of Common Pleas, 26
Court of King's Bench, 26
Courtenay family, 421
Courtenay, Henry, 290
Courtenay, Elizabeth, Countess of Devon, 331
Courtenay, Richard, Bishop of Norwich, 43
Courtenay, Thomas, 13th Earl of Devon, 183
Coventry, Co. Warwick, 151, 177-78, 180-83, 187-88, 192-93, 195-97, 268, 288, 297-98, 303, 321, 323, 336, 414
   Castle, 178
   Corpus Christi plays, 182
   Grocers' Guild, 182
   St. Mary's Guildhall, 178
   Tapestry, 178
Craon, Peter de, 10
Crécy, Battle of, 1346, 47
Crosby, Sir John, 394
Croyland (Crowland) Abbey, Lincs., 295
   Chronicle, 168, 171, 208-9, 222, 287, 318, 332-33, 340, 374, 383-84, 392, 399, 403, 412, 423, 425, 429, 432, 434-35, 429, 440-41, 446-48

Index

Crull, John, 97
Cun, Benedict, 456
Curteys, Piers, 407

Damme, Flanders, 291
Dampierre, France, Château of, 345–46
Danzig, Germany, 262, 416
Darcy, Elizabeth, Lady, 350
Dartford, Kent, 57, 75, 455
    Priory, 455, 457
Dartmouth, Devon, 27, 50, 195, 311
Daunt, John, 330
Davies, John, 134
Dean, Forest of, 298
Defoe, Daniel, 87
Deincourt, Alice, Lady Lovell, 195
De La Motte, Château of, Vannes 3, 7–8
Denbigh, Wales, 103,
    Castle, 198–99, 200, 292
Denis, St., 9, 72, 74, 81
Denmark, 49, 378
Devizes Castle, Wilts., 31
Devon, Earls of (see Courtenay, Thomas; Courtenay, John)
Dieppe, Normandy, 319
Dijon, France, 63, 109
Dissolution of the Monasteries, 263, 455
Docket, Andrew, Rector of St. Botolph's, Cambridge, 127–28, 351
Dolcereau, Maurice, 182, 192, 208
Domfront, Normandy, 50
Dominican Order, 365, 455
Doncaster, Yorks., 312, 414
Dorchester, Dorset, 19
Dordogne, River, 19
Douglas, George, Earl of Angus, 151, 201

Douglas, James, Earl of Douglas, 151, 201
Dover, Kent, 65, 67, 75, 142, 304, 319
    Castle, 304
    Straits of, 142
Dresdner, Scotland, 223
Droget, John, 428
Drogheda, Ireland, 289
Dublin, Ireland, 51, 145, 148, 182–83, 193, 289
Dudley, Lord (see Sutton, John)
Dumfries, Scotland, 200, 223
Dundas, Duncan, 200
Dunfermline Palace, Scotland, 225
Dunham Massey, Cheshire, 261
Dunstable, Beds., 211, 213, 215–16, 323
Dunstable, John, 79
Dunstanburgh Castle, Northld., 238, 240–41, 252
Durham, City of, 179, 225, 239, 251, 359
    Consorority of St. Cuthbert, 360
    Prior of, 360
    Priory (later the Cathedral), 360, 428
Dymock, Sir Robert, 409
Dynham, Sir John, 194

Earl Marshal (see Mowbray, John)
Easebourne Priory, Midhurst, Sussex, 104
East Court, Heytesbury, Wilts., 429
Eborall, John, Vicar of Paulerspury, 263
Eccleshall Castle, Staffs., 188–89, 197–98
Edgcote, Battle of, 1469, 296, 298, 302
Edinburgh, Scotland, 206, 223, 244, 366
    Blackfriars, Cowgate, 223

Edington Priory, Wiltshire, 146
Edmund "Crouchback," Earl of Lancaster, 31, 357
Edmund of Langley, Duke of York, 28
Edward of Clarence, Earl of Warwick, 368, 395, 450
Edward the Confessor, St., King of England, 25, 31, 34, 75, 159, 177, 218, 312, 324, 364
Edward, Earl of March (see Edward IV)
Edward of Lancaster, Prince of Wales, 305, 307, 332
Edward of Middleham, Earl of Salisbury, later Prince of Wales, 361, 375, 414, 432
Edward of Woodstock, the Black Prince, 27, 35, 159, 178
Edward I, King of England, 31
Edward II, King of England, 129, 406, 462-63
Edward III, King of England, 6, 26-27, 30, 40, 47, 57, 69, 136, 141, 159, 384, 416, 455
Edward IV, King of England, 24, 218, 222-24, 226, 229, 233-36, 239, 240, 244, 246, 247, 252, 257, 260-62, 269, 270, 276, 278, 280, 284, 289, 292, 297-99, 300, 305, 307, 310-15, 317, 319, 320, 322, 327-29, 332, 335-39, 342, 350, 355, 357, 363, 367, 369, 370-71, 374-76, 378-79, 380-87, 392-93, 397, 400-403, 412-13, 416-17, 420, 422, 428, 430, 447-48, 453, 456-58, 462
Edward V, King of England, 261, 380, 382-83, 385-86, 391-95, 397, 399, 400, 402, 406, 411-12, 416, 436
Edward of Westminster, Prince of Wales (see Edward V)
Edward of Woodstock, Prince of Wales ("the Black Prince"), 27, 35, 159, 178
Eleanor of Castile, Queen of England, 30, 461-30
Eleanor of Provence, Queen of England, 57, 164, 461-63
Elizabeth of Lancaster, Countess of Huntingdon, 66
Elizabeth of York, Duchess of Suffolk, 272, 396, 408
Elizabeth of York, later Queen of England, 178, 351, 413, 417, 419, 420, 422, 424, 426, 430, 433, 437-38, 440, 444-47, 449, 450, 452-53, 455-56, 458
Eltham Palace, Kent, 16, 20, 22, 25, 65, 123, 228, 377-78
Ely, Bishops of (see Bourchier, Thomas)
Isle of, 197
Emma, wife of William de Wydville, 256
English Channel, 47, 320
Eric IX, King of Denmark, 31
Ermine Street, 171
Estella, Navarre, 4-5
Estney, John, Prior of Westminster, 315
Eton College, 102, 120, 341, 351
Provost of, 275
Eugenius IV, Pope, 101
Ewelme, Oxon., 342-43
Exchequer, 112, 318, 443, 453-54, 458
Exeter, Devon, 18, 303, 311, 330, 409, 421
Duchess of (see Anne of York)
Dukes of (see Holland, John; Holland, Henry)

Fabyan, Robert, 184, 186, 262, 416
Falaise, Normandy, 50

Index

Falkland Palace, Scotland, 201
Falmouth, Cornwall, 18
Farnham Castle, Surrey, 20
Fauconberg, Lord (see Neville, William)
Ferdinand II, Archduke of Austria, 437
Ferdinand II, King of Aragon, 368
Ferdinand II, King of Naples, 437
Ferrers, Elizabeth, Lady, 258
Ferrers family, 257-59
Ferrers, Lord (see Bourchier, John)
Ferrers, William, Lord, 234
Fèvre, Raoul le, 351
FitzAlan, Joan, Lady Bergavenny, 54
FitzAlan, Richard, 4th Earl of Arundel, 18
FitzAlan, Thomas, 10th Earl of Arundel, 270
Fitzgerald, James, Earl of Desmond, 375
Fitzgerald, Thomas, Earl of Desmond, 289
  sons of, 289
FitzHugh, Elizabeth, 130
FitzHugh, Henry, Lord, 311
FitzJohn, James, 289
Flanders, County of, 58, 126, 272, 291
Flintshire, Wales, 90
Flushing (Vlissingen), Zeeland, 320
Fogge, Sir John, 271
Fortescue, Sir John, 168, 175, 201, 235-36, 245, 250, 306, 322, 334
Fotheringhay, Northants., 24, 367
  Castle, 49, 295, 338-39, 362, 367
Fountains Abbey, Yorks., 124, 414
Fox, Richard, 420
Francis II, Duke of Brittany, 236
Francis, Master, physician, 118
Francis, Sieur de Luxembourg, Viscount of Geneva, 456
Frederick III, Holy Roman Emperor, 110, 250, 368

Frederick I, King of Denmark, 378
French Revolution, 346
Froissart, Jean, 7, 13, 30

Galtres, Forest of, Yorks., 222, 413
Garter, Order and Knights of the, 6, 13, 32, 49, 69, 78, 137, 160, 165, 329, 369, 377, 450, 456-57
Gascony, France, 44, 59, 78, 150
Gate, Sir Geoffrey, 313
George II, King of Great Britain, 97
George III, King of Great Britain, 458
George, St., 28, 49, 52, 69, 72, 121, 227, 329, 369, 377, 457
George of York, Duke of Bedford, 369
Giles's Chronicle, 85
Glamorgan, Wales, lordship of, 361
Glastonbury, Somerset, 330
Glendower, Owen, 24, 86
Glengauny, Anglesey, 87
Gloucester, City of, 78, 90, 330-31, 413-14
  Dukes of (see Thomas of Woodstock, Humphrey of Lancaster, Richard III)
Goldsmiths' Company, 114, 228
Gonzaga, Anne, Archduchess of Austria, 437
Gosford Green, Coventry, Co. Warwick, 298
Gould, John, 315, 325
Grace, bastard Dr. of Edward IV, 456
Grafton, Northants., 135, 408
  The Hermitage, 263
Grafton, Richard, 256, 259, 263
Grantham, Lincs., 302
Gray, Thomas, 347
Great Ness Church, Shropshire, 121
Great North Road, 209
Great Schism, 1378, 16

Greenwich, Kent (see also Placentia), 32, 123, 137, 145, 153, 167, 172, 174–75, 228–29, 378, 411, 450, 455–56
Gregory, chronicler, 86, 252, 256
Gregory III, Patriarch of Jerusalem, 318
Grey, Catherine, 458
Grey, Sir Edward, 258
Grey, Edward, Viscount Lisle, 408
Grey, Isabella (see FitzHugh), 129
Grey, Sir John, 130, 212, 258–59, 260
Grey, Sir Ralph, 130
Grey, Sir Richard, 365, 381, 385, 427, 437, 445
Grey, Thomas, later Marquess of Dorset, 259, 271, 332, 349, 373, 376, 387, 392–93, 403, 450
Greystoke, Elizabeth, Lady Scrope, 315
Groby, Leics., 258
    Manor (Groby Hall), 258
Gruffydd, Elis, 86
Gruthuyse, Louis, Lord of, Earl of Winchester, 363–64
Guernsey, Channel Isles, 54
Guildford, Surrey, 421
Gupshill Castle, Gloucs., 331
    Manor 331, 334
Gurney, Giles (see Wigmore, Edward de)
Guy's Cliffe, Warwick, 308, 414

Hall, Edward, 130, 414
Hanseatic League, 185, 320
Hardyng, John, 101, 263
Harfleur, Normandy, 47, 70, 117, 140, 301, 310, 322, 446
Harlech Castle, Wales, 198, 252, 292
    Siege of, 1464, 252, 292
Harleian manuscripts, 408

Hastings, Sir William, later Lord, 230, 259, 264, 273, 275–76, 297, 312, 329, 332–33, 350, 363, 368, 380–84, 386, 390–92, 395–97
Hatfield, Hertfordshire, 90
Haute family, 271
Haute, Mr, 457
Haute, Sir Richard, 350, 365, 385, 387, 395, 403
Haute, Sir William, 256, 271
Havering atte Bower, Essex, 31
Hawes, Stephen, 340
Hawkins, spy, 290–91
Hazes, Jean de, 344
Hearne, Thomas, 97
Heathfield, Sussex, 147
Hedgeley Moor, Battle of, 1464, 251
Henry of Bolingbroke, Duke of Lancaster (see Henry IV, King of England)
Henry II, King of England, 139, 462–63
Henry III, King pf England, 31, 57, 203
Henry IV, King of England, 3, 12, 15–16, 18, 21, 23–26, 28, 30–32, 35–37, 99, 100, 141, 218, 266
Henry V, King of England, 24, 29, 38–39, 47, 50, 52, 55–56, 58, 62, 67, 70, 73, 76–78, 80, 85–86, 91, 94–95, 97, 112, 136
Henry VI, King of England, 24, 74, 76–79, 83–84, 91–94, 96, 98, 100, 104, 107, 112–13, 117–18, 120, 125, 132, 135–36, 140, 141, 144–45, 147, 149, 150, 154–55, 157, 166, 170, 174–78, 180, 184–86, 189, 193, 198, 201, 203–4, 206, 208, 212, 217–19, 223–26, 229, 235, 238–39, 241, 245, 251–52, 257, 263, 266, 277–78, 290, 301–2, 304–6, 308,

Index

312–18, 320, 323–24, 327–28, 335, 326, 338–39, 346, 382–84, 386, 406, 456
Henry VII, King of England, 33, 86, 95–96, 98, 100–101, 103–4, 171, 178, 180, 234–35, 297, 314, 335, 342, 346, 378, 416–17, 420, 423–24, 426, 429, 432–33, 435, 437, 446–49, 450–51, 453–54
Henry VIII, King of England, 24, 55, 226–27, 289, 436, 456
Henry of Monmouth (see Henry V)
Heraucourt, Louis de, Bishop of Toul, 114
Herbert, Maud, 234
Herbert, Sir Richard, 292
Herbert, William, Earl of Huntingdon, 340
Herbert, Sir William, later Earl of Pembroke, 179, 181–82, 187, 191, 207, 230, 234, 296–97, 316
Herbert, William, Lord Dunster, 252, 271, 282, 292–93
Hereford, City of, 182, 202, 210, 314, 325
  Beacon, 335
  Church of the Greyfriars, 211
l'Hermine, Château of, Vannes, 8, 10
Hertford, Herts., 40, 83, 90
  Castle, 77, 81, 83, 93, 175
Hesdin, France, 74, 255
Hexham, Northld., 239, 251, 300
  Battle of, 1464, 252
  Forest, 244
  Priory, 239, 252
Heytesbury, Devizes, Wilts., 429–30, 441
Heytesbury House, Wilts., 429–30, 441
Higden, Ranulf, 120
Hitchin, Herts., 156, 211
Hoccleve, Thomas, 38
Holinshed, Raphael, 40, 206, 474

Holland, Anne, Marchioness of Dorset, 271
Holland, Joan, Duchess of Brittany, 6
Holland, Margaret, Duchess of Clarence, 63
Holland, Principality of, 294, 363
Holme Park, Sonning, Berks., 31
Holy Island (Lindisfarne), Northld., 239
Holy Sepulchre, Church of the, Jerusalem, 258
Honfleur, Normandy, 140, 304
Howard, Sir John, later Duke of Norfolk, 267, 274, 276, 303, 421, 440
Howard, Thomas, Earl of Arundel, 441
Howard, Thomas, Earl of Surrey, 408
Hudson, Thomas, 261
Hull, Yorks., 199, 207–8
Humphrey of Lancaster, Duke of Gloucester, 29, 34, 56, 59, 70, 383
Hungary, Kingdom of, 109
Hungerford, Sir Walter, 86,
Hundred Years War, 23, 157, 282, 468
Hungerford, Robert, Lord, 198, 290
Hungerford, Thomas, 290
Huntingdon, Hunts.
  Dowager Countess of (see Elizabeth of Lancaster)
  Earl of (see Holland, John, Duke of Exeter)

Idley, Anne, 362
Idley, Peter, 362
Ightham Mote, Kent, 256, 421
Ipswich, Suffolk, 142
Ireland, 16, 32, 138–39, 140, 182, 192–93, 195–97, 202, 289, 314, 370, 411, 433, 450

Isabeau of Bavaria, Queen of France, 44–46, 50–52, 61, 64, 71, 82
Isabella, Duchess of Lorraine, Countess of Anjou, 155
Isabella of France, Queen of England, 8, 29, 45, 52, 129, 347, 561–62
Isabella of Luxembourg, Countess of Maine, 258
Isabella of Portugal, Duchess of Burgundy, 107–10, 115, 371
Isabella I, Queen of Castile, 268, 368, 414
Isabella of Valois, Queen of England, 12, 16, 461, 463
Isle Belle, River Seine, 51
Isle of Sheppey, Kent, 146
Islington, Middx., 278
Italy, 111, 178, 257

Jacqueline, Countess of Hainault, Holland and Zeeland, Duchess of Gloucester, 56, 67, 70, 79, 82
Jacques of Luxembourg, Seigneur de Richebourg, 274
Jacquetta of Luxembourg, Duchess of Bedford, 194, 256–58, 262, 271, 274, 299, 422
James I, King of Scots, 57, 62, 64, 66, 474
James II, King of Scots, 200
James III, King of Scots, 200, 250, 378, 451, 454–55
James IV, King of Scots, 366
Jeanne of Navarre, Viscountess de Rohan, 6
Jeanne II, Queen of Navarre, 5
Jeanne of Valois, 4
Jeanne of Valois, Duchess of Brittany, 45, 58
Jeanne of Valois, Queen of Navarre, 4
Jersey, Island of, 232

Jerusalem
 Kingdom of, 4, 34–35, 38, 73, 109, 124, 258, 318
 Siege of, 291
Jervaulx Abbey, Yorks., 414
Jeune, Robert le, 64
Joan of Arc, 91–92, 108
Joan of Navarre, Queen of England, 3–4, 24, 45, 61, 99, 236, 266, 428, 461–62
Joana of Portugal, 446
Joanna of Bavaria, Duchess of Austria, 13
Joanna II, Queen of the Two Sicilies, 109
Johanna of Bavalen, 12–13
John of Calabria, son of René, Duke of Anjou, Count of Lorraine, 108, 116, 248, 250, 286, 341
John IV, Count of Armagnac, 50, 107
John I, Duke of Alençon, 47
John IV, Duke of Brabant, 67, 82
John the Fearless, Duke of Burgundy, 33, 45–46, 52, 56, 61, 63
John of Gaunt, Duke of Lancaster, 57, 141, 160, 277, 309, 371
John of Lancaster, Duke of Bedford, 40, 53, 64, 256, 303, 369
John II, King of France, 4
John II, King of Portugal, 277
John IV de Montfort, Duke of Brittany, 5–6, 8, 13, 32, 36
John V de Montfort, Duke of Brittany, 14, 18, 27, 31–32, 37, 45, 50, 58, 77–79
John of Pontefract, 340
John I, Viscount de Rohan, 10
Johns, Sir Hugh, 258
Jones, Sir Thomas Artemus, 89
Joscelin, Château of, Brittany, 11
Juana of Aragon, Queen of Naples, 437
Juvissy, France, 437

Index

Katherine of Valois, Queen of England, 24–25, 44, 96, 132, 428, 453
Kempe, Cardinal Thomas, Archbishop of Canterbury, 146, 152–53, 165
Kendall, John, 414–15
Kenilworth Castle, Co. Warwick, 176, 181
Kennedy, James, Bishop of St. Andrews, 200
Kennington Palace, Surrey, 80
Kent, Dowager Countess of (see Visconti, Lucia)
King's College, Cambridge, 102, 341, 428
King's Langley, Herts., 73
King's Lynn, Norfolk (see also Bishop's Lynn)
  Museum, 63
"The King's Quair," 81
Kingston, Surrey, 80, 336
Kirkcudbright, Scotland
  Bay, 236, 244
  Greyfriars, 223
Knaresborough, York., 361
Koeur-la-Petite, Château of, Lorraine, 249
Kynwolmersh, William, 56
Kyriell, Sir Thomas, 182, 213

Lake District, 252
Lambert, John, 349
Lambeth Palace, London, 261
  Library, 360
Lanark, Scotland, 223
Lancaster, Duchy of, 26, 32, 77, 235
  Earls and Dukes of (see Edmund "Crouchback," John of Gaunt, Henry IV)
  House of, 11, 23, 38–39, 76, 100, 162, 170–71, 175–76, 179, 180, 200–201, 219, 270, 283, 301, 305, 309, 314, 329, 333, 335, 342, 344, 384, 417, 422, 449
Langley, Herts82, 48, 79, 82, 251
Langley, Thomas, Bishop of Durham, 43
Langstrother, Sir John, 322
Langton, Thomas, Bishop of St. David's, 433
Leeds Castle, Kent, 30, 57–58, 73, 87
  Gloriette, 30, 78
Leicester, Leics., 145, 170–71, 187, 198, 230, 258, 321, 357
Leland, John, 90
Leo, Lord of Rozmital, 281
Lilbourne, Thomas, 58
Lille, Burgundy, 247, 470
Limousin, France, 44
Lincluden Abbey, Scotland, 200, 223
Lincoln, City of, 209
  Bishop of (see Alnwick, William)
  Diocese of, 358
Lindsay, James, Provost of Dumfries, 200
Linlithgow Palace, Scotland, 223
Lionel of Antwerp, Duke of Clarence, 27–28
Lisieux, Normandy, 50
Little Malvern Priory, Worcs., 261, 335
Liverpool Cathedral, 262
Llywelyn, Howel ap, 88
Loire, River, 305
London, City of, 25, 48, 83, 120, 124, 204, 356, 425, 444
  Aldgate, 33, 216, 378
  Bishops of, 90
  Bishopsgate, 337, 394
  Blackfriars Priory, 341, 433
  Bridge, 65, 123, 223, 263, 273, 337
  Cheapside, 20, 82, 124, 278, 313
  Coldharbour, 447
  Cornhill, 124, 278
  Court of Common Council, 182, 196

London, City of (*cont.*)
  Crosby Place, Bishopsgate, 394
  The Erber, Dowgate, 355
  Great Chronicle of, 90, 333, 362, 374, 399, 444
  Knightrider Street, 269
  Leadenhall, 124, 275
  Lord Mayors of, 20, 61, 65–67, 70, 123, 152, 159, 196, 204, 213–15, 273, 291, 296, 298, 313, 336, 352, 400, 405, 409
  Ludgate Prison, 397
  Minoresses' Convent, Aldgate, 378
  Newgate, 98, 103, 278, 356
  Port of, 49
  St. John's Fields, 217
  St. Martin le Grand, College of, 356
  Smithfield, 134, 269, 270
  Southwark, 81–82, 124, 289
"Lords Appellant," 29
Lorraine, Duchy of, France, 107–9, 111, 115, 344
"Losecoat Field," Battle of, 1470, 302
Louis II, Count of Anjou, 108
Louis of Bavaria, 46
Louis IX, St., King of France, 373, 379
Louis X, King of France, 4–5
Louis XI, King of France, 233, 255, 264, 266, 268, 292–95, 301, 317, 370–72, 424
Louppy-le-Château, Lorraine, 250
Louviers, Normandy, 50
The Loveday, 1458, 184–85
Lovelace, Sir Henry, 212
Lovell, Francis, Lord, 198, 235
Lovell, Lady (see Deincourt, Alice)
Low Countries, 67, 233, 462
Low, John, Bishop of Rochester, 274
Lübeck, Germany, 185–86
Lucy, Elizabeth, 229

Ludlow, Heref.
  Castle, 148, 152–53, 180, 184, 188–89, 190–91, 207, 365–66, 379
Lund, Sweden, 31
Luton, Beds., 211
  Guild Book, 262
Luxembourg, House of, 272
Lyard Lewes, horse, 267
Lydgate, John, 38, 83, 119
Lyon, France, 126

Madeleine of Valois, 134
Magine, Théophanie la, 108
Maine, France, 60, 109, 111–13, 125, 132–34, 138, 258
Majerres, chronicler, 284
Majorca, Island of, 113
Malestroit, Jean de, Bishop of Nantes, 58
Malmesbury, Wilts., 330
Malpas Castle, Cheshire, 198
Mancini, Dominic, 227, 229, 262, 265–66, 268, 373–75, 379, 380–81, 384, 386–87, 394, 399, 403, 406, 424
Le Mans, Maine, 138
Mantes, France, 52, 70, 117
Manuel I, King of Portugal, 446
Map, Walter, 351
March, Earls of (see Mortimer, Edmund; Edward IV)
Marche, Olivier de la, 62, 227, 374
Marches, Council of the, 366, 386, 395
Marches of Wales, 170, 207, 225, 316, 320, 339, 365, 366, 385
Margaret of Anjou, Queen of England, 24, 107, 112, 178, 218, 257–58, 261, 269, 286, 305, 347, 372, 449, 461

Index

Margaret of Austria, 379
Margaret of Bavaria, Duchess of Lorraine, 108
Margaret of York, later Duchess of Burgundy, 282, 286, 288, 291, 370
Marguerite of Brittany, Viscountess de Rohan, 6
Marie of Anjou, Queen of France, 236
Marie, Countess of Eu, 3
Margaret of Anjou, Queen of England, 24, 107, 112, 178, 218, 257–58, 269, 305, 347, 372, 449, 461
Market Bosworth, Leics., 446
Market Drayton, Salop., 189
Markham, Sir John, 290
Marlow, John, Abbot of Bermondsey, 453
Marseilles, France, 110
Martin, St., 81, 113, 356
Mary of Burgundy, later Duchess of Burgundy, 370–71, 379
Mary of York, Dr. of Edward IV, 458
Maximilian of Austria, later Holy Roman Emperor, 379
McGrigor, Mary, 80
Meaux, France, 70–71
Mechtild of Hackeborn, St., 360
Melun, France, 45, 58, 63–64
Melusine, mythical ancestress of royalty, 257, 298
Mercers' Company, London, 275
  Acts of Court of, 443, 445
Merchant Adventurers' Company, London, 275
Merchants of the Staple, 65, 126
Merciless Parliament, 1388, 29
Meredith, John ap, 88, 93
Meyerbeer, Giacomo, 347
Michelle of Valois, Duchess of Burgundy, 44–46

Middleham, Yorks.
  Castle, 170, 234, 298, 359, 383, 431
  Collegiate Church of St. Mary and St. Alkelda, 432
  Prince's Tower (Round Tower), 361
Milan, Italy, 45–46, 225
  ambassadors, 111, 119, 120, 126, 167, 200, 215, 219, 220–21, 224, 230, 260, 262, 264, 283–84, 286, 304, 310, 322, 338, 360
Milano, Pietro di, 120
Milford Haven, Wales, 446
Milling, Thomas, Abbot of Westminster, later Bishop of Hereford, 312–13, 325
Minorca, Island of, 113
Minster House, Ripon, 261
Moine, Johan de, 50
Moneypenny, William, 293
Monmouth Castle, Mon., 29
Monstrelet, Enguerrand de, 51, 65, 74, 257
Montereau, France, 52, 63
Montgomery, Sir Thomas, 343–44
Montlhery, Battle of, 1465, 278
Montreuil-sur-Mer, France, 44
More, Sir Thomas, 130, 260
Mortimer, Anne, Countess of Cambridge, 28, 201
Mortimer, Edmund, 3rd Earl of March, 27
Mortimer, Edmund, 5th Earl of March, 30–31, 39, 66, 134, 152
Mortimer family, 179
Mortimer's Cross, Battle of, 1461, 210–11
Mortlake, Surrey, 32
Morton, Dr. John, later Bishop of Ely, Cardinal, Archbishop of Canterbury, 223, 238, 245, 250, 322, 334, 343, 396, 415–17, 423, 433, 449

The Mote, Maidstone, Kent, 256
Mowbray, Anne, Duchess of Norfolk and York, 372-73, 378
Mowbray, John, 4th Duke of Norfolk, 372
Much Hadham, Palace, Hertfordshire, 90
Mucklestone Church, Salop., 189

Naish Priory, Somerset, 22
Nancy, France, 108, 114, 116, 249, 283
   Battle of, 1477, 370
   Cathedral, 114
Nantes, Brittany, 6, 8-9, 13-14, 17-18, 32, 34
   Bishop of (see Malestroit, Jean de), 58
   Cathedral, 14, 32
Naples, Italy, 109-10
National Archives, Kew, 256, 269
National Portrait Gallery, London, 100
Navarre, Kingdom of, 5, 16-18, 27, 30
Nesfield, John, 413, 429
Neve, William, 261
Neville, Anne, Queen of England, 24-25, 303, 307-8, 310, 314, 318-19, 326, 332, 334-36, 355, 358, 406, 462
Neville, Cecily, Duchess of York, 156
Neville family, 162, 170, 174, 177, 230, 252, 269, 270-71, 279, 287, 294, 297, 300, 303, 308, 357, 359, 360, 370, 415
Neville, George, later Archbishop of York, 217, 271, 279, 280, 287
Neville, George, Duke of Bedford, 303, 369
Neville, Isabel, Duchess of Clarence, 293
Neville, Humphrey, 300-301
Neville, John, Lord Montagu, later Marquess of Montagu, 225, 242, 251, 272

Neville, Katherine, Dowager Duchess of Norfolk, 270
Neville, Ralph, 433
Neville, Ralph, Earl of Westmorland, 26, 28
Neville, Richard, Earl of Salisbury, 43, 91, 161, 433
Neville, Richard, Earl of Warwick, 161, 209-19, 223-25, 229-37, 239-42, 245, 255-56, 258, 263-64, 266-67, 270-72, 275-76, 278-79, 280-82, 284-88, 291-98, 300-323, 327-29, 339, 355, 357, 364-65, 368, 371, 383, 400
Neville, Robert, 433
Neville, Thomas, Bastard of Fauconberg, 311, 320, 336
Neville, William, Lord Fauconberg, 188, 197
Newark, Notts., 295
Newbottle, Northants., 258
Newbury, Berks., 421
Newcastle, Northld., 223-24, 242, 251
Newgate Prison, 98, 103, 278, 356
Newmarket, Suffolk, 126
New York Public Library, 340
Nicholas, Joan of Navarre's minstrel, 59
Norbury, John, 15-16
Norfolk, Dukes of (see Mowbray, John)
Norham Castle, Northld., 242
Norman Conquest, 1066, 31, 263
Normandy, Duchy of, France, 5, 27, 47, 50, 54-55, 60-61, 76, 90, 93, 111-12, 116-17, 132, 139, 140, 144, 147-48, 182, 208, 237, 309, 311, 319, 344, 346
North, Council of the, 430
North Sea, 245, 370
Northampton, Northants., 197-98
   Battle of, 1460, 197, 202
Northumberland, Earls of (see Percy)

Index

Northumberland House, London, 28
Norwich, Norfolk, 156, 402
  Bishop of (see Brunce, Thomas)
  Cathedral, 79
  Church of the Carmelite friars, 402
  Friars Preachers, 298
  Westwyk Gate, 298
Nottingham, Notts., 205, 295, 303, 321, 414, 429, 431
  Castle, 428, 431–32
  Earl of (see Mowbray, Thomas)

Ogle, Sir Robert, 223
Okehampton, Devon, 18
Okerlund, Arlene, 455
Oliver, Count of Penthièvre, 6, 58
Olney, Co. Warwick, 297
Orléans, Dukes of (see Louis of Valois, Charles of Valois)
  Siege of, 1428–29, 91
Ormond, Earls of (see also Butler), 269, 277, 378
Ormond Place, London, 269
Orsini, Giambattista, Cardinal, 50
Ospringe, Kent, 75
Owen, Sir David (Davy), 450
Owlpen Manor, Gloucs., 330
Oxford, Earls of (see Vere)
  Shrine of St. Frideswide, 377
  University of, 223, 371, 377, 428
Oxney, John, Prior of Christchurch, Canterbury, 304

Pamplona, Navarre, 5–7
Paris, France, 3, 5, 12, 13, 18, 30, 37, 43, 45, 46, 51–52, 64, 70–72, 92, 116–17, 120, 250, 292, 314, 318–19, 338, 346, 360, 373
  Cathedral of Notre-Dame, 71, 92, 116, 314
  Châtelet, 318
  Hôtel de Nesle, 72
  Hôtel de Saint-Pol, 12, 44, 64, 71
  Parlement, 64
  Porte Saint Antoine, 64
  Sainte Chapelle, 373
  University, 64, 318
Parliament, 64, 318
Pasche, William, 428
Paston, John, 167, 272, 301
Paston Letters, 128, 186, 327, 364
Patay, Battle of, 1429, 91
Paul II, Pope, 285
Payne's Place, Bushley, Gloucs., 334
Payntour, John, 357
Pelham, Sir John, 57
Pembroke Castle, Wales, 103, 180, 234, 335
Penmynydd, Anglesey, 86
Penthièvre, House of, 6–7, 9, 14, 58
Pepys, Samuel, 96
Percy family, 24, 28, 32, 97, 252, 293, 303
Percy, Henry, 1st Earl of Northumberland, 16, 18
Percy, Henry, 2nd Earl of Northumberland, 99
Percy, Henry, 3rd Earl of Northumberland, 170, 175, 205, 208, 219, 221, 235, 252, 296, 302
Percy, Henry, 4th Earl of Northumberland, 303, 320, 395
Percy, Sir Henry "Hotspur," 16, 25
Périgord, France, 44
Peter, Count of Luxembourg and Saint-Pol, 256–57
Peter, Duke of Alençon, 11
Peterborough, Cambs., 209
  Abbey, 79
Petrarch, Francesco, 102
Petronilla, St., 65
Pevensey Castle, Sussex, 57

Philadelphia Free Library, 59
Philip, Archduke of Austria, later Philip I, King of Castile, 378
Philip the Bold, Duke of Burgundy, 10, 45
Philip the Good, Duke of Burgundy, 45, 52–53, 61, 77, 82, 93, 107, 109, 112, 153, 184–85, 233, 241–42, 246–49, 272, 274–75, 286–87, 351
Philippa of Clarence, Countess of March, 27, 201
Philippa of Hainault, Queen of England, 461–63
Picquigny, France
Treaty of, 1475, 343, 367
Pierre of Luxembourg, 109
Pirgo Palace, Havering atte Bower, Essex, 31, 79, 99
Pisan, Christine de, 110
Pius II, Pope, 96–97
Placentia, Palace of, Greenwich, 137, 450
Plantagenet, Arthur, 229
Plantagenet, Edmund, Earl of Rutland, 205, 367
Plantagenet, Edward, Earl of March (see Edward IV)
Plantagenet, Geoffrey, Count of Anjou, 139, 463
Plantagenet, George, Duke of Clarence, 284
Plantagenet, House of, 139, 218, 257, 340, 433, 447, 456, 461
Plantagenet, Richard, Duke of Gloucester (see Richard III)
Plantagenet, Richard, Duke of York, 83, 93, 116–17, 132, 134–35, 136–39, 140–49, 150–58, 160–69, 172–99, 201–6
Plantagenet, Richard, Earl of Cambridge, 28, 83
Plantagenet, Richard, of Eastwell, 340
Plymouth, Devon, 13, 24, 50, 311, 421
Poissy, France, 45–46, 117
Poitiers, Battle of, 1356, 47
Poitou, France, 44, 182
Poland, 4
Pole, Catherine de la, Abbess of Barking, 93
Pole, John de la, later Duke of Suffolk, 230
Pole, John de la, Earl of Lincoln, 373, 430, 433
Pole, William de la, Earl of Suffolk, 93, 107, 134, 139
Pont-à-Mousson, Lorraine, Château of, 107, 110
Pont de l'Arche, Normandy, 50
Pontefract, Yorks., 206, 220, 222, 320, 367, 414
Castle, 32, 206, 387, 403, 415
Ponthieu, France, 44, 50
Pontoise, France, 52, 117
Poppelau, Sir Nicholas von, 340, 357
Poré, Martin, Bishop of Arras, 60, 62
Portchester, Hants., 118
Portsmouth, Hants., 322
God's House, 118
Portugal, Kingdom of, 277, 446
Portway, River, 331
Powys, Princes of, 32
Prévost d'Exiles, Antoine François, (the Abbé Prévost), 283, 347
Privy Council, 16, 33, 40, 75, 289, 447
Provence, County of, 108–9, 111, 270, 344
Purian, John, 30

Queenborough Castle, Isle of Sheppey, Kent, 146

Index

Queens' College, Cambridge, 127, 257, 261, 351, 160-62, 430
Queen's Gold, 291
Quercy, France, 44

Raglan Castle, Wales, 234
Raguier, Jean, 344
Randolf, John, 54-55, 58, 79
Ratcliffe, Sir Richard, 436, 444-45
Ravenspur, Yorks., 13, 320
Reading, Berks., 31, 155, 264
   Abbey, 267
Reculée, Château of, 113, 344-45
René, King of Naples and Sicily, Duke of Anjou, Count of Lorraine, 107, 112, 114, 236, 308, 345
Rennes, Brittany
   Château of, 14
Rheims, France
   Cathedral, 91
Rhineland, 59
Rhys, John, 16
Ribble, River, 278
Richard, Duke of York (see Plantagenet, Richard)
Richard, Duke of York, son of Edward IV, 365, 372, 381, 395, 398, 399
Richard of Cambridge (see Plantagenet, Richard)
Richard, Earl of Cambridge, 28
Richard II, King of England, 3, 4, 6, 11-13, 17, 19, 24-25, 27-29, 38-39, 45, 47, 52, 57, 141, 202, 218, 228, 406, 463
Richard III, King of England, 24, 341, 406, 413, 420, 429-30, 432, 441, 448, 452-53, 458, 462
Richmond, Earldom of, 11, 13, 15, 27, 33, 235, 314
   Earls of (see Tudor, Edmund; Henry VII)

Riczi, Antoine, 15, 16, 26-27
Robin of Anglesey (Robin Dhu), 87
Robin Hood, 296
"Robin of Redesdale" (see Conyers, Sir John)
Robsart, Sir Louis de, 61
La Rochelle, France, 59, 78
Rochester, Kent, 57, 75, 146-47
Rochford Hall, Essex, 28
Rohan, Viscount de (see John I, Alain X)
Rohan, Viscountess de (see Jeanne of Navarre)
Rome, Italy, 16, 257, 285
Rotherham, Thomas, Archbishop of York, 382, 390-91, 396, 440
Rotherhithe Manor, Surrey, 57
Rouen, Normandy, 64, 70, 74, 92-93, 108, 117, 139-40, 237, 287, 319, 344, 351
   Archbishops of (see William de Vienne)
   Siege of, 1418-19, 60
Rous, John, 308, 355-58, 361, 364, 381, 414, 425, 428, 431, 442, 444-46
Rous Roll, 407
Roxburgh, Siege of, 1460, 200
Royal Collection, 226, 261
Royal Library, Windsor, 227
Royal MSS, British Library, 120
Roye, Jean de, 374
Royston, Herts., 172, 209
Russell, John, Bishop of Lincoln, 382, 391
Ryton, Co. Durham, 225

Sac, Jehan le, 90, 93
Saillé, Brittany, 6
Saint-Aubin-du-Cormier, Ille-et-Vilaine, Fougères, Brittany, 11

Saint-Denis, Abbey of, Paris, 72, 74
  chronicler, 9
Saint-Malo, Brittany, 251
Saint Michiel-en-Barin, Lorraine, 249
Saint-Omer, France, 12, 242, 246–47, 255, 319
Saint-Pol, France, 12, 44, 62, 64–65, 71, 109, 247–48, 256, 265, 273
  Counts of (see Philip I; Peter, Count of Luxembourg)
St. Albans, Herts., 172, 211–15
  Abbey, 79, 100, 184, 213
  Battle of, 1455, 172–75
  Battle of, 1461, 215–16
  Verulamium, 212
St. Andrews, Bishop of (see Kennedy, James)
St. Augustine, Order of, 455
St. George, 28, 49, 52, 69, 72, 121, 227, 329, 369, 377, 457
St. John the Baptist, Church of, Henley-in-Arden, 121
St. John's Priory and Hospital, Clerkenwell, Prior of, 167
St. Leger, Sir Thomas, 421
St. Mary Overie, Priory of, Southwark, 81
St. Nicholas' Church, Calais, 12
St. Parensy, Maria, 30
St. Paul's Cathedral, London, 46, 48–49, 75, 82, 95, 124, 152, 174, 184, 196, 204, 218, 313–14, 323–24, 328, 346, 397, 447
  Bishop's Palace, 184, 199, 313, 324
  Paul's Cross, 314, 400, 457
St. Vulfran, church of, Abbeville, 74
Saintonge, France, 44
Salic Law, 4, 27
Salisbury, Countess of (see Montagu, Alice)
Salisbury, Wilts., 19, 56, 421
  Earldom of, 206
  Earls of (see Montagu, Thomas; Neville, Richard)
Salle, Antoine de la, 109
Sandal Castle, Wakefield, Yorks., 169–70, 177, 205
Sandwich, Kent, 182–83, 194–96, 304, 344
Sangatte, France, 44
Santa Clara, monastery of, Estella, 5
Sasiola, Graufidius de, 414
Sassoon, Siegfried, 429
Saumur, France, 108–11, 345–46
Savernake Forest, Wilts., 448
Savoisy, Henri de, Archbishop of Sens, 61
Scales, Elizabeth, Lady, 215
Scales, Thomas, Lord, 146, 273, 286
Scandinavia, 58
Scharf, Sir George, 97
Scotland, 81, 151, 200–201, 211, 223–25, 234–37, 240–41, 249–51, 311, 366, 378, 451, 462
Scott, Sir Walter, 97, 171
Scotus, Andreas, 234
Sebert, King of the East Saxons, 441–42
Seine, River, 51, 70, 72, 117, 304
Senlis, France, 72–74
Sens, Archbishop of (see Savoisy, Henri de)
  Siege of, 1420, 63
Sevenoaks, Kent, 145
Severn, River, 190, 329–32
Shaa, Dr Ralph, 400–401
Shakespeare, William, 24, 32–33, 35, 39, 51, 76, 131, 170, 179, 347, 396
Sheen Palace, Surrey, 288
Sheriff Hutton, Yorks.
  Castle, 206, 360, 387, 395, 430, 647
  Church, 432
Shooter's Hill, Kent, 273

Shore, Elizabeth (Jane), 349-50, 382, 397
Shore, William, 349
Shrewsbury, Salop., 207, 365
   Battle of, 1403, 25, 86
   Countess of (see Beauchamp, Margaret)
   Earl of (see Talbot, John)
   Franciscan Priory, 54
Sicily, Kingdom of, 109, 111, 345
Sigismund of Luxembourg, Holy Roman Emperor, 43, 108
Simnel, Lambert, 450
Sirego, Dr. Dominic, 280, 315, 325
Sisterhood of Silk Women, Spitalfields, 126
Sixtus IV, Pope, 258
Skinners' Fraternity of Corpus Christi, Skinners' Company, London, 343
Skipton-in-Craven Church, Yorks., 356
Sluys, Burgundy, 246
Solway Firth, 244
Somerset, Charles, 252
Somerset, Earls and Dukes of (see Beaufort)
Sorel, Agnes, 114
Southampton, Hants., 18, 70, 118, 308, 322, 445
   God's House Hospital, 118
Southwick Priory, Hants., 118
Stacey, Dr. John, of Oxford, 371-72
Stafford, Countess of (see Beaufort, Margaret)
Stafford family, 384
Stafford, Henry, 2nd Duke of Buckingham, 198, 270, 273-74, 363, 384
Stafford, Sir Henry, 234
Stafford, Humphrey, 230
Stafford, Humphrey, 1st Duke of Buckingham, 164, 170

Stafford, John, Archbishop of Canterbury, 124
Staines, Middx., 80
Stamford, Lincs., 209, 235
Stanley, Arthur Penrhyn, Dean of Westminster, 97
Stanley, Thomas, Lord, later Earl of Derby, 188-89, 274, 382, 396, 423, 446, 449
Stanley, Sir William, 335-36
Staple, Merchants of the, 65, 126
Stewart, Alexander, Earl of Ross, 457
Stewart, Sir James, 67
Stewart, Margaret, Dr. of James II, 207, 224, 244
Stillington, Robert, Bishop of Bath and Wells, 287, 376, 401-2, 408
   bastard son, 434
Stonor, Anne, 271-72
Stonor, Sir William, 269, 272
Stony Stratford, Bucks., 263-64, 387
Stow, John, 67, 87, 357, 412
Strange, John, Lord, 271
Stratford, John, 261
Stratford Langthorne Abbey, Essex, 79
Strickland, Agnes, 87, 284
Suffolk, Earl of (see Pole, William de la)
Suscinio, Château de, Sarzeau, Brittany, 10
Sutton, John, Lord Dudley, 338, 343
Sutton, William, Dean of the Chapel Royal, 343
Swynford, Katherine, Duchess of Lancaster, 141
Symonds, Richard, 450

Talbot, Eleanor, Lady Sudeley, 401
Talbot, Elizabeth, Dowager Duchess of Norfolk, 373

Talbot, John, Earl of Shrewsbury, 120, 153, 155, 157, 401
Tarascon, Château of, 109, 111
Taunton, Somerset, 330
Tchaikovsky, Pyotr Ilyich, 108
Tempest, John, 278
Tempest, Sir Richard, 278
Temple, Inns of, London, 170-71
Tetzel, Gabriel, 268, 281
Teutonic Knights, Order of, 4
Tewdwr (see also Tudor, Theodore), 85-86
Tewdwr, Maredudd (Meredith), 85
Tewdwr, Rhys ap, Prince of Deheubarth, 86
Tewkesbury, Gloucs., 190, 331, 334
  Abbey, 331-34, 368, 374
  Battle of, 1471, 331, 334-36, 339, 342,
  Chronicle of Tewkesbury Abbey, 361-62
  Margaret's Camp, 331
Thames, River, 25, 31, 83, 202, 336-37, 355, 385, 390, 453
Thérouanne, France, 65
Theodore family, 86
Thomas of Lancaster, Duke of Clarence, 64
Thomas of Woodstock, Duke of Gloucester, 28, 384
Thoresby, John, of Warwick, 371
Thwaites, Thomas, 343
Tickenhill Manor, Bewdley, Worcs., 366
Tilbury, Essex, 448
Timoléon, François, Abbé de Choisy, 45
Tiptoft, John, 30
Tiptoft, John, Earl of Worcester, 289
Titchfield Abbey, Hants., 119, 121, 123
Titulus Regius, Act of Parliament, 1484, 432, 447-48

Toledo Museum of Art, Ohio, 121
Toul Cathedral, 108, 114
Tours, France, 9, 46, 50, 112-13, 125, 301, 309
  Treaty of, 1444, 113, 125, 133
Tower of London, 20, 25, 30, 58, 65, 119, 123, 141, 149, 153, 174, 181, 184, 195, 228, 300, 311, 313, 324, 326, 337-38, 340, 372, 374, 381, 393, 412, 425, 453
  Bowyer Tower, 372
  Wakefield Tower, 338
  White Tower, 399
Towton, Battle of, 1461, 220, 223, 230, 259-60
Tredington, Gloucs., 331
Trent, River, 208, 375
Troyes, France, 50, 52, 60-63
  Abbey of Saint-Julien, 113
  Cathedral (Church of St. Martin), 113
  "La Couronne" Inn, 61
  Saint-Jean-au-Marché, church of, 62
  Treaty of, 1420
Tuchet, James, Lord Audley, 342
Tudor, Arthur, Prince of Wales, 450, 452
Tudor, Edmund, Earl of Richmond, 89, 93, 104, 153, 155-56, 164, 175, 179
Tudor, House of, 86, 97, 104, 179, 293, 393
Tudor, Jasper, Earl of Pembroke, later Duke of Bedford, 89, 93, 104, 153, 155-56, 164, 170, 292, 309, 311, 312, 314, 316, 329, 449
Tudor, Margaret, Jacinda or Tacina, 90
Tudor, Owen (Owain ap Maredudd ap Tewdwr), 85, 89, 93-94, 96, 98, 103, 175, 193, 210, 335
Tudor, Owen or Thomas (see Bridgewater, Edward)

Index

Tunstall, Sir Richard, 156, 237, 252, 278
Tutbury, Staffs, 176, 198
Tweed, River, 241–42
Twynho, Ankarette, 371–72
Tyne, River, 252
Tynemouth, Northld., 237
Tyrell, Sir James, 364, 413

Ufford, Maud de, Countess of Oxford, 24
Ursin, Jean Juvenal des, 62
Urswick, Christopher, 417

Valle Crucis Abbey, Wales, 121
Valois, House of, 5, 27, 32, 51, 62, 65
Vannes, Brittany, 3, 7–8, 10, 12, 18
   Cathedral, 422
Vatican, Rome, 309, 358
Vaudemont, Antoine de, 108–9, 111
Vaudemont, Ferry (or Frederick) de, 109, 114, 301, 341
Vaughan, Roger, 335
Vaughan, Sir Thomas, 351, 364, 366, 385, 387, 395
Vaux, Katherine, 332, 342–45
Vegetius, Publius, 414
Vergil, Polydore, 86, 90, 98, 120, 128, 171, 263, 333, 357–58, 399, 413–17, 425, 427, 440, 443–46, 448
Vere, John de, 12th Earl of Oxford, 235
Vere, John de, 13th Earl of Oxford, 235, 290
Vere, Robert de, Duke of Ireland, 24
Victoria and Albert Museum, London, 120
Victoria, Queen of Great Britain, 97
Vienne, France, 108, 470

Vignolles, Francis de, Lord of Morains, 345
Vignolles, Jean, 346
Vincennes, Château of, 71
Virgin Mary, 21, 51, 81
Visconti family, 45
Visconti, Bianca Maria, Duchess of Milan, 120
Visconti, Gian Galleazzo, Duke of Milan, 3
Visconti, Lucia, 3

Waddington Hall, Lancs., 278
Wake, Thomas, 298
Wakefield, Battle of, 1460, 205–6
Wales
   Princes of (see Edward of Woodstock, Henry V, Edward of Lancaster, Edward V)
Wallingford Castle, Berks., 40, 83, 103, 342
Walsingham, Norfolk
   Shrine of Our Lady, 79, 156
Walsingham, Thomas, 18, 39, 55, 62, 73
Wardrobe Book of Margaret of Anjou, 126, 129, 132, 151, 159
Ware, Herts., 172, 197, 211
Wark Castle, Northld., 223
Warkworth Castle, Northld., 238–39
Warkworth, John, 263, 312
Wars of the Roses, 23–24, 121, 169–71, 204, 210, 220, 232, 242, 259, 384, 461
Warwick, Co. Warwick
   Castle, 170, 177, 188, 298, 303, 322, 368, 414, 428
   Guildhall, 371
Warwick, Earls of (see Beauchamp, Thomas de; Beauchamp, Richard de; Neville, Richard; Edward of Clarence)

Watling Street, 211
Waurin, Jean de, 51, 101, 207, 242, 260
Wayneflete, William, Bishop of Winchester, 160, 180
Weever, John, 96
Weinreich, Caspar, 262, 265
Welles, Avice, 350
Welles, John, Viscount, 455, 457–58
Wells, John, Prior of Hexham, 239
Wells, Somerset, 16, 287, 330, 376
  Bishop's Palace, 330
Wenlock, Sir John, later Lord, 127, 185, 255, 264, 303, 322, 332
Weobley, Herefs., 297
Westminster Abbey, 20, 25, 34, 37, 51, 66, 75, 90–91, 94–96, 124, 160, 218, 226, 274, 281, 312, 324–25
  Abbot's House (Cheyneygates), 312, 390, 454, 451
  Chapel of St. Edward the Confessor, 34, 75, 364
  Chapel of St. Erasmus, 325, 378
  Henry VII Chapel, 96, 378
  Jerusalem Chamber, 34, 313
  Lady Chapel, 95–96
  The Queen's Diamond Jubilee Gallery, 95
  St. Edward's Shrine, 364, 408
  Sanctuary, 98, 312–13, 315, 324–25, 389–99, 400, 410, 412–13, 417, 419, 424–25, 427, 429, 451–52
Westminster Hall, 25, 26, 66, 124, 202–3, 218, 274, 407, 409, 434
Westminster, Palace of, 66, 77, 124, 159, 268, 280, 324, 359, 364, 373, 380, 390, 393, 399, 407, 434, 451
  Painted Chamber, 25, 373
  Star Chamber, 26
  St. Stephen's Chapel, 26, 280, 359, 373, 449
  White Hall, 26, 364, 407

Westmorland, Earl of (see Neville, Ralph), 26
Weymouth, Dorset, 322, 326, 330
Whethamstead, John, Abbot of St. Albans, 100, 136, 213
Whittingham, Robert, 290
Whittington, Richard, Lord Mayor of London, 67
Whittlebury Forest, Northants., 260
Widville, Anthony, later Lord Scales and 2nd Earl Rivers, 184, 194, 223, 273, 286, 304, 321, 326, 350, 385, 387–88, 391–93, 395, 403, 445
Widville, Sir Edward, 270, 373, 421, 446, 449, 450, 453
Widville, Elizabeth, Queen of England, 24, 130, 212, 256, 259–60, 262, 267, 270, 279, 289, 291, 298, 315, 317, 325, 342–43, 367, 372, 378, 401–3, 405–6, 410–12, 417–19, 420, 422–24, 426, 429–30, 432, 434, 437, 441, 447–58, 462–63
Widville family, 263, 270, 366, 374, 384, 387, 391, 393–94, 400, 412, 445, 449, 450
Widville, Jacquetta, Lady Strange, 194, 256–57, 262, 271, 298–99, 422
Widville, Joan, Lady Haute, 256, 271
Widville, John, 270, 296–98
Widville, Katherine, Duchess of Buckingham, later Duchess of Bedford, 270, 449
Widville, Lionel, Bishop of Salisbury, 270, 351, 377, 390, 421
Widville, Sir Richard, father of Richard Wydville, 1st Earl Rivers, 256–57
Widville, Sir Richard, son of Richard Wydville, 1st Earl Rivers, 421, 450
Widville, Sir Richard, later 1st Earl Rivers, 130, 256–57, 260, 267, 271, 298–99

Index

Widville, William de, 256
Wigmore, Edward de, 402
Wigmore, Herefs., 207
Wigmore, Richard, 402
William I, the Conqueror, King of England, 69, 462
William II, King of England, 25
William de Vienne, Archbishop of Rouen, 12
William of Worcester, 283, 339
William of Wykeham, Bishop of Winchester, 20
Winchester, Hants., 19-20, 81, 99, 152, 450
  Bishops of (see Beaufort, Henry; Wayneflete, William)
  Cathedral, 20, 450
Winchester Palace, Southwark, 81
Windsor Castle, Berks., 69, 81, 103, 288, 329, 342, 352, 377
  St. George's Chapel, 167, 226, 228, 341, 369, 377-78, 385, 457-59
  St. George's Hall, 69, 369
Wingfield Manor, Co. Derby, 153
Wolvesey Castle, Winchester, 19
Wood, Mary Anne, 12
Woodham Ferrers, Essex, 258
Woods, Richard, 178
Woodville (see Wydville)
Worcester, City of, 190, 192, 335
  Cathedral, 190
  Earl of (see Percy, Thomas)
  Prior of, 190
Worshipful Company of Skinners, London, 120
Wrockwardine Church, Shropshire, 121

Wychwood Forest, Oxon., 260
Wycliffe, John, 340
Wye Valley, 421
Wynne, John, 156

Yardley Gobion, Northants., 260
Ybarra, Fernando de, 13
Yolande of Anjou, 108, 115, 250, 301, 345
Yolande of Aragon, Countess of Anjou, 108, 110
York, Dowager Duchess of (see Mohun, Philippa de)
  Dukes of (see Edmund of Langley; Edward of Aumale; Plantagenet, Richard; Edward IV)
York, City of, 206, 219
  Archbishop's palace, 415
  Breckles Mill, 415
  Civic Council, 394, 414
  Civic Records, 357
  Corpus Christi Guild, 360, 415
  Creed Play the Corpus Christi Guild, 415
  Guildhall, 415
  House of, 27-28, 139, 171, 222, 230, 285, 367, 373, 375, 384, 403, 435-36
  Mayor of, 395, 415
  Micklegate and Micklegate Bar, 206, 222, 415
  Minster, 51, 71, 279, 415
Young, Thomas, 150

Zeeland, Principality of, 67, 294

About the Author

DR. ALISON WEIR is a *New York Times* bestselling author who has sold over three million books worldwide. She has published twenty-two history books, including *Eleanor of Aquitaine, The Lady in the Tower,* and *Elizabeth of York,* and her four-volume series, England's Medieval Queens. She has also written sixteen historical novels, including her Six Tudor Queens series, *The Passionate Tudor,* and *The Cardinal.*

alisonweir.org.uk
alisonweirtours.com
facebook.com/AlisonWeirAuthor
X: @AlisonWeirBooks

About the Type

This book was set in Legacy, a typeface family designed by Ronald Arnholm (b. 1939) and issued in digital form by ITC in 1992. Both its serifed and unserifed versions are based on an original type created by the French punchcutter Nicholas Jenson in the late fifteenth century. While Legacy tends to differ from Jenson's original in its proportions, it maintains much of the latter's characteristic modulations in stroke.